Location Theory and Decision Analysis

Yupo Chan

Professor & Founding Chair
Department of Systems Engineering
Donaghey College of Information Science & Systems Engineering
University of Arkansas at Little Rock

South-Western College Publishing
Thomson Learning™

Australia • Canada • Mexico • Singapore • Spain • United Kingdom • United States

Location Theory and Decision Analysis, by Yupo Chan

Publisher: Dave Shaut
Sr. Acquisitions Editor: Charles McCormick, Jr.
Developmental Editor: Alice C. Denny
Sr. Marketing Manager: Joseph A. Sabatino
Production Editor: Anne Chimenti
Manufacturing Coordinator: Sandee Milewski
Internal Design: Michael H. Stratton
Cover Design: Jennifer Lambert
Production House: Monotype Composition
Printer: RR Donnelley & Sons

Printed in the United States of America
1 2 3 4 5 04 03 02 01

For more information, contact South-Western College Publishing, 5101 Madison Road, Cincinnati, Ohio, 45227 or find us on the Internet at http://www.swcollege.com

For permission to use material from this text or product, contact us by
• telephone: 1-800-730-2214
• fax: 1-800-730-2215
• web: http://www.thomsonrights.com

ISBN: 0-324-02821-0

This book is printed on acid-free paper.

Contents

Preface

Location Theory and Decision Analysis is tailored toward upperclass and graduate-level courses that include location decision making. It includes the fundamental theories and analysis procedures of that process. With these fundamentals carefully and comprehensively compiled, it is amply suited for courses such as management science, operations research, economics, civil and environmental engineering, industrial engineering, geography, urban and regional planning and policy sciences. The book also serves as an overview of the relationship between location, transport, and land use decisions. As such it introduces more advanced topics as documented in Chan (2000) and Easa and Chan (2000).

This book is unique in that it integrates existing practical and theoretical works on facility location and land use. Instead of dealing with individual facility location or the resulting land use pattern alone, it provides the underlying principles that are behind both types of models. Of particular interest is the emphasis on counter-intuitive decisions, which are often overlooked unless deliberate steps of analysis are taken. Being oriented toward the fundamental principles of infrastructure management, the book transcends the traditional engineering and planning disciplines, where the main concerns are often exclusively physical design, fiscal, socioeconomic, or political considerations.

Employing contemporary quantitative models and case studies, the book discusses the siting of such facilities as transportation terminals, warehouses, nuclear power plants, military bases, landfills, emergency shelters, state parks, and industrial plants. The book also demonstrates the use of satellite imagery, computer-based data-retrieval technologies (such as geographic information systems), and statistical tools for forecasting and analyzing implications of land use decisions. The idea is that land use shown on a map is necessarily a consequence of individual, and often conflicting, siting decisions.

The analytical community has made significant progress in recent years in the basic building blocks of spatial analysis. Current models have captured accurately many of the bases of facility-siting decision making—proximity to demand, competition among existing facilities, and the availability of utilities and other institutional supports. Throughout this text, accessibility (as afforded by transportation) and infrastructure support (as provided by utilities and sewers) are used as determinants of location decisions. Competitive and statistical determinants that are not based on accessibility alone are also covered.

However, a novel feature of *Location Theory and Decision Analysis* is the recognition that in today's service economy, the traditional concepts of accessibility need to be broadly interpreted. Evidence indicates, for example, that half of the shopping currently done is by mail, telephone, or the Internet. Thus the definition of "a trip to the shopping mall," and hence the conventional judgment in siting a retail facility, need to accommodate such a change. "Global reach" redefines the concept of accessibility and distance in all sectors of the economy, including E-commerce, international corporations, and even the defense community. Half the globe away now means a few hours of flight time or seconds of telecommunication time. Conversely, congested streets can make cross-town travel almost impossible, and thus encourage telecommuting. Again a redefinition of accessibility and hence the conventional wisdom in office site selection is required. The theme of change carries throughout the book, serving to unify many of the spatial location models discussed.

The advances in remote sensing imagery and geographic information systems today facilitate much of spatial analysis. Electronic devices, such as satellites, sensors, computers, and telecommunications technology, make the collection and processing of data much faster, which in turn assists in the problem solving process. The book discusses how information can be stored in such a way that it can be directly translated to a format for real-time decision making. This means simple and transparent models that are database compatible and require minimal data manipulation in the solution process. These models become the tools for analysis and decision making. *Location Theory and Decision Analysis* gives the reader a comprehensive insight into the use of these tools—identifying, assembling and utilizing the important information for problem solving, rather than prescribing verbatim software instructions.

ORGANIZATION OF THE BOOK

As mentioned, this book contains a comprehensive review of the fundamental principles. Questions such as why facilities locate where they do and why population and employment activities distribute on the map as they do are answered. The first few chapters include the underlying determinants of facility location and land use, as well as the techniques that are essential to analyze these location decisions. In addition, these chapters discuss databases from remote sensing and geographic information systems (GIS), statistical tools for data analysis and forecasting, optimization procedures for choosing the desirable course of action, and multicriteria decision-making techniques to tie the entire analysis procedure together. Key concepts in economics, one of the most important disciplines in explaining the organization in space, are also reviewed.

The first five chapters — which include economics, descriptive and prescriptive techniques, and multicriteria decision making — constitute an excellent quantitatively oriented survey course in this field. If needed, the appendices provide for a review of the mathematical tools. Where there is room in the curriculum, a more advanced treatment will include the "Remote Sensing and GIS" chapter. While the first five chapters redefine location by such concepts as telecommuting, Chapter 6 drives it home. In this last chapter, new ways to store, organize, process, and transmit spatial data are reviewed.

Location Theory and Decision Analysis purposefully accommodates the different technical backgrounds and career objectives of its readers. For example, spatial economics principles are introduced in Chapter 2, allowing the non-economists to acquire the basic economic concepts that underlie much of the location literature. It serves as an excellent overview of the entire book. As another example, multicriteria decision making is reviewed in Chapter 5, with an emphasis on how it assists in location decisions. It includes discussion of state-of-the-art concepts and technology that may not be familiar to those outside the fields of management science and operations research. For example, I illustrate how an obnoxious facility, such as a noisy airport, can be located by taking into consideration all the stakeholders concerns. Most importantly, liberal numerical examples and graphics are used to get the point across. My diverse background, which spans technical consulting firms, government, academia, and the defense community, enables me to communicate with different audiences in terms of a common language. Beyond the classroom, professionals who seek an update on the fundamentals on location decisions will find this book helpful. The professional audience will find the crosscutting discussion of technical concepts in Appendix 5 particularly helpful, since it unifies the findings from different disciplines.

Exercises and case studies are used throughout the book. Rather than a set of mechanical calculations, the exercises and case studies are designed to extend many of the concepts covered in the book. They also play an important role in integrating the many diverse principles advanced in the text. One objective of the exercises is to challenge the readers creatively to use the data sets and computer software that come with *Location Theory and Decision Analysis*. While the basic exercises are well structured, readers are often asked to perform their own case studies, using the data sets if desired, and arrive at open-ended results. For the sake of synergy, all the exercises are placed together at the end of the book, rather than included separately at the end of individual chapters. To assist both instructors and students, answers to the exercises are available on my web site. Please contact me by email at ychan@alum.MIT.edu for information about the web site. Students and professionals should enter in the Subject line: REQUEST FOR SAMPLE SOLUTIONS, and instructors should enter: REQUEST FOR INSTRUCTOR'S GUIDE.

SOFTWARE

A CD-ROM provided with the text provides sample software. The main purpose of the CD is to supplement the basic ideas covered in the text. Aside from extensive databases, it contains software to implement some of the basic concepts presented. It also challenges the reader to investigate further through hands-on experiences with case studies. In view of the rapid progress in information technologies and to avoid obsolescence, the book is not specifically tied to a single generation of information technology. Rather, the book is problem-oriented and provides a set of procedures and a set of data for analysis that can transcend the technological evolution. Hands-on experiences are discussed with respect to the basic models employed, rather than the particular software or hardware.

One software program used for processing remote sensing images (courtesy of Dr. T. S. Kelso) illustrates some of the spatial statistical concepts and GIS. The remainder are software implementations of some of the facility location and land use concepts discussed in this book. While the book introduces the various analytical techniques in a pedagogic fashion, the software provides practical implementations. The programs are therefore not purely for the classroom; they have real potential for everyday, operational use.

1. All files on the CD are ASCII-text files. Where possible, both source codes and executable codes are given—mainly for the ease of execution and modification by the users. Program documentation is included as README files.

2. While references are made to supporting software for extended use of some of the programs, all programs are self-contained, and they have been developed or refined by the author and his associates. The programs do not require supporting software or language compilers.

As mentioned, sample data sets are provided to allow demonstration of the software. Most of the data are drawn from real-world case studies.

The programs have been extensively tested, but still there can be no absolute guarantee of faultlessness. It is impossible for me to provide any programming support for the software, but I am keenly interested in and would appreciate any feedback from users regarding their experiences with the programs or the book. To provide your comments, simply contact me by email at ychan@alum.MIT.edu and include in the subject line: SUGGESTIONS FOR THE BOOK.

ACKNOWLEDGEMENTS

Location Theory and Decision Analysis is a result of over two decades of work that benefited most importantly from my students but also from academic and professional colleagues around the world. The group includes reviewers of the actual manuscript.

Suraj M. Alexander, University of Louisville

Mark S. Daskin, Northwestern University

Dinesh S. Dave, Appalachian State University

Walter Fabricky, Virginia Polytechnic Institute and State University

James Farris, Golden West College

Paul Gray, Clarmont Graduate University

Ronald Klimberg, Boston University

Duane Marble, Ohio State University

Pitu B. Mirchandani, University of Arizona

Norbert Oppenheim, CUNY—City College

Stephen Robinson, University of Wisconsin

William B. Widhelm, University of Maryland

Others who aided my efforts were collaborators in various studies, such as a paper that won the 1991 Koopman Prize Award of the Institute for

Operations Research and Management Science (INFORMS). In addition to explicit references in the text, I wish to acknowledge their input. The following group by no means constitutes everyone who helped to make this book possible. However, all these people rendered invaluable guidance to this writing project.

Steven Baker, Air Force Academy; David Boyce, University of Illinois at Chicago; T. Owen Carroll, SUNY at Stony Brook; Emilio Casetti, Ohio State University; F. Stuart Chapin, University of North Carolina at Chapel Hill; Jarad L. Cohon, Carnegie Mellon University; Noel Cressie, Iowa State University; Richard deNeufville, Massachusetts Institute of Technology; John W. Dickey, Virginia Polytechnic Institute and State University; O. Day Ding, California Polytechnic State University; Kenneth J. Dueker, Portland State University; Alan G. Feldt, University of Michigan; Richard L. Francis, University of Florida; Jon Fricker, Purdue Universtiy; Richard Gagnon, North Shore Community College; William Garrison, University of California-Berkeley; Bruce L. Golden, University of Maryland; S. Louis Hakimi, University of California-Davis; Elise Miller-Hooks, Pennsylvania State University; Chin S. Hsu, Washington State University; Zhimin Huang, Adelphi University; Arthur P. Hurter, Northwestern University; John J. Jarvis, Georgia Institute of Technology; Edward J. Kaiser, University of North Carolina at Chapel Hill; Ralph Keeney, University of Southern California; Tschangho J. Kim, University of Illinois; Thomas S. Kelso, Air Force Institute of Technology; David. H. Marks, Massachusetts Institute of Technology; Edward K. Morlok, University of Pennsylvania; James G. Morris, University of Wisconsin-Madison; Srinivas Peeta, Purdue University; G. L. Peterson, Northwestern University; Peter Purdue; Naval Postgraduate School; Stehpen Putman, University of Pennsylvania; Essam Radwan, University of Central Florida; Charles Revelle, Johns Hopkins University; Brian D. Ripley, University of Washington; Morton H. Schneider, Johns Hopkins University; Thomas Sexton, SUNY at Stony Brook; Ralph E. Steuer, University of Georgia; Eric Vanmarcke, Princeton University; Steven C. Wheelwright, Harvard University; John A. White, Georgia Institute of Technology; Jeff R. Wright, Purdue University; Ping Yi, University of Akron

G. Leonardi, Instituto di Analisi dei Sistemi ed Informatica, Rome, Italy; Peter Nijkamp, Free University, Netherlands; S. Occelli, Instituto Ricerche Economico Sociali, Turin, Italy; Atsuyuki Okabe, University of Tokyo, Japan; M. B. Priestley, University of Manchester Institute of Science and Technology, United Kingdom; Peter M. Pruzan, Copenhagen Business School, Denmark; C. S. Bertuglia, Instituto Ricerche Economico Sociali, Turin, Italy; Barry Boots, Wilfrid Laurier University, Canada; Erhan Erkut, University of Alberta, Canada; Jakob Krarup, University of Copenhagen, Denmark; William H-K Lam, Hong Kong Polytechnic University, Hong Kong, China; Gilbert Laporte, University of Montreal, Canada; G. A. Rabino, Instituto Ricerche Economico Sociali, Turin, Italy; Jacque Thisse, Ecole Nationale des Ponts et Chaussees, France; Roger W. Vickerman, University of Kent at Canterbury, United Kingdom; George O. Wesolowsky, McMaster University, Canada; Alan G. Wilson, University of Leeds, United Kingdom; Maurice Yeates, Queen's University, Canada

Wayne Allison, Warren, Rhode Island; Kurt Ardaman, Fishback, Dominick, Bennett, Steper & Ardaman, Orlando, Florida; Frank Campanile, Dayton, Ohio;

Raul Meda Dooley, City Bell, Argentina; Carolyn B. Doty, Automated Sciences Group, Oak Ridge, Tennessee; A. Ruth Fitzgerald, Fitzgerald and Halliday, Hartford, Connecticut; Terry Cronin, Intelligence & Electronic Warfare Directorate, Warrenton, Virginia; Paul Guyer, Guyer Santin Inc., Sacramento, California; Walter G. Hansen, Frederick R. Harris Inc, Washington D. C.; Harvey Haack, Pennsylvania Department of Transportation; Rubin Johnson, OR Concepts Applied, Whittier, California; Frank Kudrna, Jr., Kudrna and Associates, Chicago, Illinois; Douglass B. Lee, Volpe Center, U. S. Department of Transportation; Ira S. Lowry, Housing and development consultant, Pacific Palisades, California; Robert E. Machol, Washington D. C.; Reddy Mannur, U. S. Department of Justice, Washington D. C.; David Merrill, Air Mobility Command, Scott AFB, Illinois; Larry Mugler, Denver Regional Council of Governments, Denver, Colorado; Phil D. Patterson, Department of Energy, Washington D. C.; Armando Perez, Camp Dresser & McKee Inc, Miami, Florida; Alan B. Pritsker, Pritsker and Associates, West Lafayette, Indiana; Joe H. Mize, Stillwater, Oklahoma; M. Rahman, JHK & Associates, Seattle, Washington; Earl Ruiter, Cambridge Systematics, Cambridge, Massachusetts; Howard Slavin, Caliper Corporation, Boston, Massachusetts; Bruce Spear, Volpe Center, U. S. Department of Transportation; Curtis Travis, Oak Ridge National Laboratory

I also benefited from my association with the Massachusetts Institute of Technology, Kates, Peat, Marwick & Co., Pennsylvania State University at University Park, U.S. Congressional Office of Technology Assessment, State University of New York at Stony Brook, Washington State University, and the Air Force Institute of Technology. Don Hoover is thanked for his role in editing and compiling the various iterations of this manuscript. Bradley Smith helped me with debugging the software packaged on the CD. I wish to express my gratitude to all those at South-Western College Publishing/Thomson Learning™, including Senior Acquisitions Editor Charles McCormick, Senior Development Editor Alice Denny, Senior Marketing Manager Joseph Sabatino, and Production Editor Anne Chimenti.

The strength of this work is one of synthesis — cutting across disciplines, backgrounds and experiences — precisely where this field is heading. The diverse backgrounds of these friends and colleagues in academia, government, and private industry made my job as synthesizer that much more streamlined. These people greatly assisted me in achieving the goal of informing the reader of the knowledge that falls within a specific discipline but also across other disciplines — in as readable, yet as precise and practical, a form as possible. Their assistance did not end with this volume. Chan (2000) includes these advanced topics: facility location; measuring spatial separation; simultaneous location-and-routing models; generation, competition and distribution in location-allocation; activity allocation and derivation; chaos, catastrophe, bifurcation and disaggregation; spatial equilibrium and disequilibrium; spatial econometric models; spatial time series; and spatial-temporal information. Easa and Chan (2000) includes these additional topics: trends in spatial databases, spatial decision-support systems, GIS integration with analytical models, and incorporating real-time information. It is through these additional discussions that one can fully realize the power of synergism.

YUPO CHAN

ABOUT THE COVER

This radar image shows the massive urbanization of Los Angeles, California. The complete image extends from the Santa Monica Bay at the left to the San Gabriel Mountains at the right. Downtown Los Angeles is on the right side of the textbook's cover. The complex freeway system is visible as dark lines throughout the image. Some city areas, such as Santa Monica in the upper left, appear red due to the alignment of streets and buildings to the incoming radar beam.

The image was acquired by the Spaceborne Imaging Radar-C/X-band Synthetic Aperture Radar (SIR-C/X-SAR) onboard the space shuttle Endeavour on October 3, 1994. SIR-C/X-SAR, a joint mission of the German, Italian and U. S. space agencies, is part of NASA's Mission to Planet Earth. The radar images illuminate earth with microwaves allowing detailed observations at any time, regardless of weather or sunlight conditions. The multi-frequency data will be used by the international scientific community to better understand the global environment and how it is changing. The SIR-C/X-SAR data, complemented by aircraft and ground studies, will give scientists clearer insights into those environmental changes that are caused by nature and those changes that are induced by human activity.

REFERENCES

Chan, Y. (2000). *Location, transport and land-use: modelling spatial-temporal information.* New York: Springer-Verlag.

Easa, S.; Chan, Y., eds. (2000). *GIS: Applications in urban planning and development.* Reston, Virginia: ASCE Press.

DEDICATION

To My Parents:

Susan, Arthur, and Mary

1

Introduction

"Where the telescope ends, the microscope begins. Which of the two has the grander view?"
Victor Hugo

I. OBJECTIVES

This book has three basic objectives. The first objective is *to identify the observed regularities in location decisions.* This involves examining and answering questions such as: Why do public and private facilities locate themselves the way they do? What factors do real estate developers consider when picking sites for development? Why do people live in a certain location, and why do they often work in a location different from where they live? Why are focal points such as airports, terminals, and depots situated at certain nodes in a network? Throughout this book, we will try to answer some of these questions, so that readers can judiciously locate facilities and guide development toward desired goals.

While we often take notice as to why certain facilities are placed in certain areas, we get as many explanations about such location decisions as the number of experts we ask. Each seems to offer a plausible explanation. Such explanations can be any combination of economic, technical, social, political, and behavioral reasons, not to mention such philosophies as **feng shui**—which roughly translated means "location and orientation [of a facility] with respect to the elements of nature" (Love, Morris, and Wesolowsky 1988). Are there really discernible patterns about these location decisions? Many of us have observed that ports and cities of the world are often located on major trade routes, usually at the confluence of rivers, a convenient deep sea harbor, or where railroads come together. Scientists envision future habitats in the galaxies being located at **Lagrangian points**—locations that are stable enough that space stations located there, when perturbed by slight impacts, will restore their position after reasonable oscillations. Based on these examples, it stands to reason that there may be some location patterns one can discern. These patterns, when observed to be consistently recurring in one area after another, are referred to as **regularities.** These regularities are not anywhere as precise as scientific laws, nor can they often be explained in terms of cause-effect relationships. One event does not necessarily occur because of a previous event. As a result, we have to go by the observed

patterns only and to treat those recurring patterns merely as some generally agreed upon facts. From there, analytical models can be built to reflect these premises. The first objective of this document then, is to understand, in a systematic manner, the regularity with which different location decisions are made, so that systematic procedures can be defined to anticipate similar situations that may arise in the future.

We should quickly point out there is a difference between the systematic analysis proposed here and **comprehensive,** or **holistic, planning,** which goes under different names such as **morphology, concurrency,** or **planning theory.** That body of knowledge, while extremely valuable, has been treated in excellent texts elsewhere, including those that are required reading in such professional examinations as those of the American Institute of Certified Planners (AICP), and in such documents as *Land Use* by Davis (1976). This book aims at a different area that is by definition more narrowly focused. We ask more specific questions, such as "how does transportation affect location decisions?"; "how does infrastructural support influence development of a certain area?"; or "how does transportation combined with infrastructural support affect facility location and land use?" In other words, we examine one factor at a time, one criterion at a time, and the cumulative effects rather than the simultaneous effects of all factors across all criteria. Distinction is also made between the treatment here and an approach taken by two notable publications—one by the American Society of Civil Engineers (1986), the *Urban Planning Guide,* and another by Brewer and Alter (1988), *The Complete Manual of Land Planning and Development.* The *Guide* is an excellent document that discusses a whole host of planning topics, ranging from waste to energy planning, with a design flavor as an undertone. Brewer and Alter's publication is a comprehensive description of site layout planning and design. As illustrated by examples at the end of this chapter, the focus here is on analytics, with quantitative model building as a key instrument. Thus this book serves as a useful companion to such documents as the *Guide* and represents an area that has not been covered sufficiently for many who feel the need for state-of-the-art analytic tools to make capital-intensive location decisions—the step prior to detailed design.

The second objective is *to review the operational analysis techniques that have been applied in the field.* In this regard, we report on case studies that span a number of user groups—from public and private facility location to land development. For example, we would look at the factors that go into the location of a nuclear power plant in seismically active areas in California, the location of state parks in the greater New York metropolitan area, the choice of distribution centers for military logistics, the siting of satellite tracking stations in Canada, target location in search and rescue missions, and the land development in several major North American cities, including a systematic study of bifurcation development in a medium-sized city: York, Pennsylvania. We also examine case studies around the world, including the economic impact of the Kansai International Airport outside Osaka, Japan. The common theme is how location regularities and spatial impacts can be quantified in a set of procedures or models.

The third objective—*to be able to stand back and critique some of these modeling experiences*—requires asking whether they have been successful and valid. In other words, what are the assets and liabilities of the various techniques that have been employed? Perhaps one can think of this book as a consumer's guide to location analysis and land use models. A user can look up the price tag of using a particular model, and also the benefits, specifically regarding the problem being solved. The only time that a model or analysis procedure can help is when the user is fully aware not only of its strong points, but its shortcomings as well. Only under those circumstances can an engineer, an analyst, a planner, or a manager employ the most appropriate tool toward the problem at hand, and avoid overkill with exotic technology, below-par performances with an outdated tool, and misfits between problem and analysis tools in general.

What are the more visible results and benefits from reading this text? For engineers, analysts, planners, and managers, the question is easy to answer. As long as infrastructure represents a major capital expenditure and supports economic well being and quality of life, this book serves the important role of articulating investment in these infrastructure improvements. Such infrastructure may include tracking stations, depots, terminals, roads, factories, warehouses, hazardous facilities, office buildings, and housing. Both in public decisions and in corporate planning, the analytical skills discussed in this book can mean savings or benefits in terms of a huge number of dollars. To students and researchers, this book serves as a useful compendium of spatial analysis techniques. It is a comprehensive collection, and the presentation style is pedagogic, starting from the basic building blocks to the more advanced concepts. We point out the commonalities among models used to locate facilities one at a time and to forecast the development pattern in an entire area. In this regard, it is a unified volume on **spatial science**—defined here to mean the analytical techniques that explicitly recognize the spatial elements in a study. The term spatial science, when used in this context, encompasses the traditional disciplines of facility location, transportation, logistics, land use, regional science, quantitative geography, and spatial economics. This book introduces to students and specialists in each of these disciplines the broader perspective as viewed from collective wisdom—a perspective that is absolutely essential to furthering the art of spatial science.

II. DETERMINANTS OF LOCATION

One goal of this book is to uncover the observed regularities of location decisions, in other words, the apparent underlying forces that shape development. We shall examine four major determinants of location.

A. Technological Factors

The first determinant refers to physical principles that govern location and infrastructural supports such as highways, airports, railroads, power supply, sewers, and irrigation. These supports make the functioning of the facility possible. Notice that these go beyond the availability of transportation and utilities. The example about building a space station drives this home. Only Lagrangian points in spatial mechanics will allow the location of a permanent habitat/resupply station in deep space at which spaceships can dock conveniently with the assurance that it is a stable station that can survive the impact of objects. Likewise, satellite tracking stations must be where visibility is at its best to observe the desired orbits most of the year. It stands to reason that a station too far north in the Northern Hemisphere will be unsuitable to track satellite orbits around the equator, not to mention that infrastructural support such as roadways and utilities will be scanty in these arctic regions. When the American West was developed, the railroad was the key instrument. Today, in the Midwest of the United States, one can still trace the location of towns in regular intervals along the rail lines on the prairie. They were apparently developed from water refilling stations required for the steam locomotives of the day. The separation represents the length during which all the water carried on a train evaporated—a technological factor in its truest sense.

B. Economic and Geographic Factors

A person lives at a location convenient for carrying out daily activities, both work and non-work, commensurate with the ability and willingness to pay for the corresponding residential cost. For those who cannot afford the prime locations, housing a little bit further away is the only choice. A host of theories exists to explain this phenomenon, including land rent and location theories. On a historical basis, cities have located on trade routes, perhaps due to accessibility to markets. To command a competitive edge in today's retail market, warehouses are often situated in the midst of the demand, where consumers have easy access to stored goods through the retail outlets. The most graphic example may be in emergency planning. Quick, efficient medical evacuation of the wounded dictates a judicious placement of hubs through which the injured can be quickly transported and eventually delivered to hospitals for medical care.

C. Political Factors

Zoning represents an institutionalized consensus in the community regarding the legitimate use of the land. Fiscal and jurisdictional considerations are also quite common. During the latter part of the 20th century, there have been free enterprise zones designated by the People's Republic of China to manufacture and conduct business with the free world. Some of these are located across the border from Hong Kong and Macao. These zones enjoy special jurisdictional and fiscal privileges—incentives for investment and workers. Finally, there are eminent political decisions for location as well. For example, the Dallas-Fort Worth Airport in the United States sprawls across two counties, apparently for political reasons—which in part explains its having a huge horizontal layout rather than a more vertically integrated structure. On a larger scale, many guidelines are enacted as legislation. The location of airports, for example, is subject to numerous environmental regulations. Brewer and Alter (1988) and Chapin and Kaiser (1979), among others, have a good review of the national, state, and local legislation that governs land use in general.

D. Social Factors

Dominance, gradient, and segregation, centralization and decentralization, and invasion and succession are social factors that determine location. Humans tend to congregate into communities. On the other hand, they tend to segregate themselves for certain other reasons, which results in the reservation of certain land accessible only by selected groups. Thus there are segregated regions reserved for colonial citizens in a newly discovered land to the exclusion of natives of the land. Certain public facilities are segregated between women and men for privacy reasons. Between the phenomenon of togetherness and separation, all the shades exist in between. This explains to some extent the myriad of development patterns that we see through recorded history. These social and behavioral factors vary depending on the values of the time and the context of the culture. They are somewhat difficult to quantify in a set of systematic procedures.

III. THE ROLE OF ANALYSIS

Some explanations of the perplexing issues raised can be found by the judicious employment of analysis techniques. Obviously, analysis of the problems posed above requires a set of very specialized skills. The techniques required of the analyst include **descriptive** and **prescriptive tools**. Descriptive tools are the techniques that echo location regularities that we observe around us. They are the representation of observed patterns by way of such methodologies as simulation and statistics, or more causal explanations such as regional economics. Through the use of computers, one can build a mathematical replica of the scenario and use it to test out alternative policies—much like architects will build a scale model of a building for study in a studio. Graphic display of information, afforded by today's geographic information systems, greatly facilitates such analysis (Thrall, McClanahan, and Elshaw-Thrall 1995).

Prescriptive tools, on the other hand, try to identify a course of action for decision makers. For example, to achieve the community goals and objectives, one specifies a set of policies and plans by means of goal-directed methodologies. A mathematical model can be formulated, from which one obtains a blueprint for future development. As with descriptive models, computers are often utilized to operationalize optimization models of various sorts, including those that take into account multiple criteria, echoing a pluralistic decision-making environment typical of location decisions. Advances in computational techniques have made it practical to identify desired courses of action or facility locations, which was impossible only ten years ago. While part of the advances have been due to the computational machinery, our understanding of prescriptive techniques has also made dramatic gains in the past decades.

Analysis can reveal counter-intuitive results that can easily be overlooked if such a set of rigorous thoughts are not carried out. This pertains obviously to complex situations where there are just too many factors to consider for the unaided mind to comprehend. What is more interesting is that they may arise in rather simple situations as well. We will demonstrate a couple of these below, which hopefully make a strong case for the analysis procedures advanced in this text.

A. Airport Example

Suppose a common airport is to be built to service New York City and New Haven, Connecticut—a distance of about 80 miles. Where is the best location considering the combined populations of the two cities—with approximately 14 million in New York and 2 million in New Haven? Notice the question asked here, being a narrowly focused one, is simply how to reduce the travel requirement for all the 16 million residents of the area—in terms of total **person-miles-of-travel (PMT).**

Most people who are asked the question responded by saying that the airport should be somewhere in between the two cities. Some even pointed out that it should be closer to New York than to New Haven, since New York is a larger city. The more technically minded calculated that it should be 10 miles outside Manhattan and 70 miles away from New Haven on the major highway that connects the two cities.

The correct answer in this case is that the airport, from a purely accessibility standpoint, should be as close to New York as possible. It is that location that will require the lowest PMT. To show this, just pick three possible locations:

—halfway between New York and New Haven, resulting in a travel requirement of $(40 \times 14 + 40 \times 2)$ or 640 million PMT.

—10 miles outside New York and 70 miles from New Haven, resulting in a PMT of $(10 \times 14 + 70 \times 2)$ or 280 million.

—located right at New York and a full length of 80 miles from New Haven, resulting in $(0 \times 10 + 80 \times 2)$ or 160 million PMT!

When presented with this result, people quickly pointed out that it is impossible to locate a new airport at New York, since there is simply no land. Others pointed out that environmentally speaking, no one will accept an airport close to New York City. But that was not the question. The question—which still appears in black and white above—simply focuses on one aspect: the total PMT!

We will come back to this in a case study later, where we will point out that those having knowledge of linear programming—a prescriptive technique—will readily recognize an extreme point—either New York or New Haven—as the site for the airport, not somewhere in between.[1] We will at that time bring in other considerations, including the environment, and show how the location may change as a result of these additional factors. In other words, we answer the question for the accessibility factor, then the environmental factor and so on—building up the complexity as we move along, rather than facing them simultaneously as in more holistic planning methodologies.

B. Manufacturing Plant Example

Another example equally illustrates the role of analysis as advocated here. Suppose a major manufacturer opens an additional plant in Home Town, with a payroll of 1000 workers. What will the future population and employment increase be in Home Town? We further know that each household in Home Town has 2.5 people on the average, of which there is only one breadwinner. For every five additional people, one more support service employee is required. In other words, there are multiplier effects on the economy, wherein one dollar of payroll generates more than its value in the local economy. The manufacturing employees will require support services such as shopping, medical, recreation, and so forth, involving new employees who also bring in their families who again require more services.

According to the parameters given above, a moment's reflection will show that the 1000 new manufacturing jobs will bring into town 2500 people, including dependents. These 2500 people will also require support services in

Table 1.1   ECONOMIC FORECAST OF HOME TOWN

Time increment	Basic employ	Basic employ pop	Support service emp	Support service pop	Total employ	Total pop
1	1000	2500	500	1250	1500	3750
2	—	—	250	625	1750	4375
3	—	—	125	312.5	1875	4687.5
4	—	—	62.5	156.25	1937.5	4843.75
5	—	—	31.25	78.13	1968.75	4921.88
6	—	—	15.63	39.06	1984.38	4960.94
7	—	—	. . .	. . .	. . .	. . .

Home Town and generate 500 secondary jobs. These secondary service jobs bring into town another 1250 population (500 × 2.5), including employees and family members. Now the total new employment in town is (1000 + 500) or 1500, and the total new population is 3750 (2500 + 1250). The process goes on as shown in Table 1.1, eventually stabilizing at about 2000 additional employees and 5000 additional people.

Figure 1.1 depicts the growth profile of Home Town in terms of population and employment. The growth profile stabilizes in time period 7. On the same figure is shown the growth profile when household size is increased from 2.5 to 5. In this case, the growth will perpetuate forever, as shown by the straight line of Figure 1.1. When the support service requirement is raised from 1 to 1.25 employees for every 5 people, totally uncontrolled growth will result, as shown again in Figure 1.1. Apparently, any slight increase beyond the watershed points of 5 people in a household and 1 service employee for every 5 people will fuel the fire of growth to a fury. On the other hand, family size a tiny bit smaller than 5 or service requirement less than 1 employee in 5 results in a stabilized growth in due course. The watershed point is an important piece of information for all who are interested in the future of Home Town. A technical term for the dividing line between growth versus stagnation is **bifurcation.** Without descriptive analysis such as the above, these bifurcation points are not obvious to simple, intuitive reasoning.

C. A Combined Example

Now, combining the above examples, if 1000 new jobs are added both to New Haven and to New York City, if the average family size is 2.5 people in New York and 5 people in New Haven, and if there is 1 service employee for every 5 people in both places, New Haven will experience unlimited growth while New York will be stagnating. It does not take long for the labor force of New York to see job opportunities in New Haven and respond to them in terms of reverse commuting. Nor does it take long for the unlimited growth in New Haven to outgrow its physical or infrastructural capacity. Given the growth in New Haven will have to

Figure 1.1   BIFURCATION IN POPULATION GROWTH

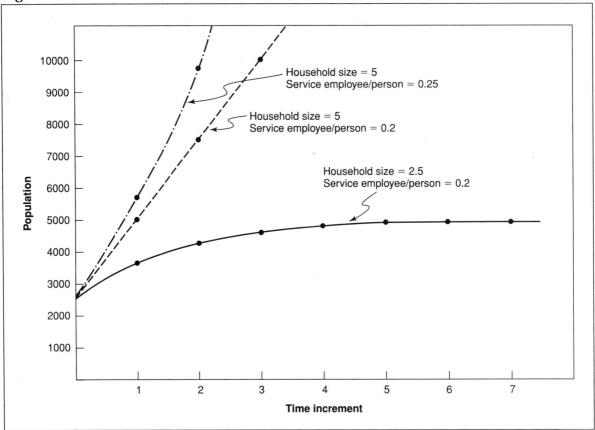

go somewhere, this will possibly mean the spread of wealth back to New York. Figure 1.2 represents this interaction between the cities schematically. The time increment is on the vertical axis and the spatial interaction is on the horizontal axis. Different growth profiles, combined with the physical limitation to unlimited growth, result in an interesting development pattern between the two cities.

With a changing demographic profile, the location of a regional airport will have to be reconsidered. We have already demonstrated that from purely an accessibility standpoint, the airport should be located at the more populated of the two cities. Now with New Haven enjoying unlimited growth while New York is stabilizing at 14,005,000, it is only a matter of time before New Haven will surpass New York in terms of population (assuming the physical limitation to growth has yet to be reached). The regional airport will eventually be located at New Haven instead of New York. The interesting, somewhat counter-intuitive, fact is that the best location for the airport will switch abruptly the minute New Haven has one person more than New York—no sooner and no later. The moment that the New Haven population exceeds New York's is a bifurcation point, at which precipitous changes occur in the fundamental behavior of the system.

Figure 1.2   ECONOMIC INTERACTION BETWEEN NEW YORK AND NEW
HAVEN OVER TIME

	NEW YORK			**NEW HAVEN**	
Time increment	**Pop increase**	**Emp increase**		**Pop increase**	**Emp increase**
0	2500	1000		2500	1000
1	3750	1500		5000	2000
2	4375	1750	Reverse commuting? ------→	7500	3000
3	4687.5	1875	Reverse commuting? ------→	10000	4000
4	4843.75	1937.5	Reverse commuting? ------→	12500	5000
5	4921.88	1968.75	←------ Population migration?	15000	6000
⋮	⋮	⋮		⋮	⋮

IV. ANALYTICAL TECHNIQUES

These examples drive home the point that analysis is an indispensable supplement to intuition in capital-intensive location decisions. These examples are merely abstractions of case studies that will be presented in detail in later chapters and in Chan (2000), where the highly simplified situations used above are protracted into the multicriteria and pluralistic decision-making process (Massam 1988) common in location debates. Suffice to say here that sophisticated analytical techniques have been developed in recent decades to perform these studies. These techniques are based—by and large—on operations research, statistics, economic analysis, and systems science. The contribution of this book is not just the collection of these techniques, but more importantly the extension of them into the spatial context. Thus the well-known extremal point optimality of linear programming (LP) is now extended from the Euclidean space of LP into the physical map of the Northeast, including the metropolis of New York and New Haven. It will be seen that when a triangle of three cities—say New York, New Haven, and Newark, New Jersey are involved, the complexity of locating a regional airport compounds many fold, resulting in the classic brain teaser: the Steiner-Weber problem. The airport can now be located—again based on proximity—at any of the three cities or in the interior point of the triangle, as will be discussed in Chapter 4. Anyone who has worked with this problem can testify to the fact that the Steiner-Weber problem is not simply an extension of LP—it goes well beyond.

The same can be argued about the Home Town development example. As seen above, the simple aspatial statement of the problem can quickly get complicated as we extend to two cities interacting with one another: say between New York and New Haven. It will be shown in sequel that the underlying theory is **input-output analysis,** a branch of knowledge economists since Leontief have developed to explain trade between such economic sectors as manufacturing, service, and housing. Including the spatial element into input-output analysis, however, compounds the model significantly, raising a whole host of conceptual and model calibration problems as evidenced in the well-publicized Lowry-Garin derivative models. When fully developed, several important factors have to be reckoned with here, including spatial competition such as in an oligopoly market consisting of several well-defined competitors, and hence supply-side investment strategies to stimulate subareal and areal economic growth. Intimately related is the fundamental assumption about factor substitution—for example, to what extent can labor be traded off against capital in the spatial production process. In other words, can labor savings be effected by better equipment and production facilities at certain sites? Simply put, the Lowry-Garin derivative models are more than just a straightforward extension of aspatial input-output analysis.

Given the complexity of including a spatial dimension, is there a fundamental basic building block of spatial interaction: the foundation that enables spatial generalization of most analysis techniques? Yes, there is, in fact, a simple spatial law, credited to Tobler (1965) which states that "Everything is related to everything else, but closer things are more related than distant things." The power lies in the beguiling simplicity of the statement, which finds its way into pervasive applications in facility location, land use, image processing, and remote sensing. It turns out that geographers, transportation planners, electro-optics researchers, and statisticians have all worried about this phenomenon for decades, if not centuries. At the core is the concept of a neighbor, which is intimately tied to the definition of proximity or **spatial separation.** Spatial separation in this case goes well beyond just the Euclidean metric or bee-line distance. It is best thought of as a price system that organizes location decisions, much as the familiar monetary price that allocates scarce resources in microeconomics; a higher price discourages consumption while a lower price stimulates consumption. Alternatively, **proximity** is the metric that establishes correlation among entities in space, such as pixels in an image. Thus accessibility in urban commuting takes on a very different light than proximity between two pixels (picture elements) in a satellite image. Yet in some ways, the fundamental principles governing both are remarkably similar in concept, namely Tobler's first law as outlined above. Furthermore, both the urban planner and the remote sensing analyst have the common goal of monitoring land use. The **gravity model,** which relates spatial interaction as a direct function of activity levels and inverse function of spatial separation, is one of the popular implementations of Tobler's law. Thus more traffic is found between high-density residential and employment centers that are close together than in lower density ones that are further apart. Likewise, satellites that monitor pollution will observe pollutants dissipating in inverse-square relationship to the point source. Calibration of the gravity model, however, is by no means simple, often necessitating a fundamental re-examination of an entire array of basic statistical principles (Sen and Smith 1995). By now, the reader should have a taste of the complexity of spatial science.

V. *CONCLUDING REMARKS*

While making facility location and land use decisions is truly an art, there appears to be an information base that can or should explain, perhaps one factor at a time, these decisions. Factors range from technological and political to economic and social. Our purpose in this book is to trace the effects of these factors, not necessarily in a holistic manner, but rather by trying to identify the consequence of each decision. Prescriptive and descriptive methodologies play a role in clarifying these decisions. For example, some of the phenomena are counter-intuitive, and an analytical framework will extend our intuition a long way toward seeing details that are not apparent to the unaided mind. The examples of airport location and the corridor development between New York and New Haven should drive this home.

Today's headlines are filled with competition for industries to locate in a certain locale, state, or nation, perhaps for both economic and political gains. In fact, facility location decisions have faced humankind throughout history. A familiar example can be found in the development of the steel industry in the United States. While iron ore was found in the convenient open pits of the Mesabi Range in Minnesota, coal was plentiful in Pennsylvania. Considering the amount of coal required, it constituted the more expensive of the two commodities to transport. Thus, we saw the historical development of steel mills in Pittsburgh, Pennsylvania; while iron ore was shipped through Duluth, Minnesota, coal was collected at Pittsburgh via the Monongahela River. Perhaps this is another example of the LP application in airport location, where the facility is located at either one of the extreme points, rather than somewhere in between.

In today's economy, where globalization and technological innovation become dominant factors, it is critical to ask how location conditions vis-a-vis structure and strategies of the firm play a part in the competitive market. When the innovation process is explained in terms of product cycle and diffusion, relevant location factors are stressed and a hierarchical pattern of innovation in space is arrived at. On the other hand, evolutionary and network theories point to the relevance of historically evolved firm structures and strategies. Empirical evidence seems to accommodate both schools of thought (Todtling 1992). In some firms, there appeared to be a pronounced differentiation of innovation across space, such as concentration of research and development and product innovation in the largest agglomerations. However, strong innovation activities, corresponding more with the evolutionary model, were in addition identified in old industrial areas and newly industrialized rural areas. It is required, more than ever, to discern the relevant factor that plays the pivoting role under these mixed development patterns, particularly when location decision becomes paramount.

Facility location and land use decisions are highly capital-intensive and highly valued. In an emergency situation, a location decision often makes the difference between security and danger. Nowhere is it more apparent than the ongoing debate on hazardous facility location, where a fine line exists between perception and reality. Recent advances in multicriteria decision-making techniques can shed some light in the debate between the proponents of and the opposition to such facilities. In short, location decisions have long-term effects on the regional and interregional economy and profound implications on the quality of life. Modern analysis techniques can shed light on the matter and can have significant rewards in more informed choices.

ENDNOTE

[1] An introduction to linear programming is contained in Chapter 4 and also in Appendix 1.

REFERENCES

American Society of Civil Engineers (1986). *Urban Planning Guide*. New York: ASCE.

Antoine, J.; Fischer, G.; Makowski, M. (1997). "Multiple criteria and land use analysis." *Applied Mathematics and Computation* 83:195–215.

Brewer, W. E.; Alter, C. P. (1988). *The complete manual of land planning and development*. Englewood Cliffs, N.J.: Prentice Hall.

Chan, Y. (2000). *Location, transport and land use: Modelling spatial-temporal information*. New York: Springer-Verlag.

Chapin, F. S.; Kaiser, E. J. (1979). *Urban land use planning*, 3rd ed. Urbana, Ill.: University of Illinois Press.

Davis, K. P. (1976). *Land use*. New York: McGraw-Hill.

Gould, J.; Golob, J. F. "Will electronic home shopping reduce travel?" *Access* (University of California Berkeley), no. 12 (spring):26–31.

Love, R. F.; Morris, J. G.; Wesolowsky, G. O. (1988). *Facilities location: Models and methods*. New York: North-Holland.

Massam, B. H. (1988). "Multi-criteria decision making (MCDM) techniques in planning." Vol. 30, Part I of *Progress in planning*, edited by D. Diamond and J. B. McLoughlin. Oxford, England and New York: Pergamon Press.

Sen, A. K.; Smith, T. E. (1995). *Gravity models of spatial interaction behavior*. Berlin and New York: Springer-Verlag.

Thrall, G. I.; McClanahan, M.; Elshaw-Thrall, S. (1995). "Ninety years of urban growth as described with GIS: A historic geography." *Geo Info Systems* (April):20–45.

Tobler, W. R. (1965). "Computation of the correspondence of geographical patterns." *Papers and Proceedings of the Regional Science Association* 15:131–139.

Todtling, F. (1992). "Technological change at the regional level: The role of location, firm structure, and strategy." *Environment and Planning A* 24:1565–1584.

Yun, D-S; Kelly, M. E. (1997). "Modeling the day-of-the-week shopping activity and travel patterns." *Socio-Economic Planning Sciences* 31, no. 4:307–309.

2

Economic Methods of Analysis

"Two and two the mathematician continues to make four, in spite of the whine of the amateur for three, or the cry of the critic for five."
James McNeill Whistler

Most of the underlying theories of facility location and land use models are basically economic concepts, and many of their input/output variables are economic measures. To understand these relationships better, a general knowledge of economic concepts and methodology is helpful. We recognize that theories have been offered by economists to explain the growth and distribution of industrial activities in an area. It is insightful to summarize their experiences—particularly the theories used in regional and interregional economics. This includes such concepts as economic-base theory (or export service theory) of gravitational interaction and theory of interregional flow. Through such a review, one sharpens the focus on the validity and limitations of these analysis methodologies.

We will also outline the basic techniques for evaluating the impact of a proposed policy on transportation systems, utility systems, and zoning codes. When an evaluation measure is often phrased in terms such as cost, benefit, equity, and efficiency, a clear understanding of these terms is necessary. Conversely, when indicators such as opportunity and quality of life are output from the model, they are much more meaningful if one can relate them to the economic theories of cost/benefit and equity/efficiency. Such an understanding would help the inquiring mind to understand the assumptions based upon which the measures are derived. Finally, for the model builder, the review of economic methods would help them configure better models and submodels.

I. ECONOMIC CONSTRUCTS FOR ACTIVITY ALLOCATION AND FORECASTING

Econometricians have been forecasting economic activities such as population and employment for a long time. Two types of forecasting methodologies can be broadly classified—forecasting on the basis of **cross-sectional data** versus that based on **time-series data.** Using cross-sectional data, models are calibrated on the current spatial distribution of activities, thus examining a "snapshot" of the population/employment distribution on the map. A time-series approach, on the other hand, would utilize not only the current pattern, but also previous patterns, which allows an observation over two or more time periods. The former is a static way of forecasting, while the latter is more dynamic. In other words, the former assumes the general activity distribution pattern will prevail over time, whereas the latter recognizes explicitly that changes over time are an integral part of the development. Aside from their important role in the development literature, the three economic concepts—economic-base theory, location theory, and input-output models—are selected for further discussion because the first two illustrate cross-sectional forecasting methodology, while the last one illustrates time-series forecasting.

A. Economic-Base Theory

The term **economic base** has many different usages and meanings so that it is necessary to clarify the definition for use here. In general, the term economic base has been applied to activities thought of as being major, fundamental, or of considerable importance in the economic structure of an area. The economic base of a community consists of those economic activities that are vital to the continued functioning and existence of that community. An economic-base study is an attempt to determine those economic activities devoted to the export of goods and services beyond the study area's borders. This activity is thought of as being the primary reason for the earning ability and economic growth of the community. Because these basic industries sell their products and services outside of the area, nonbasic or service industries can be supported within the community's boundaries. For example, barbers, dry cleaners, shoe repairers, grocery clerks, bakers, and movie operators serve others in the area who are engaged in the principal activities of the community, which may be mining, manufacturing, trade, or some other industry. These service industries have as their main function the provision of goods and services for persons living in the community.

This distinction of basic and nonbasic sectors of economic activity in an area is illustrated in Figure 2.1. Note that the income of the nonbasic sector is dependent upon the income of the basic sector so that it seems that the service industries only exist to serve basic workers and other service workers. Hence, fluctuations in income or employment in the basic sector will ultimately affect income and employment in the nonbasic sector. Since the nonbasic sector activities depend upon the basic sector, changes in the basic sector will have a net effect on the entire study area economy when some multiplier is applied to the economic-base method of analysis. The economic-base multiplier attempts to predict the change that will occur in the study area economy given a forecast of changes in certain basic activities. A significant part of the analysis involves the construction of these impact multipliers. They are numerical constants intended to impose the effects of changes in the demand for an area's goods and services upon the volume of employment or income in that region. For example, a government contract for a defense item increases employment in a firm by 2000 jobs. Indirectly both contract and job increases might generate still more work opportunities and produce a total increase in local employment two or more times a multiple of the original 2000.

Figure 2.1   CONCEPT OF BASIC VERSUS NONBASIC ACTIVITIES

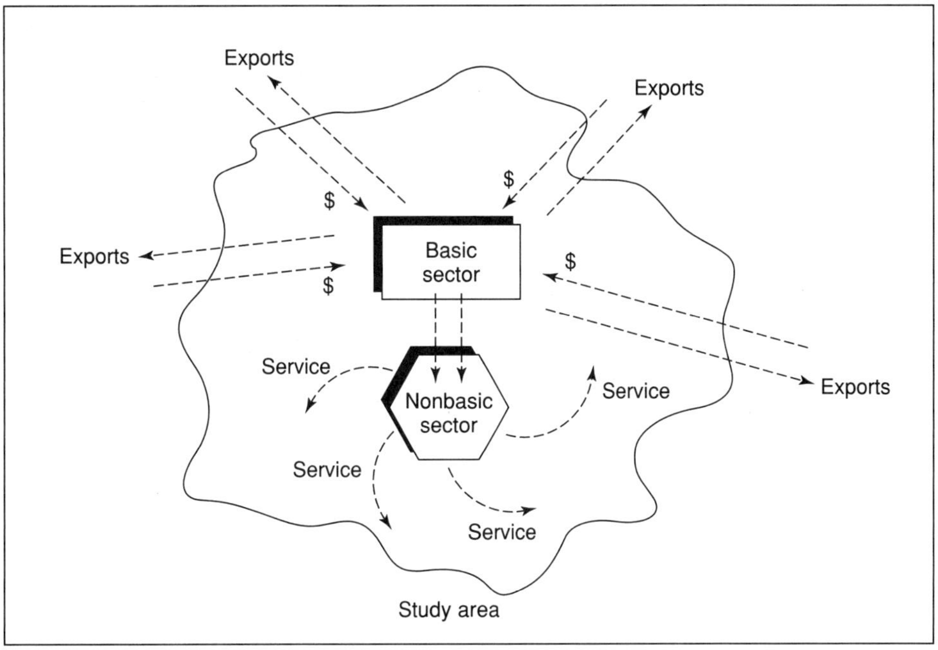

SOURCE: Adapted from Newman (1972). Reprinted with permission.

Example
Using employment as the unit of measure, classify the employment of all industries in the study area as basic or nonbasic. Establish the Normal Ratio, that relationship between basic and nonbasic employment that usually exists:

$$\text{Normal Ratio} = \frac{\text{Nonbasic Employment}}{\text{Basic Employment}} \quad \text{(Assume a 2:1 normal ratio, for example.)}$$

Total Employment = Nonbasic Employment + Basic Employment assuming the total study area employment to be 90,000. Then nonbasic employment is now 60,000 and basic employment is 30,000.

$$\text{Multiplier} = \frac{\text{Total Employment}}{\text{Basic Employment}} = \frac{60,000 + 30,000}{30,000} = 3$$

If basic employment is forecast to increase by 15,000, the total increase in nonbasic employment would be $3 \times 15,000 = 45,000$. Then the total employment for the forecast year becomes $45,000 + 90,000 = 135,000$. Since the normal ratio of 2:1 still holds, nonbasic employment is 90,000 and basic employment is 45,000. ∎

Thus, economic-base theory is to describe the development of economic activities in a typical area or region. The development of economic activities in a specific area can be explained in terms of the following four stages:

Step 1: Calculate the total population and employment and the amount of constituent basic and nonbasic (service) employment;

Step 2: Estimate the proportion of basic employment to population and that of population to service employment;

Step 3: Estimate the future trend in the basic employment; and

Step 4: Calculate the total employment and total future population on the basis of the future trend in basic employment.

In other words, basic employment has to be determined exogenously, then based on the multipliers such as labor force participation rate and population-serving ratio, which are the two proportions mentioned in Step 2, future employment and population in the region are estimated. Aside from the example above, another numerical example of the economic-base concept was given in Chapter 1 in Table 1.1.

The validity of future estimates of employment (or any other variables) depends upon the relative stability of the nonbasic-to-basic ratio developed. However, the economic-base method still has many problems to be solved. Some of these are:

1. Determining which activities are basic and nonbasic;
2. Choosing which units of measurement best represent the economy; and
3. Establishing the geographic area boundaries for which the base study is to be made.

In addition to these conceptual problems, other criticisms of the economic-base method have been registered. As the size of the study increases, the ratio of nonbasic to basic employees increases with a resultant increase in the multiplier. As a consequence, large areas have very large multipliers which do not truly reflect total economic change due to changes in the basic sector. It becomes apparent that the economic-base multiplier method is most applicable to relatively small areas and towns. Some critics challenge the premise that basic activities are more important than service activities because of the important contributions of such factors as the transportation system, communications network, and other systems serving the community. This criticism is important because planners use the basic-nonbasic distinction to emphasize which industries should be built up to improve the community's economy and to improve the balance of payments. Industries that produce goods which are presently imported would be neglected under this premise. More technical treatment of the subject will be found in Chapter 3.

B. Location Theory

Location theory, a study of the effects of space on the organization of economic activities, is a body of knowledge about the location of different activities or the rationing of different resources so as to achieve desirable spatial interaction. It has its genesis from early studies of the relative locations of plants and industry, in which the availability of raw material and the accessibility to consumer markets are of primary importance. According to the spatial price theory, transportation cost is the price for rationing resources and economic activities. For example, manufacturing plants and industries find the most convenient locations at close proximity to the input resources (both labor and raw materials) or consumer markets in order to minimize transportation costs. Another good example is a family's choice of housing location, in which a tradeoff is made between the transportation costs and other expenditures and values. If a heavy weight is placed on freedom from the noise and rush of the central city, the family locate at a distance away from the city and pay the transportation cost. In their decision, the utility of a serene environment is much higher than the utility of being close to jobs and other urban amenities.

One of the familiar location models is the **gravity model,** which states that the interaction between two subareas is proportional to their activity levels, but inversely related to their spatial separation. **Reilly's law of gravitational attraction,** for example, is based on the concept of spatial interaction. One of the first retail models was constructed out of this theory. This model uses the number of business activities, people, store sales, area, and so forth as an index of size and the fundamental measure of attractiveness of a central place. Consider a household located at I' choosing between the shopping centers at A and B as shown in Figure 2.2, or the reverse situation where a shopping center I' is to be located to serve the population at A and B. In general, the markets captured from A and B are in the ratio

$$\frac{T_A'}{T_B'} = \frac{W_A}{W_B}\left(\frac{d_B}{d_A}\right)^2 \tag{2.1}$$

where W_A and W_B are the sizes of A and B, where T_A', T_B' represent proportions of trade (percentage of sales for example) from I to A and B respectively, and d_B, d_A is the distance from B and A respectively.

From Equation 2.1 attractiveness of A and B with respect to point I', when A and B are of equal size ($W_A = W_B$), can be represented as $T_A' d_A^2 = T_B' d_B^2$. Notice the appeal of A and B is a function of both distance away and sales volume. To locate a shopping center at I' equally appealing to both the population centers A and B, or to say it the other way, to find the point I' where a shopper is indifferent between shopping centers A and B, we set $T_A' = T_B'$ in Equation 2.1 and solve for d_B. An equation can be derived that states the watershed trade area bounded between A and B, measured in miles (km) from B, is

$$d_B = \frac{d_{AB}}{1 + (W_A/W_B)^{1/2}} \tag{2.2}$$

Figure 2.2   BREAK POINT MODEL

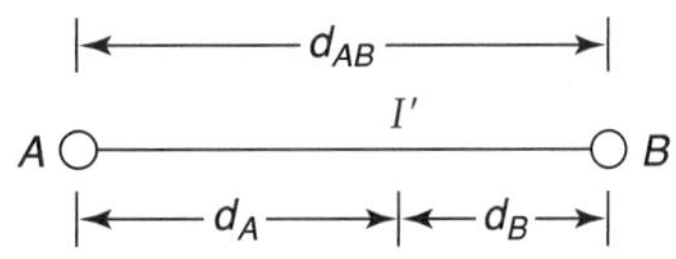

Example

Let $d_{AB} = 36$ miles (57.6 km); $W_A = 92$ retail activities, $W_B = 90$ retail activities; then $d_B = 17.8$ miles (28.5 km) from location B according to Equation 2.2. ∎

The Reilly model may be an acceptable approximation for such location decisions in rural areas where central places are rather distinguishable. In a more developed area, however, a large number of shopping centers and population centers are involved. The overlapping market areas will be too complex to be resolved by this idealized model. Another formulation of the gravity model was proposed by Lakshmanan and Hansen (1965). This model allocates retail dollars, determining the percentage of the population in subarea i that will go to the shopping center j to spend their money:

$$(expenditure)_{ij} = (expenditure)_i \frac{Wj/\tau_{ij}^{\beta}}{\Sigma_k W_k/\tau_{ik}^{\beta}}$$

where τ is the travel time and β is the positive exponent to be calibrated. This states that the total consumer retail expenditure of population in subarea i is allocated toward each shopping center j in accordance with the gravity formula. Notice travel distance d is replaced by time τ in this formulation. We will see more of this interchangeability between time and distance in subsequent discussions throughout this book. **Huff's probabilistic model** (1962) is yet another example of the gravity model, stating that the probability a consumer located at i will visit shopping center j is

$$\frac{Wj/\tau_{ij}^{\beta}}{\Sigma_k W_k/\tau_{ik}^{\beta}} \qquad (2.3)$$

Example

Suppose there are two shopping malls 5 and 10 miles (8 and 16 km) away respectively, each with 800 and 300 thousand square feet (72 and 27 thousand m²) retail floor space. According to Huff's model, the probabilities a consumer will patronize these two malls are respectively

$$\frac{(800)(1/5^2)}{(800)(1/5^2) + (300)(1/10^2)} = 0.08$$
$$\frac{(300)(1/10^2)}{(800)(1/5^2) + (300)(1/10^2)} = 0.92 \qquad (2.4)$$

assuming an exponent $\beta = 2$ (Dickey 1983). ∎

Variants of location theory are found in literature on multicommodity flow as well as short-run and long-run equilibria of economic activities. **Multicommodity-flow models** describe the simultaneous allocation of population, employment, resources and finished products between places of supply and demand. In the short run, most economic activities, including the places of supply and demand, are fixed in location. In the long run, however, they could relocate themselves somewhere else corresponding to the rationing scheme of the spatial price system. Short- and long-run multicommodity flows are often modeled by a generalized version of the gravity model and optimization models—subjects covered in Chapter 4.

C. Input-Output Models

Input-output models, developed by Leontief (1953), will be introduced with respect to two particular applications: local-impact studies and interregional-flow studies. As an example, local-impact studies reveal the possible changes in a single region. Interregional-flow studies, on the other hand, are to show the structural relationship between regions. The effect of an autonomous shock—such as the precipitous injection of basic employment into the study area as mentioned in economic-base theory—may be traced to, and through, the region under consideration. An essential part of an input-output model is an input-output table, which documents a set of economic multipliers similar to those found in economic-base theory. The input-output table (matrix) eventually gives rise to a set of simultaneous equations with production (or technical) coefficients (the multipliers) and activity variables. The set of equations can trace out, on a multi-sectoral basis, the implication of introducing a new industry into the study area (the autonomous shock). For example, if a new tourist trade is introduced into the area as a way to boost the local economy, what would be the implications on the economic activities associated with tourism such as the associated retail and entertainment industries? The set of simultaneous equations merely chain-up the sequence of effects together in a mathematical formulation through the use of a table or matrix where the rows are inputs (e.g., tourists) and the columns are outputs (e.g., retail sales). It can be thought of as a huge revenue/expenditure accounting system. The revenue side of the balance sheet shows how the output for each industry is distributed, and the expenditure side records for each industry the distribution-of-inputs per unit-of-output from all industries.

An example of such an input-output matrix is shown in Table 2.1 (Chapin and Kaiser 1979). Shown for a single region, the table records horizontally the output for each particular sector of the economy measured in terms of receipts from sales to every other sector. Thus sector 1 may be the tourist industry, sector 2 may be retail, sector 3 entertainment, and sector 4 households. Households receive

Table 2.1   EXAMPLE INPUT-OUTPUT TABLE

	Tourism sector	Retail sector	Entertainment sector	Household sector	Final demand
Tourism sector	$30	$20	$30	$25	$105
Retail sector	60	20	80	30	190
Entertainment sector	10	40	60	50	160
Household sector	40	20	30	15	105
Charges against final demand	140	100	200	120	560

SOURCE: Chapin and Kaiser (1979). Reprinted with permission.

25 million dollars during the current time period in wages as employees serving the tourist industry, the entertainment sector receives 30 million dollars from tourism, retail receives 20 million dollars, and the tourism sector spends 30 million on itself. Read vertically, the table shows input in terms of dollars spent on purchases in a particular sector from all other sectors. Thus local households as a whole spend 40 million dollars this time period on tourism, the entertainment industry spends 10 million dollars on the tourism industry as part of the intersectoral trade, and the retail industry spends 60 million dollars.

The final demand column records purchases by the tourism, retail, entertainment, and household sector—the dollar transactions after all intermediate processing and handling are completed. For example, tourists inject a total of 105 million dollars (first row sum) into the economy during this time period, divided among retail purchases, entertainment, and direct use of local labor. The charges against final demand in the bottom row are payments for tourism, retail trade, entertainment trade, and labor. Thus the fourth column (120 million) is the total wages paid to the household for supplying the labor for the remaining three sectors of the local economy, including the tourist industry, the third column is the total payment to the entertainment industry from other sectors and so on. These column totals are defined as the activity variables. To the extent that the row sums are not the same as column sums (or total purchases are not equal to payments) in Table 2.1, the final equilibrium values of these activities, taking the multiplier effects into account, are to be determined by the solution of a set of simultaneous equations.

From the dollar transactions in Table 2.1, production (or technical) coefficients are derived by dividing each input in a give column by the total of all inputs in the column. The resulting coefficients, shown in Table 2.2, are read by columns and indicate the cents-of-direct-inputs per dollar-of-output. Column 1 shows the input per dollar-value-of-output from each of all the other sectors supplying goods or services to sector 1. Thus the households contribute 29 cents toward the dollar on tourism, the entertainment sector contributes 7 cents, retail contributes 43 cents, and tourism pays itself 21 cents. The other columns show similar relationships for the retail, entertainment, and household sectors. The input-output technique, therefore, establishes a basic relationship between the volume output of any given industry in a region and the volume of input required in the production process from all other industries in this region. In this regard, the coefficients are equivalent to the labor force participation rate and population-serving ratio used in economic-base theory, except that the multipliers here are constructed out of dollar volumes rather than in terms of people. To the extent that intersectoral trade is governed by these multi-

Table 2.2   PRODUCTION (TECHNICAL) COEFFICIENTS FOR A SINGLE REGION

	Tourism sector	Retail sector	Entertainment sector	Household sector
Tourism sector	0.21	0.20	0.15	0.21
Retail sector	0.43	0.20	0.40	0.25
Entertainment sector	0.07	0.40	0.30	0.42
Household sector	0.29	0.20	0.15	0.12

pliers aside from the seed activity (or autonomous shock), the projection of the local economy, to be manifested in the final values of the activity variables, can only be determined following the four steps of economic-base theory, or alternatively solving the equivalent simultaneous equation set.

In the book, Chan (2000), more discussions of this Table can be found in the chapter on "Spatial Equilibrium and Disequilibrium."

II. ECONOMETRIC MODELING: INTERREGIONAL DEMOGRAPHIC PROJECTIONS

At the root of economic growth is population growth, for industrial wealth is nothing but a manifestation of human resources. An integral part of spatial economics is therefore the projection of population in a regional and interregional context. The demographic model is discussed here as a companion analysis to economic-base theory and input-output analysis. It also serves to illustrate economic theories, which are supplemental to classic economic theory in regional science. Three of the basic issues involved in demographic analyses are fertility, mortality, and migration. Fertility is the rate of childbirth in society. Mortality refers to the death rate in society. Migration is the population movement from one geographic location to another. Demographic analysis takes the net effect of fertility, mortality, and migration and predicts the growth or decline of population in the study area. The methods of analyzing demographic activities consist of population projection models, and matrix analyses of regional and interregional growth and distribution (Jha 1972). Population projection models are aggregate methods of extrapolating regional population growth from present trends using statistical techniques. The matrix analysis of population growth, on the other hand, is a more systemized method of projecting population growth, being more explanatory about the determinants of demographic activities.

A. Population Projection Models

Two of the key concepts used in the population projection models are comparative forecasting and extrapolation. **Comparative forecasting** is a very crude method and could be rather unreliable if performed carelessly. This forecasting method is performed by selecting two areas, A and B, which have behaved similarly in their demographic growth patterns. It is assumed that the two areas should develop similarly in the future, meaning that if A's population increases at a certain rate, B's population would increase at about the same rate. Notice that A can be a part of B geographically. Parallel attempts are made to establish population and employment growth rate for similar cities. (See the "Econometric Models" chapter in Chan [2000]).

Example
As shown in Figure 2.3, if the population growth of two areas A and B are similar in the past from t to t + 3, and if the population of A is known for the rest of the years from time period t + 4 to t + 5, we can have an idea of the population projection for area B for the corresponding years. In this method, we assume that the

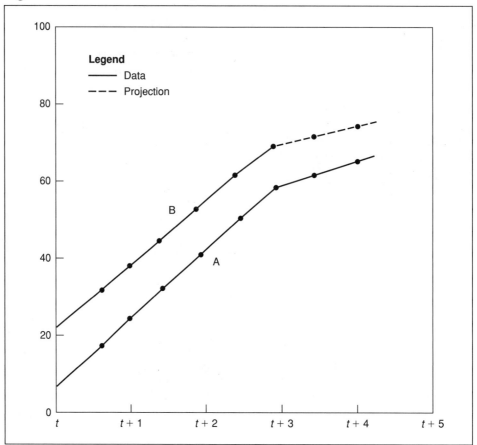

Figure 2.3   POPULATION PROJECTION BY COMPARATIVE FORECASTING

demographics of one area follow the same profile as the other. This will be true even if there is a sharp decline in growth rate occurring around time period $t + 3$. ∎

Extrapolation, on the other hand, uses statistical techniques to predict future population growth based on the trend in the same area in the past. This is the basic premise of almost all econometric models, in which the implicit assumption is that past trends prevail. It represents both the strength as well as the weakness of this type of model. It is a strength since the forecasting methodology is flexible and relatively easy to use. It is a weakness inasmuch as the underlying behavior of the study area is ignored, in preference for purely statistical correlations. The common techniques employed in comparative and extrapolation models are graphical, polynomial curves, ratio and correlation method, regression and covariance method, and inflow-outflow analysis.

1. Graphical Method. The graphical or manual technique consists of plotting points on a graph to show population growth predictions. In this method, past census data is used for plotting the graph of population versus time. Future population is obtained by extending the graph in the same way as the trend in the past. Thus in Figure 2.4, the population at $t + 5$ and $t + 6$ have been obtained by

Figure 2.4   GRAPHICAL PROJECTION OF POPULATION AT REGION C

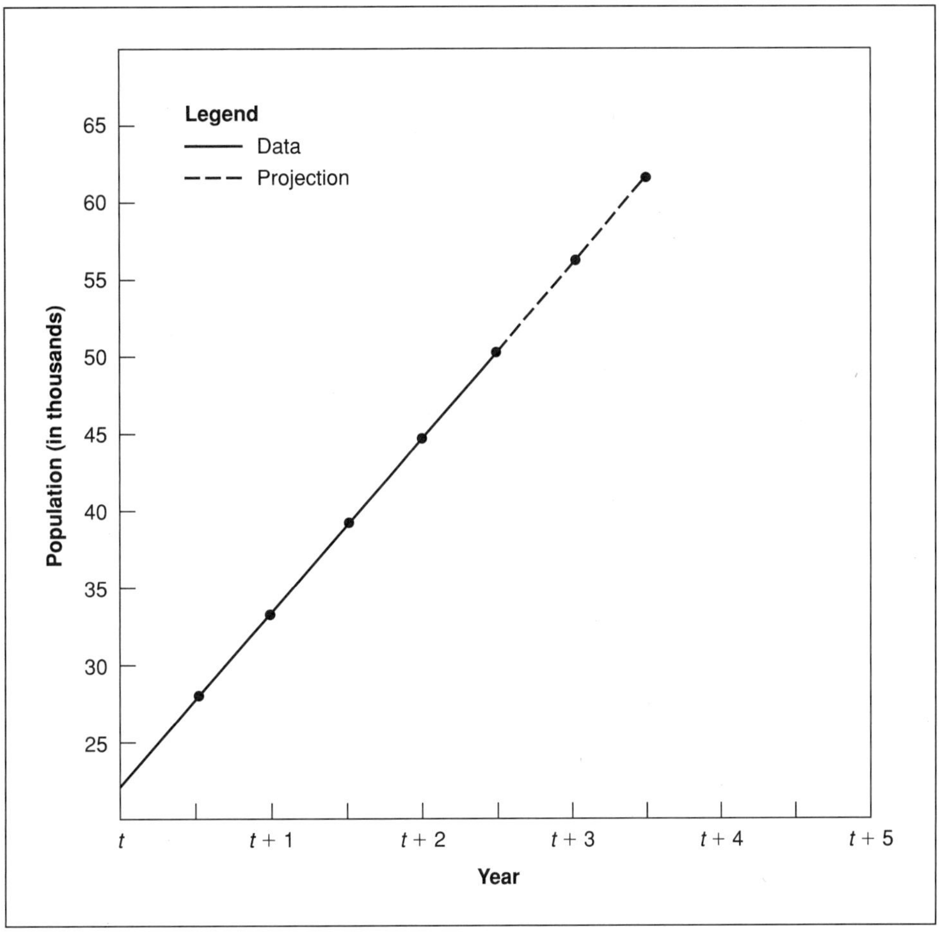

extending the graph. Simple as it may look, graphic plots of data are an essential, indispensable first step in any econometric application. They allow the modeler to get a feel of the data and more importantly to formulate a hypothesis about the structural form of the model. Pairwise plots such as those shown in Figure 2.4 are options in almost all statistical analysis software. Actual projection may not be actually performed manually, but the trend indicated by the plot is a most important piece of information for the modeler.

2. Polynomial Method. The polynomial-curve technique is a generalization of the above concept. It is built upon the following linearized formula for each forecast increment Δt: $N(t + \Delta t) + \delta N(t)\,\Delta t$, where $N(t)$ is the base-year population, Δt is the forecast period (whether it be one year, five years or ten years.), and $\delta N(t)$ is the population increase per time period Δt.

Example

If for an area, the total population in base-year t is 4500 thousand and the annual increment has been 27 thousand, then the population in $t + 10$ will be equal to $4500 + (27)(10) = 4770$ thousand. ∎

Polynomial curves are usually quite a bit more complex than the example shown above. For each time period, Δt, there exists a formal mathematical equation with a different increment as determined by the function $f(\Delta t)$: $N(t + \Delta t) = N(t) + f(\Delta t)$. Oftentimes, polynomial projections put more weight on present trends than past trends. One such weighting scheme is the **exponential smoothing technique** where the weight decays exponentially over the length of the elapsed time period, thus placing more value upon recent information. We will defer the details until the "Spatial Time-Series" chapter in Chan (2000), where formal projection methodologies will be discussed.

3. Ratio-and-Correlation Method. It might be possible that the population growth of the study area is related to the population growth of another area, or the region within which the area is located; or the population may be related to some socioeconomic factor such as employment of another area or the region. In this case, we use the ratio or coefficient of the relationship between the two areas for predicting future population, as shown in the following example.

Example
If the ratio of population at area A and any other socioeconomic factor at area B (including population) has been constant in the past years, then we can get the future area A population using this constant. Let $Z_B(t)$ represent the population or any other activity variable of area B at base year t, and suppose the ratio $N_A(t)/Z_B(t) = 0.8$.

If $Z_B(t + \Delta t) = 4000$ in the forecast year $t + \Delta t$,

then $$\frac{N_A(t)}{Z_B(t)} = \frac{N_A(t + \Delta t)}{4000} = 0.8$$

or $N_A(t + \Delta t) = (4000)(0.8) = 3200$ ∎

In other words, the ratio-and-correlation method uses another activity variable to predict population growth, if population growth can be correlated with an identifiable activity variable at a different area via a constant ratio. The reader can imagine that an example can easily be constructed for the interregional input-output model where the population in a region, being the support labor force for an industry, is simply related to the employment level at the work region by the labor-force-participation rate. The gist of this method is straightforward. If $N_i(t)/Z_j(t) =$ constant, then $N_i(t + \Delta t) = Z_j(t + \Delta t)$(constant). This model can be generalized to read

$$\frac{N_i(t + \Delta t)}{Z_j(t + \Delta t)} = f\left(\frac{N_i(t)}{Z_j(t)}, \frac{N_i(t - \Delta t)}{N_j(t - \Delta t)}, \ldots, \frac{N_i(t - n\Delta t)}{Z_j(t - n\Delta t)} \right) \quad (2.5)$$

where area i can also be area j ($i = j$), meaning that population and employment can be co-located in the same region. Here F($\cdot$) is a function showing how the constant can be determined by using historical information over n time periods. In the chapter on "Econometric Models" of Chan (2000), we will see how one can expand a great deal upon this very simple idea of ratio and correlation.

4. Regression and Covariance Analysis. This is one of the statistical calibration techniques widely used in population projection and for other activity variables as well. Here, population is taken as a dependent variable and another activity or factor is taken as an independent variable. Usually a simple bivariate regression may be represented like this: $N = a + bX$, where X is any explanatory or independent factor, a and b are calibration constants that may be obtained by fitting the model to the regional data. The companion covariance analysis, or analysis of variance, measures the quality of the statistical fit of the model to the data.

Example
If the population of a state is associated with the increase in per capita income X, and a and b have been calibrated to be 2,095,000 and 1,062 respectively. Further suppose that the forecast-year per capita income in the state is 15,000, then according to the regression equation above, future state population is projected to be $(2,095,000) + (1,062)(15,000) = 36,880,000$. ∎

In general, while the regression equation does not necessarily have to be linear to start out with, it is often to the following linear form before calibration can be performed: $N = a + b_1X_1 + b_2X_2 + ...$, where X_1, X_2 and so forth are independent variables. The regression coefficients b_1, b_2 and so forth are then calibrated for use in forecasting. Notice that the model assumes that the linear relationship between population and the independent variables will hold over time—very similar to the previous models, from comparative method to ratio-and-correlation method. The linearity assumption, and certain assumptions about the statistical distribution of the data, may impose restrictions on what is normally a very flexible modeling procedure. The technical aspects of regression and covariance analysis are discussed in Appendix 3 of this book.

5. Inflow-Outflow Analysis. The inflow-outflow analysis predicts the population of period $t + \Delta t$ into the future considering both the gain and loss of population in the area (termed **inflow** and **outflow** respectively.) The inflow is predicted by the equation

$$(inflow) = (birthrate)\, N(t) + (in\ migration)$$

The outflow, on the other hand, is predicted by

$$(outflow) = (death\ rate)\, N(t) + (out\ migration)$$

The population for the forecast year is predicted by combining the inflow and outflow results using the equation: $N(t + \Delta t) = N(t) + (inflow - outflow)$. In summary, this method relates population projection to population growth, natural increase and decrease (due to birth and death respectively), and in-and-out migration via the following equation

$$N(t + \Delta t) = N(t) + \delta^N(\Delta t) + \delta^M(\Delta t)$$

where $\delta^N(\Delta t)$ is the natural increase or decrease in time period Δt, and $\delta^M(\Delta t)$ is the net migration during period Δt. Substituting and rearranging the terms, one can write $N(t + \Delta t) = N(t) + [b(\Delta t)N(t) + \delta N^I(\Delta t)] + [d(\Delta t)N(t) + \delta N^o(\Delta t)]$ where $b(\Delta t)$,

$d(\Delta t)$ are the birthrates and death rates during period Δt respectively, and $\delta N^r(\Delta t)$, $\delta N^I(\Delta t)$ are the in-and-out migrations during period Δt.

Example

If an area had a population of 4,500 for time period t, and the birthrate and death rate per capita are 2 and 1 percent respectively and the in-and-out migrations are 234 and 198 respectively for the forecast time increment, then the forecast population is $4,500 + (2(4,500/100) + 234) - (4,500/100 + 198) = 4,581$. ■

B. Interregional Growth and Distribution

Matrix representation of population growth and distribution is convenient for estimating the growth patterns of multi-regional populations. Two methods will be introduced here: **cohort survival** and **components of change.** The cohort survival method is a way to determine population growth. **Cohort,** for this purpose, is defined as a group of people born within a given time period. The fundamental concept of this analysis is: $\mathbf{N}(t + \Delta t) = \mathbf{G}\,\mathbf{N}(t)$, where the population at a future period $\mathbf{N}(t + \Delta t)$ is related to the current period t via a matrix $\mathbf{G}$, the growth matrix. For analytical purposes, the population is broken down into cohort age groups. The matrix takes into account the death rates for each age group and incorporates them as survival ratio at the main diagonal of the matrix. On the other hand, the birthrates for each of the age groups are represented in the first row of the matrix. For example, the birthrate for age groups under childbearing age is zero, and similarly for those over the childbearing age. However, each group within the childbearing age would have a certain birthrate, suggesting their capacity to reproduce. The matrix determines the populations, by age group, for the forecast year based on survival and birthrates. The matrix also ages the base-year population into older groups for the forecast year. A group of residents in the five-to-ten-year age bracket, for example, would transition into the ten-to-fifteen-year bracket if the forecast is performed for a five-year increment. In summary, the following equation set incorporates all the above elements in a matrix notation.

$$
\begin{pmatrix}
N_1(t + \Delta t) \\
N_2(t + \Delta t) \\
N_3(t + \Delta t) \\
\cdot \\
\cdot \\
\cdot \\
N_n(t + \Delta t)
\end{pmatrix}
=
\begin{bmatrix}
0 & 0 & b_3 & b_4 & \cdot & \cdot & \cdot & b_{n-1} & 0 \\
s_{12} & 0 & 0 & 0 & \cdot & \cdot & \cdot & 0 & 0 \\
0 & s_{23} & 0 & 0 & \cdot & \cdot & \cdot & 0 & 0 \\
0 & 0 & s_{34} & 0 & \cdot & \cdot & \cdot & 0 & 0 \\
\cdot & \cdot & \cdot & \cdot & \cdot & \cdot & \cdot & \cdot & \cdot \\
0 & 0 & 0 & 0 & \cdot & \cdot & \cdot & s_{n-1\,n} & 0
\end{bmatrix}
\begin{pmatrix}
N_1(t) \\
N_2(t) \\
N_3(t) \\
\cdot \\
\cdot \\
\cdot \\
Nn(t)
\end{pmatrix}
\qquad (2.6)
$$

where b_i stands for the birthrate per person for group i, and s_{ij} stands for the surviving ratio of group i in group j.

Aside from birth-death considerations, the problem of interregional migration can be taken into account by using a migration matrix. This matrix is similar to that used to model the survival rates of cohort groups, except that net immigration and emigration rates are written in the main diagonal. Since the matrix is used to model interregional population movement alone, no birthrates are included. In the following matrix, where the row and column dimensions correspond to the different age groups, net interregional population migration is modeled:

$$
\begin{bmatrix}
0 & 0 & 0 & \cdot & \cdot & \cdot & 0 & 0 \\
m_{11} & 0 & 0 & \cdot & \cdot & \cdot & 0 & 0 \\
0 & m_{23} & 0 & \cdot & \cdot & \cdot & 0 & 0 \\
0 & 0 & m_{34} & \cdot & \cdot & \cdot & 0 & 0 \\
\cdot & \cdot & \cdot & \cdot & \cdot & & & \cdot \\
0 & 0 & 0 & \cdot & \cdot & \cdot & m_{a-1\,n} & 0
\end{bmatrix}
$$

The growth of a region is predicted by adding the birthrate, survival-rate, and migration-rate matrices, which produces a growth-rate matrix by age group

$$
G = \begin{bmatrix} \leftarrow \bar{b} \rightarrow \\ 0 \end{bmatrix} + \begin{bmatrix}
0 & 0 & \cdot & \cdot & 0 \\
s_{12} & 0 & \cdot & \cdot & 0 \\
0 & s_{23} & \cdot & \cdot & 0 \\
\cdot & \cdot & \cdot & \cdot & 0 \\
0 & 0 & \cdot & \cdot & 0
\end{bmatrix} + \begin{bmatrix}
0 & 0 & \cdot & \cdot & 0 \\
m_{12} & 0 & \cdot & \cdot & 0 \\
0 & m_{23} & \cdot & \cdot & 0 \\
\cdot & \cdot & \cdot & \cdot & \cdot \\
0 & 0 & \cdot & \cdot & 0
\end{bmatrix} \tag{2.7}
$$

Example
A simple numerical example would illustrate these matrices. Consider three age groups: 0- to 20-year-olds, 20- to 40-year-olds and 40- to 60-year-olds. These hypothetical matrices can be written:

$$
G = \begin{bmatrix}
0 & 1.5 & 0 \\
0 & 0 & 0 \\
0 & 0 & 0
\end{bmatrix} + \begin{bmatrix}
0 & 0 & 0 \\
0.9 & 0 & 0 \\
0 & 0.8 & 0
\end{bmatrix} + \begin{bmatrix}
0 & 0 & 0 \\
0.1 & 0 & 0 \\
0 & 0.1 & 0
\end{bmatrix} \tag{2.8}
$$

where the childbearing cohort group is defined as those 20 to 40 years old. We specify that 9 out of 10 people survive from the 0- to 20-year group to become 20- to 40-year-old adults. Ten percent more people in the 20-to 40-year-old group migrate into the area over 20 years—the length of the forecast period—and so on. Summing these matrices, we have the net growth matrix

$$
G = \begin{bmatrix}
0 & 1.5 & 0 \\
1.0 & 0 & 0 \\
0 & 0.9 & 0
\end{bmatrix}
$$

If the base-year population in all age groups is 10,000, the forecast population distribution (in thousands) would be

$$
\begin{pmatrix} N_1(t + \Delta t) \\ N_2(t + \Delta t) \\ N_3(t + \Delta t) \end{pmatrix} = \begin{bmatrix}
0 & 1.5 & 0 \\
1.0 & 0 & 0 \\
0 & 0.9 & 0
\end{bmatrix} \begin{pmatrix} 10 \\ 10 \\ 10 \end{pmatrix} = \begin{pmatrix} 15 \\ 10 \\ 9 \end{pmatrix} \tag{2.9}
$$

It is predicted, therefore, that in 20 years more young people than older people will be living in the study area. More precisely, there will be 15 thousand 0- to 20-year-olds, 10 thousand 20- to 40-year-olds, and only 9 thousand 40- to 60-year-olds. ∎

C. Interregional Components of Change Model

Predicting interregional population is basically the same as predicting regional population. The major differences are that instead of breaking down by age groups, we stratify by specific regions, such as the East versus West Coast. This basic concept is still used:

$$N(t + \Delta t) = N(t) + (births) - (deaths) + (migrants)$$

Symbolically, the components of change model may be stated in scalar terms for each region i as

$$\begin{aligned} N_i(t + \Delta t) &= N_i(t) + b_i(t)N_i(t) - d_i(t)N_i(t) + m_i(t)N_i(t) \\ &= [1 + b_i(t) - d_i(t) + m_i(t)]N_i(t) \\ &= g_i N_i(t) \end{aligned} \tag{2.10}$$

where b, d, and m are birth-, death and net migration rates. For example, the crude birth-, death and net migration rates from Table 2.3 give rise to the growth rate $g = 1 + 1.315 - 0.0473 + 0.0865 = 1.1707$. These are called crude because they are simply the births, deaths, and net migration over the period 1955–60 divided by the 1955 base-year population in California, without taking into consideration migration from/to the rest of the United States or any place else. In fact, proper estimation of these parameters is a subject of interest in real world applications. Chan (2000) elaborates on this topic in the "Bifurcation and Disaggregation" chapter. Usually, population, births, deaths, and migration are expressed in matrix forms, where the row and column dimensions correspond to the number of regions being modeled. The following model shows a two-region example in which the internal births, deaths, and interregional net migration are analyzed.

$$\begin{pmatrix} N_1(t + \Delta t) \\ N_2(t + \Delta t) \end{pmatrix} = \left\{ \begin{bmatrix} 1 & 0 \\ 0 & 1 \end{bmatrix} + \begin{bmatrix} b_1(t) & 0 \\ 0 & b_2(t) \end{bmatrix} - \begin{bmatrix} d_1(t) & 0 \\ 0 & d_2(t) \end{bmatrix} + \begin{bmatrix} 0 & m_{21}(t) \\ m_{12}(t) & 0 \end{bmatrix} \right\} \begin{pmatrix} N_1(t) \\ N_2(t) \end{pmatrix} \tag{2.11}$$

or in matrix notation $N(t + \Delta t) = (I + B - D + M)\, N(t) = G\, N(t)$.

Table 2.3   CALIFORNIA AND THE REST OF THE UNITED STATES (1955–60)

Region	1955 Pop	Birthrate	Death rate	Migration rate
Calif	12,988,000	0.1315	0.0473	0.0865 (~US to Calif)
Rest of the US (~US)	152,082,000	0.1282	0.0488	−0.0074 (Calif to ~US)

Example

From the data in Table 2.3, the growth matrix is the sum of the identity, birth, death, and migration matrices, where California is row/column 1 and the rest of the United States is row/column 2 of such matrices:

$$G = \begin{bmatrix} 1 & 0 \\ 0 & 1 \end{bmatrix} + \begin{bmatrix} 0.1315 & 0 \\ 0 & 0.1282 \end{bmatrix} - \begin{bmatrix} 0.0473 & 0 \\ 0 & 0.0488 \end{bmatrix} +$$
$$\begin{bmatrix} 0 & 0.0865 \\ -0.0074 & 0 \end{bmatrix} = \begin{bmatrix} 1.0842 & 0.0865 \\ -0.0074 & 1.0794 \end{bmatrix} \quad (2.12)$$

The 1960 population in California and the rest of the United States can then be computed as

$$\begin{pmatrix} N_1(1960) \\ N_2(1960) \end{pmatrix} = \begin{bmatrix} 1.0842 & 0.0865 \\ -0.0074 & 1.0794 \end{bmatrix} \begin{pmatrix} 12,988 \\ 152,082 \end{pmatrix} = \begin{pmatrix} 27,236 \\ 164,061 \end{pmatrix} \blacksquare \quad (2.13)$$

The discussion on interregional demographic model gives the reader a flavor of the basic algebra found in similar model structures as the interregional input-output model. It serves not only to introduce econometric modeling, but also to generalize to a multi-regional level a key projection concept introduced earlier in this chapter.

III. ECONOMIC CONSTRUCTS FOR COST-BENEFIT ESTIMATION

The previous sections have been devoted to the economic and econometric techniques of prediction where future activities, such as the local economy, are projected. In this section, we will concentrate on the methods of evaluation, in which a location or land use policy is analyzed or evaluated with respect to its cost and benefits. There are three economic concepts that are important to cost-benefit estimation: equity, efficiency, and externality. **Equity** is a very precise concept in economics since it connotes the distribution of income and social benefits. An example may be the equal accessibility of all segments of the population to such public services as school and recreation (Marsh and Schilling 1994). Equity can be achieved through the natural market forces, governmental intervention, or through public services and transfer payments. The price system may sometimes be inadequate to effect an equitable distribution of goods and services; it may then be necessary to subsidize schools in a less affluent neighborhood in order to render education opportunities for all.

Efficiency, in our context, means the least costly distribution of resources over space for the production of goods and services. An efficient urban structure, for example, is to have complementary goods and services to be clustered together, whereby transportation costs are minimized. Such a clustered development may mean the sacrifice of some open space that is sometimes highly valued. Efficiency, therefore, is not necessarily the only objective of urban planning; other factors need to be considered at the same time.

Externality, for the purpose of the current discussion, refers to the effects of a project other than those measured by the economic price system. In the provision of open space above, transportation cost does not accurately represent the price for the distribution of open space around the city, meaning that a precise, quantifiable price measure of the value of open space to an inhabitant is not easily obtainable. Economists have a well-defined concept about price theory, and they recognize that certain effects cannot be measured by price, including the positive benefits of open space and the negative benefits of air pollution. However, in a comprehensive accounting system, we may like to impute a cost to the community for the deprivation of open space, or the onset of pollution, both of which may be incurred in the industrial production process. This imputed cost is an example of an externality (Dahlman 1988).

Having been equipped with these basic concepts, we are prepared to examine two sets of methodologies for estimating costs and benefits. The first is **shift-share analysis,** which illustrates a technique to measure equity in a spatial context. The second is **theory of land values,** which is included here to verify the concept of efficiency.

A. Shift-Share Analysis

Shift-share analysis is a technique to divide the change in a socioeconomic measure into two or more components. For example, the population growth in an area is attributable to both the regional growth pattern and the peculiarity of the area itself. This technique can be used to measure the distribution of benefits: for instance, which subarea in the study area will receive less than its equitable share of regional growth and which will receive more. Rather than assuming a constant trend and a constant share of the regional economic activities, shift-share analysis tries to explain the change in the activity level in a particular subarea by two components. The first component is an average activity change corresponding to an aggregate regional change, while the second component is the difference between the average and actual changes in a subarea. This can be expressed by the following equation:

(subareal change) = (regional average change) + (competitive change)

For example, an urban area grows 10 percent over a five-year period, and two of its zones A and B grow by five percent and 12 percent respectively. Zone A is at a competitive disadvantage of five percent below while zone B is at an advantage of two percent above the regional average, even though both are influenced by the overall regional growth.

A general expression of shift-share analysis can be written for activity k in subarea i:

$$\Delta Z_i^k = \delta Z^k + \delta Z_i^k = \frac{\Delta Z^k}{Z^k(t)} Z_i^k(t) + \delta Z_i^k \tag{2.14}$$

which states that the total change of activity k in subarea i is due to subareal change of activity k at the regional rate, adjusted for site-specific change at the local level. Shift-share analysis is therefore a simple concept of splitting up the change in activity from time period t to $t + 1$ into two functional components. The first component indicates the norm for the region as a whole and the second the subareal deviation from the norm as mentioned. Notice that the competitive component is introduced to measure the change in a subarea relative to the regional average—showing the relative attractiveness of the subarea for the particular activity under consideration.

The competitive component of change in activity k for subarea i, δZ^k_i, can again be broken down into two components: the difference between subareal change and the regional overall growth in sector k.

$$\delta Z^k_i = Z^k_i(t)\left[\frac{\Delta Z^k_i}{Z^k_i(t)} - \frac{\Delta Z^k}{Z^k(t)}\right] \tag{2.15}$$

Putting it altogether, we can see that δZ^k in Equation 2.14 defines the change in importance of industrial sector k in subarea i over the time period, or the shift component. Equation 2.15, on the other hand, defines the increase or decrease in activity k due to the relative competitiveness of subarea i vis-a-vis other subareas, or the share component. This accounts for the name shift-share analysis.

Example

During the past five years, subarea i's manufacturing (M) sector grew less rapidly than did the region by 1.6 percent. Its commercial (C) sector, in contrast, had a growth rate that exceeded that of the region's by 3.8 percent. Regional manufacturing and commercial growth rates are given as 0.276 and 0.402 respectively (i.e., 27.6 percent and 40.2 percent), and the current subareal manufacturing and commercial activity levels are $280,000 and $180,000 respectively. Assuming a constant shift, what is the value of manufacturing and commercial trade in a projected time period?

To answer this question, we add the national growth rate to the subarea's growth rate and multiply the result by the subarea's current sectoral activity level according to Equation 2.15, yielding the projected manufacturing and commercial levels as requested:

$$\begin{aligned} \delta Z^M_i &= (-0.016 + 0.276)280 = 72.8 \\ \delta Z^C_i &= (+0.038 + 0.402)180 = 79.2 \end{aligned} \tag{2.16}$$

In this shift-share example, the first term in Equation 2.14 disappears since we assumed constant shift (Krueckeberg and Silver 1974). ∎

Figure 2.5 illustrates another example in the relationship between a regional economy and the national economy where all three components are present: national growth component, industrial mix component, and the competitive component. It shows the input data required to estimate each of these components, as well as a graphic plot of a numerical example for regional employment. Thus the drop in regional employment from 1332 to 1321 thousand is explained in terms of these components. The concepts presented in shift-share analysis, while simple, are not readily used in the field, since we never discussed how the growth rates are actually derived beyond the schematic as illustrated. Chan (2000) shows in his "Spatial Equilibrium and Disequilibrium" chapter that implementation potentials can be enhanced by including this concept within the interregional version of input-output analysis.

Figure 2.5   EXAMPLE APPLICATION OF SHIFT-SHARE ANALYSIS

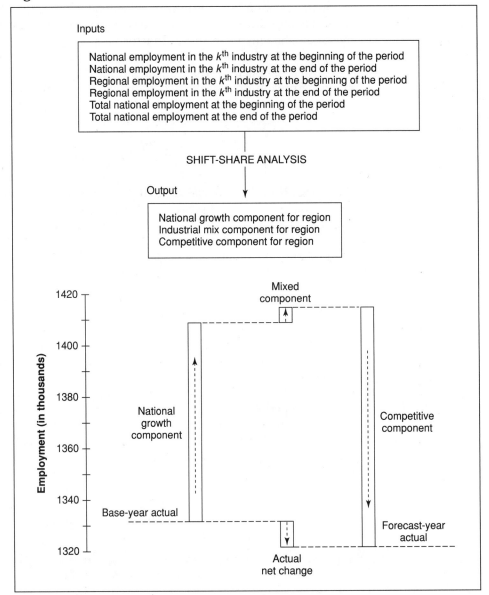

B. Theory of Land Values

Having completed our discussions on equity measurement, let us now turn to the concept of efficiency and illustrate it through the theory of land values. Land value is subject to the market forces of supply and demand and highly related to location and transportation costs. An improvement of the transportation system, such as new highway or subway construction, could affect land value significantly. Dorau and Hinman, as far back as 1928, suggested tracing land value to three additional explanatory variables: land income, rate of capitalization, and direct satisfaction from land ownership. Land income includes mortgages as well as the rent collected from tenants on the property, and in general the usefulness of the land corresponding to the various services it can render. While it may be obvious that land value depends on how potential income can be obtained from the land, it needs to be pointed out that such income includes not only those from the current time period, but also the forthcoming periods. This means that the rate of capitalization, such as interest rates, risk, and other investment preferences, are involved. The last explanatory factor—direct satisfaction from ownership—needs little explanation. It pertains to the personal rewards that are not measured by the monetary system.

Thus it can be seen that in a cost-benefit analysis, if land value is the primary measure of benefit, there are a variety of means to effect the change in land value, each of which would probably incur a cost. Improving accessibility by building highways, for instance, is a way among many others. The theory of land values helps to explain such a cost-benefit relationship, and in a practical sense, contributes toward model building. Aside from the above observations, there are several economic phenomena that are useful for model building as well. It is observed, for example, that land value or land rent declines with the distance from the central business district. The further one goes away from the central city, the lower the land value. Land rent and transportation costs are complementary. Thus in a hypothetical, circular city, the land values can be viewed as a cone in three dimensions (see Figure 2.6). If one wishes to live in the central city, the land rent is at a peak, but the transportation costs are at a minimum. On the other hand, if one locates at the fringe of the city, the land rent will be low, but the transportation cost will be high. You can either pay a high rent and be accessible, or you can pay a low rent and be comparatively inaccessible, hence having to pay more on transportation costs. Land rent is affected by transportation in another way. In the case of Philadelphia and other cities with a radial highway system, the development follows along the freeways in a finger-like manner. Suppose one adapts Burgess's classic concentric zone structure to an urban area consisting of contours of land value in rings around the city center. After a freeway is built, the development would tend to align itself along the freeway, stretching out the rings as indicated in Figure 2.7. In this case, Burgess's theory merges with Hoyt's sector theory, which suggests that there are modifications to the Burgess's concentric rings to reflect transportation corridors that induce suburban development along the corridors.

Figure 2.6   LAND RENT AND TRANSPORTATION COST

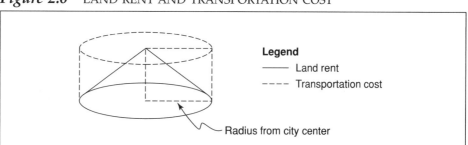

Legend
——— Land rent
- - - - Transportation cost

Radius from city center

Figure 2.7   EFFECT OF TRANSPORTATION ON LAND USE

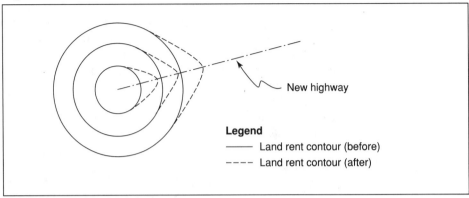

C. Consumers' Surplus

When economic efficiency is of concern, a valuation measure in spatial choice is **consumers' surplus.** The consumers' surplus is defined as the difference between what consumers might be willing to pay for a location and what they actually pay. As shown in Figure 2.8, the consumers' surplus is the area between the demand curve and the spatial price. Since the demand function expresses the users' indifference between the utility of a location and money, it can be considered as an expression of the utility of locations in terms of prices. The consumers' surplus, which is expressed in monetary units, is then a measure of the utility provided to the consumer minus the cost of production, which is reflected in the sale price to some degree. Maximization of consumers' surplus is then a close proxy of the maximization of the economic utility of the consumers. The evaluation of projects through a consumers' surplus analysis is widely, although generally only implicitly, used for large-scale public facilities. It is the only effective means of estimating economic benefits when the public facilities are so large as to effect more than marginal changes in prices.

To estimate the change in consumers' surplus brought about by any project, it is necessary to know both the price and the scale of the facility built before and after the project is completed. Figure 2.9 shows the change in consumers' surplus before and after a facility expansion from $\overline{P}_{bef}$ to $\overline{P}_{aft}$, which increases the number of consumers served from V_{bef} to V_{aft}. Algebraically, this change can be approximated by the trapezoid rule:

$$\frac{1}{2}(C_{bef} - C_{aft})(V_{bef} + V_{aft}) \qquad (2.17)$$

Measurement of the equilibrium price C can be difficult when the project is large enough to shift the demand curve by causing an income effect. Such an income effect is illustrated in Figure 2.10, where the tradeoff between housing and transportation is considered. The effective increase in income caused by a price reduction on a major facility shifts the point of maximum utility from U^*_{bef} to U^*_{aft}. The increase in income thus results in an increased demand for both transporta-

Figure 2.8   CONSUMERS' SURPLUS ILLUSTRATION

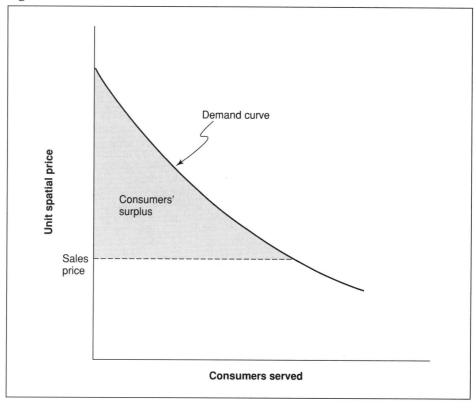

tion and housing. The income effect of a price change is only significant when major expenditure items are involved. For most families in the United States, these would be transportation, housing etc. Price changes on these items can change the level of consumption. Increased rent or housing costs could, for example, decrease the demand for travel. In developing countries, investments in basic infrastructure such as transportation, housing, and power can, by decreasing the cost of these items, significantly increase the effective income (I') of the inhabitants.

   When income effect is involved, knowledge of the income elasticity of demand $\left(\dfrac{dV}{V} \middle/ \dfrac{dI'}{I'}\right)$ is required in order to estimate the final price C_{aft}. Equation 2.17 still provides a satisfactory, although more approximate, means of calculating consumers' surplus. Chan (2000) illustrates this calculation in his "Including Generation and Distribution" chapter, where he estimates the economic value of state parks. In calculating consumers' surplus, the analyst must be careful to reckon with the effects of manipulations of the prices through a deliberated pricing policy. In systems that are publicly owned, it is possible and sometimes desirable to set prices that cover more or less than the total costs. Hydroelectric power in the western United States, for example, was subsidized below average cost to promote development. Unless the subsidies are deducted, this policy clearly increases consumers' surplus over what it might be if full cost of the service were charged. Figure 2.11 shows the total consumers' surplus made up of

Figure 2.9   CHANGE IN CONSUMERS' SURPLUS

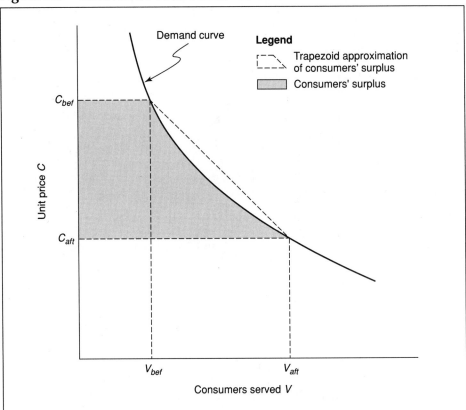

that part by the market mechanism and the other part by regulation. Such changes in consumers' surplus, effected by setting the prices of services different from their costs, are not without expenditure. The changes are indeed transfer payments that must be made up by subsidy, either from taxes or from profits in some other part of the system and deducted from the final consumers' surplus calculations of the project.

IV. UTILITY THEORY

Utility theory is a common economic concept to explain location choice and decision among alternatives in general. A view of utility functions may be developed in the following way. Each household is confronted with a choice between n different expenditures, including savings or dis-savings, within an income budget. This can be expressed by the following equation where p_i and x_i refer to the price and quantity of the ith expenditure: $I' = \Sigma_{i=1}^{n} p_i x$. On the other hand, the household derives a certain amount of satisfaction from the quantities of each commodity it purchases, and this degree of satisfaction, when added up, provides a total utility. This utility may be expressed as a function of the vector of purchases of com-

Figure 2.10   THE INCOME EFFECT

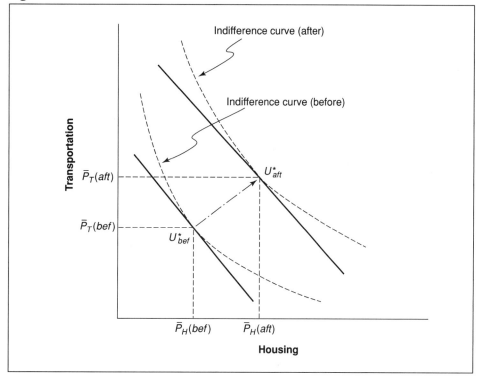

Figure 2.11   SUBSIDY AND TRANSFER PAYMENT

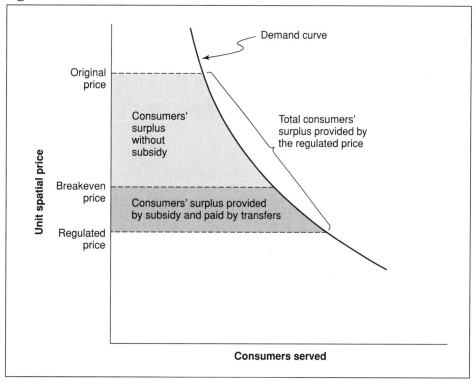

modities and services **x**: $v = f(\mathbf{x})$; but this expression is vacuous until we specify the form of the function $f(\mathbf{x})$. One may assume, for example, that it could be linear:

$$v = \sum_{i=1}^{n} w_i x_i \qquad (2.18)$$

This says that utility is the weighted sum of the purchases. This turns out to be not a very satisfactory idea because if a household tried to maximize its utility under this simple form, the whole budget would be spent on the commodity or service for which w_i/p_i was a maximum. Thus if the weight on travel was high and transportation cost was low, a family might spend its entire income on travel, which is somewhat absurd.

It would not help very much if we retain the linear model of Equation 2.18, but placed a requirement on the minimum consumption of each x_i. This would result in every commodity being consumed at its minimum level with the exception of the most cost effective one. A more complicated model can easily be devised in which various needs are each satisfied by a linear combination of commodities, and minimum values are set for the satisfaction of each need. This model is still unrealistic in that the minimum level of needs has to be set exogenously. Normally within the household, choices are made between the levels of satisfaction of various broad classes of needs—the need for housing, accessibility, non-housing, and non-location goods and services. Any linear model would force us to make decisions about these tradeoffs outside the model.

What makes tradeoff and consumption both possible and necessary is the fact that, for most goods, increasing quantities provide increasing satisfaction, but at a decreasing rate. Thus if twice the space is available to a household by moving further away from the city, the increased space may not double the housing satisfaction. In some cases, it might even decrease it. If we assume that increasing amounts of a commodity always add something to a household's utility, or at least never subtract from it. Suppose we also assume that the increase in satisfaction for each additional unit of a given commodity is diminishing, we have familiar economic statements about utility functions which are usually expressed mathematically:

$$\begin{aligned} \partial v/\partial x_i &\geq 0 & i &= 1, 2, \ldots, n \\ \partial^2 v/\partial x_i^2 &\leq 0 & i &= 1, 2, \ldots, n \end{aligned} \qquad (2.19)$$

An example function is

$$v = \sum_i a_i \ln x_i \qquad (2.20)$$

or alternatively

$$v = \prod_{i=1}^{n} x_i^{a_i} \qquad (2.21)$$

A form of the utility function corresponding to these two is extremely useful for our discussion here because we are dealing with commodities which are, in the western culture, absolutely essential. Every family must have housing, access to employment, and other commodities such as food and clothing. If one of these commodities is reduced to zero in Equation 2.21, the level of utility falls to zero. A utility function of this type leads to tradeoffs that give adequate weight to extreme deprivation of any of the essential commodities of life. While Equations 2.20 and 2.21 are useful utility-function forms, alternative approaches exist to quantify a decision maker's values. In Chapter 5 the multiattribute utility theory will be introduced, which is based more on behavioral grounds.

A. Estimating Bid-Rent via Utility Function

Before utility can be measured, the terms of the utility function must be defined. Part of the satisfaction from a particular residential location may be associated with the accessibility to work and/or recreational facilities in an area. Another may be connected to the availability of schools or pleasantness and quiet of the community. Let us now see how these are actually being quantified. First, we stratify the population by income, family size, and other socioeconomic factors, not only to detect different behaviors, but also to be sure that we are dealing with relatively uniform levels of housing and related expenditures. In the discussion that follows, it should be understood that income is fixed at a class mean, or at least falls within a relatively narrow range as a result of the stratification of individual households.

Alonso (1970) has the idea of measuring utility with reference to income, whereby the utility function takes into consideration the total available income. In a family's budget, let us define M' as the non-location expenditures, which include items such as food, clothing, and education. M' also includes savings at a bank. Another expenditure is rent (r), which includes mortgage payments, rent, and utility bills. Then we have transportation cost represented by T. Collectively r and T are referred to as location expenditures. These budget components can be broken down further, but the way we are doing it now satisfies our purpose. All these expenditures must fit into the budget I': $I' = M' + r + T$, which says certain parts of the income go to location and another to non-location expenditures. The simple equation above also underlines the complementary relationship between transportation outlay and rent, as covered earlier in this chapter when we discussed land rent theory.

We will now assume a particularly simple form of the utility function referenced as Equation 2.20:

$$v = \ln M' + \alpha_1 \ln H + \alpha_2 \ln A + \alpha_3 \ln C' \tag{2.22}$$

Here, M' stands for the consumption of all non-location goods as discussed above, while H, A, and C' stand respectively for the expenditure on providing housing, accessibility, and community amenities. In Equation 2.22, α_1, α_2, and α_3 are coefficients defining the relative importance of housing, accessibility, and amenities. We now introduce a basic assumption of overriding importance, whose application to this problem is due to Alonso (1964, 1970). We assume that for a particular set of households of homogeneous tastes, utility is uniform wherever they are located in the metropolitan area. We cannot, of course, be sure that by defining homogeneous socioeconomic groups, we have actually defined groups whose preferences in the housing market are also homogeneous. Given some uniformity in tastes, however, the assumption of equal utility is based on elementary economic considerations. If the utilities being enjoyed are in fact not equal and if there are locations in which a particular group could enjoy a higher utility, members of that group will bid up the price of land and housing at that location. The higher cost of the housing package in this preferred area will, via the budget constraint, reduce the amount of money available for purchase on non-location commodities and thus reduce the level of utility enjoyed. Given freedom to move in search of better housing opportunities, this type of bidding will raise demand in some locations and lower it in others to the point where all utilities for this group have been equalized. This implies that there is a competitive equilibrium and the assumption for freedom to move is again important in achieving this equilibrium. See household groups *A*, *B*, and *C* of a high income class trading off their preference between housing, accessibility, and amenities expenditures in Figure 2.12(a). This contrasts with two households *B* and *X* in a high and low income class respectively shown in Figure 2.12(b).

Given that the utilities of any particular locating group are fixed at any particular point in time, the *v* which appears in Equation 2.22 is a constant, and we redefine it as

$$v = \ln I' + \ln F \tag{2.23}$$

Since we are dealing with a homogeneous income group, $\ln I'$ is a constant and *F* is an arbitrary constant whose role will appear below. If we now substitute

Figure 2.12   UTILITY FUNCTION AND BUDGET

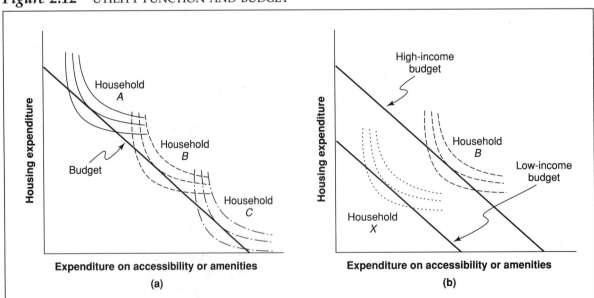

$M' = I' - r - T$ and Equation 2.23 in Equation 2.22 and rearrange terms, we arrive at the following expression:

$$\ln \left([I' - r - T]/I' \right) = \ln F - \alpha_1 \ln H - \alpha_2 \ln A - \alpha_3 \ln C' \qquad (2.24)$$

This is an estimating equation which can be empirically tested and which expresses the proportion of non-location expenditures undertaken by each family as a function of housing, accessibility, and community amenities in each location. This equation has two essential properties. First, all the variables in it can be observed for a number of different household classes in a number of different locations, and consequently it can be determined. The level of non-location expenditures can be estimated from this equation and then, since I' and T are known, the rent which would be offered can be estimated using this equation.

We will show how this important procedure can be achieved. If we exponentiate Equation 2.24, we get $(I - r - T)/I' = FH^{-\alpha_1}A^{-\alpha_2}C'^{-\alpha_3}$. Rearranging terms, we can isolate rent on the left-hand side of the equation. We show this value of rent as an estimated value:

$$r = I' - T - I'FH^{-\alpha_1}A^{-\alpha_2}C'^{-\alpha_3}$$

This is equivalent to the form of the budget equation $r = I' - T - M'$. These values of r are bid-rents discussed by Alonso in his development of the theory of location behavior. Expressing $\ln (1 - [r + T]/I')$ in Equation 2.24 in series, and recognizing that $(r - T)/I'$ is a fraction, an approximation can be made only by taking the first term of the series expansion[1]:

$$\ln \left(1 - \frac{r + T}{I'} \right) \approx - \frac{r + T}{I'} \qquad (2.25)$$

This says that our dependent variable is approximately equal to the (negative) fraction of income spent on rent and transportation combined. This is analogous to the dependent variable of many of the housing market analyses: the rent-income ratio.

Notice the location expenditure is small compared to the rest of the budget for a majority of the population. The fraction of income spent on location expenditures can be estimated by this simple formula; it serves as an approximation for the dependent variable in the Equation 2.24. The above analysis indicates that there is substantial uniformity in the behavior among groups that have been defined on socioeconomic grounds. This behavior can be characterized through utility functions of a fundamentally simple nature. Data are available in the census and elsewhere for providing values for these estimates. All of the relevant variables that we suggested on a priori basis turn out to be statistically significant. The uses to which this analysis can be put must be discussed in conjunction with modeling the market clearing mechanism for housing. (See the Herbert-Stevens model in Chapter 4.)

B. Minimum-Cost Residential Location

Alonso's model of residential location would hold that households are located to minimize the cost of housing and travel. For a monocentric metropolis, this cost is expressed simply as $C(d) = H + r(d) + a'Vd/l'$, where $C(d)$ is the total location cost as a function of distance from the metropolitan area's center, the land area desired for the parcel of land is assumed constant, $r(d)$ is the cost of a unit-of-land as a function of location, a' is the unit cost of commuting (cost per unit-of-distance-traveled), d is the location's distance from the workplace at the metropolitan center, l' is the real discount rate on commuting trips due to such modern day conveniences as telecommuting, and V' is the number of one-way commuting trips taken per year (Lund and Mokhtarian 1994).

Since households are assumed to minimize this cost in their location decisions,

$$\dot{C}(d^*) = \dot{r}(d^*) + a'V/l' = 0 \qquad \text{or} \qquad \dot{r}(d^*) = -a'V/l' \qquad (2.26)$$

where the derivatives are evaluated at d^*, the least-cost residential location. Inasmuch as land prices tend to decrease with distance from the metropolitan center, $\dot{r} < 0$. So long as this relationship holds and to the extent that telecommuting lessens the number of work trips per year ($V_1 < V_0$), telecommuting is associated with a more gentle land-rent gradient:

$$\dot{r}(d^*)V_0 < \dot{r}(d^*)V_1 < 0 \qquad (2.27)$$

Assuming that land prices follow a conventional exponential decay, then $r(d) = r_0\exp(-Kd)$, where r_0 is the land price at the metropolitan area center and K is a decay constant. Therefore,

$$\dot{r}(d) = -r_0K\exp(-K_0) \qquad (2.28)$$

Combining Equations 2.26 and 2.28 yields $r_0K\exp(-Kd^*) = a'V/l'$. This results in the least-cost residential location

$$d^* = (l/K)\ln[l'r_0K/a'] - (\ln V)/K \qquad (2.29)$$

Notice that this relationship consists of a constant term that does not vary with commuting trips per year, minus a term that increases logarithmically with the number of annual commuting trips.

How would residential location change with the onset of telecommuting? To examine this, we define the change in least-cost location,

$$\Delta d^* = d^*(V_1) - d^*(V_0)$$

Replacing Equation 2.29 into this definition yields

$$\Delta d^* = [\ln V_0 - \ln V_1]/K = \ln(V_0/V_1)/K$$

Figure 2.13   CHANGE IN RESIDENTIAL LOCATION WITH TELECOMMUTING

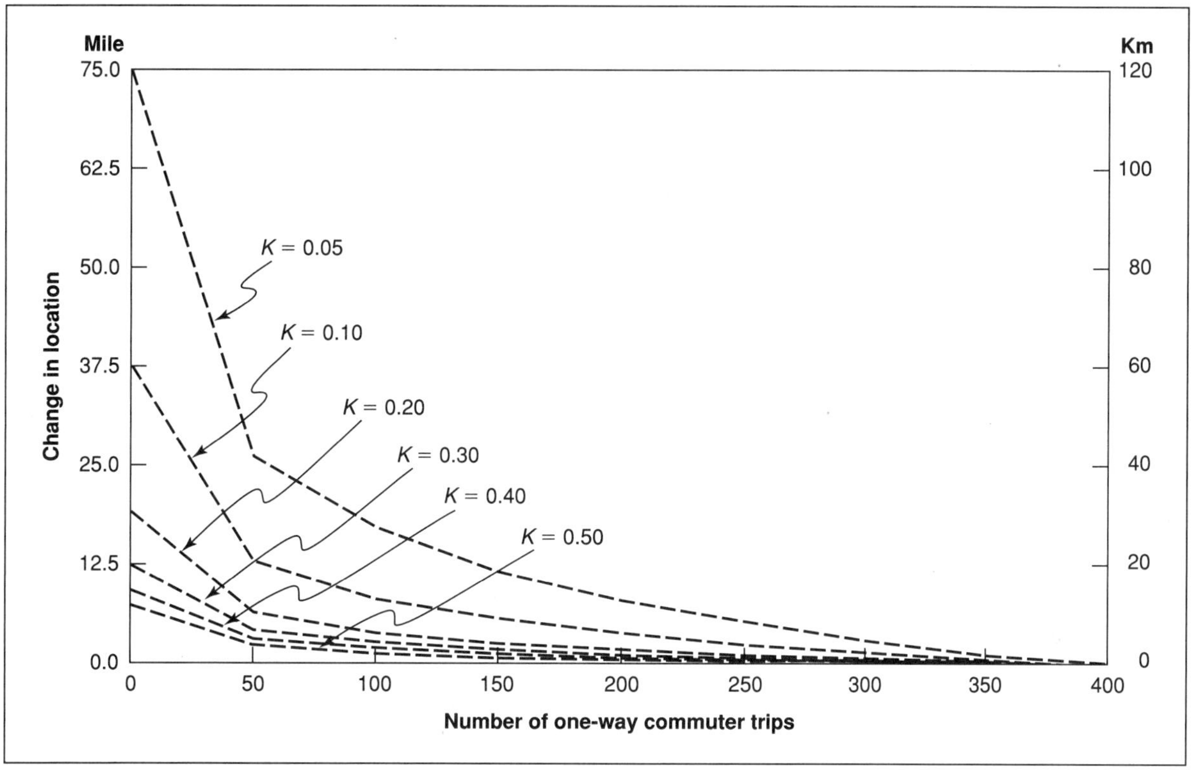

SOURCE: Lund and Mokhtarian (1994). Reprinted with permission.

Note that this change in equilibrium location is affected by only the change in commuting trips and the decay constant of land prices. Other factors entering into the initial location decision do not affect the magnitude of change in the equilibrium least-cost location.

Example
Consider a household initially located 6.25 miles (10 km) from the metropolitan center ($d_0^* = 6.25$ mi) where 400 one-way commuting trips are made annually ($V_0 = 400$). Land prices decay exponentially at a constant rate ranging from 8 percent to 80 percent per mile (5 percent to 50 percent per km) or $K = 0.08$ to 0.8 per mi. Figure 2.13 shows the change in equilibrium residential location as a function of the number of commuting trips and land prices. It confirms the theoretical and intuitively appealing finding in Equation 2.27, that residential location is affected most by telecommuting in a sprawling city with long commuting distances. ∎

V. THE LOCATION DECISION

The above residential location discussions, particularly Equation 2.26, can be carried over to industrial activities.[2] Assume that all activity takes place on a featureless plain consisting of land of equal quality. The rent that any producer will be prepared to pay for a given unit of land i, r^i, will be determined by its output (the number of customer visitations) V, the price per unit at the market, γ, direct cost of production, c, the transport rate per unit of distance a', and d_i, distance from the market:

$$r^i = V(\gamma - c) - Va'd_i \qquad (2.30)$$

Here V, γ, c, and a' are assumed constant under conditions of perfect competition. This maximum rent, also referred to as bid-rent by Alonso (1960), is determined uniquely by the location of the site.

A. Bid-Rent Curves

Thus far we have assumed a single activity. If we introduce a second activity, it is obvious that V, γ, and c will not be constant and also it is likely that a' will vary according to weight or any special carriage requirements of the product. However, since perfect competition and freedom of entry prevail, we would not expect the profitability at the most favored location, which we can assume to be arbitrarily close to zero, to differ. The reason is that it and all producers would change production with consequent changes in price to restore an equality of profit. Hence the only change to be made if we have more than one activity is to introduce a', the transport rate, as a determinant of r^i. It is then obvious that by knowing the transport rates for commodities we can derive the location pattern of production about the market. High transport cost activities will locate at a close distance and low transport cost activities will take locations further away. We can determine a relationship between r and d for each a'; the maximum r^i payable at each d_i will determine the activity which will locate there.

Following Alonso (1964), this is best illustrated with a series of bid-rent curves as shown in Figure 2.14. Each bid rent curve $r^i d_i$ is defined by the linear Equation 2.30. Points d' and d'' define important switch points in land use between activities with different bid-rents. The piecewise linear line highlighted in bold is the revealed rent function for the area on the basis that land is allocated to the highest bidder.

B. Industrial Location

Weber (Friedrich 1929) also started with the basic premise that particular locations do not have cost advantages in the actual manufacture of goods. However, in addition to land, most manufacturing industry requires inputs of more than one factor of production and, unlike land, these other factors cannot be assumed to be uniformly distributed in general. The location of a plant will therefore depend on the relative pulls of the various material locations and the market. Weber assumes these to be points rather than areas for simplicity. Assuming that for a particular product these various points are not coincident, the critical factors to be considered will be the relative weights of inputs and outputs and the distances over which these relative weights of input and outputs must be moved. Since transport rates depend on these two factors, the main interest was whether industries would locate nearer the market or to the source of materials and this could be related, through the transport costs, to whether the production process was weight losing or weight gaining. The materials index, the ratio of material

Figure 2.14   BID-RENT CURVES

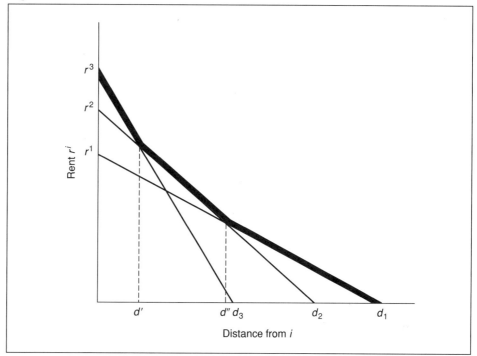

weight to product weight, is a crude measure. It suggests that high values would involve a location dominated by sources of materials and low values (less than unity) would involve market domination, while values of about one would suggest location indifference.

The basic location criterion is thus minimizing total transport costs, assuming that market price of the product and prices of factor inputs are given and independent of location. The optimal location involves finding a set of distances

Figure 2.15   WEBER'S INDUSTRIAL LOCATION MODEL

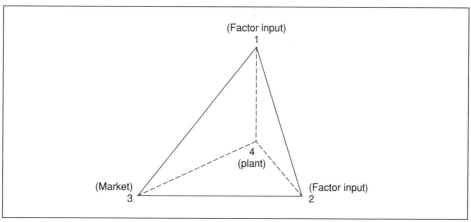

d^i the inputs must be moved and distance-to-the-market D: $w_1 d_1 + w_2 d_2 + \ldots + w_n d_n + D$. Here w_1 and w_2, are the inputs required per unit of output. Figure 2.15 illustrates the simplest case of such a model. The figure shows a location triangle relating the market, node 3, to the two factor inputs at 1 and 2. The distances 3-1, 3-2, and 1-2 are geographic distances between the points. The optimal location for a plant at node 4 depends on the effective forces represented by the lines linking it to each corner. These forces are proportional to the relative weights of inputs or outputs as taken into account in the materials index. Node 4 can be found by constructing circles representing isocost lines centered on each corner of the triangle and examining their intersections. The most interesting result from this model is the dominance of end-points, many of which appear optimal, in-between points are of little importance. Numerical examples of this result are shown in Chapter 4.

C. Residential Location Models

According to Alonso (1964), the consumer looking for a housing location maximizes a utility function $v = v(x, s', d)$ where x is the quantity of a composite consumption good representing other activities engaged in by the consumer, s' is the average-size of site, and d is again the distance from the subarea of interest. In his/her location decision, the consumer is constrained by his/her available budget b^u, $p''x + r^i s_i' + a'd_i \le b^u$, where p'' is the price of the composite consumption good. It is from this model that the bid-rent function for each individual can be derived as the maximum amount a person is willing to pay for a site that would be just as desirable as another.

If we interpret the value of r^i in the above model as being the bid-rent for that location, then from the maximization exercise, we derive

$$\frac{\partial r}{\partial d} = \frac{p''}{s'}\frac{U_d}{U_x} - \frac{1}{s}\frac{\partial(a'd)}{\partial d} \tag{2.31}$$

where U_d and U_x are the appropriate marginal utilities of location and the composite consumption good. Rearranging Equation 2.31 in terms of marginal rates of substitution, we obtain

$$\frac{U_d}{U_x} = \frac{1}{p''}\left[s'\frac{\partial r}{\partial d} + \frac{\partial(a'd)}{\partial d}\right]$$

The above equation states the following: The incremental satisfaction from relocation (in terms of movement outward), which is obtained by substituting travel for goods, must be exactly equal to the cost of that relocation in terms of changing rent costs and changing travel costs. For simplicity we can assume that the good x has a price of unity such that $1/p'' = 1$. Furthermore, since the marginal rate of substitution is assumed to be conventionally negative and since transport costs will increase with distance, the land costs term must be negative. Obviously sites must always have a non-negative size and hence $\partial r/\partial d < 0$; we thus have the basic result that rents must decline with distance and hence the normal assumed shape of the bid-rent curve of Figure 2.16. In this figure, the lines r^i-d_i represent

Figure 2.16   HOUSEHOLD LOCATION MODEL

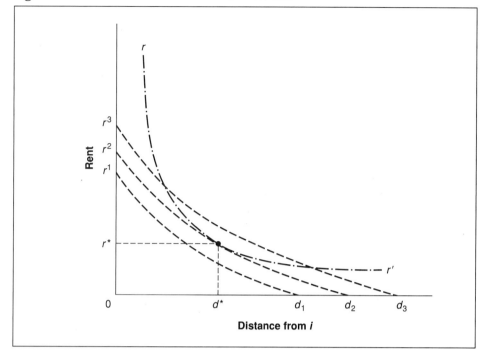

bid-rent curves for an individual household. The higher the curve, the lower the level of satisfaction. The curve r-r' is the equilibrium rent function for the city formed as an envelope curve to the various bid-rent lines of Figure 2.14. The equilibrium rent and location for this household is represented by (d^*, r^*).

VI. SCALE AND NUMBER OF PUBLIC FACILITIES

Consider a homogeneous service to be distributed over some spatially distributed population. Let us assume that the service is distributed from a point-representable system of approximately up to four facilities—p_1, p_2, p_3 or p_4—each having an identical scale $\overline{P}$ measured in terms of capacity, capital outlay, or some other metric. The service is consumed by individuals who travel to the facilities for this purpose, and the service is priced at zero, meaning a public service provided by government to the citizens in the area. Total consumption Q of the service is the measure of effectiveness.

A. Static Short-Run Equilibrium

Now total consumption Q is a function of scale P and the number of facilities p

$$Q = Q(\overline{P}, p) \tag{2.32}$$

Total cost of the system C_t is made up of capital cost C_s and operating cost C_o, $C_t = C_s + C_o$, where

$$C_s = C_s\,(\overline{P}, p) \tag{2.33}$$

and

$$C_o = C_o(V) \tag{2.34}$$

In other words, capital cost depends on the number and scale of facilities built, while operating cost is related to the number of consumers served (V). The spatial pattern of facilities for a given ($\overline{P}$, p) is that pattern for which V is maximized. There exists a fixed budget b^u between capital and operating expenditures.

Figure 2.17, Figure 2.18, and Figure 2.19 illustrate some likely properties of Equations 2.32 through 2.34. Since the service is zero-priced, there is presumably some upper limit V^* to the amount that a population might be expected to consume. Holding the number of facilities constant in Figure 2.17, positive variation in scale may be expected to produce first increasing then decreasing positive variations in demand. The curves in Figure 2.17 actually represent a family of sections through the surface of Equation 2.32. They are therefore demand or consumer coverage curves for the service, given a fixed number, p_k, of facilities at varying scales. Scale expenditures play a role of negative prices or subsidies. An exactly analogous diagram could be made for the number of facilities, holding scale constant. The general character of V ($\overline{P}$, p) is thus a function monotonically increasing to some asymptote V^*. It would look like a curved surface climbing away from the origin.

Figure 2.17   COVERAGE OF CONSUMERS

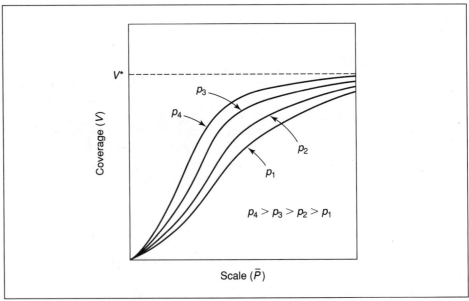

Figure 2.18   CAPITAL COSTS

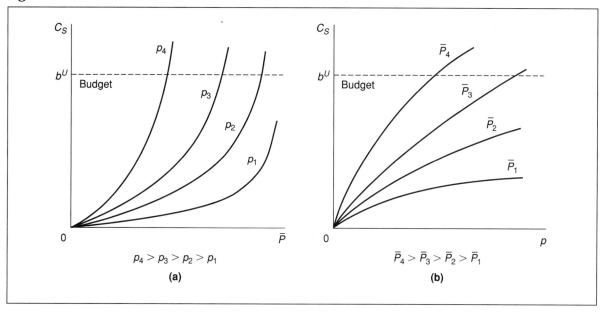

Cost relationships may be handled in a similar way. Figure 2.18 presents a pattern of capital cost variations for constant levels-of-scale and number of facilities respectively. Although we assume that increase in scale eventually incurs higher marginal cost, there seems to be no reason for such an increase with the replication of facilities. Rather, the reverse seems to hold. The capital cost surface, C_s, may be generated from the families of sections in Figure 2.18. In short, increase in scale results in lower marginal cost compared with construction of new facilities in the beginning, and reverses itself as the system expands to full size.

Figure 2.19   OPERATING COST

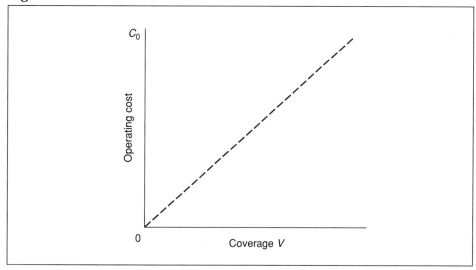

For operating cost, C_o, several problems arise. We have made it a function of total demand on the assumption that the marginal product for any variable input to a given system does not vary with the form of the system itself, but only with the aggregate quantity of services demanded and produced. The reason for the distinction between capital and operating costs should be clear. The latter depends upon demand, representing the variable cost of responding to demand at the level induced by the former. In part, this may be an artificial distinction. Demand for a service does respond to the level of variable inputs insofar as it determines convenience and quality of service. We will avoid this complication for the moment by assuming that variable inputs are added to maintain some constant level of quality. For simplicity, this relationship is represented as generally linear in Figure 2.18, although it should be noted that in terms of the variables of Figures 2.17 and 2.18, it is likely to be nonlinear.

With appropriate assumptions about continuity and well-behaved functions, the problem may now be formulated as a constrained maximization: *Max* $V = V(\overline{P}, p)$ subject to $C_t = b^u$. The Lagrangian for this problem is $z = V(\overline{P},p) - \lambda[C_s(\overline{P}, p) + C_o(V) - b^u]$ for which the conditions for maximization become:

$$\frac{\partial z}{\partial \overline{P}} = \frac{\partial V}{\partial \overline{P}} - \lambda\left[\frac{\partial C_s}{\partial \overline{P}} + \frac{\partial C_o}{\partial V}\frac{\partial V}{\partial \overline{P}}\right] = 0$$

or

$$\frac{\partial V}{\partial \overline{P}} = \left[\lambda \bigg/ \left(1 - \lambda\frac{\partial C_o}{\partial V}\right)\right]\frac{\partial C_s}{\partial \overline{P}} \tag{2.35}$$

Similarly

$$\frac{\partial V}{\partial p} = \left[\lambda \bigg/ \left(1 - \lambda\frac{\partial C_o}{\partial V}\right)\right]\frac{\partial C_s}{\partial p} \tag{2.36}$$

and

$$\frac{\partial z}{\partial \lambda} = C_s(\overline{P}, p) + C_o(V) = b^u \tag{2.37}$$

Combining Equations 2.35 and 2.36, we obtain the maximization condition

$$\frac{\partial V}{\partial \overline{P}} \bigg/ \frac{\partial V}{\partial p} = \frac{\partial C_s}{\partial \overline{P}} \bigg/ \frac{\partial C_s}{\partial p} \tag{2.38}$$

The equilibrium condition basically says that the maximal coverage is attained by a combination of scale expansion and new facility construction as justifiable by the marginal costs of the two ways to provide capacity. The consequences of our assumption about variable operating cost show up immediately in Equation 2.38. The equilibrium condition for demand maximization includes only system variables. If this seems peculiar, we might reflect that operating cost appears in Equation 2.37, which says that the cost for service coverage and system capacity expansion is limited by the budget available. Given our assumption that a given increase in demand generates the same operating cost no matter whether it derives from the scale or number of system components, its absence from Equation 2.38 is less surprising. Whether that assumption is tenable is another matter.

More significantly, this formulation evades the problem of location via its cost structure, which is totally dependent upon scale and number of facilities and has no spatial cost components. So far the researchers have been unable to incorporate the location problem into a pure analytic model. In view of the numerous mathematical programming and heuristic approaches to this type of problem, there would seem to be advantages to structuring the total problem as a computer model. In analytical terms, this raises the problem of our assumption of continuity in the variable p. Using a calculus-based model, we cannot simultaneously assume it would be continuous for scale analysis and discrete for a location-effective algorithm. Perhaps an iterative estimation process is the way around this problem, but the theoretical result is less precise. In any case, it seems probable that the location problem for public facility systems must be attacked in tandem with system structure and scale. Several problems still remain. Introduction of variable facility scales in a single system is clearly necessary. As soon as this is done, then questions of hierarchy begin to arise.

The static equilibrium treated above is general in the sense that it deals with simultaneous location and scale of all components of a facility system. The equivalent partial problem might be formulated in several ways. If an increment to a budget for an existing system is given, then we might be interested in determining the optimal addition to the system. This does not necessarily mean that any new components are added. The entire budget increment could be spent on scale changes. If the problem is to achieve a specified incremental gain in some effectiveness measure, the same qualifications would apply. In these circumstances it is not clear how a partial form should be specified. Possibly, it should hold the present facility location structure constant and allow only scale changes and new facility locations. Again, advances in more sophisticated methods than simple calculus are necessary for addressing such problems.

B. Dynamic Long-Run Equilibrium

To analyze systems of facilities with static equilibrium analysis is to ignore a most important characteristic: their changes over time. Facility systems are usually built quite slowly, reacting to changes both in the size of the broader systems they serve and in technology and social preferences. If the broader system is a growing city, then there may be conflict between static and dynamic system optima. This may be especially true if, for whatever reason, decisions early in a system's development can effectively close off options for later forms. A geometric illustration of a dynamic system conflicting with static solutions is offered by a simple model. Consider the circular and generally symmetric city represented in Figure 2.20. At this particular size and for some local service, the optimal number of facilities is one, and it is located at the center, *A*. The city grows symmetrically both in density and at its outer margin until it reaches the size shown in Figure 2.21. At this new level the static-equilibrium solution, taking into account a probable larger budget for the service, calls for two identical facilities, *B*. If they are located symmetrically, there is no path of growth for this

Figure 2.20   FACILITY EXPANSION IN A CIRCULAR AND SYMMETRIC CITY

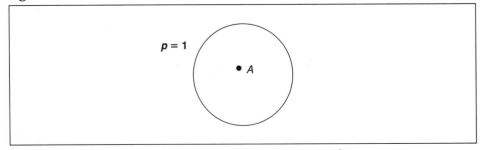

Figure 2.21   LARGER CITY WITH TWO FACILITIES

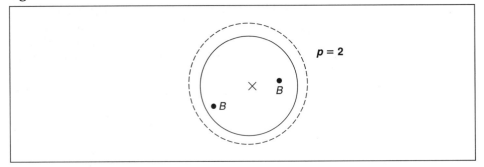

facility system from stage 1 to stage 2 that does not call for removal of *A*. Whether that is likely depends on the rate of growth and the fixed capital investment in *A*.

The example is made artificial by the assertion of identical facilities. In practice, accommodation may be partially achieved by variations in scale among facilities. For example, the equivalent problem for three components might be to approximate a symmetric uniform scale optimum by a variable scale but still symmetric three-component system (see Figures 2.22 and 2.23 respectively). In the latter, the original facility is retained at a larger scale than the others. Without specifying particular forms for the relationships between spatial pattern, scale, and demand, we cannot say much more than this.

The dynamic long-run equilibrium discussion above suggests two modeling approaches. We may look for possible system growth paths through time under varying constraints and criteria for effectiveness and try to identify stages at which such paths coincide with static equilibrium solutions, or we may set up static equilibrium solutions and try to construct minimum cost paths to connect them. Since most facility system analyses are likely to start with an existing set of components, most of which incur high relocation costs, either form could be employed. The choice is perhaps yet another version of the process/end-state conflict in planning models, in this case with both forms involving specific criteria for choice since the decisions are public. Very little work in this direction has been done. Chan (2000) discusses growth paths of land use, rather than facility location, in his chapter on "Bifurcation and Disaggregation." The continuous generalization of facility location—land use—is easier to model

Figure 2.22   THREE FACILITIES AT UNIFORM SCALE

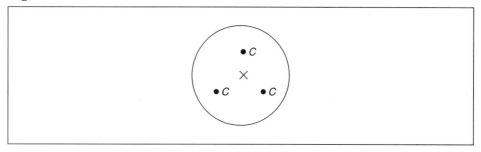

Figure 2.23   THREE FACILITIES AT VARIABLE SCALE

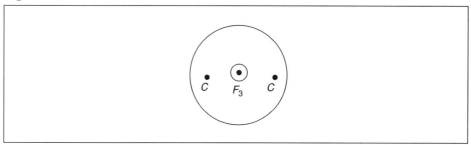

inasmuch as it avoids the discreteness or lumpiness that prevents smooth transition from stage to stage, although bifurcation models do allow for precipitous happenings to take place. Again computer models seem to be most promising given the mathematical complexity of any reasonable looking structure for analysis. One such program, the Garin-Lowry model, is included on the CD under the YI-CHAN folder.

The main problem of locating public services, as can be seen, is choosing the scale and the number of facilities at specified geographic locations that would be most adequate to provide the public services for the budget allocation. The theoretical exposé, while addressing most of the key considerations in planning for public services, has to be further refined for specific applications. Associated with the scale and location considerations, for example, are the ways and means to make the public service available to the community. In this regard, the spatial location of a facility becomes as important as the scale and the number of facilities.

VII. SPATIAL LOCATION OF A FACILITY

Consider the triangular network *ABC* as shown in Figure 2.24, where there are three highways represented by the three edges of the triangle. A facility, for instance, a shopping mall, is to be located on the highway system so that the distance to the farthest population center *A, B,* or *C* is minimized. The demand at *A, B,* or *C* does not enter into the picture in this example; only distances are considered.

Figure 2.24   TRIANGULAR NETWORK *ABC*

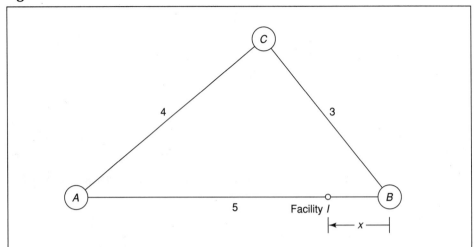

A. Center of a Network

Suppose for the time being the facility is to be located among candidate sites on a highway between nodes *A* and *B*, which has a separation of 5 miles (8 km). Let us place a facility at point *I* at a distance of x from node *B*. The distance function between node *A* and point *I* is 5 − x, and the distance function between node *B* and *I* is simply x. These distance functions are shown in Figure 2.25 (Ahituv and Berman 1988). We are supposed to find the one center location, or the location which minimizes the farthest point away. The maximum distance is shown on the upper envelope of Figure 2.25. The minimum occurs at x = 2.5 miles (4 km) from *A*, or halfway between *A* and *B*, which is located at the lowest point on the envelope. This is sometimes referred to as the **mini-max** solution.

Unfortunately, the problem is more involved, since there is node *C* as well. Let us examine the distance between points on link (*A*, *B*) and node *C*. If the facility is located at node *B*, the shortest distance to node *C* would be 3 miles (4.8 km). When we move point *I* along the link (*A*, *B*) from *B* toward *A*, the shortest distance function becomes 3 + x. This, however, stops when x reaches 3 miles from node *B*, because at that point it is better to approach node *C* via node *A*. The distance function from *I* to *C* becomes 9 − x, where 9 is the sum of the distances of links (*B*, *A*) and (*A*, *C*), and x remains to be the distance of point *I* from node *B*. The complete distance function is given by

$$d_{I3} = \begin{cases} 3 + x & for\ 0 \le x \le 3 \\ 9 - x & for\ 3 \le x \le 5 \end{cases} \qquad (2.39)$$

The function is shown in Figure 2.26.

In Figure 2.27, we have combined the distance functions to nodes *A* and *B* from Figure 2.25 with the distance function to node *C* in Figure 2.26. A new upper envelope is drawn, which describes the maximum distance from *I* to nodes *A*, *B*, and *C*, depending on the location of *I* on link (*A*, *B*). The minimum of the maximum distance is obtained when the facility is placed at a distance of x = 1 mile (1.6 km) from *B*. At this facility location, the maximum distance to demands

Figure 2.25   DISTANCE FUNCTIONS BETWEEN A FACILITY AND DEMANDS
AT *A* AND *B*

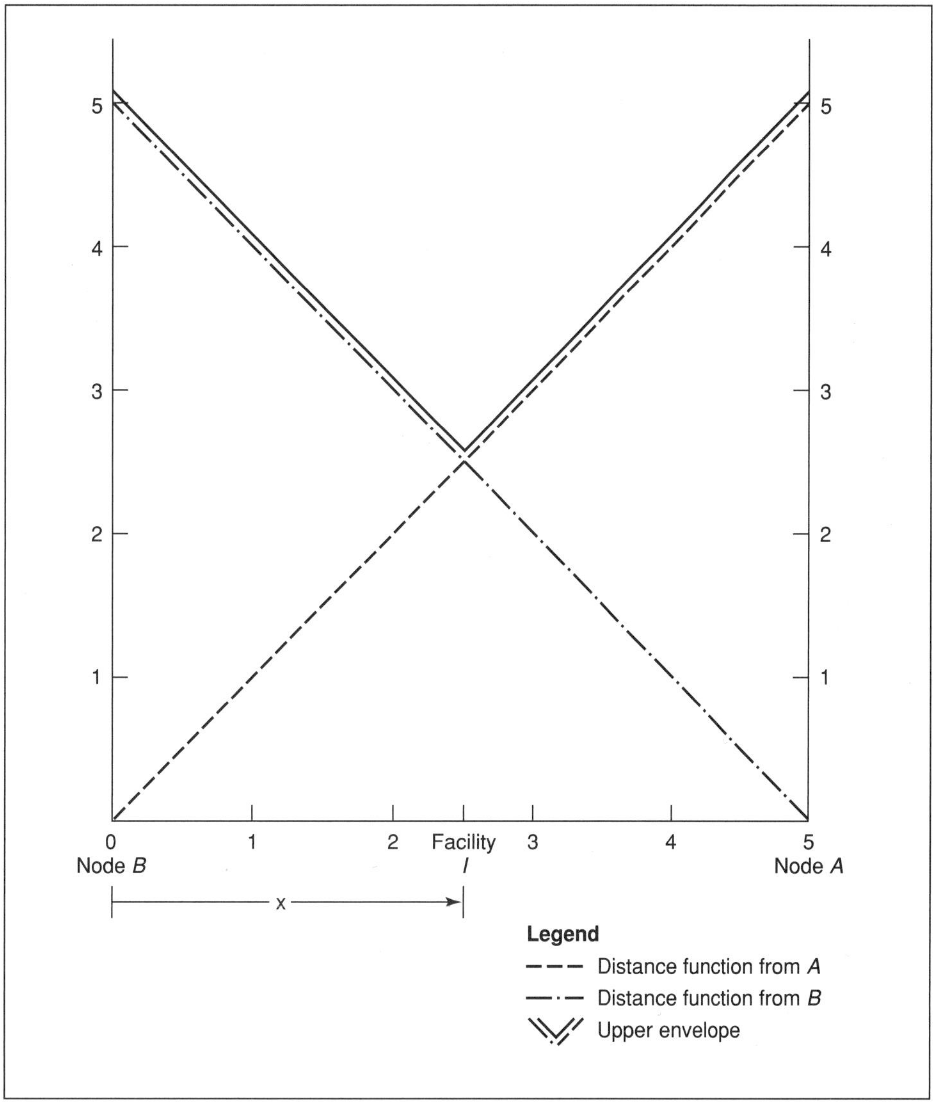

SOURCE: Adapted from Ahituv and Berman (1988). Reprinted with permission.

at A, B, and C is minimized at a value of 4 miles (6.4 km). In a similar fashion, we proceed to inquire about the distance functions between points of link (*B, C*) and node A, then link (*C, A*) and node *B*. The process is in fact quite tedious. More efficient algorithms are available to circumvent this exhaustive search procedure, but they are beyond the scope of this text. Interested readers are referred to the "Facility Location" chapter in Chan (2000).

B. Median of a Network

Suppose we are to locate a facility such that the average distance from a demand node to the nearest facility is minimized—the minimum-of-the-weighted-sum **(mini-sum)** solution. It has been shown (Hakimi 1964) that such a facility has to

Figure 2.26 CENTER DISTANCE FUNCTION FOR LOCATING FACILITY IN A NETWORK

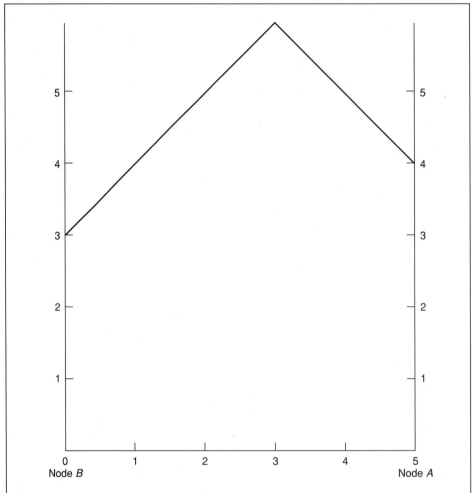

SOURCE: Adapted from Ahituv and Berman (1988). Reprinted with permission.

be located at a node. This is distinctly different from the center problem above, in which the facility can be anywhere on an arc (including the two nodes that define the arc also.) To show this nodal optimality condition for one median, we examine the network consisting of only one link, as depicted in Figure 2.26 (Ahituv and Berman 1988). A and B represent the two demand nodes, which are separated by a distance d_{AB}. The demand proportion generated at node A is T'_A, while that at node B is $T'_B = 1 - T'_A$. Suppose we place the facility at I on link (A, B). Assume d_A is the distance between node A and the facility I. The average weighted distance for delivering the service from I to the consumers, or for the consumers to access the facility, is

$$T'_A d_A + (1 - T'_A)(d_{AB} - d_A) = T'_A d_A - d_{AB} - d_A - T'_A d_{AB} + T'_A d_A =$$
$$d_{AB}(1 - T_A) + d_A(2T'_A - 1) \qquad (2.40)$$

Figure 2.27   COMBINED DISTANCE FUNCTION FOR FACILITY IN A NETWORK

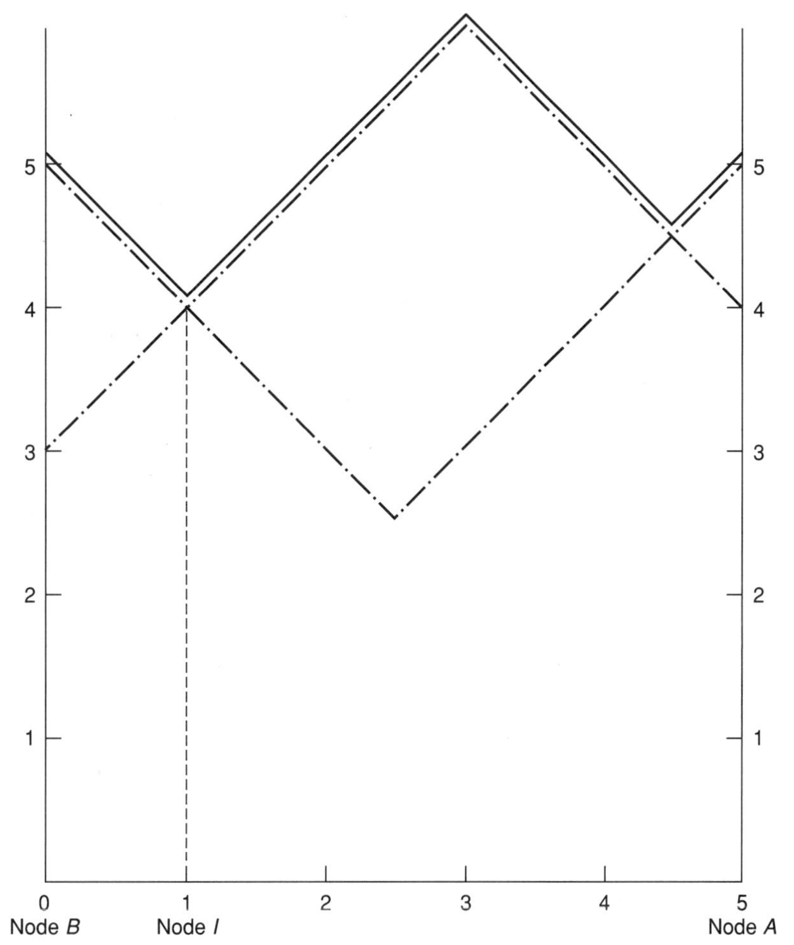

The first term of the above equation is constant; it does not depend on the location of I. The second term is a function of the location of I, or d_A. Now suppose node A generated more demand than node B, thus $T_A' > 1/2$. Hence $(2T_A' - 1) > 0$ and Equation 2.40 is minimized when $d_A = 0$, or when the facility is located at A. However, if node B generated more demand than A, namely $T_A' < 1/2$ and $(2T_A' - 1) < 0$, Equation 2.40 is minimized when d_A assumes its biggest possible value d_{AB}. In this case we will place the facility at node B. If the two nodes generate equal demand, facility I may be located anywhere on link (A, B) including the two nodes. Figure 2.28 illustrates the above problem graphically. The average distance as represented by Equation 40 is plotted as a function of the distance from node A to the facility I, d_A. For $T_A' < 1/2$, the median should be located at A, where the average distance is minimized. For $T_A' = 1/2$, the median can be anywhere between A and B and the travel distance is the same. For $T_A' < 1/2$, the facility should be located at B. Figure 2.28 contrasts sharply with Figure 2.25 in that upper

Figure 2.28   AVERAGE DISTANCE AS A FUNCTION OF MEDIAN LOCATION

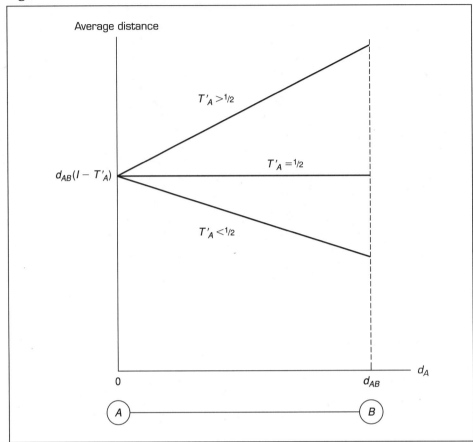

SOURCE: Ahituv and Berman (1988). Reprinted with permission.

envelope in the latter has a kink in the middle while the former is a monotonically increasing or nondecreasing function. The former identifies a nodal optimum at either A or B, while the latter locates an optimum in between the two nodes A and B.

This problem will be discussed again in Chapter 4, where the same problem will be formulated as a linear program, which yields the nodal optimality results directly from the properties of a linear program. From the gravity model, center and median discussions, it is quite clear that depending on the figure of merit for evaluation, a facility can be located at very different places. It is therefore important to properly define an evaluation measure from the beginning of an analysis.

C. Competitive Location and Games

Let us now illustrate competitive location decisions on a network. Suppose there are already p facilities located. We wish to locate r new facilities that are to compete with the existing facilities for providing service to the customers at the nodes. All demands are perfectly inelastic and the consumers' preferences are binary. We assume customers will change their habits and use the closest new facility if and only if it is closer to them than the closest old facility. Ties are broken in favor of an old facility. Suppose there are two competitors, where both players wish to control as large a share of the market as possible. The first player selects p points for his facilities; the second player, having knowledge of the competitor's decision, selects r points. As the problem is presently stated, each player has exactly one move and has to make the best move possible. This is especially true in situations where the facilities are expensive to construct, and once the facilities are constructed no further moves can be contemplated. The first player knows that once the p sites are selected, the second player will then select the best possible r sites for the facilities. One may pose two possible scenarios for this game to continue beyond the first move by each player (Hakimi 1990).

> **(a)** The facilities are mobile but for each player it takes a certain amount of time to respond to the other player's choice of sites (move), assuming that the players do have the computational power to make the best move at each step.

> **(b)** The first player does not have the computational power to find r centers while each player does have the capability of finding r medians or p medians. For both cases, the question arises about where the two players will end up.

Example 1

In the example shown in Figure 2.29(a), we assume $p = r = 1$, the payoff at each node to be 1, and the arc lengths are all 1. In Figure 2.29(b) both players' first moves are indicated, where $y_1(1)$ is the mid-point on the edge (2, 3) which is a 1-median. At this stage, it is the first player's turn to move. That move ($x_1(2)$) and the second player's response to it ($y_1(2)$) are shown in Figure 2.29(c). Finally, Figure 2.29(d) indicates the third move of the first player and the second player's response. At this stage, it is clear that the game will continue indefinitely. Whichever player quits first is the loser and will control exactly one-third of the market, leaving the rest to the other player. This example illustrates a situation where the game does not reach an equilibrium, that is, where each player finds that continuing to move is the only way to avoid being limited to the one-third share of the market. Note that in the above example, the first move by the first player, that is the choice of $x_1(1)$, is a 1-center of the network. ∎

Figure 2.29 NON-EQUILIBRIUM EXAMPLE

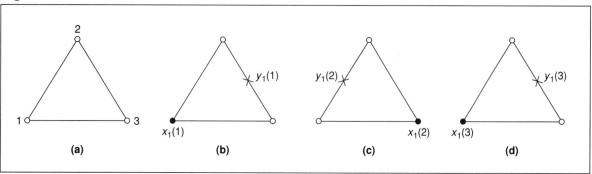

(a) (b) (c) (d)

SOURCE: Hakimi (1990). Reprinted with permission.

Figure 2.30   EQUILIBRIUM EXAMPLE

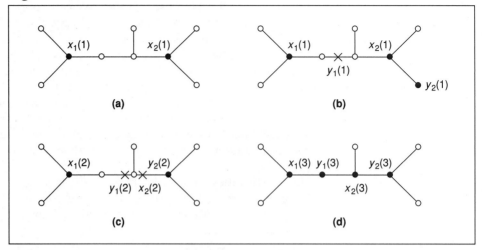

SOURCE: Hakimi (1990). Reprinted with permission.

Example 2

Let us now consider the network of Figure 2.30(a). Assume the payoff at each node is 1, $p = r = 2$, and the arc lengths are all 1. The first player's move $\{x_1(1)\ x_2(1)\}$ and the second player's response $\{y_1(1), y_2(1)\}$ are shown in Figure 2.30(b). The first player's second move $\{x_1(2), x_2(2)\}$ and, correspondingly, the second player's second move $\{y_1(2), y_2(2)\}$ are shown in Figure 2.30(c). The players' third moves $\{x_1(3), x_2(3)\}$ and $\{y_1(3), y_2(3)\}$ are again shown in Figure 2.30(d). Now it is the first player's turn again. He or she knows, of course, of the positions of his or her competitor and finds that his or her present location is at a 2-median. Thus he or she will not move from his or her present position which implies that the second player also will not move and the game is over. Thus the game terminates in an equilibrium state. We note in passing that the first player's position constitutes a 2-center location of this tree network as well. ∎

D. Imperfect Information

It can be seen that the spatial games illustrated above is based in part on the players' lack of perfect information. We start with a single player making a decision on the basis of a known set of information. The first decision to make is whether the player is in the best situation achievable. If he or she is not then he or she must take action. However, there are two problems: one is a lack of perfect information, such that what the player perceives is not necessarily true and because of this ignorance additional information might be needed. Secondly, the player recognizes that even if the adjustment to improve the situation is made, that might not be achieved in a given decision period. In general, our decision maker is assumed to be extremely myopic, to the extent that the system state does not change as a result of his or her decision. We have a situation reminiscent of early attempts to solve classic models of oligopoly markets, in other words, markets dominated by several players. Under these assumptions, the market solution could be shown to be stable, as in the Cournot case where the rival's output is assumed constant in each decision period, and one adjusts his or her output to maximize profit accordingly. Or the market may be unstable, as in the Bertrand or Edgeworth case, where the rival's spatial prices are assumed constant, and the price is adjusted to under cut the rival.[3] In these cases we need to examine two features, whether a full stable equilibrium will be reached and, if so, the speed at which this will take place. The critical factors will be the adjustment to the assumed optimal position and the possible error in making that assumption. Oftentimes, we are concerned less with the final equilibrium itself and more with the path leading to it. In this regard, we are particularly interested in individual players' reactions in each period (Vickerman 1980).

A more realistic model would need to relax the assumed myopia of individuals and introduce strategic reactions of the type adopted in game theory, in which perfect knowledge is assumed. Starting with pure zero-sum games, for example, a conservative player is maximizing minimum gain while the other equally conservative player is minimizing maximum loss. As implied in a zero-sum game, gain to one player matches the amount of loss to the other. In general, individuals are concerned not only with their own attempts to optimize but also with any reactions of conflicting parties to their own actions. A simple example will illustrate the complexities introduced here. A supermarket chain siting a new store will recognize that other shops will be responding to the same stimuli (for example, relative proximity to a new residential area) and that this may generate additional benefits such that the precise site cannot be planned independently. It also realizes that competitors will also respond in an attempt to secure new markets themselves. The calculation depends additionally on the assumptions made about the response of customers, both existing and potential. In the absence of collusion, all of these responses have to be given ahead of time, but the final solution will depend on how good those assumptions are. Once again we shall need to be concerned with whether the path converges ultimately to a stable equilibrium and the speed at which the adjustment takes place. In this case it is not sufficient simply to take assumed responses and examine the behavior of the system, since non-myopic individuals concerned with improving their situations will also learn from revealed responses and accordingly may modify their responses in subsequent decisions. Hence, we also require a learning process within the model.

It will be clear even from this simple description that a representative model of this type will be unavoidably complex. While it would be possible to proceed with continuous functions in a model, there is much to be said for taking a programming approach—an approach which involves systematic computational procedures (often using a computer.) Many of the decisions are of a discrete nature and may involve thresholds and discontinuities that are awkward for a continuous model. The use of discrete time periods also accommodates varying degrees of myopia in adjustment. It is also important that we should stress the operation of the economy as a series of explicitly individual but interdependent decisions. The most useful approach to this type of problem is **recursive programming,** in which a relationship between given system states and expected actions is established, and so are the attempts to simulate a sequence of expected actions through time (Nelson 1971).[4]

There are two possible assumptions about how the markets move into equilibrium at the end of each period. One way is to require the markets to clear period by period, so that a sequence of temporary equilibria is formed, or so that disequilibrium can exist. This was illustrated in Section VI of this chapter, where the transition between one, two and three facilities in a growth environment is anything but continual. An assumption of equilibrium appears unrealistic and almost contrary to the logic of an adaptive model that depends on the independent, albeit linked, reactions of different individuals. Unrealistic as it may be, it does have a number of convenient, simplifying properties. For example, it raises the question of whether individuals attempt to move into full equilibrium. If experience teaches them to modify their behavior, it should also reveal the degree of success of such modification. Given these behavioral adaptations, a policy of suboptimizing may be less costly than an attempt at complete optimization. The sets of reactions might incorporate information about this learning process in a full disequilibrium, wherein it is a conscious decision of individuals that causes the failure to achieve market equilibrium.

It will be apparent that this approach enables a considerable degree of flexibility in the structure and design of a model of the urban, and general spatial, system. At this level of generality it is not possible to draw even qualitative conclusions about whether the results will differ substantially from those of an equilibrium model. It does, however, seem reasonable to expect that, freed from a requirement of a dynamic equilibrium path or even a period by period establishment of equilibrium, the spatial economy may well exhibit a rather different structure. The next step is therefore to use simple versions of this model to simulate the development and structure of urban areas under, for example, different reaction schedules. Such an approach may form an empirical base in the examination of the performance and structure of urban economies under practical planning regimes. A further question is the extent to which such a model can be used to evaluate urban changes, given most evaluation procedures are based on equilibrium metrics. For further details, see chapters starting with "Generation, Competition and Distribution" and ending with "Spatial Equilibrium and Disequilibrium," in Chan (2000).

VIII. ECONOMIC BASIS OF THE GRAVITY-BASED SPATIAL ALLOCATION MODEL

In the traditional literature, the most common location technique for land use (as contrasted with facility location) is the gravity model. Here we will derive the various forms of the gravity model based on the assumption that individuals maximize their net benefits in choosing a destination facility (Cochrane 1975). The trade proportions among competing shopping centers, for example, reflect the overall probability of trips being made on the basis of the attractiveness and convenience of the shopping center. Various forms of gravity models have been proposed. They are reviewed below in preparation for later parts of this book.

A. The Singly Constrained Model

Singly constrained gravity model is one in which the number of trips originating in any subarea is assumed determined and fixed. These trips are being made to any of the competing facilities that offer the service. In addition, the model assumes that at each destination there exists some quantity of activities that attracts consumers to patronize that facility. Thus the activity at a shopping mall may be the size of the mall measured in retail floor space. We do not know the precise value a trip maker might place on any particular trip, since tastes are individual.

Figure 2.31   PROBABILITY DENSITY FUNCTION OF TRIP UTILITY

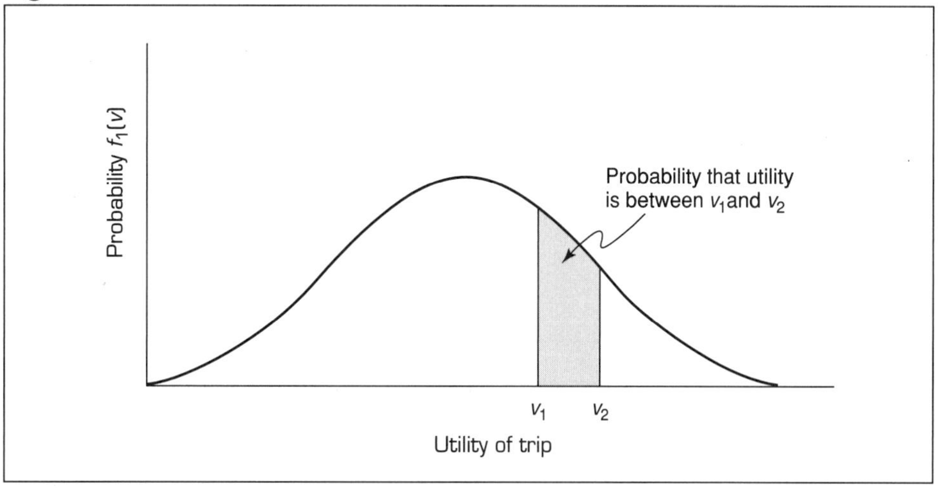

SOURCE: Cochrane (1975). Reprinted with permission.

However, we hypothesize that we can assign a probability that this value will fall between trip utilities v_1 and v_2 (see Figure 2.31.) Define consumers' surplus as the net benefit of any trip after the trip cost has been subtracted from the basic value or utility. Since we can estimate the cost of any particular trip, we can estimate the probability that the surplus lies between any two values.

The central assumption of the present derivation of the gravity model is that the probability that a particular trip maker from one subarea will travel to a facility is the probability that the trip to that facility offers a surplus greater than that of a trip to any other facilities. The probability of an individual trip to a facility being optimal increases with the activity or opportunity at that facility and decreases with travel distance, since the net benefit is reduced by a greater cost. We consider the effect of the number of opportunities offered by a facility. Since we are interested in the probability that the trip to the facility is the best choice, we first estimate the probability of the utility of the optimal (highest utility) trip lying within particular bounds. The cumulative distribution function of the largest v among n independent samples from a common underlying distribution is given by $\Phi(v) = [F(v)]^n$ where $F(v)$ is the cumulative distribution function of the common underlying distribution. The reason is that the cumulative distribution function is the probability that the value is less than or equal to v, and the probability that the best of n is in this range is identical to that of all n being less than or equal to v. Now provided n is moderately large (in double figures at least), $\Phi(v)$ is scarcely affected by the shape of the underlying distribution outside the upper tail (see Figure 2.32.) It is possible to develop an asymptotic (large n) expression of $\Phi(v)$ based only on the shape of the upper tail. If the upper tail can be approximated by a simple exponential function, as indicated in Figure 2.32, $\Phi(v)$ rapidly approaches the simple asymptotic form

$$\Phi(v) = \exp[-ne^{-b(v-\bar{v})}] \tag{2.41}$$

where $\bar{v}$ is the average trip utility.

Figure 2.32 CUMULATIVE DISTRIBUTION FUNCTIONS OF TRIP UTILITY

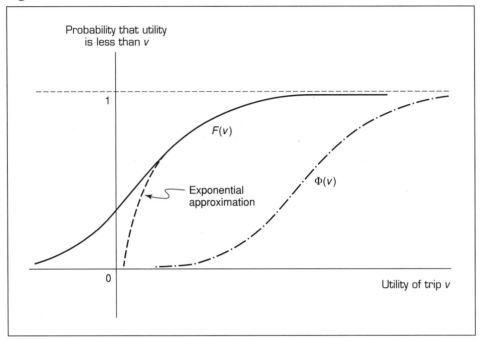

SOURCE: Cochrane (1975). Reprinted with permission.

Provided that we assume only that the underlying distribution is approximately exponential in the upper tail, the probability density function for the utility of the best trip in any subarea is given by the differential of Equation 41. This distribution is indicated in Figure 2.33. It is a positively skewed distribution whose skewness is independent of b, $\bar{v}$ and n. The mean is

$$\bar{v} + \frac{1}{b}[\ln(n) + 0.577]$$

and the standard deviation is $\sigma = \pi/\sqrt{6b}$. As n increases, the distribution remains identical in form, but moves to the right of a distance proportional to $\ln(n)$. It may be argued that we do not know the activity at a facility that attracts trips. For our purpose, it is in fact only necessary to assume that the proportion of trips ending up in facility j, $T_j'n$, is proportional to W_j, activity at facility j: $T_j'n = c'W_j'$ where c' is a proportionality constant. Hence for trips to facility j, $\Phi(v) = \exp[-c'W_j e^{-b(v-\bar{v})}]$.

We can now calculate the surplus (or net benefit) offered to a trip maker from subarea i by the optimal trip to facility j. We define this surplus as the difference between the probabilistic utility v (the gross benefit of making the trip) and a deterministic trip cost C_{ij} incurred in making the trip. C_{ij} is a generalized cost incorporating direct payments, time costs, and so forth. The surplus is therefore given by $S_{ij}' = v_i - C_{ij}$, and by substitution, we can obtain the probability that the surplus will attain any particular value S':

Figure 2.33   PROBABILITY-DENSITY FUNCTION FOR THE UTILITY OF THE
BEST TRIP

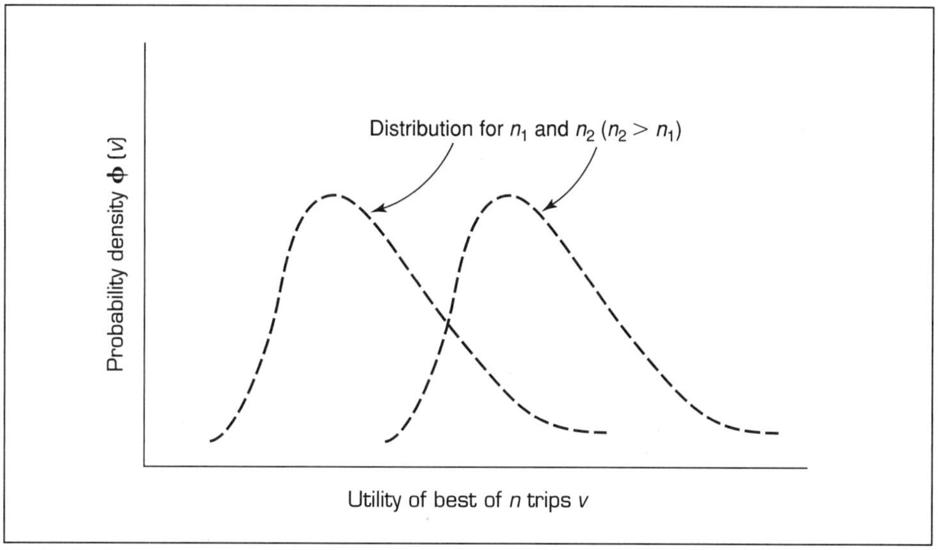

SOURCE: Cochrane (1975). Reprinted with permission.

$$\Phi_{ij}(S') = \exp\left[-c'W_j e^{-b(s'-\bar{v}+C_{ij})}\right] \tag{2.42}$$

where $\Phi_{ij}(S')$ is the cumulative distribution function of the surplus accruing from
the preferred (optimal) trip between subarea i and facility j. Our basic assumption
throughout is that a trip maker will choose the trip from his origin subarea that
maximizes personal surplus. The probability that this trip from subarea i will be
to facility j is the probability that the highest surplus offered by a trip possibility
in facility j is greater than the highest surplus offered by any other facility. This
probability is given by

$$\int_{-\infty}^{\infty} \phi'_{ij}(S')\left[\prod_{r\neq j}^{J} \Phi_{ir}(S')\right]dS' \tag{2.43}$$

This equation considers all the joint probabilities that "the surplus result-
ing from the trip to facility j has a value in the neighborhood of S' ($\Phi_{ij}(S')$) and that
"the surplus resulting from a trip to another facility is less than S'." Integrating
from $-\infty$ to ∞ assumes that the trip will always be made even if the surplus is negative. However, if the cost determines which trip is made rather than whether a
trip is made at all, the probability of the surplus being negative is very low and
we can approximate with these limits of integration, which is simpler computationally.

Equation 2.43 can be rewritten as

$$\int_{-\infty}^{\infty}\left[\frac{\phi'_{ij}(S')}{\Phi_{ij}(S')}\left(\prod_j \Phi_{ij}(S')\right)\right]dS' \tag{2.44}$$

Differentiating Equation 2.42, we obtain

$$\phi'_{ij}(S') = bc'W_j\exp\left[-b(S'-\bar{v} + C_{ij})-bW_je^{-b(-\bar{v}+ C_{ij})}\right] \tag{2.45}$$

Substituting Equations 2.42 and 2.45 into Equation 2.44, we obtain

$$\frac{W_je^{-bC_{ij}}}{\Sigma_jW_je^{-bC_{ij}}}$$

which is the same as the gravity model of Huff, as indicated in Equation 2.3, except a power function of travel time is now replaced by a negative exponential function of generalized spatial cost. Since the total number of trips originating from subarea i is V_i, the expected number of trips V_{ij} from subarea i to facility j is

$$\frac{V_iW_je^{-bC_{ij}}}{\Sigma_jW_je^{-bC_{ij}}} \tag{2.46}$$

which is the customary form of the singly constrained gravity model. We can calculate the total surplus arising from the trips actually made. The calculation uses methods unfamiliar outside statistics (see Cochrane [1975] for derivation):

$$\frac{1}{b}\sum_i V_i\left[0.577 + \ln\left(c'e^{b\bar{v}}\sum_j W_je^{-bC_{ij}}\right)\right] \tag{2.47}$$

We are normally only interested in the change in surplus resulting from a change in trip costs from C^0 to C', which can be represented by

$$\frac{1}{b}\Sigma_i V_i\ln\left[\frac{\Sigma_jW_je^{-bC'_{ij}}}{\Sigma_jW_je^{-bC^0_{ij}}}\right] \tag{2.48}$$

as shown in Equation 2.17 and illustrated in Figure 2.9.

Example
With the appropriate average-trip-utility $\bar{v}$, $W_j = 1$ and a single trip origin $V_i = 1$, Equation 2.46 can be simplified to read $\theta_{ij} = \exp(-bC_{ij})/\Sigma_j\exp(-bC_{ij})$, Equation 2.47 becomes $S_i' = \frac{1}{b}\ln\Sigma_i e^{-bC_{ij}}$ and Equation 2.48 becomes

$$\frac{1}{b}\ln\left[\sum_j \exp(-bC'_{ij})\Big/\sum_j \exp(-bC^0_{ij})\right]$$

Notice that if the travel-choice set has only one option, the summation sign vanishes and $S_i' = C_i = \bar{v}$. Suppose $b = 0.2$, $C_{i1} = 5$ and $C_{i2} = 8$ for the base-year and $C_{i1} = 5$, $C_{i2} = 8$ and $C_{i3} = 12$ for the forecast year after an accessibility improvement. These three expressions can be evaluated as shown in Table 2.4 and

Table 2.4   SAMPLE BENEFIT MEASURES BEFORE ACCESSIBILITY
            IMPROVEMENT

C_{ij}	b	$\exp(bC_{ij})$	θ_{ij}	$\bar{v}$	S_i'
$C_{i1} = 5$	0.2	0.3679	0.6457	6.0629	2.8126
$C_{i2} = 8$		0.2019	0.3543		
Total		0.5698	1.0000		
$C_{i1} = 5$	0.6	0.0498	0.8581	5.4257	4.7450
$C_{i2} = 8$		0.0082	0.1419		
Total		0.0580	1.0000		

SOURCE: de la Barra (1989). Reprinted with permission.

Table 2.5. The second expression S_i'—representing the utility or benefit (actually a
dis-utility or dis-benefit in this case) from origin i—is evaluated at 2.8126 for the
base-year, and 2.0738 for the forecast-year. The third expression, representing the
difference in benefit attributable to accessibility improvement, is evaluated at
$(1/0.2) \ln [0.6605/0.5698] = 0.7386$ (de la Barra 1989).

  If $b = 0.6$, the surplus from origin i is evaluated at $S_i' = 4.7450$ for the
base-year and 4.7227 for the forecast-year. The consumers-surplus increase is now
0.0228 (instead of 0.7386.) Remember that the $b = 0.2$ represents a low-sensitivity
group while $b = 0.6$ a high-sensitivity group, where sensitivity in this case
refers to responsiveness to cost. Thus the lower sensitivity group perceives a
lower disutility from the same travel choice set when compared with the high-
sensitivity group (2.81 against 4.75 in the base-year). For the consumer-surplus
increase, the low-sensitivity group clearly benefits more from the accessibility

Table 2.5   SAMPLE BENEFIT MEASURES AFTER ACCESSIBILITY
            IMPROVEMENT

C_{ij}	b	$\exp(bC_{ij})$	θ_{ij}	$\bar{v}$	S_i'
$C_{i1} = 5$	0.2	0.3679	0.5570	6.8772	2.0738
$C_{i2} = 8$		0.2019	0.3057		
$C_{i3} = 12$		0.0907	0.1373		
Total		0.6605	1.0000		
$C_{i1} = 5$	0.6	0.0498	0.8472	5.5092	4.7227
$C_{i2} = 8$		0.0082	0.1401		
$C_{i3} = 12$		0.0008	0.0127		
Total		0.0588	1.0000		

SOURCE: de la Barra (1989). Reprinted with permission.

improvement (0.7386 versus. 0.0228). These results show the importance of these surplus indicators in evaluating policy options. Traditionally, transport-related projects have been evaluated with a cost and time criterion, assuming that the preferred project will be the one producing the lowest average-travel-cost. The numerical example above shows that this is clearly a fallacy—$\bar{v}$ has increased from 6.06 to 6.88 and from 5.43 to 5.51, respectively, after accessibility improvement!

Using consumers' surplus, accessibility improvement will always produce benefits, however small, and these benefits will not be the same throughout various population groups. It can be seen, for example, that for the population with a low sensitivity to cost, the percentage of trips destined for the nearest zone, corresponding to $C_{ii} = 5$, is 0.6457. By contrast, for the population with a high-sensitivity to cost, the percentage rises to 0.8581. As a result, the average-cost $\bar{v}$ paid by the high-sensitivity group will be lower than that of the low-sensitivity group (5.43 against 6.06). In the forecast-year (after accessibility improvement), 14 percent of the low-sensitivity group can now access the distant zone 3, against only 1 percent of the high-sensitivity group. Correspondingly, the average-cost $\bar{v}$ of the former group rises from 6.06 to 6.88, while the latter group only moves from 5.42 to 5.51. The average utility indicators S_i' show in both cases an improvement when the new accessibility option is introduced, but they also show that the low-sensitivity group benefits more, because the dis-utility moves from 2.81 to 2.07 while the high-sensitivity group hardly moves from 4.75 to 4.72. Hopefully, this numerical example drives home the usefulness of interpreting the gravity model in terms of economic benefits.

B. The Doubly Constrained Model

Aside from a fixed number of trips originating from i, the doubly constrained gravity model also restricts the number of trips ending in j. This model is appropriate for work trips where the number of trips emanating from the origin residential subarea every morning is perfectly inelastic, and these trips are heading toward employment centers that have a specific number of jobs, at least in the short run. If there is no constraint on trip ends, there will be some employment centers j in which the number of unconstrained trip ends will exceed the number of jobs available. We assume that under these conditions competition will lead to the jobs being taken up by those trips for which the surplus available is greatest. This will occur either because the utilities of the set of trip ends are bid down or because the costs are bid up. In either case we may represent the effect as the addition of an extra cost r_j to the trip, these additional costs are set such as to restrict demand to the jobs available.[5]

We then rewrite Equation 2.42 as

$$\Phi_{ij}(S') = \exp\left[-c'W_j e^{-b(S'-\bar{v} + C_{ij} + r_j)}\right].$$

Substituting in Equation 2.44 and integrating as before, we obtain the probability of a trip ending up in employment center j:

$$\frac{W_j e^{-b(r_j + C_{ij})}}{\Sigma_j W_j e^{-b(r_j + C_{ij})}} = \frac{W_j e^{-br_j} e^{-bC_{ij}}}{\Sigma_j W_j e^{-br_j} e^{-bC_{ij}}} \tag{2.49}$$

The number of trips from i to j is correspondingly

$$V_{ij} = V_i \frac{W_j e^{-br_j} e^{-bC_{ij}}}{\Sigma_j W_j^{-br_j} e^{-bC_{ij}}}$$

where r_j is the calibration constant chosen such that $\Sigma_i V_{ij} = V_j = c'W_j$ for all j as mentioned. It is clear that this model is equivalent to the conventional doubly constrained model

$$V_{ij} = V_i \frac{W_j a_{j0} e^{-bC_{ij}}}{\Sigma_j W_j a_{j0} e^{-bC_{ij}}}$$

where $a_{j0} = e^{-br_j}$ with both a and r representing a calibration constant. A numerical example of the doubly constrained gravity model is found in Chapter 3. The change in surplus resulting from a change in trip costs is given by

$$\frac{1}{b}\Sigma_i V_i \ln\left[\frac{\Sigma_j W_j e^{-br_j} e^{-bC'_{ij}}}{\Sigma_j W_j e^{-br_j} e^{-bC^0_{ij}}}\right]. \tag{2.50}$$

In order to balance the number of trip destinations with the number of origins over the entire area, some of the additional facility costs r_j will be positive and some will be negative. These values will result in a_{j0}'s less than and greater than one respectively. It should also be noted that the surplus expression represents the benefit received solely by trip makers.

C. The Unconstrained Model

The unconstrained model is the most difficult of the gravity models discussed so far, where the trip generation at origin is modeled in addition to trip distribution. A partially constrained model is suggested by Cochrane (1975) in which it is assumed that there exists an upper limit to the number of trips generated by any subarea—as the trip costs rise, some of the trips are no longer made. When integrating Equation 2.43 above, we took the limits of integration from $-\infty$ to ∞. The low value was used because when the distribution of maximal surplus is very much greater than zero the probability of a negative value of surplus is negligible and we can obtain a simple integral by using these limits. This assumption implies that the primary economic force bringing about trip making is stronger than those that decide the choice between destinations. If this is not the case, we should integrate more precisely between limits of 0 and ∞. This implies that the trip maker decides not to make even the optimal trip if the surplus is not positive. Where the utility of the trip is only of the same order as the cost, this is an important consideration. Certain social and recreational trips are likely to come into this category, although trips such as work trips do not. More will be said about this in the "Location-Allocation" chapter of Chan (2000).

Integrating Equation 2.43 between the new limits leads to

$$[1-\exp(-b'\Sigma_j W_i e^{-bC_{ij}})]\frac{W_j e^{-bC_{ij}}}{\Sigma_j W_j e^{-bC_{ij}}} \tag{2.51}$$

where $b' = -c'e^{b\bar{v}}$. Trips executed V_{ij} can be expressed in terms of this uncon-strained model by

$$V_{ij} = V_i(W_i, W_j, b', b, C_{ij})\Theta(W_j, b, C_{ij}) \tag{2.52}$$

where V_i is the trip-generation term and Θ is the trip distribution term. Each of these two terms can be equivalenced to Equation 2.51 by setting

$$V_i = W_i[1-\exp(-b'\Sigma_j W_j e^{-bC_{ij}})]$$

and

$$\Theta_{ij} = \frac{W_j e^{-bC_{ij}}}{\Sigma_j W_j e^{-bC_{ij}}}$$

The trip-generation term constrains the total trips made in response to increases in the cost of trip making. Hence, if costs rise on particular links, the total number of trips changes in accordance with the trip-generation term to a certain limit, and the allocation of trips among destinations changes in accordance with the gravity trip-distribution term meanwhile. Again, we will further develop this model in the "Location-Allocation" chapter of Chan (2000).

D. The Intervening Opportunity Model

Besides the gravity model, another common spatial allocation model is the inter-vening opportunity model (IOM). The IOM is based on a probabilistic formula-tion, which states that the probability, dP, that a trip will terminate in a destina-tion is the joint probability that no termination point has been found among the total number of opportunities n visited so far and that the trip ends up in the cur-rent destination which offers an additional dn number of opportunities: $dP = [1-P(n)] L' dn$. Here $P(n)$ is the probability that a termination point is found in the volume of destinations n, and L' is a constant probability that the subarea visited is in fact the termination point for the trip. Solving the differential equation for $P(n)$, the probability of finding a termination point in the n subareas visited is $P(n) = 1-e^{-L'n}$. The expected number of trips from i, V_i, that will terminate in j, V_{ij}, is obtained by multiplying the total number of trips originating at i by the proba-bility that the trip will terminate amid the n_j additional opportunities found in subarea j $V_{ij}=V_i[P(n+n_j)-P(n)]$. Substituting the value of $P(n)$ in the above equa-tion, the usual form of the IOM is

$$V_{ij} = V_i[e^{-L'n}-e^{-L'(n+n_j)}] \tag{2.53}$$

The basic theory of IOM states that (a) all opportunities are ordered by in-creasing distance from the origin and (b) the probability of an activity to be lo-cated at a particular destination is equivalent to a series of Bernoulli trials, where an activity is more likely to be located closer by than further away, everything else being equal. Thus in the residential location example in Figure 2.34,

Figure 2.34   DEFINITION OF OPPORTUNITIES IN THE INTERVENING
OPPORTUNITY MODEL

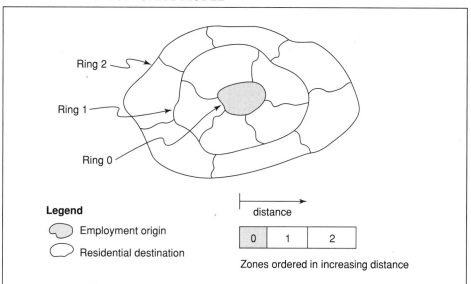

- the probability of locating in destination $0 = L'$
- the probability of locating in destination 1 but not in destination $0 =$ $L'(1-L')$; and
- the probability of neither locating in destinations 0 nor 1 but locating in destination $2 = L'(1-L')(1-L')$.

In this example, there are five residential zones at a certain distance away from the employment zone, and there are seven zones yet further away. Here the number of zones within annular ring 0, 1, and 2 are $n_0 = 1$, $n_1 = 5$ and $n_2 = 7$. The zones are identified only by the annular ring in which they are located and all zones are assumed to be of equal size to denote that each offers the same residential opportunities. Alternatively, one can think of the destinations being ordered in increasing distance from the employment origin, each with 1, 5, and 7 opportunities respectively as shown in the lower part of the figure. If the probability of residential location in a zone, L', is $1/2$, we can compute the relative frequency of residential activity distribution as

- percentage of population living in origin $0 = e^0 - e^{-(1/2)(1)} = 0.390$
- percentage of population living in destination $1 =$ $e^{-(1/2)(1)} - e^{-(1/2)(6)} = 0.556$
- percentage of population living in destination $2 =$ $e^{-(1/2)(6)} - e^{-(1/2)(13)} = 0.048$

and so on.

The simple numerical example illustrates not only the computational mechanics of Equation 2.53, but also the problem of calibration. For example, we observe that assigning the value of $1/2$ to L' is merely arbitrary; its value needs to be calibrated from available trip-length-frequency data. Second, defining residential opportunity as the physical land area may be convenient, but a more workable definition is likely to be problem specific and requires more effort. Finally, it is noted that the population allocation percentages up to the second annular rings do not add up to 100 percent. But if one considers additional annular rings ad infinitum, the sum of the percentages has to be unity according to Equation 2.53. Some practitioners prefer this model on the grounds that it can be developed from a defined set of statistical assumptions. Others have been concerned by the fact that the IOM has no intrinsic cost elements, and in particular does not distinguish the case where the subsequent opportunity is marginally more distant.

Curiously, it is possible to derive the IOM as a special case of the gravity model. We derive these models by assuming a relationship between the cost of transport between two points and the number of intervening opportunities. If we assume this to be of a power form:

$$n = b''[C_{ij}]^{\beta} \tag{2.54}$$

then $C_{ij} = [b'']^{-1/\beta} n^{1/\beta}$ where travel cost is not a function of distance as alluded to previously. In the singly constrained gravity model, we can write

$$V_{ij} = V_i \frac{n_j \exp(-b[b'']^{-1/\beta} n^{1/\beta})}{\Sigma_j n_j \exp(-b[b'']^{-1/\beta} n^{1/\beta})} \tag{2.55}$$

Substituting $b[b'']^{1/\beta} = b_0$

$$V_{ij} = V_i \frac{n_j \exp(-b_0 n^{1/\beta})}{\Sigma_j n_j \exp(-b_0 n^{1/\beta})}$$

and using the incomplete gamma function $\Gamma'[x, y]$, Cochrane (1975) evaluated Equation 2.55 as

$$V_{ij} = V_i \left\{ \frac{\Gamma'[\beta, b_0(n + n_j)1/\beta] - \Gamma'[\beta, b_0 n^{1/\beta}]}{\Gamma'[\beta, b_0 n'^{1/\beta}]} \right\} \tag{2.56}$$

where n' is the total number of opportunities in the study area. The gamma function can be considered as a set of related functions of the second variable, the particular function to be used being indicated by the first variable, which in this case is β. If the number of opportunities is directly proportional to the cost as indicated in Equation 2.54, β is equal to one and the incomplete gamma function becomes the negative exponential function. We then obtain

$$V_{ij} = V_i \left[\frac{e^{-b_0 n} - e^{-b_0(n + n_j)}}{1 - e^{-b_0 n'}} \right]$$

If n' is large, the usual form of IOM results: $V_{ij} = V_i [e^{-b_0 n} - e^{-b_0(n + n_j)}]$. This derivation illustrates a very important concept in the analysis of spatial-temporal information. Through spatial cost transformation, apparently unrelated models can be equivalenced. We will have many other examples later on in this book and in Chan (2000) to illustrate this point.

IX. CONCLUDING REMARKS

In this chapter we have reviewed many of the basic economic concepts of facility location and activity allocation. We saw that the determination of spatial patterns—both in discrete facility locations and continuous land-use developments—can be explained in a set of common terms. These common constructs range from median to center models, from input-output analysis to the gravity model—all developed from basic economic concepts such as utility theory. Modern-day econometrics also allows empirically based approaches to be used to forecast future activity patterns. This is performed independent of the classic economic concepts, as illustrated in the interregional demographic projection section. In a fairly readable manner, it illustrates the basic building blocks of spatial-temporal information. To be sure, analysis of spatial-temporal information involves not only economic or econometric techniques, but the well-established economic concepts are convenient and familiar points of departure for many who work in this field.

In the next few chapters, we will provide the ways and means to further operationalize some of these concepts. In Chapter 3, we lay out the statistical procedures; while in Chapter 4, we outline the optimization algorithms. These techniques help to implement what were up to now theoretical constructs in terms of solid operational procedures. Recent advances in both descriptive and prescriptive tools allow us to realize some of the goals that our predecessors can only dream of. We then introduce a more recent paradigm for location decisions, multi-criteria decision making, which departs from traditional economics in several ways. First, it is behaviorally based rather than structurally based, complete with its own version of multi-attribute utility theory. Second, it broadens our concepts of ranking locations and shows that some counterintuitive results regarding transitivity and intransitivity among candidate sites may occur. For example, we demonstrate that site *A* preferred to site *B*, and site *B* preferred to site *C* does not necessarily mean site *A* is preferred to site *C*. Such recent advances in behavioral and mathematical sciences allow for a more innovative approach to modeling spatial decisions in general. It is one of our objectives to report these exciting developments here in this volume.

ENDNOTES

[1] The series expansion for ln $(1 + x)$, where $-1 \leq x \leq 1$, is $x + x^2/2 + x^3/3 + ...$
[2] Much of the discussion in this section is taken from Vickerman (1980).
[3] These two cases will be analyzed in detail in later chapters when we construct models of market equilibrium.
[4] Recursive programming is explained in Appendix 2. Chan (2000) also illustrated application of recursive programming in his "Location-Routing Models" chapter. A software example is included on the attached CD under the RISE folder.

[5] Chan (2000) discussed alternate ways to effect this reallocation in his "Lowry-based Models" and "Bifurcation and Disaggregation" chapters. The readers may also wish to experiment with the software on the attached CD under the LOWRY and YI-CHAN folders.

REFERENCES

Ahituv, N.; Berman, O. (1988) *Operations manual of distributed service networks—A practical quantitative approach.* New York: Plenum Press.

Alonso, W. (1964). *Location and land use: Toward a general theory of land rent.* Cambridge, Massachusetts: Harvard University Press.

Alonso, W. (1970). "Equilibrium of the household." In *Urban analysis: Readings in housing and urban development,* edited by A. N. Page and W. R. Siegfried. Glenville, Illinois.: Scott, Foresman and Co., 168–177.

Alonso, W. (1960). "A theory of the urban land market." *Paper and Proceedings of the Regional Science Association* 6:149–157.

Anderson, S. P.; Never, D. J. (1991). "Cournot competition yields spatial agglomeration." *International Economic Review* 32:793–808.

Chapin, F. S.; Kaiser, E. J. (1979). *Urban land use planning,* 3rd ed. Urbana, Illinois.: University of Illinois Press.

Chan, Y. (2000). *Location, transport and land-use: Modelling spatial-temporal information.* New York: Springer-Verlag.

Cochrane, R. A. (1975). "A possible economic basis for the gravity model." *Journal of Transport Economics and Policy* 9:34–49.

Dahlman, C. J. (1988). "The problem of externality." In *The theory of market failure,* edited by T. Cowen. Fairfax, Virginia: George Mason University Press, 168–177.

de la Barra, T. (1989). *Integrated land use and transport modelling: Decision chains and hierarchies.* Cambridge, England: Cambridge University Press.

Dickey, J. W. (1983). *Metropolitan transportation planning,* 2nd ed. New York: McGraw-Hill.

Dorau, H. B.; Hinman, A. G. (1928). *Urban land economics.* New York: The Macmillan Co.

Friedrich, C. J., ed. (1929). *Alfred Weber's theory of the location of industries.* Chicago: Chicago University Press.

Hakimi, S. L. (1990). "Location with spatial interactions: Competitive locations and games." In *Discrete location theory,* edited by P.B. Mirchandani and R. L. Francis. New York: Wiley-Interscience, 439–478.

Hakimi, S. L. (1964). "Optimal location of switching centers and the absolute centers and medians of a graph." *Operations Research* 12:450–459.

Huff, D. L. (1962). Determination of intraurban retail trade areas. Real Estate Research Program. University of California at Los Angeles. Los Angeles.

Jha, K. Demographic models. Working Paper. Department of Civil Engineering. Pennsylvania State University. University Park, Pennsylvania.

Krueckeberg, D. A.; Silver, A. L. (1974). *Urban planning analysis: Methods and models.* New York: Wiley-Interscience.

Lakshmanan, T. R.; Hansen, W. G. (1965). "A retail market potential model." *Journal of the American Institute of Planners* 31, no. 2:134–143.

Leontief, W. W. et al. (1953) *Studies in the structure of the American economy.* New York: Oxford University Press.

Lund, J. R.; Mokhtarian, P.L. (1994). "Telecommuting and residential location: Theory and implications for commute travel in the monocentric metropolis." *Transportation Research Record* 1463, pp. 10–14.

Mai, C-C. (1986). "Random input transport rate and optimum location of the firm." *Transportation Planning Journal* (Taiwan, Republic of China) 18:311–331.

Marsh, M. T.; Schilling, D. A. (1994). "Equity measurement in facility location analysis: review and framework." *European Journal of Operations Research*, 74, No. 1:1–17.

Mokhtarian, P. L.; Meenakshisundarum, R. (1999). "Beyond tele-substitution disaggregate longitudinal structural equation modeling of communication impacts." *Transportation Research* 7:33–52.

Mokhtarian, P. L.; Varma, K. V. (1998). "The trade off between trips and distance traveled in analyzing the emissions impacts of center-based telecommuting." *Transportation Research* 3:419–428.

Nelson, J. (1971). "An interregional recursive program model of production, investment, and technological change." *Journal of Regional Science* 11: 33–47.

Newman, E. E. (1972) Economic concepts and models. Working Paper. Department of Civil Engineering. Pennsylvania State University. University Park, Pennsylvania.

Papageorgiou, Y. Y. (1990). *The isolated city state: An economic geography of urban spatial structure.* New York: Routledge (Chapman and Hall).

Van Lierop, W. (1986). *Spatial interaction modelling and residential choice analysis.* Hants, England: Gower.

Vickerman, R. W. (1980). *Spatial economic behaviour: The microeconomic foundations of urban and transport economics.* New York: St. Martin's Press.

Yeates, M.; Garner, B. (1980). *The North American city,* 3rd ed. San Francisco: Harper and Row.

3

Descriptive Tools for Analysis

"Most of the fundamental ideas of science are essentially simple and may, as a rule, be expressed in a language comprehensive to anyone."
Albert Einstein

A distinction is made in our discussion between descriptive versus prescriptive analysis techniques. A **descriptive model** is one that replicates the location and land use decisions made in a study area, while a **prescriptive model** starts out with a premise of existing practice and concentrates on the steps to arrive at a recommended course of action. Put in another way, a descriptive model summarizes the set of observed data and tries to explain these observations in a systematic manner. A prescriptive model, on the other hand, takes the view that the model has been constructed, and the model is used to choose a desirable course of action. In Chapters 3 and 4, we will review these analysis tools, paving the way for further analyses. The discussions here are geared toward problem solving; the development is therefore more intuitive than algorithmic or axiomatic in nature. We supplement these discussions with more methodological background materials attached as appendices of this book, where the readers will find self-contained reviews on optimization, stochastic process, statistics, and systems theory.

I. AN EXAMPLE

Three cities in Ohio—Cincinnati, Columbus, and Dayton—are planning a regional airport for their residents. By pooling resources, these cities will obtain a superior facility not possible without such cooperation. It is postulated that such an airport will have to be contained within the triangle defined by the three cities (Hurter and Martinich 1989). Within this triangle, it is not clear where the best location should be. The reader may recognize this as a Weber problem, as introduced in Chapter 2. If all three cities are equally important, one approach is to locate the airport in a central point convenient to all three cities. Such a location may be the common point of the angle bisectors to the triangle defined by the three cities, as illustrated in Figure 3.1. The total travel time among the three cities is 27.63 + 53.51 + 44.31 = 125.46 minutes. This reflects the airport location most convenient for any citizen, irrespective of where he or she lives.

What happens to the location if each city is weighted differently, or if the siting decision is made by a central authority that has the aggregate interest of the entire region in mind? Assuming 125 minutes is the optimum, one would expect that the total travel distance will be larger than 125, since parochial interests—interests that stand in the way of the common good—are now taken into consideration depending on the weight placed on each city. Similar to the bisector case, each city pair would have combined airport travel times longer than the straight line between them, inasmuch as the airport may be located toward the third city, rather than along the corridor between the city pair concerned. Based on this reasoning and the above calculations, we can describe the candidate airport location more precisely as a set of inequalities:

$$x_1 + x_2 \geq 70$$
$$x_1 + x_3 \geq 60$$
$$x_2 + x_3 \geq 90$$
$$x_1 + x_2 + x_3 \geq 125$$
$$x_1, x_2, x_3 \geq 0$$

The above set of equations is by no means the only, nor is it necessarily the best, description of this location problem. An advantage of this descriptive model is its simplicity, which allows the construction of a prescriptive model by superposing

Figure 3.1   A LOCATION DETERMINED BY ANGLE BISECTORS

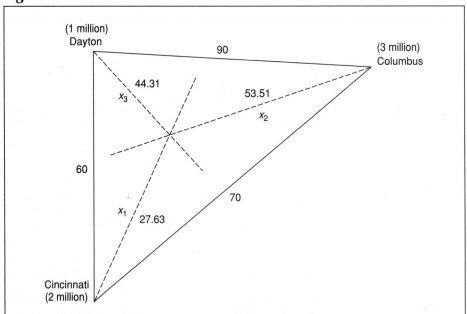

SOURCE: Claunch, Goehring, and Chan (1992). Reprinted with permission.

an objective function such as minimizing the person-minutes-of-travel: Min $2x_1 + 3x_2 + x_3$, where the set of weights are the population sizes on each city. This example, simple as it may be, may bring out the difference between what we mean by a descriptive versus a prescriptive model.

II. DESCRIPTIVE TECHNIQUES: ANOTHER EXAMPLE

In the example cited in Chapter 1, the relationship between basic and secondary economic activities in New York City and New Haven is identified, and a model is built to reflect the observed phenomenon. The relationship can often be displayed graphically in a flow chart as a first step of the analysis. To operationalize the flow chart, parameters such as the average size of a family in the study area need to be calibrated. In Chapter 1, we have already sketched out a flow chart entitled "Economic Interaction between New York and New Haven Over Time" and assumed some calibration parameters. The generic term, descriptive techniques, is used to include logical flow charts and calibration. Such tools are the ways and means to construct a model replicating the study area.

Generally speaking, there are six steps in building a descriptive model. Again using the New York-New Haven development example,

Step 1:   identifies the system components. In this example, there are three economic sectors: basic, service, and household. They are related in a pairwise manner in Figure 3.2. Basic employment refers to the new jobs introduced to either New York or New Haven. The household sector initially encompasses all the dependents of the workers brought into the area. Correspondingly, service employment consists of additional jobs required to support the households that are now located in the area.

Figure 3.2   BLOCK DIAGRAM OF THE NEW YORK-NEW HAVEN DEVELOPMENT EXAMPLE

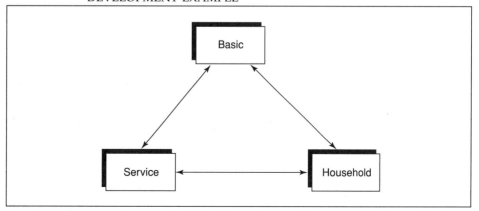

Step 2: follows with a definition of what goes into these economic sectors. One may define, for example, all support services including such services as medical, fire, education, shopping, food, and entertainment, under a single service sector rather than seperating them into the public service sector (e.g., medical, fire and education) and the private service sector (e.g., shopping, food, entertainment).

Step 3: defines specific variables corresponding to the sectors or subsystems. For example, one needs to define the basic employment as E^B, service employment E^R, and population N. Attention is paid to geographic or spatial attributes too, such as the population and employment in New York versus New Haven. Finally, we distinguish the activities in the base year versus the forecast year—in which case a temporal attribute is associated with the variables. In this example, five time periods were modeled.

Step 4: delineates the mechanisms of change or casual structure of the system. Using the New York-New Haven example again, basic employment is isolated as the seed for other dependent developments, such as service employment and population. Furthermore, the population and employment in New York and New Haven interact with each other, as shown in the commuting pattern between the two cities, in which the population of one city may find employment in another.

Step 5: One decides between a descriptive versus prescriptive application, that is to say, whether the model is to be used primarily to answer what-if type questions or in plan specification. A descriptive formulation strives to capture the development pattern of the study area as a primary focus. For a prescriptive formulation, on the other hand, specific goals and objectives of the community need to be explicitly modeled on top. In the New York-New Haven example, a descriptive, rather than prescriptive, model is constructed.

Step 6: One assembles all the aforementioned elements into a coherent model. This means the variables defined in *Step 3* are related to each other in a set of equations or other mathematical framework relating the logical structure identified in *Step 4* and in light of the application intent of *Step 5*. In subsequent discussions, we will see how this is accomplished for the New York-New Haven example.

There will be many occasions in an analysis professional's career when a model, whether descriptive or prescriptive, needs to be constructed. The above six steps will become a handy checklist for model building. This chapter will focus on descriptive techniques. These types of analysis tools will be discussed: simulation, queuing, econometrics, and calibration. They will be introduced in an order that parallels our discussions on model building. The sequence also starts with the less complex and progresses toward the more sophisticated.

III. SIMULATION

Perhaps no other tool can illustrate a descriptive model better than simulation, since a simulation model simply replicates the existing phenomenon in the study area. **Simulation** is a familiar analysis tool since it is easy to understand and apply. Notice this does not make the claim that people invariably apply it correctly; in fact, the contrary is true. There are more misuses than valid uses of simulation. It makes it so much more important, therefore, to put this analysis tool in perspective.

In the first stage of building a simulation model, components of the system and their interrelationships need to be identified. These interrelationships may be preliminary postulations that are subject to verification and validation in later stages. The basic components of a system are best displayed in a block diagram. We have already discussed the example illustrated in Figure 3.2. In this figure, the interdependency among the basic, service, and household sectors is shown by the use of arrows. Thus in a visual manner, one can see these economic sectors are tied together. The next step in this type of descriptive modeling involves a logic flow chart. The flow chart details the aggregate relationship identified in the block diagram, in which one examines the precise casual chain of events. Figure 3.3 illustrates such a chart for the New York-New Haven example. Basic employment generates dependent population. The population requires services, thus bringing in service employment. The service employees in turn have their dependent population brought into the area. Figure 3.3 clearly identifies basic employment as the seed of the subsequent activities. Furthermore, it highlights the cyclical generation of population and service employment.

Simulation can be deterministic or stochastic. **Deterministic simulation** can be best described as the modeling of the average condition of the system, ignoring the transient and time-varying behavior. **Stochastic simulation,** on the other hand, specifically gears toward the random fluctuation of the system. The New York-New Haven example is a good illustration of deterministic simulation. If we ignore the spatial interaction between the two cities, a simple model can be constructed. Suppose the variables are: basic employment E^B, population N,

Figure 3.3   LOGIC FLOW CHART OF THE NEW YORK-NEW HAVEN EXAMPLE

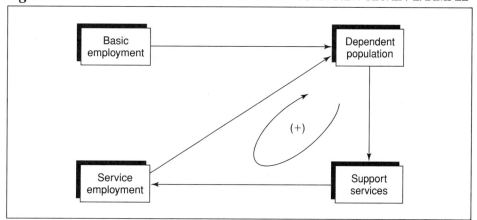

Table 3.1   ILLUSTRATION OF A DETERMINISTIC SIMULATION ON REGIONAL ECONOMIC DEVELOPMENT

Time n	Basic emp E^B	Basic emp pop	Support service emp E^R	Support service pop	Total emp E	Total pop N
1	E^B	$f E^B$	$af E^B$	$af^2 E^B$	$(1 + af)E^B$	$f(1 + af)E^B$
2			$a^2 f^2 E^B$	$a^2 f^3 E^B$	$(1 + af + a^2 f^2)E^B$	$f(1 + af + a^2 f^2)E^B$
3			$a^3 f^3 E^B$	$a^3 f^4 E^B$	$(1 + af + a^2 f^2 + a^3 f^3)E^B$	$f(1 + af + a^2 f^2 + a^3 f^3)E^B$
...			...	...	...	...
∞			0	0	$(1 + af + a^2 f^2 + a^3 f^3 + ..)E^B$	$f(1 + af + a^2 f^2 + a^3 f^3 + ..)E^B$

average household size f, and service employment multiplier a (defined as the number of service jobs generated from one resident.) The economic development of either New York or New Haven (without commuting between the two cities) can be modeled by Table 3.1. which is basically a quantification of the numerical calculations documented in Table 1.1 in Chapter 1 in which the increase in basic employment generates subsequent development through multiplier effect. The reader may wish to view the two tables side by side for comparison purposes.

It can be seen that such a procedure points toward an employment increment of $a^n f^n EB$ and a population increment of $a^n f^{n+1} E^B$ in the nth iteration. In other words, each iteration through the loop between dependent population, support services, and service employment in Figure 3.3 generates another increment of activities. As iterations progress, which can be thought of as time progresses in this example, the amount of activities generated can become smaller and smaller, remain the same, or increase, depending on the household size f and the population serving ratio a. Thus the simulation will either yield dampened growth or unlimited growth depending on the total employment series $(1 + af + a^2 f^2 + a^3 f^3 + ...)E^B$ and the total population series $f(1 + af + a^2 f^2 + a^3 f^3 + ...)E^B$.

Recognizing the similarities to a geometric series

$$1 + x + x^2 + x^3 + ... = \frac{1}{1 - x} \qquad (x < 1), \qquad (3.1)$$

the series above have analytical solutions if $af < 1$, where the total employment series sums up to $E^B/(1-af)$ and the total population series sums up to $fE^B/(1-af)$. Thus in the New York-New Haven example in Chapter 1, where $f = 2.5$ and $a = 0.2$, the total employment is $1000/[1 - (0.2)(2.5)] = 2000$, and the total population is $(2.5)(2000) = 5000$. The series will have no immediate closed form solution for $af = 1$ and $af > 1$. Thus simulation is a more versatile tool than analytical solutions in general, in that simulation can provide a solution where analytical methods fail.

Another example of deterministic simulation is the **limits to growth model** (Meadows et al. 1972). Following the procedures of this model, the feedback loop flow diagram of Figure 3.3 can be illustrated by using a positive sign, meaning that there is a reinforcement effect among the variables, as is typical of the multiplier effect in a regional economy. In a world forecasting model, Meadows et al. constructed a flow diagram consisting of both positive and negative feedback loops, depicting the interactions among the various sectors of the world economy. For example, population is positively related to the birthrate, and negatively related to the death rate, meaning that an increase in the birthrate will further increase the population, whereas an increase in the death rate will accelerate a decline in the population:

$$POPULATION = F_1(BIRTHRATE, DEATH\ RATE)$$

Birth- and death rates are again dependent upon the industrial economy well-being, agricultural food production, and the environmental condition:

$$BIRTH\text{-}DEATH\ RATE =$$
$$G(INDUSTRIAL\ OUTPUT\ PER\ CAPITA,\ FOOD\ PER\ CAPITA,\ POLLUTION)$$

In a similar manner, the feedback loops in Figure 3.4 can be represented in the remaining set of equations:

Figure 3.4   LIMITS TO GROWTH MODEL

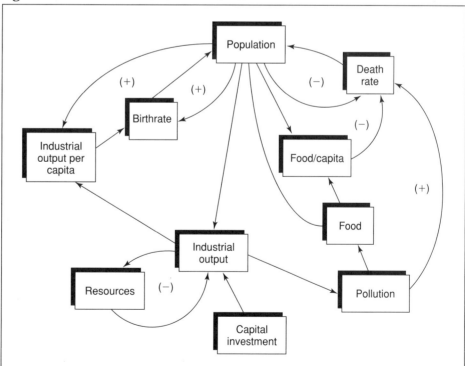

INDUSTRIAL OUTPUT = F₂(CAPITAL INVESTMENT, POPULATION, RESOURCES)

POLLUTION = POLLUTION OF PREVIOUS YEAR +
$\qquad\qquad$ *(POLLUTION-GENERATION RATE) (INDUSTRIAL OUTPUT)*

RESOURCES = FIXED AMOUNT − (YEARLY RATE OF USE) (INDUSTRIAL OUTPUT)

FOOD = F₃(POLLUTION, POPULATION)

$\qquad$ Clearly, this logic-flow diagram is much more complex than the economic-base model for New York-New Haven. The relationship needs to be expressed in the language of the computer to make the model feasible for use. In the following computer run, the inputs to the model consist of:

$\qquad$ birthrate = 0.035 (or 35 in 1000) per year

$\qquad$ death rate = 0.015/year

$\qquad$ food production rate = 1 percent growth per year

$\qquad$ resource use rate = 0.4 percent/year

$\qquad$ industrial output rate = 4 percent/year

$\qquad$ pollution generation rate = 0.3 percent/year.

$\qquad$ Starting out with these world statistics in 1970:

$\qquad$ population (P) = 3.6 billion

$\qquad$ food-production rate (F) = 1 unit/person (the average of 2000 calories
$\qquad\qquad\qquad\qquad\qquad\qquad$ per person per day)

$\qquad$ world resource (R) = 1 unit

$\qquad$ industrial output (O) = 1 unit (equivalent to 2 trillion dollars)

$\qquad$ pollution generation rate (X) = 1 unit.

$\qquad$ The model in turn forecasts these statistics in the world through the year 2100. The highly publicized doomsday result is sketched in Figure 3.5. After some transient phenomena, the steady state condition is reached where resources are depleted and the world population dwindles to a few.

$\qquad$ Other global simulation models include World Integrated Model, Latin American World Model, United Nations Input-Output World Model, and Global 2000, just to name some of the major ones (Congressional Office of Technology Assessment 1982). Worthy of note is that spatial elements are totally absent in all these models, including the limits to growth model. In other words, the entire world is treated as an entity and one does not distinguish between the continents, countries, states/provinces, and regions. We will see how such deficiencies can be redressed in subsequent discussions.

Figure 3.5   WORLD FORECAST THROUGH 2100

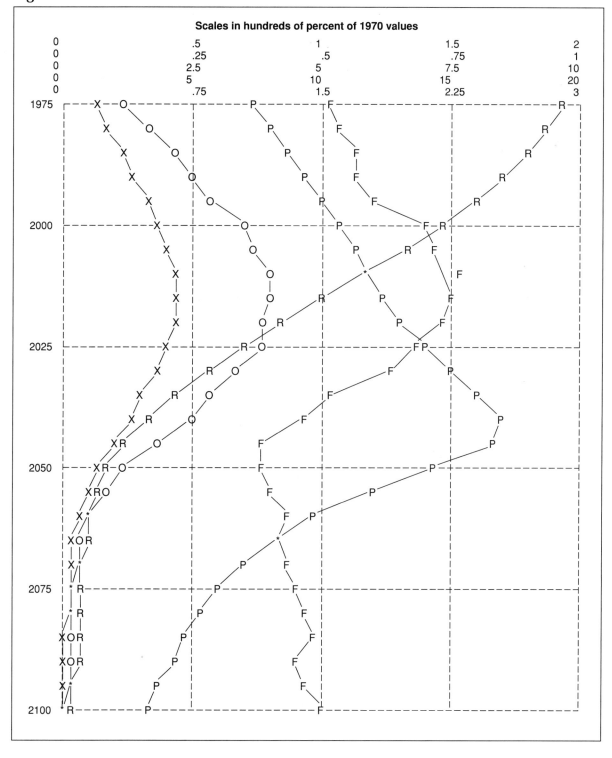

IV. STOCHASTIC SIMULATION

While deterministic simulation serves as a good introduction, much of simulation modeling involves uncertainty, which is an integral part of the model. Stochastic simulation has its Monte Carlo variety and discrete event variety. Here, we define **Monte Carlo simulation** as the model which addresses uncertainty through random number generators, which effectively generates probability distributions through much the same idea as a roulette wheel. Thus the probability of certain events taking place is determined by spinning such a roulette wheel. A clock may be used to keep track of time increments, as was done in the limits to growth model. At each time increment, an event may or may not happen depending again on the random number generator that serves as the roulette wheel in the computer. Discrete event simulation, on the other hand, goes one step further in sophistication. It goes from the current event to the next event in sequence, with the clock updated as it processes the next event. Most people associate this branch of simulation with computer languages, including GPSS, SIMSCRIPT, GASP, SLAM (Pritsker 1986) and SIMAN. Recent advances in computer science call for object-oriented simulation languages that allow for model execution efficiency. Discrete event simulation has not been as widely used as regular Monte Carlo simulation in facility location and land use, simply because of the more aggregate nature of location decisions. Recent requirements of a service economy, however, have changed this practice dramatically, as we will see in Section V.

The best way to illustrate Monte Carlo simulation is still through examples. Many land use games are used to introduce students of planning to the many political and institutional factors in development. One of these is the **Community Land Use Game (CLUG)** developed by Feldt (1972). The decision-making process on urban development is often characterized by conflicting interests seeking social, political, and financial gain. Short of actual experience (which sometimes turns out to be costly), the use of games is one of the best ways to highlight the issues. CLUG is usually played by three or more teams, each of which consists of two or more members. A community is represented on a square with a grid of secondary road network and spines of primary roads. A utility plant, denoted by a circle, is set up, but without any distribution and collection facilities (see Figure 3.6). The game board represents the site of a community yet to be developed by the players. The local economy is connected with the outside world through a transportation terminal (marked as a square at the waterfront). The game simulates the development of a brand new community, as catalyzed by the initial location of basic industries (or export service industries). In other words, external investment starts the development of the local economy.

Parallel to the concept of the economic-base theory, there are three economic sectors represented in the game:

1. **Basic industries,** consisting of full industries (FI) and partial industries (PI);
2. **Residential sector,** where the housing density ranges from sparse to dense, as represented by single residence (R1), double residence (R2), triple residence (R3), and quadruple residence (R4);
3. **Service sector,** which is exemplified by the central store (CS), local store (LS), and office unit (O). Each of these economic units is characterized by its construction cost, income, number of employees,

Figure 3.6   THE CLUG PLAYING BOARD

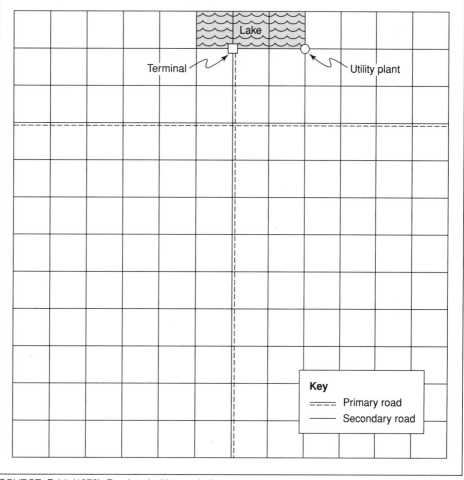

SOURCE: Feldt (1972). Reprinted with permission.

payroll, service costs and so forth. Corresponding to these sectors are also the land-use parcels (represented as a cell or square on the board) on which development can take place.

Aside from these players, someone serves as a city manager, who represents the community to the outside world, particularly in its financial management. He is the exogenous party who constructed the transportation system connecting the community with the outside world, thus laying the groundwork for future developments in the local community. The community develops the industries that occupy the land *ab initio* and that provide a tax base for the construction of the utilities. The industries, in turn, employ the labor forces from the residential population. In accordance with the economic-base theory, secondary activities such as the retail services are attracted into the city. The monetary flow between these sectors serves as a link between the various activities, and the community pays for their public utilities and other public services through taxes.

The development sequence is simulated by the following steps in the game:

1. **Purchase land.** Each team is an entrepreneur from the outside world who is contemplating land purchase investment in the study area. A bidding process is conducted, and the highest bidder on a parcel of land will be awarded its ownership.
2. **Provide utilities.** Since only the power plant exists in the beginning, power lines have to be constructed before further development is possible. Power lines have to be provided for at least one side of a parcel before that land can be developed. A majority consensus determines the precise location of a line. The construction of utility systems is to be paid for from the general tax coffers of the community.
3. **Renovate.** If this is the second or higher round of the game, the study area would have been built up already, consisting of a number of existing buildings. During the useful life of an existing building, there is a chance that the building will be lost, and the chance increases with age. Table 3.2 determines the probability of loss via the use of a pair of dice or a random number generator. For example, when the building is 10 years old, it is condemned if the equivalent numbers on a pair of dice are 5, 6, 7, or 8, which is equivalent of a loss probability of 0.556. In the event that a building is condemned, it can be demolished during the construction step of any round, in other words, at the next step.
4. **Construct building.** New construction is now considered on all lands owned by an entrepreneur, as long as utilities are available for the site. Two chances are given to each team to either construct or pass. Any construction decision should weigh income potential against cost.

Table 3.2   PROBABILITY OF BUILDING LOSS

Age of building	Probability of loss	Losing numbers
0	0.056	3
1	0.111	5
2	0.167	7
3	0.195	2, 7
4	0.250	2, 7, 11
5	0.306	2, 7, 9
6	0.362	3, 7, 8
7	0.417	5, 7, 8
8	0.445	6, 7, 8
9	0.500	3, 6, 7, 8
10	0.555	5, 6, 7, 8

5. **Designate employment.** A contractual agreement is to be made between the industry/service sectors and the household sector about the commitment of labor forces to employment opportunities. Thus both the full and partial industries, stores, and the offices bid on the existing labor pool, culminating in contracts being signed.

6. **Set prices in local store (LS), central store (CS) and office (O).** An arrangement is to be worked out between the LS and CS with the residential sector about the price of goods. Similarly, contracts are signed between the office/industries and stores in regard to the purchase of goods and services from one another. While the unit price can be negotiated with the stores and offices in the community, a fixed price is charged for goods and services purchased from the outside world through the city manager.

7. **Receive income.** In order to start the process, some incentives have to be provided to the industries to start production. The city manager gives income to the industries for putting people to work, a process simulating receiving gross earnings from the manufactured goods. The income is set above the wage rate in order to show a profit margin above labor cost. This is the only money paid by the city manager to the players; all other income is generated through payments among teams for payrolls, payments to stores, and so forth.

8. **Pay employees.** Each team owning a land use which employs people from residential units owned by another team pays that team a labor wage.

9. **Pay LS, CS and O.** Upon completing the exchange of payments for meeting payrolls to employees, each team owning residential units must make payments to the local and central stores with which they are trading at the agreed-upon price. Notice that each residential unit must make payment to two kinds of stores, both local and central, corresponding to the two types of market baskets purchased. Similarly, offices are paid for the services rendered.

10. **Pay transportation.** For each industry, the players compute the cost of shipping to the terminal by counting the number of units of distance traveled, distinguishing the different unit costs between a major highway and a secondary road. If the industry is shopping at an office on the board, the weighted distance to this unit should be computed similarly. Then players take each residential unit in turn and compute their transportation costs to work or shop also. Finally, they finish off with the LS or CS, who also use the roads to deliver their goods. These figures are then summed to yield the total transportation cost for each team.[1]

11. **Pay taxes.** Tax is levied against the real estates as a percentage of the respective assessed values. Charges are also made against the community for construction of new utility lines, for maintenance of old lines, and for social services for each residential unit. The comparison of this cost to total taxes raised can be shown to yield the community surplus or deficit for the current round. When an individual team cannot meet its tax obligations, the city manager will begin foreclosing until sufficient value has been received to meet the required tax debt.

These 11 steps illustrate the parallel between CLUG and the real world. Particularly worthy of note is the renovation portion of the simulation, where the probabilistic statement of the simulation comes in. This example shows graphically the use of Monte Carlo simulation in land use games and the similarity between certain aspects of gaming and simulation.

V. DISCRETE EVENT SIMULATION

To properly understand discrete event simulation, some background on queuing and time-dependent random process (stochastic process) is necessary.[2] Suppose a fleet of vehicles is responding to service requests in a network. A model developed by Larson, as cited by Ahituv and Berman (1988), aids in assessing the system performance under normal operating conditions (or under steady state of the system). **Larson's hypercube model** assumes that demands can be represented by different independent point sources. The point sources are represented by a **centroid,** a regular node in the network where all demands around the vicinity are supposed to originate. Calls for service arrive at the centroid according to a **time-homogeneous Poisson process,** a random pattern that averages at a given arrival rate λ'':

$$P(k) = \frac{\lambda''^{k} e^{-\lambda''}}{k!} \qquad k = 0, 1, 2, \ldots \qquad (3.2)$$

where k is the random number of actual demand-requests per unit-time. The service time τ, setting aside the enroute travel time, for each vehicle unit is assumed to be negative exponentially distributed—again a random process with a given mean $1/\mu'$: $f_\tau(\tau) = \mu' e^{-\mu'\tau}$, where τ denotes the random variable for service time.

A. Stochastic Process

Each vehicle server, say a fire truck that helps to put out a fire, may be in two possible states, busy or free. When a call arrives, a single vehicle unit is chosen from those that are free and is immediately assigned to provide service. In the event that all servers are busy, the call is either lost (in other words, passed to a nearby jurisdiction for service) or queued until a unit becomes available. We call the former **zero capacity queue** (or the **loss system model**) and the latter **infinite capacity queue.** The hypercube model provides a steady-state analysis as an approximation to time non-homogeneity. With the model, many performance measures of system effectiveness can be derived. Among the important measures are the expected service unit response time, service unit dispatch frequencies, service unit workload, and the workload of a particular unit relative to the other units. To demonstrate the model, refer to the sample network of Figure 3.7. We assume that service stations (depots) are located at nodes 2 and 5. At each station, there is only one vehicle. Whenever there is a call, the dispatcher will assign the closest available vehicle to serve the calling node. The dispatching center can assign only stationary vehicles while they are at their depots. The center cannot contact a moving vehicle. When all units are busy, a special service unit from another

Figure 3.7   SAMPLE NETWORK FOR HYPERCUBE MODEL

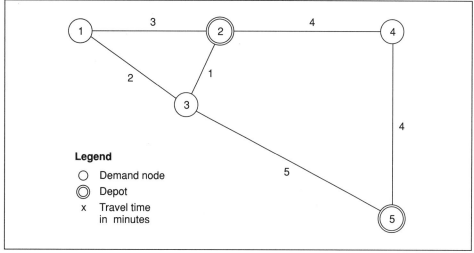

SOURCE: Ahituv and Berman (1988). Reprinted with permission.

jurisdiction will be dispatched (assuming a zero capacity queue). In addition, we know that calls for service are issued, on the average, every $1/3$ minute ($\lambda'' = 3$). The average service takes 1 minute ($\mu'' = 1$). The length of the links is measured in time units. The server's speed of travel is constant, and the demand for service, k, is equally divided among the centroids (i.e., the fraction of demand among the centroids is $f_1 = f_2 = f_3 = f_4 = f_5 = 1/5$.)

Knowing that there is only one server vehicle at each depot, we may say that at any time a depot either possesses an idle vehicle or it does not. We will denote it by 0 or 1, respectively. A state of the system is defined to be a vector of two components. The first component indicates the status (free or busy) of the server at node 2, and the second component indicates the status of the server at node 5. Since there are only two depots in the example, the entire network can be in any of the following four states:

(0, 0)   the two vehicles are available at both nodes 2 and 5;

(0, 1)   only the vehicle from node 2 is available;

(1, 0)   only the vehicle from node 5 is available;

(1, 1)   no vehicle is available from either node 2 or node 5.

Now based on the shortest distance, we can devise a dispatching table for the network, recalling that the policy is always to dispatch the closest available unit and to do nothing if both vehicles are busy (ties can be broken arbitrarily). Table 3.3 describes the dispatching rules for each of the four states:—✔ designates "dispatch," —designates "do not dispatch." It is easily seen from the table that the closest vehicle is dispatched whenever both vehicles are available [state (0, 0)]. In other states, there is only one dispatching possibility; thus, there is no dilemma as to which unit to dispatch.

Now that we have established the dispatching rules, we would like to investigate the process by which the network changes from one state to another. For

Table 3.3   DISPATCHING RULES FOR THE HYPERCUBE NETWORK

State	Server vehicle location	Demand node				
		1	2	3	4	5
(0, 0)	2	✔	✔	✔	—	—
	5	—	—	—	✔	✔
(0, 1)	2	✔	✔	✔	✔	✔
(1, 0)	5	✔	✔	✔	✔	✔
(1, 1)				not relevant		

instance, when the network is in state (1, 0) at a certain time interval, it can either change to state (1, 1) if the vehicle at node 5 is assigned to a call, or it can enter into state (0, 0) if the vehicle stationed at node 2 has been released from a previous service call (and is back at node 2). The network cannot change directly from (1, 0) to (0, 1) owing to the Poisson arrival and negative exponential service. In other words, a transition from (1, 0) to (0, 1) would imply that two events can occur in a very short time interval dt—the vehicle at node 5 is assigned while the server at vehicle 2 is being freed at the same time. Figure 3.8 depicts the transitions from one state to another. By observing Figure 3.8, we can use the information about the service rate y_1 and the call rate λ'' to derive the rate of the various transitions. For instance, when the network is in state (0, 1), it will change to state (1, 1) at a mean rate of 3 per minute, because on the average there is a call every 1/3 minute. On the other hand, the transition from (0, 1) to (0, 0) is at a mean rate of 1 per minute, since the average service time is 1 minute. A similar computation can be preformed for state (0, 0). If a call arrives from node 1, 2, or 3, the vehicle from node 2 will be dispatched. Since the rate of calls is 3 per minute and nodes 1, 2, and 3 each assume one-fifth of the overall demand, the transition rate from state (0, 0) to state (1, 0) is

$$\left(\frac{1}{5} + \frac{1}{5} + \frac{1}{5}\right) (3) = 1.8$$

Similarly, the transition rate from (0, 0) to (0, 1) is

$$\left(\frac{1}{5} + \frac{1}{5}\right) (3) = 1.8$$

These transition rates are again summarized in Figure 3.8.

Now we assume the network is in balance (steady state); namely, it makes transitions from one state to another with a regularity that reflects an equilibrium between demand for and supply of services. This implies that there are steady-

Figure 3.8   TRANSITION BETWEEN STATES IN A HYPERCUBE MODEL

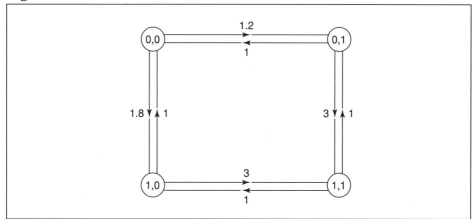

SOURCE: Ahituv and Berman (1988). Reprinted with permission.

state probabilities for being in the various states. We will denote them by $P_{(0,0)}$, $P_{(0,1)}$, $P_{(1,0)}$, and $P_{(1,1)}$. Equilibrium implies that the expected rate of leaving a state is equal to the expected rate of entering into the same state. For example, the expected rate by which the network departs from state $(0, 1)$ is $3 P_{(0,1)} + 1 P_{(0,1)}$. The first term refers to a transition to $(1, 1)$ while the second term refers to a transition to $(0, 0)$. Similarly, the expected rate at which the network arrives at state $(0,1)$ is a weighted sum of all the transition rates from states that can transition into $(0, 1)$; specifically, $1.2 P_{(0,0)} + 1 P_{(1,1)}$. Since in the steady state there should be a balance between the expected rates of entering and leaving a certain state, we may write a balance equation for $(0, 1)$:

$$3 P_{(0,1)} + 1 P_{(0,1)} = 1.2 P_{(0,0)} + 1 P_{(1,1)}$$

Similarly, we can obtain balance equations for all the other states. For $(0, 0)$, we will obtain

$$1.8 P_{(0,0)} + 1.2 P_{(0,0)} = 1 P_{(0,1)} + 1 P_{(1,0)}$$

For $(1, 0)$, we will obtain

$$1 P_{(1,0)} + 3 P_{(1,0)} = 1 P_{(1,1)} + 1.8 P_{(0,0)}$$

For $(1, 1)$, we obtain

$$1 P_{(1,1)} + 1 P_{(1,1)} = 3 P_{(1,0)} + 3 P_{(0,1)}$$

In addition to these balance equations, we know that the state probabilities should add to 1:

$$P_{(1,1)} + P_{(1,0)} + P_{(0,1)} + P_{(0,0)} = 1$$

Now we have five equations to find a solution for four unknown probability values. Any three of the balance equations and the last one will do:

$$
\begin{aligned}
-1.2\,P_{(0,0)} & & +4\,P_{(0,1)} & & & & -1\,P_{(1,1)} & & =0 \\
3\,P_{(0,0)} & & -1\,P_{(0,1)} & & -1\,P_{(1,0)} & & & & =0 \\
-1.8\,P_{(0,0)} & & & & +4\,P_{(1,0)} & & -1\,P_{(1,1)} & & =0 \\
P_{(0,0)} & & +P_{(0,1)} & & +P_{(1,0)} & & +P_{(1,1)} & & =1
\end{aligned}
$$

The solution to these equations provides the steady-state probabilities for the network: $P_{(0,0)} = 0.1176$, $P_{(0,1)} = 0.1676$, $P_{(1,0)} = 0.1853$, and $P_{(1,1)} = 0.5295$. The results indicate that more than 50 percent of the time the two vehicles will be *busy* [$P_{(1,1)}$]. Around 11 percent of the time, the two servers will be idle [$P_{(0,0)}$]. The expected response time for this example is (where R' is the required time in dispatching a special reserve unit from a neighboring jurisdiction.)

$$
P_{(0,0)}\left[\sum_{i=1,2,3} f_i d^{2,i} + \sum_{i=4,5} f_i d^{5,i} \right] + P_{(0,1)} \sum_{i=1}^{5} f_i d^{2,i} + P_{(1,0)} \sum_{i=1}^{5} f_i d^{5,i} + P_{(1,1)} R' \tag{3.3}
$$

With $R'=10$ and all time separations d^{kl} obtainable from the shortest paths on the Figure 3.7 network, the above expression can be verified to be $(0.1176)[(0.2)(3 + 0 + 1 + 4 + 0)] + (0.1676)[(0.2)(3 + 0 + 1 + 4 + 6)] + (0.1853)[(0.2)(7 + 6 + 5 + 4 + 0)] + (0.5295)(10) = 6.7677$. The workload of the vehicle at node 2 is $P_{(1,1)} + P_{(1,0)} = 0.7148$ or this vehicle is busy about 71 percent of the time. The workload of the vehicle at node 5 is $P_{(1,1)} + P_{(0,1)} = 0.6971$. The fraction of dispatches that send the vehicle from node 2 to node 1 is $f_1[P_{(0,0)} + P_{(0,1)}] = (0.2)(0.1176 + 0.1676) = 0.0570$.

B. Simulation

The memory and execution time required to solve the hypercube model equations roughly doubles with each additional server. In other words, the procedure requires solving $2^{Q'}$ equations, where Q' is the number of servers. This can amount to huge computational requirements. Among ways to overcome this is discrete event simulation, which has become an efficient tool. This is made possible by the availability of very user-friendly simulation languages. Instead of solving simultaneous equations, the simulation processes each demand-request through the network. The term **discrete event** refers to examining the next event, whether it be another demand generated, a demand ready to be served, and so on. The program turns the clock on and eventually tallies up the performance statistics as computed analytically above.

It is not until recently that discrete event simulation has played a significant role in facility location. The City of Baltimore, for example, conducted a study to locate Emergency Medical Services (EMS). A validated discrete event, stochastic simulation model, Ambulance System Site Inspection Simulation Technique (ASSIST), was used to measure the performance of the EMS, pointing toward a city wide response time of 5 minutes; 95 percent of the demand was responded to within 10 minutes. Though these statistics indicated a well-run system, the EMS administrators requested a study because of perceived inequities in the spatial distribution of service, outlying areas tended to have higher response times than areas in the center of the city. ASSIST was used to validate the location of EMS by an optimization model (Heller et al. 1989). Parameter estimation of the optimization model was based on the same data used in the simulation and, where necessary, deterministic estimation of random variables. Emergency travel times were approximated in the simulation using two databases: (1) two travel time matrices, representing peak and off-peak (8-hour time intervals each) traffic conditions for travel between the activity centroids of any two nodes in the 207-node transportation network, and (2) about 4200 medic-unit run tickets that documented the spatial and geographic history of the response. The travel time parameters in the location model, τ_{ij}, were defined by the average of the estimated peak and off-peak emergency travel times.

EMS has been simulated as a non-homogeneous Poisson process, with arrival rates defined for 24 call zones and for 6 four-hour intervals. In other words, different arrival rates are defined for each zone and each four-hour interval, rather than a homogeneous process characterized by a single average arrival rate. For the optimization model, mean daily demand at depot node j was estimated as

$$f_j(i) = P(j \mid i) \sum_{t=1}^{6} \lambda''_{it}$$

where j and i are depot and call nodes respectively, and λ''_{it} is the tth arrival rates for call node s. Historical and simulated average daily demand for EMS service system wide were both about 200 calls per day. Since there were 16 medic-units (depots) in the historical system, this average was used to define a maximum workload for any medic-unit. Perfectly balanced utilization would be achieved at about 12.5 calls per day per unit. A total of 28 current and potential medic-unit locations or home depots had been defined in the original study and were retained. A prescriptive model can be constructed by optimizing the figure of merit as defined by Equation 3.3, including equity among call zones.

Let $\Gamma(W, p) = \{j \mid y_j = 1\}$ be the siting result from the optimization of the location model with binary location-variable y_j, maximum workload for a medic-unit W, and p medic-units relocated. Solutions were generated for workloads $W = \infty$, and $W = 18, 16$, and 14. When the least constrained optimization was solved ($W = \infty$), it was found that the maximum number of units relocated was 6; thus the **relocation model** was solved for $p = 1, \dots, 6$. Example formulations of such an optimization model can be found in the "Facility Location" and "Measuring Spatial Separation" chapters of Chan (2000). Configuration solutions $\Gamma(w, p)$ to the various optimizations were obtained and, where possible, system performance measures for the configurations were compared using statistical inference. The optimization measures are deterministic and do not lend themselves to statistical comparison. All differences must be assumed to be significant since the average is all that is available. Simulation, however, also provides sample variance so the t-test[3] could be used to compare mean response times, $M(W, p)$, which were found by simulating the optimization solutions, $\Gamma(W, p)$. Here, t-values were calculated to compare $M(W, p)$ among themselves and with the base case.

The t-statistics indicate that the optimization solutions produced the desired effect of mean response time reduction in the simulated system. At about the 15 percent significance level, solutions to reduce mean response time were found by the optimization model. However, the simulated $W = \infty$ solutions, when compared to the base case, do not result in statistically significant mean response time changes, even at the 20 percent significance level. This result is quite different from the optimization results, in which up to a 0.14 minute mean response time reduction was achieved. Furthermore, if the significance level was reduced to 30 percent, it is possible that the solution, $\Gamma(\infty, p)$, for $p = 3$ and 6 results in increases in mean response time (t-values of 1.21 and 1.16 respectively). Finally, if significance levels were restricted to at least 10 percent, the t-values indicate that configuration solutions from the $W = \infty$ solution to relocate 3 to 6 units produced simulated mean response times significantly higher than the corresponding location solutions with maximum workload set at 16 and 18 respectively. These differences between simulation and optimization models can possibly be attributed to a homogeneous versus non-homogeneous assumption.

With the exception of these aberrations, optimal solution to the location of EMS has been verified against simulation results overall. Simulation was shown to be important and necessary for designing and verifying location models. Without the use of simulation, the effects projected from solutions produced by deterministic optimization models may be erroneous or not statistically significant. In the following section and the next chapter, we will describe in more detail the basic philosophy behind optimization models, so that the reader can better appreciate the statements made above. It should also be noted that this example illustrates that simulation has its proper place in spatial-temporal analysis. It can supplement stochastic process when the problem is too big to be solved analytically. It is also a good verification tool when real world data are not available for model validation.

With the advantage of several years, a similar verification study was performed by Repede and Bernardo (1994). An optimization model that maximizes the expected demand coverage was constructed. Demand variations over time or non-homogeneity was explicitly modeled in both the optimization and simulation models in the study. The siting and fleet size (or the number of ambulances) decisions obtained from the optimization model were input to a simulation model that detailed the performance of the location and fleet size decisions. The computational cycle between the two models formed a decision support system for the city of Louisville, Kentucky, with the optimization location model prescribing the siting and the simulation model evaluating the siting decision. In this case, validation data were available to gauge the quality of both the conventional static optimization model and the dynamic decision-support systems model proposed here. The decision-support system, which explicitly recognized non-homogeneity, was found to yield better agreement with field data. Better still, the decision-support system arrived at improved location decisions, corresponding to a 13-percent increase in coverage and 36 percent decrease in response time. This study again reinforces the role of stochastic process—and simulation in particular—in location analysis.

VI. INVENTORY CONTROL USING
MARGINAL ANALYSIS

In facility location, siting of warehouses is often of interest. The intent is to place a warehouse so that the transportation cost of resupplying its inventory is lowest, and so is the delivery cost to the stores or customers. Simulation and stochastic process can be used in inventory analysis, wherein the decision to reorder can be reached systematically to avoid stockout and excessive storage costs. A common approach is to employ **marginal analysis,** which shows how a descriptive tool can be used for optimization in special cases (Lapin 1975, Winston 1994). When the demand for the inventory in the warehouse is uncertain and its life-time is limited, we have an example of the newsboy problem.[4] Similar to selling newspapers at the newsstand, the objective of the newsboy problem is to decide how many items should be ordered at the beginning of each inventory cycle. The **uncertain demand** during the period $d\xi$ expresses the number of items that customers will require during this period. Two types of outcomes may occur. If demand is no larger than the order quantity (z), sales will equal the quantity demanded $d\xi$. If demand is greater than the initial order, sales will be limited to the order quantity z.

Three cost elements are considered: C is the unit cost of surplus inventory, and c is the unit opportunity cost due to shortage. Let $F(\xi)$ be the cumulative demand-function where ξ is the random variable for demand. To obtain the expected cost, we will assume that the probabilities for possible levels of demand $dF(\xi)$ is known. For an order quantity z and when demand is $d\xi$, the total cost is

$$
\begin{aligned}
C(z - d\xi) \quad & \text{if } d\xi \leq z \\
c(d\xi - z) \quad & \text{if } d\xi > z
\end{aligned}
\tag{3.4}
$$

The expected total cost is $\varphi = CP(z \geq d\xi) + cP(z < d\xi)$. Such a cost function is plotted in Figure 3.9. Equation 3.4 says that if demand is less than the order quantity, we have overstocked at a per-unit cost of C, and if demand is higher than the order quantity, we have understocked at a per-unit cost of c. Should we order one additional unit dz, the surplus cost will be increased by C, but the stockout cost will be reduced by c (or a $-c$ change). This marginal cost can be represented by the difference between overstocking cost and the reduction in stockout cost:

$$
\varphi(z + dz) - \varphi(z) = CP(z \geq d\xi) - cP(z < d\xi)
$$

To order the optimal quantity, we order until the marginal cost is equal to zero, assuming that we have the common situation of a convex cost function as shown in Figure 3.9. In other words, starting out with having economy of scale, we order until it starts to change over to dis-economy of scale:

$$
CP(d\xi \leq z) - c(1 - P[d\xi \leq z]) \geq 0
$$

The optimal order quantity z^* is the smallest level z such that

$$
CP(d\xi \leq z) - c(1 - P[d\xi \leq z]) = (C + c)\,P(d\xi \leq z) - c \geq 0
\tag{3.5}
$$

or

$$
P(d\xi \leq z) = F(z) \geq \frac{c}{C + c}
\tag{3.6}
$$

This tells us that we need to calculate only the above ratio using the unit costs given for the problem and establish the cumulative probability for demand. The smallest demand z^* with a cumulative probability that exceeds this ratio is the order quantity that minimizes total expected cost.

Figure 3.9   A CONVEX EXPECTED TOTAL COST FUNCTION

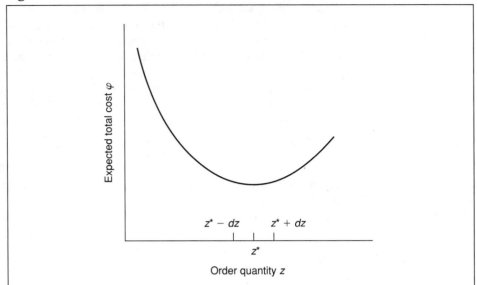

Example

Instead of direct substitution of numbers, we illustrate in this example how such a result as shown in Equation 3.6 can be useful in parametric analysis (Faneuff, Sterle, and Chan 1992). It also shows that marginal analysis has its analytic properties, thus surpassing simulation in the modeling process in limiting cases. Let demand be a uniform probability density function $f(\xi) = 0.002$. The cumulative function is then correspondingly $F(\xi) = 0.002\xi$. Suppose the current inventory stands at 100 units, and the warehouse has a storage capacity of 500. Also the expected total cost $\varphi(z)$ for an inventory cycle is parametric on Ω and ρ: $2600 - (8 + \Omega + \rho)z$. The unit costs of over- and under stocking (C and c) can be determined as a function of Ω and ρ by solving this equation:

$$2600 - (8 + \Omega + \rho)z = \int_{100+z}^{500} c(0.002d\xi) + \int_{0}^{100+z} C(0.002d\xi) \qquad (3.7)$$

where $dF(\xi) = 0.002d\xi$ as mentioned. The right-hand side of the above equation boils down to $(0.8c + 0.2C) + (0.002C - 0.002c)z$, which as a function of z consists of the intercept $(0.8c + 0.2C)$ and the slope $(0.002C - 0.002c)$. By equating them to the corresponding intercept and slope on the left-hand side of Equation 3.7 respectively, we have two equations and two unknowns C and c:

$$0.8c + 0.2C = 2600$$
$$0.002(C-c) = -8-\Omega-\rho$$

This result is $C = -400(\Omega + \rho) - 600$ and $c = 100(\Omega + \rho) + 3400$.

According to Equation 3.5, the marginal cost is set at zero, $\dfrac{d\varphi(z)}{dz} = 0$, for an optimal order quantity z^*, or $\dfrac{d\phi(z)}{dz} = (C + c) \, F(z) - c = 0$. Substituting the values for C, c and $F(z)$ from above,

$$\frac{d\varphi(z)}{dz} = (5.6 - 0.6\Omega - 0.6\rho)z - 100(\Omega + \rho) - 3400 = 0 \tag{3.8}$$

which determines the optimal order quantity in terms of the parameters Ω and ρ

$$z^* = \frac{100(\Omega + \rho) - 3400}{5.6 - 0.6\Omega - 0.6\rho} \tag{3.9}$$

In locating a warehouse, order quantity is specified for each location. This is illustrated in the "Simultaneous Location-Routing" chapter of Chan (2000). Here Ω is the parameter to account for the given warehouse capacity and ρ for each delivery vehicle capacity—capacity that is needed to deliver supplies to a demand location. ∎

VII. BAYESIAN ANALYSIS

Similar to inventory control, many facility location and land use analyses require a rule to help make sound decisions. A descriptive tool to accomplish this is **Bayesian analysis,** which includes the latest information on top of past knowledge in formulating the decision rule. We will describe this method via an example of constructing nuclear power plants on a proposed site considering safety and other environmental conditions. Based on site-specific environmental studies, we can summarize the results in terms of two states of nature: (a) geotechnical condition ideal and (b) condition marginal. Historical record of site-specific studies have shown that one out of 10 sites in the study area shows up as suitable, or $P(\text{ideal}) = 0.1$. This means that $P(\text{marginal}) = 0.9$, or nine out of 10 sites are not suitable. Now the decision maker faces two actions to consider for the construction project: (a) to build or (b) not to build at the proposed site. A payoff matrix can be written for the savings in millions of dollars for each nuclear power plant corresponding to the various decisions and states of nature:

	ideal	marginal
build	1.3	−0.2
not-to-build	0	0

This payoff matrix says that if we decide to build at the site, and the site turns out to be ideal, $1.3 million will be saved. On the other hand, if the site turns out to be marginal, remedial engineering will cost an additional $200,000. Obviously, a decision not to build does not incur any savings or cost. The expected return for each decision can now be computed:

$$\begin{aligned} build: \ & 0.1(1.3) + 0.9(-0.2) = -0.05 \\ not\text{-}to\text{-}build: \ & 0.1(0) + 0.9(0) = 0 \end{aligned} \tag{3.10}$$

Based on these numbers, the not-to-build decision should be the course of action since it is less costly.

A. Bayesian Update

Instead of making the final decision based on historical records, it is decided that additional information is to be gathered in order to have better knowledge about the site. The immediate decision then involves having additional borings drilled at $100,000 each or no additional work at (naturally) no cost. The boring may result in a positive statement about the suitability of the site or a negative statement. From experience, the accuracy of boring tests are as follows:

$$P(positive \mid ideal) = 0.7 \qquad [\text{or } P(negative \mid ideal) = 0.3]$$
$$P(positive \mid marginal) = 0.2 \qquad [\text{or } P(negative \mid marginal) = 0.8]$$

This says that the chance that a boring will tell the true story when the site is suitable is 70 percent and the chance that it will tell the wrong story is 30 percent. Likewise, the chance of telling the truth when the site is not suitable is 80 percent and telling a lie 20 percent.

The reliability of the boring test can be represented by graphical means in terms of events and sample elements. The following diagram summarizes the possible outcomes:

	ideal	*marginal*
positive	*iiiiiii*	*mm*
negative	*iii*	*mmmmmmmmm*

$$m = 9\,i$$

This indicates that the chance that the test will turn out to be positive given the site is ideal (*i*) is seven out of 10, and that the test will turn out to be negative is three out of 10. Similarly, the chance that the test will show up negative when the site is marginal (*m*) is eight chances out of 10, while the chance that it will show up positive is two out of 10 times. For every ideal site, there are nine marginal sites. This event diagram is a convenient way of keeping track of sample elements. With this diagrammatic representation, the **Bayes' rule** can be easily explained and summarized by the following equation

$$P(ideal \mid positive) = \frac{P(ideal \ and \ positive)}{P(positive)} \qquad (3.11)$$

This equation shows how to compute the chance that the site is ideal given a positive result of a boring test, when all the information is available on the right-hand side of the equation. Assuming the probability of a site being ideal given that a positive boring test is not available, such a calculation is necessary to arrive at a build or not-to-build decision. Intuitively, if the boring test is positive, we tend to infer the site is ideal, which can lead toward a build decision. Obviously, this inference can be made only under the following condition: The probability of the site being ideal given a positive test is high. Thus the decision is made easy by evaluating the above equation or assembling all the information on the right-hand side of the equation.

The assemblage of this general set of information is expedited by the application of Bayes' rule, which can be represented conveniently by Figure 3.10, a companion to the event diagram above. Assisted by the figure, these calculations can be made by further breaking down the right-hand side of Equation 3.11 in terms of the given information:

$$P(ideal \text{ and } positive) = P(ideal)P(positive \mid ideal)$$
$$= (0.1)(0.7)$$
$$= 0.07$$

$$P(positive) = P(ideal \text{ and } positive) + P(marginal \text{ and } positive)$$
$$= P(ideal)P(positive \mid ideal) + P(marginal)P(positive \mid marginal)$$
$$= (0.1)(0.7) + (0.9)(0.2)$$
$$= 0.25$$

which lead toward $P(ideal \mid positive) = (0.07)/(0.25) = 0.28$. These calculations can be confirmed by the event diagram above by counting the sample elements row-wise and then column-wise for the event of interest. Thus the probability of being ideal *and* positive is

$$7i/(7i + 3i + 2m + 8m) = 7i/(7i + 3i + 2[9i] + 8[9i]) = 0.07 \text{ and so on}$$

B. Bayesian Decisions

Given the result of an additional boring is positive, the new payoff matrix, after inclusion of the boring cost in dollars, is

	ideal	marginal
build	1.2	−0.3
not-to-build	−0.1	−0.1

Figure 3.10   GRAPHIC REPRESENTATION OF BAYES' RULE

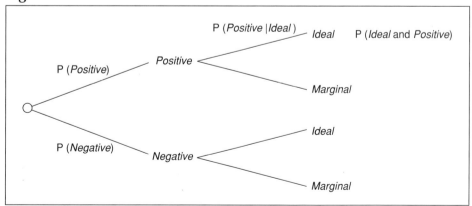

The expected return (in dollars) of the decision to build can be computed as

$$P(ideal \mid positive)(1.2) + P(marginal \mid positive)(-0.3)$$
$$= (0.28)(1.2) + (0.72)(-0.3)$$
$$= 0.12.$$

Since the expected return of the not-to-build decision is -0.1, the decision is clearly to build if boring results are positive. Next is to decide between build or not-to-build if the test is negative. Again, employing Bayes' rule:

$$P(ideal \mid negative) = \frac{P(ideal \text{ and } negative)}{P(negative)}$$

and following the same calculations as in the case of a positive boring result, it can be shown that this conditional probability is evaluated at 0.04. The expected return of building a plant is -0.24, and the expected return of the not-to-build decision is -0.1. Thus the decision is clearly not-to-build if the test result is negative.

The next logical question is: Should tests be conducted? In other words, can we arrive at the same decision without the extra expense and trouble of boring tests? To answer this question, we calculate the expected return if testing is conducted:

$$P(positive)(Payoff \text{ of a positive result}) + P(negative)(Payoff \text{ of a negative result})$$
$$= (0.25)\{P(ideal \mid positive) [1.2] + P(marginal \mid positive)[-0.3]\} +$$
$$(0.75)\{P(ideal \mid negative) [-0.1] + P(marginal \mid negative)[-0.1]\}$$
$$= (0.25)[0.28(1.2) + 0.72(-0.3)] + (0.75)[0.04(-0.1) + 0.96(-0.1)]$$
$$= -0.045.$$

Likewise, we calculate the expected return if testing is not conducted, which is the same as the expected return of the not-to-build decision as computed in Equation 3.10:

$$P(ideal)(payoff \text{ from an ideal condition}) +$$
$$P(marginal)(payoff \text{ from a marginal condition})$$
$$= (0.1)(0) + (0.9)(0)$$
$$= 0$$

Compared with incurring a cost of $100,000 to conduct a test, the decision is obviously not to test.

C. Decision Tree

The best way to review the entire problem is by way of a **decision tree,** which summarizes all the possible decisions and outcomes. Referring to the decision tree of Figure 3.11, these with the given data are displayed. (a) The payoff matrices are laid out in the *Payoff* column. (b) The cost of a test is 0.1 million dollars. This means the cost of constructing a power plant is $(0.3 - 0.1) = 0.2$ million dollars. With the previous calculations summarized in the same figure, it can be verified that the expected return of building the plant, given testing is positive, can be easily computed from the information contained in Figure 3.11: $E(build\,|\,positive) = (\$0.03)/0.25 = \$0.12$, which says that the expected return given a boring test turns out to be positive is \$120,000. Similarly, the expected return of a not-to-build decision given a test is positive is:

$$E(not\text{-}to\text{-}build\,|\,positive) = (-\$0.025)/0.25 = -\$0.1$$

which amounts to a cost of \$100,000. In the same way,

$$E(build\,|\,negative) = (-\$0.18)/0.75 = -\$0.24.$$
$$E(no\text{-}build\,|\,negative) = (-\$.075)/0.75 = \$-0.1.$$

Figure 3.11   BAYESIAN DECISION TREE

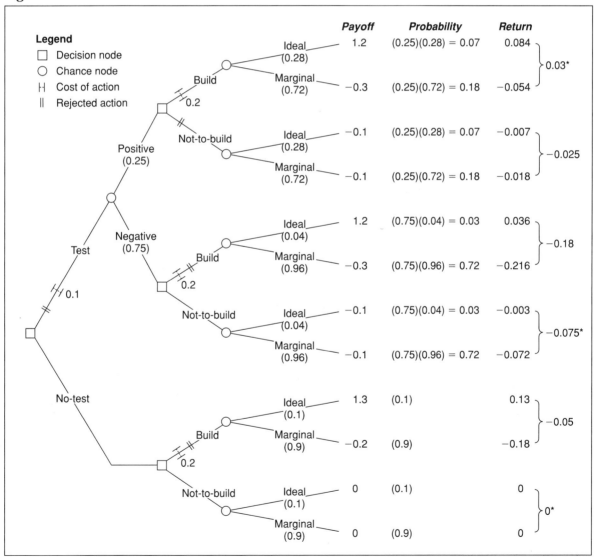

Notice from the decision tree that it is meaningless to ask for the expected return of a build decision, $E(build)$, without the qualification of "given the test is positive," "given the test is negative," or "given there is no test." However, it is very meaningful to calculate the expected return of conducting a test. Thus following the logical paths in the decision tree, $E(test)$ can be easily evaluated: $E(test) = (\$0.03) + (-\$0.075) = -\$0.045$. Following a similar path on the other side of the decision tree, the expected return of the no-test decision, $E(no\text{-}test)$, is obviously 0 even without any computation.

To round out the discussion on Bayesian decision making, we like to ask the question: "How much is the boring worth in terms of the additional information it buys?" This is referred to as the expected value of sample information, and can be computed as

(expected value of optimal decision with sample info) −
(expected value of optimal decision without sample info)
$$= \$[(-0.045) - (0)]$$
$$= \$0.045$$

Thus, the decision maker should be willing to pay up to \$45,000 for an additional boring test (sample information). Since the test actually costs \$100,000, we conclude that the test is not worthwhile. Consequently, following the logical path to its logical conclusion on the decision tree, building the plant at the proposed site is undesirable.

D. Bayesian Classifier

The reader may be so convinced by the nuclear power plant example above that it is possible to formalize a rule to classify go versus no-go decisions. But what about situations where there are more than two decisions—for instance, "go," "no-go," and "wait"—and is there a more compact way to characterize the decision in such situations? Here we have a general classification problem, deciding which logical decision among K decisions (where $K > 2$) we should commit ourselves to given certain payoffs and probabilities of outcomes. A classification exists that is optimal in terms of expected payoffs, and also yields the lowest expected probability of committing classification errors (Gonzalez and Woods 1992).

Instead of a single attribute (such as dollars in the above siting example), let a decision be made based on a vector of attributes $\mathbf{x} = (x_1, x_2, \ldots)$ where x_1 may be cost, x_2 may be risk, and so on. The probability that a particular vector of attributes $\mathbf{x}$ logically belong to class G_i is denoted by $P(G_i \mid \mathbf{x})$. If a classifier decides that $\mathbf{x}$ logically belonged to G_j when it actually belonged to G_i, it incurs a classification error, which is manifested in terms of a loss measure L_{ij}. As attribute vector $\mathbf{x}$ may belong to any of K classes under consideration, the average loss incurred in assigning $\mathbf{x}$ to class G_j is

$$L_j(\mathbf{X}) = \sum_{k=1}^{K} L_{kj} P(G_k \mid \mathbf{x})$$

Using Bayes' rule, or $P(A \mid B) = [P(A)P(B \mid A)]/P(B)$, the above equation can be rewritten as

$$L_j(\mathbf{x}) = \frac{1}{P(\mathbf{x})} \sum_{k=1}^{K} L_{kj} P(\mathbf{x} \mid G_k) P(G_k) \tag{3.12}$$

where $P(\mathbf{x} \mid G_k)$ is the probability that the attribute or feature vector really comes from class G_k and $P(G_k)$ is the probability of occurrence of class G_k. Since $1/P(\mathbf{x})$ is common to all the loss measures $L_j(\mathbf{x})$, $j = 1,2, \ldots, K$; it can be dropped from Equation 3.12 without affecting the relative order of these functions from the smallest to the largest value. The expression for the average loss then reduces to

$$L_j(\mathbf{x}) = \sum_{k=1}^{K} L_{kj} P(\mathbf{x} \mid G_k) P(G_k) \tag{3.13}$$

The classifier has K possible classes to choose from for any given feature vector x. It computes $L_1(\mathbf{x})$, $L_2(\mathbf{x})$, $\ldots$, $L_K(\mathbf{x})$ and assigns the feature vector to the class with the smallest loss. In many decision problems, the loss for a correct decision is zero, and it has the same non-zero value (for example, 1) for any incorrect decision. Under these conditions, the loss function becomes

$$L_{ij} = 1 - z_{ij} \tag{3.14}$$

where the indicator variable $z_{ij} = 1$ if the vector has been properly classified ($i = j$). On the other hand $z_{ij} = 0$ if it is improperly classified ($i \neq j$). Equation 3.14 indicates a loss of unity for incorrect decisions and zero loss for correct decisions (as indicated by the indicator $z_{ii} = 1$ or in vector notation $\mathbf{Z}_i = (z_{ii}, z_{ij})^T = (1,0)^T$). Substituting this equation into Equation 3.13 yields

$$\begin{aligned} L_j(\mathbf{x}) &= \sum_{k=1}^{K} (1 - z_{kj}) P(\mathbf{x} \mid \mathbf{z}_k) P(\mathbf{z}_k) \\ &= P(\mathbf{x}) - P(\mathbf{x} \mid \mathbf{z}_j) P(\mathbf{z}_j) \end{aligned} \tag{3.15}$$

The Bayes' classifier then assigns a feature vector $\mathbf{x}$ to class G_i if $L_i(\mathbf{x}) < L_j(\mathbf{x})$, or

$$P(\mathbf{x}) - P(\mathbf{x} \mid \mathbf{z}_i) P(\mathbf{z}_i) < P(\mathbf{x}) - P(\mathbf{x} \mid \mathbf{z}_j P(\mathbf{z}_j) \tag{3.16}$$

This is equivalent to

$$P(\mathbf{x} \mid \mathbf{z}_i) P(\mathbf{z}_i) > P(\mathbf{x} \mid \mathbf{z}_j) P(\mathbf{z}_j) \qquad j = 1, 2, \ldots, K; j \neq i \tag{3.17}$$

Thus we can see that the Bayesian classifier for 0-1 loss functions is nothing more than implementation of decision function of the form

$$L_j'(\mathbf{x}) = P(\mathbf{x} \mid \mathbf{z}_j) P(\mathbf{z}_j) \qquad j = 1, 2, \ldots, K \tag{3.18}$$

where a feature vector $\mathbf{x}$ is assigned to class G_i if $L_i'(\mathbf{x}) > L_j'(\mathbf{x})$ for all $j \neq i$.

As an example, consider a scalar attribute x involving two classifications ($K = 2$) governed by Gaussian **probability-density functions (PDFs)**, with means μ_1 and μ_2 and standard deviations σ_1 and σ_2 respectively. From Equation 3.18, the decision function has the form

$$\begin{aligned} L_j'(x) &= P(x \mid \mathbf{z}_j) P(\mathbf{z}_j) \\ &= \frac{1}{\sqrt{2\pi}\sigma_j} \exp\left[-\frac{(x - \mu_j)^2}{2\sigma_j^2} \right] P(z_j) \qquad j = 1, 2 \end{aligned} \tag{3.19}$$

Figure 3.12 shows a plot of the PDF for the two classes. The boundary between the two classes is a single point, x_0, such that $L_1'(x_0) = L_2'(x_0)$. If the two classes are equally likely to occur, $P(z_1) = P(z_2) = 1/2$, and the decision boundary is the value of x_0 for which $P(x_0 \mid z_1) = P(x_0 \mid z_2)$. This point is the intersection of the two PDFs, as shown in Figure 3.12. When $\mu_1 = 0$, $\mu_2 = 1$, and $\sigma_1 = \sigma_2 = \sigma$, for example, $x_0 = 1/2$. Any feature attribute to the right of $x_0 = 1/2$ is classified as belonging to class G_1. Similarly, any feature attribute to the left of $x_0 = 1/2$ is classified as belonging to class G_2. For computational ease, logarithm is often applied toward the decision function:

$$
\begin{aligned}
L_j'' &= \log L_j' \\
&= \log [P(\mathbf{x} \mid \mathbf{z}_j)P(\mathbf{Z}_j)] \\
&= \log P(\mathbf{x} \mid \mathbf{z}_j) + \log P(\mathbf{z}_j)
\end{aligned}
\tag{3.20}
$$

In the case of the scalar Gaussian PDF above, this simplifies to

$$
\log P(\mathbf{z}_j) - \log \sigma_j - \frac{(x - \mu_j)^2}{\sigma_j^2}
\tag{3.21}
$$

after leaving out the common constant term such as $-1/2(\log 2\pi)$.

Now let us compare and contrast two classification possibilities by taking the ratio

$$
\log \left[\frac{P(z_{1j} = 1 \mid \mathbf{x}, \mathbf{z}_j)}{P(z_{2j} = 1 \mid \mathbf{x}, \mathbf{z}_j)} \right].
$$

For known parameters μ_1, μ_2, and σ_2, we have from Bayes' theorem:

Figure 3.12   DEFINING A DECISION BOUNDARY

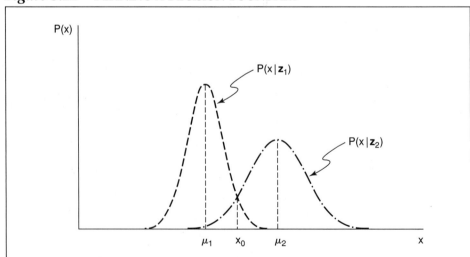

$$P(A \mid BC) = P(ABC)/P(BC) = P(ABC)/[P(B \mid C)P(C)] =$$
$$P(A \mid C)P(C)P(B \mid AC)/[P(BC)P(C)] = P(A \mid C)/[P(B \mid C)/P(B \mid AC)]$$

that

$$\log\left[\frac{P(z_{1j} = 1 \mid \mathbf{x}, \mathbf{z}_j)}{P(z_{2j} = 1 \mid \mathbf{x}, \mathbf{z}_j)}\right] = \log\left[\frac{P(z_{1j} = 1 \mid \mathbf{z}_j)/(P(\mathbf{x} \mid \mathbf{z}_j)/P(\mathbf{x} \mid z_{1j} = 1, \mathbf{z}_j))}{P(z_{2j} = 1 \mid \mathbf{z}_j)/(P(\mathbf{x} \mid \mathbf{z}_j)/P(\mathbf{x} \mid z_{2j} = 1, \mathbf{z}_j))}\right]$$

$$= \log\left[\frac{P(z_{1j} = 1 \mid \mathbf{z}_j)}{P(z_{2j} = 1 \mid \mathbf{z}_j)}\right] + \frac{1}{x_j}\left[-\frac{(x_j - 1)^2}{\sigma^2} + \frac{(x_j - 0)^2}{\sigma^2}\right] \quad (3.22)$$

$$= \log\left[\frac{P(z_{1j} = 1 \mid \mathbf{z}_j)}{P(z_{2j} = 1 \mid \mathbf{z}_j)}\right] - \frac{\left(x_j - \frac{1}{2}\right)}{\sigma^2}$$

Notice that

$$\frac{P(\mathbf{x} \mid \mathbf{z}_j)/P(\mathbf{x} \mid z_{1j} = 1, \mathbf{z}_j)}{P(\mathbf{x} \mid \mathbf{z}_j)/P(\mathbf{x} \mid z_{2j} = 1, \mathbf{z}_j)} = \frac{P(\mathbf{x} \mid \mathbf{z}_j)P(\mathbf{x} \mid z_{2j} = 1, \mathbf{z}_j)}{P(\mathbf{x} \mid \mathbf{z}_j)P(\mathbf{x} \mid z_{1j} = 1, \mathbf{z}_j)}$$

$$= \left[\frac{(\exp[-(x_j - 0)^2/2\sigma^2])^{1/xj}}{(\exp[-(x_j - 1)^2/2\sigma^2])^{1/xj}}\right] \quad (3.23)$$

which shows that when $x_j = 1/2$, we have $P(\mathbf{x} \mid \mathbf{z}_j)^2$ in both the numerator and denominator, corresponding to the joint probability of being in either group $j = 1$ or $j = 2$. On the other hand, when $x_j > 1/2$, the probability of being in group $j = 2$ is enhanced, and when $x_j < 1/2$, the probability of being in group $j = 1$ is enhanced. For those interested in a numerical illustration beyond the power plant example, please refer to the "Spectral versus Spatial Pattern Recognition" section in Chapter 6.

VIII. ECONOMETRIC APPROACH

The above described model building philosophy can be visualized as an approach wherein the casual sequence of events are chained together in a manner reflecting the process in real life, hence the terms decision analysis, simulation, and probabilistic models. Thus in decision analysis, we update a prior probability using sample information and based on the updated information define a decision boundary to classify a multiattribute observation. In a stochastic model, one schedules service vehicles in response to time varying demands. Finally in simulation, we replicate the sequence of events in which a previous event leads toward a subsequent event. A parallel approach, to be discussed here, does not claim to have an explicit understanding of the causal chain. Rather, it examines a set of historic data and tries to postulate a structural relationship that explains the observed data. If history repeats itself, or if the structural relationship prevails, one can forecast the future. Such an approach, as applied in facility location and land use, is termed the **econometric method.** Its components are explained below.

Figure 3.13   ARROW DIAGRAM FOR ECONOMIC-BASE EXAMPLE

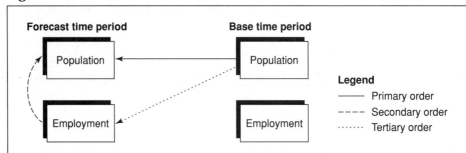

A. Arrow Diagram and Path Analysis

The first step in an econometric approach is the construction of arrow diagrams. An **arrow diagram** is a graphic aid to postulate the relationships between a number of factors. These may be a primary, secondary, or tertiary order correlation. Note that an arrow diagram shows structural relationships and unlike its analogue, the logic flow chart, no casual pattern is implied. Thus in Figure 3.13, a relationship is postulated between the population in the base-year and the forecast-year (with an arrow pointing from base- to forecast-year), which expresses correlation and not causation. The distinction is really apparent if one compares it to the logic flow diagram that traces service activities to basic employment. While one may suspect that the population in the forecast period would continue to be large if population in the base period is large (a correlation), it is not the same as the more close ties between basic and nonbasic activities (a causation). Primary, secondary, and tertiary ordering (or relationship) between two factors is defined to reflect a decreasing degree of correlation. In the example shown in Figure 3.13, the most important correlation, according to the postulation of the model builder, exists between the base-year and the future-year population. The least dominant correlation, on the other hand, is that between base-year population and forecast employment.

Path analysis is a refinement of the arrow diagram technique. While the arrow diagram quantifies the correlation between two factors such as employment and population, path analysis defines the relationship more precisely by confirming the arrow from employment to population is in fact correct or vice versa, as shown in Figure 3.14. Putting the discussion in more familiar experi-

Figure 3.14   PATH ANALYSIS FOR THE ECONOMIC-BASE EXAMPLE

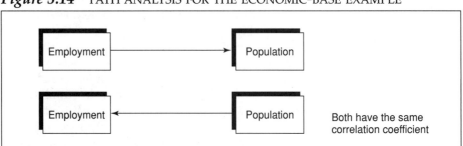

ences, path analysis addresses the chicken-and-egg phenomenon, where the initiating factor is to be identified. Citing a popular example, we may have found a high correlation between the number of medical doctors and the number of sick people in an infected community. A distinction is to be made between the sequence of events as to whether the infirm triggered the arrival of the doctors or the doctors caused the epidemic. The answer is quite obvious in this example. It is, however, less so in many other circumstances. Back to the economic base example we have been using, it is not entirely clear which is the initiating event: employment or population. As illustrated above in the economic base example, employment and population serve as the initiator alternatively. Path analysis can be used to resolve these nebulous situations because it is a means to check internal consistency—thus pointing out contradictory structural ordering. We will come back to this a bit later.

B. Econometric Models

Thus far, only the qualitative relationship between factors has been discussed. To quantify this relationship, we need to place a numerical value between each pair of factors. This is termed the **correlation coefficient,** which assumes a value from zero through unity[5] (Figure 3.15). A value close to unity would denote a high degree of association, while a value close to zero would indicate a lack of association between two factors. Once the correlation coefficient between population and employment (r_{PE}) is defined, mathematical expressions can be written for the arrow model we examine above: (employment) $\alpha\, r_{EP}$(population), or (population) $\alpha\, r_{PE}$(employment); where $r_{EP} = 1/r_{PE}$.

Once the correlation coefficients are defined, it is rather straightforward to recognize that the arrow diagram shown in Figure 3.13 can be quantified as the following set of equations:

$$(forecast\ pop) = a(forecast\ emp) + b(base\text{-}yr\ pop)$$
$$(forecast\ emp) = c(forecast\ pop) + d(base\text{-}yr\ emp)$$

(3.24)

Figure 3.15   CORRELATION COEFFICIENTS

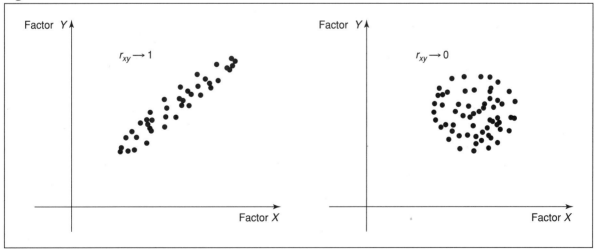

Here a, b, c and d are **calibration coefficients,** showing that future-year population is correlated both to base-year population and future-year employment. Now we are at a position to come back to the use of path analysis to validate a postulated set of relationships, which so far has been nothing but a hypothesis in the mind of the modeler. Application of path analysis to the 2-arrow models as shown in Table 3.4 results in the necessary conditions shown in Table 3.5. These tables illustrate two points. First, there are subsets of models where predicted relationships are mutually contradictory. Second, several models should, if valid, satisfy the same necessary conditions on the correlation coefficients.

The two tables constructed for 2-arrow models demonstrate that path analysis can be a useful means to discriminate between some models and can help the analyst reject some models that are obviously false. For example, in order for the "X-in-the-middle" (and the corresponding econometric models) to be valid, the correlation coefficients r_{XY} and r_{XZ} must be non-zero. If any one of these two correlation coefficients happens to be zero, the "X-in-the-middle" model is proven to be invalid and some of the corresponding pointing directions of the arrows may need to be reversed (as in the "Z-in-the-middle" models). The results also show that correlation coefficients are not a useful guide for the positive identification of the best model. Many models with contradictory implications may satisfy the same correlation requirements. Table 3.5 shows, for example, that one cannot distinguish statistically between the "Z-in-the-middle" models: $X \leftarrow Z \rightarrow Y$, $X \rightarrow Z \leftarrow Y$, $X \rightarrow Z \rightarrow Y$ and $X \leftarrow Z \leftarrow Y$. To distinguish between these possibilities, the modeler must rely upon his understanding of the situation being modeled.

Table 3.4   TYPOLOGY OF 2-ARROW MODELS

Model type	Arrow diagram	Econometric equations
Both X and Z independently affect Y.	$X \searrow \quad Z \swarrow$ to Y	$X = b_1$ $a_{21} X + Y + a_{23} Z = b_2$ $Z = b_3$
X, partially caused by Z, causes Y.	$Z \downarrow X \downarrow Y$	$X + a_{13} Z = b_1$ $a_{21} X + Y = b_2$ $Z = b_3$
The primary variable X causes both Z and Y.	$X \swarrow \searrow$ to $Z \quad Y$	$X = b_1$ $a_{21} X + Y = b_2$ $a_{31} X + Z = b_3$
The secondary variable Z intervenes between X and Y.	$X \downarrow Z \downarrow Y$	$X = b_1$ $Y + a_{23} Z = b_2$ $a_{31} X + Z = b_3$
The primary variable X and the supposedly dependently variable Y are correlated but not casually connected.	$Z \swarrow \searrow$ $X \quad Y$	$X + a_{13} Z = b_1$ $Y + a_{23} Z = b_2$ $Z = b_3$

SOURCE: De Neufville and Stafford (1971). Reprinted with permission.

Table 3.5   RESULTS OF PATH ANALYSIS

Grouping of models	Arrow diagram	Path analysis prediction	Condition
Y in the middle	$X \searrow \quad \swarrow Z$ Y	$r_{XZ} = 0$	$r_{XY} \neq 0$ $r_{YZ} \neq 0$
X in the middle	$Z \downarrow X \downarrow Y$ $X \swarrow \searrow$ $Z \quad Y$	$r_{XY} = \dfrac{r_{YZ}}{r_{XZ}}$	$r_{XY} \neq 0$ $r_{XZ} \neq 0$
Z in the middle	$X \downarrow Z \downarrow Y$ $Z \swarrow \searrow$ $X \quad Y$	$r_{XY} = r_{XZ} r_{YZ}$	$r_{XZ} \neq 0$ $r_{YZ} \neq 0$

SOURCE: De Neufville and Stafford (1971). Reprinted with permission.

IX. CALIBRATION

In the above discussions, we have presented two parallel methodologies to construct a descriptive model, one based on casual relationships while the other is founded upon correlation inferences. We call them, for convenience, simulation and econometric models respectively. In order to make either one of these models operational, a calibration process has to be carried out. This is to estimate the parameters of the model, such as the average number of dependents per employee (or the reciprocal of labor force participation rate)—an economic-base example we are familiar with—or the coefficients a and f in Table 3.1.

A. Ordinary Least Squares

The calibration procedure is expedited if one deals with a linear relationship, since there are more software packages available for linear than nonlinear relationships. Nonlinear relationships can often be converted to linear ones as shown in the example below—as we have demonstrated in Equations 3.20 and 3.21.

> *Nonlinear form:* $W = aX^b Y^c Z^d$
> *Log-linear form:* $\log W = \log a + b \log X + c \log Y + d \log Z$

Once a log-linear equation is obtained, the linear statistical techniques can be applied when one treats the logarithm of a variable as the observations. When carrying out such a procedure, however, care must be exercised in observing the normal distribution assumptions on error terms in linear-regression calibration techniques, as explained in Appendix 3.

There are about five categories of goodness of fit statistical techniques, ranging from the less sophisticated to the more involved. The first to be discussed is the manual procedure. Here, the ratio between the two variables may be used to estimate the parameter. For example, to estimate the average size of the household, the total population in the study area is divided by the number of households. To estimate the labor force participation rate, the number of employees is divided by the total population and so on. The next technique is **ordinary least squares (OLS)**, where a graphical plot of the pair of variables of interest is used to determine an equation, from which the values of parameters can be obtained. For example, industrial development may be directly related to accessibility in a linear equation: *development* = *a*(*access*) + *b*. A plot such as Figure 3.15 will have development as the Y axis and accessibility as the X axis. Linear regression will yield the numerical values of *a* and *b*, as explained in Appendix 3.

Where there is more than one equation to be fitted, **indirect least squares** and **two-stage least squares** are the appropriate methods. For illustration purposes, let us examine the following simultaneous equation set, where *a*, *b*, and *c* are to be calibrated:

$$(forecast\ pop) = a(forecast\ emp) + b(base\text{-}yr\ pop)$$
$$(forecast\ emp) = \qquad\qquad\quad + c(base\text{-}yr\ pop).$$

It is to be noted that the equation set is a realization of the second block of arrow diagrams in Table 3.4 and Figure 3.13. The special property of such a set of equations allows simplification to be made on the structural form. The second equation can be readily substituted into the first one, resulting in a reduced form: *forecast pop* = *d*(*base-yr pop*) + *e*, where the coefficients *d* and *e* can be calibrated using ordinary least squares techniques. The substitution in effect removes the coupling between the forecast employment variable that appears on the left-hand side of the second equation and the right-hand side of the first equation. The name indirect least squares refers to the fact that through the reduced form straightforward regression can be performed on a single equation instead of the simultaneous set. In general, an exactly identified set of structural equations can be reduced to a number of uncoupled equations, which can then be calibrated independent of one another.

B. *Two-Stage Least Squares*

If an arrow diagram results in the following equations:

$$(forecast\ pop) = a(forecast\ emp) + b(base\text{-}yr\ pop)$$
$$(forecast\ emp) = c(forecast\ pop) + d(base\text{-}yr\ pop) \qquad (3.25)$$

then a less straightforward procedure called two-stage least squares (2SLS) needs to be employed. The basic idea of 2SLS is to replace the endogenous explanatory variables $\mathbf{Y}$ in each equation with an estimated matrix $\hat{\mathbf{Y}}$ based on the regression of the variables in the **Y**-vector on all of the predetermined (exogenous) variables, the **X** matrix in the model. This is referred to as stage 1 of the calibration. The second stage then involves ordinary least squares estimation of each Y_i based on $\hat{\mathbf{Y}}$ and $\mathbf{X}^6$. For example, in the set of equations labeled 3.25 above, one can define the *forecast pop* and *forecast emp* as endogenous variables **Y** and *base-yr pop* as exogenous variable **X**. Then stage one of 2SLS estimates a matrix of the two forecast variables $[\hat{Y}_{pop}, \hat{Y}_{emp}]$ based on the regression of these forecast variables on the base-year population. In the second stage, forecast variables, $\mathbf{Y}_{pop}$ and $\mathbf{Y}_{emp}$ are regressed against the estimated forecast-variables $[\hat{Y}_{pop}, \hat{Y}_{emp}]$ and the (*base-yr pop*) variable **X**.

Mathematically, this process is shown by first moving all Y's to the left-hand side of the equation so that $\mathbf{D'y''} = \mathbf{B'x'} + \mathbf{A}$, where **D'** is the calibration-coefficient matrix, **B'** is the calibration-coefficient matrix and **A** is the disturbance or error vector. In this case **D'** is 2×2 matrix $\begin{bmatrix} 1 & -a \\ -c & 1 \end{bmatrix}$, **y** is 2×1 vector (*forecast pop, forecast emp*)^T, **B'** is the 2×2 matrix $\begin{bmatrix} b & 0 \\ 0 & d \end{bmatrix}$, **x'** is a 2×1 vector (*base-yr pop, base-yr pop*)^T, and **A** is a 2×1 vector $(A_1 \ A_2)^T$. Solving this equation results in $\mathbf{y''} = \mathbf{D'^{-1}B'x'} + \mathbf{D'^{-1}A}$, or what is commonly referred to as the reduced form of the original structure $\mathbf{y''} = \mathbf{Cx} + \mathbf{D'^{-1}A}$ where $\mathbf{C} = \mathbf{D'^{-1}B'}$. Then using ordinary least squares, estimates of the coefficients $\hat{\mathbf{C}}$, or **C**, can be determined for each of the reduced form equations such that $\hat{\mathbf{Y}} = \hat{\mathbf{C}}^T\mathbf{X}$ where $\hat{\mathbf{Y}}$ is the estimated values of the endogenous variables. Here **C** is 2×2, **x** is 2×1, and $\hat{\mathbf{Y}}$ is 2×1. In the second stage, ordinary least squares is applied to the model

$$Y_i = \mathbf{a}^T\hat{\mathbf{Y}} + \mathbf{b}^T\mathbf{x'} + A_i \tag{3.26}$$

to find asymptotically unbiased estimates of the parameters **a** and **b**. Here $\hat{\mathbf{Y}} = (Y_{pop}, \hat{Y}_{emp})^T$ and $\mathbf{a} = (a_1, a_2)$ and $\mathbf{b} = b$. In evaluating the significance of the model, similar measures to those employed in OLS can be used, *viz*, the Student-t test, the *F*-test, and the coefficient of multiple determination R^2. However, a word of caution is in order: Since both $\hat{\mathbf{Y}}$ and $\mathbf{y''}$ are used to compute R^2 in Equation 3.26, negative values can result. Therefore R^2 should not be used directly as a measure of the variation explained by the model. In addition, it follows from OLS that when there is high correlation between the explanatory variable, such as $\hat{\mathbf{Y}}$ and $\mathbf{x'}$ in Equation 3.26, the structural parameters **a** and **b** will be imprecise and have a high standard error.

C. Example of Two-Stage Least Squares

A linear urban model based on a set of simultaneous equations was developed for a twenty-three zone study area in central Berkshire, England. The calibration process involves running the regression model a number of times, testing for the significance of the variables, checking that the regression assumptions have not been violated, and interpreting the regression coefficients. The following equations set were postulated initially

$$\begin{aligned} \Delta N &= c_1 + a_1\Delta E^R + b_1\Delta E^B + b_2\Delta N + b_3N + b_4E^R + b_5E^B + b_6t' \\ \Delta E^R &= c_2 + a_2\Delta N + b_1\Delta E^B + b_8N + b_9E^R + b_{10}u \end{aligned} \tag{3.27}$$

Here N is zonal population, E^B is zonal basic employment, E^R is zonal service employment, t' is accessibility-to-employment, and u is accessibility-to-population. The Δ increments refer to changes over a five-year period. Using off-the-shelf econometric computer programs, the first stage of the calibration is to calculate the reduced form estimates for population and service employment changes from multiple regression equations expressing each as a function of all the exogenous variables. The second stage entails using these reduced form estimates as the explanatory variables on the right-hand sides of the simultaneous equations and performing multiple regression on each of the equations individually. This determines the coefficients c_1 to c_2, a_1 to a_2, and b_1 to b_{10}. At prediction, the coefficients of the reduced form equations and the coefficients of the simultaneous equations will be used in the same two-stage procedure to predict population and service employment changes over some future time period (Foot 1981).

Trial 1 of the calibration process produces the following result:

$$\Delta N = 2514.51 + 27.702\Delta\hat{E}^R - 15.415\Delta E^B + 0.129N - 5.830E^R + 2.822E^B - 0.073t'$$
$$\Delta E^R = 80.611 - 0.037\Delta\hat{N} + 0.555\Delta E^B - 0.0003N + 0.153E^R + 0.0045u \tag{3.28}$$

where the reduced form estimates of population and service employment changes are denoted by ΔN and ΔE^R respectively. The R^2 for the first equation is 0.733, and the R^2 for the second is 0.998. The t-values for the coefficients associated with each explanatory variable in the first equation are respectively 0.973, 0.952, 1.344, 1.109, 1.529, and 0.503. Those for the second equation are 3.663, 12.614, 0.083, 38.25, and 2.647. To test the level of significance of the variables, the theoretical t-value at the 5 percent level for the first equation is $t = 2.114$, and for the second equation, $t = 2.106$.

It can be seen that many of the variables in both equations are not significant (particularly in the first equation), and this can largely be explained by the interrelationships between some of the variables which show up in the correlation matrix (Table 3.6). By inspection of this matrix and the level of significance of the coefficients, accessibility to employment was removed from the first equation and base-year population from the second equation, because of their high correlation with other variables in the equation. When the models were re-computed, service employment at the calibration year in the first equation was still not significant and, therefore, removed. The removal of these three variables lead to an increased level of significance of the other variables and, on re-computation, produced a simultaneous equation set containing only significant variables:

$$\Delta N = 44.745 - 3.844\Delta\hat{E}^R + 2.372\Delta E^B + 0.144N + 0.924E^B$$
$$\Delta\hat{E}^R = -80.099 - 0.037\Delta\hat{N} + 0.555\Delta E^B + 0.152E^R + 0.0044u \tag{3.29}$$

The first equation commands an R^2 of 0.700, while the second equation 0.998. The t-values in the first equation are 5.547, 2.174, 2.571, and 2.897; and for the second equation 4.625, 12.907, 50.667, and 3.508. It can be seen that service-employment change is almost perfectly reproduced by the model, and population change, significantly. The overall R^2 values have been reduced only slightly by removing the non-significant variables from the model. This latter, more parsimonious model

Table 3.6   CORRELATION MATRIX BETWEEN VARIABLES IN THE CENTRAL
BERKSHIRE MODEL

	N	E^R	E^B	ΔN	ΔE^R	ΔE^B	u
E^R	0.6722						
E^B	0.7284	0.9028					
ΔN	0.1892	−0.3478	−0.0167				
ΔE^R	0.7042	0.9885	0.9113	−0.3026			
ΔE^B	0.5747	0.4634	0.6423	0.2719	0.5801		
u	0.8455	0.5413	0.5331	0.1559	0.5697	0.3929	
t'	0.8063	0.5342	0.4937	0.0859	0.5609	0.3613	0.9821

SOURCE: Foot (1981). Reprinted with permission.

satisfies the regression assumptions relating to the independence of the exogenous variables far better.[7]

The main problem with the final model is the negative coefficients, which in the first equation suggest that as service employment increases in a zone, population decreases. Similarly in the second equation, as population increases service employment decreases. This is due to the data used for calibration. With just the exogenous variables available in producing the reduced form estimates, the two-stage regression model cannot cope with extensive re-development that took place downtown in which shops and office buildings replaced substandard housing. Because of the large number of shops and offices downtown, the effects of this downtown re-development dominate over other zones in the entire study area. Exogenous variables relating to re-development must be included in the first stage of the regression to improve the explanation and provide more reasonable coefficients. In spite of this common problem among two-stage least squares, the calibrated model is statistically significant enough to be used for prediction in five-year increments, as long as the forecast is not over-extended into the future. For an example of this forecasting procedure, see the "Econometric Model" chapter in Chan (2000).

D. Maximum Likelihood

Another econometric technique to be discussed here is the maximum likelihood estimation procedure. It is a calibration procedure that estimates the unknown parameters by maximizing the probability, that the sample drawn is a true representation of the population, given the population distribution and sampling frame. An example of the gravity model is the best way to illustrate this model fitting technique. Suppose a consumer is choosing between two shopping malls ($k = 1$ or 2) to go to on Saturday morning. A sample of three shoppers ($n = 1, 2, 3$) has been included in a survey. Each shopper was asked about his individual travel time to a shopping mall k ($k = 1, 2$), τ_{nk}, and the final choice of the mall. The individual survey results are tabulated in Table 3.7. An examination of the table shows that the individuals surveyed chose a location mainly based on proximity.

Table 3.7   DISAGGREGATE CALIBRATION OF A MAXIMUM LIKELIHOOD
MODEL

Individual n	Time to location 1 τ_{n1} (min)	Time to location 2 τ_{n2} (min)	Locational choice k
1	5	7	1
2	4	6	1
3	6	4	2

SOURCE: Kanafani (1983). Reprinted with permission.

Consider a model such as the following for an individual's discrete location decision as derived by consumers' surplus maximization in Chapter 2:

$$P(n, k) = \frac{\exp(\alpha_k \tau_{nk})}{\sum_{i=1}^{2} \exp(\alpha_i \tau_{ni})} \qquad k = 1, 2; n = 1, 2, 3 \tag{3.30}$$

A likelihood function L is defined as the probability that in a sample of three persons, one person chooses location 2 and two persons location 1. Thus the likelihood that the first two persons choose location 1 while the third location 2 is $P(1,1)P(2,1)P(3,2)$. There are three possible ways that the sample can have the one-person/location 2, two persons/location 1 split:

- the first person goes to shopping mall 2 while the second and third go to mall 1,
- the first and third go to mall 2 while the second goes to mall 1,
- the first and second go to mall 2 while the third goes to mall 1.

The likelihood function L now looks like

$$\frac{3!}{2!1!}P(1, 1)P(2, 1)P(3, 2). \tag{3.31}$$

It is computationally convenient to take the logarithm of the likelihood function

$$\ln L = \ln 3 + \ln P(1,1) + \ln P(2,1) + \ln P(3,2). \tag{3.32}$$

which can be written as

$$K + \ln\frac{\exp(5\alpha_1)}{\exp(5\alpha_1) + \exp(7\alpha_2)} + \ln\frac{\exp(4\alpha_1)}{\exp(4\alpha_1) + \exp(6\alpha_2)} + \ln\frac{\exp(4\alpha_1)}{\exp(6\alpha_1) + \exp(4\alpha_2)} \tag{3.33}$$

where K is a constant. After collapsing of some terms

$$ln\ L = K + (4\alpha_2 + 9\alpha_1) - \{ln[exp(5\alpha_1) + exp(7\alpha_2)] +$$
$$ln[exp(4\alpha_1) + exp(6\alpha_2)] + \quad (3.34)$$
$$ln[exp(6\alpha_1) + exp(4\alpha_2)]\}$$

The values of α's are simply determined by solving these two simultaneous equations.

$$\frac{\partial(\ln L)}{\partial\alpha_1} = 0;\quad \frac{\partial(\ln L)}{\partial\alpha_2} = 0 \qquad (3.35)$$

These equations seek the values of α's that maximize the value function. The estimation typically involves the hill-climbing numerical technique, which is tangential to the development here and will be covered in Chapter 4, which summarizes prescriptive techniques.

Skipping over the computational details and getting at the results, the above two equations boil down to

$$9 - \frac{5\ exp(5\alpha_1)}{exp(5\alpha_1) + exp(7\alpha_2)} + \frac{4\ exp(4\alpha_1)}{exp(4\alpha_1) + exp(6\alpha_2)} + \frac{6\ exp(6\alpha_1)}{exp(6\alpha_1) + exp(4\alpha_2)} = 0 \quad (3.36)$$

and

$$4 - \frac{7\ exp(7\alpha_2)}{exp(5\alpha_1) + exp(7\alpha_2)} + \frac{6\ exp(6\alpha_2)}{exp(4\alpha_1) + exp(6\alpha_2)} + \frac{4\ exp(4\alpha_1)}{exp(6\alpha_1) + exp(4\alpha_2)} = 0 \quad (3.37)$$

Numerical solution of these two equations and two unknowns is performed, yielding $\alpha_1 = -14.434$ and $\alpha_2 = -14.211$. The reader should note the negative value of the α parameters. Compared with the OLS procedure discussed above, the maximum likelihood procedure typically is more efficient with data, but it requires knowledge of the underlying distribution of the basic random variable. It provides an unbiased estimator, rather than an asymptotically unbiased one. While the calibration procedure appears straightforward in this example, solutions to Equation 3.35 may be very difficult to find. When the errors are normally distributed, the maximum likelihood estimators of the regression coefficients are the least squares estimators.

X. AGGREGATE VERSUS DISAGGREGATE MODELING

The same shopping location example can be modeled using an aggregate format, which is simpler in many regards. Instead of addressing each individual's decision, the shoppers of the entire study area are modeled. Consider the case of three shopping centers from which the shoppers can choose. Table 3.8 shows the average travel cost and time to each of these centers, as well as the number of patrons that end up there. The objective is to calibrate an aggregate, instead of disaggregate, location choice model. The model specification will look like

$$P_k = \frac{\exp(a\tau_k + bc_k)}{\Sigma_i \exp(a\tau_i + bc_i)}$$ (3.38)

where τ_k and c_k are the travel time and cost via mode k, and a, b are calibration constants. Notice that instead of location-specific calibration parameters α_1 and α_2, a single set is used across all centers, indicating a homogeneous behavior among the shoppers. The above is often referred to as a multinomial logit model. The maximum likelihood function looks like

$$L = \frac{100!}{50!\ 40!\ 10!} P_1^{50} P_2^{40} P_3^{10}.$$

Let X be the denominator for P_1, P_2, and P_3 (see Equation 3.38). Then $\ln L = 50(15a + 3b) + 40(10a + 4b) + 10(20a + 7b) - 100 \ln X$ in which values for τ_k and c_k are obtained from Table 3.8.

$$\frac{\partial(lnL)}{\partial a} = 1350 - (100/X)\ [15\exp(15a + 3b) + 10\exp(10a + 4b) + 20\exp(20a + 7b)] = 0$$ (3.39)

and

$$\frac{\partial(lnL)}{\partial a} = 380 - (100/X)[3\exp(15a + 3b) + 4\exp(10a + 4b) + 7\exp(20a + 7b)] = 0$$ (3.40)

Solution of these simultaneous equations yields $a = -0.02868$ and $b = -0.36640$. Again, the readers should note the negative signs for the parameters a and b.

There are several implications from aggregate, rather than disaggregate, modeling. The straightforward one is that the calibration procedure is more simple. The more noteworthy one is that aggregate and disaggregate modeling have very different behavioral assumptions. This point is best shown by the following replication test, where the calibrated model is used to reproduce the observed data, as a descriptive model should. To show the replication test, one

Table 3.8 DATABASE FOR CALIBRATING AN AGGREGATE LOCATION CHOICE MODEL

Shopping center k	Average time τ_k	Average cost c_k	No of patrons at center k
1	15	3	50
2	10	4	40
3	20	7	10

Table 3.9   REPLICATION TEST DATA FOR LOGIT MODEL

Shopper	Time to location 1 τ_1 (min)	Time to location 2 τ_2 (min)	$\delta\tau = \tau_1-\tau_2$ (min)	Cost to location 1 c_1 ($)	Cost to location 2 c_2 ($)	$\delta c = c_1-c_2$ ($)	Locational decision
1	25	30	−5	3.00	1.00	2	1
2	10	15	−5	1.00	1.00	0	1
3	50	40	10	5.00	1.00	4	2
Average	—	—	0	—	—	2	—

should be aware of the fact that a logit choice model discussed above can be represented as

$$P_1 = \frac{1}{1 + \exp\Delta} \quad \text{and} \quad P_2 = \frac{\exp\Delta}{1 + \exp\Delta} \tag{3.41}$$

for the two shopping center cases, where $\Delta = \beta\,(\delta\tau) + \gamma\,(\delta c) + \alpha$ in which $\delta\tau = \tau_2-\tau_1$ and $\delta c = c_2 - c_1$. Suppose a disaggregate model is calibrated with $\beta = -293.2$ $\gamma = -71.3$ and $\alpha = 1.93$ based on time-unit of hours and cost in $ \times 10^{-2}$. This means that for the data shown in Table 3.9, an entry of 17 minutes should be translated to 0.293 hours and $2.16 should be translated to 0.0216 before they are substituted into the model formulas. Using the model consistently in disaggregate prediction will yield $\Delta_1 = -293.2(.02) - 71.3(.0833) + 1.93 = 2.0053$, $\Delta_2 = 7.869$ and $\Delta_3 = -21.705$. These values, when substituted into Equation 3.41, yield P_2 of 0.1187, 0.00038 and 1.000 for shoppers 1, 2, and 3 respectively. The average of these three P_2s is .373, which agrees with the observed data in Table 3.9:

$$P_2 = \frac{(2\ shopper\ at\ 2)}{(a\ total\ of\ 3\ shoppers)} = 0.333$$

On the other hand, misuse of the model by using average travel time and cost will lead toward totally erroneous predictions. Thus substituting aggregate data $\Delta = -293.2(0.02) - 71.3(0) + 1.93 = -3.93$ into Equation 3.41 will result in $P_1 = 0.02$ and $P_2 = 0.98$, which is far from reality. Thus, care must be exercised in the calibration and consistent use of aggregate versus disaggregate models. As long as aggregation across individuals is handled with care, it need not be a major source of error in the forecasting process.

XI. THE GRAVITY MODEL REVISITED

We have described above the calibration of a location choice model as represented in Equations 3.30 and 3.38. It will be shown here that the aggregate version of the two models can be developed from first principles other than consumers' surplus maximization (as discussed in Chapter 2), and they can be calibrated with a method other than maximum likelihood. We start with the functional form $V_{ij} = V(\mathbf{S}_{ij}, \mathbf{A}_j)$ where $\mathbf{S}_{ij}$ is the vector of level-of-service variables between i and j as measured in accessibility. (Recall that accessibility is an inverse function of travel cost, travel time, and other spatial-separation metrics.) $\mathbf{A}_j$ is a vector of socioeconomic variables representing such activities as population and employment.

A. Singly Constrained Gravity Model

Let us use F_{ij} to denote an accessibility factor, defined as an inverse function of travel cost in a form such as $\exp(-bC_{ij})$ and C_{ij}^{-b}. Let us also use V_j to denote the attraction at destination j, where the attraction may be employment opportunities, or in this case simply the trips terminating at the destination zone V. A model can now be constructed bearing the form $V_{ij} = MV_iF_{ij}V_j$ where M is a calibration constant. Since the sum of the originating trips have to add up to the production, or $\Sigma_j V_{ij} = V_i$, we can write $\Sigma_j MV_iF_{ij}V_j = V_i$. Canceling the V_i term from both sides of the equation and extracting the calibration constant M from the summation sign, we have $M\Sigma_j F_{ij}V_j = 1$ or $M = 1/(\Sigma_j F_{ij}V_j)$. Substituting this calibration constant M back to the original equation, we have

$$V_{ij} = \frac{V_iF_{ij}V_j}{\Sigma_j F_{ij}V_j}$$

which is the familiar singly constrained gravity model.

Consider a region consisting of four zones 1, 2, 3, and 4. Residents in zones 1 and 2 are considering shopping at zones 2, 3 and 4. The existing travel pattern is represented in Table 3.10. As can be seen, there are 1000 potential trip productions emanating from zone 1 and 1400 from zone 2. The trip attractions at zones 2, 3, and 4 are 1300, 300, and 800 respectively. The travel costs (as represented in minutes of travel times) between the zones, C_{ij}, are shown in Table 3.11. A travel accessibility function of $F_{ij} = C_{ij}^{-2}$ is assumed, or the calibration parameter b is set to 2 initially. This means a set of $F(C_{ij})$s that appears as follows:

Table 3.10   EXISTING INTERZONAL TRAVEL

From/to	Zone 1	Zone 2	Zone 3	Zone 4	V_i
Zone 1		500	200	300	1000
Zone 2		800	100	500	1400
Zone 3					
Zone 4					
V_j		1300	300	800	2400

SOURCE: Dickey (1983). Reprinted with permission.

Table 3.11   INTERZONAL TRAVEL TIMES (IN MINUTES)

From/to	Zone 1	Zone 2	Zone 3	Zone 4
Zone 1	3	8	5	10
Zone 2	8	3	10	5
Zone 3	5	10	3	20
Zone 4	10	5	20	3

SOURCE: Dickey (1983). Reprinted with permission.

C_{ij}	3	5	8	10
$F(C_{ij})$	0.111	0.0400	0.0156	0.0100

Now the interzonal trips can be estimated by

$$V_{12} = 1000 \left[\frac{(1300)(0.0156)}{(1300)(0.0156) + (300)(0.0400) + (800)(0.0100)} \right] = 503 \quad (3.42)$$

Similarly, $V_{13} = 298$, $V_{14} = 199$, $V_{22} = 1127$, $V_{23} = 23$, and $V_{24} = 250$. Since $V_{12} + V_{22} = 1630 \neq 1300$, calibration of the model is necessary in order to replicate the existing data more closely. The need for calibration is best shown by a trip distribution plot such as Figure 3.16, where trips of a certain duration, say 3, 5, 8, and 10 minutes are plotted. It can be seen that the observed curve is significantly different from the estimated. To bring the estimated and observed trip distribution curves together, the accessibility factors $F(C_{ij})$ can be adjusted by scaling the points on the curve according to the observed data. For example,

$$F'(3) = F_{22}' = F_{22}(800/1127) = (0.1111)(800/1127) = 0.0789$$
$$F'(5) = F_{13}' = F_{24}' = (0.04)(700/548) = 0.0511$$
etc.

This also yields $F'(8) = F_{12}' = 0.0155$ and $F'(10) = F_{14}' = F_{23}' = 0.0180$. From these accessibility factors, new estimates can be made on interzonal travel. For example,

$$V_{12}' = 1000 \left[\frac{(1300)(0.0155)}{(1300)(0.0155) + (300)(0.0511) + (800)(0.0180)} \right] = 404 \quad (3.43)$$

Similarly, it can be shown that $V_{13}' = 307$, $V_{14}' = 289$, $V_{22}' = 965$, $V_{23} = 51$, and $V_{24}' = 385$. Based on these estimated trips, the trip distribution plot is shown again in Figure 3.16.

The process is repeated until the third iteration, when the two distribution curves seem to agree with one another, as shown in Figure 3.16. At this iteration, $V_{12}''' = 457$, $V_{13}''' = 245$, $V_{14}''' = 298$, $V_{22}''' = 857$, $V_{23}'' = 79$, and $V_{24}''' = 463$.

Figure 3.16   TRIP DISTRIBUTION PLOTS

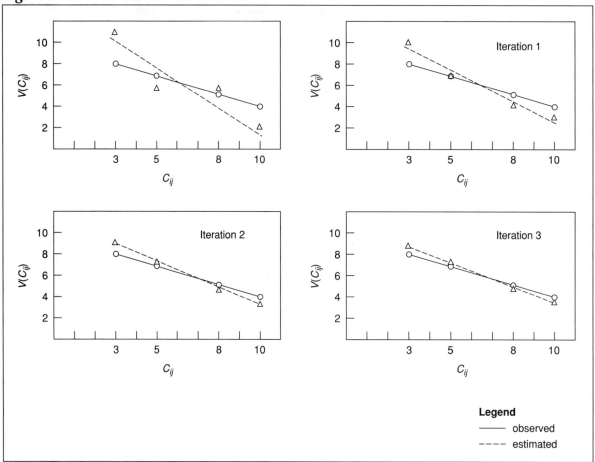

The goodness of fit between the two curves can be shown formally by the chi-square test. To explain this test, the step-by-step computation is organized around Table 3.12. The degree of freedom is $n - 1 = 4 - 1 = 3$. From a chi-square table of any statistics text, χ^2 to a 0.95 significance level with 3 degrees of freedom is

Table 3.12   CHI-SQUARE TEST

Time Interval (min)	3	5	8	10
Observed y_i	800	700	500	400
Estimated $\hat{y}_i$	857.28	707.90	457.40	377.00
$(y_i - \hat{y}_i)$	−57.28	−7.90	42.60	23.00
$(y_i - \hat{y}_i)^2$	3281.00	62.41	1814.76	529
$(y_i - \hat{y}_i)^2/\hat{y}_i$	3.83	0.09	3.97	1.40
$\Sigma_i(y_i - \hat{y}_i)^2/\hat{y}_i$	3.83	3.92	7.88	9.29

$\chi^2(0.05,3) = 7.815$. The fact that chi-square statistic of 9.29 from Table 3.12 is bigger than 7.815 means that the fit between the trip distribution curves is not statistically significant.

Recall that we hypothesized a coefficient of $b = 2$ in the accessibility factor $F(C_{ij}) = C_{ij}^{-b}$ initially for the model, but found that it was not giving the best fit to the data in the trip distribution curve initially. Over the three iterations, we have modified sufficiently the calibration parameter b by adjusting the F values. At the termination of the algorithm, we have a set of F values, from which the final calibrated parameter b can be recovered. To do this, we first take the logarithm of $F(C_{ij}) = C_{ij}^{-b} : \ln F = -b \ln C$. $\ln F$ is then regressed against $\ln C$ using the following set of data, with the stipulation that the regression line will go through the origin.[8] The slope of the regression line is then simply the b value we are looking for.

	$\ln F$	$\ln C$
$F(3) = 0.0583$	-2.8422	1.0986
$F(5) = 0.0512$	-2.9720	1.6094
$F(8) = 0.0221$	-3.8122	2.0794
$F(10) = 0.0234$	-3.7550	$2.3026.$

Result of the regression shows that $b = 1.874$ at an R^2 of 0.9958. In other words, the slope of the trip distribution curve should be gentler than first hypothesized, as illustrated in Figure 3.16.

B. Doubly Constrained Model

It is quite obvious that the above model is not easy to calibrate since a number of ad hoc procedures need to be strapped together to achieve the desired goodness of fit. A simpler alternative is to formulate a doubly constrained model that explicitly takes into account the constraints placed on the number of trip attractions in addition to the number of productions (Oppenheim 1980). Consider the following model for a study area consisting of n' zones $V_{ij} = k_i l_j V_i V_j F(C_{ij})$ such that

$$\sum_{i=1}^{n'} V_{ij} = V_j \qquad j = 1, \ldots, n'$$

$$\sum_{j=1}^{n'} V_{ij} = V_i \qquad i = 1, \ldots, n' \tag{3.44}$$

Notice that instead of one calibration constant M, two constants k_i and l_j are introduced. By substitution of these constraints into the initial equation for the model, we have

$$\sum_{i=1}^{n'} k_i l_j V_i V_j F(C_{ij}) = V_j \qquad j = 1, \ldots, n'$$

$$\sum_{j=1}^{n'} k_i l_j V_i V_j F(C_{ij}) = V_i \qquad i = 1, \ldots, n' \tag{3.45}$$

These reduce to

$$l_j \sum_{i=1}^{n'} k_i V_i F(C_{ij}) = 1 \qquad j = 1, \ldots, n'$$

$$k_i \sum_{j=1}^{n'} l_j V_j F(C_{ij}) = 1 \qquad i = 1, \ldots, n'$$

(3.46)

after canceling V_j on both sides of the first equation, and likewise for V_i of the second. The calibration constants can now be determined:

$$l_j = \frac{1}{\displaystyle\sum_{i=1}^{n'} k_i V_i F(C_{ij})} = 1 \qquad j = 1, \ldots, n'$$

$$k_i = \frac{1}{\displaystyle\sum_{j=1}^{n'} l_j V_j F(C_{ij})} = 1 \qquad i = 1, \ldots, n'$$

(3.47)

Notice the two equation sets are coupled together, in that k appears on the right-hand side of the first equation set, and l appears on the right-hand side of the second. An iterative solution strategy is anticipated. A numerical example will make this clear.

Example
Given these interzonal travel times

$$[C_{ij}] = \begin{bmatrix} 2 & 4 & 8 \\ 5 & 1 & 7 \\ 7 & 6 & 3 \end{bmatrix}$$

the following accessibility factors can be derived for a particular functional form and an assumed value of the calibration constant b:

$$[C_{ij}] = \begin{bmatrix} 2 & 4 & 8 \\ 5 & 1 & 7 \\ 7 & 6 & 3 \end{bmatrix}$$

The observed values of interzonal travels are shown in Table 3.13.

Table 3.13   OBSERVED INTERZONAL TRAVEL OF A DOUBLY CONSTRAINED
MODEL

From/to	$j = 1$	$j = 2$	$j = 3$	V_i
$i = 1$	1,800	3,100	100	5,000
$i = 2$	3,100	1,500	400	5,000
$i = 3$	15,100	25,400	4,500	45,000
V_j	20,000	30,000	5,000	55,000

SOURCE: Oppenheim (1980). Reprinted with permission.

Table 3.14   CALIBRATION OF A DOUBLY CONSTRAINED MODEL

		Iteration Number			
		1	2	3	4
k_1	1		0.9148	0.9125	0.9125
k_2	1		1.3312	1.3437	1.3437
k_3	1		0.9833	0.9824	0.9824
l_1		0.1187^a	0.1164	0.1164	
l_2		0.1058	0.1073	0.1073	
l_3		0.0965	0.0961	0.0961	

[a] All these nine l values are to be multiplied by 10^{-4}. For example, 0.1187 is actually 0.1187×10^{-4}.

SOURCE: Oppenheim (1980). Reprinted with permission.

We wish to solve the six equations and six unknowns for k_1, k_2, k_3, l_1, l_2, and l_3 as represented by Equation 3.47 where $n' = 3$ in this case. Suppose we start with the arbitrary values of 1 for the k's. Substituting 1's in the formulas will yield $l_1 = 0.1187 \times 10^{-4}$, $l_2 = 0.1058 \times 10^{-4}$, $l_3 = 0.0965 \times 10^{-4}$. Now substitute these l values into the formulas for the k's in Equation 3.47, one will find that these new values for the k's are no longer l's. We continue this process until a consistent set of ks and ls are obtained, as shown in Table 3.14. It can be seen that we obtain convergence within four iterations.

Based on these values of k and l, $\hat{V}_{ij}$s can be estimated as shown in Table 3.15. Also shown in the same table is the percentage error between estimated ($\hat{V}_{ij}$) and observed interzonal travel (V_{ij}^*): $(\hat{V}_{ij} - \hat{V}_{ij})/\hat{V}_{ij}$. To reduce the error further, another functional form for the accessibility factor may be in order, either by changing from a power function C_{ij}^{-b} to exponential function $\exp(-bC_{ij})$ or vice versa (among other possible functional forms), or changing the initial value of b. Such a decision can be assisted by examining the plots of the trip distribution curves, as illustrated in the singly constrained gravity model example. ∎

Table 3.15   ESTIMATED INTERZONAL TRAVELS IN A DOUBLY CONSTRAINED MODEL

From/to	$j = 1$	$j = 2$	$j = 3$	V_i
$i = 1$	1,563 $(-15.2)^a$	3,178 $(+2.5)$	257 $(+61.1)$	4,998
$i = 2$	3,209 $(+3.4)$	1,313 (-14.3)	478 $(+16.3)$	5,000
$i = 3$	15,238 $(+1.0)$	25,498 $(+0.4)$	4,265 (-5.51)	45,001
V_j	20,010	29,989	5,000	54,999

[a] Numbers in parentheses indicate the percentage errors between observed and estimated interzonal travel.

SOURCE: Oppenheim (1980). Reprinted with permission.

XII. SPATIAL INTERACTION

As can be seen from the gravity model calibration, one of the major steps in spatial-temporal analysis is to enrich our information about the study area based on partially observable data. We have seen from the numerical examples above that an $n' \times n'$ matrix of trip movements is to be constructed from given row and column sums, often referred to as the trip productions and attractions (or more properly the origin trips and destination trips). In this case, we wish to estimate n'^2 pieces of information from $2n'$ pieces of data when certain statements can be made about travel behavior, as manifested in the trip distribution function showing the relative trip lengths in the area. In short, we wish to provide more complete activity distribution information from scanty observations. There are two formal methods to do this: minimum information theory and entropy maximization.

A. Information Theory

Here, let us concentrate on a facility location example. Suppose a firm is about to locate in one of the n' zones of a region. A land developer has studied the firm and its needs, and concludes that the probability of the firm locating in zone 1 is Q_1, in zone 2 is $Q_2, \ldots$, and more generally, of locating in zone i is Q_i. The number Q_i is the developer's guess about the likelihood of the firm locating in zone i. Alternatively expressed, the ratio $Q_i/(1 - Q_i)$ is the odds on the firm choosing zone i. Clearly, probabilities cannot be negative (so the non-negativity requirement applies: $Q_i \geq 0$) and the firm must locate somewhere (so the sum of the sub-areal shares must be unity: $\Sigma_i Q_i = 1$). Perhaps the developer then receives inside information that one member of the board favors a particular zone, say j. The developer is therefore forced to revise his/her estimates so that the estimated probability of the firm locating in zone i is now P_i. The insider message has evidently caused the developer to change his or her mind about the likely outcome of the event and has therefore imparted improved information (Webber 1984; Gonzales and Woods 1992). The question is: How much more information than before?

The developer starts with the probability distribution $\mathbf{Q} = (Q_1, Q_2, \ldots, Q_{n'})$, and changes this opinion to $\mathbf{P} = (P_1, P_2, \ldots, P_n')$. Let the extra information contained in the insider message which updates the probabilities $\mathbf{Q}$ to $\mathbf{P}$ be denoted by $I(\mathbf{P};\mathbf{Q})$. Five desiderata are now associated with the measure $I(\mathbf{P};\mathbf{Q})$ and we need to address these five specifications for $I(\mathbf{P};\mathbf{Q})$. First, the two probability distributions may in fact be one and the same ($\mathbf{P} = \mathbf{Q}$). In this case, the message does not change the developer's mind. This means the information is worthless or $I(\mathbf{P};\mathbf{Q}) = 0$.

Second, it is reasonable to require that the information conveyed by the message does not depend on the order in which zones are listed or labeled, say from zone 1 to zone n'. In other words, it does not matter whether, for instance, the downtown zone is labeled as zone 1, zone 2, or zone 3 and so on.

Third, it is required that the metric $I(\mathbf{P};\mathbf{Q})$ be continuous. Thus, if the message has only a small effect in updating the probabilities (or $\mathbf{P}$ is very similar to $\mathbf{Q}$), only a little information is gained in the process of updating $\mathbf{P}$ to $\mathbf{Q}$. In other words, $I(\mathbf{P};\mathbf{Q})$ is very small or nearly zero, slight differences in probability distributions are associated with marginal information.

Fourth, suppose that the developer has only the knowledge on the zones in which the firm will not locate. Lacking further information, the developer believes that each of the remaining zones is equally likely to be chosen. Three special cases can be defined for this situation:

(a) One initially believed the n' zones were feasible, but reduced this to $(K + 1)$ when given a message, where $0 < K < n'$. This means that $\mathbf{Q} = (1/n' + 1/n', \ldots, 1/n')$, and $\mathbf{P} = (1/(K + 1), 1/(K + 1), \ldots, 1/(K + 1))$ where $P_i \geq Q_i$.

(b) One believed that n' zones were feasible, but reduced them to K upon receipt of insider information: $\mathbf{Q} = (1/n', 1/n', \ldots, 1/n')$, $\mathbf{P} = (1/K, 1/K, \ldots, 1/K)$. Here $P_i > Q_i$.

(c) One initially believed that $(n' + 1)$ zones were feasible, but reduced that number to K when given insider information (remembering $K < n'$): $\mathbf{Q} = (1/(n' + 1), 1/(n' + 1), \ldots, 1/(n' + 1))$, $\mathbf{P} = (1/K, 1/K, \ldots, 1/K)$. Here $P_i >> Q_i$.

In terms of the number of zones taken out of contention by the insider's message, (a) has received the least information and (c) the most, and $I(\mathbf{P};\mathbf{Q})$ is required to satisfy this ordering of information contents. In other words, as one progresses from (a) to (c), P_i becomes larger (or the location of the firm becomes more definite) as more information is available.

Fifth and last, the zones may be classified into two groups: $1, 2, \ldots, K$, and $K + 1, K + 2, \ldots, n'$. The location question then becomes: what are the probabilities that the firm will locate in group 1 or group 2, and given that any one group is chosen, what is the probability that the firm will choose a particular zone in that group? Let (Q_1^*, Q_2^*) and (P_1^*, P_2^*) be the prior and posterior probabilities of choosing each group, and let $\mathbf{Q}_1$ and $\mathbf{Q}_2$ (or $\mathbf{P}_1$ and $\mathbf{P}_2$) be the prior (or posterior) probabilities of choosing a zone within each group. Then an insider's message provides information about group membership (or changes $\mathbf{Q}^*$ to $\mathbf{P}^*$) and about specific zone location given the group has been identified (or changes $\mathbf{Q}_1$ and $\mathbf{Q}_2$ to $\mathbf{P}_1$ and $\mathbf{P}_2$ respectively). In this case, the expected total amount of information is $I(P_1^*, P_2^*; Q_1^*, Q_2^*) + P_1^* I(\mathbf{P}_1; \mathbf{Q}_1) + P_2^* I(\mathbf{P}_2, \mathbf{Q}_2)$, or the combined information of group identification and zone location.

These five desiderata are posed on the measure of information. Together the five uniquely specify the mathematical measure of the information provided by the insider message that changes probabilities from $\mathbf{Q}$ to $\mathbf{P}$:

$$I(\mathbf{P}; \mathbf{Q}) = \sum_{i=1}^{n'} P_i \ln \frac{P_i}{Q_i} \tag{3.48}$$

The fundamental premise of information theory is that the generation of information can be modeled as a probabilistic process that can be measured in a manner that agrees with intuition. In accordance with this supposition, a random event A that occurs with probability $P(A)$ is said to contain $I(A) = \ln(1/P(A)) = -\ln P(A)$ units of information. The quantity $I(A)$ is often called the **self-information** of A. Generally speaking, the amount of information attributed to event A is inversely related to the probability of A. If $P(A) = 1$ (that is, the event occurs with certainty), $I(A) = 0$ and no information is attributed to it. In other words, because no uncertainty is associated with the event, no information would be imparted by communicating that the event has occurred. However, if $P(A) = 0.99$, communicating that A has occurred conveys some small amount of information.

Communicating that A has not occurred conveys much more information, because this outcome is much less likely, $P(\sim A) = 0.01$. Thus in Equation 3.48, $\ln(P_i/Q_i) = -(\ln P_i - \ln Q_i)$ is the information gained from the insider message about locating the firm in zone i. Weighing each zone by the current probability P_i and summing the zonal information gain over n' zones provides the mathematical expression for minimum discrimination information over the entire study area. Most importantly, it can be shown that this expression possesses all the five desired properties outlined above.

A common way to operationalize the metric in Equation 3.48 is the entropy measure[9]. If $\mathbf{Q}$ is a uniform distribution in Equation 3.48 (i.e., if $Q_i = 1/n'$ for every $i = 1,2, \ldots, n'$) then

$$I(\mathbf{P},\mathbf{Q}) = \sum_i P_i \ln\frac{P_i}{1/n'} = \sum_i P_i \ln(P_i n') = \sum_i P_i \ln P_i +$$
$$\sum_i P_i \ln n' = \sum_i P_i \ln P_i + \ln n' \qquad (3.49)$$

Consider a firm choosing a location among n' zones to open business. A priori, it is believed that the probability that a firm should be located in zone i is Q_i, for each $i = 1,2, \ldots, n'$. Some structural or aggregate data are now obtained that describe the locational decision at hand; call these data D'. The problem is to describe the spatial distribution of firms (or the probability that any one firm locates at each zone), given that D' alone are insufficient to provide such detailed information. The logical inferential method of solving this problem is called **minimum information principle**. As beliefs are changed from $\mathbf{Q}$ to $\mathbf{P}$, it reflects that an amount of extra information is gained to effect the change; different $\mathbf{P}$'s correspond to different amounts of information. The minimum information principle requires that a value of $\mathbf{P}$ is chosen that minimizes the apparent information given by the data D', but subject to the requirement that $\mathbf{P}$ is consistent with D'. Thus the method asserts that the phenomena should be described in the way which deviates least from the original beliefs, apart from the modifications dictated by D'.

B. Entropy

Now let the journey-to-work trip distribution be $\mathbf{P} = \mathbf{V} = [V_{ij}]$ be chosen with minimum information from a priori distribution $\mathbf{Q} = [Q_{ij}]$ (Putman 1978; Cesario 1975). Notice here, that without violating any of the arguments above, V_{ij} and Q_{ij} are no longer probabilities. In terms of information theory, this can be represented as choosing $\mathbf{V}$ to minimize

$$I(\mathbf{V};\mathbf{Q}) = \sum_{i=1}^{n'} \sum_{j=1}^{|J|} V_{ij} \ln\frac{V_{ij}}{Q_{ij}} \qquad (3.50)$$

subject to given data D'. Here n' stands for the number of origin zones and $|J|$ the number of destination zones. To the extent that $\mathbf{Q} = [Q_{ij}]$ is given, the above expression is equivalent to

$$\text{Min } \Sigma_i \Sigma_j V_{ij} \ln V_{ij} - \ln Q_{ij} \qquad \text{or} \qquad \text{Min } \Sigma_i \Sigma_j V_{ij} \ln V_{ij} \qquad (3.51)$$

To interpret this, let us examine a simple example due to Senior (1973). Imagine six employed persons living in one residential zone $i = 1$, and commutes to three work zones $j = 1, 2, 3$. Suppose that the six workers are named A,B,C,D,E, and F. We may now specify the origins and destinations of the work trips for each worker. Each possible, fully described, system of (a) one origin, (b) three destinations, and (c) six total work trips with their specified origins and destinations may be called a **microstate** of the system. Six of these possible microstates are shown in Figure 3.17. There are obviously many more since there are very many such microstates of even this simple system.

Let us now consider microstate 1 where the number of trips between i and $j = 1$ is 3; the number between i and $j = 2$ is 2; and the number between i and $j = 3$ is 1. Microstate 6 may also be seen to have this same distribution of trips: from i to $j = 1$ there are 3 trips, from i to $j = 2$ there are 2, and from i to $j = 3$, there is 1. Clearly there are many microstates that could be drawn that would

Figure 3.17   SYSTEM MICROSTATES

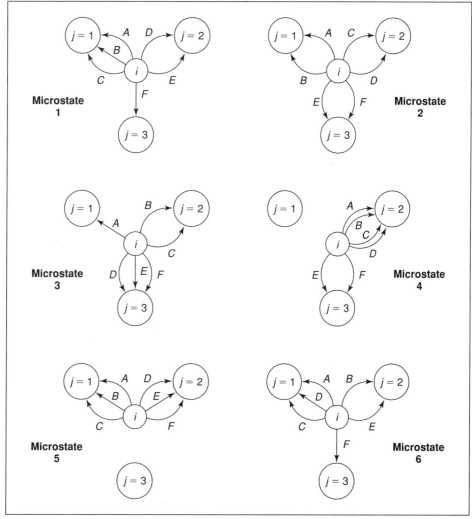

SOURCE: Putman (1978). Reprinted with permission.

have this same arrangement of total trips. This particular arrangement of zone to zone trips, if described independently of which worker is making which trip, may be called the **mesostate** of the system. Four mesostates of the system are shown in Figure 3.18. Comparing Figures 3.17 and 3.18, it can be seen that the microstates 1 and 6 are two possible manifestations of mesostate A. Microstate 2 is a possible manifestation of mesostate B, but microstate 5 is *not* a possible manifestation of mesostate D. Thus each mesostate describes a specific set of possible microstates.

If we now consider that there might be several residential zones in addition to the one which has been used in this example, then a more aggregate description of the system would be the total trips leaving each origin and the total trips arriving at each destination. Let us assume that two workers live in zone $i = 2$, and four workers live in zone $i = 3$ in addition to the six already defined as living in $i = 1$ (and we equate one worker with one work trip as we have been doing). Further assume that these additional workers are named G, H, I, J, K', and M. A microstate of this newly expanded system would be a list of the origins and destinations of the work trips for each of the 12 workers, $V_{ij}(k); k = A, B, \ldots, M$. A mesostate of this system would be a list of the total number of work trips from each origin zone to each destination zone Q_{ij} or V_{ij}. Finally, a **macrostate** of this expand system is a list of the total trips leaving each origin and the total trips arriving at each destination, V_i. Figure 3.19 shows four macrostates of the expanded system.

Referring to Figure 3.19, macrostates 1 and 2 with 6 trips leaving $i = 1$ contain all the previous examples of microstates and mesostates. Macrostates 2 and 3, with the trips leaving $i = 1$ not equal to six, correspond to other system states which do not include the microstates and mesostates given as examples. We

Figure 3.18   SYSTEM MESOSTATES

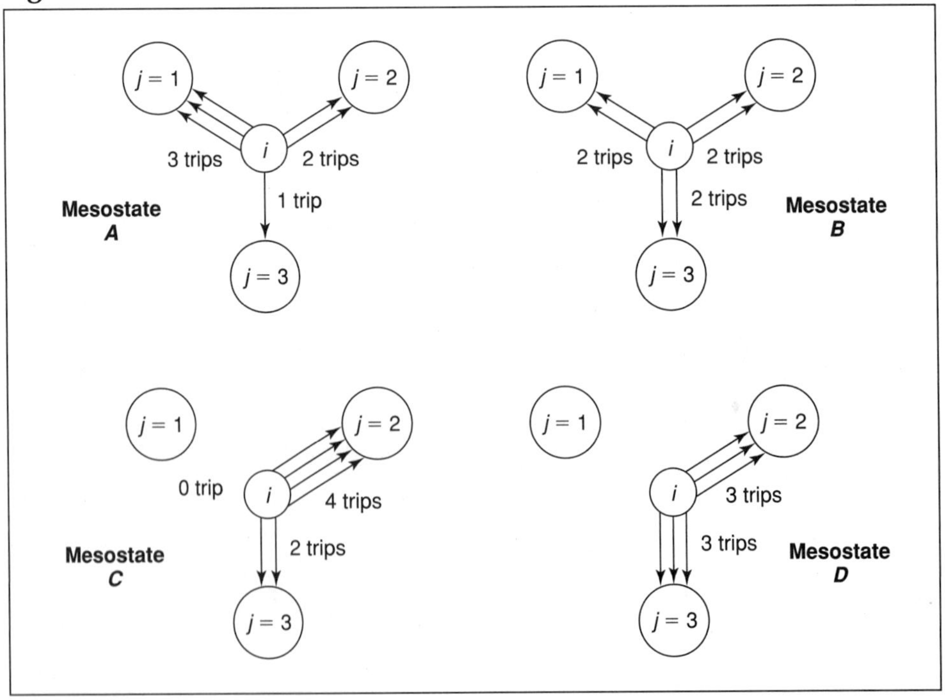

SOURCE: Putman (1978). Reprinted with permission.

Figure 3.19   SYSTEM MACROSTATES

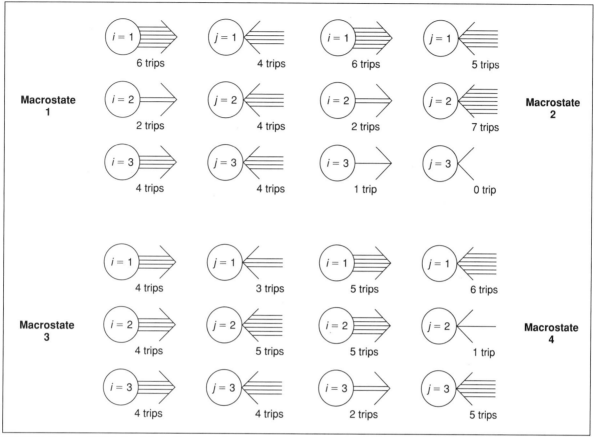

SOURCE: Putman (1978). Reprinted with permission.

should also note in passing that one could have defined a macrostate for the example of a single origin used at the start of this discussion. This would have been, in a sense, a degenerate case, as the trips leaving the single origin would always have been equal to six. The microstates as defined here in this discussion correspond to a disaggregate model as referred to in Section V; mesostates correspond to aggregate modeling; and macrostates are the given conditions for calibrating a gravity model. The entropy formulation deals with the meso- and macrostates and requires two key assumptions. First, all microstates are assumed to be equally probable. Second, the most likely mesostate or macrostate is assumed to be the one with the greatest number of possible microstates. We refer to this second assumption as **entropy maximization.**

We may now develop a spatial interaction model for the mesostate level using entropy, rather than gravity model formulation. The given information could consist of the origin trips V_i and the destination trips V_j where $\Sigma_j V_{ij} = V_i$ and $\Sigma_i V_{ij} = V_j$, or the total number of trips $Q = \Sigma_i V_i = \Sigma_j V_j = \Sigma_{ij} Q_{ij}$. Let us examine the microstates $V_{ij}(k)$ for a given Q. For the example in Figure 3.17, $i = 1, j = 1, 2, 3$ and $V = 6$, the microstates consist of $V_{11}(k)$, $V_{12}(k)$ and $V_{13}(k)$. Stripping the traveler designation k, $V_{11} + V_{12} + V_{13} = Q$. V_{11} trip makers can be selected from Q in $Q!/[V_{11}!(Q - V_{11})!]$ ways, according to the familiar combinatorial formula of statistics. Now if we ask in how many ways it is possible to select V_{12} out of the remaining $(Q - V_{11})$ travelers in each case, it is given by $(Q-V_{11})!/[V_{12}!(Q - V_{11} - V_{12})!]$. The total number of ways of selecting V_{11} out of Q *and* V_{12} out of $(Q - V_{11})$ is given by the product of the two combinatorial formulas, or $Q!/[V_{11}!V_{12}![(Q - V_{11} - V_{12})!]$. Continuing on in this way, we see that the total number of ways in which we can select a particular distribution $\mathbf{V} = [V_{ij}]$ distribution from Q is

$$\frac{Q!}{V_{11}!V_{12}!V_{13}!} \quad \text{or} \quad \frac{Q!}{\Pi_{ij}V_{ij}!} \tag{3.52}$$

The combinatorial formula above results regardless of the order in which the entries in $\mathbf{V}$ are considered. In other words, it is independent of the way we label the zones.

Applying this formula, the number of microstates of mesostate A in Figure 3.18 is $6!/[(V_{11}!)(V_{12}!)(V_{13}!)]$ or $6!/[(3!)(2!)(1!)] = 60$. The number of microstates of mesostate B is $6!/\{(2!)(2!)(2!)\} = 90$. By trial and error, one may substitute values for V_{11}, V_{12} and V_{13} in the denominator of the equation and discover that the minimum value of the denominator (subject to the constraint that the sum of all the trips equal six) is at $2!2!2!$. This corresponds to the maximum number of microstates 90, which suggests that in the absence of any further information about our example (such as the number of trips originating at a zone and terminating at a zone), the most probable mesostate is when the six trips are evenly distributed to the three destinations. In general, the most probable mesostate is when the number of microstates is to be maximized or max $[Q!/\Pi_{ij}V_{ij}]$. Stirling's approximation for large values of x yields $\ln(x!) = x \ln(x) - x$. Applying such approximation to the logarithm of the above maximization expression results in Equation 3.51, remembering that $Q = \Sigma_{ij}Q_{ij}$ in this case. Thus entropy maximization is shown to be equivalent to the minimum information principle.

XIII. QUALITY OF A MODEL CALIBRATION

In this chapter, we have discussed the various ways to describe the scenario under analysis. We call this descriptive modeling. After all the above work has been performed, the final question arises as to how good the model is in replicating the real world. Obviously, the answers vary depending on whom you ask, and most importantly, the end use of the model. However, here are some scientific measures of merit, which form part of the information on the quality of the model calibration.

A. Chi-Square Test

The chi-square test, for example, can be used to determine how well theoretical probability distributions (such as an assumed normal distribution) fit empirical distributions (in other words, those obtained from sampled data). In general, the chi statistic measures the discrepancy between the estimated and observed frequencies. It is used to test whether a set of estimated frequencies differ from a set of observed frequencies sufficiently to reject the hypothesis under which the expected frequencies were obtained. The formula generally used for the chi-square statistic is,

$$x_2 = \sum_{i=1}^{n} \frac{(y_i - \hat{y}_i)^2}{\hat{y}_i}$$

where y_i is the observed data and $\hat{y}_i$ is the estimated. If there is a close agreement between the estimated and observed frequencies, χ^2 will be small. If the agreement is poor, χ^2 will be large. A numerical example has been worked out in Section XI-A in connection with the singly constrained gravity model.

Using the chi-square idea, it can be shown that the maximum entropy explanation of spatial distribution can be used to calibrate the parameters such as α's in Equation 4.30. This can be accomplished by the **minimum discrimination information statistic** $2V\Sigma_i\Sigma_j V_{ij}\ln(V_{ij}/Q_{ij})$, which has an asymptotic chi-square distribution with $(n'J - L')$ degrees of freedom. Here, L' is the total number of control totals placed on the number of trips made plus the number of parameters to be calibrated (Oppenheim 1995). For example, when the given data D' consist of the number of origin trips V_i, the number of destination trips V_j, (or the equivalent statement about the total number of trips in the study area V), and the total travel cost in trip minutes or trip miles, $L' = n' + |J| + 1$ corresponding to the number of origin zones, the number of destination zones and the b coefficient for the trip distribution curve $\exp(-bC_{ij})$, as shown in Section XI-B. The statistic takes on a value of zero when the model is perfect, in other words, when all predictions V_{ij} are equal to the corresponding observations Q_{ij}, and a positive value for less than perfect model fit. The statistical significance of the model performance may then be tested by comparing the value of the statistic with the threshold value from the chi-square table with appropriate number of degrees-of-freedom at the chosen level of confidence. If the former is greater than the latter, the hypothesis that the distri-bution of predicted values is not significantly different from that of the observed values must then be rejected. In other words, the calibration needs to be further refined to effect closer agreement between the predicted and observed trips.

B. Variance Reduction

Irrespective of the calibration techniques used, a common measure to compare an estimated model with the observed model is the sum of squared errors:

$$\sum_{i=1}^{n}(y_i - \hat{y}_i)^2 \tag{3.53}$$

This measure can be normalized by the number of observations n (where n is a large number), turning it to what is often referred to as the **residual variance:**

$$\frac{1}{n}\sum_{i=1}^{n}(y_i - \hat{y}_i)^2$$

Similarly, the square root can be taken to further normalize the measure

$$\sqrt{\frac{1}{n}\sum_{i=1}^{n}(y_i - \hat{y}_i)^2}$$

which is sometimes called the **standard error of estimate**.

All the above are absolute measures. Depending on the units used in the variables Y, the figures obtained from these formulas will be different. To truly normalize to a relative scale, we first define the worst case as the variance about the mean:

$$\sqrt{\frac{1}{n}\sum_{i}(y_i - \overline{Y})^2}$$

The ratio of Equation 5.53 and the above variance is then a more workable measure of the relative size of the actual variance. We call this ratio ρ. In other words

$$\hat{\rho}^2 = \frac{\sum_i (y_i - \hat{y}_i)^2}{\sum_i (y_i - \overline{Y})^2}$$

The variance reduction due to the model is simply $1 - \hat{\rho}^2$ The more variance the model can account for, the better. For this reason, it is preferable to have the above equation approaching unity.

The reader will detect the parallel concepts in linear regression, although the above development is, in our opinion, more general and goes well beyond linear models. Thus the model can be calibrated by any calibration technique, particularly when a combination of techniques are used, the measure of merit still readily applies to the combined model, while more specialized measures are only good for each individual model.

Example
As an example, consider the nonlinear doubly constrained gravity model in Section XI-B discussed previously. Here, the $\hat{\rho}^2$ is

$$\frac{\sum_{i=1}^{3}\sum_{j=1}^{3}(y_{ij} - \hat{y}_{ij})^2}{\sum_{i=1}^{3}\sum_{j=1}^{3}(y_{ij} - \overline{Y})^2}$$

Based on the data contained in Table 3.14 and Table 3.15, we have the relative size of the estimation variance $\hat{\rho}^2 = 3.843 \times 10^{-4}$. The variance reduced by the model is thus $1 - \hat{\rho}^2 = 0.9996$, which is quite impressive. ∎

XIV. CONCLUDING REMARKS

We have provided in this chapter a summary of pertinent analysis tools that are useful in describing the context of a facility location/land use decision. The methods are diverse, but they are all spatial extensions of simulation, probabilistic models, and statistical analysis. We also introduce specialized techniques used to analyze spatial interactions, as exemplified by the gravity model, information, and entropy theories. To the extent that warehouses are built to store the appropriate amount in anticipation of deliveries to potential demand points, we review the marginal analysis that governs inventory control over a network. This will help to locate facilities and to make timely delivery of goods and services. Together with the basic building blocks reviewed in appendices to this book, we will have a self-contained set of background tools for the reader. The discussions in these methodological chapters differ from that in the appendices in terms of context. While the appendices are purely applied mathematics, the treatment here is applications-oriented model building. Thus examples are drawn from the subject matter of this book, even though they have to be simplified to achieve the transparency desired. In later chapters, in the CD software, and in Chan (2000), case studies will be presented wherein we show how the more fully developed models are used to come up with real world decisions.

ENDNOTES

[1] A numerical example is worked out in Chapter 4 for illustration.

[2] A methodological review of stochastic process may be found in Appendix 2.

[3] For an explanation of the t-statistic, see Appendix 3. Paired t-tests are used here, which test the hypothesis that there is no significance between two sample means, m_1 and m_2, or the difference between the sample means is zero. $m_d = m_1 - m_2 = 0$. Traditional statistical tests are character ized by significance levels, or the confidence one would place on the test results.

[4] A better term is the "News vendor" problem.

[5] The correlation coefficient is defined in Appendix 3.

[6] The matrix notation is adopted here for ease of explanation only, it is not essential for development. For a formal introduction to the matrix representation of linear regression, refer to Appendix 3

[7] For a discussion of the statistical and practical considerations in selecting a regression equation, see Appendix 3. A parsimonious model has the proper balance between practicality and statistical significance.

[8] This is referred to as constrained regression.

[9] Entropy originates from the Greek and roughly means change or transformation.

REFERENCES

Ahituv, N.; Berman, O. (1988). *Operations management of distributed service networks: A practical approach.* New York: Plenum Press.

Al-Mosaind, M. A.; Ducker, K. J.; Strathman, J. G. (1993). "Light rail transit stations and property values. A hedonic price approach." (Presentation Paper 930806). Paper presented at the 72nd meeting of the Transportation Research Board, Washington D. C.

Black, W. R. (1991). "A note on the use of correlation coefficients for assessing goodness-of-fit in spatial interaction models." *Transportation* 18:199–206.

Cesario, F. J. (1975). "A primer on entropy modeling." *AIP Journal* (January):40–48.

Chan, Y. (2000). *Location, transport and land-use: Modeling spatial-temporal information.* New York: Springer-Verlag.

Claunch, E.; Goehring, S.; Chan, Y. (1992). Airport location problem: Three and four city cases. Working Paper. Department of Operational Sciences. Air Force Institute of Technology. Wright-Patterson AFB, Ohio.

Cliff, A. D.; Ord, J. K. (1975). "Space-time modeling with an application to regional forecasting." *Transactions—Institute of British Geographers* 66:119–128.

Congressional Office of Technology Assessment (1982). *Global models, world futures, and public policy.* Washington, D. C.: U. S. Congress.

De Neufville, R: Stafford, J. (1971). *Systems analysis for engineers and managers.* New York: McGraw-Hill.

Dickey, J. W. (1983). *Metropolitan transportation planning,* 2nd ed. New York: McGraw-Hill.

Duann, L-S.; Chang, C-C. (1992). "A study of the development of disaggregate residential location choice models." *Transportation Planning Journal* (Taiwan, Republic of China) 21, no. 4:401–422.

Fanueff, R.; Sterle, T.; Chan, Y. (1992). A warehouse location, inventory allocation problem. Working Paper. Department of Operational Sciences. Air Force Institute of Technology. Wright-Patterson AFB, Ohio.

Feldt, A. G. (1972). CLUG: *Community Land Use Game.* New York: Free Press.

Foot, D. (1981). *Operational urban models: An introduction.* New York: Methuen.

Golan, A. (1998). "Maximum entropy likelihood and uncertainty: A comparison." In *Maximum entropy and Bayesian methods,* edited by G. J. Erikson. Boston: Kluwer Academic Publishers.

Gonzalez, R. C.; Woods, R. E. (1992). *Digital image processing.* Reading, Massachusetts: Addison-Wesley.

Guy, C. M. (1991). "Spatial interaction modelling in retail planning practice: the need for robust statistical methods." *Environment and Planning B* 18: 191–203.

Heller, M.; Cohon, J. L.; Revelle, C. S. (1989). "The use of simulation in validating a multi-objective EMS location model." *Annals of Operations Research* 18: 303–322.

Hurter, A. P.; Martinich, J. S. (1989). *Facility location and the theory of production.* Boston: Kluwer Academic Publishers.

Kalaba, R.; Moore, J. E.; Xu, R.; Chen, G. (1995). A new perspective on calibrating spatial interaction models: An application to shopping centers. Working Paper. School of Urban and Regional Planning. University of Southern California. Los Angeles.

Kanafani, A. (1983). *Transportation demand analysis.* New York: McGraw-Hill.

Lapin, L. (1975). *Quantitative methods for business decisions with cases,* 4th ed. Orlando, Florida: Harcourt Brace Jovanovich.

Lee, S-Y.; Haghani, A. E.; Byun, J. H. (1995). Simultaneous determination of land use and travel demand with congestion: A system dynamics modeling approach. (Presentation Paper 950716). Paper presented at the 74th meeting of the Transportation Research Board, Washington D. C.

Meadows, D. H.; Meadows, D. L.; Randers, J.; Behrens, W. W., III (1972). *The limits to growth.* New York: Signet.

Oppenheim, N. (1980). *Applied urban and regional models.* Englewood Cliffs, New Jersey: Prentice Hall.

Oppenheim, N. (1995). *Urban travel: Demand modeling.* New York: Wiley-Interscience.

Pritsker, A. B. (1986). *Introduction to simulation and SLAM,* 3rd ed. New York: Halsted Press.

Putman, S. (1978). The integrated forecasting of transportation and land use. In *Emerging transportation planning methods,* edited by W. Brown. Washington D. C.: Office of University Research. Research and Special Programs Administration. U. S. Department of Transportation, 119–147.

Repede, J. F.; Bernardo, J. J. (1994). "Developing and validating a decision support system for location emergency medical vehicles in Louisville, Kentucky." *European Journal of Operational Research* 75:567–581.

Rubenstein, B.; Zandi, I. (1998). An evaluative tool for solid waste management. Working Paper. Department of Information Systems. University of Maryland at Baltimore County. Baltimore, Maryland.

Senior, M. S. (1973). "Approaches to residential location modeling 1: Urban ecological and spatial interaction models (a review)." *Environment and Planning* 5: 165–197.

Thompson, G. L.; Weller, B.; Terrie, E. W. (1993). New perspectives on highway investment and economic growth. (Presentation Paper 930597). Paper presented at the 72nd meeting of the Transportation Research Board, Washington D. C.

Webber, M. J. (1984). *Explanation, prediction and planning: The Lowry model.* London: Pion.

Willemain, T. R. (1981). *Statistical methods for planners.* Cambridge, Massachusetts: MIT Press.

Winston, W. L. (1994). *Operations research: Applications and algorithms,* 3rd ed. Belmont, California: Duxbury Press.

4

Prescriptive Tools for Analysis

*"The mathematical sciences particularly exhibit order, symmetry
and limitation, and these are the greatest forms of the beautiful."*
Aristotle

This chapter will follow our discussion on the two methods of analysis identified
in our taxonomy, focusing now on prescriptive instead of descriptive techniques.
By way of a definition, prescriptive technique is generally used in system design,
where a stated goal or objective is to be achieved. In the context of this book, the
function of a prescriptive model then, is to configure a facility location or land use
plan to achieve this goal or objective. For example, if one is to stimulate residential development in an area, the model, after it has been set up, will prescribe
a land use plan that will provide all the utilities, transportation, and zoning that
will best facilitate such a development. To the extent that we often wish to provide
the best design, optimization procedures are an integral part of the prescriptive
tool kit. Here in this chapter, we will introduce the basic building blocks of
prescriptive analysis (including optimization concepts), deferring most of the
implementation and computational details to subject focused chapters throughout
this book and the appropriate book appendices. Included in the latter category
are such appendices as "Optimization Schemes" (Appendix 1) and "Control,
Dynamics, and System Stability" (Appendix 4).

I. A TYPICAL PRESCRIPTIVE MODEL

As always, examples are the best way to introduce a new concept. We will build
upon the three-sector urban economy example from Chapter 3, namely, an economy made up of the residential, basic, and service employment sectors. Three fundamental steps are involved in effecting a prescriptive model: defining goals and
objectives, representing the system, and then putting them together in a single
model. Inasmuch as step two calls for system representation, clearly prescriptive
techniques are not mutually exclusive of descriptive techniques. A prescriptive

model can be thought of as an extension of a descriptive model, in which goals and objectives are added on top.

A. Goals and Objectives

First, let us discuss the goal or the objective one tries to optimize, which is an important part of a prescriptive model. Two examples of the objective function may be cited from Chapter 2: efficiency and equity. Efficiency may mean the least costly way to provide quality housing, while equity may be concerned with constructing housing in such a manner that it is equally accessible to all the population. Oftentimes, the objective function is also referred to as the **figure of merit.** Thus the efficiency figure of merit in the example is the total cost, which is to be minimized. Accessibility may become the equity measure for the example, which is to be maximized. One way to do this may be to formulate a land use/transportation plan that would guarantee accessibility to housing within 15 minutes of travel time from work for all the urban population. The question now becomes: Can we configure a land use plan that will achieve both efficiency and equity?

Another feature of a prescriptive model can be cited. Suppose one has a parcel of land on which he or she wishes to build housing or offices in order to maximize the utility of the land but there are a number of encumbrances, one of which may be the development density allowable by zoning codes. Thus in an area zoned for single family units, the parcel cannot be developed into a multiple dwelling apartment building no matter how much the developer wants it to be. Thus a prescriptive model has to include the representation of the scenario under which one operates, including the many constraints such as zoning density. We have already seen in Chapter 3 how these constraints can be modeled. To the extent that descriptive techniques are adept in system representation, it is relatively straightforward to build a prescriptive model on top of a descriptive model by simply adding objective functions. We will illustrate how this is performed.

B. Representation of the System

The scenario under study and the interrelationship between all the components are first represented in a flow chart or a set of simultaneous equations. These equations are formulated in a manner similar to those introduced in the descriptive modeling discussion. The simulation approach, for example, requires a flow chart to represent the system. The econometric approach, on the other hand, is formulated in a set of simultaneous equations. Again, some examples may be useful. A flow chart of a basic economy may include the relationship between manufacturing, retail, and household sectors in an algorithmic set of steps, as shown in the economic-base example in previous chapters. A correlative model, on the other hand, may start with an arrow diagram showing primary, secondary, and tertiary relationships among all the variables. The relationships are then formalized into a set of simultaneous equations, with the coefficients *a, b, c,* and *d* to be calibrated by econometric techniques. We review an example initiated in Chapter 3 below:

$$(\textit{forecast pop}) = a \ (\textit{forecast emp}) + b \ (\textit{base-yr pop})$$
$$(\textit{forecast emp}) = c \ (\textit{forecast pop}) + d \ (\textit{base-yr emp})$$

(4.1)

Here the coupling effects between population and employment are explicitly recognized, in that employment needs to be supported by a labor force, and at the same time, dependent population often follows employment.

C. A Prescriptive Formulation of the Economic-Base Concept

Now we can show how the familiar descriptive formulation of the economic-base theory can be converted to a prescriptive format by the introduction of objective functions. The economic-base model deals with four types of land use: retail, residential, manufacturing, and undeveloped, all of which are to be placed within the available land. In accordance with economic-base theory, basic manufacturing land is exogenously determined and hence a constant. Undevelopable land is the same way. This leaves us with two decision variables, retail land use and residential land use. All the development has to be contained within the available land. Our example problem then can be represented by the first of several constraint equations, where, once again, the retail and residential land use are decision variables, while manufacturing and undevelopable land are treated as constants.

$$(\textit{retail land use}) + (\textit{residential land use}) \leq (\textit{developable land})$$

Another constraint deals with density and zoning, that the maximum development density as permitted by zoning cannot be exceeded:

$$(\textit{no. of dwelling units})/(\textit{res. land use}) \leq (\textit{max allowable density}) \qquad (4.2)$$

The last constraint is worthy of mention. It models the often observed fact that in order to establish any retail activity in a zone, one shall have a minimum threshold of viable activities, often referred to as the critical mass, or the smallest amount of activities that can sustain the business:

$$(\textit{retail emp density})(\textit{retail land use}) \geq (\textit{threshold}) \qquad (4.3)$$

Now if one adds an objective function on top of the set of equations, which represent the system, a prescriptive model is obtained. Instead of the efficiency and equity objectives, a plausible objective may be to maximize the development of the land, which may be measured in terms of the total employment and population in the area:

$$\max[(\textit{retail emp density})(\textit{retail land}) + (\textit{res density})(\textit{res land})] \qquad (4.4)$$

As can be seen, a distinguishing feature of the example model is that it consists of a set of simultaneous equations. In real life, it may not be possible to model the system as analytically as shown here. It is entirely conceivable that simulations is the only means to represent the complex operations of the system under discussion. Still, objective functions can be imposed on top to effect a prescriptive model in this situation.

II. HEURISTIC SOLUTION TECHNIQUES

Having fixed some fundamental ideas about a prescriptive model, let us proceed to survey some of the tools for solving such a model. We have categorized prescriptive tools into two classes. One is heuristic and the other analytical. **Heuristic techniques** refer to a set of methodologies that are not strictly mathematical. They may consist merely of a number of clever or intuitive computational procedures. **Analytical techniques,** on the other hand, are more mathematically rigorous and have a transparent or traceable relationship between the constituent components. Heuristic techniques consist basically of a set of carefully specified computational schemes that are usually programmed into the computer to yield good solutions. These techniques are devoid of the nice, transparent properties that characterize analytical procedures, and an optimal solution is not often guaranteed. Three types of heuristic techniques will be discussed here: the manual approach, the enumerative, and the direct search.

A. Manual Approach

The **manual approach** is a very simple approach. It involves formulating alternative plans that represent the various zoning and transportation policies, for instance, then performing the forecast as a second step, and finally picking the plan that yields the best figure of merit. Another example would be to pick two candidate locations for a facility, evaluate the merits of both, and pick the better of the two. Take the Community Land Use Game (CLUG) discussed in Chapter 3. Three economic sectors parallel to economic-base theory are represented: the basic sector consisting of full industries and partial plants, the residential sector consisting of R1, R2, R3, and R4 housing (in order of higher development-density), and the service sector as exemplified by Central Store (CS) and Local Store (LS).

Referring to Figure 4.1, among the many factors that shape the community development is accessibility to the export market through the harbor terminal. Let us say an entrepreneur is deciding between two sites for his partial industry (PI), as marked by PI-1 (grid point 6-72) and PI-2 (grid point 12-72) on the playing board shown in Figure 4.1. The residential quarters of his labor force is located at R2 (12-58). With the given road system, transportation terminal, and the required utility line already in place and paid for, which is the preferred site location judging purely on transportation cost?

Site PI-1: accessibility to population = (6)(1) + (2)(2) = 10
accessibility to export market = (6)(1) = 6
total transportation cost = 16;

Site PI-2: access to population = (6)(2) = 12
access to market = (6)(1) + (2)(2) = 10
total transport cost = 22

Based on the above manual analysis, PI-1 is the best choice because it has a lower transportation cost altogether.

Figure 4.1 LOCATIONAL CHOICE USING A MANUAL PRESCRIPTIVE TECHNIQUE

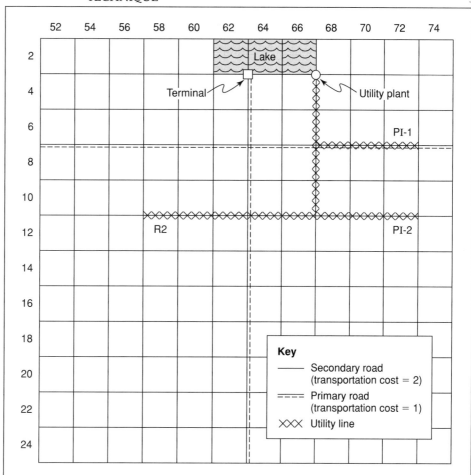

B. Enumerative Method

The **enumerative method** is often used when the options can be represented in discrete integer variables. For example, four divisions of a company *A, B, C,* and *D* have a choice among four sites, 1, 2, 3, and 4, to locate a plant. A prescriptive model is used to assign each division to a site according to some figure of merit such as overall cost to the company. The integer variable x_{ij} assumes the value of 1 when industrial plant *i* is located at site *j*. Consider the costs associated with locating four plants in four sites as shown in Table 4.1. The assignment of a plant to a site would be made according to the lowest total cost, where each site can take only one plant and no more. Such an assignment can be computed after a combinatorial programming model, such as the following, has been formulated:

$$\min \sum_{i=1}^{4} \sum_{j=1}^{4} c_{ij} x_{ij}$$

$$\text{s.t.} \sum_{j=1}^{4} x_{ij} = 1 \qquad i = A, B, C, D$$

$$\sum_{i=1}^{4} x_{ij} = 1 \qquad j = 1, 2, 3, 4 \tag{4.5}$$

$$x_{ij} = \{0,1\}$$

where the c_{ij}'s are defined in the cost table.

While there are more efficient solution methods, such a problem can be solved by an enumerative scheme such as **branch and bound** (B&B). Here we describe a general B&B procedure (Hillier and Lieberman 1990). The algorithm is described for both maximization and minimization problems, with the former described in the general text and the latter in parenthesis:

Step 0: *Initialization.* $z_L(z_U)$ = value of best known feasible solution. (If none, $z_L[z_U] = -\infty\ [+\infty]$.) Go to Step 2.

Step 1: *Branch.* Based on some rule, select unfathomed node and partition it into two or more subsets (subproblems/nodes).

Step 2: *Bound.* For each new subset (subproblem/node), find an upper (lower) bound $z_U^i(z_L^i)$, for example, by solving a relaxed subproblem for the objective function value of feasible solutions in the subset.

Step 3: *Fathom.* For each new subset i, exclude i from further explicit enumeration if
  a) $z_U^i(z_L^i) \le (\ge)z_L(z_U)$;
  b) Subset i cannot have any feasible solutions; and
  c) Subset i has a feasible solution. If $z_U^i(z_L^i) > (<)z_L(z_U)$, set $z_L(z_U) = z_U^i(z_L^i)$ and store as the incumbent solution.

Step 4: *Stopping rule.* Reapply test (a) to all live (unfathomed) nodes. If no unfathomed nodes remain, stop. Incumbent solution is optimal. Else, return to step 1.

Alternatively, let $z_L^*(z_U^*) = \max_i z_L^i (\min_i z_U^i)$. Stop when $z_L(z_U)$ is within ϵ percent of optimal solution.

There are two problem specific rules that need to be supplied to the general algorithm (Hillier and Lieberman 1986):

Table 4.1   SITE LOCATION OF COST INDUSTRIAL PLANTS

		Sites			
		1	2	3	4
Plants	A	9	5	4	5
	B	4	3	5	6
	C	3	1	3	2
	D	2	4	2	6

Branch. Look at all possible ways of assigning next plant to unassigned site. Use best bound.

Bound. At any node, add lowest cost assignment to current solution whether feasible or not, in other words, for all unassigned industries, assign the lowest cost site. The only exception is where assignments have already been made, then the plant cannot be assigned a second (additional) site.

The B&B tree is shown in Figure 4.2. At each node of the tree, lower and upper bounds z_L and z_U need to be computed. In the initial node 0, for example, the lower bound is simply to assign plants to sites irrespective of the rule that says "one plant, one site." Thus the popular plants have the choice of more than one site: for example, plant D can locate in both sites 1 and 3, C in both 2 and 4. On the other hand, if the one-plant-one-site rule is followed, an easy way to assign is to have plant A assigned to site 1, B to 2, C to 3, and D to 4. While the former way of assigning will achieve an overall cost lower than reality, the latter will certainly be more costly than necessary; hence the former and latter constitute the lower and upper bounds respectively. The upper and lower bounds define the range within which the final solution will reside.

At node A of iteration 1, the lower bound can be evaluated by working with the cost table by striking out the row and column denoting the commitment

Figure 4.2   BRANCH AND BOUND TREE

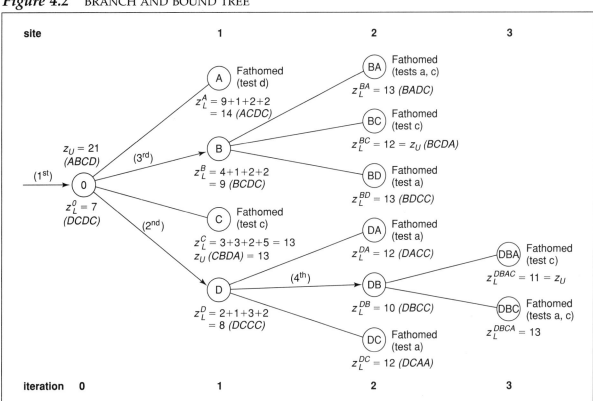

Table 4.2   MODIFIED SITE LOCATION COST DURING BRANCH AND BOUND

		Sites			
		1	2	3	4
Plant	A	(~~9~~)	~~3~~	~~4~~	~~5~~
	B	~~4~~	3	5	6
	C	~~3~~	(1)	3	(2)
	D	~~2~~	4	(2)	6

of a plant to a site. In Table 4.2, for example, row A and column 1 are struck out. With the remaining cells in the table, a lowest cost assignment is again obtained, irrespective of whether it is a feasible assignment or not; in other words, whether or not the "one plant, one site" rule has been violated. Hence the lower bound is to assign plant C to site 2, D to 3, and again C to 4 (inasmuch as C is popular). We call this solving the relaxed subproblem. Node B in iteration 1 is evaluated similarly.

At node C, a feasible solution is obtained. According to Step 3(c) of the B&B algorithm, the node has been fathomed in the sense that an incumbent solution has been obtained. Also, a new upper bound is obtained by setting $z_U = z_L = 13$. Intuitively, it says that we will not accept solutions that are worse (bigger) than 13 in the objective function value from this point on, inasmuch as we already have an incumbent solution with this overall cost. Hence node A is now eliminated from further consideration by way of fathoming rule 3(a), which says, "Prune the branch that has a overall cost bigger than the current upper bound."

The algorithm proceeds until all possible assignment combinations have been implicitly enumerated through the fathoming rules. The iterations can be summarized by the following table, which documents the steady improvement of the incumbent solution in terms of a lower total cost:

Iteration	z_U	z_L	Assignment
0	21	7	ABCD
1	13	8	CBDA
2	12	10	BCDA
3	11	11	DBAC

This table can be referenced against Figure 4.2. The iterations refer to figure columns for z_U amd branching sequence for z_L. The optimal solution, shown at node DBA in iteration 3, is $x_{A3} = x_{B2} = x_{C4} = x_{D1} = 1$ with the rest of the decision variables equal to zero. This means plant A is to be located in site 3, plant B in 2, C in 4, and D in 1.

C. Direct Search Technique

When the decision variable is continuous rather than discrete, a **direct search technique** is very common in optimization. For example, we wish to build the optimal mileage of highways to obtain the most accessibility for the entire region as a whole. Given the relationship between accessibility and highway miles as shown in Figure 4.3, a direct search procedure can be used to identify the highway miles which provide the best accessibility for a fixed budget. The direct search technique simply explores the shape of the objective function (which is accessibility in this case) experimentally. We have shown two possible shapes of the function in Figure 4.3 depending on whether the problem is constrained by the budget or when congestion sets in at some point. In the latter case, Figure 4.3(a) shows that any additional highway miles built beyond the congestion point will decrease accessibility rather than increase it.

The shape of the function as shown in Figure 4.3(a) is a concave function between 150 and 475 miles of constructed highway. Maximizing a concave function over a convex region such that the mileage ranging from 150 to 475 will yield the unique optimum of 400. This is shown in Part (a) of the figure. On the other hand, if the new addition in highway mileage is limited by the budget to 300 as suggested above, it becomes a constrained optimization problem (figure 4.3(b)). The optimum in this case will be at 300 instead. Maximizing a concave objective function over a convex region—such as the continuous line segment from 150 to 300 or 475—is termed a convex programming problem. Barring special circumstances, uniqueness of the optimum may be guaranteed. Should the range be expanded now to 0–475 in Part (a) of the figure and 0–300 in Part (b) of the figure, the objective function for accessibility is no longer concave, since the function over the range 0 to 150 is convex. The change from a convex to concave function occurs at the inflection point of 150 as shown.

Oftentimes, the shape of the objective function is unknown, although we have a good assurance that it has only one mode. In other words, there is only one maximum point rather than several optimal points, consisting of a global optimum. By **global** or **local optima** we mean the "mountain top" and other "hilltops" respectively. In this case, the Fibonacci search technique will locate the

Figure 4.3   A DIRECT SEARCH TECHNIQUE

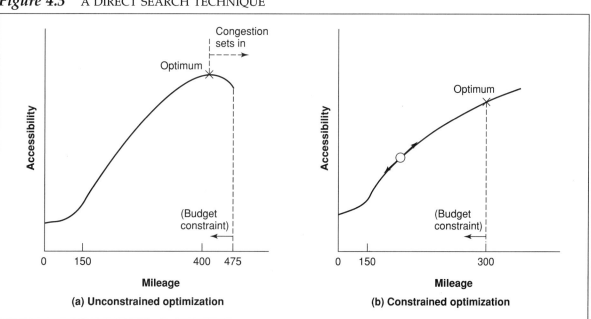

(a) Unconstrained optimization

(b) Constrained optimization

optimum quite efficiently. **Fibonacci search** is one of the most efficient ways to allocate m allotted search points for this function. The method consists of computing the value of $g(x)$, the objective function to be optimized, in m points. Each of the m points is chosen in such a way that having obtained the result for each new point, we can eliminate a subinterval—as large as possible—of the current interval. This process ensures that the optimum will not be located within the subinterval.

A special Fibonacci procedure called the method of golden section will serve to introduce this technique, where m is variable, instead of fixed. We wish to locate the optimum in as few trial points as possible. The logic behind the method of Golden Section is based on elimination of the range of search based on the results of existing search points covered. Suppose $g(x)$ is defined between a and d:

$$
\begin{array}{ccccc}
 & & & c & \\
|\!-\!\!-\!\!-\!\!-\!\!-\!| \!-\!\!-\!\!-\!\!-\!\!- \; x \; -\!\!-\!| \\
a & & b & & d
\end{array}
$$

If searches have been conducted in b and c, due to unimodality and another provision, and $g(b) < g(c)$, one can discard ab. The points to search are based on a fixed ratio:

$$\frac{whole}{larger} = \frac{larger}{smaller} = constant = 1.618$$

For example, for the interval ad shown above, the search points b and c are determined by

$$\frac{ad}{bd} = \frac{bd}{ab} = 1.618$$

This ratio and its reciprocal 0.618 have a long history of use in design, particularly in architecture.

D. The Golden Section Algorithm

An example will illustrate the **Golden Section algorithm.** Suppose a retailer is to locate a shop to capture as large a market as possible among the competitors. The retailer is considering a stretch of highway 60 miles (96 km) in length, within which the shop is to be located. Such a problem can be solved by the Golden Section method, a special application of Fibonacci search. Throughout the algorithm, we will refer to Figure 4.4, showing an unknown unimodal function representing the market potential along the highway.

Initialization:
We define the search range to be $[a, b] = [0, 60]$, with the end points 0 and 60 included in the search. We decide on the first search point by applying the golden section ratio $1/1.618$:

$$b_1 = a + r(b - a) = 0 + 1/1.618(60 - 0) = 37.08.$$

Figure 4.4   UNIMODAL FUNCTION WHOSE PRECISE SHAPE IS UNKNOWN

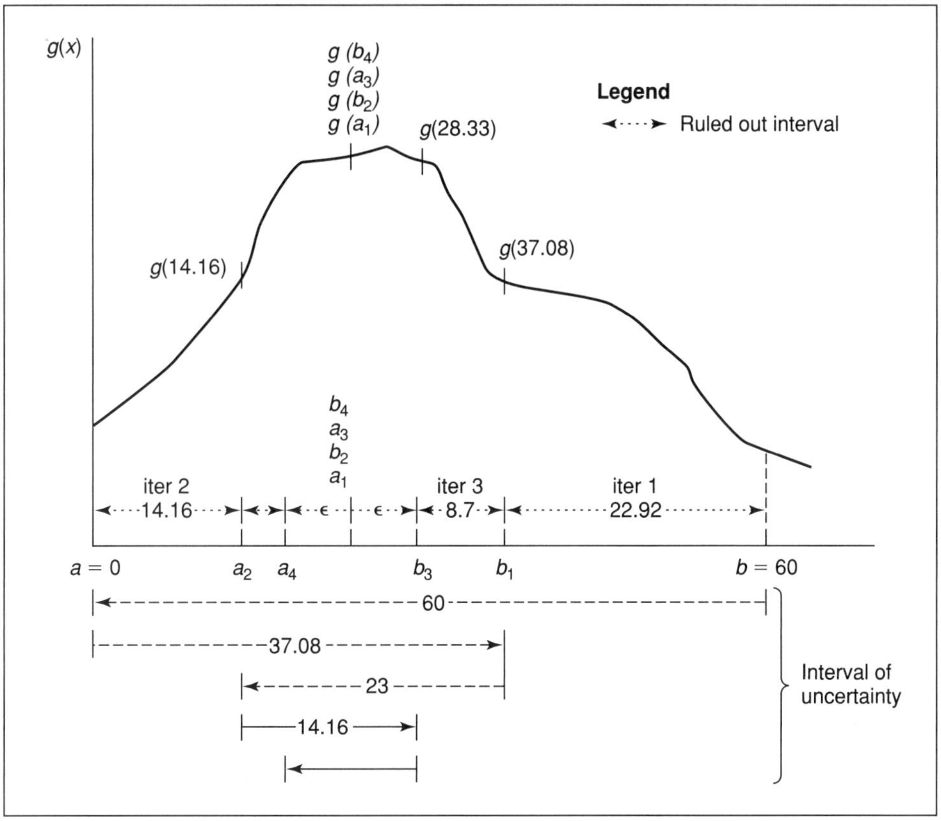

Iteration 1:

Evaluation at the search point b_1 and another search point a_1 yields the following result: $g(a_1)) > g(b_1)$, which means the optimal point has to be left of b_1, i.e., $x^* < b_1$. We discard the segment bb_1 from further consideration. The search point a_1 is defined as the proximal point to the left of b_1 generated from a golden section ratio distance from b, $a_1 = b - 0.618(b - a)$, where $0.618 = 1/1.618$. Notice the evaluation at the search point can be determined in a number of ways, including relatively subjective comparison between the two proximal search points, b_1 and a_1, regarding the preference between them, or a more formal market survey conducted for the two hypothetical locations. (See the airport location example in Section IV of Chapter 5.) But locating a_1 according to the Golden Section ratio would yield best results.

Our convention is to name the left point of the search interval a and the right point b. Here we switch our attention to the next poke point a_2 from our current position b_1: $b_1 \rightarrow a_2$, where the subscripts 1 and 2 denote the iteration number. Since our interval has been reduced from 60 to 37.08, we label b_1, the right end point of the search interval as b: $b = b_1 = 37.08$ and

$$a_2 = b - r(b - a) = 37.08 - 0.618(37.08 - 0) = 14.16.$$

Now we repeat this set of procedures iteratively.

Iteration 2:

$g(b_2) > g(a_2)$ means $x^* > a_2$, where b_2 is the proximal point to the right of a_2. The next poke point is $a_2 \to b_3$. The left end point is $a = a_2 = 14.16$, and $b_3 = a + r(b - a) = 14.16 + 0.618(37.08 - 14.16) = 28.33$.

Iteration 3:

$g(a_3) > g(b_3)$ means $x^* < b_3$, where a_Δ is the proximal point. The next poke point is $b_3 \to a_4$. The right end point is $b = b_3 = 28.33$, and $a_4 = b - r(b - a) = 28.33 - 0.6318(28.33 - 14.16) = \ldots$

Notice the interval of uncertainty regarding the location of the optimum retail location reduces steadily from 60: $60 \to 37.08 \to 23 \to 14.16 \to \ldots$

Stopping Rule:
When the interval of uncertainty gets down to a certain point, the algorithms stops. If we set the tolerance limit (or the error) to be ϵ, $b - a = 2\epsilon$ since the optimum is likely to be in the middle of the interval, everything else being equal. As an example: if ϵ is set at 0.04, stop when $b - a = 0.08$. When the interval of uncertainty gets down to this level, we terminate the algorithm. In this example, the retail shop location needs only be identified within 0.08 of a mile or 141 yards (127 m) along the highway.

E. Fibonacci Search Procedure

As mentioned previously, a more general procedure where the number of searches is limited is called Fibonacci search. Instead of positioning the search at a golden section ratio, we have a sequence of ratios for the first search point, the second search point, the third, and so on. Consider the following recursive relationship that generates an infinite series of numbers C_n which in turn determines such ratios:

$$C_n = C_{n-1} + C_{n-2} \quad n = 2, 3, \ldots$$

Define $C_0 = 1$ and $C_1 = 1$. The above equation generates a series of numbers that are known as Fibonacci numbers:

Sequence k	Identifier	Fibonacci No. F_k
0	C_0	1
1	C_1	1
2	C_2	2
3	C_3	3
4	C_4	5
5	C_5	8
6	C_6	13
7	C_7	21
.	.	.
.	.	.

It can be shown that the Fibonacci search is an optimal search technique in the minimax sense. In other words, in a sequence of m functional evaluations, it will yield the minimum maximum interval of uncertainty.

Let Δ_k be the interval of uncertainty after k functional evaluations, and x_n be the decision variable x for which we seek an optimal value after k functional evaluations ($k = 1, 2, \ldots, m$). Unlike the Golden Section method, ϵ represents the given minimum separation allowed between any two points over the interval, instead of half the interval of uncertainty. In other words, ϵ represents the resolution that can be obtained experimentally between x_k and x_{k-1}. The initial interval is $\Delta_0 = b - a$. The evaluations at a and b, $f(a)$ and $f(b)$, yield no knowledge of where the optimal solution lies, preventing us from eliminating any region from the search interval. This means that the interval of uncertainty remains the same at the second iteration, or $\Delta_1 = b - a$. (In some ways, this is reflected through the first two Fibonacci numbers of 1.)

One can prove that the length of the interval of uncertainty after the first two functional evaluations is given by the following relationship:

$$\Delta_2 = \frac{1}{C_m}[\Delta_0 \, C_{m-1} + \epsilon(-1)^m] \qquad (4.6)$$

The length of the final interval of uncertainty (which may not be less than ϵ) can also be shown to be given by the following equation:

$$\Delta_k = \frac{\Delta_0}{C_m} + \epsilon\frac{F_{k-2}}{C_m}$$

Notice the final interval of uncertainty is a function of the number of experimental evaluations (m), the allowable resolution (ϵ), and the initial search interval (Δ_0). The final interval will converge to zero as the number of functional evaluations increases to infinity, provided that ϵ is allowed to be infinitely small.

Finally, one can prove that the following evaluation is valid throughout the search procedure:

$$\Delta_k = \Delta_{k-2} - \Delta_{k-1} \qquad k = 3,4,\ldots, m \qquad (4.7)$$

Example
The Golden Section example was a good illustration, but it represents a rather symmetrical objective function $g(x)$ about the optimal location (x^*). Here we show another function which is a bit more skewed, just to demonstrate that the search technique can handle both situations, including the one illustrated in Figure 4.3(b). Let us get back to the example in which the accessibility measure is a function of mileage. We wish to maximize the calibrated accessibility function $f(x) = -3x^2 + 21.6x + 1.0$ between the interval [0, 25], with a minimum resolution of 0.50 and a search budget of six functional evaluations (Ravindran et al. 1987). In other words, the best accessibility is obtained somewhere between 0 and 2500 miles (4000 km) of additional highway built in the study area. Notice that such functions are not generally obtainable explicitly. It is given here for illustration purposes only.

From equation 4.6,

$$\Delta_2 = \frac{1}{13}[25(8) + 0.50] = 15.4231$$

The first two functional evaluations will be conducted over the range [0,25] symmetrical within this interval, where $b_1 = a + \Delta_2 = 0 + 15.4231 = 15.4231$ and $a_2 = b - \Delta_2 = 25 - 15.4231 = 9.5769$. This results in $f(b_1) = -379.477$ and $f(a_2) = -67.233$. Since the figure of merit is smaller at b_1 than at a_2, Figure 4.5 shows that the region to the right of $b_1 = 15.42$ can be eliminated. Note that $\Delta_0 = \Delta_1 = 25$. Hence $\Delta_3 = \Delta_2 - \Delta_2 = 25 - 15.4231 = 9.5769$ using Equation 4.7.

Symmetrical within the present interval of uncertainty, the two new points will be $b_3 = 9.5769$ and $a_4 = 5.8462$, and $f(b_3) = -67.233$, $f(a_4) = 24.744$. Notice that one of the new functional evaluations corresponds to one of the old functional evaluations. The current evaluation allows for the elimination of the region to the right of $b_3 = 9.5769$. The current interval of uncertainty is $\Delta_4 = \Delta_2 - \Delta_3 = 15.4231 - 9.5769 = 5.8462$. If we continue the process, convergence is obtained at the 6th iteration when the interval of uncertainty $\Delta_6 = 2.115$, and the resolution is $\epsilon = b_7 - a_6 = 4.2304 - 3.731 = 4994$, which is less than the specified minimum resolution of 0.5. In other words, the search now terminates since an answer within 50 miles (80 km) is tolerable. Thus the best accessibility was obtained when 373 to 423 miles (597 − 677 km) of new highway are built. ■

Figure 4.5   INTERVAL OF UNCERTAINTY IN FIBONACCI SEARCH

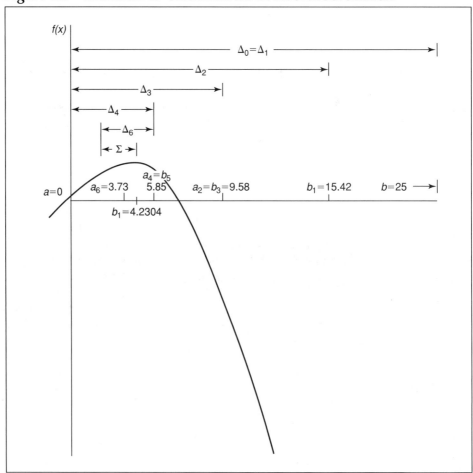

From Equation 4.6

$$\underset{\substack{m \to \infty \\ \epsilon \to \infty}}{Lim}(\Delta_2) = \Delta_0[F_{m-1}/F_m]$$

One can show that in the limit the ratio F_{m-1}/F_m goes to 0.618, which is the golden section ratio 1/1.618. It is important to reemphasize once more that we do not need to know the precise form of the objective function in Fibonacci search. It is equally worthwhile to point out again that the evaluation of the figure of merit is often-times very difficult, even though we have assumed away the problem by having an analytical expression for the figure of merit $f(x)$. This is where a search technique such as this comes in. In the two examples used, for instance, all that is necessary to evaluate the objective function is to compare it at two proximal points, and the only answer required is which is the better figure of merit, not by how much is it better. In the accessibility example, we simply perform traffic flow simulations at two proximal points to see which provides better area-wide accessibility. In the retail store location example, expert opinions can be used to compare the competitiveness of a store at one location vis-a-vis another, without explicitly quantifying the market share. Few optimization techniques would have this level of robustness and simplicity regarding the knowledge on the objective function.

III. ANALYTICAL SOLUTION TECHNIQUES

Analytical techniques, unlike the heuristic procedures, are subject to more rigorous mathematical treatment. They are usually solvable in closed form, rather than a process of trial and error (as was used in heuristic and direct search procedures). We have included here examples ranging from calculus to nonlinear programming.

A. Calculus

A familiar example of the analytical techniques is calculus. In this case, the objective function is expressible in a differentiable function, and the problem is subject to solutions by a well-defined set of theorems and procedures. It is required that there should be a peak or valley within the defined range of the variables. The reader might have already figured out that the accessibility maximization example above can easily be determined by setting the first derivative to zero: $\dot{f} \in (x) = 6x + 21.6 = 0$, or $x^* = 3.6$, which checks out with the previous solution using the Fibonacci search.

Instead of such an explicit functional form, an implicit function can be defined after the constraints are merged into the objective function, as is typically done in the **Lagrangian procedure.** Again the best way to illustrate this is through an example (Au and Stelson 1969). Suppose one is given a rope of *2s* feet (meters) and is to tie each end to a tree and to rope off an area as large as possible by locating a pole somewhere in the clearing, as illustrated in Figure 4.6. Where should the pole be placed? According to geometry, the area of a triangle A is defined in terms of its three sides—a, b, c—and the perimeter $2s$ according to the following expression, which we maximize: max $f(b,c) = A^2 = s(s-a)(s-b)(s-c)$. The only limitation is the length of the rope:

Figure 4.6   ROPING OFF AN AREA

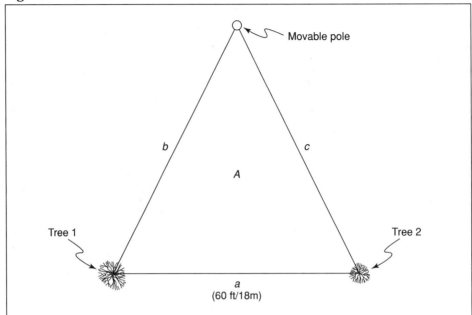

$$g(b,c) = a + b + c - 2s = 0 \qquad\qquad (4.8)$$

The Lagrange procedure calls for the formation of a **Lagrangian function,** which is the linear combination of the objective and constraint, to be maximized:

$$\max L(b,c,\lambda) = f(b,c) - \lambda g(b,c) = s(s-a)(s-b)(s-c) - \lambda(a+b+c-2s)$$

where λ is called the **Lagrange multiplier** or the **dual variable.**

Taking the first derivative of the Lagrangian function with respect to the three variables b, c and λ, we have

$$\dot{L}(b) = 0 \text{ yields } -s(s-a)(s-c) - \lambda = 0$$
$$\dot{L}(c) = 0 \text{ yields } -s(s-a)(s-b) - \lambda = 0$$
$$\dot{L}(\lambda) = 0 \text{ yields } a+b+c-2s = 0.$$

Solving these three equations for three unknowns b, c, λ: $b = s-a/2$, $c = s-a/2$, and $\lambda = -as(s-a)/2$. Thus if the rope is 200 feet (60 m) in length, and the two trees are 60 ft (18 m) apart, an equilateral triangle should be formed as shown in Figure 4.6, where the two sides b and c each measures $(100)-(60/2)=70$ ft (21 m). The area so enclosed is 1897 sq ft (171 m²). As indicated by the Lagrange multiplier or (dual variable), $\lambda = \Delta z/\Delta c = \Delta z/\Delta b$ a movement of the pole to the left or the right of the existing position by one foot (0.3 m) of rope length will decrease the enclosed area by $[(60)(100)(100-60)/2]^{1/2} = 346$ sq ft (10.4 m²).

In the section below and also in Appendix 1, we will discuss another analytical solution technique, linear programming. It will be shown that λ has the same interpretation as the dual variable in LP, meaning the effect of changing the resources on the right-hand sides (RHS) of the constraint equations (in this case 0) by $+\Delta$ or $-\Delta$ (where Δ is nonnegative in value). If $-\Delta$, the rope is lengthened according to Equation 4.8, and the area of the triangle will increase. On the other hand, if $+\Delta$, the rope is shortened, and the area will decrease instead. The interesting point is that $\lambda = \Delta^{-z}/\Delta^{s}$ is always nonnegative. The amount of increase or decrease is $\lambda \Delta$. Similar interpretation can be made for the distance between the trees a. In this case λ would be unrestricted in sign.

B. Linear Programming

There are other types of analytical techniques, including linear and nonlinear programming. First, let us discuss **linear programming** (LP), an optimization method involving a set of linear simultaneous equations. A classic LP model in the early development of urban modeling is the **Herbert-Stevens residential model** (Herbert and Stevens 1960). The model structures a market clearing mechanism to allocate residential bundles among the wealthy and the poor (for example, $i = 1,2$) over the zones k in an urban area (for example, $k = 1,2$). We will use this model to illustrate the LP optimization technique. The first index in identifying variables and input parameters in the model is a household group i, distinguishing residents with different budgets and tastes ($i = 1,2$ for the rich and poor as mentioned). Instead of recognizing specific families, certain groups (containing more than one family) with the same budget and tastes are considered. Next to be considered are certain types of amenities h associated with the housing, which may refer to the amount of green space or public services such as schools and hospitals ($h = 1,2$). For a family type i, they are interested in the residential bundle with amenity level h in a specific zone k of the city, with an associated cost c_{ih}^{k}. Included in the aggregate cost c_{ih}^{k} are transportation expenditures considering the number of trips and the associated length of each trip, but excluding the site rent paid to the landlord.

Now let us discuss the land rent paid by group i for residence h. There are two types of rents, total site rent and unit site rent. Total site rent is the amount paid for the total housing while the unit site rent is just the amount of rent per unit acre (0.4 ha), where s_{ih}' stands for the acreage for housing type h considered by household type i. The former will be used in the primal version of the model while the latter will be used in the dual (the terms primal and dual will be explained below). Both of these costs are exclusive of the house and the travel cost; they refer to the land alone. Finally, the distinction between residential bundle and the market basket needs to be made. A residential bundle is simply an aggregate of the quality of the house, how nice the surroundings are, and the transportation cost. The market basket, on the other hand, is the residential bundle plus other commodities that can be fit into the residential budget, including land rent.

The LP model decides who is going to obtain a particular piece of land. In the allocation process, it recognizes that people try to economize and obtain the best for their residential budget b_{ih}, in other words, maximizing their savings ($b_{ih} - c_{ih}^{k}$). The savings can be applied toward paying site rent to the landlord, or it could be a net savings if land is free in an economic context (as in zones where a surplus of land is available). Thus we have made savings synonymous with rent paying ability—a household can afford to pay the landlord site rent only if it has savings. The objective function of the LP seeks to maximize aggregate rent paying ability over the entire study area. The final allocation is based on a tradeoff between how much one can afford and what one is looking for. These concepts can be formalized in the set of equations below.

Decision variables: $(\leftarrow x_{ih}^{k} \rightarrow)^{T}$ = transpose vector containing the number of households of group i using residential bundle h located in zone $k = (x_{11}^{1} x_{12}^{1} x_{21}^{1} x_{22}^{1})$ and $(x_{11}^{2} x_{12}^{2} x_{21}^{2} x_{22}^{2})$; it goes without saying that these variables in the two vectors should ideally be integers.

Input Coefficients: $(\leftarrow b_{ih} \rightarrow)^{T}$ = transpose vector of the residential budget (in 10,000 dollars) allocated by group i to bundle $h = (b_{11} b_{12} b_{21} b_{22}) = $ (5 4 3 2); $(\leftarrow c_{ih}^{k} \rightarrow)^{T}$ = transpose vector of annual cost (in 10,000 dollars) to group i who chooses bundle h in area k, exclusive of site cost (land rent) = $(c_{11}^{1} c_{12}^{1} c_{21}^{1} c_{22}^{1})$ and $(c_{11}^{2} c_{12}^{2} c_{21}^{2} c_{22}^{2}) = $ (4 3 2 1) and (3 2 1 0.5) respectively; $(\leftarrow s'_{ih} \rightarrow)^{T}$ = transpose vector of the number of acres (ha) in the site used by a household of group i if it uses residential bundle $h = (s'_{11} s'_{12} s'_{21} s'_{22}) = $ (0.9 0.8 0.6 0.5).

Right-Hand Sides: $(\leftarrow L^{k} \rightarrow)^{T}$ = transpose vector of acres (ha) of land available for residential use in zone $k = (L_1 \ L_2) = $ (20 15); $(\leftarrow N_i \rightarrow) = $ transpose vector of the number of households of group i that are to be located in the study area = $(N_1 \ N_2) = $ (15 10).

Now we can write out the set of constraint equations. For land availability, we have:

$$0.9x_{11}^{1} + 0.8x_{12}^{1} + 0.6x_{21}^{1} + 0.5x_{22}^{1} \leq 20 \qquad \text{in zone 1}$$

$$0.9x_{11}^{2} + 0.8x_{12}^{2} + 0.6x_{21}^{2} + 0.5x_{22}^{2} \leq 15 \qquad \text{in zone 2;}$$

Demand for housing can be written as:

$$x_{11}^{1} + x_{12}^{1} + x_{11}^{2} + x_{12}^{2} = 15 \qquad \text{for household group 1}$$

$$x_{21}^{1} + x_{22}^{1} + x_{21}^{2} + x_{22}^{2} = 10 \qquad \text{for household group 2.}$$

Finally we write the objective function:

$$\text{Max } (\textit{savings in rent}) = \ (5-4)x_{11}^{1} + (4-3)x_{12}^{1} + (3-2)x_{21}^{1} + (2-1)x_{22}^{1} +$$
$$(5-3)x_{11}^{2} + (4-2)x_{12}^{2} + (3-1)x_{21}^{2} + (2-0.5)x_{22}^{2}$$

While this "toy example" is constructed for illustration purposes, its generalization to m residential bundles, n household groups and U' zones can be readily inferred. For the specific example above, the solution assigns 3.75 and 11.25 households in group 1 to residential bundle 1 in zone 1 and bundle 2 in zone 2 respectively, and 10 in group 2 to bundle 1 in zone 2. In other words, $x_{11}^{1} = 3.75$, $x_{12}^{2} = 11.25$, and $x_{21}^{2} = 10$ and all other decision variables are zero.[1] Thus housing type 1 is popular among residents in this area, and so is zone 2 as a place to live (Vernon et al. 1992). The latter appears reasonable since the cost coefficients for zone 2 are smaller than those in zone 1, resulting in the greatest increase in savings, defined, once again, as $(b_{ih} - c_{ih}^k)$. Thus the model allocates as many house-holds as possible in zone 2 and meets the remaining demand through the use of zone 1. An area-wide rent savings of $462,500 is achieved.

The above is called the **primal formulation** of the LP. The **dual formula-tion** is the mirror image of the primal and can be written after defining two dual variables written for the land-availability constraint and the demand-for-housing constraint respectively:

$$r^k = \text{rent per unit-of-land in zone } k \ (k = 1,2)$$

$$v'_i = \text{subsidy per household in group } i \ (i = 1,2)$$

Now the dual LP looks like:

$$0.9r^1 - v'_1 \geq (5 - 4)$$
$$0.8r^1 - v'_1 \geq (4 - 3)$$
$$0.6r^1 - v'_2 \geq (3 - 2)$$
$$0.5r^1 - v'_2 \geq (2 - 1)$$
$$0.9r^2 - v'_1 \geq (5 - 3)$$
$$0.8r^2 - v'_1 \geq (4 - 2)$$
$$0.6r^2 - v'_2 \geq (3 - 1)$$
$$0.5r^2 - v'_2 \geq (2 - 0.5)$$

$$\text{Min } 20r^1 + 15r^2 - 15v'_1 - 10v'_2$$

While the rs are positive, the sign for the vs can be both positive or negative, since these dual variables are associated with the equality constraints defined for the demand for housing (as contrasted with the inequality constraints for land avail-ability)—a point which will be elaborated shortly below.

The dual LP determines the rent in each zone k and the subsidy paid to each household group i. Let us explain more in detail. Landlords at each zone k can receive at least as much site rent per residential bundle h as the highest bidder of household group i is willing to pay. Please note the actual cost to a household is the rent a household i pays after accounting for the subsidy received by the household or a taxation on the household group (when v'_i is negative). The dual program min-imizes total land rent paid to landlords in all the zones k, minus the subsidy to all household groups i—i.e., the net rent paid. Notice this may mean a certain amount of subsidy has to be paid to household group i in order to guarantee a location at a particular bid-rent. The availability of subsidy to household group i enables that household to locate a residential bundle h in neighborhood k—a location which would be impossible without the subsidy. A poorer household can in fact be the highest bidder per unit of land as long as the household bids on small lots. Likewise, subsidy may be assigned to a wealthy household to ensure a residential bundle location also. The use of subsidy variable v' sometimes presents a problem as one goes back and forth between the dual and the primal formulations. Take the primal formulation first: There may be situations where all of one household group i cannot be located in zone k due to the capacity constraint on the land L^k—under the primal objective function of maximizing total savings in location rents. The remaining households of group i have to be located elsewhere (in zone k' for instance). Relocating these group i households in k' zone, however, would involve a subsidy (viewing from the dual formulation). Because of the LP formulation, this subsidy v_i' must be assigned to *all* households in group i. This may lead to excessive high rents in the favorite zones, when the actual cost to a household is the net of actual rent minus the subsidy.

      Solution to the dual LP yields $r^1 = 0$, $r^2 = 1.25$, $v_1' = -1.00$ and $v_2' = -1.25$. This says that surplus land is available in zone 1, resulting in rent per unit-of-land being zero in this zone.[2] The taxation for household group 1 is $10,000 while that for household group 2 is $12,500, being the wealthier of the two groups. It can be seen that the wealthy residents, similar to their less affluent counterparts, both want their desired housing type and location and are willing to pay for it. But the consumers' surplus, or the difference between the maximum amount that the consumer would pay and the amount the consumer actually pays, is distinctly different among the two. As expected in an LP, the dual solution of net rent paid over the study area is identical to the primal solution of total savings in land rent. Both are valued at $462,500.

C. Primal and Dual Linear Programs

The LP discussion highlights the most interesting relationship between the primal formulation of an optimization problem and its dual. For the same housing example, one can review the key features of this relationship by constructing the LP tableau contained in Table 4.3. In the tableau, it is clear that the dual formulation is simply the transposed primal tableau. The cost coefficients in the primal objective function become the right-hand side of the dual LP, and the right-hand side of the primal becomes the cost coefficients of the dual objective function. While we used to maximize in the primal, now we minimize in the dual. Each constraint of the primal has a dual variable assigned to it. Dual variables assigned to an inequality are positive in sign, while those assigned to equality constraints are unrestricted in sign as mentioned.

      Certain duality theorems govern the solutions of the primal and dual LPs:

    (a) If both the primal and dual problems have feasible solutions, the primal problem has an optimal solution with a figure of merit equal to the dual problem.

Table 4.3   PRIMAL AND DUAL TABLEAU EXAMPLE

Primal →	x_{11}^1	x_{12}^1	x_{21}^1	x_{22}^1	x_{11}^2	x_{12}^2	x_{21}^2	x_{22}^2	Min ↓
r^1	0.9	0.8	0.6	0.5					≤ 20
r^2					0.9	0.8	0.6	0.5	≤ 15
v_1'	-1	-1			-1	-1			$= -15$
v_2'			-1	-1			-1	-1	$= -10$
Max →	$\geq$	$\geq$	$\geq$	$\geq$	$\geq$	$\geq$	$\geq$	$\geq$	↑ Dual
	$(5-4)$	$(4-3)$	$(3-2)$	$(2-1)$	$(5-3)$	$(4-2)$	$(3-1)$	$(2-.5)$	

(b) Whenever a constraint in either one of the problems holds as a strict inequality so that there is slack (or surplus) in the constraint, the corresponding variable in the other problem equals zero. Otherwise a strict equality is obtained, together with the corresponding unrestricted variables in the other problem. This is usually referred to as primal and dual **complementary slackness.**

Based on statement (b) above, the dual variable, nonnegative in value, can be interpreted as the opportunity cost associated with the limited resource. In other words, r' corresponds to the additional contribution to the savings or rent figure of merit should land in zone 1 be increased by one unit. Thus both r^1 and r^2 can be interpreted as the additional net rent from an additional unit-of-land in zone 1. Parallel interpretation can be made regarding the dual variables associated with equality constraints, such as v_i'. In this case, the dual variable can be either positive, negative, or zero. In the Herbert-Stevens model above, for example, v_i' is negative and is interpreted as the taxation paid by household group i. Should v_i' be positive, it corresponds to subsidy, as mentioned previously. Both taxation and subsidy point toward the inherent valuation of group i toward their housing demand. Notice the dual variables are similar to the Lagrange multiplier in the discussion of calculus as an optimization technique. In fact, the Lagrange multipliers are the names given to dual variables in nonlinear differentiable functions through historical practice. The dual variable v_i' has a similar interpretation as the Lagrange multiplier λ in the example on roping off an area, as discussed under Section III-A. Both reflect the increase or decrease in objective function value should the strict equality constraint be relaxed.

D. Solution of Linear Programs

There are a number of ways to solve LP on the computer, ranging from traditional **simplex procedures** to newer techniques such as the **interior-point (projective)** method, from general procedures for regular tableaux to specialized techniques that exploit special structures of the tableau (See Appendix 1 or Bazaraa, Jarvis, and Seral 1990). While the simplex algorithm is illustrated in Appendix 1, it is not the intent of this chapter to summarize all possible solution algorithms, nor are we in fact capable of doing so in such a limited space. Rather, we would like to highlight the salient points that will hopefully guide the location/land use analyst toward formulating a problem in an LP, selecting the appropriate computer package for the problem at hand, understanding the implications of the computer outputs, and perhaps most important of all, discerning abnormalities in the modeling process, if any, in a timely fashion. Let us use the same example we used in Chapter 1—the airport-location problem. Instead of the New York City area, let us move to the Midwest of the United States. Suppose an airport is to be built between Dayton, Ohio (population one million) and Cincinnati (population two million)—with a time separation of 60 minutes (min) on Interstate Highway 75. We wish to locate the airport solely in such a way that the travel (measured in person-minutes) for all residents of the two cities is to be minimized. Where should we build the airport?

Let the airport be located x_1 min away from Cincinnati (C) and x_2 min from Dayton *(D)*. The following LP can be constructed to model this problem: Min $\{2x_1 + x_2 \mid x_1 + x_2 \geq 60\}$, where the $\geq$ sign is used in the constraint to include the construction of an airport away from the Interstate Highway 75 that directly connects the two cities. The solution to this LP, in spite of its somewhat counter intuitive nature, is at either one of the extreme points C or D, in accordance with basic theorems in LP. This is shown below and in Figure 4.7, where the feasible region and objective function are plotted out in full. In this case, the airport is to be located at Cincinnati, $x^* = (0, 60)^T$, resulting in a minimum of 60 million total person-minutes of travel, $z^* = 60$.

$$|\longleftarrow\!\!x_1\!\!\longrightarrow|\longleftarrow\!\!x_2\!\!\longrightarrow|$$
$$C\text{\textemdash}\!\!\text{\textemdash}\!\!\text{\textemdash}\!\!\text{\textemdash}\!\!\text{\textemdash}D$$
$$\text{60 min}$$

       Should the Dayton population grow to two million and the Cincinnati population remain at existing level, the LP now looks like: Min $\{2x_1 + 2x_2 \mid x_1 + x_2 \geq 60\}$. The multiple solution is shown in Figure 4.7. In this case, the airport can be anywhere between Dayton and Cincinnati on Interstate 75. Except for degeneracy, an LP solution algorithm amounts to an efficient way of implicitly (instead of exhaustively) evaluating the objective function at all possible extreme points and picking the very best. As mentioned, the simplex algorithm is described in Appendix 1.

       Such an analysis can be carried over to the case of three cities (Cincinnati, Columbus, and Dayton) and four cities (Cincinnati, Columbus, Dayton, and Indianapolis). With Columbus' population at three million, Indianapolis at 3.5 million and the door-to-door times (after transportation improvement) as shown in Figure 4.8, these LPs were solved with the decision variables x_1, x_2, x_3, and x_4, corresponding to the time from Cincinnati, Columbus, Dayton, and Indianapolis

Figure 4.7   GRAPHICAL SOLUTION OF AN AIRPORT LOCATION PROBLEM

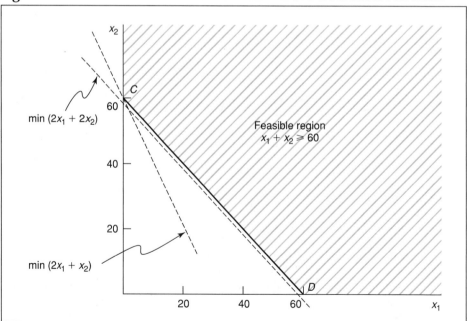

respectively (Bartholomew, Brown, and Chan 1990; Cameron, O'Brien, and Chan 1990; McEachin, Taylor, and Chan 1992; Harry et al. 1992).

For the three-city case:

$$\text{Min } (2x_1 + 3x_2 + x_3)$$
$$\text{s.t. } x_1 + x_2 \geq 70$$
$$x_1 + x_3 \geq 60$$
$$x_2 + x_3 \geq 90$$
$$x_1 + x_2 + x_3 \geq 125$$

(4.9)

where the last constraint shows minimum total time from each of the vertices of a triangle to a common point, as determined by the intersection of three angle bisectors (Claunch, Goehring, and Chan 1992). For the four-city case:

$$\text{Min } (2x_1 + 3x_2 + x_3 + 3.5x_4)$$
$$\text{s.t. } \quad x_1 + x_2 \geq 70$$
$$x_1 + x_3 \geq 60$$
$$x_2 + x_3 \geq 90$$
$$x_3 + x_4 \geq 120$$
$$x_1 + x_4 \geq 150$$
$$x_2 + x_4 \geq 206.62$$
$$x_1 + x_2 + x_3 + x_4 \geq 266.62$$

(4.10)

where the last constraint represents the minimum total travel time from the four vertices to a common point, as determined by the bisectors from Cincinnati–Dayton, Columbus, and Indianapolis.

Figure 4.8   THREE- AND FOUR-CITY EXTENSION OF THE AIRPORT
LOCATION PROBLEM

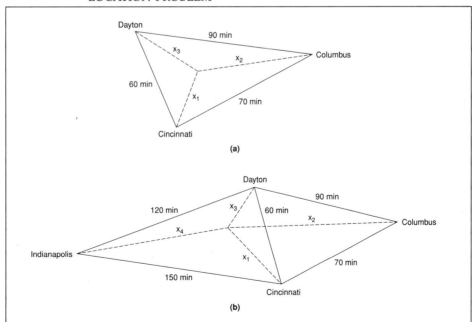

It was found that multiple solutions are again obtained in the three-city case, inasmuch as the combined Dayton and Cincinnati population exactly amounts to the Columbus population. Should one additional baby be born in Columbus, making Columbus the most populous city by just a shade, the airport would now be located in Columbus! In the case of four cities with the populations shown, the airport location changes to Cincinnati. Again the multiple solution is obtained when the population at all three or four of the cities are the same, where the multiple solutions occur at the inside of the convex hull formed by the cities as marked by the wedges.

Population (in millions) at

Cincin	Columb	Dayton	Indianap	Airport location	Obj function value
2	3	1		$x_1 = 35$, $x_2 = 35$, $x_3 = 55$ or wedge *LD* in Figure 4.9 or $x_1 = 20$, $x_2 = 0$, $x_3 = 90$	*230* person-min
2	3	1	3.5	$x_1 = 6.69$, $x_2 = 63.31$, $x_3 = 53.31$, $x_4 = 143.31$ or wedge *LD* in Figure 4.10	*758.21* person-min

In Figures 4.9 and 4.10, the figure legends suggest that each solution is qualified by a solution method and a model, each of which is denoted by a capital letter. Among the solution methods are LP, nonlinear program (NLP), direct search, and NLP version of the direct search. Among the models are the baseline solution with the given metropolitan population and both the multiple solutions when the combinations of populations are equal and when noise considerations are taken into account. Solutions to these LPs are very sensitive to the precise for-

Figure 4.9   SOLUTIONS TO THE THREE-CITY CONFIGURATION

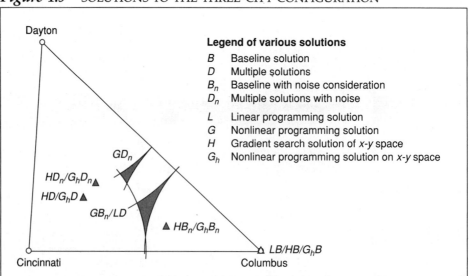

Legend of various solutions

B Baseline solution
D Multiple solutions
B_n Baseline with noise consideration
D_n Multiple solutions with noise

L Linear programming solution
G Nonlinear programming solution
H Gradient search solution of *x-y* space
G_h Nonlinear programming solution on *x-y* space

Figure 4.10   SOLUTIONS TO THE FOUR-CITY CONFIGURATION

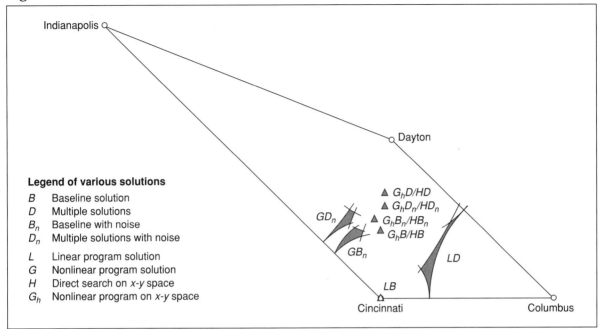

mulation and numerical errors, illustrating two key concerns in LP solution algorithms. Overall, these results are consistent with findings by Hurter and Martinich (1989), who reported studies in this Fermat or Steiner-Weber problem in the general context of industrial plant location.

Sensitivity analysis was performed by Leonard, McDaniel, and Nelson (1991), who changed the travel times between the cites slightly in the three-city problem. The travel times between Cincinnati–Columbus and Columbus–Dayton were reversed. The general result regarding extreme point and interior point solutions does not change. It appears that the driving force seems to be the populations rather than the travel times. Sensitivity analysis of the population coefficients of the three-city problem reinforces the observation that a city with a population larger than that of the remaining cities will host the airport. As mentioned, any increase in the Columbus population, which equals the combined populations of Cincinnati and Dayton, will make Columbus the optimal airport location. As another example, as soon as the Cincinnati population slightly dominates over Columbus and Dayton combined, the airport is located at 5 miles (8 km) outside the city. Sensitivity analysis on the four-city problem yields similar results. Finally, sensitivity experiments with the set of constraints yield interesting results. By deleting the last constraint of the three-city problem, a different and larger wedge of alternate solutions results. On the other hand, when the last constraint was removed in the four-city problem, the solution space did not change. Further examination shows that the last constraint is redundant and, hence, is not needed.

Before we conclude our discussion on linear programming, let us comment further on the computational aspects. Suffice to say that LP software has been perfected over the years. Numerical round-off errors involved in solving the linear set of equations has been an active area of investigation, resulting in steady improvements. Receiving equal attention is the storage requirement for intermediate data in large-scale problems, particularly regarding the basic feasible solutions corresponding to the various extreme points. Most recent advances have concentrated on input-output convenience (sometimes referred to as user friendliness). It is clear that the future generation of LP software (as well as nonlinear program software) will be those with symbolic-processing capabilities, including inputs expressed in algebraic forms such as equations and vector/matrix mathematical symbols (Brooke, Kendrick, and Meeraus 1995). In Chapter 6, we include an elementary example of such an input stream expressed in a set of equations. Equally viable is a parallel effort to link algorithmic procedures to data storage, as evidenced in spread sheet based procedures (Winston 1994).

E. Nonlinear Programming

When the objective function and/or the constraints are no longer linear functions, we have a **nonlinear program.** An example of a nonlinear objective function is the example used in Fibonacci search, where accessibility is given as a quadratic function of the highway mileage. Another example is the calculus optimization problem where the area enclosed by a rope is a nonlinear function of the rope length. These two examples can be considered special cases of nonlinear programming. Here we will examine the more general case and discuss a robust way of solving the general class of nonlinear programming problems. Again, we will use an example to introduce these concepts. Continuing the three-city airport study mentioned in the sensitivity analysis above, we introduce noise abatement as an additional concern (Leonard, McDaniel, and Nelson 1991). Here a simple representation of noise pollution is taken: *pollution = (constant)(population)(distance)*$^{-2}$. Following this assumption, the noise pollution at each city i is Kx_i^{-2}, where K is the calibration constant, same for all three cities. This term is added to the LP objectives of Equations 4.9 and 4.10, resulting in Equation 4.11. Different values of K were experimented with and at $K = 2{,}150$, the nonlinear objective function is equal to the linear at the halfway point between Dayton and Cincinnati in the two-city case. The constant K controls the effect of noise on the objective function. For very large K, the noise persists for a very long distance away from the airport. Conversely, as K approaches zero, the noise effect on the objective function becomes nonexistent. For values of K larger than 2150, two optimum locations were found, each located between the cities, symmetrically left and right of the center line (Interstate Highway 75). As K is reduced below 2,150, McEachin et al. (1992) found multiple optimal solutions. As a result of these experiments, the constant 2150 is used throughout the three- and four-city cases.

The three-city case now has the objective function

$$\text{Pollution} = 2(x_1 + Kx_1^{-2}) + 3(x_2 + Kx_2^{-2}) + (x_3 + Kx_3^{-2}) \qquad (4.11)$$

Notice the objective function is a nonlinear function of the travel time decision variables. The airport location is now in the interior of the triangle defined by the three cities, at a point away from the three populations. When the populations at the three cities are equal, the airport location is at a point equally far away from each of the three cities. This interior point result is again consistent with Hurter and Martinich's general finding. Extensive computational results were obtained by McEachin et al. (1992) for the three- and four-city cases, as summarized in Figure 4.9 and Figure 4.10. Aside from an LP and NLP, a gradient search, or hill climbing algorithm was directly used to verify the results. A gradient search procedure is a general numerical way of solving nonlinear programs based on "climbing up the hill" in the steepest ascent direction in each step. The search was conducted directly on the triangle as defined in the x-y Euclidean space. The region within which the search is conducted is delineated by the three cities, or the four cities. An example of the gradient search solution for the three-city case is shown in Figure 4.11, complete with the combined noise and travel cost contours. Here one can see the optimum occurs at the "bottom of the valley" as defined by the contour 392 in this minimization example. Notice once again that the x-y space defines the feasible region for the search to be conducted, rather than the x_1, x_2 and x_3 decision-variable space used in both the LP and NLP models.

Similar to the linear case, the "legs" x_1, x_2, and x_3, as defined by the constraints shown in Equation 4.9 are not long enough to meet at a point in the three-city baseline configuration. The solution is somewhere within the triangular wedge as indicated by the symbol GB_n in Figure 4.9. The multiple solution where combinations of cities have the same population, is also shown as a similar wedge, labeled as GD_n. These solutions are obtained via two different solution methods. The first is an off-the-shelf, NLP solver GINO (Lasdon and Warren 1986).

Figure 4.11   GRADIENT SEARCH SOLUTION TO THREE-CITY
CONFIGURATION WITH NOISE

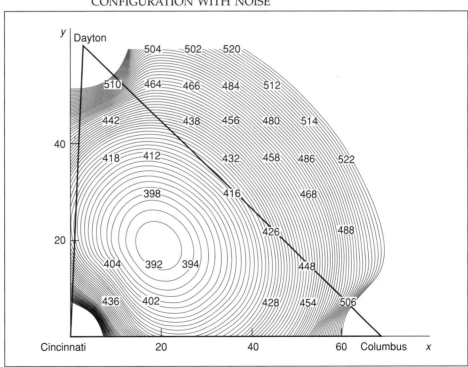

The second is the direct method of gradient search (Russell, Wang, and Berkhin 1992). The optimal NLP and direct search solutions of the baseline case diverge slightly. Their objective function values are close, at 239.47 and 248.12 respectively. The direct search solution is about six minutes away from the wedge defined by the NLP solution. Similar discrepancies are found between the multiple solutions. In our judgment, this reflects the numerical round-off errors by different algorithms, caused mainly by the difference between the feasible region defined by the x-y Euclidean space and the x_1, x_2, and x_3 space. To verify this point the analytical models were solved again using the NLP technique on the x-y space, rather than the x_1, x_2, and x_3 space. Both the direct search and NLP yield identical solutions. For completeness, we also include here the solutions for a four-city case in Figure 4.10, which exhibit many of the same phenomena.

F. Solution of a Nonlinear Program

We will illustrate two general types of solution algorithms. The first is a nonconvex programming solver based on the method of steepest ascent. This is intended for unconstrained optimization problems. Then we introduce the more general method to solve constrained problems.

1. Method of Steepest Ascent. As illustrated in Figure 4.12, the ideas behind the **method of steepest ascent** is quite simple. Starting with any initial point x^0, one hikes up the mountain in the direction of steepest ascent. One keeps moving forward to the top of the ridge, at which time one reassesses the steepest ascent direction, which involves a 90-degree turn as shown at x^1. Having re-established the steepest ascent direction, one again moves up to the top of the ridge at x^2, takes another 90-degree turn and proceeds to move forward. If this procedure is repeated, one would eventually arrive at the top of the hill at x^*. Notice we are on top of the hill instead of the mountain mainly because of the starting point x^0. Should we start at $x^{0'}$ instead of x^0, one would have hiked up the top of the mountain at x^{**}. We call x^* a local optimum and x^{**} a global optimum. Notice what we have performed is an unconstrained optimization. If one places a constraint such as $x_1 = x_2$ on this problem, the optimization result would have been different, the global maximum would have to be at x^* instead of x^{**} along the line $x_1 = x_2$.

The general algorithm proceeds as follows:

1. Select a starting point $x^k = x^0 = (x_1^0, x_2^0, ..., x_n^0)$ and set $k = 0$.
2. Find a direction to move $d^k = \nabla f(x^k)$ which will improve (increase/decrease) the function at iteration k, where $d^k = (d_1^k, d_2^k, ..., d_n^k)^T$
3. Move a distance t^k in the direction d^k to a new point $x^{k+1} = x^k + t^k d^k$ where t^k is the nonnegative step size at iteration k, to be determined by (a) a line search (Golden Section for example), or (b) analytic technique (parametric in t^k).
4. Check for local optimality, for instance

$$\left. \frac{\partial f}{\partial x_j} \right|_{x = x^k} < \epsilon \quad j = 1, 2, \ldots, n \tag{4.12}$$

If stopping criteria are not met, $k \to k + 1$, go to step 2, otherwise, stop.

Figure 4.12 EXAMPLE SEARCH

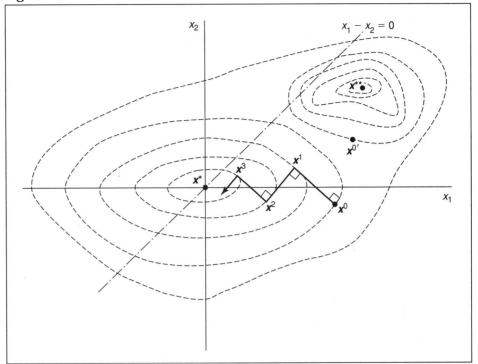

Note: Gradient is perpendicular to objective function contour at $\mathbf{x}^k$ and tangent at $\mathbf{x}^{k11}$ ($k = 0, 1, 2$).

Example

Suppose we wish to maximize the function $f(x) = 2x_1x_2 + 2x_2 - x_1^2 - 2x_2^2$. The two components of the gradient are: $d_1 = \dot{f}(x_1) = 2x_2 - 2x_1$ and $d_2 = \dot{f}(x_2) = 2x_1 + 2 - 4x_2$, or $\mathbf{d}^0 = (d_1^0, d_2^0) = \nabla f(x^0) = \nabla f(0, 0) = [\dot{f}(x_1 = 0, x_2 = 0), \dot{f}_{x2}(x_1) = 0, x_2 = 0)] = (0, 2)$. For $k = 1$, set $x_1^1 = 0 + t(0) = 0$, $x_2^1 = 0 + t(2) = 2t$. Then $f(\mathbf{x}^1) = t[x^0 + t\nabla f(x^0)] = f(0, 2t) = 2(0)(2t) + 2(2t) - (0)^2 - 2(2t)^2 = 4t - 8t^2$. Maximization of $f(x_1)$ over t yields $t^* = 1/4$, and correspondingly $\mathbf{x}_1 = (0,0) + 1/4(0, 2) = (0, 1/2)$. Since $d_i = 2(1/2) - 2(0) = 1$, it is clear that more iterations are necessary. Thus the iteration continues when we repeat what was applied toward $\mathbf{x}^0$ previously. ∎

2. Karash-Kuhn-Tucker Conditions. Solution of a constrained nonlinear program is governed by the **Karash-Kuhn-Tucker (KKT) conditions,** which can be thought of as a generalization of the Lagrangian method discussed earlier. Consider the following optimization problem expressed in decision variable vector of n dimension in cartesian space:

$$\text{Max/Min } f(\mathbf{x})$$
$$g_i(x) = b_1' \qquad i \in I' = \{1, 2, \ldots, m\}$$

The Lagrangian method, as applied to equality constraints, can be represented in matrix algebra as

$$\nabla f(\mathbf{x}^*) -/+ \sum_{i \in I'} \lambda_i \nabla g_i(\mathbf{x}^*) = 0 \tag{4.13}$$

with the negative sign corresponding to the maximization problem and the positive sign minimization problem. This is sometimes referred to as the dual feasibility condition. Here $(\mathbf{x^*}, \boldsymbol{\lambda})$ is an optimal solution with unrestricted signs, in other words, both $\mathbf{x}$ and $\boldsymbol{\lambda}$ can assume either a positive or negative value. A complementary slackness relationship can also be written, similar to the relationship between a primal and dual LP:

$$\lambda_i [b_1' - g_i(\mathbf{x^*})] = 0 \qquad \textit{for all } i \in I \tag{4.14}$$

These form the essence of the KKT conditions. Variants of these two equations can be written for nonnegative requirements on the variable $\mathbf{x}$ and $\boldsymbol{\lambda}$.

Consider the mathematical program P'

$$\text{Max/Min } f(x)$$
$$g_i(x) \le b_i' \qquad i \in I' = \{1, 2, \ldots, m\}$$

If $f(x)$, $g_i(x)$s are differentiable functions satisfying certain local regularity conditions such as non-singularity and convexity, then $\mathbf{x^*}$ can be an optimal solution to problem P' only if there exist nonnegative λ_i $(i \in I')$ such that the same conditions as the case with equality constraints apply. If $\mathbf{x^*}$ is to be nonnegative also,

$$\nabla f(\mathbf{x^*}) - / + \sum_{i \in I'} \lambda_i \nabla g_i(\mathbf{x^*}) \le / \ge 0 \tag{4.15}$$

These necessary KKT conditions can be interpreted as a saddle point, as illustrated in Figure 4.13. Note Equations 4.13 and 4.14 hold for strict equality constraint irrespective of the sign of $\mathbf{x}$ and $\boldsymbol{\lambda}$ as in the Lagrangian, and according to Figure 4.13, partial derivatives with respect to x and λ are zero. On the other hand, for truncated xs and λs due to nonnegativity, we may fall short of the saddle point or the saddle point may not be reached.

The equivalent dual complementary slackness condition can be written in long hand as:

$$x_j \left[\frac{\partial f}{\partial x_j} - \sum_{i=1}^{m} \lambda_i \frac{\partial g_i}{\partial x_j} \right] = 0 \qquad j = 1, 2, \ldots, n \tag{4.16}$$

In the case of equality constraints, the dual feasibility condition (Equation 4.15), when expressed in long hand, becomes

$$\frac{\partial f(\mathbf{x})}{\partial x_j} \le 0 \qquad j = 1, 2, \ldots, n \tag{4.17}$$

for maximization problems. The dual complementary slackness condition (Equation 4.16) above, in the case of equality constraints, would simply be

$$x_j \frac{\partial f(\mathbf{x})}{\partial x_j} = 0 \qquad j = 1, 2, \ldots, n \tag{4.18}$$

For illustration, one can check these KKT conditions against a two-variable LP.

Figure 4.13   MAX IN x AND MIN IN λ

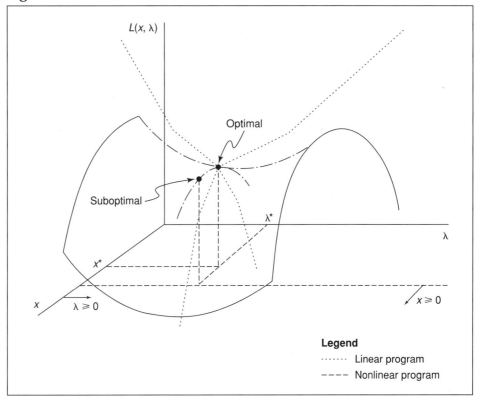

$$\text{Max } f(x) = c_1 x_1 + c_2 x_2$$
$$g_i(x) = a_{i1} x_1 + a_{i2} x_2 - b'_i \le 0 \qquad (i = 1, 2)$$
$$x, \lambda \ge 0.$$

The first KKT equation (Equation 4.13) becomes the dual feasibility condition:

$$\begin{bmatrix} c_1 \\ c_2 \end{bmatrix} \ge \lambda_1 \begin{bmatrix} a_{11} \\ a_{12} \end{bmatrix} + \lambda_2 \begin{bmatrix} a_{21} \\ a_{22} \end{bmatrix} = \overline{\mathbf{A}}^T \lambda \qquad (4.19)$$

Pre-multiplying by $\mathbf{x}$, we obtain the weak duality $x^T c \ge x^T \lambda^T \lambda = b'^T \lambda$ and the strong duality. In the former case, the primal objective function value is not less than the dual. In the latter case, the primal solution (z_x^*) is the same as dual solution (z_λ^*) at optimality. The complementary slackness Equation 4.14 simply reads

$$\lambda_1 (b'_1 - a_{11} x_1 + a_{12} x_2) = 0$$
$$\lambda_2 (b'_2 - a_{21} x_1 + a_{22} x_2) = 0$$

3. Frank-Wolfe Method. Now that the KKT conditions have been briefly reviewed, let us go to NLP solution methods that build upon this primal dual relationship. Obviously, there are quite a few solution algorithms for an NLP. Some of them have been reviewed in the discussions on enumeration and calculus already. A classic and rather robust method is that of **Frank-Wolfe** (F-W).

For a continuously differentiable function $f(x)$, suppose we want to solve the NLP with linear constraints: Max/Min $\{f(\mathbf{x}) \mid A\mathbf{x} = \mathbf{b}, \ \mathbf{x} \geq 0\}$. Here, $\mathbf{A}$ is an $m \times n$ tableau of coefficients, $\mathbf{x}$ is a vector of n decision variables and $\mathbf{b}'$ is the right-hand-side vector m long. The F-W algorithm linearizes the nonlinear objective function and turns it into an LP at each linearization. The algorithm converges to a solution after solving a series of LPs.

In detail, an iterative, primal method generates a sequence of points $\mathbf{x}^o,\ldots,\mathbf{x}^k \epsilon \ X = \{\mathbf{x} \mid \overline{A}\mathbf{x} = \mathbf{b}', \ \mathbf{x} \geq 0\}$ where $\mathbf{x}^{k+1}$ is found from $\mathbf{x}^k$ as follows: Set $k = 0$, start by solving the LP

$$\text{Max/Min} \ \nabla f^T(\mathbf{x}^k)\cdot\mathbf{x}$$
$$\text{s.t.} \qquad \overline{A}\mathbf{x} = \mathbf{b}' \qquad \qquad \text{PL}(x^k)$$
$$\mathbf{x} \geq 0$$

where $\nabla f^T(\mathbf{x}^k)$ is nothing more than the tangent at $\mathbf{x}^k$. It can be shown that the KKT dual complementary-slackness conditions—the mirror image of the primal ones outlined above in Equation 4.14—are included in the above LP: $[\nabla f^T(\mathbf{x}^o) -/+ \sum_{i\in I'} \lambda_i \nabla g_i(\mathbf{x}^o)]x^o = 0$ which, when $\mathbf{x}$ is non-zero, is equivalent to $\nabla f^T(\mathbf{x}^o)\mathbf{x}^o = \mathbf{b}'^T\boldsymbol{\lambda}$ and $\mathbf{c}^T\mathbf{x} = \mathbf{b}'^T\boldsymbol{\lambda}$ at optimality. Let $\mathbf{x}^k_{LP}$ be a vertex of X, an optimal solution of PL$(\mathbf{x}^k)$. Then $\mathbf{x}^{k+1}$ is chosen so as to maximize or minimize f in the interval $[\mathbf{x}^k, \mathbf{x}_{LP}]$. Figure 4.14 below will illustrate the algorithm, including the steps to convergence. It will be clear that the solution may be suboptimal—rather than globally optimal—depending on the starting point at which the algorithm is initiated.

In Figure 4.14, illustration of the generalized Frank-Wolfe algorithm is provided for a one-dimensional case, mainly for illustration clarity. We wish to maximize the accessibility function $f(x)$ over the interval of K miles (km) of additional highway. The starting point is x^0, where a tangent $\nabla f(x^0)x$ is constructed. It intersects the upper limit of our search interval K at x^0_{LP}—an extreme point of the LP. Our search interval now reduces from K to $[x^0, x^0_{LP}]$. Moving on to the first iteration of the algorithm, call this extremal point x^1. Again a tangent is constructed $\nabla f(x^1)x$, which intersects the tangent from the previous iteration $\nabla f(x^0)x$ at x^1_{LP} $(k = 1)$. Again, the interval reduces to $[x^1_{LP}, x^1]$. A tangent is constructed once more at this point, which we now rename x^2. The process simply continues until the peak at x^k_{LP}/x^{k+1} is reached. It is not hard to see that the peak so reached is a global maximum. On the other hand, an alternate starting point, say at $x^{0'}$, might end up at a local optimum such as $x^{k'}/x^{k'+1}$, with a tangent $\nabla f(x^{k'})x$ that is horizontal. Simple as it may be, this example illustrates how one can covert an NLP into a series of LP's and iteratively arrive at an optimum. Most important, this is a rather general procedure for a large number of situations, so long as $f(x)$ is differentiable. We will illustrate this procedure once more using the airport location problem in Chapter 5, where the one-dimensional example will be generalized.

IV. INTEGER OR MIXED-INTEGER PROGRAMMING

The next type of prescriptive technique to be discussed is **integer programming** (IP) or **mixed-integer programming** (MIP), where all integer solutions are required in IP while only some of the variables are required to be integer-valued in

Figure 4.14 ONE-DIMENSIONAL ILLUSTRATION OF GENERALIZED FRANK-WOLFE ALGORITHM

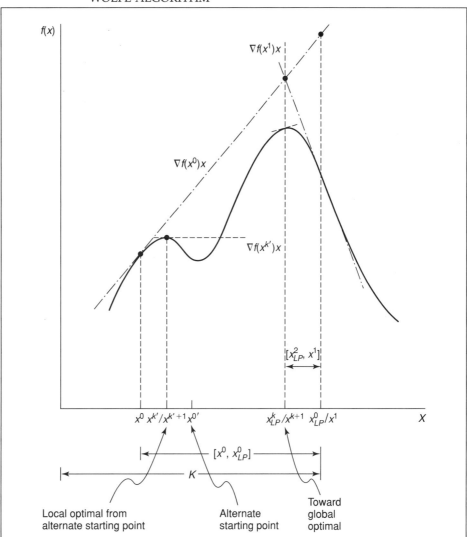

MIP. With this type of optimization, everything looks the same as an LP or NLP except a subset of the decision variables need to be discrete in the final answer. Examples of these have been given already in terms of housing location and industrial plant location. One recalls that in the Herbert-Stevens model, we ended up with integer value for only some of the households assigned to a particular housing type and a neighborhood. Should the answers be required in strict integers, it may be necessary to integerize them by a B&B procedure, where the branching rule is simply $\lceil x \rceil$ and $\lfloor x \rfloor$, corresponding to rounding a fractional variable to the next higher integer and next lower integer respectively. We will not discuss the details of the integerization routines inasmuch as they are all automated in IP or MIP codes. The logic is very much similar to the B&B procedure discussed previously in Section II-B when binary branches are constructed, wherein one branch fixes the fractional variable to the next higher integer and another branch the next lower integer as mentioned. A subproblem is defined as an LP corresponding to a relaxed version of the original IP or MIP, dropping its integrality requirements. Each of these subproblems is evaluated at each node of the B&B tree. In a nutshell, we solve the LP first and then fix the fractional variables, if they exist, by rounding the variable up or down. For this reason, the procedure is sometimes referred to as **LP relaxation,** to the extent that we relax the integrality requirement in the beginning. While this works reasonably well with small linear IPs or MIPs, the procedure is usually not advisable for large size problems, anywhere beyond several hundred integer variables at the time of writing. Neither does it work for NLPs where integer values are required, since the bounding rules become very nondiscriminating in such NLPs, thus resulting in a huge combinatorial space to be enumerated.

A. Total Unimodularity

Let us now turn to the IP example corresponding to the location of industrial plants and look for ways other than B&B to generate integer solutions. We are required to have 0-1 variables x_{ij} in that example, corresponding to plant i being assigned to location j. The solution is guaranteed to be integer if one should solve the model simply as an LP since there are some inherent properties of this type of IP that are of interest: A matrix $\bar{A}$ is said to be **totally unimodular (TU)** if and only if every subdeterminant of $\bar{A}$ equals 1, -1, or 0. A maximization (minimization) linear program with the constraint $\bar{A}x \leq (\geq)b'$ and $x \geq 0$ has an integer optimum solution for any arbitrary integer vector b' provided that the matrix $\bar{A}$ is totally unimodular. It turns out that the tableau of the industrial plant location problem has the very exact TU property to make the solution integer, as one can see from the corresponding simplex tableau ($\bar{A}$ matrix) for the industrial plant location problem in Table 4.4. This problem is related to the general class of transportation/allocation problems and the linear assignment problems.

In fact, we can characterize the problem as a network problem as well, since the problem can be represented as a bipartite network shown in Figure 4.15, with plants appearing in the left group of nodes and potential sites appearing on the right-hand side group (hence the term bipartite). A network tableau is by definition a TU matrix. Being able to cast a problem into a network model has addi-

Table 4.4   MATCHING TABLEAU FOR INDUSTRIAL PLANT LOCATION

Node	$(A, 1)$	$(A, 2)$	$(A, 3)$	$(A, 4)$	$(B, 1)$	$(B, 2)$	$(B, 3)$	$(B, 4)$	...	$(D, 4)$	RHS
A	1	1	1	1	1	1	1	1			1
B											1
C											1
D											1
1	−1				−1						−1
2		−1				−1					−1
3			−1				−1				−1
4				−1				−1		−1	−1

tional computational advantages. Efficient codes exist for the solution of network models, particularly ones such as this, which are classified as pure min-cost flow problems. Here one seeks the minimum cost flow from source s to sink t, directing four units of flow from left to right of the figure. Execution of these codes, including SAS/OR (1985, 1991) and CPLEX, will yield a solution such as the one shown in Figure 4.15. In the figure, unitary flows are found in the paths leading from s to t_n, valuating, among others, x_{A3}, x_{B2}, x_{C4}, and x_{D1} at unity. This assignment is identical to the one arrived at by B&B earlier in the chapter (in Section II-B).

Likewise, it can be shown that the Herbert-Stevens model can be cast into a network formulation. Raulerson, Bowyer, Zornick, and Chan (1994) have demonstrated that the problem can be structured as a bipartite graph as shown in Figure 4.15 by assigning the left group of nodes as the rich and poor resident groups and the right group of nodes as the housing types in each residential zone. The arc costs will simply be $(c_{11}^1, c_{12}^1, c_{11}^2, c_{12}^2)$ emanating from the first left node and $(c_{21}^1, c_{22}^1, c_{21}^2, c_{22}^2)$ emanating from the second node. In this case, there are two nodes on the left column and four on the right. In other words, the two columns no longer have the same number of nodes as in the plant location problem. A much faster execution time was observed in a sample problem for the Dayton, Ohio using the SAS/OR and CPLEX network software, rather than LP software.

B. Network Software

Many location problems can be formulated as flow and matching models, as alluded to above. These flow and matching models can in turn be solved efficiently when represented in terms of graphs and networks. We have already seen the efficacy of min-cost-flow and assignment models in solving the industrial plant location problem above. By way of a definition, a **graph** is defined as a set of vertices or nodes V' connected by edges. A **network** is simply a graph with flow(s)

Figure 4.15   MATCHING NETWORK FOR INDUSTRIAL PLANT LOCATION

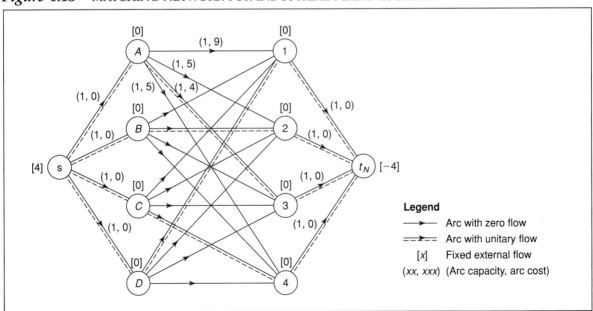

on it. A directed graph has directionality placed on the edges, which are now referred to as arcs $\underline{A}$. When flow is placed on a directed graph (hence turning it into a network), the arcs are also called links. If a problem can be represented as a network, it can be solved readily by off-the-shelf network software, much like an LP can be solved by a variety of ready-made codes. Network problems also have physical analogues that one can relate to, such as the interpretation of dual variables v_i' as nodal potentials or odometer readings at node i (see Appendix 1).

Experiences with network software will show that the input is quite user-friendly. It follows a convention separate from regular LP. The arcs in the network, for example, are input in a head-to-tail format rather than the equivalent tableau format as shown in Table 4.4. An example for our industrial plant network in Figure 4.15 is given below.

From	*to*	*Cost*	*Capacity*
s	A	0	1
s	B	0	1
.	.	.	.
.	.	.	.
A	1	9	1
A	2	5	1
.	.	.	.
.	.	.	.
3	t_n	0	1
4	t_n	0	1

It can be shown that such a representation is equivalent to a specialized LP tableau **A** called node-arc incidence matrix. Such a matrix has been illustrated in Table 4.4 without the links from the source and without the links leading toward the sink. When represented in terms of a network, it is not surprising that a node-arc incidence matrix is TU. Most network codes use a set of terms that need to be explained. Several of these appear in Figure 4.15:

> $[x]$ = fixed external flow, a positive number means the injection of flow into the network while a negative number depletion;
> (xx, xxx) = (arc capacity, arc cost).

These network terms have close parallels to the equivalent LP. For example, fixed external flows correspond to the **RHS** vector of an LP tableau. In Table 4.4, for example, an equivalent representation of the network similar to Figure 4.15, without the arc emanating from source s and incident upon sink t_N, have fixed external flow of +1 and −1 at the individual sources A, B, C, D and sinks 1, 2, 3, 4 shown as the RHS. A master source and sink, while not necessary, are generally constructed for convenience—to make the problem solvable by generic, off-the-shelf network codes—as shown in Figure 4.15.

The arc costs in a network model correspond to the cost vector in the LP objective function. Thus a minimum cost flow will effectively represent the optimal solution to the equivalent minimization LP, with arc flow replacing the decision variables in the computation process. Arc capacity $\overline{u}_{ij}$, on the other hand, is the upper bound of a decision variable. Since the decision variables are 0-1 valued, it is not hard to see why a capacity of 1 is placed at each arc in the network model. Other equivalences can be established as well, but we will not have the space to go into them here. Interested readers may wish to consult Appendix 1 and excellent treatments of the subject in such texts as Ahuja et al. (1993) and Bertsekas (1991).

Aside from a network tableau, it is often not clear whether a large problem is TU, since the definition given above is far from an operational test. Experience has shown, however, that many sparse tableaux of mainly 0-1 entries often yield integer solutions as long as the right-hand side is integer. This is an important observation for the practitioners inasmuch as many facility location problems have exactly such a type of tableaux. Notice this means that a problem can be entered into a regular LP code with a good chance of obtaining an integer solution[3]. Modern codes such as CPLEX has the advanced feature to discern any network structure within a tableau and exploit it by employing network algorithms. The result is then combined with the non-network part of the tableau to provide the overall solution to the original problem. We have a detailed explanation of a network with side constraints algorithm in Appendix 1, where the side constraints refer to the non-network part of the tableau.

C. Network with Gains

Pure network flow models, functional as they may be, have only limited applications. Take the example of a material handling plant in which four products *A, B, C, D* are manufactured. These products can be made at any one of five work-stations 1, 2, 3, 4, and 5. Each work-station has a limited number of hours available for production and a specific unit cost of production. A minimum production quota is set for each product, a unit of which is valued at a certain amount. A network with gain flow model is used to solve the problem, with the intent of obtaining a most effective operation, in which the cost of manufacturing is minimized and the value of products is maximized. In Figure 4.16, the parameters at the supply nodes on the left column represent the maximum hours available at a work-station and the unit cost of production, while those at the demand nodes in the right column represent the maximum output potentials and the value of a product. The manufacturing plant operates for 20 eight-hour days each month (160 hours total) at the maximum. The arcs connecting the left column to the right column in this bipartite graph convert the flow in hours of production into units of product. This is accomplished by the gain parameter, which converts the hours of each work-station *i* to products at node *j*. The value of a product is expressed as a negative cost and the maximum number of production is expressed as a slack external flow.

This allocation model assigns work-stations to products so as to maximize value of production and minimize cost:

$$\text{Min} \left(\Sigma_i w_i x_i + \Sigma_j w_j x_j \right)$$

$$\text{s.t.} \quad \Sigma_j x_{ij} = x_i \leq 160 \qquad \text{for all } i$$

$$\Sigma_j a_{ij} x_{ij} = x_j \leq b_j \qquad \text{for all } j$$

Figure 4.16   NETWORK WITH GAIN MODEL OF PRODUCT ALLOCATION

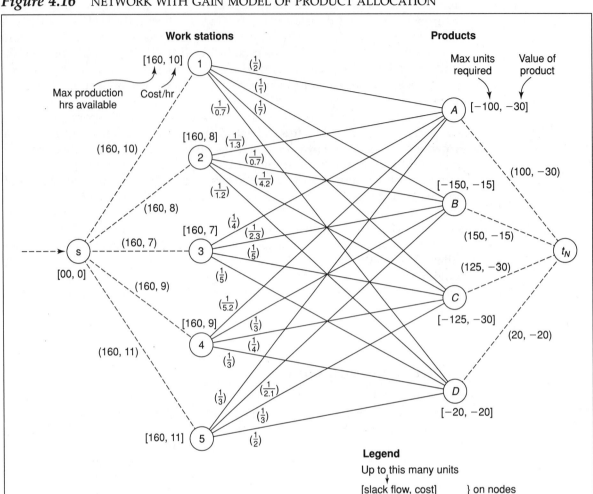

where w_i is the cost/hr of work-station i, w_j is the value of product j (expressed in negative values), and $b'_j = 100, 150, 125, 20$ corresponding to production requirement for product type $j = A, B, C, D$. Notice $\Sigma_i x_i \neq \Sigma_j x_j$, hence the term network flow with the a_{ij} gain parameters (in this case it is actually loss). The total flow terminating at the sink t_n is less than the total flow emanating from the source s, in other words, conservation-of-flow no longer applies. The linear programming model above can be cast into a min-cost-network-flow problem:

$$\text{Min} \sum_{(i,j)\in A} w_{ij} x_{ij}$$
$$\text{s.t.} \sum_{j\in\delta^+(i)} x_{ij} - \sum_{j\in\delta^-(i)} a_{ji} c_{ji} = b'_i \quad \text{for all } i \in V'$$
$$0 \leq x_{ij} \leq \bar{u}_{ij} \quad \text{for all } (i,j) \in \underline{A}$$

where w replaces c as the symbol for costs, V' is the set of nodes and $\underline{A}$ a set of links, $\delta^+(i)$ is the set of nodes reachable from i, $\delta^-(i)$ is the set incident upon i, and $\overline{u}_{ij}$ is the capacity on arc (i,j). This is a more general network flow model than pure min-cost-flow. For $a_{ji} = 1$, it reduces to the traditional pure min-cost-flow model as discussed in the above section. On the other hand, when $a_{ji} \neq 1$, it represents a network with gain, as illustrated by the manufacturing example being discussed.

Let A be the matrix of constraint coefficients, the matrix formulation for this problem becomes $\text{Min}\{\mathbf{w}^T\mathbf{x} \mid A\mathbf{x} = \mathbf{b}',\ 0 \leq \mathbf{x} \leq \overline{\mathbf{u}}\}$. Notice that $\mathbf{A} = [\mathbf{A}_B, \mathbf{A}_N]$, where the node-arc incidence matrix written in terms of the basic and nonbasic parts, is no longer TU. As shown in Appendix 1, $\mathbf{A}_B$ is the basis matrix of $m - 1$ linearly independent columns, and $\mathbf{A}_N$ is the remaining nonbasic columns. $\mathbf{x}_B$ is a vector of basic flow variables in the same order as columns of $\mathbf{A}_B$, while $\mathbf{x}_N$ is the vector of nonbasic variables in the same order as columns of $\mathbf{A}_N$:

$$\mathbf{A}\mathbf{x} = \begin{bmatrix} \mathbf{A}_B, \mathbf{A}_N \end{bmatrix}\begin{bmatrix} \mathbf{x}_B \\ \mathbf{x}_N \end{bmatrix} = \mathbf{b}'$$

$$\mathbf{A}_B\mathbf{x}_B + \mathbf{A}_N\mathbf{x}_N = \mathbf{b}'$$

and $\mathbf{x}_B = \mathbf{A}_B^{-1}[\mathbf{b}' - \mathbf{A}_N\mathbf{x}_N]$ through the **network simplex procedure,** which is explained in Appendix 1 in terms of the pure network flow version. In essence, the basis is represented via a tree consisting of $m - 1$ arcs. Instead of performing an algebraic basis inversion, we accomplish this through the tree graph. The fact that rank $\mathbf{A}$ = rank $(\mathbf{A}_B) = m - 1$ means $\mathbf{x}_B$ is unique.

Procedurally, the network with gain network algorithm will start with adding a node, called the slack node, and a number of additional arcs that enter or leave the slack node, called slack or artificial arcs. The slack node, usually numbered one greater than the number of nodes in the original network, can serve the dual function of a super source/sink. The flows associated with the slack node may not obey flow conservation (as amply illustrated by the current manufacturing example). The artificial arcs perform the function of the artificial variables of linear programming, and the slack arcs represent the slack external flows provided in the original model. As part of the network-simplex procedure, we already mentioned that the basis of the network flow LP is represented as the spanning tree of $m - 1$ nonzero arc flows, shown equivalently as $m - 1$ linearly independent columns of the node-arc incidence tableau. Here the basis of the LP is $m - 1$ in rank. Let us now review the basic terms in a network with gains model. These definitions are best referenced against the manufacturing example illustrated in Figure 4.16: **External flow** enters or leaves a network, where **fixed external flow** b_i' at node i enters the network at (supply) node i if positive, and leaves the network (as a demand node) if negative. **Slack external flow**—a variable to be determined as part of the optimization procedure—is, once again, similar to slack variables in LP. A negative slack variable means extra supply available at node i to satisfy excess demands (as represented by the sum of flows incident upon i, $(\sum_{j\in\delta^-(i)} x_{ji})$, while a positive slack variable means extra demand available at node i to draw off excess supply $(\sum_{j\in\delta^+(i)} x_{ji})$. For a positive (negative) slack flow $x_{s''i}$ $(x_{is''})$ {or the external flow representations $[+x_{s''i}]$ $([-x_{is''}])$}, an arc is constructed from (to) the slack node s'' to (from) node i. The capacity of the arc is the absolute value of the slack flow capacity $|b_{s''i}|$, and the cost on the arc is $w_{s''i}$. The $b_{s''i}$s and $w_{s''i}$s are given (complete with positive and negative signs such as the network with gain example in Figure 4.16). If $b_{s^r i}$ is positive (negative) $x_{s^r i}$ enters (leaves) the network as external flows. We will further illustrate the usefulness of this convention in Appendix 1. Case studies are documented in the "Facility Location" chapter of Chan (2000).

    The **generalized network flow problem** is significantly more difficult to solve than the pure min-cost-flow problem. The **generalized network simplex algorithm** is the fastest available algorithm for solving the generalized network flow problem in practice (Ahuja et al. 1993). The generalized network simplex algorithm is an adaptation of the LP simplex. This adaptation is possible because of the special topological structure of the basis. The basis of the generalized network flow problem is a **good augmented forest,** to be defined as follows: In the spanning tree with an extra arc called the root arc[4], an augmented forest is a collection of node disjoint augmented trees that span all the nodes of the graph. We define a **good augmented tree** as one whose cycle is formed by a gainy extra arc (in other words, an arc with a_{ij} associated with it) to the tree. A good augmented forest is consisted of nothing but good augmented trees. It can be shown that the basis of the generalized network flow problem is a good augmented forest. Good augmented forests play the same role in the generalized network simplex algorithm. Instead of one tree representing the basis, we have now more than one tree to span the nodes, depending on the number of gainy arcs involved. While the nodal potential equations are similar, the optimality conditions for a good augmented forest has a slightly different definition of the reduced cost, as defined by $w_{ij} - v_i + a_{ij}v_j$ (which is equivalent to $c_j - z_j$ in a regular simplex, with $c_j = w_{ij}$ and $z_j = v_j' - a_{ij}v_j$ in this case). Notice the equivalent pure-network-flow reduced cost is $w_{ij} - v_i' + v_j'$, where v_i', v_j' are the dual variables at rows i and j of the node-arc incidence matrix. v_i' can be interpreted as nodal potentials at node i, or alternatively as "odometer readings" in the context of measuring spatial separations. In the latter interpretation, a reduced cost of $w_{ij} - v_i' + v_j' \le 0$ or $w_{ij} \le v_i' - v_j'$ indicates a faster way to go from i to j via link (i,j), and hence the link should be used.

V. DECOMPOSITION METHODS IN FACILITY LOCATION

Consider this special MIP

$$\text{Min } (c^T x + g^T y)$$

Subject to

$$\sum_{j=1}^{n} x_{ij} = 1 \qquad i = 1, \ldots, m \tag{4.20}$$

$$x_{ij} \le y_j \qquad i = 1, \ldots, m; \quad j = 1, \ldots, n \tag{4.21}$$

$$\sum_{j=1}^{n} y_j = p$$
$$x_{ij} \ge 0 \qquad i = 1, \ldots, m; \quad j = 1, \ldots, n \tag{4.22}$$
$$y_j = \{0, 1\} \qquad j = 1, \ldots, n$$

In this model, the continuous variable x_{ij} denotes the fraction of customer demand at node i that receives service from a facility at node j, while the 0-1 discrete variable y_j signifies whether or not a facility is built (Magnanti and Wong 1990). In network flow terminology, the forcing constraints Equation 4.21 restricts the flow to only those nodes j that have been chosen as facility sites. Finally, constraint Equation 4.22 restricts the number of facilities to a prescribed number p. This model is often referred to as the p-median problem, where c_{ij} denotes the cost of serving demand from node i by a facility at node j. It is conventional to set $\mathbf{g} = \mathbf{0}$, since oftentimes only the number of facilities, rather than their explicit facility costs, are of importance. The reader will recognize this as a special case of Benders' decomposition as discussed in Appendix 1, in which the decision variables can be decomposed into two groups: continuous and discrete. For reasons that will become clear, **Benders' decomposition** is also referred to as resource directive decomposition since it starts with a set of initial dual variables and adjust the common resource availability by fixing certain decision variables.

A. Resource Directive Decomposition

Consider the five-node, two-median example where the costs are defined   as

$$[c_{ij}] = \begin{bmatrix} 0 & 5 & 9 & 11 & 12 \\ 5 & 0 & 4 & 6 & 7 \\ 9 & 4 & 0 & 2 & 3 \\ 11 & 6 & 2 & 0 & 1 \\ 12 & 7 & 3 & 1 & 0 \end{bmatrix}$$

where the entries specify the costs of serving the demand at node i from a facility located at node j. Suppose we have a current configuration with facilities located at nodes 2 and 5 (in other words, $y_2 = y_5 = 1$), the minimum cost objective function for this configuration is obtained by examining the minimum unit costs in columns 2 and 5. It is evaluated in this case at $(5 + 0) + (3 + 1 + 0) = 9$, suggesting that facility 2 serves demands at nodes 1 and 2 and facility 5 serves demands at 3, 4, and 5. Relative to the current solution, let us evaluate the reduction in the objective function cost if facility 1 is opened and all other facilities retain their current open-close status. This new facility would reduce the cost of servicing the demand at node 1 from $c_{12} = 5$ to $c_{11} = 0$. In other words, demand 1 will be served by facility 1 instead of facility 2, resulting in a cost reduction. Therefore the saving for opening facility 1 is 5 units. Similarly, by opening facility 3 we would reduce, relative to the current solution, cost of serving node 3 from $c_{35} = 3$ to $c_{33} = 0$. The saving is 3 units. Finally, opening facility 4 would reduce node 3 cost from 3 to 2 and node 4 cost from 1 to 0, for a total saving of $1 + 1 = 2$. Since facilities 2 and 5 are already open in the current solution, there is no saving for opening any of them.

Note that when these savings are combined, the individual assignments as computed above might overestimate possible total savings since the computation often double counts the cost reductions for any particular demand node. For example, our previous computations predict that opening both facilities 3 and 4 would reduce the cost of serving node 3 and give a total reduction of $3 + 1 = 4$ units, even though the maximum possible reduction is clearly 3 units, which is the cost of servicing node 3 in the current solution. (A demand can only be served by one facility, not both facilities.) With this savings information, we can bound the cost z of any feasible configuration y from below by

$$z \geq 9 - 5y_1 - 3y_3 - 2y_4 \tag{4.23}$$

Notice that specifying a different current configuration would change our savings computations and permit us to obtain a different lower bound function. For example, the readers can verify that configuration $y_1 = y_3 = 1$ would produce a lower bound inequality

$$z \geq 9 - 4y_2 - 4y_4 - 4y_5 \tag{4.24}$$

Each of these two bounding functions is always valid. By combining them we obtain an improved lower bound for the optimal two-median cost. Solving the following mixed integer program would determine the best location of the facilities that uses the combined lower bounding information:

$$\begin{aligned} \text{Min } & z \\ \text{s.t. } \quad & z \geq 9 - 5y_1 \qquad\quad - 3y_3 - 2y_4 \\ & z \geq 9 \qquad - 4y_2 \qquad\quad - 4y_4 - 4y_5 \\ & y_1 + y_2 + y_3 + y_4 + y_5 = 2 \\ & y_j = \{0, 1\} \quad j = 1, \ldots, 5 \end{aligned} \tag{4.25}$$

This yields a lower bound of $z' = 5$, obtained by setting $y_1' = y_2' = 1$ and $y_3' = y_4' = y_5' = 0$. Alternatively, one can set $y_1' = y_4' = 1$, or $y_1' = y_5' = 1$, or $y_3' = y_4' = 1$, and all other $y_j' = 0$ in each case. This bounding procedure is the essence of Benders' decomposition. In this context Equation 4.25 is referred to as a Benders' master problem and Equation 4.23 and Equation 4.24 are called Benders' cuts. When applied to an MIP with integer variables $\mathbf{y}$ and continuous variables $\mathbf{x}$, Benders' decomposition repeatedly solves a master problem like Equation 4.25 in the integer variables $\mathbf{y}$. At each step, the algorithm uses a simple savings computation to refine the lower bound information by adding a new Benders' cut to the master problem. Each solution $(z', \mathbf{y}')$ to the master problem yields a new lower bound z' and a new configuration $\mathbf{y}'$. For p-median problems, with the facility locations fixed at $\mathbf{y}'$, the resulting allocation problem becomes a trivial LP, viz, to assign all demand at node i to the closest open facility, or minimize c_{ij} over all j with $y_j' = 1$. It is in this resource allocation context that we refer to Benders' procedure as resource-directive decomposition. The optimal solution $\mathbf{x}'$ to this LP generates a new bound on the optimal objective function value of the p-median problem. As one will see in Appendix 1, the savings from any current configuration $\mathbf{y}'$ can be viewed as dual variables of this LP. Therefore, in general, the solution of an LP would replace the simple savings computation. The method terminates when the current lower bound z^* equals the cost of the best (least-cost) configuration $\mathbf{y}^*$ found so far. This equality implies that the best upper bound z equals the best lower bound z^* and so $\mathbf{y}^*$ must be an optimal configuration, with the associated optimal allocation $\mathbf{x}^*$. Again, the full Benders' decomposition algorithm is explained in Appendix 1.

B. Price Directive Decomposition

As contrasted with resource directive procedures, the dual variables of a price directive decomposition (or Lagrangian relaxation) are priced out in a Lagrangian, which decides on the next set of decision variables to be engaged. Lagrangian relaxation offers another type of decomposition technique that produces lower bounds. Consider the above *p*-median problem once again. As an algorithmic strategy for simplifying the problem, suppose we remove the constraints Equation 4.20, weighting them by Lagrange multipliers (dual variables) λ_i, and placing them in the objective function. We obtain the Lagrangian relaxation problem, namely

$$z_{LR}(\lambda) = \min \left[\sum_{i=1}^{5} \sum_{j=1}^{5} c_{ij} x_{ij} + \sum_{i=1}^{5} \lambda_i \left(1 - \sum_{j=1}^{5} x_{ij} \right) \right] \tag{4.26}$$

subject to the remaining constraints. Each penalty term $\lambda_i (1 - \sum_{j=1}^{5} x_{ij})$ will be positive if λ_i has the appropriate sign and the *i*th constraint Equation 4.26 is violated. Therefore, by adjusting the penalty values λ_i, we can discourage Equation 4.26 from having an optimal solution that violates the constraints Equation 4.20.

Note that since the penalty term is always zero for all λ_i whenever **x** satisfies Equation 4.20, the optimal relaxation problem cost $z_{LR}(\lambda)$ is always a valid lower bound for the optimal *p*-median cost. The primary motivation for adopting this algorithmic strategy is that Equation 4.26 is very easy to solve. Let us set $x_{ij} = 1$ only when $y_j = 1$ or maintain feasibility of Equation 4.21. The modified cost coefficient $(c_{ij} - \lambda_i)$ of x_{ij} is nonpositive in Equation 4.26. thus summing over all nodes *i*, the optimal benefit of setting $y_j = 1$ is $z_j = \sum_{i=1}^{5} [\min (0, c_{ij} - \lambda_i)]$ and we can rewrite Equation 4.26 as

$$z_{LR}(\lambda) = \min \left[\sum_{j=1}^{5} z_j y_j + \sum_{i=1}^{5} \lambda_i \right] \tag{4.27}$$

subject to Equation 4.22, including the integrality and nonnegativity requirements. This problem is solved simply by finding the two smallest z_j values and setting the corresponding variables $y_j = 1$. For example, letting $\bar{\lambda} = (3, 3, 3, 3, 3)^T$ for the time being, Equation 4.27 becomes

$$z_{LR}(\bar{\lambda}) = \min (-3y_1 - 3y_2 - 4y_3 - 6y_4 - 5y_5 + 15) \tag{4.28}$$

The corresponding optimal solution for Equation 4.26 has a Lagrangian objective function value $z_{LR}(\bar{\lambda}) = 15 - 6 - 5 = 4$; the solution has $y_4 = y_5 = 1$, $x_{34} = x_{44} = x_{45} = x_{54} = x_{55} = 1$, and all the other variables set to zero. Notice that this solution for the Lagrangian problem is not feasible for the *p*-median problem. Indeed, for any $i = 1, 2, \ldots, 5$, it does not satisfy the demand constraint Equation 4.20—hence the term relaxation in that certain constraints are ignored.

For another dual variable vector $\lambda^* = (5, 5, 3, 2, 3)^T$, Equation 4.27 becomes $z_{LR}(\bar{\lambda}) = \min (-5x_1 - 5x_2 - 4x_3 - 5x_4 - 4x_5 - 18)$. Its optimal objective-function value $z_{LR}(\bar{\lambda}) = 8$ is a tight lower bound since the optimal *p*-median cost is also eight. This example illustrates the importance of using good values for the dual variables λ_i in order to obtain strong lower bounds for the Lagrangian relaxation problem. In fact, to find the sharpest possible Lagrangian lower bound, we need to solve the optimization problem $\max_{\lambda} z_{LR}(\overline{\lambda})$. This optimization problem in the variables λ has become known as the Lagrangian dual problem to the original facility location model. (See Appendix 1 for a step-by-step algorithm to solve the Lagrangian relaxation problem.)

VI. SPATIAL INTERACTIONS: THE QUADRATIC ASSIGNMENT PROBLEM

In many locational problems the cost associated with placing a facility at a certain site depends not only on the distances from other facilities and the demands, but also on the interaction with other facilities (Burkard 1990; Francis, McGillis, Jr., and White 1992). In this section we examine a class of discrete location models that permit us to address certain interaction between facilities. The basic concepts can best be illustrated by an example: A manufacturing cell is being designed with manual material handling between work-stations. Figure 4.17 presents a schematic of the possible locations of the work-stations along the aisle. The objective is to minimize the total distance that material moves. The following distance matrix shows the separation between station locations a, b, c, d (in inches for example):

$$[d_{ij}] = \begin{bmatrix} 0 & 340 & 320 & 400 \\ 340 & 0 & 360 & 200 \\ 320 & 360 & 0 & 180 \\ 400 & 200 & 180 & 0 \end{bmatrix}$$

and material flow between the stations A, B, C, D themselves (in pounds for example) is represented by

Figure 4.17   LOCATION CONFIGURATION FOR WORK-STATIONS

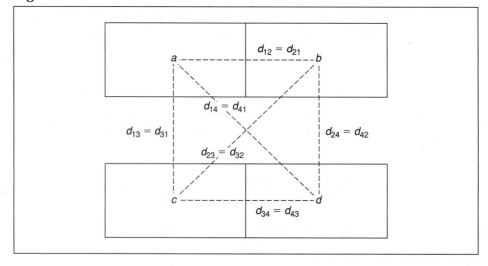

$$[c_{kl}] = \begin{bmatrix} 0 & 80 & 40 & 30 \\ 80 & 0 & 30 & 20 \\ 40 & 30 & 0 & 10 \\ 30 & 20 & 10 & 0 \end{bmatrix}$$

What is the best assignment of work-stations to locations?

A. Nonlinear Formation

Define the discrete variable x_{ki} = 1 or 0, depending on whether work-station k is assigned to location i. Similarly, x_{lj} denotes whether work-station l is assigned to location j. Consider a piece of material moves from work-station k to work-station l, the total material movement (in, for instance, lb-ft or kg-m) per unit-time is to be minimized:

$$\text{Min} \sum_{k=1}^{3} \sum_{l=1}^{3} \sum_{i=1}^{3} \sum_{j=1}^{3} c_{kl} \, d_{ij} \, x_{ki} \, x_{lj}$$

Notice that the material flow between two locations i and j would depend on what work-stations are placed there. Since every work-station must be assigned to a location and every location must have a work-station, these constraints must be imposed:

$$\sum_{i=1}^{3} x_{ki} = 1 \qquad k = 1, 2, 3$$

$$\sum_{k=1}^{3} x_{ki} = 1 \qquad i = 1, 2, 3 \tag{4.29}$$

$$x_{ki} \in \{1, 0\} \qquad k = 1, 2, 3; \quad i = 1, 2, 3$$

If we assume that station A is placed at location a, station B on location b, C on c, and D on d, then the objective function will assume the value

$$(2)[(340)(80) + (320)(40) + (400)(30) + (360)(30) + (200)(20) + (180)(10)] = 137{,}200$$

corresponding to the upper or lower triangle of the matrices $[d_{ij}]$ or $[c_{kl}]$. On the other hand, if we assume A is placed at d, B at b, C at c, and D at a, then we have

$$(2)[(340)(20) + (320)(10) + (400)(30) + (360)(30) + (200)(80) + (180)(40)] = 112{,}000$$

This comparison drives home the point that the cost of placing a work-station depends on the interaction with the other work-stations. In this case, the second configuration is better than the first since the amount of material movement is less.

B. Linear Formulation

This nonlinear program is computationally demanding. It has been shown that the model can be simplified to a linear integer program

$$\text{Min} \sum_{k=1}^{n} \sum_{l=1}^{n} \sum_{i=1}^{n} \sum_{j=1}^{n} r_{klij} \, y_{klij} \tag{4.30}$$

where $r_{klij} = c_{kl}d_{ij}$ and $y_{klij} = x_{ki}x_{lj}$. Notice the quadratic term $x_{ki}x_{lj}$ has now been replaced by a new binary variable y_{klij}. The constraints are the same as before except for two additional ones that govern the relationship between the x and y variables:

$$x_{ki} + x_{lj} - 2y_{klij} \geq 0 \qquad k, l, i, j = 1, \ldots, n$$
$$y_{klij} \in \{0, 1\} \qquad k, l, i, j = 1, \ldots, n \qquad (4.31)$$

Although the linear binary program was easy to implement, it has some worrisome properties. Along with the optimal solution for x_{ki}, we obtain the solution at the optimum for $y_{klij} = 0$. The objective function for the model, in turn, is zero. We are then required to take the optimal values of x_{ki}, $x_{14} = x_{25} = x_{32} = x_{41} = 1$ and substitute them into the original nonlinear objective function to obtain the final solution of 110,000 lb-ft (15,208 kg-m). This means that A is placed at d, B is at c, C on b and D on a.

For non-negative coefficients r_{klij}, the model can be recast into an MIP:

$$\text{Min} \sum_{k=1}^{n} \sum_{l=1}^{n} u_{kl},$$

where

$$u_{kl} = x_{ki} \left(\sum_{i=1}^{n} \sum_{j=1}^{n} r_{klij} x_{lj} \right).$$

The constraints are the same as the original quadratic assignment problem, with these two additional ones that govern the relationship between x and u:

$$s_{kl} x_{ki} + \sum_{i=1}^{n} \sum_{j=1}^{n} r_{klij} x_{lj} - u_{kl} \leq s_{kl} \qquad k, l = 1, \ldots, n$$
$$u_{kl} \geq 0 \qquad k, l = 1, \ldots, n \qquad (4.32)$$

where

$$s_{kl} = \sum_{i=1}^{n} \sum_{j=1}^{n} r_{klij}.$$

Note that we can assume $r_{klij} \geq 0$ without loss of generality, since adding a constant to all cost coefficients does not change the optimal solution.

C. Comments

Many well-known combinatorial optimization problems can be formulated as quadratic assignment problems (QAP), including the linear assignment problem and traveling salesman problem (TSP). If a linear assignment problem with cost matrix $[c_{ij}]$ is given, let us define

$$r_{klij} \leftarrow \begin{cases} c_{ij} & \text{for } (i, j) = (k, l) \\ 0 & \text{otherwise} \end{cases} \qquad (4.33)$$

or that the work-stations are permanently fixed at a unique location. Then the objective function of the given linear assignment problem is equivalent to the QAP objective (Equation 4.30). Because of space limitations presently, the readers are referred to Chan (2000) for the latter relationship between QAP and TSP. Suffice to say here that the TSP is defined as the least costly tour among *n* cities starting and ending in the same city, which on the surface bears little resemblance to the QAP, inasmuch as TSP is a routing problem and QAP is a location problem. The formal relationship between them and an extended explanation of TSP is offered in Chan (2000) under the chapters on "Routing" and "Location-and-Routing."

The QAP is discussed here for several reasons. It illustrates how a seemingly complex nonlinear formulation can be simplified by linearization. Indirectly, it also shows the importance of proper formulation to the solution algorithm, to the extent that a linear integer program or mixed integer program is much easier to solve than a nonlinear one. Thus while we laid out the various prescriptive techniques such as linear and nonlinear programming in this chapter, the distinction becomes blurred when we start solving problems in earnest. This does not mean the taxonomy proposed here is superficial, it simply argues for a deeper understanding of spatial temporal problems than the level exposed in general operations research textbooks. On the side, we suggested that different types of location and routing problems can be equivalenced also through transformation. Thus the linear assignment problem, the QAP and TSP all belong the same family. It will not be the first time we will see this type of discussion. In fact, a major focus of this book and Chan (2000) is to point out the mathematical equivalence between seemingly diverse physical spatial problems, including the land use model discussed in Section VIII.

VII. PRESCRIPTIVE ANALYSIS IN FACILITY LOCATION: DATA ENVELOPMENT ANALYSIS

Data Envelopment Analysis (DEA) is a linear programming technique to measure efficiency of a **decision-making unit** (DMU), interpreted here as alternative facility location (Thomas 1995; Winston 1994). One of the major drawbacks of the traditional DEA formulation is that there is a separate formulation for each individual DMU. In other words, each site is separately modeled, and the results are then compared. Here we formulate a combined model that can assess the efficiency of several alternatives all at once. To complete the re-formulation of the traditional DEA model, additional variables must be introduced. One new variable x_i ($i = 1, 2, 3$) is the efficiency score of each facility. It carries a value between zero and one. A value close to one indicates an efficient DMU, or that a site is a viable alternative. The binary variable y_i ($i = 1, 2, 3$) indicates the selection of an alternative in the output. If an alternative i will not be included into the output, $y_i = 0$; otherwise it is unitary valued. Let b_{ki} denote the weights placed on the kth benefit of the ith alternative, and the weights c_{li} the lth cost for the ith alternative. The key is to note that b_{ki} and c_{li} will have a nonzero value only if $y_i = 1$. In the following facility-siting example, we will have three alternatives corresponding to three sites, three output benefit measures and two input cost measures. DEA simply picks the most efficient facility based on the benefit cost ratio.

The objective function now looks like

Maximize

$$x_1 + x_2 + x_3 + 0b_{11} + 0b_{21} + 0b_{31} + 0b_{12} + 0b_{22} + 0b_{32} + 0b_{13} + 0b_{23} + 0b_{33} +$$
$$0c_{11} + 0c_{21} + 0c_{12} + 0c_{22} + 0c_{13} + 0c_{23} + 0y_1 + 0y_2 + 0y_3$$

which seeks the highest, combined efficiency score among all three facilities, or $x_1 + x_2 + x_3$. The second step is to bound the efficiency scores by some large number M. In this example, M is set equal to 100. The number acts as a ceiling on each efficiency scores and prevents an unbounded answer.

$$x_1 \le 100 \qquad x_2 \le 100 \qquad x_3 \le 100$$

This problem has only three solutions. Thus $y_1 = 0$, $y_2 = 0$, and $y_3 = 1$ is one of three solutions.

There needs to be some indication of the number of facilities to be included in the analysis. In this particular case, only one facility (the most efficient one) will be chosen:

$$y_1 + y_2 + y_3 = 1$$

The next set of constraints is used to compute the efficiency score of the facility in consideration. Here the benefits of each facility are evaluated. For example, facility 1 has 9 units of benefit 1, 4 units of benefit 2, and 16 units of benefit 3, and so on. Notice that the efficiency scores x_is are bounded above and below through the 0–1 ranged weights b_{kl}s and c_{li}s.

$$x_1 - 9b_{11} - 4b_{21} - 16b_{31} \ge 0 \qquad\qquad x_1 - 9b_{11} - 4b_{21} - 16b_{31} + 100y_1 \le 100^\#$$
$$x_2 - 5b_{12} - 7b_{22} - 10b_{32} \ge 0 \qquad\qquad x_2 - 5b_{12} - 7b_{22} - 10b_{32} + 100y_2 \le 100$$
$$x_3 - 4b_{13} - 9b_{23} - 13b_{33} \ge 0 \qquad\qquad x_3 - 4b_{13} - 9b_{23} - 13b_{33} + 100y_3 \le 100^\&$$

Inasmuch as the costs are bigger than benefits, the following set of constraints assures that the efficiency score for any efficient facility cannot exceed a value of 1. Notice that each facility has its own unique weighting system through the b_{ki}s and c_{li}s:

For facility 1

$$-9b_{11} - 4b_{21} - 16b_{31} + 5c_{11} + 14c_{21} \ge 0^@$$
$$-5b_1 - 7b_{21} - 10b_{31} + 8c_{11} + 15c_{21} \ge 0$$
$$-4b_{11} - 9b_{21} - 13b_{31} + 7c_{11} + 12c_{21} \ge 0^\%$$

For facility 2

$$-9b_{12} - 4b_{22} - 16b_{32} + 5c_{12} + 14c_{22} \ge 0$$
$$-5b_{12} - 7b_{22} - 10b_{32} + 8c_{12} + 15c_{22} \ge 0$$
$$-4b_{12} - 9b_{22} - 13b_{32} + 7c_{12} + 12c_{22} \ge 0$$

For facility 3

$$-9b_{13} - 4b_{23} - 16b_{33} + 5c_{13} + 14c_{23} \geq 0$$
$$-5b_{13} - 7b_{23} - 10b_{33} + 8c_{13} + 15c_{23} \geq 0$$
$$-4b_{13} - 9b_{23} - 13b_{33} + 7c_{13} + 12c_{23} \geq 0$$

The next three constraints act as the scaling equations, which ensure that the weights are 0–1 ranged. The scaling is dependent upon whether or not the binary variable y_i is turned on or not. Thus if y_1 is unitary valued, the weights c_{11} and c_{21} are adjusted to convert the sum of the two costs associated with facility 1 (5 and 14) to be unity.

$$5c_{11} + 14c_{21} - y_1 = 0$$
$$8c_{12} + 15c_{22} - y_2 = 0$$
$$7c_{13} + 12c_{23} - y_3 = 0^*$$

Finally, the constraints which make this whole apparatus work are the weight forcing constraints. The constraints are either-or in nature and assure that the weights for a facility cannot be greater than zero unless the facility is turned on ($y_i = 1$). In addition, if the facility is turned on, it assures that each weight will be greater than a very small number. In the example, the number is assumed to be 0.0001.

Weight forcing constraints for facility 1

$b_{11} - 100y_1 \leq 0$	$-b_{11} + 100y_1 \leq 99.9999$
$b_{21} - 100y_1 \leq 0$	$-b_{21} + 100y_1 \leq 99.9999$
$b_{31} - 100y_1 \leq 0$	$-b_{31} + 100y_1 \leq 99.9999$
$c_{11} - 100y_1 \leq 0$	$-c_{11} + 100y_1 \leq 99.9999$
$c_{21} - 100y_1 \leq 0$	$-c_{21} + 100y_1 \leq 99.9999$

Weight forcing constraints for facility 2

$b_{12} - 100y_2 \leq 0$	$-b_{12} + 100y_2 \leq 99.9999$
$b_{22} - 100y_2 \leq 0$	$-b_{22} + 100y_2 \leq 99.9999$
$b_{32} - 100y_2 \leq 0$	$-b_{32} + 100y_2 \leq 99.9999$
$c_{12} - 100y_2 \leq 0$	$-c_{12} + 100y_2 \leq 99.9999$
$c_{22} - 100y_2 \leq 0$	$-c_{22} + 100y_2 \leq 99.9999$

Weight-forcing constraints for facility 3

$b_{13} - 100y_3 \leq 0$	$-b_{13} + 100y_3 \leq 99.9999$
$b_{22} - 100y_3 \leq 0$	$-b_{23} + 100y_3 \leq 99.9999$
$b_{33} - 100y_3 \leq 0$	$-b_{33} + 100y_3 \leq 99.9999$
$c_{13} - 100y_3 \leq 0$	$-c_{13} + 100y_3 \leq 99.9999$
$c_{23} - 100y_3 \leq 0$	$-c_{23} + 100y_3 \leq 99.9999$

For purpose of explanation, consider the weight forcing constraints for facility 1. The first five constraints in the set assure that the input and output weights will not be greater than zero unless $y_1 = 1$. If y_1 does indeed equal one, then the first five constraints also act as an acceptable upper bound on the expected values of the weights. Once again, an M value of 100 has been assumed. The second five constraints in the set for facility 1 assures that if the cost and benefit weights are turned on ($y_1 = 1$), they will be greater than or equal to 0.0001. The model output is very straightforward. Recall that the cap of 100 has been placed on all of the efficiency scores. Based on the number of facilities that are to be included in the analysis, the program will pick the facility or facilities that maximize the sum of the efficiency scores. For example, if only one facility is to be chosen, then only the most efficient facility will have its efficiency score calculated. The other efficiencies will be set to 100 (the upper bound), thereby indicating that the facility is not as efficient as the facility that was picked.

The linear programming solver confirmed the following results. The maximum objective function value is 201 (by definition). The problem has multiple optima. $y_1 = y_2 = 0$ and $y_3 = 1$ is one of the two optimal solutions. The weight-forcing constraints imply that $b_{11} = b_{21} = b_{31} = c_{11} = c_{21} = 0$, and $b_{12} = b_{22} = b_{32} = c_{12} = c_{22} = 0$. Efficiency-score-computation constraints and upper bounds on x_is imply that $x_1 = x_2 = 0$. The scaling equation (marked by *) implies that $7c_{13} + 12c_{23} = 1$. Constraints marked by # and & imply that $4b_{13} + 9b_{23} + 13b_{33} = x_3$. Hence the original problem with 55 constraints and 21 variables is reduced to the following problem:

$$\text{Max} \quad 4b_{13} + 9b_{23} + 13b_{33}$$
$$\text{s.t.} \quad 5c_{13} + 14c_{23} \geq 9b_{13} + 4b_{23} + 16b_{33}$$
$$8c_{13} + 15c_{23} \geq 5b_{13} + 7b_{23} + 10b_{33}$$
$$7c_{13} + 12c_{23} \geq 4b_{13} + 9b_{23} + 13b_{33}$$
$$7c_{13} + 12c_{23} = 1$$

Now the question is: "Can we find weights for benefits and costs so that benefits are less-than-or-equal-to costs for all three facilities, and the benefits of facility 1 are equal to its costs (= 1)?" If the answer is affirmative, then the solution is called efficient. Here, the optimal objective-function-value is equal to 1, and thus the solution (locate at site 3) is efficient. In order to identify all efficient solutions, one must be able to identify all multiple optima to this LP. Notice DEA is a good illustration of a prescriptive model. The weights b and c are not determined through a consensus building process, but by prescription to push the efficiency envelope as far as possible. Further discussion of DEA in Facility Location is found in Chan 2000 under the "Spatial Separation" chapter.

Example
Solution of the above MIP suggests that facility 2 is inefficient and facilities 1 and 3 are efficient. Both x_1 and x_3 are unitary-valued. When one examines the optimal relaxed LP, the dual prices give us great insight into facility 2's inefficiency. Consider all facilities whose efficiency constraints have non-zero dual-prices. (In our example, facilities 1 and 3 have non-zero dual prices.) If we form the weighted average of the output vectors and input vectors for these facilities (using the absolute value of the dual price from each facility as the weight), we obtain the

following. Taking the dual variables from the weighting equations for each facility, namely Equations marked by @ and % above:

$$\text{Averaged output-vector} = 0.26094\,(9\ 4\ 16)^T + 0.66003\,(4\ 9\ 13)^T$$
$$= (4.98858\ 6.98403\ 12.75543)^T$$

$$\text{Averaged input-vector} = 0.26094\,(5\ 14)^T + 0.66003\,(7\ 12)^T = (5.92491\ 11.57352)^T$$

Suppose we create a composite facility by combining 0.26094 of facility 1 with 0.66003 of facility 3. The averaged output-vector tells us that the composite facility produces close to the same amount of outputs 1 and 2 as facility 2 (5 and 7), but the composite facility produces $(12.75543 - 10) = 2.75543$ more of output 3. From the averaged input-vector for the composite facility, we find that the composite facility uses less of each input than does facility 2. We now see exactly where facility 2 is inefficient. ∎

VIII. PRESCRIPTIVE TECHNIQUES IN LAND USE

Thus far, we have concentrated on discrete facility-location models, which lend themselves readily to prescriptive modeling. While the development is not as natural, it can be shown that prescriptive models can be constructed for land use planning as well. To show this, we will point out the linkage between the site location model of Equation 4.5 and a basic building block of land use models: the gravity model. It will be shown that when the spatial cost function of the gravity model assumes a particular form, it becomes the site location model mentioned above. The relationship is obvious and not-so-obvious. It is quite apparent once one recognizes that the decision process to site a facility is the same as that involved in making travel plans. It is not so obvious so far as historical development is concerned, since the two models come from very different professional groups who are not familiar with each other's work until recently.

A. Entropy Maximization Model

Take the doubly constrained gravity model discussed in Chapter 3 for allocating economic activities among available land (Wilson, Coelho, MacGill, and Williams 1981). Such a model can be derived from a mathematical program of the following form:

$$\text{Max} - \Sigma_i \Sigma_j v_{ij} \ln V_{ij} \tag{4.34}$$

subject to

$$\begin{aligned} \Sigma_i V_{ij} &= V_i \\ \Sigma_j V_{ij} &= V_j \\ \Sigma_i \Sigma_j V_{ij} C_{ij} &= C \\ V_{ij} &\geq 0. \end{aligned} \tag{4.35}$$

As pointed out in Section XII-B of Chapter 3, this is the well-publicized Stirling approximation of the entropy maximization model in which C is the total observed travel cost expended in the trip travel pattern $\{V_{ij}\}$. The optimal solution results in a most probable distribution of activities consistent with all known information. Such information is associated with the cost and constraints placed on the interactions generated from origin i and attracted to destination j.

The Lagrangian associated with this mathematical program is

$$L\,(\mathbf{V},\boldsymbol{\alpha},\boldsymbol{\gamma},\boldsymbol{\beta}) = -\Sigma_i\,\Sigma_j\,V_{ij}\ln V_{ij} + \Sigma_i\,\alpha_i\,(V_i - \Sigma_j\,V_{ij})$$
$$+\Sigma_j\,\gamma_j\,(V_i - \Sigma_j\,V_{ij}) + \beta\,(C - \Sigma_i\,\Sigma_j\,V_{ij}\,C_{ij}) \tag{4.36}$$

and L is to be maximized over non-negative values of the trip interactions V_{ij}. The maximization problem results in non-zero values for each V_{ij} for finite values of β. The optimal solutions

$$V_{ij}^* = \exp\,[-\,\alpha_i^* - \gamma_i^* - \beta^* C_{ij}]$$

result, where the optimal Lagrange multipliers $\boldsymbol{\alpha}$, $\boldsymbol{\beta}$, and $\boldsymbol{\gamma}$ are shown with an asterisk (*). By defining

$$k_i = \frac{\exp\,[-\,\alpha_i^*]}{V_i},\text{ where }l_j = \frac{\exp\,[-\,\gamma_j^*]}{V_j},$$

the doubly constrained gravity model

$$V_{ij} = k_i\,l_j\,V_i\,V_j\,F_{ij} = k_i\,l_j\,V_i\,V_j\,\exp\,(-\,\beta C_{ij}) \tag{4.37}$$

is obtained, as defined in Section XI-B in Chapter 3.

B. Relationship to the Allocation Model

As the parameter β tends to infinity, the model Equation 4.37 tends to the solution of the allocation model Equation 4.5 when the interactions x_{ij} are generalized from $\{0,1\}$ all-or-nothing assignment to any number instead. Correspondingly, the number of assignments at i is generalized to V_i and at j to V_j (Wilson et al. 1981). Introducing the non-negativity constraint $V_{ij} \geq 0$, the appropriate first order KKT conditions for the Lagrangian Equation 4.36 are given by the dual complementary slackness [Equation 4.18], dual feasibility [Equation 4.17], and non-negativity conditions below:

$$V_{ij}\frac{\delta L}{\delta V_{ij}} = 0,\qquad \frac{\delta L}{\delta V_{ij}} \leq 0,\qquad V_{ij} \geq 0 \tag{4.38}$$

and it is necessary to consider the possibility of boundary solutions. Because $\delta L/\delta V_{ij}$ is not defined at the boundary $V_{ij} = 0$, an appropriate limiting process must be invoked to solve Equation 4.38.

To show this, consider the following Lagrangian variant of the model defined by Equations 4.34 and 4.35:

$$\text{Max}_{V_{ij}} -\frac{1}{\beta^*}\Sigma_i\ \Sigma_j\ V_{ij}\ln V_{ij} - \Sigma_i\ \Sigma_j\ V_{ij}C_{ij} \tag{4.39}$$

subject to

$$\begin{aligned} \Sigma_j\ V_{ij} &= V_i \\ \Sigma_i\ V_{ij} &= V_j \\ V_{ij} &\geq 0 \end{aligned} \tag{4.40}$$

for the value of β^* which satisfies the travel cost constraint in the set of constraints Equation 4.35. The optimal Lagrange multipliers $\hat{\alpha}_i^*\hat{\gamma}_i^*$ of the resulting Equation 4.36, $V_{ij} = \exp\ [-\beta^*(\hat{\alpha}_i^* + \hat{\gamma}_j^* + C_{ij})]'$ are related to those associated with the entropy maximizing model by $\beta^{\cdot}\hat{\alpha}^* = \alpha^*$ and $\beta^*\hat{\gamma}^* = \gamma^*$. The model as defined by Equations 4.39 and 4.40 is now seen as a member of a family, parameterized by β^*. Variation in β^* in the entropy maximizing model corresponds to the variation of the total travel cost C. As β^* becomes very large the relative contribution of the dispersion term $\frac{1}{\beta^*}\Sigma_i\ \Sigma_j\ V_{ij}\ln V_{ijl}$ becomes small compared with that from interacting costs. In the limit as β^* tends to infinity, the nonlinear program becomes the linear allocation model associated with facility location. Thus it can be seen that a basic building block of land use model, the gravity model, is just a generalization of a basic building block of facility location, the linear allocation model.

C. Optimal Control Models of Spatial Interaction

All the prescriptive models discussed so far in this chapter are static models, in which the time element is explicitly absent. Spatial dynamics has become an issue of great interest in recent decades, mostly for its capacity to model the evolution of land use over time (Nijkamp and Reggiani 1992). More specifically, an optimal control model[5] based on a cumulative entropy-function is used to establish correspondence between macro/aggregate dynamic models for spatial interaction and micro/disaggregate choice models. All trips V_{ij} are time dependent in this case. In such a control problem, state variables can be defined as the number of trips generated from zone i; V_i. A control variable may be V_{ij}, suggesting the possibility of influencing spatial movements through such means as physical restraints or user-charge incentives. It can be seen also that a spatial interaction model corresponds to a logit model. This is explained in the "Activity Allocation and Derivation" chapter of Chan (2000).

A distinct advantage of the dynamic extension is its capability in examining order and chaos. A stochastic-control formulation further suggests that under the conditions of a catastrophe behavior, the stochastic disturbances do not affect evolution of the dramatic changes—an interesting result indeed. An important corollary question is whether there exist types of models capable of generating complexity in dynamic phenomena while retaining extreme simplicity in their structure. Another corollary question is whether it is possible to empirically verify the evolution through empirical time-series data. We will tackle these cogent questions in the "Chaos" and "Spatial-Temporal Information" chapters in Chan (2000).

IX. CONCLUDING REMARKS

We have reviewed in this chapter the pertinent prescriptive techniques used in facility location/land use models. To the extent possible, we try to illustrate with examples rather than formal theoretical development, leaving much of the algorithmic procedures to Appendix 1. Classic examples include the Herbert-Stevens model, the Steiner-Weber location problem, the p-median problem, and the gravity model. Within the limited space available, hopefully we have outlined the main ideas behind a variety of heuristic and analytical methods of optimization. Included in the survey is the central notion of convergence and duality that governs many of the algorithms we use and provide much of the insights we can gain from applying prescriptive models. We also begin to show the relationship between location/allocation models, location/routing models, and spatial interaction models through such formulations as the quadratic assignment problem and entropy maximization. We conclude with some of the newest techniques available. These include the DEA evaluation model, which rank orders alternative facility locations, assuming the most efficient use of each site. An optimal control formulation extends the static spatial-interaction model to yield the evolution pattern over time. Best of all, it shows the implications of judicious intervention policies. In short, this chapter paves the way for many of the topics that build upon these elementary tools.

ENDNOTES

[1] Solution algorithms are explained in Section III-D below and in Appendix 1.
[2] This is in accordance with the complementary slackness conditions in LP, where a non-zero dual variable value is associated with a tight primal constraint (that is a constraint satisfied strictly at equality or land is developed 100 percent). Reversely, a dual variable is zero-valued at constraints that are strict inequalities, which is the case in point when there is surplus land. The following section will elaborate on this point.
[3] See the satellite tracking station placement examples within the last sections of the "Facility Location" chapter in Chan (2000).
[4] A root arc corresponds to an artificial variable in regular LP, making up a full rank of m in a node-arc incidence matrix of rank m − 1. (See Appendix 1 for more details.)
[5] For an introduction to optimal control theory, please see Appendix 4. Also consult the dynamic programming example in Appendix 2.

REFERENCES

Ahuja, R. K.; Magnanti, T. L.; Orlin, J. B. (1993). *Network flows: Theory, algorithms, and applications.* Englewood Cliffs, New Jersey: Prentice-Hall.

Au, T.; Stelson, T. E. (1969). *Introduction to systems engineering: Deterministic models.* Reading, Massachusetts: Addison-Wesley.

Bartholomew, A.; Brown, S.; Chan, Y. (1990). Airport location problem: Initial formulation. Working Paper. Department of Operational Sciences. Air Force Institute of Technology. Wright-Patterson AFB, Ohio.

Bazaraa, M. S.; Jarvis, J. J.; Sherali, H. D. (1990). *Linear programming and network flow.* New York: Wiley.

Bersekas, D. P. (1991). *Linear network optimization: Algorithms and codes.* Cambridge, Massachusetts: MIT Press.

Brimberg, J.; Chen, R.; Chen, D. (1998). "Accelerating convergence in the Fermat-Weber location problem." *Operations Research Letters* 22:151–157.

Brooke, A.; Kendrick, D.; Meeraus, A. (1995). *GAMS: Release 2.25.* (Scientific Press Series). Boston: Boyd and Fraser.

Burkard, R. E. (1990). "Locations with spatial interactions: The quadratic assignment problem." In *Discrete facility location theory,* edited by P. Mirchandani and R. L. Francis. New York: Wiley-Interscience.

Cameron, D. M.; O'Brien, D. L.; Chan, Y. (1990). Airport location problem: Alternative formulation. Working Paper. Deptartment of Operational Sciences. Air Force Institute of Technology. Wright-Patterson AFB, Ohio.

Chan, Y. (2000). *Location, transport and land-use: Modeling spatial-temporal information.* New York: Springer-Verlag.

Chen, P. C.; Hansen, P.; Janmard, B.; Tuy, H. (1998). "Solution of the multisource Weber and conditional Weber problems by D.-C. programming." *Operations Research* 46, No. 4:548–562.

Claunch, E.; Goehring, S.; Chan, Y. (1962). Airport location problem: Three- and four-city cases. Working Paper. Deptartment of Operational Sciences. Air Force Institute of Technology. Wright-Patterson AFB, Ohio.

Francis, R. L.; McGinnis Jr., L. F.; White, J. A. (1992). *Facility layout and location: An analytical approach.* Englewood Cliffs, New Jersey: Prentice Hall.

Hamerslag, R.; Van Berkum, E. C.; Repolgle, M. A. (1993). A model to predict the influence of new railways and freeways on land use development. (Presentation Paper 930875). Paper presented at the 72nd annual meeting of the Transportation Research Board, Washington, D. C.

Hansen, P.; Mladenovic, N.; Taillard, E. (1998). "Heuristic solution of the multisource Weber problem as a p-median problem." *Operations Research Letters* 22:55–62.

Harry, D.; Farmer, R.; Chan, Y. (1995) Airport location problem: Comparison of algorithms. Working Paper. Department of Operational Sciences. Air Force Institute of Technology. Wright-Patterson AFB, Ohio.

Hillier, F. S.; Lieberman, G. J. (1986). *Introduction to operations research.* San Francisco, California: Holden-Day.

Hillier, F. S.; Lieberman, G. J. (1990). *Introduction to mathematical programming.* New York: McGraw-Hill.

Hurter, A. P.; Martinich, J. S. (1989). *Facility location and the theory of production.* Boston: Kluwer Academic Press.

Kent, B.; Bare, B. B.; Field, R. C.; Radley, G. A. (1991) "Natural resource land management planning using large-scale linear programs: The USDA forest experience with FORPLAN." *Operations Research* 39:13–27.

Lasdon, L.; Warren, A. (1986) *GINO: General interactive optimizer.* (Scientific Press Series). Femcraftvillage, Massachusetts: Boyd and Fraser.

Leonard, R.; McDaniel, P.; Nelson, R. (1991). Airport location problem. Working Paper. Deptartment of Operational Sciences. Air Force Institute of Technology. Wright-Patterson AFB, Ohio.

Magnanti, T.; Wong, R. T. (1990). "Decomposition methods for facility location problems." In *Discrete facility location theory,* edited by Mirchandani, P. and Francis, R. L. New York: Wiley-Interscience.

McEachin, R.; Taylor, G.; Chan, Y. (1992). Airport location problem: Linear and nonlinear formulations and solutions. Working Paper. Department of Operational Sciences. Air Force Institute of Technology. Wright-Patterson AFB, Ohio.

Nijkamp, P.; Reggiani, A. (1992). *Interaction, evolution and chaos in space.* Berlin and New York: Springer-Verlag.

Raulerson, J.; Bowyer, R.; Zornick, J.; Chan, Y. (1994). The Herbert-Stevens residential model. Working Paper. Department of Operational Sciences. Air Force Institute of Technology. Wright-Patterson AFB, Ohio.

Ravindran, A.; Philips, D. T.; Solberg, J. (1987). *Operations research: Principles and practices,* 2nd ed. New York: Wiley.

Russell, D. M.; Wang, R.; Berkhin, P. (1992). *HiQ reference manual.* Los Gatos, California: Bimillennium Corporation.

SAS Institute Inc. (1991). *Changes and enhancements to SAS/OR software,* (Release 6.07). Preliminary documentation. Cary, North Carolina.

SAS Institute Inc. (1991). *SAS/OR user's guide.* (Version 5). Cary, North Carolina.

Thomas, P. C. (1995). Using locational and data envelopment analysis models to site municipal solid waste facilities. Master's Thesis. Department of Environmental Engineering and Management. Air Force Institute of Technology. Wright-Patterson AFB, Ohio.

Vernon, R.; Lanning, J.; Chan, Y. (1992). The residential allocation prediction model: A linear-programming/network-flow problem. Working Paper. Department of Operational Sciences. Air Force Institute of Technology. Wright-Patterson AFB, Ohio.

Wilson, A. G.; Coelho, J. D.; Macgill, S. M.; Williams, H. C. W. L. (1981). *Optimization in locational and transport analysis.* Chichester, England: Wiley.

Winston, W. L. (1991). *Operations research: Applications and algorithms,* 3rd ed. Belmont, California: Duxbury Press.

5

Multicriteria Decision Making

"I have hardly ever known a mathematician who was capable of reasoning."
Plato

While most of us have practiced **multicriteria decision making (MCDM)** in our business and personal life, it is relatively recent that the knowledge base for such a procedure has been organized and quantified into a formal set of methodologies. In some ways, it represents the amalgamation of descriptive and prescriptive models in the context of behavioral sciences. Descriptive models were defined in Chapter 3 to include such techniques as the conventional use of simulation and statistics that replicate the real world scenario. Prescriptive models, on the other hand, refer to procedures, such as optimization, which go one step further to arrive at a desirable course of action. We will show in this chapter that through the integration of both descriptive and prescriptive procedures, the role of quantitative analysis becomes clear in a pluralistic society with many interests and aspirations.

First, we try to capture the fundamental ideas behind MCDM, particularly as it is applied toward location decisions (Massam 1988). Because of page limitations, this chapter may not be as comprehensive a treatment as the excellent methodological texts such as Chankong and Haimes (1983), Goichoechea, Hansen, and Duckstein (1982), Seo and Sakawa (1988), Yu (1985), and Zelany (1982). The main ideas behind these comprehensive treatments, however, are hopefully reported in a summarized format, with liberal examples drawn from location decisions to bring alive the concepts. This document also differs from others in introducing MCDM from a prescriptive framework, rather than a descriptive framework. Unlike most books on this subject, we approach the subject from **multicriteria optimization,** while most texts start with decision analysis. An advantage of this approach is that a deterministic view of the world is adopted in the beginning. Only at a later stage do we assume knowledge of probabilistic concepts. This is judged to be more intuitive in our opinion. A second advantage is that we tend to view the MCDM process as a whole very early in the discussion. Thus the basic concepts are put immediately at the front end. While this may violate the scientific tradition of axiomatic development, we hope the style is more compatible with the application oriented standpoint, in which the question of "what MCDM does for me?" is answered in the first few pages. Such a way of thinking appears to be endorsed by Goichoechea et al. (1982) and Kirkwood (1997).

I. PREFERENCE STRUCTURE

We like to introduce MCDM in terms of the X, Y', and Z' space. X is often referred to as the **alternative set** or the **decision space.** Y' is the criterion set or the outcome space, and Z' is the preference structure. For example, sites A and B are military bases that are candidates for closure. A decision is to be made to close one of the two. Thus in the X-space, we defined a vector of two binary variables $\mathbf{x} = (x_1, x_2)$, where the binary variables take on the unitary value when base A and B are closed, and zero otherwise. The impact of a base closure may be measured in terms of a peace dividend and the defense posture in case of war, as represented by the two entries of the vector $f(\mathbf{x}) = (f_1(\mathbf{x}), f_2(\mathbf{x}))$ respectively. This criteria set can be written compactly as $\mathbf{f} = (y_1', y_2')$, where y_1' may be quantified in terms of dollar cost savings in peace time, and y_2' is readiness in case of war, measured, for instance, by the number of emergencies reachable within a travel radius (i.e., geographic coverage in hours of flight time). The vector $\mathbf{y} = (y_1', y_2')$ in this case is defined in the Y' space. Out of the y_is, the alternative with the best figure of merit $\mathbf{y}'^*$ is picked by the decision maker(s) according to some preference structure Z'. Let us say that it corresponds to alternative $\mathbf{x}^*$, which is the vector $(1,0)$ when $\mathbf{y}'^*$ is mapped back to the X space via the inverse function $\mathbf{x}^* = f^{-1}(\mathbf{y}'^*)$, indicating that base A, rather than B, should be closed. All MCDM problems evolve around such mapping between X, Y' and Z' space. We hasten to add that while the mapping between X and Y' is relatively straightforward, the mapping between Y' and Z' (or the preference structure), tends to tax the limitation of the state of the art.

A. The Importance of Preference Structure

Quantifying the preference structure is the most taxing part of MCDM. It is in fact the heart and soul of the modeling procedure. To illustrate the Z space, let us elaborate on the above example and further suggest that of the two bases slated for closure, A is a scientific base while B is a tactical base, meaning that B is closely linked to combat while A is somewhat removed from it. Let us further consider the decisions in the context of two different philosophical outlooks: pessimistic and optimistic. Here we show the payoffs of the two alternative decisions—or utility measures by which we have put cost savings and geographic coverage in the same scale. The common scale ranges in this case from 0 (worst) to 100 (best):

	Criteria set f: Utility if there is			
	peace $f_1(\mathbf{x})$	war $f_2(\mathbf{x})$	min payoff	max payoff $\mathbf{y}'$
Alternative Set X				
base A closure ($x_1 = 1$)	50	90	(50)	(90)
base B closure ($x_2 = 1$)	100	30	(30)	(100)
	$\overset{\uparrow}{Y'}$			

The data show that if base A is closed, it will look ill-advised (50 points in a 100) if peace is maintained. The reason is that the scientific know-how generated from base A, aside from being a long-term defense investment, could have spinoffs in the civilian economy. In conducting a war on a real-time basis, however, it is much more astute to keep the tactical base B while scientific base A appears to have little bearing upon the day-to-day fighting. Considering these tradeoffs, the question is again: Should A or B be closed—assuming only one of the two bases is to be closed?

A pessimistic decision maker will plan for the worst and will look at the worst possible outcome corresponding to each of the two decisions. This is between closing A or B, with a minimum payoff of 50 and 30 respectively. In other words, should A be closed, the decision maker wants to anticipate the worst result or the minimum payoffs that correspond to a peace outcome. Should B be closed, on the other hand, the decision maker would like to plan for the war outcome. On the other hand, an optimistic decision maker will plan for the best possible outcomes or maximum payoffs, war if A is closed and peace if B is closed, corresponding to scores of 90 and 100 respectively. Both decision makers are trying to make the best of the situation, or maximizing the respective payoffs. The pessimist (who is going to maximize the minimum payoffs) will close A while the optimist (who is going to maximize the maximum payoffs) will close B. In other words, based on the same set of data, different preference structures will lead toward an entirely different decision.

Suppose now we have three locations to consider—A, B, and C—instead of two. Let us rank them in order of preference. In a general case, the ranking can be compiled for base closing, for warehouse location, or for siting of a manufacturing plant. Let us say PQR Corporation is considering three states for building a new manufacturing plant. The candidate sites in States 1, 2, or 3 are evaluated by three criteria (Yu 1985):

Scores

Criteria	$\mathbf{y}^1$	$\mathbf{y}^2$	$\mathbf{y}^3$
Labor force	6	7	8
Transport	7	8	6
Tax breaks	8	6	7

where each score y_{ij} is between 0 and 10, with 10 being the most desirable. Each score is specified for candidate site j on criterion i. For example, on labor-force availability, State 3 ranks the highest, State 2 ranks second, and State 1 is last. Here $Y' = \{\mathbf{y}^1, \mathbf{y}^2, \mathbf{y}^3\}$, with the score for each State $\mathbf{y}^1 = (6, 7, 8)^T$, $\mathbf{y}^2 = (7, 8, 6)^T$ and $\mathbf{y}^3 = (8, 6, 7)^T$.

Now suppose PQR Corporation adopts the following preference structure arbitrarily. It decides that a State is preferred to another if at least in one out of three criteria, the State is leading by 2 or more points, and in the remaining two criteria, the State is not inferior to the others by more than 1 point. Put it in another way, State 1 is preferred to State 2, or $\mathbf{y}^1 > \mathbf{y}^2$, if and only if State 1 offers at least one criterion i in which $y_i^1 - y_i^2 \geq 2$ and $y_k^2 - y_k^1 < 2$ for the remaining criteria $\{k \neq i\}$. One can now picture the resulting ranking as a cyclic relationship: $\mathbf{y}^1 > \mathbf{y}^2$, $\mathbf{y}^2 > \mathbf{y}^3$ and $\mathbf{y}^3 > \mathbf{y}^1$ (instead of $\mathbf{y}^1 > \mathbf{y}^3$ as one would expect from transitivity)[1]. Aside from non-transitivity, this example emphasizes the important role preference structure plays in ranking alternatives. It is conceivable that if another preference structure be adopted, transitivity may result.

B. Paired versus Simultaneous Comparison

Instead of a pairwise comparison between alternatives, another way is to simultaneously compare the alternatives against an ideal, where an ideal point has the best components in the outcome space. For example, one wishes to rank the four alternatives pictured in Figure 5.1, where the two-criteria measurements of an alternative—labor availability and transport—are displayed. Thus site A has a labor force availability rating of 42 out of a best of 100 and a transportation index of 49. The ideal score is 91 for both labor availability and transport defining an ideal alternative X^* of (91, 91). If preferences are measured in terms of the Euclidean beeline distance displacement from the ideal, then the order of preference is $A > B > D > C$ as one can visually inspect from Figure 5.1. Here ranking is obtained by a simultaneous comparison among all alternatives (Zelany 1982).

Assume that an increase in shipping rates has caused a shift from D: (14, 91) to D':(14, 56), or transportation is now no longer as convenient as before. This shifts the ideal point X^* to (91, 56), as shown in Figure 5.2. The new ranking now—again based on Euclidean-distance displacement—is $B > A > C > D'$. Notice the preference ranking between A and B has been reversed as a result, as has C and D'. Suppose another site with the same characteristics as the original site D is now being considered. Call this site E. Introducing site E:(14, 91) into the

Figure 5.1   IDEAL SITE AND RANKING AMONG LOCATIONS

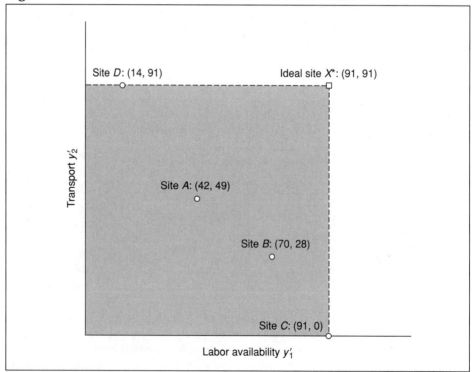

Figure 5.2   DISPLACEMENT OF THE IDEAL

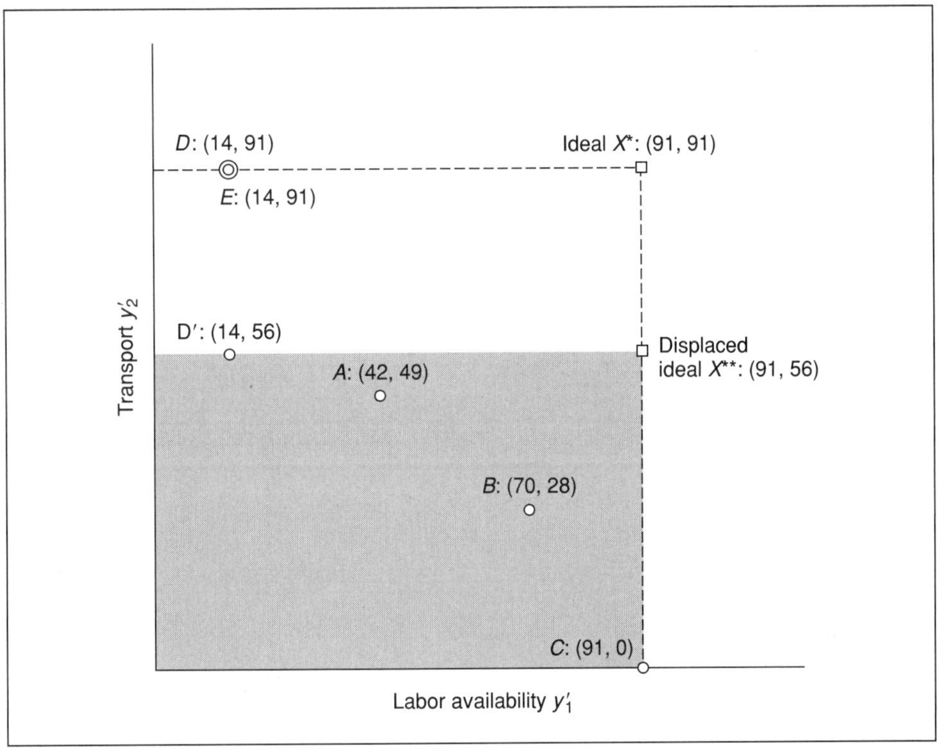

SOURCE: Zelany (1982). Reprinted with permission.

candidate set changes the ranking to $A > B > E > D' > C$. A nonoptimal alternative A has been made optimal by adding E, the replacement for D, back to the feasible set X. This is somewhat contradictory to traditional decision analysis, which assumes a definite utility associated with each alternative, and the alternative with a higher utility is always preferred.

Instead of continuing with a simultaneous comparison among the alternatives, we will now return to paired comparisons, just to show another point. In comparing A with B, the decision maker uses X^* as a point of reference. A is compared with X^* and B is compared with X^*, each separately. The comparison between A and B is an indirect consequence of this process. Now consider the very first case once more. We shall explore a particular triad of options, say $\{A, B, D\}$, shown in Figure 5.3. After comparing between B and D, one concludes that $D > B$. Next, observe that between A and D, $A > D$. Now that D has been exhaustively compared with A and B, it can be discarded from consideration ("out of sight, out of mind"). This leads to the pairwise comparison between A and B, resulting in $B > A$ because the removal of D has induced the displacement of X^* to X^{**}. The net result is: $A > D$, $D > B$, and $B > A$, which—similar to the plant-location example—is again not transitive. If we start the process with the paired comparison between A-D, it will result in $A > D$. We then establish that $A > B$ by comparing A and B, and finally $D > B$, resulting in a fully transitive relationship $A > D > B$. This shows the order we ask questions in a survey can bias the results.

Figure 5.3 SEQUENTIAL CHOICE AMONG THREE ALTERNATIVES

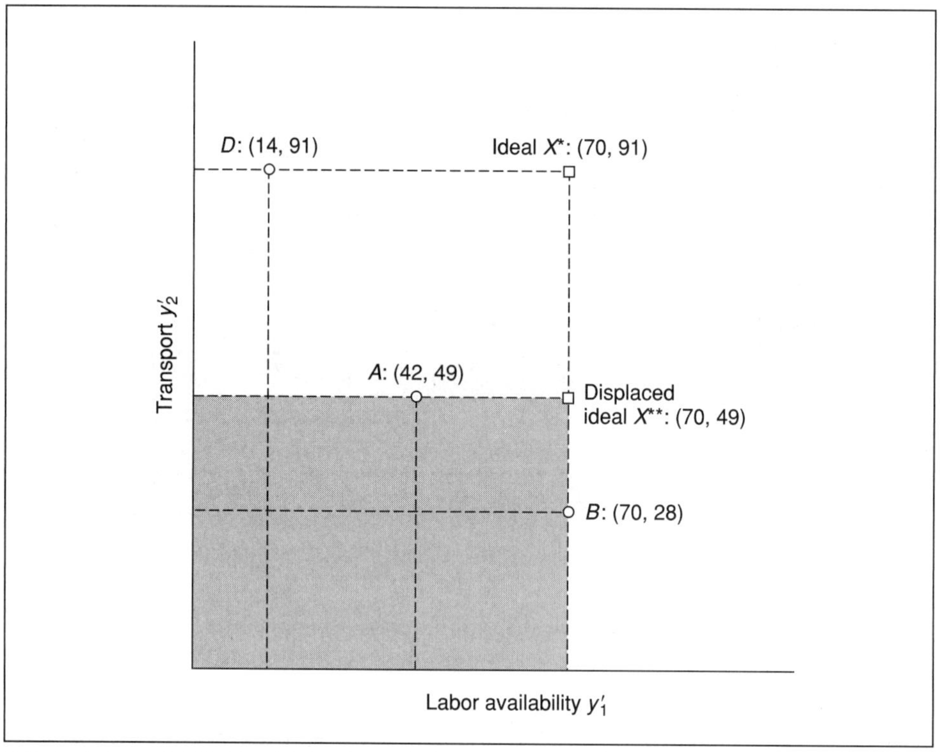

SOURCE: Zelany (1982). Reprinted with permission.

It can be seen that, depending on the sequential process assessing preference among alternatives, the resulting ordering is different. In situations involving sequential displacements of the ideal, the order of preference can be changed significantly. There is also a possibility of intransitivity, when a sequence of pairwise comparisons are performed. Thus the preference structure, which is often represented by the utility or value function $v(\mathbf{y}')$, is in fact the most difficult procedure in MCDM. Depending on the way one valuates the outcomes, such as comparing them against a current ideal or viewing them in an optimistic or pessimistic light, the ranking of alternatives can be very different.

II. SIMPLE ORDERING

Given the difficulties with preference structures, are there any guidelines and procedures ready for making decisions? The answer is a resounding yes, and that is where a discussion such as the current one may become useful to the readers, not only in giving warnings about the danger of performing analyses incorrectly, but also in providing guidelines for the correct procedures.

The most straightforward case of MCDM is simple ordering among alternatives, where no preference structure is required. In other words, we work strictly in the X and Y' space, requiring no resolution among incompatible criteria in the Z space. In other words, we dispense with the "apples versus oranges" tradeoff. It also avoids the pitfalls associated with many surveys based on paired comparisons in which the order in which questions are asked results in very different rankings among alternatives, as we pointed out earlier. It turns out that using simple ordering, one can readily rule out a large percentage of the alternatives, leaving only very few to consider. As such, this is a very useful analysis technique on many occasions.

Assuming that we all agree upon "the more the merrier" philosophy, the concept of dominance then comes in naturally as a simple ordering tool. In the above example, if site A is better than site B in all the criteria: labor availability, transportation and tax breaks, few would disagree with the choice of A over B. Such a dominance relationship among alternatives is often referred to as **Pareto preference.** An outcome **y'** is said to be Pareto optimal if and only if it is a non-dominated solution (or it is an N-point). A Pareto optimal solution is also called an **efficient, noninferior, non-dominated,** or **admissible solution.** For example, the ideal solutions illustrated in Figure 5.3 and Figure 5.1 are nondominated solutions because they are equal or better than all the other alternatives in the two criteria considered: labor availability and transportation. Straightforward as it may appear, the concept of dominance is a rather robust tool. The set of N-points offers preference determination under conditions of ignorance (about how to compare incommensurate attributes such as y_1' and y_2'.) Thus there is no requirement to make difficult tradeoffs. In Figure 5.1, Figure 5.2, and Figure 5.3, for example, regardless of the exact value of utility/value function definition, $v(y_1', y_2')$, its maximum will be the N-point X^*: $v^*(y_1'^*, y_2'^*) \geq v_i(y_{1_i}', y_{2_i}')$, where $y_1'^* \geq y_{1_i}'$ and $y_2'^* \geq y_{2_i}'$.

It makes sense to explore Y' and characterize its set of N-points before engaging in the assessment of v. It is possible an alternative will emerge such as shown in Figure 5.4, which is often known as the conflict-free solution. Put it in the context of Figure 5.3, Figure 5.2, and Figure 5.1, such a "win-win" solution represents the "ideal." Even though such situations seldom arise, it is well-advised to recognize them when they appear, since it saves a good deal of negotiation and hard work.

Figure 5.4   CONFLICT-FREE SOLUTION

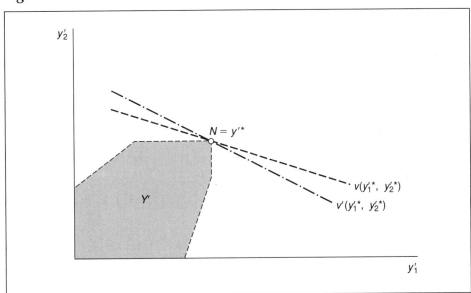

III. EXPLORING THE EFFICIENT FRONTIER

Perhaps one of the best ways to explore the efficient frontier and to illustrate the X, Y' and Z' space of MCDM is still through a **multicriteria linear program** MCLP. Consider this example (Yu 1985): A corporation is deciding how much company housing to provide the employees (x_1) and the amount of 'commercial housing' from the free market (x_2)—with the amount of housing measured in square footage. The corporation in this case has to balance between welfare to the employees f_1 and the corporate goal f_2—both of which the company wants to maximize: Max $f_1(x_1, x_2) = 4x_1 - x_2$ and Max $f_2(x_1, x_2) = 2x_1 + 5x_2$. Here, the first criterion is the employee welfare, which is enhanced by the availability of company housing, since it is cheaper to the employees than commercial housing. The second is the corporate goal, which refers to the bottom line, wherein commercial housing is less expensive on the company's pocketbook. Obviously the two criteria are not necessarily congruous and hard decisions have to be made regarding the trade-offs between these incompatible objectives.

Now only a certain amount of housing subsidy is obligated by the company to each employee for use in both company and commercial housing. A company and commercial dwelling unit has different costs associated with them, with commercial housing one and a half times more expensive for the family pocketbook: $2x_1 + 3x_2 \le 12$. Only a certain amount of commercial housing is available within commuting distance from the company: $x_2 \le 3$. It is corporate policy to at least provide an amount of company housing somewhat commensurate with the commercial housing available—at one third of the footage: $3x_1 - x_2 \ge 0$. Finally, nonnegativity applies to the decision variables since they represent footage of housing: $x_1, x_2 \ge 0$.

In order to solve this multicriteria LP, a proven method is to convert one of the two criterion functions, say $f_2(x)$ into a constraint, which is added to the existing constraint set $x \in X$:

$$\text{Max } f_1(x_1, x_2) = 4x_1 - x_2$$
$$\text{s.t. } x \in X,$$
$$f_2(x_1, x_2) = -2x_1 + 5x_2 \ge r_2$$

where r_2 is a satisficing level for f_2, say the acceptable company profit. By graphically minimizing and maximizing f_2 over X, the feasible region defined by the original constraint set, we find $-12 \le f_2(x) \le 13$. Solving the above LP with r_2 varying from -12 to 13, we can find all N-points:

r_2	(x_1, x_2)	(f_1, f_2)
-12	A (6, 0)	A' (24, −12)
-7	B (5.06, 0.63)	B' (19.63, −7)
-2	C (4.13, 1.25)	C' (15.25, −2)
3	D (3.19, 1.88)	D' (10.88, 3)
8	E (2.25, 2.50)	E' (6.50, 8)
12	G (1.50, 3)	G' (3, 12)
13	F' (1, 3)	F' (1, 13)

as illustrated in the X-space (Figure 5.5) and the Y'-space. Notice by virtue of the computation shown in tabular form above, the (f_1, f_2) column and the corresponding points in the figure, A–F in the X-space and A'–F' in the Y-space constitutes an efficient frontier which dominates over all points $y' \in Y'$. Such an

Figure 5.5   THE DECISION AND OUTCOME SPACE

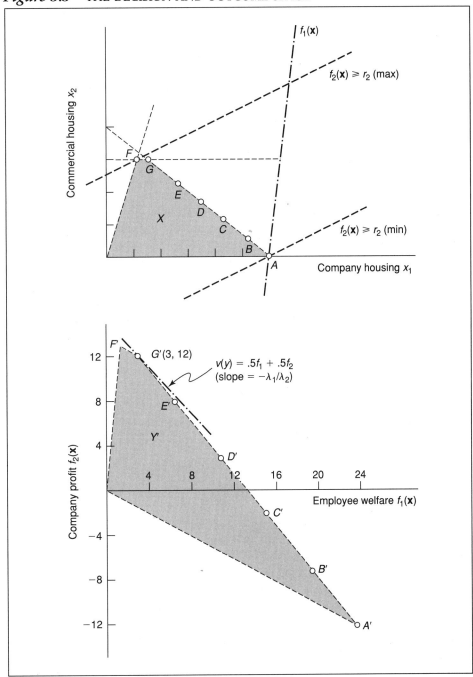

SOURCE: Yu (1985). Reprinted with permission.

N-set is generated by the **constraint reduced feasible region method,** where one of the two criterion functions has been eliminated by converting it into a constraint (Steuer 1986).

A logical question to ask at this point is: What (λ'_1, λ'_2) would make A', B', ... , or F' a maximum point of $v(\mathbf{f}) = \lambda'_1 f'_1 + \lambda'_2 f'_2$ over Y'? Consider the existing maximum $\mathbf{G}'$ for instance. All λ's satisfying $\boldsymbol{\lambda}'(\mathbf{y}' - \mathbf{G}') \geq 0$, $\mathbf{y}' \in Y'$, or $(\lambda'_1, \lambda'_2)\begin{bmatrix} y'_1 - 3 \\ y'_2 - 12 \end{bmatrix} \leq 0$, can—among other conditions—shift the maximum point of $\boldsymbol{\lambda}'\mathbf{f}$, or $(\lambda'_1, \lambda'_2)\begin{bmatrix} f_1 \\ f_2 \end{bmatrix}$ to F. Specifically, the weights in $\boldsymbol{\lambda}'$ must satisfy $(y'_2 - 12)/(y'_1 - 3) \leq -\lambda'_1/\lambda'_2$, to cause a shift, where the y's are the points within the feasible region Y', or the set of feasible outcomes. One can see the similarity between this and the optimality test used in regular LP.

Let us denote these conditions as the **weight cone** $\Lambda(G')$. The table below illustrates examples of $\Lambda(G)$ and $\Lambda(F)$, given $\lambda'_1 + \lambda'_2 = 1$ by convention:

λ'_1	λ'_2	y'^*	f_1^*	f_2^*
0.5	0.5	G'	3	12
0.333	0.667	$F'-G'$	1–3	12–13
0	1	F'	1	13
.	.	.	.	.
.	.	.	.	.
.	.	.	.	.

Another way of thinking about this concept is to examine a linear, additive value-function $v(\mathbf{f}) = \lambda'_1 f_1 + \lambda'_2 f_2$, which is rotated with a pivot at G', the table above simply records the "break points" at which an extreme point such as G' is no longer the "optimal" with regard to the value function under consideration, as the weights in the value function change. One can think of this tradeoff—or some kind of sensitivity analysis—between λ'_1 and λ'_2 taking place in the Z'-space.

In the context of this housing example, the multicriteria LP (or MCLP) sketches out the entire efficient frontier consisting of the illustrative points A' through G', which are members of the N-set. Irrespective of the valuation placed upon employee welfare vis-a-vis company profit, the nondominated solutions are the only ones worthy of further examination. When more weight is placed upon the employee's welfare, a solution such as A' will make sense, which when translated back to the decision space X, means that the company would provide all employee housing. On the other hand, when company profit is valued over employee welfare, F' and F will become the viable solution, and commercial housing will provide the bulk of the living quarters for the employees. A solution such as F, for instance, shows 3 units of commercial housing and one unit of company housing. The criteria $f_1(\mathbf{x})$ and $f_2(\mathbf{x})$, which are realized as outcomes y'_1 and y'_2, are shown as A' and F' which are $(24, -12)$ and $(1, 13)$ respectively. Thus the company suffers a loss if it places too much emphasis on employee welfare. On the other hand, it makes a large profit if the bottom line is closely guarded.

IV. MULTICRITERIA SIMPLEX (MC-SIMPLEX)

While the above example illustrates the basic concepts behind MCLP, formalization of the above problem is necessary for solving realistic size problems. Before we provide a solution algorithm, some terms need to be defined: $X = \{\mathbf{x} \in R^n \mid {}^A\mathbf{x} \leq \mathbf{b}, \mathbf{x} \geq \mathbf{0}\}$, where $\overline{A}$ is a matrix of order $m \times n$. In other words, $\mathbf{x}$ vectors are n-dimensional nonnegative real numbers within the region defined by the constraints ${}^A x \leq \mathbf{b}$. Let $\mathbf{C}$ be a q by n matrix with its kth row denoted by $\mathbf{c}^k$ so that $c^k\mathbf{x}$, $k = 1, \ldots, q$, is the kth criterion function. The criteria space is thus given by $Y' = \{\mathbf{Cx} \mid \mathbf{x} \in X\}$. The objective function of the mathematical program now looks like max $z = \boldsymbol{\lambda}^T \mathbf{Cx}$, which is sometimes referred to as vector optimization. Thus in the previous example,

$$\overline{\mathbf{A}} = \begin{bmatrix} 2 & 3 \\ 0 & 1 \\ -3 & 1 \end{bmatrix}, \mathbf{b} = (12, 3, 0)^T, \mathbf{C} = \begin{bmatrix} 4 & -3 \\ -2 & 5 \end{bmatrix} \text{ and } z = \lambda'_1(4x_1 - x_2) + \lambda'_2(-2x_1 + 5x_2). \text{ Indeed,}$$

many MCLP's have been solved using such a combined objective function z, which in effect assumes an additive-linear-value function $v(\mathbf{f}) = \lambda'_1 f_1 + \lambda'_2$. By changing the weights λ', the efficient frontier is sketched out, as already alluded to above. Such a **weighted-sum method** has its intuitive appeal, and can be made operational quite readily in many analysis offices inasmuch as it needs only a regular LP computer code. Its generality, however, is more questionable, since it may miss efficient solutions in integer-programming problems where decision variables are required to be discrete—a point we will come back to in sequel.

A. The MC-Simplex Algorithm

To formally solve an MCLP, we need an MC-simplex algorithm. For the purpose of this discussion, the best is to illustrate the basic concepts of this algorithm through a numerical example, and then refer the reader to some software that can take care of the computation on a day-to-day level. Consider the following MCLP (Zelany 1982):

$$\text{Max } f_1(\mathbf{x}) = 5x_1 + 20x_2$$
$$\text{Max } f_2(\mathbf{x}) = 23x_1 + 32x_2$$
$$\text{s.t. } 10x_1 + 6x_2 \leq 2500$$
$$5x_1 + 10x_2 \leq 2000.$$

with the normal nonnegativity constraints on the decision variables. For comparison and illustration purposes, graphical solution to the problem is given in Figure 5.6 which will be explained via the following algebraic procedures.

As a readily operational procedure, we can form a tableau corresponding to $z = \lambda'^T \mathbf{f}$, or that we solve the LP starting out with the combined objective function for a particular value of λ', with $0 \leq \lambda_i \leq 1$. By working with the following tableau:

current basis J_k	x_1	x_2	x_3	x_4	RHS
	$5\lambda'_1 - 23\lambda'_2$	$-20\lambda'_1 - 32\lambda'_2$	0	0	0
x_3	10	6	1	0	2500
x_4	5	10	0	1	2000

Figure 5.6   GRAPHICAL SOLUTION OF A MULTICRITERIA LINEAR PROGRAM IN X AND Y' SPACE

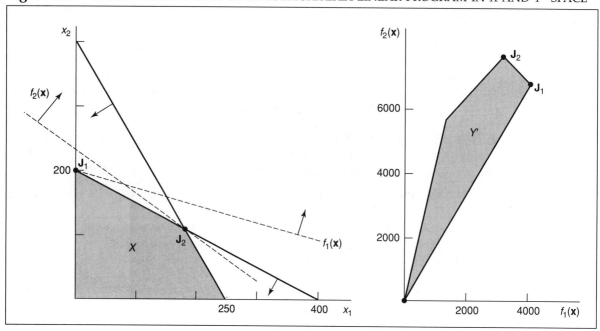

It can be seen from the combined $(z_j - c_j)$s in the first row why this is called the weighted-sum approach.

Now instead of solving this as a single objective LP, the MC-simplex calls for writing the first line as two lines and carrying out the simplex procedure, say the primal simplex. Thus the first line of the tableau now looks like:

criterion	−5	−20	0	0	0
rows	−23	−32	0	0	0

We are at a position to carry out the pivoting procedures.[2] Since the second variable x_2 will benefit both of the criterion functions more so than x_1, it is introduced into the basis. Notice this is an example of **dominance**: x_2 dominates over x_1. The result of this pivot is shown below:

criterion	5	0	0	2	4000
rows	−7	0	0	$3^1/_5$	6400
x_3	7	0	1	$-^3/_5$	1300
x_2	$1/_2$	1	0	$1/_{10}$	200

It can be seen that the entry rules of a regular simplex are modified to include dominance. As another example, if the criteria row looks like

0	0	0	2	4000
-7	0	0	$3\frac{1}{5}$	6400

instead of the above, introducing x_1 into the basis—thus effecting an alternate solution—would not hurt the first criterion function, but will improve the second by 7 per unit of increase in x_1. This implies that the existing solution with respect to the first criterion function is a dominated solution—that it is inferior to the alternate solution with x_1 in the basis. We call this alternate solution an efficient solution, N-point, or Pareto optimum. In fact, the definition of a Pareto optimum is that it gains at the expense of nobody else.

Now back to the original problem, the solution after the first pivot is an N-point $\mathbf{J}_1$, in that one of the criteria rows, the $(z_j - c_j)$s for $f_1(\mathbf{x})$, are all nonnegative; meaning that on the first criterion, the solution $\mathbf{J}_1$ dominates. Continuing the simplex, the other N-point obtained is:

criterion	0	0	$-5/7$	$17/7$	$21500/7$
rows	0	0	1	$13/5$	7700
x_1	1	0	$1/7$	$-3/35$	$1300/7$
x_2	0	1	$-1/14$	$1/7$	$750/7$

where the second criterion function, $f_2(\mathbf{x})$, is optimized, at the expense of the first. This example contrasts nicely with the made-up criteria rows as shown above where *both* criteria can be improved by another pivot—or at least not degraded by the pivot. It can be shown that any additional pivot performed on the tableau corresponding to the second N-point will revert back to the tableau corresponding to the first N-point. Thus we have established all N-points, defined once again as the extreme points where at least one of the criteria is optimized, for a given minimum value of the other criterion, r_k. The collection of N-points have the property of dominating over all other points in Y.

If there are two possible pivot columns to choose from, then the concept of dominance again comes into play—the column that will improve $f_k(\mathbf{x})$ the most and degrade $f'_k(\mathbf{x})$ the least $(k \neq k')$ is the one to use. For example, consider the following criteria rows:

criterion	5	0	0	6	4000
rows	-7	0	0	$-3\frac{1}{5}$	6400

It is clear that x_1, rather than x_4, should be pivoted in, since the introduction of x_1 will degrade $f_1(\mathbf{x})$ the least, but will improve $f_2(\mathbf{x})$ the most. On the other hand, the following criteria rows show a 'tie' between x'_1 and x_4 as the pivoting column, inasmuch as x_1 will benefit $f_2(\mathbf{x})$ at the expense of $f_1(\mathbf{x})$ while x_4 will upgrade $f_1(\mathbf{x})$ at the expense of $f_2(\mathbf{x})$:

criterion	5	0	0	-2	4000
rows	-7	0	0	$3\frac{1}{5}$	6400

This latter example is similar to finding the J_1–J_2, Pareto optimum in the original example.

Referring back to the first pivot tableau containing the combined objective-function, it can be seen that solution J_1 or x^1 will stay optimal if the z_j-c_j entries remain nonnegative—the typical optimality condition for simplex tableaux:

$$z_1(\lambda') = 5\lambda_1' - 7\lambda_2' \geq 0$$
$$z_2(\lambda') = 2\lambda_1' + (3\text{-}1/5)\lambda'2 \geq 0$$

Alternatively,

$$\lambda(J_1) = \{\boldsymbol{\lambda}' | \lambda\tau \begin{bmatrix} 5\,0\,0\,2 \\ -7\,0\,0\,3\frac{1}{5} \end{bmatrix} \geq 0\}.$$

Similarly, we can write

$$\lambda(J_2) = \{\boldsymbol{\lambda}' | \boldsymbol{\lambda}'^T \begin{bmatrix} 0\,0\,-\frac{5}{7}\,\frac{17}{7} \\ 0\,0\,1\,\frac{13}{5} \end{bmatrix} \geq 0$$

It is often convenient to display these two conditions graphically. Figure 5.7 shows the plot of the λ-space (or what we have been referred to as the Z'-space). This figure illustrates a few cogent points. For example, it clearly shows that there is at least one point $\lambda' = (7/12, 5/12)^T$ common to both $\Lambda(J_1)$ and $\Lambda(J_2)$, where z reaches its maximum at both x_1 and x_2. With this λ',

$$z(x^1) = (5\lambda_1' + 23\lambda_2')x_1 + (20\lambda_1' + 32\lambda_2')x_2 =$$
$$[5(7/12) + 23(5/12)]0 + [20(7/12) + 32(5/12)]200 = 5000.$$

Similarly, $z(x^2) = 5000$ as expected. In the same figure is shown the values of λ that will make the basis J_1 optimal and the range that will make J_2 optimal, as defined by the nonnegativity requirements outlined above. We call $\Lambda(J_1)$ and $\Lambda(J_2)$ the weight-cones. This two-dimensional case is quite graphic, introducing the concepts that can easily be carried over to higher dimensional cases.

The numerical and graphical explanation of the solution procedure has one advantage. It shows quite clearly that such a multiplex algorithm for multicriteria LP is nothing but an extension of the single objective simplex algorithm. Theoretically, one can solve multiplex models that are just as large as the largest single objective models that may be solved (Ignizio and Cavalier 1994). Obviously, the computation associated with higher dimensional cases is best performed by specialized computer software. To date, such software is still in the developmental stage. An example software is distributed under the name of ADBASE (Steuer 1986), which has been extended by Shields and Chan (1991). Interactive visualization programs have also been implemented, such as one by

Figure 5.7   THE z'-SPACE CONTAINING THE WEIGHT CONES

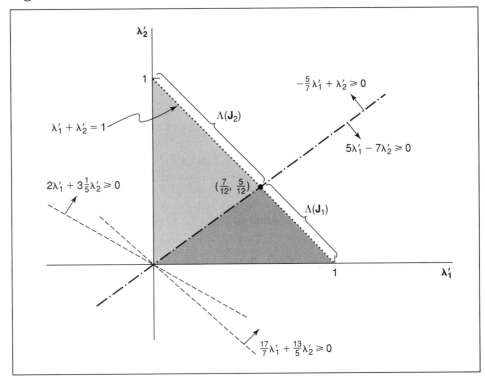

Korhonen and Laakso (1986), marketed under the trade name VIG, which solves nonlinear programming problems in addition to LP. Such interactive techniques represent an exciting area of research for these types of multicriteria optimization problems (Buchanan and Daellenbach 1987).

B. Nonlinear and Integer Programming

The ideas introduced in MCLP can be carried over to nonlinear programming (NLP) and integer programming (IP) as well. Consider the illustration in Figure 5.8, where a nonlinear multicriteria optimization problem is shown. Although somewhat transparent from the figure, it needs to be reemphasized that not all convex combinations of the extreme points in the efficient solutions $N_{ex} = \{A, B, C\}$ can be non-dominated, and that the optimal solution can be any N-point, not just the extreme points N_{ex}. It is not necessarily an N_{ex}-point. An example of the latter case is shown in point D in the nonlinear programming illustration in Figure 5.8. These two facts are further driven home by an integer program, where discrete points, rather than the feasible Y' region as shown, are the candidates for the optimum. In the case of IP, the efficient points may be unsupported in that they are not on the efficient frontier A-B-C in general. Another complication is that to locate these efficient N-points, the constraint reduced feasible region method as described in the introductory section on MCLP is mandatory. The weighted-sum approach, which combines the criterion functions into one, will end up missing N-points on the frontier, as illustrated by the point E.

Figure 5.8   A MORE GENERAL MULTICRITERIA OPTIMIZATION PROBLEM

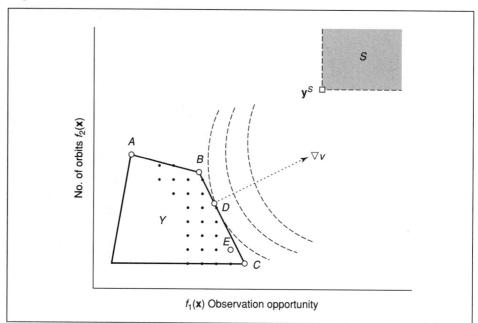

At D, the value function v represents the tradeoff of criterion y'_1 with another y'_2. The correct weights would cause the composite-z gradient $\Delta_v^T = \left(\dfrac{\partial v}{\partial y'_1}, \dfrac{\partial v}{\partial y'_2} \right)$ to point in a direction normal to BC. This concept is akin to linear programming (LP), in which the gradient of the objective-function z is indicated by the vector $\mathbf{c}$, in other words, $\nabla^T z = \left(\dfrac{\partial z}{\partial x_1}, \dfrac{\partial z}{\partial x_2}, ..., \dfrac{\partial z}{\partial x_n} \right) = (c_1, c_2, ..., c_n)$. Take the tangent at point D: $v = \lambda'_1 y'_1 + \lambda'_2 y'_2 = constant$. The slope of the tangent bears resemblance to the relationship derived for the linear additive value function:
where

$$\frac{\partial v}{\partial y'_1} = \lambda'_1, \ \frac{\partial v}{\partial y'_2} = \lambda'_2 \tag{5.1}$$

hence

$$\frac{\lambda'_1}{\lambda'_2} = \left(\frac{\partial v}{\partial y'_1} \Big/ \frac{\partial v}{\partial y'_2} \right) \tag{5.2}$$

In multicriteria nonlinear optimization, solution procedures are by and large built upon this gradient concept when the criterion functions and/or value functions are no longer linear. This concept can be further extended to the case when the constraints are nonlinear in addition (Li and Wang 1994).

In general, the state of the art in multicriteria nonlinear and integer programming is not at all as developed as MCLP, which in and of itself is already complex. In an MCLP problem of any size, the N-set is often huge, so much so that wading through the set is no trivial task. Imagine now that we proceed to the integer and nonlinear cases, which further introduce complexity of their own to the problem (Karaivanova et al. 1992; White 1990). However, real world problems of facility location, however, often belong to the integer and nonlinear cases. We will illustrate each of these subsequently.

C. An Interactive Frank-Wolfe Example

A prominent way of performing **multicriteria nonlinear programming** is the interactive Frank-Wolfe approach. Building upon the piecewise linear concept outlined in Chapter 4, this approach assumes the existence of an underlying preference function, but never actually requires this preference function to be identified explicitly. The basic idea is that even if the decision maker cannot specify an overall preference function, he or she can provide local information regarding a preference at a particular situation. The iterative approach moves from an initial feasible solution toward optimal solution by finding the direction of steepest ascent and the optimal step size in that direction. Again, explicit knowledge of the overall preference function is not essential. Only local information concerning the preference of the decision maker is required, and this, in turn, is sufficient to determine the direction and step size.

Refer to the airport location problem discussed in Chapter 4. The airport location problem calls for the selection of a site between the two cities of Cincinnati and Dayton, Ohio—with populations of two and one million respectively—so that both travel time and noise impact are minimized. To apply the F-W method to this problem, two criterion functions, travel cost $f_1(\mathbf{x})$ and noise impact $f_2(\mathbf{x})$, are known. The following condition must exist: all $f_i(\mathbf{x})$, $i = 1, 2, ...,$ q, are convex and continuously differentiable in their respective domains, and the constraints form a convex and **compact set** (i.e., a contained region to prevent unboundedness). Here, $q = 2$, and $f_1(\mathbf{x})$ is the travel time and $f_2(\mathbf{x})$ is the noise. By formulating the airport location problem as minimizing travel and noise, we rewrite the two-city case as

$$\text{Min } v(f_1(\mathbf{x}), f_2(\mathbf{x})) = v(2x_1 + x_2, 2x_1^{-2} + x_2^{-2})$$
$$\text{s.t.} \quad x_1 + x_2 \geq 60$$
$$x_i \geq 0 \quad (i = 1, 2)$$

where x_1 is the distance from Cincinnati and x_2 is the distance from Dayton. Taking the gradient of value function $v(\mathbf{f}) = \lambda_1' f_1(\mathbf{x}) + \lambda_2' f_2(\mathbf{x})$ yields

$$\nabla_x v(\mathbf{f}) = \frac{\partial v}{\partial f_1} \begin{bmatrix} \frac{\partial f_1}{\partial x_1} \\ \frac{\partial f_1}{\partial x_2} \end{bmatrix} + \frac{\partial v}{\partial f_2} \begin{bmatrix} \frac{\partial f_2}{\partial x_1} \\ \frac{\partial f_2}{\partial x_2} \end{bmatrix} \tag{5.3}$$

which is evaluated at the sequence of locations $\mathbf{x}^0, \mathbf{x}^1, \mathbf{x}^2, ...$ and so forth. The initial gradient at the halfway point between Cincinnati and Dayton $\mathbf{x}^0 = (30, 30)^T$, for example, is

$$\nabla_x v(f(\mathbf{x}^0)) = \lambda_1' \begin{bmatrix} 2 \\ 1 \end{bmatrix} + \lambda_2' \begin{bmatrix} -4x_1^{-3} \\ -2x_2^{-3} \end{bmatrix}_{x^0 = (30, 30)} = \begin{bmatrix} 2\lambda_1' - 0.00015\lambda_2' \\ 1\lambda_1' - 0.00007\lambda_2' \end{bmatrix} \quad (5.4)$$

and the LP to be solved is simply

$$\text{Min } \nabla_x^T v\, (f(\mathbf{x}_0))\, \mathbf{x} = \text{Min } (2\lambda_1' - 0.00015\lambda_2', \lambda_1' - 0.00007\lambda_2') \begin{bmatrix} x_1 \\ x_2 \end{bmatrix} \quad (5.5)$$
$$\mathbf{x} \in X \qquad\qquad \mathbf{x} \in X$$

where $\mathbf{x} \in X$ is a shorthand notation for $x_1 + x_2 \geq 60$ and $x_i \geq 0$. Suppose the decision maker decides that the **marginal rate of substitution** is fifty-fifty, or $\lambda'/\lambda' = -1$, through local linearized indifference curves such as the one shown in Figure 5.9. In this figure, the decision maker is asked about the increment of travel cost $\Delta f_1(\mathbf{x})$ for which he or she is willing to trade off against a decrement of aircraft noise $\Delta f_2(\mathbf{x})$. The slope of this indifference curve is precisely $-\lambda_1'/\lambda_2'$, which in the case of equal weights assumes the value of -1. Without loss of generality, let us set $\lambda_1' = 1$, which means $\lambda_2' = 1$ in this example. (Here $\lambda_1' + \lambda_2' \neq 1$.) Now by the following LP, the optimal solution $\mathbf{x}^* = (0, 60)^T$ is determined: Min $\{2x_1 + x_2 \mid x_1 + x_2 \geq 60; x_i \geq 0\}$. Thus at this initial iteration of the algorithm we are moving the airport toward Cincinnati from the halfway point between the two cities according to the steepest ascent direction $\mathbf{d}^0 = \mathbf{x}^* - \mathbf{x}^0$, where $\mathbf{x}^0 = (30, 30)^T$ and $\mathbf{x}^* = (0, 60)^T$ or $\mathbf{d}^0 = (-30, 30)^T$.

The decision maker now determines the step size α to move along this direction $\mathbf{x}^0 + \alpha^0\mathbf{d}^0$. The decision maker, assisted by tabular or graphic displays of the function $f(\mathbf{x}^0 + \alpha^0\mathbf{d}^0) = (f_1(\mathbf{x}^0 + \alpha^0\mathbf{d}^0), f_2(\mathbf{x}^0 + \alpha^0\mathbf{d}^0))$, determines the step size α^0 between 0 and 1. One possible way to obtain the best step size α is to display the values for the two criterion functions $f_i(\mathbf{x}^0 + \alpha^0\mathbf{d}^0)$ for $i = 1$ and 2 as a function of α over the selected values of α in a tabular or graphic way. Example of the curves are shown in Figure 5.9. The decision maker then determines a value of α for the most preferred values of the corresponding criterion functions. In short, the following optimization problem is solved: Min $v(f(\mathbf{x}^0 + \alpha\mathbf{d}^0)$. Read off the $f_1(\mathbf{x})$ and
$0 \leq \alpha \leq 1$
$f_2(\mathbf{x})$ values on Figure 5.10. From these f_is, the λ_1' and λ_2' values can be determined in Figure 5.9 by reading off the slope λ_1'/λ_2' at $(f_1(\mathbf{x}_0), f_1(\mathbf{x}_0))$. The λs facilitate the next iteration. Suppose $\lambda^0 = 0.5$. We are now at $\mathbf{x}^1 = \mathbf{x}^0 + \alpha^0\mathbf{d}^0 = (30, 30)^T + 0.5(-30, 30)^T = (15, 45)^T$ and the iterations continue until the incremental ascent of the preference function v is minuscule, as with most hill-climbing algorithms as explained in Chapter 4.

Assuming equal weights among the two criterion functions and a constant step size of 0.5, a series of iterations were performed, with the following results (Staats and Chan 1994):

Iteration k	airport location $\mathbf{x}^k$
0	$(30, 30)^T$
1	$(15, 45)^T$
2	$(7.5, 52.5)^T$
3	$(3.75, 56.25)^T$
4	$(1.875, 58.125)^T$
5	$(0.9375, 59.0625)^T$
6	$(30.46875, 29.53125)^T$
.	.
.	.

Figure 5.9   DETERMINATION OF MARGINAL RATE OF SUBSTITUTION

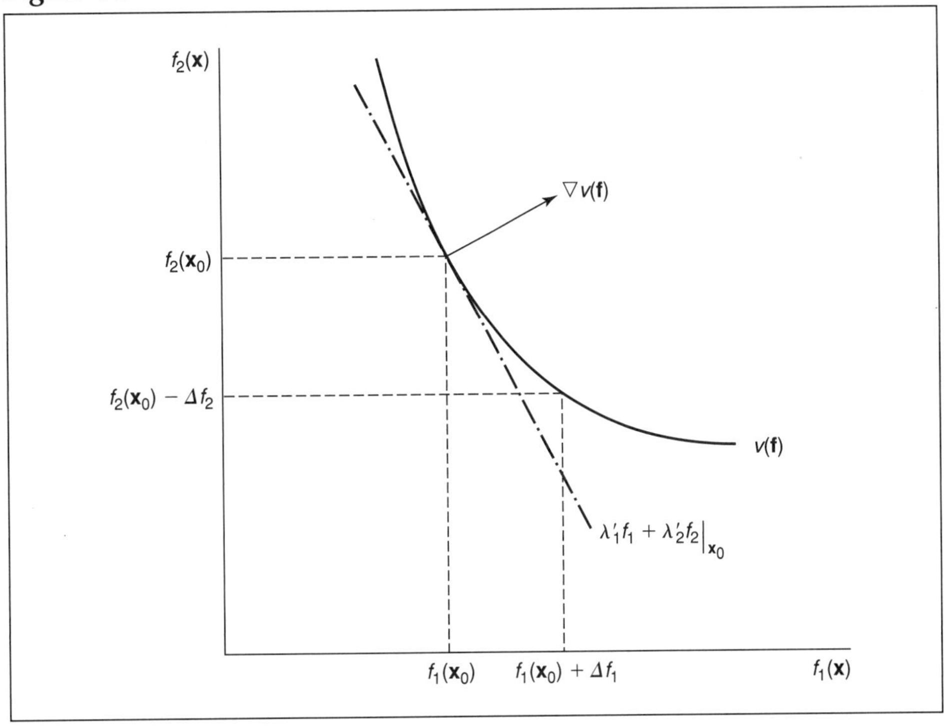

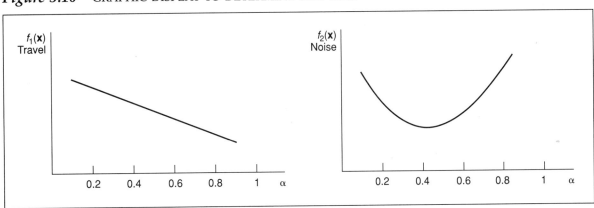

It can be seen that while the airport steadily moves toward Cincinnati in the first five iterations, starting at iteration 6, there is a direction reversal toward Dayton. If we make subsequent iterations, it will begin moving toward Cincinnati again. However, there is a limit to this westward movement—namely at a point east of the previous reversal point $(0.9375, 59.0625)^T$. This point is further from Cincinnati and closer to Dayton, or $x_1 > 0.9375$ and $x_2 < 59.0625$. As this point subsequently moves east toward Dayton again, there is once again a limit to its movement. In this case, it falls short of $(30.46875, 29.53125)$. Thus the airport location bounces back and forth within a shrinking interval, eventually converging toward a final

Figure 5.10   GRAPHIC DISPLAY TO DETERMINE STEP SIZE

equilibrium point. This point can be determined by a shortcut method for this case of equal weights ($\lambda_1' = \lambda_2' = 1$). This is the point where the objective function of the LP as shown in Equation 5.5 is minimized for both x_1 and x_2, which occurs when the gradient $\nabla_x v$ is $(1, -1)^T$, or when the coefficient for x_1 is the same as x_2 in the objective function: $2\lambda_1' + \lambda_2'(-4/x_1^2) = \lambda_1' + \lambda_2'(-2/x_2^3)$. Thus for $\lambda_1' = \lambda_2' = 1$, we solve the equation set consisting of $2 - 4/x_1^3 = 1 - 2/x_2^3$ and $x_1 + x_2 = 60$, where $x_1 + x_2 \geq 60$ has to be satisfied at strict equality. This equation set yields $x_1 = 1.5873$ and $x_2 = 58.4127$. This says that for equal weights placed on the two criteria, the decision maker is indifferent about noise and travel at an airport located at (1.5873, 58.4127), or about 1.6 miles (2.56 km) outside Cincinnati.

It can be shown that the above iterative procedure is a special case of a more unified interactive multiple objective programming procedure (Gardiner and Steuer 1993). This airport example has been solved previously in Chapter 4. The solution obtained here is consistent with and close to the previous solution. Because of the peculiarity of the criterion functions $f_1(\mathbf{x})$ and $f_2(\mathbf{x})$, the gradient of $f_2(\mathbf{x})$, $\begin{bmatrix} -0.00015 \\ -0.00007 \end{bmatrix}$, is small for the $\mathbf{x}^0$ chosen in comparison with $f_1(\mathbf{x})$, $\begin{bmatrix} 2 \\ 1 \end{bmatrix}$. For this reason, the example does not fully illustrate the importance of properly determining λ_1' vis-a-vis λ_2' well. Perhaps a better example is to solve the equivalent problem

$$\text{Max } v(f_1(\mathbf{x}), f_2(\mathbf{x})) = v(-2x_1 - x_2, 2x_1^2 + x_2^2)$$
$$\text{s.t.} \qquad x_1 + x_2 \geq 60$$
$$x_i \geq 0 \quad (i = 1,2)$$

where $f_1(\mathbf{x})$ and $f_2(\mathbf{x})$ are concave and a maximization objective replaces a minimization. This will illustrate the interactive F-W procedure better, when the decision maker participates—in a more significant way—in determining the direction of climb and the step size. Most interestingly, the solution to this new problem is diametrically opposite to the previous minimization formulation, given the same λ' and α values, and given that the noise function $f_2(\mathbf{x})$ so formulated is different from the one used in the previous $f_2(\mathbf{x})$. In this case, the airport is located at $(59.50, 0.5)^T$ or half a mile (0.8 km) outside Dayton.

Readers interested in more detailed discussions of interactive multi-objective programming can consult Seo and Sakawa (1988) and Gardiner and Steuer (1993). It is apparent from the above example that interactive programming of this sort is highly numerical in nature. Aside from convergence issues, different functional forms may give rise to drastically different solutions, as one can see clearly from the airport-location problem above. In practice, however, such an extreme result is unlikely to occur. Remember that the above results are built upon the rather indefensible assumption of $\alpha = 0.5$ and $\lambda_1' = \lambda_2' = 1$ throughout the iterations. This simplifying assumption is made mainly for our computational convenience. In fact, the entire foundation of interactive procedures of this sort is to explore the decision maker's revealed preferences, guided by charts and tables, at various situations. Correspondingly, his or her reactions, as reflected by values of α and λ's—are expected to be different at each iteration. Convergence in this case is obtained not so much from numerical properties as it is from the decision-maker's behavioral changes. The behavioral change from one iteration to another, reflecting sharpening of the decision maker's focus, should more than compensate for the dilemma that apparently arose from different functional forms for the travel and noise criterion functions $f_1(x)$ and $f_2(x)$, leading toward a consistent location for the common airport between Cincinnati and Dayton.

D. Comments

The most challenging (and interesting) part of MCDM is still the Z'-space, where the criteria are to be traded against one another. Generally, there have to be at least two criteria for decision making to occur, since a single criterion means simply "take it from the top" on a uni-dimensional scale–a laborious exercise at best. In spite of the seemingly elaborate effort made above, let us conclude this section by reiterating an important point. It is necessary to have good measurement units for the metric used. Advanced computational algorithms are also necessary for efficient search, but they are not sufficient for decision making in the presence of multiple criteria. The crux of MCDM lies in the Z'-space, making participatory, interactive techniques so much more attractive as a solution tool.

We have illustrated the interactive procedure for NLP above using the F-W method. A body of knowledge exists for evaluating a finite set of discrete alternatives. One such procedure is ELECTRE (Roy 1977), which is a robust technique that does not necessarily assume transitivity of preferences. Of the variants to the method, Chankong and Haimes (1983) recommended the sequential (interactive) elimination procedure inasmuch as it furnishes opportunities to gain greater understanding and appreciation of what is being done, and more importantly, what levels of risk are involved when eliminating certain alternatives. Chan (2000) discusses this method in the "Facility Location" chapter, but he uses a deterministic, outranking elimination procedure.

V. GOAL SETTING

The type of problems we have been solving above are often referred to as **goal seeking,** where "the more the merrier" is the modus operandi. **Goal setting,** on the other hand, refers to an environment in which there is a standard against which alternatives can be compared. For example, in locating a satellite tracking station, there are minimum standards one sets for observational opportunity and coverage of the various orbits. A station location either satisfies this minimum standard or it does not. Thus goal setting is defined as the procedure of identifying a satisficing set S such that, whenever the decision outcome is an element of S, the decision maker will be happy and satisfied and is assumed to have reached the optimal solution.

A. Compromise Programming

We now refer to the example in Figure 5.8 again. Assuming the decision maker defines his satisficing set by $S = \{(y_1', y_2') \mid y_1' \geq 20, y_2' \geq 10\}$, meaning that the minimal standard for observational opportunity is 20 (in say a maximum of 100) and the station needs to track at least 10 orbits. The graphical depiction clearly shows that no satisficing solutions exist, since the region Y' and S do not intersect. The logical solution is to look for the second best, similar to the examples shown in Figures 5.1, 5.2 and 5.3, where deviation from the threshold standard $\mathbf{y}^s = (20, 10)^T$ is to be minimized here. The goal-setting (GS) program now looks like

$$\begin{aligned} v &= \min\,(d_1 + d_2) \\ f_1(\mathbf{x}) + d_1 &\geq 20 \\ f_2(\mathbf{x}) + d_2 &\geq 10 \end{aligned}$$

with the feasible region $\mathbf{x} \in X$ as defined previously for this example. Notice here v assumes a particular goal setting value function, in which the two criteria, $f_1(\mathbf{x})$ and $f_2(\mathbf{x})$ (and hence the deviational variables, d_1 and d_2) are in different units. The total displacement from S, defined here as the simple sum (rather than say the weighted sum) of the two deviations, is minimized (Lai et al. 1994).

There is no station locations that can satisfy the minimal standard, or $S \cap Y' = \varnothing$ and $v > 0$. To find a satisficing solution, we must restructure the feasible region X in the decision space, change the criterion vector $\mathbf{f}$ and/or alter the standards that define S. In other words, we must either examine more locations for the tracking station, or improve the tracking capabilities for an existing site, or our expectation for observational opportunities and orbit coverage must be lowered. If X and **f** are fairly fixed, we may need to change S. For example, the goals of $y_1' \geq 20$ and $y_2' \geq 10$ must come down. This is another example of an interactive process between the decision maker and the analyst.

Thus far, we have ignored the precise way used to measure deviation. We simply stated that it is the sum of two different scales, one measured in the horizontal and the other in the vertical dimension of the outcome space. This **Manhattan metric** is distinctly different from the Euclidian metric used in Figures 5.1, 5.2, and 5.3 (Saber and Ravindran 1996). The natural question then is: what is the proper measure?

B. Deviational Measures

Different problems dictate the use of different deviational measures, since the way the compromise is measured defines the value function. It so turns out that both of these deviation metrics—Manhattan and Euclidean—can be accommodated within the l_p-metric, which also includes the weights placed on y_1' and y_2'. The metric assumes the functional form of

$$r'(\mathbf{y}'; p, \mathbf{w}') = \left\| \mathbf{y}' - \mathbf{y}'^{*} \right\|_{p,\mathbf{w}'} = \left[\Sigma_i \mathbf{w}'^{p}_i \left| \mathbf{y}_1' - \mathbf{y}_i' \right|^{p} \right]^{1/p} = \left[\Sigma_i \mathbf{w}'^{p}_i d_i^p \right]^{1/p} (1 \leq p \leq \infty)$$

In the above expression, it can be seen that it reduces to the Manhattan and Euclidean metrics when $p = 1$ and 2 respectively. In the case of l_∞-metric, the above expression is simply $\max_i \left[w_i' d_1 \right]$ When $\mathbf{w}'$ is not specified, the usual convention is to assume $w_i' = 1$ for all i's.

In general, as p is increased from 1 to 2, the emphasis shifts toward the more prominent of the Ith $\mathbf{y}'$ component. In the extreme case when $p = \infty$, only the more prominent component counts, with the less prominent, albeit just a shade less prominent, totally overwhelmed. We refer to this case as the totally noncompensatory situation. Using the example above about satellite tracking stations, it may turn out that $f_2(\mathbf{x})$, the number of orbits covered, may be the criterion that the decision maker really cares about whenever there is a site that has an $f_2(\mathbf{x})$ advantage over $f_1(\mathbf{x})$ (the number of observational opportunities). This phenomenon should then be modeled as a compromise program with an l_∞-metric.

In location models, the l_∞-metric is of particular interest. If y'_1 and y'_2 represent distances demands 1 and 2 are from a facility, it can be shown that it can be modeled as a special case of a compromise program with the l_∞-metric. In this case $r'(\mathbf{y}'; \infty, 1)$ boils down to the further of the two distances. In emergency facility location, such as the siting of a fire station, for example, it is common to minimize the furthest distance away, so that the worst situation can be covered—in case a fire breaks out at the furthest house from the station. Again, such a way of fighting fire reflects a philosophical viewpoint of caring for the most geographically disadvantaged household in the community. An equally valid figure of merit may be to minimize the average response time to all the households in the area. If this is the case, the Manhattan metric is definitely a viable measure in a city with a square grid street system. It can further be argued that the weights should not be equal among all parts of town, that highly populated areas should receive more attention than the wilderness. Thus the weights w come in besides the parameter p. The geometric interpretation of l_∞-metric is found in Chan (2000) under the "Facility Location" chapter.

C. Goal-Setting Example

To close out the discussion on goal setting, a numerical example may be in order. Consider the compromise program:

$$
\begin{aligned}
\text{Goal 1:}\quad & f_1(\mathbf{x}) = x_1 \geq 8 \\
\text{Goal 2:}\quad & f_2(\mathbf{x}) = x_2 \geq 9 \\
\text{s.t.}\quad & 3x_1 + x_2 \leq 24 \\
& 2x_1 + 7x_2 \leq 35
\end{aligned}
$$

all xs positive.

(a) Graph the X space, Y' space and the satisficing set S.

The identical X and Y' spaces are sketched in Figure 5.11, complete with the satisficing set S and the extreme points of X and Y: $\mathbf{J}_1 = (0, 5)$, $\mathbf{J}_2 = (7, 3)$, and $\mathbf{J}_3 = (8, 0)^T$.

(b) Assuming both goals at the same priority level, specify the point in both X and Y' that minimizes the maximum deviation.

This corresponds to minimizing the l_∞-metric or more specifically Min $[r'(\mathbf{y}'; \infty, \mathbf{1})$ = Max $\{(8 - y'_1), (9 - y'_2)\}$ = max $(d_1, d_2)]$. It can be verified that this amounts to point $N = (28/9, 37/9)$, which is obtained by drawing a square box centered at $(8,9)$ that barely touches $(\mathbf{J}_1, \mathbf{J}_2)$. The square box is the contour of the l_∞-norm, whose horizontal edge is the locus of $d_1 > d_2$ and the vertical $d_2 > d_1$. The watershed is the 45^0 diagonal.

(c) Specify the point in both X and Y' space that solves the preemptive model with the goals ranked in the order in which they are listed. What is the solution point if we reverse the priorities?

Figure 5.11   GOAL-SETTING EXAMPLE

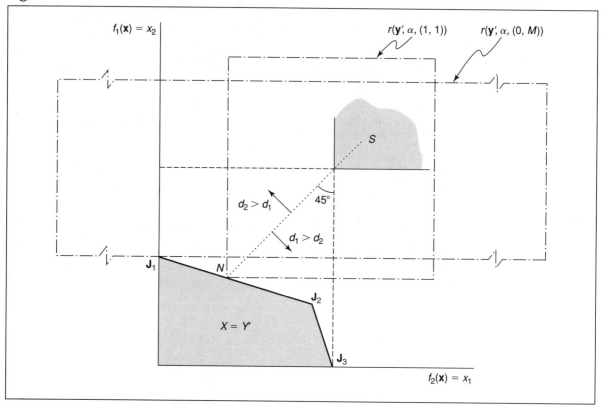

The lexicographic ordering between the first and second goal, or $f_1(\mathbf{x})$ and $f_2(\mathbf{x})$ respectively, can be thought of as placing a very large weight M on $f_1(\mathbf{x})$ in comparison to $f_2(\mathbf{x})$. This amounts to Min $[r'(\mathbf{y}'; \infty, (M, 0) = \text{Max}\{M(8 - \mathbf{y}_1'), 0(9 - \mathbf{y}_2')\} = \text{Max } (8 - y_1')]$. This yields the non-dominated point $\mathbf{J}_3$. By reversing the order, we write Min $[r'(\mathbf{y}', \infty, (0, M) = \text{Max}\{0(8 - \mathbf{y}_1'), M(9 - \mathbf{y}_2')\} = \text{Max } (9 - y_2')]$, resulting in another non-dominated point $\mathbf{J}_1$. Again, these two points can be located geometrically by drawing two boxes, with the first one greatly elongated vertically, while the second elongated horizontally, touching X or Y' at $\mathbf{J}_3$ and $\mathbf{J}_1$ respectively.

Now imagine gradually shifting the weight between the two extreme values of 0 and M. A series of boxes can be drawn between $\mathbf{J}_1$ and $\mathbf{J}_3$ that sketch out the entire efficient frontier (or N-set) of X and Y', with the intermediate point N corresponding to equal weights among f_1 and f_2. In other words, minimizing the l_∞-metric as a quasi-convex function can generate any non-dominated solution point between $\mathbf{J}_1$ and $\mathbf{J}_3$, including $\mathbf{J}_2$. Notice applying the l_∞-metric to the example shown in Figure 5.8 will similarly sketch out the N-set along A-B-C.

VI. VALUE FUNCTIONS

Thus far, we have been alluding to value functions through our discussion of the Z'-space and the deviational measures such as the l_p-norm. We also have been promulgating the fact that the heart of MCDM lies in dealing with the value function. We certainly have arrayed some useful tidbits about MCDM without facing the hard problem! Maybe it is time for us to face the central issue by giving a formal definition: A value function $v(\mathbf{y}')$ on Y' is a metric that alternative 1 is preferred to 2, or $\mathbf{y}^1 > \mathbf{y}^2$, if and only if $v(\mathbf{y}^1) > v(\mathbf{y}^2)$. Utility function is a special case when uncertainty in the outcomes y_i's is involved, through which the risk perception of a decision maker is elicited. While value functions can be used as an ordinal scale to rank order alternatives, utility function is a cardinal scale to compare the merit of one alternative to another. For the purpose of this book, we use the generic term value function to include both ordinal and cardinal measurements. More will be said about this later.

A. Additive versus Multiplicative Form

A value function represents revealed preference information. A multi-attribute value function $v(\mathbf{y}'_1, ..., \mathbf{y}'_3)$ assumes some kind of attribute independence among y_i's. If the random variables y_i's ($i = 1, ..., q$) are statistically independent, the joint density function

$$P(y'_1, ..., y'_n) = P(y'_q)...P(y'_q) \tag{5.6}$$

where $P(y_i)$ is the marginal (univariate) density function of y'_i. Hence the assessment of a q-dimensional function is simplified to that of q one-dimensional functions: $v(y'_1, ..., y'_q) = g[v_1(y'_1), ..., v_q(y'_q)]$. Notice the cross terms $v(y'_1, y'_2)$, $v(y'_1, y'_3)$, and so forth, are absent in the $g(.)$ function. Thus the independence property greatly simplifies the determination of multi-attribute value functions. As will be shown, additive value functions look like $w_1v_1(y'_1) + w_2v_2(y'_2) + w_3v_3(y'_3)$, while multiplicative value functions look like $w_1v_1(y'_1) + w_2v_2(y'_2) + w_3v_3(y'_3) + kw_1w_2v_1(y'_1)v_2(y'_2) + kw_1w_3v_1(y'_1)v_3(y'_3) + kw_2w_3v_2(y'_2)v_3(y'_3) + k^2w_1w_2w_3v_1(y'_1)v_2(y'_2)v_3(y'_3)$, where ws are generalized weights, and ks are scaling constants (Sainfort and Deichtman 1996). In previous examples of the value function, we have assumed $v_i(y'_i) = y'_i$, which greatly simplifies the expressions for both additive and multiplicative value functions.

Value functions v_is are scaled from 0 to 1, and the role of k in a multiplicative value function is to assure that this compound value function v will also assume value in the interval 0 to 1. If $w_i = \lambda'_i$, or $\Sigma_i w_i = 1$, then $k = 0$, and the multiplicative form reduces to the additive form. Only when $w_i \neq \lambda'_i$ does $k \neq 0$, hence the need for a multiplicative value function. While there are a whole host of equations to represent a value function, the advantage of the additive and multiplicative forms is that most conceivable shapes of the function can be accommodated within the order of q calibration constants ws and ks.

Again, we like to emphasize that the ranking among alternatives will be the same whether an additive or multiplicative function is used, as long as they are strategically equivalent. The units of a value function—to be differentiated now from a utility function—have no intrinsic meaning inasmuch as we are dealing with ordinal ranking. Any value function can be transformed by a monotonic function, and the result will represent exactly the same preferences as before. An example is $v(y'_1, y'_2) = y'_1 y'_2$. Taking a logarithm of the value function will yield another value function $v'(y'_1, y'_2) = (\ln y'_1) + (\ln y'_2)$. Both v and v' will give the same preference ranking among alternatives since a logarithmic function is a monotonic transformation. The time we worry about the exact functional form is when cardinal measurements, sometimes referred to as the preference intensity, are required. It also follows from this discussion that the establishment of a value function implies transitivity of preference. Value functions, where only ordinality is involved, are not measured directly. This is a consequence of the observation that quite different functions may be strategically equivalent and that units of value have no intrinsic meaning as mentioned. For the purpose of evaluation, the information contained in a value function can be obtained indirectly, and this is done by estimating the decision maker's revealed preferences at sampled situations. An example is in the interactive Frank-Wolfe method discussed earlier, where the exact form of the value function is not known, only attribute and criterion tradeoffs at local situations are assessed.

B. Univariate Utility Function Construction

Measurement of utility for an alternative is based on the axiom

$$E(v(\mathbf{y}')) = \Sigma_j P^j v(\mathbf{y}^1) \tag{5.7}$$

This says that the utility of an alternative is the sum of the utility of each of the possible outcomes $\mathbf{y}^j$ weighted by the probability of occurrence P^j. Consider a decision maker (DM) playing a lottery. The DM's choices in this lottery can be illustrated in a decision tree, which is shown in Figure 5.12. If the probability of losing the lottery is P, winning is $1-P$, the amount he or she loses in the lottery is y^1, and the amount he or she wins is y^2, the decision maker has either option II of taking the lump sum $Py^1 + (1 - P)y^2$, or option I of playing the lottery, with an expected return of $Pv(y^1) + (1 - P)v(y^2)$.

The classic illustration of this concept is to consider the situation when there is only a single attribute $\mathbf{y}'_i$ for three probabilistic scenarios: risk-averse, risk-prone and risk-neutral. To measure a multi-attribute value function, whether additive or multiplicative, involves defining these unidimensional or univariate utility functions $v(\mathbf{y}'_i)$ as a first step. The independence property among y_is facilitates straightforward aggregation of these univariate utility functions into the multi-attribute form. To simplify the notation, we write y in lieu of y'_i in the discussions here.

Figure 5.12   DECISION TREE FOR UNIVARIATE UTILITY FUNCTION

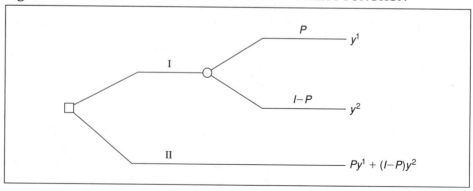

1. Risk-aversion example. To start out, we illustrate construction of a univariate utility function for a DM who is risk-averse. Being a conservative, the DM prefers the expected monetary value of a nondegenerate[3] lottery $y(II)$ to the lottery itself $y(I)$. In other words, he or she is not willing to take a chance and prefers option II to I or $y(II) > y(I)$, which when translated into utility, means $v[y(II)] > v[y(I)]: v[Py^1 + (1 - P)y^2] > Pv(y^1) + (1 - P)v(y^2)$. This results in a strictly concave utility function as illustrated in Figure 5.13. Here, the utility of the expected sum of money $v(Py^1 + (1 - P)y^2)$ is greater than the expected value of the utility of winning and losing, $Pv(y^1) + (1 - P)v(y^2)$.

2. Risk-prone example. Conversely, suppose the DM prefers the lottery $y(I)$ to the expected monetary value of a nondegenerate lottery $y(II)$, or $y(I) > y(II)$, $v[y(I)] > v[y(II)]$. This results in $Pv(y^1) + (1 - P)v(y^2) > v[Py^1 + (1 - P)y^2]$. The optimistic DM is then characterized by a strictly convex utility function, as shown in Figure 5.14. It follows without saying that a risk-neutral DM will have a utility function that is simply a straight line. Notice that all these univariate functions can be represented by the function $v(y) = a + be^{-cy}$, where a, b, and c are calibration constants, and c represents the degree of risk aversion. For $v(0) = 0$ and $v(1) = 1$, $v(y) = (1 - e^{-cy})/(1 - e^{-c})$. As the positive parameter c increases, the utility function becomes more convex, indicating higher risk aversion.

3. Certainty equivalent. A certainty equivalent of a lottery is an amount such that the DM is indifferent between the lottery and the amount $\hat{y}$ for certain. Therefore, $\hat{y}$ is defined by $v(\hat{y}) = E[v(\overline{y})]$, or $\hat{y} = v^{-1}\{E[v(\overline{y})]\}$, where $\overline{y}$ is the uncertain outcome of a lottery. Notice that the certainty equivalent is not the same as the value

Figure 5.13   A STRICTLY CONCAVE UTILITY FUNCTION

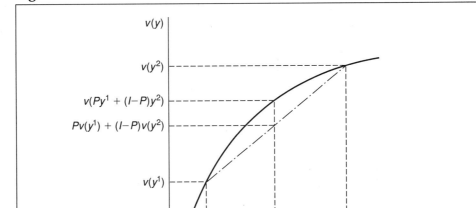

Figure 5.14   A STRICTLY CONVEX UTILITY-FUNCTION

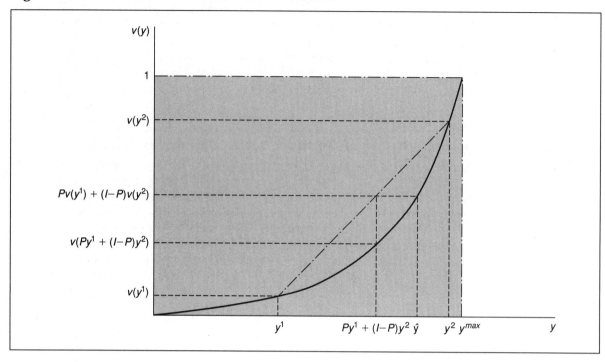

of the expected return $v[Py^1 + (1 - P)y^2]$ except for a risk-neutral DM. By way of notation, it is common to write the certainty equivalent in terms of the loss and win in a lottery, y^1 and y^2 respectively: $P(y^1) \oplus (1 - P)(y^2) \sim \hat{y}$. The certainty equivalent of the convex utility function is overlaid in Figure 5.14, so is the 0–1 normalization for v common among utility functions.

Suppose we set $v(y^1) = 0$ and $v(y^2) = 1$, where $y^1 = y^{min} = 0$ and $y^2 = y^{max}$ in Figure 5.15. Keeping the same probability of win and loss, the point $\hat{y}$ is now placed between the loss and win amounts of the lottery and another certainty equivalent defined as: $P(y^1) \oplus (1 - P)(\hat{y}) \sim \hat{y}'$. Then we find yet another certainty equivalent by examining the interval between $\hat{y}$ and y^2, resulting in $\hat{y}''$. $P(\hat{y})) \oplus (1 - P)(y^2) \sim \hat{y}''$. The result is $v(\hat{y}') = Pv(y^1) + (1 - P)v(\hat{y}) = (1 - P)^2$ and $v(\hat{y}'') = Pv(\hat{y}) + (1 - P)v(y^2) = P(1 - P) + (1 - P) = (1 - P)(1 + P)$. Subsequent points are obtained by substituting $\hat{y}'$ and $\hat{y}''$ in the binary lottery for $[y^1, \hat{y}]$ and $[\hat{y}, y^2]$ in turn. The process can be repeated as often as desirable or practical to sketch out the full function $v(y)$. We illustrate this process in Figure 5.15. It can be seen that the process is particularly simple for $P = 0.5$—a probability most people can associate with the common experience of coin flipping. The certainty equivalents so obtained also divide the utility range into halves, quarters, and so on. For this reason, this method is often called the fractile method. We will illustrate this method step by step later on in this chapter.

C. Independence Among Criterion Functions

To conclude this section, let us see when a multi-attribute value function can be aggregated from a constituent set of univariate value functions constructed

Figure 5.15   THE FRACTILE METHOD OF MEASURING UTILITY FUNCTION

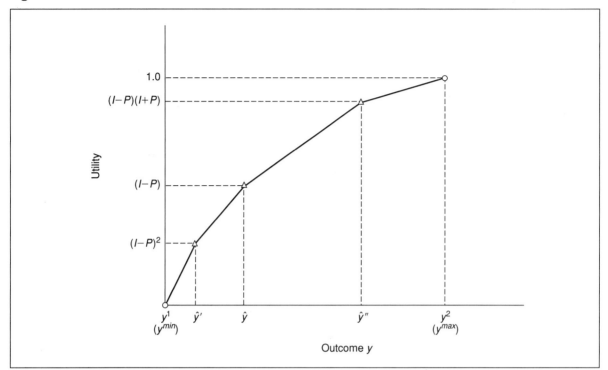

above, and when it is invalid to do so. Take a residential location problem. A family selects a house on the basis of purchase cost y_1', floor space y_2', maintenance cost (utilities and upkeep) y_3', appreciation (%) y_4', and appeal y_5'. The family constructs a value function for each candidate housing alternative assuming an additive value function:

$$v(\mathbf{y}') = w_1 v_1(y_1') + w_2 v_2(y_2') + ... + w_5 v_5(y_5') \qquad (5.8)$$

where $v_i(y_i')$s are uni-dimensional value functions.

We check the independence of attributes by asking the following mathematical question for a \$150,000 home: $v_1(\$150,000)$ = constant (say 0.6) for both a maintenance cost of y_3' = \$3000 or 2000/year? Given that both purchase cost and maintenance expenses relate to overall residential expenses, they may not be independent. The answer to the above question is "no." Equation 5.6 is violated. Hence the overall value function cannot be formed from the constituent univariate value-functions as suggested. Including both y_1' and y_3' in a multi-attribute value function as shown in Equation 5.8 appears not justified. (See Figure 5.16.)

What happens if two criteria $f_i(\mathbf{x})$ and $f_j(\mathbf{x})$ used in an analysis are correlated? Obviously, the above two-step process of (a) measuring a univariate function and (b) aggregating univariate functions into a multivariate one will no longer be valid. More complicated analysis will have to go into forming a multi-attribute value function. In multicriteria optimization, where we have derived the individual criterion functions $f_i(\mathbf{x})$'s, not all $f_i(\mathbf{x})$'s in the objective function

Figure 5.16   TEST OF STATISTICAL INDEPENDENCE AMONG ATTRIBUTES

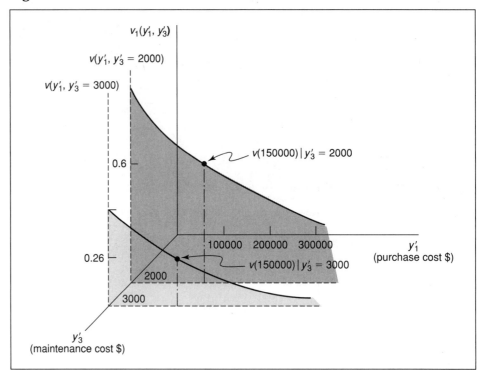

$v(f_1(\mathbf{x}), ..., f_q(\mathbf{x}))$ can be independent. Independence in this context would mean that the $f_i(\mathbf{x})$s are orthogonal. Consider two criteria $f_i(\mathbf{x})$ and $f_j(\mathbf{x})$. A measure for the correlation between the Ith and jth criterion is similar to its statistical analogue. The angle between the two criterion vectors is defined between the gradients $\mathbf{c}^i$ and $\mathbf{c}^j$

$$\cos^{-1}\left[\frac{(\mathbf{c}^i)^T\mathbf{c}^j}{||\mathbf{c}^i||_2||\mathbf{c}^j||_2}\right] \tag{5.9}$$

An ideal angle, as mentioned, is 90 degrees when the two criteria are totally independent. The more the criteria are correlated, the smaller the angle.

Take the MC-simplex example from Section IV-A in this chapter, where $\mathbf{c}^1 = (5, 20)^T$ and $\mathbf{c}^2 = (23, 32)^T$ and the angle between them is computed by Equation 5.9 as 21.67 degrees. This angle agrees with the graphical plot of Figure 5.6. The angle here is too small in comparison with an ideal orthogonality of 90 degrees, indicating there is a fair amount of correlation between the two criterion-functions. For high correlations, seemingly good weighting among the criteria—λ' weights in accordance with the decision maker's priority—produce non-optimal points. On the other hand bad weights may produce an optimal point. This result is completely analogous to the statistical discussion above where the lack of independence (or spurious correlations) will result in a highly complex modeling task.

D. Summary

To put all the concepts together regarding value functions, we would like to conclude this section with a numerical example. You are using multi-attribute utility theory to analyze a two-alternative, three-attribute decision-making problem involving uncertainty. The alternatives (possible outcomes and probability distributions) are described below:

Alternative	Possible outcomes $(\mathbf{y}_1', \mathbf{y}_2', \mathbf{y}_3')$/probabilities p		
Site A	$(20, 60, 100)/0.6$	$(10, 80, 40)/0.4$	
Site B	$(30, 50, 80)/0.3$	$(40, 40, 60)/0.2$	$(20, 70, 50)/0.5$

Individual single-attribute utility functions, and the overall multiple-attribute utility function are represented by: $v(y_1', y_2', y_3') = 0.3v_1(y_1') + 0.5v_2(y_2') + 0.2v_3(y_3')$ and the graphical sketches as shown in Figure 5.17.

Figure 5.17 EXAMPLE UNIVARIATE UTILITY FUNCTIONS

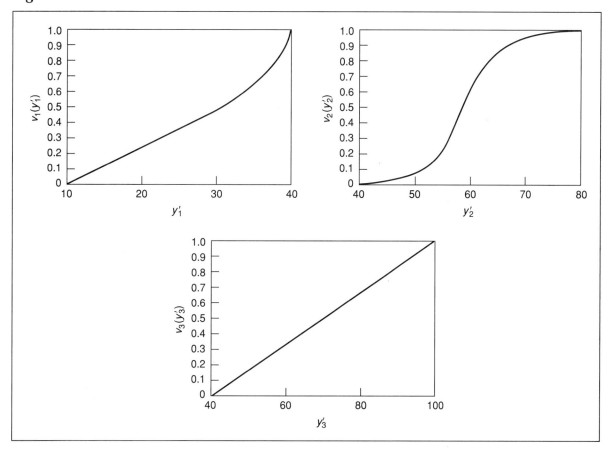

(a) What site should the DM select and why?

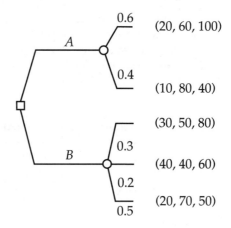

$$v(A) = 0.3[0.6v_1(20) + 0.4v_1(10)] + 0.5[0.6v_2(60) + 0.4v_2(80)] + 0.2[0.6v_3(100) + 0.4v_4(40)]$$
$$= 0.3[0.6(0.23) + 0.4(0)] + 0.5[0.6(0.6) + 0.4(1)] + 0.2[0.6(1) + 0.4(0)]$$
$$= 0.54$$

$$v(B) = 0.3[0.3v_1(30) + 0.2v_1(40) + 0.5v_1(20)] + 0.5[0.3v_2(50) + 0.2v_2(40) + 0.5v_2(70)]$$
$$+ 0.2[0.3v_3(80) + 0.2v_3(60) + 0.5v_3(50)]$$
$$= 0.3[0.3(0.5) + 0.2(1) + 0.5(0.25)] + 0.5[0.3(0.1) + 0.2(0) + 0.5(0.95)]$$
$$+ 0.2[3(0.7) + 0.2(0.35) + 0.5(0.2)]$$

$$= 0.48$$

Hence $A > B$, or Site A is preferred to Site B.

(b) What properties about the preferences of the DM did the decision analyst need to demonstrate in order to show that the form of the total utility-function is theoretically correct?

Following the discussion in Section VI-C directly above, one needs to show independence among all combinations of y_i's.

It can be seen that value functions can be used to rank order alternatives according to Equation 5.7. In the case where univariate utility functions are available and the exact form of the value function is known, as shown in the numerical example directly above, the ranking is cardinal. Thus alternative A is exactly $0.54/0.48 = 1.13$ times more preferable to alternative B. A premise of such a statement is that the constituent attributes are independent. In the section immediately below, we will further discuss independence among y_i's in some detail.

VII. VALUE-FUNCTION MEASUREMENT STEPS

Should preference intensity be required, the precise form of the univariate utility functions and their aggregation into a value function are required, as already alluded to above. This involves the calibration coefficients, ks and ws. It also brings us face to face with the core of MCDM. A five-step process is prescribed to carry out this task (Zelany 1982):

1. Familiarize DM with the concepts and techniques of value function measurement.
2. Identify the appropriate value decomposition form, $v(\mathbf{y}')$.
3. Measure component value functions $v_i(y_i')$.
4. Determine the ks and ws.
5. Validate the consistency of $v(\mathbf{y}')$ against DM's observed rankings.

First and foremost, the DM and the stakeholders must be involved with the definition of value function, or what we have been referred to as the Z'-space. After all, the value function is supposed to reflect the DM's way of looking at the world. The simplest of all value functions has only linear terms, $v = w_1 y_1' + w_2 y_2'$, where the $v_i(y_i') = y_i'$. However, this simple form is the exception rather than the rule in real world applications. Should we be forced to decide between an additive versus multiplicative function, the discriminant is the type of independence between the attributes y_i's. An additive value function requires that the attributes be **preferentially independent,** while mutual utility independence is necessary in addition for **multiplicative utility** models. Limiting the value function to these two decomposition forms has the computational advantage of calibrating only in the order of q coefficients as mentioned.

A. Preferential versus Utility Independence

The pair of attributes y_1' and y_2' is preferentially independent of attribute y_3' if the value tradeoff between y_1' and y_2' is not affected by a given level of y_3'. Formally stated, if $[(y_1^{\text{I}}, y_2^{\text{I}}) | y_3'] > [(y_1^{\text{II}}, y_2^{\text{II}}) | y_3']$, then $[(y_1^{\text{I}}, y_2^{\text{I}}) | y_3''] > [(y_1^{\text{II}}, y_2^{\text{II}}) | y_3'']$, where $y_3'' \neq y_3'$. Following the example on locating a plant among candidate states, labor availability, transportation, and tax advantages are considered. The value tradeoff between labor availability and transportation at two locations I and II may not depend on the tax advantage. In this case, we say that labor availability and transportation is preferentially independent of tax advantage, and location I is preferred to II in terms of labor transportation considerations irrespective of tax differences. Preferential independence concerns ordinal preferences among attributes. Should all pairwise attributes pass this preferential independence test, it is conceivable then that the plant location problem could be modeled using a linear, additive value function. Simply stated, preferential independence means the tradeoffs between any two attributes are governed by the unique indifference curve between these two attributes regardless of the values of other attributes (Ang and Tang 1984). If attribute 1 is preferentially independent of attribute 2, and attribute 2 is preferentially independent of attribute 1, then attribute 1 is mutually preferentially independent of attribute 2. If a set of attributes $y_1', \ldots, y_n'$ is mutually preferential independent, the decision maker's preferences can be represented by an additive value function. Notice preferential independence is a necessary but not sufficient condition for an additive value function.

Utility independence, on the other hand, says the relative utility of y_i' remains the same regardless of other y_i''s. In other words, the utility of each of the y_i''s can be separately determined. Attribute y_1' is utility independent of attribute y_2' when conditional preferences for lotteries on y_1', given y_2', do not depend on the particular level of y_2'. As an example let y_1' be the anticipated percentage improvement owing to investments on sites 1 and 2 (with $y_1^1 = 35\%$ and $y_1^2 = 10\%$), also the probabilities of success are $P^1 = P^2 = 0.5$. Let y_2' be the initial capital needed, with $y_2^1 = y_2^2 = \$100$ million; the certainty equivalent in this case is 15%. Now let the initial investment be $y_2^{1'} = y_2^{2'} = \$200$ million. If the certainty equivalent remains the same (in other words, it depends solely on the percentage improvements y_1^1 and y_1^2 and not on any fixed investment value y_2') then attribute y_1' would be utility independent of y_2'. This example is illustrated in Figure 5.18.

Utility independence is directional: y_1' is utility-independent of y_2' does not mean that y_2' is utility independent of y_1'. Attributes $y_1', y_2', \dots , y_q'$ are said to be mutually utility independent, if every subset of the attribute set is utility independent of its complement. As an example, let us consider this decomposable value function $v(y_1', y_2') = g[v_1(y_1'), v_2(y_2')]$. Mutual utility independence is established among the attribute set $\{y_1', y_2'\}$ *if and only if* y_1' is utility independent of y_2' and y_2' utility-independent-of y_1'. To establish mutual utility independence is

Figure 5.18   ILLUSTRATING UTILITY INDEPENDENCE

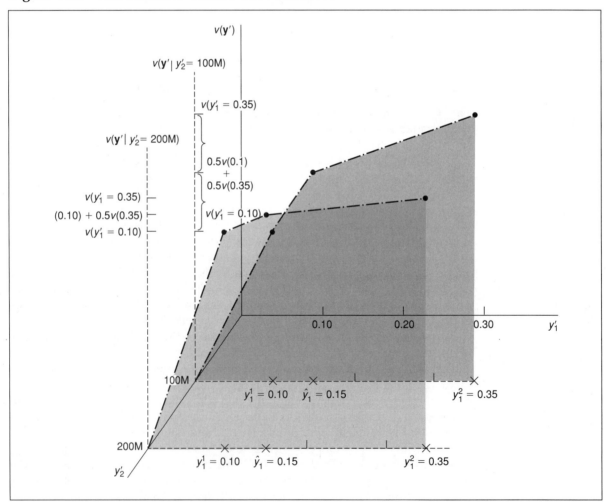

therefore complex, it requires formal lottery surveys to be conducted on uncertain outcomes in order to address the cardinal scale required of utility functions. Through these surveys, it is possible to measure the way utility changes over one dimension, independent of all other attributes. These independent measurements can then be combined to give the multi-attribute utility function. An informal way of explaining mutual utility independence is to say that the shape of the utility function $v_i(y_i')$ over $\mathbf{y}'$—whether risk-averse, risk-prone or risk-neutral—is the same irrespective of the level of all other attributes. An example of univariate functions of the same shape is shown in Figure 5.18. Notice here the two utility functions at $y_2' = 100$ million dollars and $y_2' = 200$ million look dissimilar, but they have the same indifference statement: $0.5(0.10) \otimes 0.5(0.35) \sim 0.15$. In other words, both curves indicate that the decision maker is indifferent between the certainty equivalent of 15 percent improvement and "achieving 35-percent-improvement with 50 percent chance" and getting only "10 percent improvement 50 percent of the time." (Notice that stating that two functions have the same shape is different from saying that two functions are strategically equivalent.) If we reverse y_1' and y_2' and are able to show utility independence between y_2' and y_1', then, y_1' and y_2' are mutually utility independent.

The extra amount of work associated with establishing mutual utility independence yields a much more useful metric. Instead of the mere rank order guarantee obtained from preferential independence, mutual utility independence quantifies the intensity of preference. To sum up the discussion on preferential and utility independence, let us review the basic concepts once again (Ang and Tang 1984). Effectiveness of an alternative is measured by several attributes via multi-attribute value functions. It is obvious that each of these attributes will require its respective unit of measurement, such as dollar costs, minutes of time, and parts-per-million of pollutants. Similar to Equation 5.7 the expected utility of an alternative $E(v(\mathbf{y}'))$ and the associated probability density function $P(\mathbf{y}')$ will, therefore, be multidimensional:

$$E(v)(\mathbf{y}')) = \int_{y_1'}\!\!...\int_{y_q'} v(y_1', \, ..., \, y_q') \, P(y_1', \, ..., \, y_q') \, dy_1'...dy_q' \qquad (5.10)$$

where y_1' to y_q' are random variables of the q respective attributes associated with each alternative. Determining these *joint* utility and density functions requires the evaluation of the conditional utility and probability functions. Moreover, these functions may have to be developed entirely or largely on the basis of subjective judgments and interviews, and they have to be performed for all the alternatives. This would generally be impractical if not impossible. Appropriate assumptions have been proposed in the above sections to exploit statistical independence among attributes, particularly preferential and utility independence. The assumptions of mutual preferential independence and mutual utility independence together imply that the joint utility function may be expressed as a function of the marginal (univariate) utility functions, namely the form $v(y_1', \, ..., \, y_q') = g[v_1(y_1'), \, ..., \, v_q(y_q')]$ where the $v(\cdot)$ is decomposable into function $g(\cdot)$ as defined by the following multiplicative expression (Keeney and Raiffa 1976)

$$kv(\mathbf{y}') + 1 = \prod_{i=1}^{q} [1 + kw_i v_i(y_i')] \qquad (5.11)$$

Notice this follows Equation 5.6 in which a joint probability density function (PDF) is broken into univariate PDFs. Here $v(\mathbf{y}')$ and $v_i(y_i')$ are 0–1 ranged univariate utility functions (of the exponential form $v(y) = a + be - e^{-cy}$ for instance) as defined previously. The reader can check that $v(y')$ boils down to the familiar two- and three-dimensional multiplicative, decomposed form by setting $\mathbf{y'} = (y_1', y_2')$ and $\mathbf{y} = (y_1', y_2', y_3')$:

$$kv(\mathbf{y'}) + 1 = [1 + kw_1v_1(y_1')][1 + kw_2v_2(y_2')][1 + kw_3v_3(y_3')]$$
$$kv(\mathbf{y}) + 1 = 1 + kw_1v_1(y_1') + kw_2v_2(y_2') + kw_3v_3(y_3') + k^2w_1w_2v_1(y_1')v_2(y_2') + k^2w_2w_3v_2(y_2')v_3(y_3')$$
$$+ k_2w_1w_3v_1(y_1')v_3(y_3') + k^3w_1w_2w_3v_1(y_1')v_2(y_2')v_3(y_3')v(\mathbf{y'}) = w_1v_1(y_1') + w_2v_2(y_2') + w_3v_3(y_3')$$
$$+ kw_1w_2v_1(y_1')v_2(y_2') + kw_2w_3v_2(y_2')v_3(y_3') + kw_1w_3v_1(y_1')v_3(y_3') + k^2w_1w_2w_3v_1(y_1')v_2(y_2')v_3(y_3')$$

After the univariate utility functions have been obtained, the function g may be determined by scaling $v_i(y_i')$ with respect to other utility functions such that they are consistent with one another and that $0 \leq v(y) \leq 1$. Consider the two-dimensional case (Ang and Tang 1984). It is obvious the outcomes (y_1^{min}, y_2^{min}) and (y_1^{max}, y_2^{max}) are the least and most desirable ones for the two-attribute utility function. In accordance with normal practice, we set $v(y_1^{min}, y_2^{min}) = 0$ and $v(y_1^{max}, y_2^{max}) = 1$. Then from Equation 5.11, the utility function with y_1' set at the least desirable state and y_2' at the most desirable state is given by

$$1 + kv(y_1^{min}, y_2^{max}) = [1 + kw_1v_1(y_1^{min})][1 + kw_2v_2(y_2^{max})] = 1 + kw_2$$

or   (5.12)

$$w_2 = v(y_1^{min}, y_2^{max})$$

and by symmetry, it can be shown that $w_1 = v(y_1^{max}, y_2^{min})$. Moreover, by substituting $v(y_1^{max}, y_2^{max})$ into Equation 5.11, we obtain

$$1 + kv(y_1^{max}, y_2^{max}) = [1 + kw_1v_1(y_1^{max})] [1 + kw_2v_2(y_2^{max})]$$

or   (5.13)

$$1 + k = (1 + kw_1)(1 + kw_2)$$

Now the value of $v(y_1^{max}, y_2^{min})$ can be determined from a pair of indifferent lotteries as shown in Figure 5.12, where the payoff $\mathbf{y}^1$ is now (y_1^{max}, y_2^{max}), $\mathbf{y}^2$ is (y_1^{min}, y_2^{min}), and $P\mathbf{y}^1 + (1 - P)\mathbf{y}^2$ is set at (y_1^{max}, y_2^{min}). Suppose the decision maker is indifferent between alternatives I and II at probability $P_1 = v(\hat{\mathbf{y}}_1) = v(y_1^{max}, y_2^{min})$; then from Equation 5.12 $w_1 = P_1$, and $w_2 = v(\hat{\mathbf{y}}_2) = v(y_1^{min}, y_2^{max}) = P_2$ (by symmetry). From Equation 5.13

$$k = (1 - w_1 - w_2)/w_1w_2 = (1 - P_1 - P_2)/P_1P_2$$

Hence the two-attribute utility function is calibrated to be

$$v(y_1', y_2') = w_1v_1(y_1') + w_2v_2(y_2') + kw_1w_2v_1(y_1')v_2(y_2')$$
$$= P_1v_1(y_2') + P_2v_2(y_2') + (1 - P_1 - P_2)v_1(y_1')v_2(y_2')$$

The multiplicative utility function above is the most general representation of a multi-attribute utility function in consideration for the efficiency with which such functions can be calibrated. We recall that when $k = 0$, the multiplicative function reduces to the simple additive form, with $w_1 + w_2 \ldots + w_q = 1$. We say that the y_is exhibit **additive independence** in this case. We will illustrate the procedure of calibration in the following numerical examples, namely steps 2 through 4 of the five-step value function measurement process.

B. Examples of Utility Function Calibration

We will illustrate the calibration of a multi-attribute utility function via two examples. The first will show an additive function where the weights w_i are to be determined. The second will show a multiplicative function where both the weights wi and the scaling constant k are to be determined.

Example 1: Determination of Weights
Suppose for the time being, the component univariate utility functions have been determined as $v_1(y_1') = 3/2\, y_1' - 1/2\, y_1'^2$, $v_2(y_2') = 3/4\, y_2' - 1/8\, y_2'^2$, and $v_3(y_3') = y_3' - 1/4\, y_3'^2$. Also the value function is determined to be additive, meaning that $k = 0$, and $\Sigma_i w_i = 1$. An interview with the decision maker yields the indifference relationships when the multivariate value function assumes different attribute levels for y_1', y_2' and y_3': $(0, 1, 1) \sim (1, 0, 1)$ and $(1, 1, 1) \sim (0, 2, 2)$. Now substitute the indifference results from the interview into the composite value function, or $v[(0, 1, 1)] = v[(1, 0, 1)]$ We solve for the w_is: $5/8\, w_2 + 3/4\, w_3 = w_1 + 3/4\, w_3$ or $w_1 = 5/8\, w_2$. Similarly, setting $v[(1, 1, 1)] = v[(0, 2, 2)]$ yields $w_1 + 5/8\, w_2 + 3/4\, w_3 = w_2 + w_3$. Solving these two equations together with $w_1 + w_2 + w_3 = 1$, we yield $(w_1, w_2, w_3) = (5/21, 8/21, 8/21)$ (Yu (1985)]. ∎

Example 2: Two-Attribute Utility Function Calibration
For a large urban area, landfill (L) and incinerators (I) are alternatives for solid-waste disposal. The univariate utility functions for each option are shown in Figure 5.19, where up to eight landfills or incinerators are considered (de Neufville 1990). Lotteries unveil these indifference relationships:

$$0.7(L = 8, I = 8) \otimes 0.3(L = 0, I = 0) \sim (L = 8, I = 0)$$
$$0.4(L = 8, I = 8) \otimes 0.6(L = 0, I = 0) \sim (L = 0, I = 8).$$

The first line says the following: The population is indifferent between a lottery at "70-percent probability of having all the 8 landfills and 8 incinerators built, and 30-percent none at all," vis-a-vis "building all 8 landfills and zero incinerator." The second line shows the indifference between "40-percent having all facilities built" vis-a-vis 60-percent "all incinerators only." From this lottery, one can conclude

$$v(L=8, I=0)=0.7\,v(L=8, I=8)+0.3\,v(L=0, I=0)=(0.7)(1)+(0.3)(0)=0.7$$
$$v(L=0, I=8)=0.4\,v(L=8, I=8)+0.6\,v(L=0, I=0)=(0.4)(1)+(0.6)(0)=0.4.$$

Thus $w_1 = 0.7$ and $w_2 = 0.4$. $k = (1 - 0.7 - 0.4)/(0.7)(0.4) = -0.1/(0.7)(0.4)$ according to Equations 5.12 and 5.13 respectively. The two-attribute utility function now looks like

$$v(L, I) = 0.7\, v_L(L) + 0.4\, v_I(I) - 0.1\, v_L(L)\, v_I(I).\ ∎$$

Figure 5.19   TWO-ATTRIBUTE UTILITY-FUNCTION CALIBRATION EXAMPLE

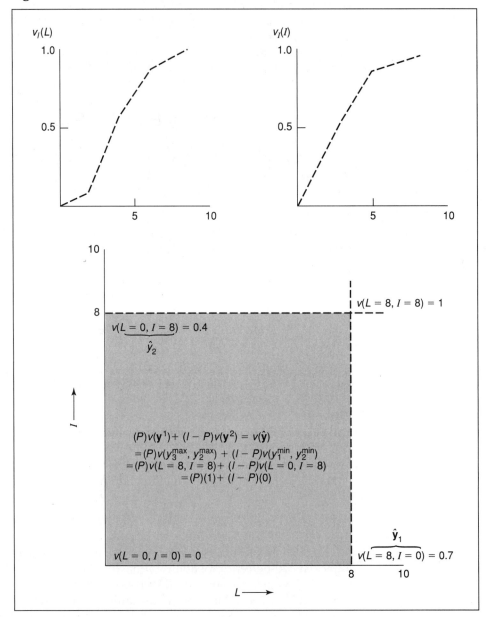

Example 3: Determination of 3-Attribute Utility Function

A client has asked you to help him compare three commercial land development projects and choose the best one. Each project is to develop a shopping
center. The client can fund only one of these efforts and must begin development as soon as possible. Each project has been evaluated by the client in terms
of cost, time to completion, and effectiveness for each of two possible growth
scenarios. However, the type of growth profile is not known. The growth profile will be one of two types—high or low—and each is equally likely.

The performance of the three projects for a high and low growth profile is determined in Table 5.1. You decide to construct a multi-attribute utility function v to help evaluate the three projects after obtaining the following information from the client. The three attributes—cost, time to completion, and effectiveness—have the following ranges:

cost	20–40 (less is preferred)
time to completion	10–30 (less is preferred)
effectiveness	40–60 (more is preferred)

Armed with this information, you solicit the following indifference and lottery data from the client, where the three entries in parenthesis refer to cost (C), time to completion (T), and effectiveness (E) respectively.

Indifference set 1:	$(30, 20, 60) \sim (35, 17, 60) \sim (20, 25, 60)$
	$(30, 20, 40) \sim (35, 17, 40) \sim (20, 25, 40)$
Indifference set 2:	$(40, 20, 50) \sim (40, 25, 60) \sim (40, 17, 45)$
	$(20, 20, 50) \sim (20, 25, 60) \sim (20, 17, 45)$
Indifference set 3:	$(30, 30, 50) \sim (25, 30, 45) \sim (35, 30, 55)$
	$(30, 10, 50) \sim (25, 10, 45) \sim (35, 10, 55)$
Indifference set 4:	$(40, 30, 60) \sim (20, 30, 40)$
Indifference set 5:	$(40, 20, 40) \sim (20, 30, 40)$
	$(40, 20, 40) \sim (40, 30, 60)$
Lottery set 6:	$0.8(40, 30, 40) \otimes 0.2(20, 10, 60) \sim (20, 30, 40)$

Here, $\mathbf{y}^i \sim \mathbf{y}^j$ means project i is indifferent from project j, and $P \otimes Q$ stands for a lottery between the outcomes P and Q. We have also assumed that the utility function of the DM is multiplicative with constant parameters w_1, w_2, w_3, and k. Obviously, such an assumption needs to be justified as will be shown later. It is prudent to start with a multiplicative form since the additive form can be thought of as a special case when $k = 0$.

Then the following information is used to specify single-attribute utility functions using the quartile method. For example, $0.5(20) \otimes 0.5(40)$ means a lottery in which there is a 50–50 chance of obtaining a score of 20 or 40.

Table 5.1   PERFORMANCE OF PROJECTS FOR HIGH- AND LOW-GROWTH PROFILES[4]

Project	High			Low		
	Cost y_1	Time y_2	Effect y_3	Cost y_1	Time y_2	Effect y_3
A	20	30	40	25	20	40
B	30	10	50	30	15	45
C	25	20	60	30	20	50

Set 7: Lotteries over C, given $T = 10$, $E = 60$ and $T = 30$, $E = 40$,
$$0.5(20) \otimes 0.5(40) \sim 30$$
$$0.5(30) \otimes 0.5(40) \sim 35$$
$$0.5(30) \otimes 0.5(20) \sim 25.$$

Set 8: Lotteries over T, given $C = 40$, $E = 40$ and $C = 20$, $E = 60$,
$$0.5(10) \otimes 0.5(30) \sim 20$$
$$0.5(20) \otimes 0.5(30) \sim 25$$
$$0.5(20) \otimes 0.5(10) \sim 15.$$

Set 9: Lotteries over E, given $C = 40$, $T = 30$ and $C = 20$, $T = 10$,
$$0.5(40) \otimes 0.5(60) \sim 50$$
$$0.5(50) \otimes 0.5(40) \sim 45$$
$$0.5(50) \otimes 0.5(60) \sim 55.$$

Notice the above lotteries show utility independence. In other words, preferences for lotteries involving different levels of costs do not depend on the levels of time and effectiveness. Preferences for lotteries involving different levels of time do not depend on the levels of cost and effectiveness. Finally, preferences for lotteries involving different levels of effectiveness do not depend on the levels of cost and time.

Now what should the client do regarding project selection? Specifically,

(a) Which data set establishes that preferences in T-C space are preferentially independent of E?

Set 1 establishes that $\{C, T\}$ is preferentially independent of $\{E\}$, inasmuch as effectiveness level is held constant in this set.

(b) Which set establishes that preference in T-E space are preferentially independent of C?

Set 2 establishes that $\{T, E\}$ is preferentially independent of $\{C\}$.

(c) Which set establishes that E is utility independent of C and T?

Set 9 establishes that $\{E\}$ is utility independent of $\{C, T\}$.

(d) Draw and label the single-attribute utility functions for C, T and E. Specify the set that was used in constructing each of the three utility functions.

The single-attribute utility functions are shown to be all risk-neutral in Figure 5.20. To summarize, mutual preferential and mutual utility independence are established for these attributes:

Set 1 establishes that $\{C, T\}$ is preferentially independent of $\{E\}$ and $\{T, C\}$ preferentially independent of $\{E\}$;
Set 2 establishes that $\{T, E\}$ is preferentially independent of $\{C\}$ and $\{E, T\}$ preferentially independent of $\{C\}$;
Set 3 establishes that $\{C, E\}$ is preferentially independent of $\{T\}$ and $\{E, C\}$ preferentially independent of $\{T\}$;
Set 7 establishes that $\{C\}$ is utility independent of $\{E, T\}$;

Set 8 establishes that {T} is utility independent of {C, E};
Set 9 establishes that {E} is utility independent of {C, T}.

Since cost, time to completion, and effectiveness are mutually utility independent, this means that the multi-attribute utility function is in fact multiplicative. Remember that mutual utility independence is a necessary and sufficient condition for a multiplicative functional form.

(e) Calculate the weights and scaling constant for the multiplicative utility-function. Show and explain your work.

According to set 4, $v(40, 30, 60) = v(20, 30, 40)$ or $v(y_1^{min}, y_2^{min}, y_3^{max}) = v(y_1^{max}, y_2^{min}, y_3^{min})$, which means $w_3 = w_1$ according to the three-attribute expansion of Equation 5.11. From set 5, $v(40, 20, 40) = v(20, 30, 40)$ or $v(y_1^{min}, y_2^{between}, y_3^{min}) = v(y_1^{max}, y_2^{min}, y_3^{min})$. Hence $w_1 = w_2 v_2(20)$, or $w_1 = 0.5w_2$. From set 5 again, $v(40, 20, 40) = v(40, 30, 60)$ or $v(y_1^{min}, y_2^{between}, y_3^{min}) = v(y_1^{min}, y_2^{min}, y_3^{max})$. Therefore $w_2 v_2(20) = w_3$, or $w_3 = 0.5w_2$. From set 6,

$$(20, 30, 40) \sim \left\{ \begin{array}{ll} 0.8 & (40, 30, 40) \\ 0.2 & (20, 10, 60) \end{array} \right. \tag{5.14}$$

or

$$(y_1^{max}, y_2^{min}, y_3^{min}) \sim \left\{ \begin{array}{ll} 0.8 & (y_1^{min}, y_2^{min}, y_3^{min}) \\ 0.2 & (y_1^{max}, y_2^{max}, y_3^{max}) \end{array} \right. \tag{5.15}$$

Hence $v(y_1^{max}, y_2^{min}, y_3^{min}) = w_1 = 0.8(0) + (0.2)(1) = 0.2$. This leads to $w_2 = 0.4$ and $w_3 = 0.2$. Substituting these values of w into the three-attribute expansion of Equation 5.11 when $v(\mathbf{y}^{max}) = 1$ and $v_i(y_i^{max}) = 1$, $1 = w_1 + w_2 + w_3 + k(w_1w_2 + w_1w_3 + w_2w_3) + k^2(w_1w_2w_3)$ yields $0.016k^2 + 0.20k - 0.2 = 0$ or $k = 0.9307$. The

Figure 5.20   UNIVARIATE UTILITY FUNCTIONS FOR COST, TIME, AND EFFECTIVENESS

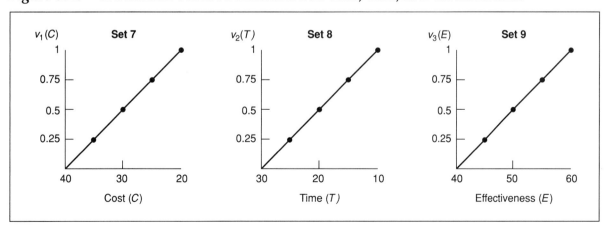

multivariate function now assumes the form $v(y'_1, y'_2, y'_3) = 0.2v_1(y'_1) + 0.4v_2(y'_2) + 0.2v3(y'_3) + 0.0745v_1(y'_1)v_2(y'_2) + 0.0372v_1(y'_1)v_3(y'_3) + 0.0745v_2(y'_2)v_3(y'_3) + 0.0139v_1(y'_1)v_2(y'_2)v_3(y'_3)$.

It should be noted that there is a numerical relationship between the scaling factor k and the weights w_is. $\Sigma_i w_i < 1$ implies $k > 0$, $\Sigma_i w_i > 1$ implies $-1 < k < 0$, and as already mentioned, when $\Sigma_i w_i = 1$, $k = 0$. The weights w_i represent the multi-attribute utility of y'_i when y'_i is at its best level and all other y_js $(j \neq i)$ at their worst. In order to calibrate a multi-attribute utility function, a survey needs to include enough questions to assess the indifference relationships between utilities of special combinations of the criteria levels $(y'_1, ..., y'_q)$, whereby sufficient equations are obtained for the determination of w_i.

(f) Calculate the expected utility of each development project.

Given the high- and low-growth profiles are equally likely, the expected utilities of the three projects A, B, and C can be readily calculated:

$$E(v(\mathbf{y}^A)) = 0.5v(20, 30, 40) + 0.5v(25, 20, 40) = (0.5)(0.2) + (0.5)(0.3779) = 0.2890.$$
$$E(v(\mathbf{y}^B)) = 0.5v(30, 10, 50) + 0.5v(30, 15, 45) = (0.5)(0.6873) + (0.5)(0.4979) = 0.5926.$$
$$E(v(\mathbf{y}^C)) = 0.5(v(25, 20, 60) + 0.5v(30, 20, 50) = (0.5)(0.6483) + (0.5)(0.4482) = 0.5482.$$

(g) Which project should the client choose if your utility function does in fact represent his/her preferences? Explain.

To maximize expected utility, the client should choose project B. ∎

Readers interested in details of multi-attribute utility theory can find further reading in Keeney and Raiffa (1976), Zelany (1982), and Seo and Sakawa (1988). Empirical calibration procedures are outlined in de Neufville (1990) and Bana e Costá (1990).

C. Validation

To illustrate the rest of the five-step value function measurement process, suppose the value function has a simple additive form $v(y) = w_1 v_1(y_1) + ... + w_q v_q(y_q)$ and a DM has determined a weight ratio to show the importance for every possible pair of criteria:

criteria	1	2	3
1	w_1/w_1	w_1/w_2	w_1/w_3
2	w_2/w_1	w_2/w_2	w_2/w_3
3	w_3/w_1	w_3/w_2	w_3/w_3

Thus $w_{12}=w_1/w_2$ shows the relative importance of criterion 1 against criterion 2. In general $w_{ij} = w_i/w_j$ in the matrix $W=[w_{ij}]_{q \times q}$. An interview matrix **W** is *consistent* if $w_{ij} = w_{ji}^{-1}$ and $w_{ij} = w_{ik}w_{kj}$, or criterion i is preferred to j the same way as j is preferred to i. This consistency in part validates a value function as specified in step 5 of the five-step process. Now given the pairwise-comparison ratios w_{ij}, the weights w_i should satisfy the following set of equations:

$$w_{11}w_1 + w_{12}w_2 + w_{13}w_3 = q'w_1$$
$$w_{21}w_1 + w_{22}w_2 + w_{23}w_3 = q'w_2$$
$$w_{31}w_1 + w_{32}w_2 + w_{33}w_3 = q'w_3$$

q' is the eigenvalue and $\mathbf{w}$ is the eigenvector in the above equation set $\mathbf{Ww} = q'\mathbf{w}$ or $(\mathbf{W} - q'\mathbf{I})\mathbf{w} = \mathbf{0}$.

Notice q' can be uniquely determined, considering we have a fourth equation $w_1 + w_2 + w_3 = 1$. In the above example, for instance, $q' = 3$ if everything is consistent. If an interview with the DM yields a matrix $\mathbf{W}'$ (instead of $\mathbf{W}$), and the eigenvalue is 3.5, the weights by the DM are inconsistent. The bigger the eigenvalue is, the larger the inconsistency. The same set of simultaneous equations can be defined for analyzing the univariate value functions $v_i(\mathbf{y}_i')$, where the weight eigenvector $\mathbf{w} = (w_1, ..., w_q)^T$ is now replaced by the scores of alternatives j on criterion i $\mathbf{v}_i = (v_i^1, ..., v_i^{|J|})^T$, where $|J|$ is the number of alternatives (in lieu of q, the number of criteria), and $0 \leq v_{ij} \leq 1$ (just like $0 \leq w_i \leq 1$). An example is shown later in which a three alternatives, A, B, and C, are evaluated in terms of risk, performance, and schedule compliance. Figure 5.21 illustrates this point graphically, particularly where the univariate risk-criterion utility function v_R is expressed in terms of the utilities of the three alternatives A, B, and C: $v_R = w_R^A v_R^A + w_R^B v_R^B + w_R^C v_R^C$. Here $(v_R^A, v_R^B, v_R^C)^T$ is the eigenvector to be determined, and w_R^A, w_R^B and w_R^C have been obtained from the interview. We will step through these calculations subsequently. Suffice to say here that when contrasting this approach with the lottery method described previously, one can see that the current approach tends to assume additive decomposition all the way, not only in the multi-attribute value function between risk (R), performance (P), and schedule compliance (S), $v = w_R v_R + w_P v_P + w_S v_S$, but also in determining the univariate functions v_R, v_P and v_S of these criteria. Instead of estimating a full univariate utility function, a point estimate is made. Saaty's (1980) widely disseminated *The Analytic Hierarchy Process* is based on the above concepts.

In general, for a system of equations such as $(\mathbf{W} - q'\mathbf{I})\mathbf{w} = \mathbf{0}$, if $w_{ii} = 1$, then $\Sigma_{k=1}^a q_k' = q$ for all eigenvalues q_k' that satisfy the equations. The eigenvalues q_k' constitute a measure of consistency of the AHP. If the answers of DM are totally consistent, the principal eigenvalue $q_{max}' = q$ and $q_k' = 0$ for all other ks. Should one perturb the perfect entries w_{ij} by a small amount (which often occurs in actual interviews with decision makers), the eigenvalues $q'(-\infty \leq q \leq \infty)$ change by small amounts also. Small variations in w_{ij} keep the q_{max}' close to q and the rest close to 0, some of which may be slightly less than 0. The result $q_{max}' \geq q$ always holds. A consistency index (CI), $(q_{max}' - q)/(q - 1)$, will measure the closeness to consistency. In general, a CI less than 0.1 is considered acceptable. Notice again that the process consists of normalizing w's, or setting the equation $\Sigma_i w_i = 1$, perturbations on the $\mathbf{W}$ matrix will yield $q' \geq q$ even for a perfectly symmetrical $\mathbf{W}$ matrix.

Example
The **analytic hierarchy process** (AHP) is used to assess hazardous facility siting. The best site is evaluated with respect to the risk (R), performance (P), and schedule-of-completion (S), resulting in the following tradeoff weights $[w_{ij}]$:

Best site:	risk	perf	sched
risk	1	$1/3$	2
perf	3	1	3
sched	$1/2$	$1/3$	1

Similarly, the three candidate sites A, B and C are compared among themselves with respect to the three criteria: risk, performance, and schedule, resulting in the weights $[w_{ij}]$:

risk	A	B	C	perf	A	B	C	sched	A	B	C
A	1	1	2	A	1	3	9	A	1	3	$1/9$
B	1	1	2	B	$1/3$	1	$1/7$	B	$1/3$	1	$1/7$
C	$1/2$	$1/2$	1	C	$1/9$	7	1	C	9	7	1

The graphical representation of this problem is shown in Figure 5.21, which has a two-level hierarchy, with **w** to be determined in the first level, and $\mathbf{v}_i$ the second level.

(a) Compute the weight eigenvector $\mathbf{w} = 5\,(w_R, w_P, w_S)^T$ and eigenvalue q'_{max} for the best site.

$$
\begin{aligned}
1\,w_R + 1/3\,w_P + 2\,w_S &= q'w_R \\
3\,w_R + 1\,w_P + 3\,w_S &= q'w_P \\
1/2 w_R + 1/3\,w_P + 1\,w_S &= q'w_S \\
w_R + w_P + w_S &= 1
\end{aligned}
$$

Here $\mathbf{w} = (0.249, 0.593, 0.158)$, $q'_{max} = 3.053$ and CI = 0.026.

(b) Now write a composite value-function of additive form to include all the component univariate value functions of risk (R), performance, (P) and schedule (S).

$$
v = 0.249v_R + 0.593v_P + 0.158v_S
$$

(c) Compute the eigenvector $\mathbf{v}_i = (v_i^A, v_i^B, v_i^C)$ and eigenvalue for each of the criteria $i = R, P,$ and S.

$$
\begin{aligned}
1\,v_R^A + 1\,v_R^B + 2\,v_R^C &= q'_R v_R^A \\
1\,v_R^A + 1\,v_R^A + 2\,v_R^C &= q'_R v_R^A \\
1/2 v_R^A + 1/2 v_R^A + 1 v_R^C &= q'_R v_R^A \\
v_R^A + v_R^B + v_R^C &= 1
\end{aligned}
$$

Figure 5.21   ANALYTIC HIERARCHY PROCESS EXAMPLE

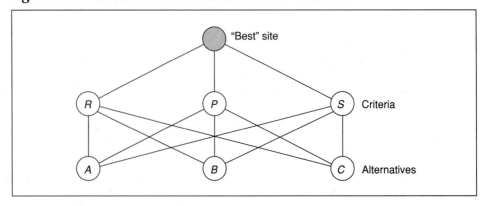

Hence $\mathbf{v}_R = (v_R^A, v_R^B, v_R^C) = (0.4, 0.4, 0.2)$, $q'_{Rmax} = 3$, and CI $= 0$.

$$
\begin{aligned}
1\,v_P^A + 3\,v_P^B + 9\,v_P^C &= q'_P v_P^A \\
1/3\,v_P^A + 1\,v_P^B + 1/7\,v_P^C &= q'_P v_P^B \\
1/9\,v_P^A + 7\,v_P^B + 1\,v_P^C &= q'_P v_P^C \\
v_P^A + v_P^B + v_P^C &= 1
\end{aligned}
$$

It follows that $\mathbf{v}_P = (v_P^A, v_P^B, v_P^C) = (0.701, 0.084, 0.215)$, $q'_{Pmax} = 4.12$, and CI $= 0.56$.

$$
\begin{aligned}
1v_S^A + 3v_S^B + 1/9v_S^C &= q'_S v_S^A \\
1/3v_S^A + 1v_S^B + 1/7v_S^C &= q'_S v_S^B \\
9v_S^A + 7v_S^B + 1v_S^C &= q'_S v_S^C \\
v_S^A + v_S^B + v_S^C &= 1
\end{aligned}
$$

Therefore $\mathbf{v}_S = (v_S^A, v_S^B, v_S^C) = (0.138, 0.072, 0.79)$, $q'_{S\,max} = 3.205$, and CI$=103$.

(d) Based on the composite value-function defined in (b) and the eigen-vectors $v_i=(v_i^A, v_i^B, v_i^C)$ computed in (c), rank order the preference among sites A, B, and C.

$$
\begin{aligned}
v^A &= 0.249v_R^A + 0.593v_P^A + 0.158v_S^A = 0.537 \\
v^B &= 0.249v_R^B + 0.593v_P^B + 0.158v_S^B = 0.161 \\
v^C &= 0.249v_R^C + 0.593v_P^C + 0.158v_S^C = 0.302.
\end{aligned}
$$

Therefore site A is preferred to C, which is in turn preferred to B. Notice here that we need not determine the precise form of the univariate utility functions v_R, v_P, and v_S. Only point estimate v_i's are necessary.

(e) Based on the eigenvalues in (c) above—q_R, q_P, and q_S—comment on the consistency of the DM and hence the validity of the rank order derived in (d).

With the exception of the risk criterion, the interviews yield rather inconsistent result, with the performance inconsistence and schedule inconsistency exceeding the CI maximum of 0.1 set by Saaty (1980). One can also argue that the schedule consistency is marginally acceptable. A poor consistency index reflects a number of problems. Here it may reflect the validity of the DM's responses during the interview. The consistency index also measures the independence among criteria, a concept somewhat parallel to that of preferential independence in multi-attribute utility theory. In this case, an overall CI of 0.026 suggests that the three criteria—risk, performance, and schedule—appear to be independent of each other. Too high a set of CIs can put into question the reliability of the ranking among alternatives. If the CIs are deemed unacceptable, the analyst needs redefine the criterion and to conduct the performance interview again to obtain a more reliable ranking.

The final step in the five-step process also calls for field validation of the rank order obtained above, which is a normal conclusion to value function modeling. Unless the ranking obtained from this set of value functions agrees with the observed ones, the process is not complete and more iterations through the five steps is required. Even though this is understood, one can be amazed at the number of applications where this last validation step is not carried out. ∎

In general, multi-attribute utility analysis is a useful tool for decision making. However, the key lies in the conduct of the interviews with DM's. Pairwise comparisons and lottery questions typically are cumbersome to administer, which discounts to a large extent the usefulness of these techniques (Islam 1996). While there are constant debates over the correct theoretical underpinnings, it appears that the ultimate test is the ability of the procedure to reproduce and predict the DM's ranking simply and consistently. For example, the concept of strategic equivalence allows an additive value-function to replace a more complex one for ranking alternatives (see Section IV-A of the current chapter). If an ordinal ranking is sufficient, the procedure is certainly attractive in a problem-solving environment. In our strive toward perfection, this point should not be forgotten (Luce and von Winterfeldt 1994; Tiley 1994).

VIII. MULTICRITERIA DECISION MAKING AND FACILITY LOCATION

Facility locations are typically evaluated on the basis of multiple criteria. For example, Hegde and Tadikamalla (1990) report on the use of AHP in solving a facility location problem faced by a large multinational corporation. The problem is that of deciding where to locate service terminals for the spare parts division. The AHP was introduced and successfully used to solve the problem. The managers in this case developed a sense of ownership in the findings of the study because the AHP facilitates their involvement at every level. This results in the implementation of the findings from the study. As another example the placement of a landfill has to take into consideration all these factors among others: capital cost, operating cost, environmental impact, and the not-in-my-backyard syndrome (Erkut and Moran 1991). The question is how these criteria can be incorporated into an objective function, if such an exercise is deemed desirable. Here we will demonstrate a way this can be carried out using the MCDM procedures introduced in this chapter.

A. The X, Y', and Z' Spaces in Facility Location

In general, three types of objective functions have been used most in the literature concerning location decisions. Covering models locate facilities such that the demands are covered within a pre-specified critical time or distance. Thus express package carriers locate their hubs in such a way in order to capture as much of the market share as possible, while at the same time guaranteeing a specific delivery time. Median or mini-sum models locate facilities in such a way that the average distance between the facilities and the demands served is minimized. An example is the placement of regional distribution warehouses, whereby all the retail outlets are supplied from these warehouses in the most expeditious manner. Center or mini-max models locate facilities to minimize the weighted maximum distance from the facilities to the demands. For example, in locating fire stations, a meaningful criterion is to be able to take care of the fire furthest away from the station as rapidly as possible. Chan (2000) discussed these objectives in detail in his "Facility Location" chapter.

A number of MCDM techniques have been reviewed in this chapter to locate facilities, including MCO, interactive programming, compromise programming, multi-attribute utility theory (MAUT), and AHP. Many of these modeling approaches will again be discussed more substantively in sequel. For the time being, we illustrate the usefulness of AHP, MAUT, and MCO in viewing the role of MCDM in location modeling. The MCDM location model can be structured as shown in the typical AHP tree of Figure 5.22, which is seen to be totally consistent with the X, Y' and Z' spaces advocated by the author for viewing MCDM. MCO requires first of all an explicit definition of the alternative space (X) and the outcome space (Y'), in order to define the efficient frontier. Where desirable, it may further require the objective function (Z') to be identified before an optimal solution can be found. Interactive programming relaxes the last requirement in that the decision maker can progressively articulate preferences as he or she explores the efficient frontier. MAUT, on the other hand, requires a two-step process of first quantifying the utility function, from which alternatives can then be rank-ordered according to the "common currency of exchange," utiles. Finally, AHP is a self-contained procedure to rank-order alternatives.

We have shown that an MCDM problem can be decomposed into the X, Y' and Z' levels. The relationship between the alternative space (X) and the outcome space (Y') or the objective space (Z') is relatively straightforward, in as much as it amounts to a bookkeeping process once data become available. However, it is much more challenging to provide the relationship between levels Y' and Z' (Beroggi and Wallace 1995). We would like to illustrate this interaction via a multi-criteria optimization case study of locating fire stations (Mirchandani and Reilly 1987). We will show how MAUT can reduce a MCDM problem into a single objective optimization problem by way of utiles. From there on, the problem can be solved as a median (or center) problem, defined between the X space and the Z' space. To obtain a direct relationship between the response time of fire units (the Y' space) and the property or casualty damage (the Z' space) is quite difficult for several reasons, most of which have to do with data availability. Problems also exist owing to uncertainty about when and where a fire might occur, and how DMs value the levels of achievement of various performance measures. Even if it were known how location decisions influence the level of achievement of these performance measures, subjective assessment of the relative

Figure 5.22   LEVELS OF HIERARCHY FOR THE LOCATION PROBLEM

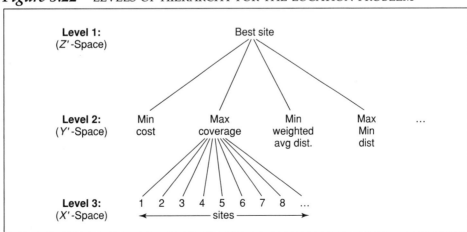

SOURCE: Haghani (1991). Reprinted with permission.

values of the attributes associated with these measures would have to be made. An alternative to obtaining an empirically derived cost benefit function is to use utility analysis. This method uses the experience of fire fighting professionals to make the tradeoffs of the various attributes, incorporating uncertainties in the exact future location, number of fires, and response times.

B. Multi-Attribute Utility and Optimization

Let us temporarily assume that the arrival time of the fire trucks fully determines all adverse consequences of fires. Thus a fire truck arriving promptly on the scene results in the least property damage and casualties, and a late arrival results in the worst damage and casualties. Each siting plan yields a probability density function (PDF) for the fire unit's response time, where the PDF takes into account the uncertainties regarding where a fire might occur. Rather than minimizing the expected value of its response time, utility theory suggests that the DM maximizes some function of the distribution of response time, called the expected utility, which is defined as $E[v(\tau)] = \int_0^\infty P_i(\tau)v(\tau)\,d\tau$ according to Equation 5.10 where $P(\tau)$ is the PDF of the response time to a random fire, and $v(\tau)$ is the utility of response time τ. Notice the utility of response time needs not be a univariate linear function. For example, a fire chief might prefer a 3-minute expected response time with a low variance to a to 2-minute response time with a high variance.

If we partition the study area into n' zones, the expected utility can be represented as

$$E[v(\tau)] = \sum_i^{n'} f_i \left[\int_0^\infty P_i(\tau)v(\tau)\,d\tau \right]$$

where f_i is the proportion of fires in zone i, and $P(\tau)$ is the PDF response time τ to the random fire in zone i. Note that $P_i(\tau)$ depends on the location of the closest fire truck unit to zone i. Thus suitable location criterion for the scenario is to maximize the expected utility, $E[v(\tau)]$, by optimally placing the required p units among the available n' sites.[5] The practice of a typical fire department calls for dispatching a pre-assigned number of units from pre-specified locations to a fire. The philosophy is that more than one fire truck is often required to put out a fire. In this case, we assume that the first two fire trucks dispatched are the most critical to the outcome of a fire. It is likely that the response time of the second arriving unit will have some effect as the first on the damage caused by a fire. We need a multi-dimensional utility function $v(\tau_1, \tau_2)$, where τ_1 is the first unit response time and τ_2 is the second unit response time. The expected utility resulting from a given set of fire station locations can now be represented as

$$E[v(\tau_1, \tau_2)] = \sum_{i=1}^{n'} = 1 f_i \left[\int_0^\infty \int_0^\infty P_i(\tau_1, \tau_2)\, v(\tau_1, \tau_2)\,d\tau_1\,d\tau_2 \right] \tag{5.16}$$

where $P_i(\tau_1, \tau_2)$ is the joint PDF of the first- and second-unit response times to a random fire in zone i, and $v(\tau_1, \tau_2)$ is the bivariate utility function of the first and second unit response times.

The Taylor series expansion of $v(\tau_1, \tau_2)$ around $(\bar{\tau}_1, \bar{\tau}_2)$, the mean values of respective response times, is

$$v(\tau_1, \tau_2) = v(\bar{\tau}_1, \bar{\tau}_2) + v_{10}(\bar{\tau}_1, \bar{\tau}_2)(\tau_1 - \bar{\tau}_1) + v_{01}(\bar{\tau}_1, \bar{\tau}_2)(\tau_2 - \bar{\tau}_2) +$$
$$\tfrac{1}{2}v_{20}(\bar{\tau}_1, \bar{\tau}_2)(\tau_1 - \bar{\tau}_1)^2 + \tfrac{1}{2}v_{02}(\bar{\tau}_1, \bar{\tau}_2)(\tau_2 - \bar{\tau}_2)^2\, v_{11}(\bar{\tau}_1, \bar{\tau}_2)(\tau_1 - \bar{\tau}_1)(\tau_2 - \bar{\tau}_2) + \cdots$$

(5.17)

where $v_{ij}(\tau_1, \tau_2)$ are the partial derivatives corresponding to the kth and jth order:

$$v_{ij}(\tau_1, \tau_2) = \left(\frac{\partial}{\partial \tau_1}\right)^i\left(\frac{\partial}{\partial \tau_2}\right)^j v(\tau_1, \tau_2)$$

Since $\bar{\tau}_1, \bar{\tau}_2$ are the mean values of τ_1, τ_2 respectively, then $E(\tau_1 - \bar{\tau}_1) = 0$ and $E(\tau_2 - \bar{\tau}_2) = 0$, and the expected value of $v(\tau_1, \tau_2)$ can be approximated by

$$v(\bar{\tau}_1, \bar{\tau}_2) + \tfrac{1}{2}E[v_{20}(\bar{\tau}_1, \bar{\tau}_2)(\tau_1 - \bar{\tau}_1)^2] + \tfrac{1}{2}E[v_{02}(\bar{\tau}_1, \bar{\tau}_2)(\tau_2 - \bar{\tau}_2)^2]$$
$$+ E[v_{11}(\bar{\tau}_1, \bar{\tau}_2)(\tau_1 - \bar{\tau}_1)(\tau_2 - \bar{\tau}_2)]$$

(5.18)

or equivalently

$$v(\bar{\tau}_1, \bar{\tau}_2) + \tfrac{1}{2}v_{20}(\bar{\tau}_1, \bar{\tau}_2)\sigma_1^2 + \tfrac{1}{2}v_{02}(\bar{\tau}_1, \bar{\tau}_2)\sigma_2^2 v_{11}(\bar{\tau}_1, \bar{\tau}_2)\, cov\,(\tau_1, \tau_2)$$

(5.19)

The above expression gives the expected utility of a siting plan as a function of the means, variances (σ), and the covariances (cov) of the response times of the two first arriving units.

Through a series of structured interviews with an official of the Albany, New York Fire Department, Mirchandani and Reilly (1987) developed a utility function of the response times for the first two engines arriving at a fire. To start out, single-attribute utility functions were assessed. The multi-attribute utility functions were then constructed from these univariate functions. To illustrate, consider the utility function for the first engine response time to low-risk fires. The fire department official revealed that he was constantly risk averse. A generic form to represent risk-averse univariate function is $v(\tau) = a - be^{c\tau}$, where a, b and c are positive calibration constants. During the interview, the official indicated that he would be indifferent between a 50-50 lottery of "1-minute and 5-minute response times" and a "response time of 3.75 minutes with certainty." The utility functions were assessed by conducting such lotteries over a range of 0–10 min. By assigning the following arbitrary utility values to the two extreme outcomes, $v(0) = 1$ and $v(10) = 0$, the following utility function results for the first and second engines that arrive, respectively,

$$v_1(\tau) = 1.016 - 0.016e^{0.415\tau}$$

and

$$v_2(\tau) = 1.079 - 0.079e^{0.262\tau}$$

By assuming mutual preferential and utility independence, the multi-attribute utility-function $v(\tau_1, \tau_2)$ can be shown as

$$0.971v_1(\tau_1) + 0.763v_2(\tau_2) - 0.734v_1(\tau_1)v_2(\tau_2)$$

Details of the study are documented in Reilly (1983). The discussion above simply illustrates that MAUT can be used in a practical scenario to formulate a single objective function, with which a conventional integer program between the X and Z' space can then be formulated and possibly solved, using a median formulation in this case. Thus the two seemingly disparate bodies of knowledge of MCDM, MAUT and MCO, can in fact be integrated productively into a single package for real world applications. This simple case study amply illustrates emergency facility location problems that are found not only in providing urban services, but also in such sectors as the defense community, where tactical operations are often judged on the basis of timeliness in response.

IX. A TAXONOMY OF METHODS

In the above brief review of MCDM, we regard the DM's underlying problem as one of selecting an alternative y' from the set of alternatives Y' in criteria space so as to best achieve his/her objectives as reflected by the value function, $v(\mathbf{y}')$: $\max\{v(\mathbf{y}') \mid \mathbf{y} \in Y'\}$. To the extent that information is decentralized and not immediately available, an educational process is required on both the part of the DM and the analyst in order to gain insights into the problem. Examples abound in both interactive mathematical programming and multi-attribute value function definition. Table 5.2 shows such an educational process (Bogetoft and Pruzan 1991).

In this table, it is clear that considerable interaction between the DM and the analyst is a prerequisite for a successful MCDM process. Both the DM and the analyst will have to be willing to assume part of the responsibility in either initiating or responding to a particular MCDM procedure. Thus a procedure can be directed by either one of the two parties. The type of interaction can be either one-way or two-way, as shown by the arrows in the table. Obviously, a two-way interaction is by definition more involved than one-way, resulting in an iterative process.

Table 5.2   TAXONOMY OF INTERACTIVE MCDM PROCEDURES

Type of investigation	DM directed	Analyst directed
Phased	Prior articulation of alternatives	Prior articulation of preferences
	(DM ← Analyst)	(DM → Analyst)
Iterative	Progressive articulation of alternatives	Progressive articulation of preferences
	(DM –q→ analyst)	(DM←q– analyst)
	←a–	–a→

A. *Prior Articulation of Alternatives*

The analyst can undertake an extensive investigation of the set of feasible alternatives, Y', and submit them as a set of proposals to the DM. The DM inspects the set of proposals, clarifies his own preferences and makes a choice. Throughout this chapter, we have pointed out simple ordering as a key concept in organizing the alternative set, particularly in defining the efficient frontier. This value free Pareto concept allows some powerful computational procedures to be followed in MCO. While the weighted sum procedure is readily operational with many off-the-shelf LP software, its application is mainly limited to problems amenable to LP model formulations. The constraint reduced feasible region method is likely to be more versatile in solving integer programming and nonlinear programming models. To the extent facility location decisions are discrete, integer programming is a key technique in the tool box of the analyst and so is the constraint reduced feasible-region method.

B. *Prior Articulation of Preferences*

In this model, the DM's preferences $v(\mathbf{y}')$ is constructed by the analyst based on studying the DM's behavior through surveys (for example). In this process, the objectives, criteria and attributes of the stakeholders need to be first defined, say, in a multi-attribute value function. The preference structure of the DM is then subsequently established in terms of such verifiable properties as transitivity of preferences and preferential and utility independence among attributes. These properties will point toward a particular way that alternatives can be rank ordered, including ordinal, cardinal, and lexicographic ranking. If transitivity is established, for example, value/utility functions can possibly be calibrated to operationalize the repertoire of techniques under MCO or **multi-attribute decision analysis** (MADA), with the latter defined here as the generalization of single-attribute Bayesian decision with the latter theory.

C. *Progressive Articulation of Alternatives*

Instead of a one-way interaction, either directed by the DM or the analyst, this process is now iterative. In each iteration, the DM asks the analyst about the set of alternatives, the analyst answers and the DM evaluates the answer. The DM then decides either to continue the search by posing new questions or to stop the search and choose one of the alternatives identified so far. Compromise programming is one of the ways that such iteration can take place. If no satisficing solutions exist, the goal setting process can compromise between the goals and the set of feasible alternatives. The set of alternatives, as reflected through the criterion space, or the Y'-space, can be greatly expanded—for example—upon the availability of additional resources, including monetary, technological, or managerial. This will allow satisficing solutions to be generated to meet the expectations of the goals set forth by the DM.

D. *Progressive Articulation of Preferences*

In each iteration, the analyst poses questions to the DM about his preferences and the DM answers. If the analyst now knows sufficiently about the DM's preferences to make a choice from the concrete set of alternatives, he/she proposes a choice.

Otherwise, the questioning continues. In MCLP, for example, the analyst can assist the DM to "travel along" the efficient frontier, wherein the DM goes back and forth between the relevant adjacent efficient extreme points (See Section IV-C on the interactive Frank-Wolfe algorithm.) Through this process, the analyst and the DM both sharpen their insights into the problem, allowing for a coordinated effort in decision making (Huang and Li 1994). As part of the progressive articulation of preferences, it is entirely possible that the domination structure of the DM falls outside the paradigm of Pareto preference and value function. Both of these concepts are indeed very restrictive, and a large gap exists between the two (as will be explained immediately below). While this will nullify a fair amount of the formal methodology presented above, it nevertheless allows the DM to obtain the most important product of the process: insights into the problem at hand.

X. DOMINATION STRUCTURES

Pareto preference is the simplest kind of preference, which allows MCO to be operationalized. On the other hand, the assumptions of a value function representation or the existence of preference relationship $\{>\}$ certainly are very restrictive. The gap between the assumption of Pareto preference and that of the preference having a value function representation is very large. Let us give an example (Yu 1985). A landowner is willing to sell the land adjacent to his or her home for at least $50,000/acre (125,000/ha). Let f_1 be the extra leisure time in hours he or she would spend in his homestead should he or she retain the adjacent land and f_2 be the additional income in dollars generated from the land sale. In terms of the weight cone, he or she requires $df_1/df_2 = -\lambda_2'/\lambda_1' \geq 50$ in $v(\boldsymbol{\lambda}) = \lambda_1'f_1 + \lambda_2'f_2$ for a sale to occur. Figure 5.23 shows his or her domination structure. Observe that unless Y' is convex, the non-dominated set cannot be obtained using maximization of the value function $v(\boldsymbol{\lambda}')$. In other words, the final solution may not be obtainable by maximizing additive or multiplicative value functions.

Can we somehow make transformations to the criteria f_1 and f_2 that will allow us to derive a value function that we can maximize? The landowner reveals that he or she is happy to sell for at least $50,000 per acre. The question here is that for $50,000 an acre; is the landowner willing to give up one, two, three, or more acres? What about $60,000 per acre? In this problem, the landowner has only a preference, while a value function attempts to create cardinality among these one-, two-, or three-acre land sales. In this case, he or she is willing to sell for more than 50,000 an acre, but is not sure how much land to sell. For example, at $50,000 per acre, he or she might be willing to sell one acre. At that point the $50,000 might no longer be worth missing any additional acres. However, at $100,000 per acre, he or she might be willing to sell more, because now he or she would be earning enough additional money to further improve and expand on the existing home (even though there is less surrounding land to enjoy.) Questions such as these offer insights into the marginal rate of substitution between leisure hours and extra income. We typically plot a marginal rate of substitution curve as convex function with which a convex Y' region can be applied, and an optimal solution can be identified (See illustration in Figure 5.23.) With the information given, however, it is not clear whether the marginal rate of substitution curve is concave or convex, and as a result, no optimal solution can be obtained.

Figure 5.23   WEIGHT CONE FOR ALTERNATIVE DOMINATION STRUCTURE

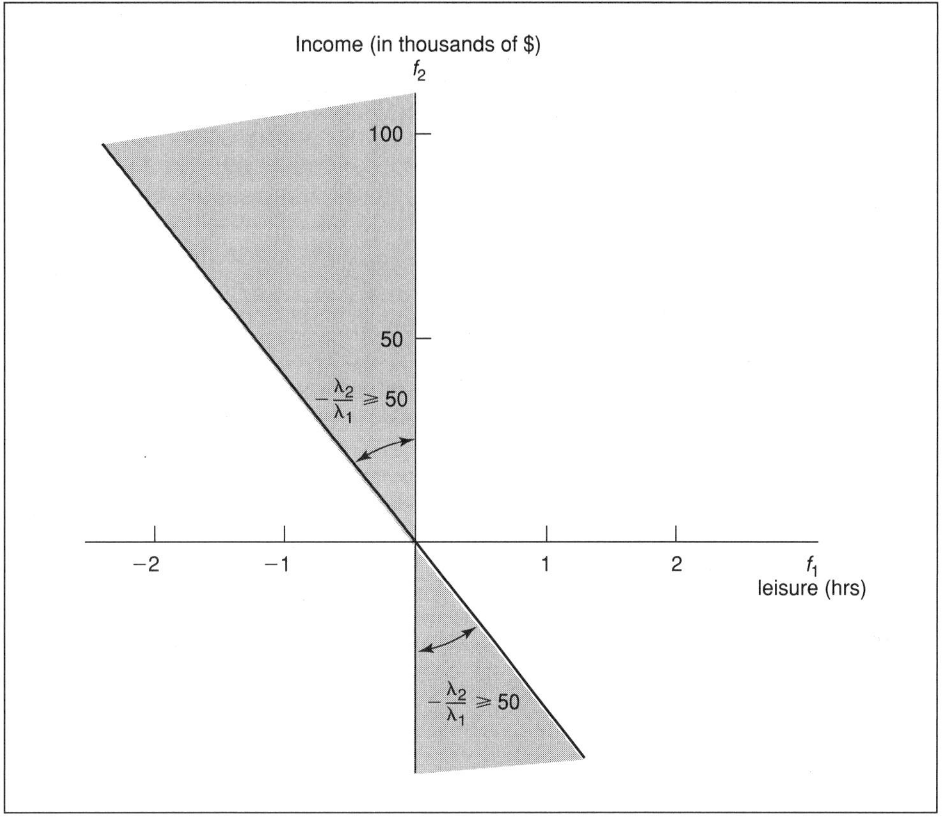

In summary, the information available from the DM is only sufficient to give a rank order, in other words, $51,000 per acre is preferred to x hours of additional leisure hours at the homestead. Even this is dubious, since we cannot valuate x. We cannot derive a value function because we cannot derive the univariate utility function for leisure time and extra income. In other words, the model fails because the revealed preference does not predict the DM's answer if we ask a question such as: "Would you sell *five* acres for $50,000 an acre?," which by the way is a legitimate question for the buyer to ask.

XI. COLLECTIVE DECISION MAKING

Following the same line of reasoning, the design that is best overall for a group of individuals with different interests often cannot be found analytically either. There cannot be any universally acceptable analytic solution because people place enormously different values on products. The utility/value function for a group is known formally as a group utility/value-function (GUF), which is an aggregation of individual values $\text{GUF} = f(v^1, ..., v^n)$. How does the aggregation of individual value functions into GUF take place? Should it be simply the weighted sum, $\text{GUF} = \Sigma_i w^i v^i$? But how about equity among the individuals that make up the group—that every one should achieve some minimal level of satisfaction, and we should discount a disproportionately excessive individual level of utility? Perhaps $GUF = \Sigma_i w^i exp(-[v^i - E(v)])$ may be more appropriate?[6] Keeney and Kirkwood (1975) define a **group utility function** (GUF) as an extension of the multi-attribute utility function specified in Equation 5.11. The additional weights w^i represent value tradeoffs of the decision makers. According to the authors, the GUF can be specified by a dictator who picks weights impartially to incorporate the preferences of all group members into the decision, or by using the collective response of the group to define the weights. In the first case, the process is similar to the technique used to determine parameters for a single DM. The second case involves a combination of the individual's utility functions and evaluation of the **individual group utility function** (IGUF) for each member of the group. The GUF is then constructed as a weighted aggregation of the IGUFs. This process includes interpersonal comparison of preferences and requires the measurement of the strength of individual preferences. Given complexities associate with the above method, it can be difficult to determine the overall GUF.

A. Arrow's Paradox

The difficulty of group decision making is well-publicized by the Arrow's paradox (Arrow 1963), which highlights these salient points:

1. The choices a group makes depend on its internal rules of decision-making; for example, its voting rules.
2. No one voting rule or decision-making process is intrinsically best.
3. The choices made by a group are therefore necessarily an ambiguous reflection of its preferences, so that we cannot rely on a group's choices to construct its GUF.

A voting procedure illustrates ambiguity of choice. Consider a family of three persons evaluating three different houses to buy, with their individual assessments looking like the following (de Neufville 1990).

Following our discussion in Section I in the current chapter, suppose the family agrees to select its home by successively comparing pairs of options until it has ranked them all. Thus comparing A against B, home A is preferred to home B ($A > B$) by a 2:1 majority according to the tabulation above. If home A is then retained as a preferred option and compared to home C, we find $C > A$ also by a 2:1 majority. Having compared all three options, can we conclude $C > A > B$?

To answer this question, we can check the results by comparing B and C, wherein $B > C$ by a 2:1 majority. Thus one can conclude that $C > A > B > C$,

Ranking of housing locations	Family member		
	Husband	Wife	Dependent
First	A	C	B
Second	B	A	C
Third	C	B	A

which is an intransitive result! This example shows that we cannot rely on the choices expressed by a group to reflect its GUF. The actual choice may depend critically on the precise way a voting or consensus building procedure is applied. This again reinforces the conclusion reached from another location decision example documented in Section I-A of the current chapter. Research into this difficult problem is continuing, as evidenced by Leitmann (1976).

B. Game Theory

A group decision-making process is sometimes modeled by game theory, which tries to capture the pluralistic decision-making process (Silberberg 1990). A historic game-theoretic model of interaction between market participants is Cournot's analysis of a duopoly, or a market in which exactly two suppliers produce identical goods or services. Let V_i^s be the output of firm i ($i = 1, 2$), let $C_i(V_i^s)$ be that firm's cost function, and let $D(V^d)$ represent the industry inverse-demand curve, or the price-schedule expressed as a function of the firms' total output V^d, where $V^d = V_1^s + V_2^s$. A downward sloping demand function is assumed. If the firms were able to collude perfectly, that is, act as monopolist, they could achieve maximum profit since between the two of them they have cornered the market. Cournot considered the case where such collusion was impossible. He postulated that, at any moment, each firm would maximize its profits assuming the other firm's output as given. In other words, a firm's decision is based on the other firm's output decision from (yesterday), fully convinced that this other firm will behave the same manner (tomorrow). Each firm maximizes its profits based on this somewhat naive assumption. In this way, the firms continually adjust their outputs until each firm has no further incentive to do so.

Take the example of the demand curve $D(V^d) = 30 - V^d = 30 - V_1^s - V_2^s$ and the constant-cost curves $C_1(V_1^s) = C_2(V_2^s) = 6$. For firm 1 therefore, the profit-maximization objective function would look like $\max_{V_1^s} I_1 = [D(V_1^s + V_2^s)V_1^s - C_1(V_1^s)]$ with a similar expression for firm 2. In our example, the profit to be maximized is $I_1 = (24 - V_1^s - V_2^s)V_1^s$. When the other firm's output is taken as parametric, the first-order conditions for optimization are obtained simply by the partial derivatives

$$V_1^s \dot{D} (V_1^s + V_2^s) + D - \dot{C}_1(V_1^s) = 0 \ and \ V_2^s \dot{D}(V_1^s + V_2^s) + D + \dot{C}_2(V_2^s) = 0 \ respectively$$

In this example, we are taking the partials as the following:

$$\frac{\partial I_1}{\partial V_1^s} = 24 - 2V_1^s - V_2^s = 0 \ and \ \frac{\partial I_2}{\partial V_2^s} = 24 - 2V_2^s - V_1^s = 0$$

Solving each equation in terms of the other firm's output yields the reaction functions

$$V_1^s = V_1^*(V_2^s) \quad V_2^s = V_2^*(V_1^s) \tag{5.20}$$

For this example, the reaction functions are $V_i^s = 12 - V_j^s/2$ ($i = 1, 2$), as illustrated in Figure 5.24. For the general case where the demand function is nonlinear, the reaction functions are shown in Figure 5.25 as curvilinear curves. Both of these reaction curves, whether linear or curvilinear, indicate the profit

Figure 5.24   NASH EQUILIBRIUM IN A COURNOT DUOPOLY

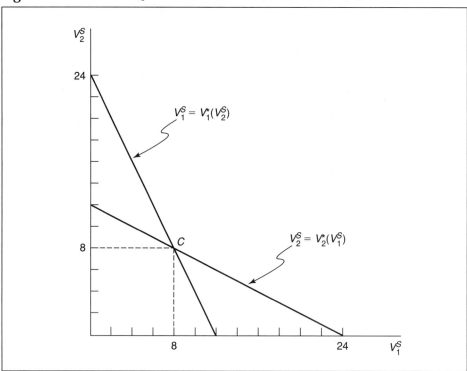

maximizing output of each firm, for parametric values of the other firm's output. The intersection of the firm-1 and firm-2 curves, point C, is the Cournot solution to the duopoly market. In our example, $V_1^s = V_2^s = 8$, or the firms will provide 8 units of output each, at a market price of 14 units, and yielding a net profit of 64 units.

This solution is also called a **Nash equilibrium,** defined as the more general equilibrium condition in which neither firm will change its decision under the assumed behavior. However, it is not a Pareto solution, since further gains from trade could exist with a lower price. For that reason, each firm has a wealth-maximizing incentive to cheat on this arrangement. It can be seen from the demand and profit functions of this numerical example that firm 1 can raise its profit I_1 by lowering it price $D(V^d)$ and increasing its production. Thus by lowering its price to 13, for example, firm 1 can capture the entire market and now increase its profit from 64 to $(7)(17) = 119$ units. For this reason, there are variants to this model. Bertrand and Edgeworth, for example, constructed a similar model in which price, instead of output, is assumed fixed in the duopolistic competition. Stackelberg proposes that one firm, say firm 2, assumes that firm 1 will react in a Cournot manner to firm 2's output decision, according to the reaction function (Eqation 5.20). Firm 2 then chooses output assuming the above relation for V_1^s. In other words, it does not assume, as in the Cournot model, that firm-1's output will be fixed. Rather, firm-2 anticipates firm-1's Cournot behavior. Firm 2 in this case is the Stackelberg leader; firm 1 is the follower. Depending on the cost functions, different solutions emerge. Both firms could choose to be leaders, in which case Stackelberg warfare results.

In general, game theory describes the complex behavior of these DMs in a pluralistic setting. It can be shown that game theory, a complicated body of knowledge in and of itself, can become overwhelmingly complex by the introduction of multiple criteria. Building on the work of Cook (1976), Hannan (1982), and Zelany (1976), Patterson, Horton, and Chan (1994) and Payne (1995) experimented with the simple case of a two-person zero-sum game, the solution of which corresponds to the primal and dual solutions of an LP assuming maximum gain for one team and minimum loss for the other. The term zero sum here refers to the condition that one team's gain is exactly equal to the other team's loss. As soon as two criteria or two payoff metrics are involved there appeared to be more than one equilibrium, considering both local and global optima. Finding these equilibria is often a trial-and-error process. By now, one should be totally convinced that the analysis of pluralistic decision making is in fact beyond the state-of-the-art in modeling.

C. Recommended Procedure

Since there is no analytic way for a group to choose among options, we can only recommend a procedure for dealing with the problem (de Neufville 1990). The purpose of the procedure then would assist in the meeting of the minds:

1. Model the physical alternatives
2. Define the noninferior options, or sometimes referred to as the production possibility frontier, or trace out the reaction functions
3. Determine individual preferences
4. Explore the possible tradeoffs
5. Negotiate toward a collectively satisfactory solution.

Step 4 unveils the differences between individual's tradeoffs among attributes, thus offering the possibility of mutually beneficial exchanges. In Step 5, the negotiation takes place in the consequences of the alternatives and their cost benefit distribution among the stakeholders.

A compromise alternative in the production possibility frontier may then be identified. A mutually beneficial distribution may result in sharing, instead of monopolizing, the cost-benefits. Figure 5.25 illustrates such a possibility, where the best alternative for a group involves finding both the best alternative and the best way to allocate its cost-benefits. Thus a production possibility frontier is constructed as an envelope of maximum utility curves among all pairs of individuals i and j. The best alternative is then defined as the one that satisfies both the GUF and the production possibility frontier—if a GUF can be defined of course. In lieu of a production possibility frontier, one can think of a triopoly instead of a duopoly and progressively toward an oligopoly market, which collectively define a utility possibility frontier based on individual maximum utility reaction functions $v^i = v^{i*}(v^j)$.

Lewis and Butler (1993) described and evaluated an iterative technique to facilitate multi-objective decision making by multiple DMs. The proposed method augments an interactive MCO procedure with preference ranking tool and a consensus-ranking heuristic. Computational experience suggests that the proposed framework is an effective decision-making tool. The procedure quickly located

Figure 5.25   UTILITY PRODUCTION FRONTIER AND THE GUF

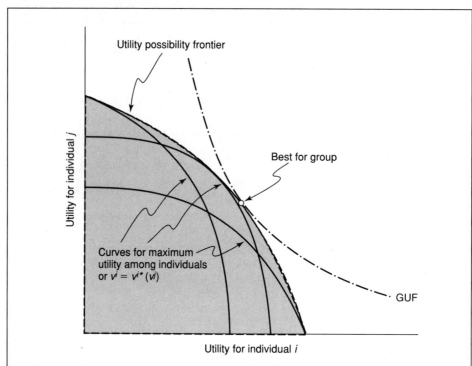

excellent compromise solutions in a series of test problems with hypothetical DMs. In addition, a real-world resource allocation study yielded positive feedback from the participants.

XII. CONCLUDING REMARKS

The relative newness of multiple-criteria decision making (MCDM) brings with it a host of competing approaches. The purpose of this chapter is to expose the reader to a wide variety of techniques. The discussion is organized around the paradigm of the X, Y' and Z' space, which allows us to introduce the concepts of decisions, criteria, and value functions systematically, and cover both multple-attribute decision analysis and multiple-criteria optimization (MCO). It has been shown that Pareto preference is the simplest kind of option ranking requiring little articulation of the decision-makers' preference structure. There is a large gap between this and ranking based on a value function, where the DM's articulation of preference has to be clearly understood. Understanding the DM's value function has to be the most interesting and challenging aspect of the field of MCDM. Once the X, Y' and Z' spaces have been defined, the process of MCDM can be carried out. Recent research points toward an interactive procedure to do this, which represents a prominent direction the field is moving.

What are the challenges facing MCDM in the foreseeable future? Zionts (1992) suggests viewing MCDM to be made up of four different subareas: multicriteria mathematical programming, multi-criteria discrete alternatives (including integer MCO), multi-attribute utility theory, and negotiation theory. On the macro level, he sees negotiation as a fruitful area of research, since there is but a dearth of understanding in this important subject presently. Before and even after rigorous theories are established, approximations to the theory, possibly along the line of an expert system, may be very useful. He cited the example of MAUT, where additive utility functions are often calibrated in practice even though preferential independence cannot be rigorously proven. An expert system is helpful in helping negotiators understand and structure their own positions, even though a theory of negotiation is far from complete. On a micro level, Zionts suggests examining these topics: A Tshebycheff-, or l_∞-norm, is a good proxy utility function since it can generate all non-dominated solution points. More precisely, minimizing the norm as a quasi-convex function can generate any non-dominated solution points (Gardiner and Steuer 1995). Cone dominance can also be exploited by using nonexistent or dummy solutions, such as an ideal, for comparison purposes. The advantage is to increase the information learned as a result of asking preference questions of DMs. A visual display, possibly through computer graphics, will greatly assist the DMs in performing MCDM analysis. We have seen such an example in Figure 5.10.

Dyer et al. (1992) also provide some collective thoughts on the future of MCDM. Utility functions that go beyond the additive format as explained in this chapter are judged to be worthy of further investigation (Fishburn; 1988; Wakker 1989). There is also a need for eclectic approaches that synthesize the meritorious among existing theories and practices to improve MCDM procedures. Interactive MCO, an important area of research identified previously, needs consolidation so that procedure switching can take place as the decision process progresses (Buchanan 1994). To this list we would like to add integer MCO, which is an important application area not supported by adequate computational algorithms (Narula and Vassilev 1994).

Korhonen (1992) outlines his observation regarding recent developmental trends. Recent techniques tend to have these features in common:

1. They do not cramp the DM's style and involvement;
2. They have interactive feedback mechanisms including graphics (El-Mahgary and Lahdelma 1995; Antunes and Climaco 1994);
3. They have a built-in evolutionary process, allowing modification of the model as the analysis progresses;
4. DMs are provided with fast turnaround analysis techniques.

Based on this prognosis, it is clear that MCDM (or sometimes called multi-criteria decision aid [Vincke 1992]) is a most needed analysis technique. Because of its developmental nature, however, it also represents an active area of further research.

ENDNOTES

[1] A ranking among alternatives is transitive $A > B$, $B > C$ means $A > C$.
[2] For a review of the simplex procedure, see Appendix 1.
[3] A nondegenerate lottery means that the lottery will have two distinct outcomes, thus discounting the special case where the two outcomes are identical.

[4] Cost is in millions of dollars, time to complete is in years, and effectiveness is the number of shoppers attracted per month (in thousands).

[5] While the p-median problem was introduced in Chapter 4, the "Facility Location" chapter in Chan (2000) discusses the conventional p-median problem in detail.

[6] Notice the exponential form for v^i is simply written for conceptual clarity, the real function should be $1 - \exp(-[v^i - \bar{v}])$.

REFERENCES

Ang, A; Tang, W. H. (1984). *Probability concepts in engineering planning and design. vol. II: Decision, risk and reliability.* New York: Wiley.

Arrow, K. (1963). *Social choice and individual values.* New Haven, Connecticut: Yale University Press.

Askoy, Y.; Butler, T. W.; Minor, E. D. III (1994). Comparative studies in interactive multiple objective mathematical programming. Working Paper. A. B. Freeman School of Business. Tulane University. New Orleans, Louisiana.

Antunes, C. H.; Climaco, J. (1994). "Decision aid for discrete alternative multiple criteria problems: A visual interactive approach." *Information and Decision Technologies* 19:185–193.

Balling, R. J.; Taber, J.; Brown, M. R.; Day, K. (1998). Multiobjective urban planning using a genetic algorithm. Working Paper. Department of Civil and Environmental Engineering. Brigham Young University. Provo, Utah.

Bana e Costà, C. A. (1990). *Readings in multiple criteria decision aid.* Berlin, Germany and New York: Springer-Verlag.

Bana e Costà, C. A.; Enslin, L.; Zanella, I. J. (1998). "A real-world MCDA application in cellular telephony systems." In *Trends in multicriteria decision making,* edited by T.J. Stewart and R. C. van den Honert. Berlin, Germany and New York: Springer-Verlag, 412–423.

Beroggi, E.G.; Wallace, W.A. (1995). "Operational control of the transportation of hazardous material: An assessment of alternative decision models." *Management Science* 41:1962–1967.

Bogetoft, P.; Ming, C.; Tind, J. (1994)."Price-directive decision making in hierarchical systems with conflicting preferences." *Journal of Multi-Criteria Decision Analysis* 3: 65–82.

Bogetoft, P.; Pruzan, P. (1991). *Planning with multiple criteria: Investigation, communication, choice.* Amsterdam, The Netherlands: North-Holland.

Briggs, T. H.; Kunsch, P.L.; Mareschal. B. (1990). "Nuclear waste management: An application of the Multicriteria PROMETHEE methods." *European Journal of Operational Research* 44:1–10.

Buchanan, J.T.; Daellenbach, H.G. (1987). "A comparative evaluation of interactive solution methods for multiple objective decision making." *European Journal of Operational Research* 29:353–359.

Buchanan, J.T. (1994). "An experimental evaluation of interactive MCDM methods and the decision-making process." *Journal of the Operational Research Society* 45:1050–1059.

Chan, Y. (2000). *Location, transport and land use: Modelling spatial-temporal information.* New York: Springer-Verlag.

Chankong, V.; Haimes, Y. Y. (1983). *Multiobjective decision making—Theory and methodology.* Amsterdam, The Netherlands: North-Holland.

Cook, W. D. (1976). "Zero-sum games with multiple goals." *Naval Research Logistics Quarterly* 23, No. 4:615–622.

de Neufville, R. (1990). *Applied systems analysis: Engineering planning and technology management.* New York: McGraw-Hill.

Dyer, J. S.; Fishburn, P. C.; Steuer, R. E.; Wallenius, J.; Zionts, S. (1992). "Multiple criteria decision making: Multiattribute utility theory: The next ten years." *Management Science* 38, No. 5:685–654.

El-Mahgary, S.; Lahdelma, R. (1995). "Data envelopment analysis: Visualizing the results." *European Journal of Operational Research* 85:700–710.

Erkut, E.; Moran, S. R. (1991). "Locating obnoxious facilities in the public sector: An application of the analytic hierarchy process to municipal landfill siting decisions." *Socio-Economic Planning Sciences* 5, No. 2:89–102.

Fishburn, P. C (1988). *Nonlinear preference and utility theory.* Baltimore, Maryland: Johns Hopkins University Press.

Gardiner, L. R.; Steuer, R. E. (1993). "Unified interactive multiple objective programming." *European Journal of Operational Research* 71:1244–1259.

Gardiner, L. R.; Steuer, R.E. (1995). Range equalization scaling and solution dispersion in the Tchebycheff method: A preliminary study. Working Paper. Department of Management. Auburn University. Alburn, Alabama.

Goicoechea, A.; Hansen, D. R.; Duckstein, L. (1982). *Multiobjective decision analysis with engineering and business applications.* New York: Wiley.

Haghani, A. E. (1991). "Multicriteria decision making in location modeling." *Transportation Research Record* 1328:88–97.

Hannan, E. L. (1982). "Reformulating zero-sum games with multiple goals." *Naval Research Logistic Quarterly* 29, No. 1:113–118.

Hegde, G. G.; Tadikmalla, P. R. (1990). "Site selection for a sure service terminal." *European Journal of Operational Research* 48:77–80.

Huang, Z.; Li, S. (1994). "The role of cardinal utilities in multiple objective programming." *American Journal of Mathematical and Management Sciences* 14:301–325.

Hokkanen, J.; Lahdelma, R.; Salimer, P. (1999). "A multiple criteria decision model for analyzing and choosing among different development patterns for the Helsinki Cargo Harbor." *Socio-Economic Planning Sciences* 33:1–23.

Ignizio, J. P.; Cavalier, T. M. (1994). *Linear programming.* Englewood Cliffs, New Jersey: Prentice Hall.

Islam, R.; Biswal, M. P.; Alam, S. S. (1996). Clusterization of alternatives in analytic hierarchy process. Working Paper. Department of Mathematics. Indian Institute of Technology. Kharagpur, India.

Karaivanova, J.; Korhonen, P.; Narula, S.; Wallenius, J.; Vassiler, V. (1992). A reference direction approach to multiple objective integer linear programming. Working Paper. Institute of Informatics. Sofia, Bulgaria.

Keeney, R. L.; and Raiffa, H. (1976). *Decisions with multiple objectives: Preferences and value tradeoffs.* New York: Wiley.

Keeney, R. L.; Kirkwood, C. W. (1975). "Group decision making using cardinal social welfare functions." *Management Science* 22, No. 4:430–437.

Keeney, R. L. (1994). "Using values in operations research." *Operations Research* 42:793–813.

Kirkwood, C. (1997). *Structural decision making.* Belmont, California: ITP Duxbury.

Korhonen, P. (1992). "Multiple criteria decision support: The state of research and future directions." *Computers and Operations Research* 19:305–307.

Korhonen, P.; Laakso, J. (1986). "A visual interactive method for solving the multiple criteria problem." *European Journal of Operational Research.* 24:277–287.

Lai, Y-J.; Liu, T-Y.; Hwang, C-L. (1994) "TOPSIS for MODM." *European Journal of Operational Research* 76:486–500.

Leitmann, G. Ed. (1976). *Multicriteria decision making and differential games.* New York: Plenum.

Lewis, H. S.; Butler, T. W. (1993). "An interactive framework for multi-person, multiobjective decisions." *Decision Sciences* 24:1–22.

Li, Z.F.; Wang, S. Y. (1994). "Lagrange multipliers and saddle points in multi-objective programming." *Journal of Optimization Theory and Applications* 83:63–81.

Lieberman, E. R. (1991). *Multi-objective programming in the USSR.* Boston, Massachusetts: Academic Press.

Luce, R. D.; von Winterfeldt, D. (1994) "What common ground exists for descriptive, prescriptive, and normative utility theories?" *Management Science* 40:263–279.

Massam, B. H. (1988). "Multi-criteria decision making MCDM techniques in planning." Vol. 30, Part I of *Progress in planning,* edited by D. Diamond and J. B. McLoughlin. Oxford, England and New York: Pergamon Press.

Mirchandani, P.; Reilly, J. (1987). "Spatial distribution design for fire-fighting units." In *Spatial analysis & location-allocation models,* edited by A. Ghosh and G. Rushton. New York: Van Nostrand Reinhold, 186–223.

Moulin, H. (1986). *Game theory for the social sciences,* 2nd and Rev. ed. New York: New York University Press.

Narula, S. C.; Vassilev, V. (1994) "An interactive algorithm for solving multiple objective integer linear programming problems." *European Journal of Operational Research.* 79:443–450.

Patterson, K.; Horton, K. G.; Chan, Y. (1994) Games with multiple payoffs. Working Paper. Department of Operational Sciences. Air Force Institute of Technology. Wright-Patterson AFB, Ohio.

Payne, R. (1995). Games with multiple payoffs: A rejoinder. Working Paper. Department of Operational Sciences. Air Force Institute of Technology. Wright-Patterson AFB, Ohio.

Reilly, J. (1983). Development of a fire station placement model with consideration of multiple arriving units. Doctoral Dissertation. Rensselaer Polytechnic Institute. Troy, New York.

Rinquest, J. L. (1992). *Multiobjective optimization: Behavioral and computational considerations.* Boston, Mass.: Kluwer Academic Publishers.

Roy, B. (1977) "A conceptual framework for a prescriptive theory of 'decision aid'." *TIMS Studies in the Management Science* 3:55–64.

Saaty, T. L. (1980). *The Analytic hierarchy process.* New York: McGraw-Hill.

Saber, H. M.; Ravindran, A. (1996) "A partitioning gradient based algorithm for solving nonlinear goal programming problems." *Computers and Operations Research* 23: 141–152.

Sainfort, F.; Deichtmann, J. M. (1996). "Decomposition of utility functions on subsets of product sets." *Operations Research* 44: 609–616.

Seo, F.; Sakawa, M. (1988). *Multiple criteria decision analysis in regional planning.* Dordrecht, Holland: Reidel.

Shields, M.; Chan, Y. (1991). The extended ADBASE program. Working Paper. Department of Operational Sciences. Air Force Institute of Technology. Wright-Patterson AFB, Ohio.

Staats, R.; Chan, Y. (1994). Numerical examples of multiple criteria decision making. Working Paper. Department of Operational Sciences. Air Force Institute of Technology. Wright-Patterson AFB, Ohio.

Steuer, R. E. (1986). *Multiple criteria optimization: Theory, computation, and application.* New York: Wiley.

Stewart, T. J. (1999). "Evaluation and Refinement of Aspiration Based Methods in MCDM." *European Journal of Operational Research* 113:643–652.

Tiley, J. S. (1994). Solvent substitution methodology using multiattribute utility theory and the analytical hierarchical process. Master's Thesis. AFIT/GEE/ENS/945–3. Air Force Institute of Technology. Wright-Patterson AFB, Ohio.

Van Herwijnen, M.; Janssen, R. (1998). "The use of MCDM to evaluate trade-offs between spatial objectives." In *Trends in multicriteria decision making,* edited by T. J. Stewart and R. C. van den Honert. Berlin, Germany and New York: Springer-Verlag, 303–312.

Van Herwijnen, M.; Rietveld, P. (1999). "Spatial dimensions in multicriteria analysis." In *Spatial multicriteria decision making and analysis,* edited by J.-C. Thill. Brookfield, Vermont: Ashgate, 77–102.

Vincke, P. (1992). *Multicriteria decision aid.* Chichester, England: Wiley.

Wakker, P. P. (1989). *Additive representation of preferences: A new foundation of decision analysis.* Boston: Kluwer Academic Publishers.

White, D. J. (1990). "A bibliography on the applications of mathematical programming multiple-objective methods." *Journal of the Operational Research Society* 41:669–691.

Yu, P. L. (1985). *Multiple criteria decision making.* New York: Plenum Press.

Zelany, M. (1976). "Games with multiple payoffs." *International Journal of Game Theory* 4, No. 4:179–191.

Zelany, M. (1982). *Multiple criteria decision-making,* New York: McGraw-Hill.

Zionts, S. (1992). "Some thoughts on research in multiple criteria decision making." *Computers and Operations Research* 19:308–311.

6

Remote Sensing and Geographic Information Systems

"Give me to learn each secret cause;
Let number's, figures, motion's laws
Reveal before me stand;
These to great Nature's scene apply
and round the Globe, and through the sky
Disclose her working hand."
      Mark Akenside

Locational and land use studies rely heavily on the availability of data. While one can argue that data are never complete enough to perform analyses, there is also a tendency to collect too much information (or at least collect irrelevant information). Data collection has been facilitated greatly by remote sensing devices such as satellites and computer-based data organization tools such as geographic information systems. With the technological advances in remote sensing and geographic information systems, the data collection effort can theoretically be streamlined. But they also underline a more urgent need to match data against information requirements, such that the relevant data are collected and that they are in the correct format and in sufficient quantity. In this chapter, we wish to review the data base that is required in facility location and land use, mainly from the angle of matching data with analysis requirements. Also included is the processing of such data to bring out the information in as useful a form as possible for application-oriented purposes.

I. DATA IN SPATIAL-TEMPORAL ANALYSIS

Depending on the type of application, the data to be collected would vary. Table 6.1 shows sample data requirements for performing land use modeling in an

Table 6.1   TYPICAL DATA REQUIRED IN URBAN PLANNING APPLICATIONS

Data Items

- total population by place of residence
- population by age-sex groups by place of residence
- population by family size groups by place of residence
- population by annual family income groups by place of residence
- population by industry groups by place of residence
- population by occupational groups by place of residence
- total labor force by place of residence
- total employment by place of work
- employment by industry groups by place of work
- employment by occupational groups by place of work
- employment by income groups by place of work
- total annual retail sales by place of sale
- annual retail sales by retailing groups by place of sale
- total value of manufactured products by place of manufacture
- value of manufactured products by industry groups by place of manufacture
- total government expenditures by place of agency
- capital and operating government expenditures
- government expenditures, capital and operating, by agency
- total person trips by place of destination
- total person trips by land-use groups by place of destination
- total market value of land by small area
- market value of land by land-use groups by small area
- total market value of land and buildings by small area
- market value of land and buildings by structural-type groups by small area
- total housing units by small area
- housing units by type of structure by small area
- housing units by density class by small area
- housing units by condition of structure by small area
- housing units by age of structure by small area
- total floor area by small area
- floor area by land-use groups by small area
- land area by land-use groups by small area
- accessibility to region by small area
- distance (time or cost) to all parts of the region or to the center of the region by small area

urban setting. As one can see, a lot of data need to be gathered. Moreover, such data often need to be collected consistently over more than one period of time to observe a trend. Generally, obtaining this amount of data is costly. The advances in collection and data processing devices do not diminish this resource requirement, even though the cost per unit of information may be lowered. This apparent contradiction is traceable to the fact that a lot of information is often collected superfluously, either due to the ease with which the collection and processing devices work or the lack of care taken in the conduct of such procedures. Invariably, only a tiny fraction of the information gathered is useful, and the information that is really needed is left out. It is essential therefore to be selective in accordance with what data is really required, as suggested above.

A. Resource Requirement

There were reported price tags associated with collecting each piece of information listed in Table 6.1, and many of them signify much time and effort. It is necessary before data collection to assess the resource at hand and to perform a careful tradeoff analysis between the worth of a piece of information and its cost. There are three general categories of costs in facility location and land use modeling: data assembly, model calibration, and analysis and forecasting. In urban applications, for example, data assembly is the most costly, taking up to 30–50 percent of the study budget. This figure can perhaps be generalized to other applications as well. Much of the data assembly cost is attributable to manpower. Taking all requirements into consideration, the time required to collect data is about 4 to 6 person-months in each urban application. This assumes the availability of public domain data sources such as the census and remote sensing data such as that from LANDSAT. The cost of collecting data will become prohibitive, if such data need to be collected from original sources.

When new technology such as geographic information system (GIS) and remote sensing are introduced, the data collection resource requirement picture can become much more complex. Oftentimes, there is an enormous overhead involved in such an introduction. More often than not, the problem boils down to the need to properly match technology against the problem at hand, and the institution has to have the correct environment to foster change. Even though this appears obvious, case after case can be cited where well-intentioned people got burned in the automation process.

B. Assembly of Data Sources

In the context of this book, there are essentially five different categories of data required. The first is labeled **activity,** which includes population and employment in urban applications for example. The second is **land use,** which is a physical description of the site(s). The third is **transportation,** which addresses the accessibility issue that governs the way population and employment distribute themselves in the study area. Transportation goes well beyond facilities such as roads, rail, and terminals to include travel time, distance, and costs in general. The fourth is **infrastructure,** which includes public utilities and other supporting elements. A final category includes information on the **environment,** which pertains to water quality, air quality, noise, and so forth. The source of the first category of information—population and employment, is typically the census, which is conducted by the Bureau of Census in the Department of Commerce every 10 years in the United States and updated every five years. The employment statistics are tabulated by the Standard Industrial Classification (SIC) code. Population is compiled by census tract, while education information may be collected by school districts, although there are recent trends to put them on a more consistent geographic sub-units, as afforded by the advent of GIS.

The second category information, land use, is traditionally survey data, supplemented by aerial photos. In the United States, the information is often coded according to the Standard Land Use Coding Manual published by the Department of Housing and Urban Development. Part of the land use information is the permissible development densities, which deal with (among other items) the height of buildings that are in certain zones. In urban applications, such information is often encoded in zoning maps available from metropolitan planning agencies. In recent years, we have seen the introduction of satellite imagery that greatly expands the type of land use information that is available. In rural applications, land use refers to anything from landform and soils to ecological and vegetative classifications.

The third category information, transportation, is traditionally encoded in highway networks for urban applications. Standard computer programs are available to extract the necessary travel time information between two points in a study area. Trip frequency is needed, that is, information on what percentage of trips taken are of a particular duration. For example, 30 percent of the trips may be under 10 minutes in duration, 50 percent between 10 and 20 minutes, with the remaining over 20 minutes. Transportation or highway agencies are the best source of such information. In rural applications, interregional commodity flows are often required, representing trading that takes place via air, highway, or waterways.

Fourth, the infrastructure information—sewers, water supply, and power—is usually dispersed among the various political jurisdictions and utility companies. Individual communities, states, and countries are often the custodians of these records. Inasmuch as utility companies are highly regulated in the United States, these public agencies often need to be consulted before utility companies are willing to release information beyond basic factual data.

Finally, environmental information of interest lies in a variety of stakeholders: for instance, industries that pollute and those that do not, governmental agencies that oversee public health and safety, and advocacy citizen groups who are watchdogs for conservation. While site-specific and interest-group-specific data gathering is indispensable, remote sensing has increasingly played a more important role in environmental monitoring in recent years. It provides accessible information irrespective of political jurisdiction.

C. Use and Display of Information

In view of the cost of data collection, a cogent question to ask is: "What is the minimum information set, or the absolutely necessary amount of information out of the comprehensive set, that will allow us to do the analyses?" The main idea is to identify substitutes in case a particular piece of information is not available. For example, work trips can be substitutes for employment, and housing can serve as a proxy for population. A desirable strategy is to have information that is readily observable, such as from satellites, instead of from secondary sources. Remote sensing technology has developed to such an extent now that this strategy has become quite feasible.

It is widely agreed that a key element of a GIS is graphical display. There are specifications as to the way that a display should be presented and used. For example, it should be problem-oriented, and it should provide just the appropriate amount of information for the occasion—no more and no less. Figure 6.1 and Figure 6.2 show some rather interesting three dimensional plots of population information in York, Pennsylvania—a focal case study area in the "Exercises and Problems" appendix and the accompanying compact disc. Two graphs are displayed—the **proximal graph** by zone (Figure 6.1) and the **contour graph** by continuous distribution (Figure 6.2). Proximal maps are usually graphed for land use

Figure 6.1   PROXIMAL MAP OF DEVELOPABLE RESIDENTIAL LAND IN
YORK, PENNSYLVANIA

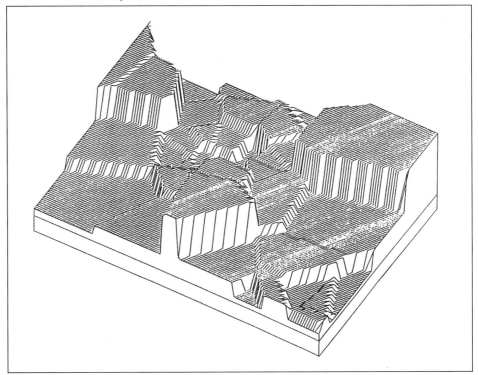

Figure 6.2   CONTOUR MAP OF POPULATION IN YORK, PENNSYLVANIA

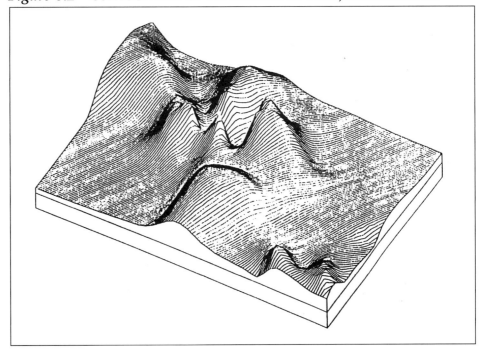

information, while contour maps are used for activities such as population and employment. For example, residential land use in thousands of square feet (m^2) can be plotted, delineated by the boundaries of tesselations that approximate traffic zones, as shown in Figure 6.1. Population, on the other hand, is considered to be ubiquitous among developable land and hence represented here as continuous distribution.

Information over time can also be displayed as well (Langran 1992). Zonal population or employment over the base-year and forecast-year can be displayed side-by-side as bar charts in Figure 6.3. Such a plot shows the spatial variation of population or employment activities temporally; it is effective in displaying the regional impacts of a policy over a planning horizon. Obviously, many other variations are possible, including overlays, and there are quite a few graphics packages today that have extensive display capabilities such as virtual reality in which realistic images are constituted by the user for experimentation. Thus existing capabilities in data retrieval and imagery enhancement allow a great deal of flexibility in information display. Perhaps an area for further improvement and exploitation may be a concerted effort to bring the user and the analysis communities together through these graphical displays, so that the analyst can provide the user with what is really needed rather than what the analyst thinks is needed.

Figure 6.3   BASE-YEAR ZONAL EMPLOYMENT, YORK, PENNSYLVANIA

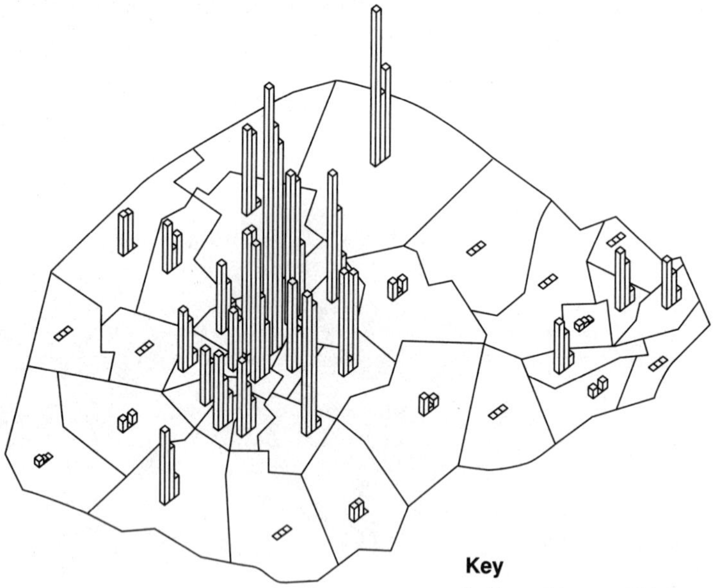

Key

Left-most bar – Total employment
Middle bar   – Basic employment
Right-most bar – Nonbasic employment

II. GEOGRAPHIC CODING SYSTEMS

According to Werner (1974), the two major structural elements of all geographic coding systems are a concept of areal division, classification, or definition; and some form of coding logic. In recent years, overt emphasis has been given to the automated aspects of geocoding logic and data storage, retrieval and display in large, geographically referenced information systems. This has resulted in a popular tendency to assume that a legitimate geocoding system must be computer-based and requires a fairly sophisticated coding structure. Broadly conceived, systematic geographic coding has had a long and diverse history that includes many classifications other than coding-oriented systems of geographic reference.

A. Central Place Theory

Historically, there exists a well-publicized scheme regarding a natural geographic classification hierarchy. It was believed that central places were developed from distribution points for goods and services in order to serve a surrounding hinterland (for instance, an agricultural region). The central place evolves later on as a political and social center for the region, serving a diverse number of interest groups and concerns beyond farmers. A central place may be developed from a transport focus or break bulk point. For example, Chicago, besides being a central place for the distribution of agricultural goods, is also a natural waterways center and a rail hub for manufacturing industries. It is a distribution and collection center for all commodities passing through the Great Lakes and the Midwest of the United States in general. Specialized function settlements constitute yet another type of central places: for example, coal mining in Scranton/Wilkes-Barre, Pennsylvania. There are many parallel cases of this kind, including resorts, spas, and other natural resource centers.

One can identify a hierarchy of central places. A hamlet is a local center, a village is a neighborhood center; town is a community center; a city is a regional center; and a metropolis and a megopolis may be described as cosmopolitan gathering places. Industrialized nations seem to become more and more urbanized. For this reason, this hierarchical geographic classification scheme may be applicable to a number of industrialized nations. It forms a logical scheme for storing geographic information. Thus one can look up the population and employment in a hamlet versus a village versus a town and all the way up to a megalopolis. Recent analysis techniques organize spatial data around tile-like tessellations that approximate these natural settlement patterns.[1]

B. Concentric Zone, Sector, and Multi-Nuclei City Structures

Aside from these broad classifications of central places, there are some observed regularities in the internal structure of an urban area, upon which finer geographic subdivisions can be discerned. As far back as 1923, Burgess postulated a structure of **concentric rings** around the central business district corresponding to belts of different activities (see Figure 6.4(a)). The central business district, which forms the core of the onion-ring structure, is the focus of commercial, social, and civic activities as well as the transportation system. Outside the central business district is a transition zone where residential and light manufacturing activities

Figure 6.4 CONCENTRIC ZONE, SECTOR, AND MULTI-NUCLEI STRUCTURES OF A CITY

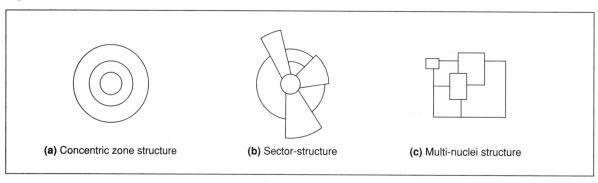

(a) Concentric zone structure **(b)** Sector-structure **(c)** Multi-nuclei structure

are found. Further out, there is the zone for blue-collar workers' homes. Then comes the ring of higher income residences, including the better apartments and single-family dwellings. Finally, on the outer fringe is the commuters' zone in which suburbs and satellite towns are found.

The **sector city structure,** suggested by Hoyt as far back as 1939, is a modified version of the above in that it incorporates transportation factors more explicitly. The influence of transportation routes in guiding urban growth is modeled along corridors (or sectors) in addition to the ring structure (see Figure 6.4(b)). This structure recognizes that growth occurs along transportation routes since they facilitate the movement of people and freight. Also incorporated is the fact that high-income residential activities tend to move out from the city center as a result of better transportation to and from the central business district.

Finally, the **multi-nuclei structure** recognizes that a disparate group of centers grow to merge into a multi-nucleated urban area. Certain heavy industries may have located themselves in certain parts of town. At the same time mutually exclusive facilities are likely to separate one from the other. Thus quality residences tend to locate themselves away from the industries for environmental reasons. As a result, several central places evolve within the same urban area. An illustration of this concept is again shown in Figure 6.4(c).

There are other postulated geographic structures of a city, but those described above represent the classic ways to classify a city into subregions for geographic reference. It would seem that a GIS should be able to take into consideration such a classification scheme. In reality, however, most GIS tend to organize their classification scheme along arbitrary geographic boundaries of census tracts, school districts, voting precincts, and traffic zones. They bear little resemblance to the logical scheme as outlined above. In recent years, districting models have been proposed to divide a community into logical subdivisions (Benabdallah and Wright 1992; Bennion and O'Neill 1994; Ahituv and Berman 1988). This represents a revived interest in the structure of human settlements. More will be said on district clustering in Section XII of this chapter.

C. Dual Independent Map Encoding System

The fundamental urban data classification used in practice goes to a level of detail way beyond the internal city structure schemes above. In a way, it also goes beyond the census tracts, school districts, voting precincts, and traffic zones. In the United States, the requirement for a continuing metropolitan planning process in the 1960s created an increased demand upon the Bureau of the Census to provide a small area data and expanded data-user services. This, in turn, led to the initiation of the Census-Use Study, which was to improve methods for relating census data to local agency data at a fine geographic scale. By the 1970s, a fairly standardized universe of urban geographic base files utilizing the Dual Independent Map Encoding (DIME) system, based on block-face coding, had been implemented in almost all standard metropolitan statistical areas.

The 1970 census instituted a computerized procedure that incorporated many of the advances developed in the studies in the 1960s. As mentioned, the major geocoding innovation was DIME. A DIME geographic base file is essentially a description of block boundaries defined by its nodes (or vertices). Figure 6.5 illustrates this technique through a series of illustrations. Many of the steps in the traditional geocoding process are eliminated by the use of specially prepared

Figure 6.5   ILLUSTRATING THE DIME FILES

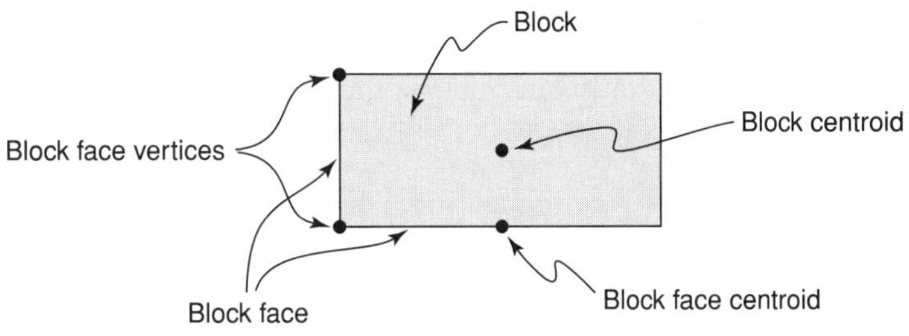

(a) Alternative ways of coding data at city block level.

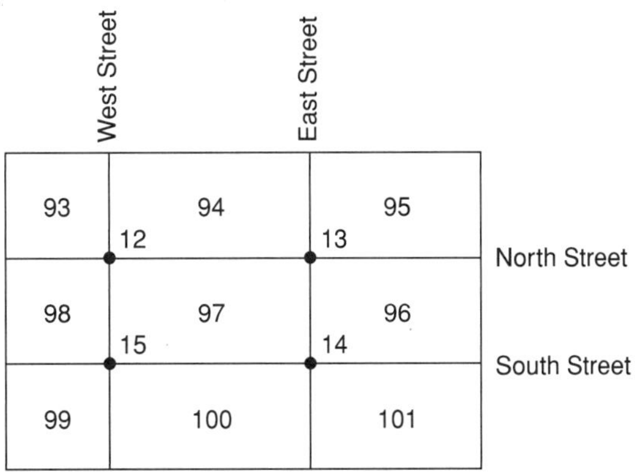

Segment name	Nodes		Block number		Address			
	From	To	Left	Right	Left		Right	
					Low	High	Low	High
North Street	12	13	94	97	133	229	134	230

(b) Form of segment records in a DIME file.

SOURCE: Hutchinson (1974). Reprinted with permission.

master-coding-maps and the keying of census files to coding maps through the geographic identifiers. The construction of noded map, map-resources lists, block numbering-schemes, field work and Address Coding Guide (ACG) preparation may now be unnecessary. Use of standard DIME/ACG files entails the construction of the arterial network in the DIME system, the reconstruction of census data to fit traffic zones, and the addition of local transportation and land use files to the modified DIME Census-file. The arterial network can be reconstituted from DIME. To do this, however, a DIME file must be adjusted for transportation-system applications. That task will include creating a new network file, adding data on traffic direction, capacity, pavement width, etc. (See Figure 6.5(b)). To reconstruct census data by traffic zones, it is necessary to provide a table of equivalents between census areas and traffic zones. Similarly, the addition of local codes allows use of the DIME file in the analysis of local and census data as they relate to local areas.

The use of DIME files is based on the fact that the city block is one of the smallest, most standard and relatively permanent urban areal units. Block face is the lowest common-denominator unit for urban geographic base files because, in general, cities are made up of blocks. With data gathered and recorded by blocks, data sets can be aggregated or disaggregated to conform to any number of special area boundaries, for instance, school districts, traffic zones, or police precincts. Thus, only one geographic coding system is required to meet the varied demands of many users.

D. Topologically Integrated Geographic Encoding and Referencing

Unlike the urban environment, there is no analogous common-denominator unit for national geographic base files. A nation's geography encompasses a far more heterogeneous mix of land use patterns, natural areas, governmental entities, and other spatial orderings than that which characterizes metropolitan geomorphology. While many national geocoding systems are based on county units or units compatible with county boundaries, there are important exceptions, such as zip code zones and congressional districts. These do not necessarily aggregate to the county level. There is a lack of definition, both semantic and geographic, of sub-county units. There is the problem of variation between urban and rural land use, settlement patterns, and population densities which create great disparities in the size of the spatial units coded both within a single system and among the various systems (Schweiger 1992; Gryder 1992).

As part of the 1990 census, the U.S. Department of Commerce, Bureau of the Census, developed an automated geographic database, known as the Topologically Integrated Geographic Encoding and Referencing (TIGER) system. TIGER provides coordinate-based digital-map information for the entire United States, Puerto Rico, the U.S. Virgin Islands, and the Pacific Territories over which the United States has jurisdiction. The TIGER system has significantly improved the accuracy of the 1990 census maps and geographic reference products. Extract files from the TIGER system permit users with appropriate software to perform such tasks as linking the statistical data in the 1990 Census of Population and Housing: displaying selected characteristics on maps or a video display screen at different scales and with whatever boundaries they select for any geographic areas of the country. For example, a map for a particular county may be displayed showing the distribution of the voting age population by city block. The Bureau makes the information, called TIGER/Line™ files, available to the public on CD-ROM. A program, available from some of the most widely circulated GIS software, allows the users to display the information in a graphic form.

TIGER data is the most widely used spatial data used to geographically define a local area or region available today. They replace the 1980 GBF/DIME (Geographic Base File/Dual Independent Map Encoding) files, and contain these data elements:

1. Census map features such as road, railroad and rivers
2. Feature names and classification codes
3. Alternate feature names
4. Associated 1980 and 1990 census geographic area codes
5. Federal Information Processing Standard (FIPS) codes
6. Latitude and longitude coordinates
7. For areas formerly covered by DIME files: address ranges and zip codes

Other TIGER-related products that may be helpful for specific applications include:

1. TIGER/DataBase™—containing point, line, and area information from TIGER's internal data base, including additional information not available in the TIGER/Line™ files;
2. TIGER/Boundary™—containing coordinate data for specific 1990 census tabulation area boundary sets; for instance, a file containing all state and county boundaries, and another containing all census tract and block-numbering area boundaries;
3. TIGER/Tract comparability™—providing information for 1980 and 1990 census tracts.

Klosterman (1991) gives an excellent introduction to the TIGER system, emphasizing applicational considerations. Also included are a glossary of terms and contacts for further information.

E. Other Data Sources

In the United States, data from National Aeronautics and Space Administration (NASA), National Oceanic and Atmospheric Administration (NOAA), and Department of Interior through the U.S. Geological Survey (USGS) have been particularly important supplements to data from the Bureau of Census. Specific examples of data here included remotely sensed, land use, land cover, and digital elevation data (Star and Estes 1990; Schweiger 1992). Table 6.2 presents examples of digital data sets, produced on a routine basis, that are available (or are being made available) from the U.S. government. Data from USGS can be used to define street networks. USGS offers Digital Line Graphs (DLGs) through the National Digital Cartographic Data-Base (NDCDB). DLGs are files of cartographic data primarily made by digitizing point locations and line and polygon outlines from map separation materials. (See example in Figure 6.11.) The spatial data are topologically structured. Spatial relationships, such as adjacency and

Table 6.2   DIGITAL DATA AVAILABLE FROM THE UNITED STATES
GOVERNMENT

Data Type	Data Source
Topography: Digital elevation model Digital terrain data	U.S. Geological Survey (National Mapping Division) Defense Mapping Agency
Land use and land cover: Ownership and political boundaries Transportation Hydrography	U.S. Geological Survey (National Mapping Division) Note: Department of Energy also has transportation data
Socioeconomic and demographic data: Census tract boundaries Demographic data Socioeconomic data	U.S. Department of Commerce (Census Bureau)
Soils	U.S. Department of Agriculture (Soil Conservation Service)
Wetlands	U.S. Fish and Wildlife Service
Remotely sensed data	National Aeronautics and Space Administration National Oceanic and Atmospheric Administration

SOURCE: Star and Estes (1990). Reprinted with permission.

connectivity among data elements, are explicitly encoded. In addition, DLG data elements may have coded attributes. An improved data model, called Digital Line Graph-Enhanced (DLG-E), will be available soon. DLG-E provides for the explicit representation of individual cartographic features, such as roads, counties, buildings and streams, in addition to the topologically structured spatial data provided in the current DLG. This enhancement also provides a more extensive set of attributes and relationships for these features than exists in a DLG. Other data which are available from USGS include digital elevation model data, land use and land cover data, and geographic names data, as suggested earlier and shown in Table 6.2. Remote-sensing data will be discussed in a later section of this chapter.

There is a long-range effort in the U.S. Government to create a NDCDB. This is based on the work of an interagency coordinating committee, to set standards for the format and content of digital spatial data throughout the government. The layers to be included in this database include hypsography (topographical relief), hydrography (surface water for navigation), land surface cover, surface features including vegetation, boundaries, positional control, transportation, other man-made structures, and the Public Land Survey System. One commercially available source of spatial data is EtaMaps®, available through Etak, Inc. They contain centerline street data, address ranges, political and statistical boundaries, and zip codes. They come in two formats: as ASCII format which can be read by the leading GIS software products such as ARC/INFO, AutoCAD, IGDS, INFORMAP and others and a compressed format, making EtakMaps® usable with other Etak software products. Many of the GIS software vendors provide data sources as well. We will survey these GIS software in a later section.

The United Nations Environment Programme (UNEP) is a spatial data user as well as a producer. Through the newly established Global Resources Information Database, with existing centers at the UNEP offices in Geneva, Switzerland, and Nairobi, Kenya, efforts are under way to collect and disseminate important spatial data sets for the globe, as well as provide certain kinds of assistance in spatial data collection and processing to less-developed countries. Sample data sets in the archives now include range and endangered species distribution for parts of the world, as well as small scale global data sets of soils and vegetation.

Shaw, Maidment, and Arimes (1993) reported a computer-based regulatory information system for site planning. The concept of jurisdiction is used to separate the regulations and permit requirements applicable to a particular development from those that are not. It is a useful tool for providing early feedback to prospective permit applicants. In sites with rapidly changing regulations, updating and maintaining current information may require substantial effort. To use GIS in concert with regulatory information is a feasible solution, although this has its cost implications as well. Finally, this concept can be carried over to hazardous waste regulations, environmental permitting, and appropriative water-right laws.

III. GEOGRAPHIC INFORMATION SYSTEMS (GIS)

Computer-based GIS is characterized by its ability to integrate layers of spatially oriented data through a variety of analytical approaches. The end result, if carefully executed, is productive sharing of information for multiple problem solving. Among the general advantages of GIS are (Lee and Zhang 1989):

(a) The ease of data retrieval;

(b) The discovery and display of information gained by observing interaction between location and land use attributes;

(c) The capacity to process a large amount of data for spatial evaluation;

(d) The ability to make scale and projection changes, remove distortions, and perform coordinate rotation and translation; and

(e) The analysis of spatial relationships through the application of empirical and quantitative models.

A. Data Organization and Structure

The choice of a particular **spatial data structure** is one of the important decisions in designing a GIS (Star and Estes 1990). Each type of spatial data or theme in a GIS is referred to as a data layer or data plane. In each of these data layers, there are three primitive geometrical entities to encode: points, lines, and polygons or planes. **Points,** such as the locations of oil and water wells, and **lines,** such as the centerlines of roadways or streams, are key elements of this breakdown. When we consider bounded regions, such as the borders of a subdivision or the edges of a lake, we often focus on the boundary lines called the enclosed region **polygons.** We use the term to include curved boundaries in addition to straight line boundaries. Not all GISs can work directly with curves as such. More often than not, they permit a curved line to have interior digitized points in addition to the end points. Thus a curve is approximated by straight line segments. Besides geometric information, equally important is the non-spatial or attribute data. For a simple spatial object such as a well, the essential spatial information is the geodetic or geographic location of the well. Ancillary information may include its depth, date of drilling, production volume, ownership, and so forth. (See examples in Figure 6.11 and Figure 6.12.)

1. Raster Data Structure. The data structure of a GIS can be broadly classified into two types: raster and vector. In a raster structure, a value for the parameter of interest, for example, elevation above datum, land use class, and plant biomass

Figure 6.6 RASTER DATA STRUCTURE EXAMPLE

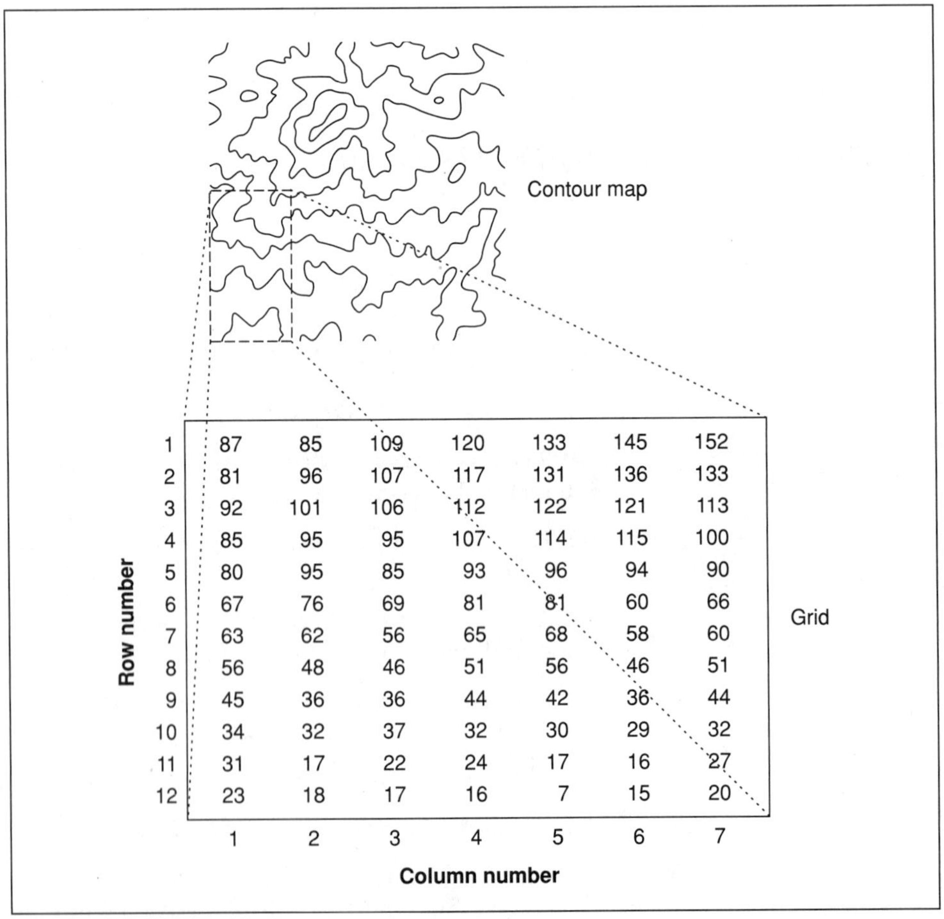

Row number	1	2	3	4	5	6	7
1	87	85	109	120	133	145	152
2	81	96	107	117	131	136	133
3	92	101	106	112	122	121	113
4	85	95	95	107	114	115	100
5	80	95	85	93	96	94	90
6	67	76	69	81	81	60	66
7	63	62	56	65	68	58	60
8	56	48	46	51	56	46	51
9	45	36	36	44	42	36	44
10	34	32	37	32	30	29	32
11	31	17	22	24	17	16	27
12	23	18	17	16	7	15	20

SOURCE: Star and Estes (1990). Reprinted with permission.

Figure 6.7   DEFINITION OF SPATIAL NEIGHBORHOOD

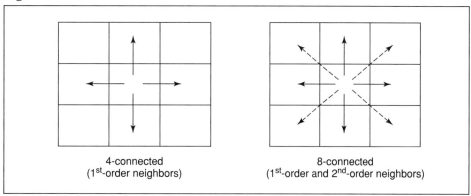

4-connected
(1st-order neighbors)

8-connected
(1st-order and 2nd-order neighbors)

SOURCE: Star and Estes (1990). Reprinted with permission.

density, is developed for every cell in a grid over space. In Figure 6.6, elevation in meters has been recorded from a contour map on a regular grid, where each cell is referenced by the row and column numbers. Thus at the position represented by the first cell (1, 1), the land is 87 meters (290 feet) above sea level, and so forth.

One consequence of this grid system is that a cell has either four or eight adjoining neighbors, depending on one's preference, as shown in Figure 6.7. Notice that the 4-connected neighbors are closer than the 8-connected neighbors inasmuch as the diagonal elements are 1.41 times further away than the immediate 4-connected ones. The former is called **first-order neighbors** and the latter **second-order neighbors.** (See the "Spatial Time Series" chapter in Chan [2000] to see how the order of neighbors affects spatial analysis.)

Consider a development as shown in Figure 6.8(a). A map from a local planning agency shows the legal property boundaries, streets, and restrictions on construction and development due to easements of public utilities. Figure 6.8(b) shows a raster converted representation of the map. The numbers in each

Figure 6.8   A SUBDIVISION MAP AND ITS RASTER REPRESENTATION

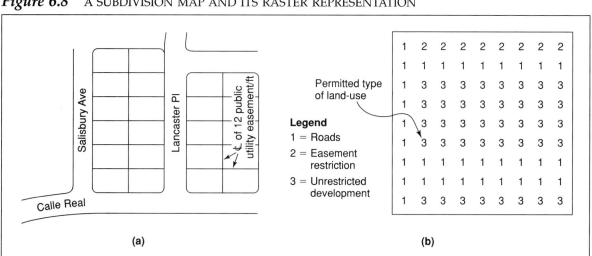

SOURCE: Star and Estes (1990). Reprinted with permission.

cell indicate the permitted land use for each cell, using a majority rule in case of ambiguity due to the coarseness of the grid overlay on the subdivision map. By adding up the number of cells in each category, we can determine the percentage area coverage of each land use category:

Land use category	Class	Total cells	Percent of total
Roads	1	33	41
Easement-restriction	2	8	10
Unrestricted-development	3	40	49

Raster data sets in practice can be very large. When dealing with such large data sets, there are several algorithms used to compress the data. Aside from the obvious method of increasing the coarseness of the grid, one way of compressing the data uses chain codes. **Chain codes** consider a map as a set of spatially referenced objects placed on top of a background. The coordinates of a starting point on the border of an object (for example, a lake) are recorded, and then the sequence of cardinal directions of the cells that make up the boundary are stored. As shown in Figure 6.9, the shaded area is represented, beginning from the starting point (1, 1), by 3 units north, 1 east, 1 south, 2 east, 1 south, 1 west, 1 south, and 2 west. This may be an efficient way to store areas, particularly since each spatial object is kept as a separate entity in the data base. However, some kinds of processing will be required so that the entire raster array can be reconstituted, a complex task that may amount to an unacceptable cost.

2. Vector Data Structures. The second major type of data structure in a GIS is the vector format. In a description of spatial data based on vectors, we make the assumption that an element may be located at any location, without the positional constraints of a raster array. Vector data structures are based on elemental points whose locations are known to arbitrary precision, in contrast to the approximate raster data structures described above. As a simple example, to store a circle in

Figure 6.9   A CHAIN CODE REPRESENTATION

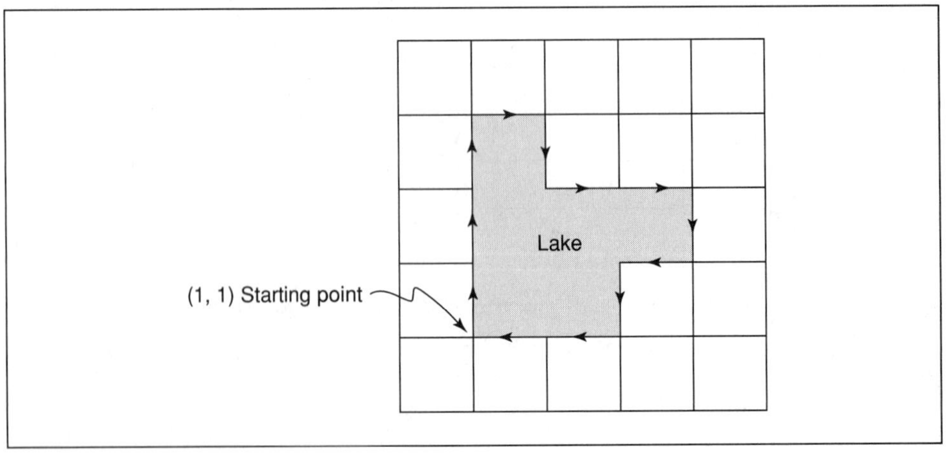

(1, 1) Starting point

Lake

one of the raster data structures, we might find and encode all the raster cells whose locations correspond to the boundary of the circle. This is often called a low-level description of the circle. A high-level description, on the other hand, might efficiently store the circle by recording a point location for the center of the circle, and specifying the radius. In this example, the high-level description based on a vector representation is more efficient in terms of the amount of data required, as well as more precise.

Several forms of vector data structures are in common use. In a **whole polygon structure,** each layer in the data base is divided into a set of polygons such as the one shown in Figure 6.10. Each polygon is encoded in the data base as a sequence of locations that define the boundaries of each closed area in a specified coordinate system (sometimes called a boundary loop). Each polygon is then stored as an independent feature. There is no explicit means in this system to reference areas that are adjacent. This is, to some extent, comparable to the chain-coded raster discussed above, in that for both a whole polygon structure and a chain-coded raster, the emphasis is on the individual polygonal areas, where each discrete area is stored separately. Thus the three regions in Figure 6.10 appear as

Polygon I	*Polygon II*	*Polygon III*
1, 4	2, 2	6, 4
4, 3	4, 2	7, 2
4, 2	4, 0	6, 1
2, 2	1, 0	4, 0
		4, 2
		4, 3

Figure 6.10   EXAMPLE OF A WHOLE POLYGON STRUCTURE

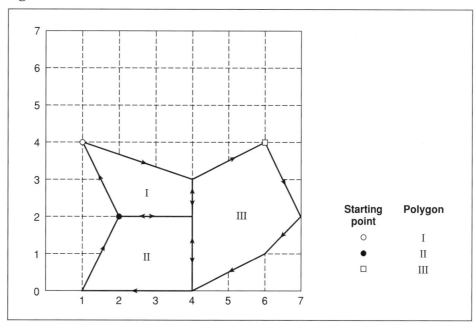

SOURCE: Star and Estes (1990). Reprinted with permission.

Attributes of the polygons, such as land cover or ownership, may be stored with the coordinate list. Please note that by maintaining each polygon as a separate entity this way, the topological organization of the polygons is not maintained. By topology is meant the relationships between different spatial objects: which polygons share a common boundary, which points fall along the edge of a particular polygon, and so on. In a whole polygon structure, line segments that define the common edges of polygons are recorded twice, once for the polygon on each side of the line. Similarly, points that are shared by several polygons, such as location (4, 2) in the example, will also be represented several times in the data base. With this organization, editing and updating the database without corrupting the data structure can be difficult.

One of the best known standard vector file formats is the previously mentioned DLG of the USGS. The agency is producing these vector files based on the source materials used to compile the USGS 7.5-Minute and 15-Minute Topographic Maps Series. A separate set of DLG data files is based on 1:2,000,000-scale map products. The data contents of the DLG files are subdivided into different thematic layers. One layer consists of boundary information, including both political and administrative boundaries in the region. A second layer is for hydrographic features. A third layer is for the transportation network in the area. Finally, the fourth layer is based on the Public Land Survey System, which has as its focus a survey system administered by the U.S. Bureau of Land Management.

The essential data elements of the DLG level-3 structure are similar to the other vector data structures discussed in connection with DIME files. Nodes represent either end points of lines or line intersections, while additional points are used where required to indicate significant features along lines. Lines have starting and ending nodes, and as such, they permit us to specify a direction along the line as well as the areas on the left and right sides of the line. A special degenerate line is defined as a line of zero length and is used to define features that are indicated on the map as a point. Degenerate lines are recognizable because they have the same starting and ending node. Areas in the DLG format are completely bounded by line segments. Each area may have an associated point that represents the characteristics of the area; the point location is arbitrary and may not even be within the area. The point, line, and area elements provide information about topology and location. In addition, there is an extensive system for coding attribute information for the elements. The attribute codes are based on those features represented on USGS topographic maps. Attribute codes are structured in a specified way, with both major and minor code components, where a major code may signify surface cover for example and a minor code may contain more specific descriptors.

3. Relational Vector Structure Graphical approaches utilize cartographic principles—for example, symbols, line weights, and color—for characterizing spatial features and their type and magnitude. Relational databases contain an ordered set of information grouped together in two-dimensional tables known as relations. Users define the relation that is appropriate to the query whether the tables are already available or need to be constructed by the controlling program. Relational databases have the advantage that their structure is very flexible and can meet the demands of all typical queries that can be formulated. Figures 6.11 and 6.12 present examples of such a data structure. Illustrated in these examples are representations of areas, lines, and points, as well as their attributes, stored as alphameric mirror images of the graphical counterpart. The example here shows

Figure 6.11   CHAIN AND POLYGON DATA RECORDS FOR GIS

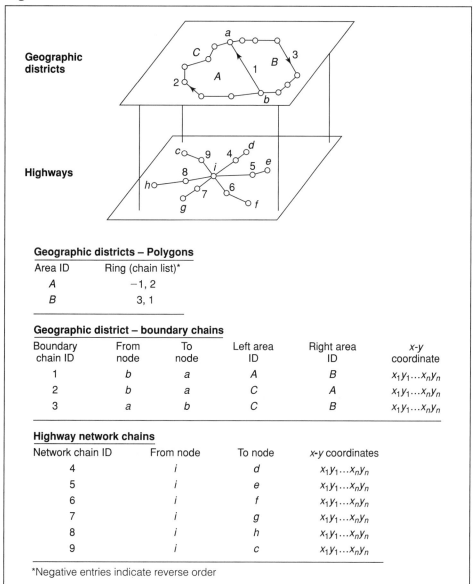

Geographic districts – Polygons

Area ID	Ring (chain list)*
A	−1, 2
B	3, 1

Geographic district – boundary chains

Boundary chain ID	From node	To node	Left area ID	Right area ID	*x-y* coordinate
1	b	a	A	B	$x_1y_1...x_ny_n$
2	b	a	C	A	$x_1y_1...x_ny_n$
3	a	b	C	B	$x_1y_1...x_ny_n$

Highway network chains

Network chain ID	From node	To node	*x-y* coordinates
4	i	d	$x_1y_1...x_ny_n$
5	i	e	$x_1y_1...x_ny_n$
6	i	f	$x_1y_1...x_ny_n$
7	i	g	$x_1y_1...x_ny_n$
8	i	h	$x_1y_1...x_ny_n$
9	i	c	$x_1y_1...x_ny_n$

*Negative entries indicate reverse order

SOURCE: Nyerges and Dueker (1988). Reprinted with permission.

highway network attributes, including travel times and traffic volumes. In summary, these are the advantages of a relational organization:

(a) All data structures can be normalized (such as a unit-square representation of a rectangular map)[2];

(b) Spatial consistency is insured across entities (as key points are geocoded in *x-y* coordinates);

Figure 6.12   LOCATIONAL DATA LINKED TO ATTRIBUTE DATA

Highway-network chains			
Network chain ID	**From node**	**To node**	**Coordinates**
4	*i*	*d*	$x_1 y_1 \ldots x_n y_n$
5	*i*	*e*	$x_1 y_1 \ldots x_n y_n$
6	*i*	*f*	$x_1 y_1 \ldots x_n y_n$
7	*i*	*g*	$x_1 y_1 \ldots x_n y_n$
8	*i*	*h*	$x_1 y_1 \ldots x_n y_n$
9	*i*	*e*	$x_1 y_1 \ldots x_n y_n$

Locational data

Highway-network data			
Chain ID (control section ID)	**Travel time (min.)**	**Traffic volume (veh./day)**	**Other attributes**
4	15	5,000	…
5	20	10,000	…
6	17	4,000	…
7	14	6,000	…
8	22	11,000	…
9	18	3,000	…

SOURCE: Nyerges and Dueker (1988). Reprinted with permission.

(c) Spatial relations are compact (see, for example, the district specification in Figure 6.11) and isolated from non-spatial relationships (in Figure 6.12);

(d) Features can be attached to multiple spatial entities inasmuch as these entities are referenced against one another; and

(e) Multiple geobases can be attached to the same application database.

B. Location Reference System and Data Structure

As seen from Figures 6.11 and 6.12, GIS queries can be spatial, non-spatial (attribute), or a combination of the two through the establishment of suitable linkages. When spatial information is desired, data must be established within a coordinate system that can serve as a spatial reference system. In addition to the reference control scheme, data are generally related to a map base that maintains good horizontal and vertical control. USGS 1:24,000- and 1:62,500-scale quadrangles have been employed in a number of GIS studies. The USGS 1:100,000-scale maps are gaining popularity and utility because of the useful scale for a variety of small-scale GIS investigations and because of the current U.S. Census TIGER files that utilize data from that map series. USGS map series provide, in general, good topographic, transportation, hydrographic, political boundary, and spatial control on each base map to serve as the locational reference for GIS analyses. Global Positioning Systems, afforded through satellite technology, are gradually providing a mechanism to secure accurate survey coordinate information with time and cost savings.

As mentioned, closely related to location referencing is topological information. Topological information allows one to describe not only an object's position, but also its spatial relationships with respect to neighboring objects. Some kind of topological information is implicit in spatial data. In a simple raster structured data file, for example, there is a specified spatial organization for the data. The regularity in the array provides an implicit addressing system. This permits rapid random access to specified locations in the database. Thus we know immediately those cells that are adjacent to any target location, and we can easily find and examine those regions that bound a specified group of cells. Topological information in vector structures is often coded explicitly in the database. Line segments with DIME files, for example, have identifiers and codes for the polygon on either side. When topological relationships are not explicitly coded in vector data structures, it can be relatively expensive and time-consuming to constitute them.

The advantages and disadvantages of raster versus vector spatial data structures hinge on data volume (or storage efficiency), retrieval efficiency, robustness to perturbation, data manipulation efficiency, data accuracy, and data display. While some of these have been discussed in the previous section, there are fundamental differences between the two systems that make comparison irrelevant: raster is quasi-continuous, while vector is clearly discrete; raster representation may be considered more dense than vector because more unique values are stored. On this basis, the two systems are geared toward different applications, and they have their respective roles to play. To illustrate how difficult the comparison job really is, consider comparison of processing efficiency in modern GIS systems. Traditionally, overlay operations are thought to be more efficient in raster systems. In current data processing technology, however, there may be an efficient means to determine the approximate locations of polygons by maintaining a separate index database. Using such an index to structure a search through the spatial data, a comparison of raster and vector data structures based on processing speed may be more sensitive to the spatial data itself than to the choice between the two data structures. If forms of both raster and vector structures are found in a GIS, as well as structure conversion routines and appropriate analysis tools for each data type, then the data could be stored in their natural form to both optimize geographic specificity and minimize conversion costs and attendant bias. This also permits analytic procedures to operate on a data structure where efficiency or accuracy is highest. While this strategy is more complex than one in which all data are stored and manipulated in a single data structure, efficient software and hardware for vector/raster conversion can significantly reduce the size of the problem.

Because of today's prevailing philosophy of data sharing between various organizations, federal agencies have begun distributing spatial data using Topological Vector Profile (TVP) as part of the Spatial Data Transfer Standard (SDTS). The most notable of these applications is USGS's conversion of all 1:100 000 -scale and 1:2 000 000-scale DLG-3 data to TVP and making TVP available free of charge on the Internet. Lazar (1996) provided a primer on using the TVP. SDTS will eventually cover all aspects of spatial-data transfer, including the conceptual modeling of spatial data itself. These encompass the definition of 32 vector and raster spatial objects. SDTS would have specifications for data quality reports, logical specifications for transferring data (what items can be transferred and how they are organized), and the physical field format of the data transfer. Currently, TVP requires several spatial objects to exist in every data set. One feature of TVP is that it provides a common dictionary to unify hitherto diverse spatial object terminologies. For example, the following spatial objects are defined:

(a) **planar node:** a zero-dimensional object that is a topological intersection or endpoint of one-dimensional objects,

(b) **complete chain:** a one-dimensional object that reference starting and ending nodes and left and right two-dimensional objects,

(c) **GT-polygon:** a two-dimensional object, where the GT stands for geometry and topology, and

(d) **universe polygon:** the special GT-polygon that covers the rest of the universe outside of other GT-polygons; there is always exactly one universe polygon.

An SDTS data set is referred to as a transfer. A **transfer** consists of a group of files encoded. In the TVP, all files for a particular transfer will be in a single, separate directory for any medium with a directory structure. There is also an ASCII text README file associated with it. Part of the file name refers to a logical grouping of related information. For example, it may facilitate the transfer of one-dimensional spatial objects such as complete chains. It should be noted the system is still evolving and additional features are being implemented, often at the suggestion of the users.

C. Geographic Information Systems Technology

While the computer is just a tool, GIS is often thought of as computer systems for managing a spatial data structure (Lee and Zhang 1989). The main hardware factors that influence the performance and capacity of a computer system are word length, main memory size, processing speed, size of external storage, and data transfer rate between external and main memories. The cost of software development is generally high. Current software packages include management systems, logic programming, object-oriented programming, and object-oriented databases. The complexity lies in the need to integrate geometric and non-geometric data and the need for a distributed system.

There are five essential elements in a GIS according to Star and Estes (1990): **data acquisition, preprocessing, data management, manipulation** and **analysis,** and **product generation.** We have addressed data acquisition already, and more will be said under the section on remote sensing. The remaining four components of the system are intimately related to the way hardware and software are configured. Preprocessing involves manipulating the data in several ways so that they may be entered into the GIS. Two of the principal tasks of preprocessing include data format conversion and identifying the locations of objects in the original data in a systematic way. The first involves converting paper maps and transparent overlays to computerized data sets. Modern day scanners and digitizers greatly assist in the process, but much of the work, as is usually the case, still rests with the human. The second task is to determine the characteristics of any specified location in terms of the data layers in the system. It is clearly a labor-intensive and skill-intensive effort to ensure that the resulting database can be of maximum value to the user.

Data management functions govern the creation of, and access to, the database itself. These functions provide consistent methods for data entry, update, deletion, and retrieval. Modern database management systems isolate the users from the technical details of data storage, such as the particular data organization on a mass storage medium. When the operations of data management are executed well, the users usually do not notice, nor do they care, about the intricacies of the information processing technology. When they are done poorly, however, everyone notices the slowness of the system, the cumber with which the system operates, and the frequent disruption. Finally, data management concerns include issues of security. Procedures must be in place to provide different users with different kinds of access to the system and its database.

Manipulation and analysis are often the focus of a system user's attention. Many users believe, incorrectly, that this module is all that constitutes a GIS. In this portion of the system are the analytic operators that work with the database contents to derive new information. For example, we may need to move data from our GIS to an external system where a particular numerical model is available, and then transport the derived results back into the spatial database inside the GIS. This kind of modularity is useful, and at the same time challenging, for the designer of a GIS. It is of particular interest here so far as this book is mainly concerned with analysis.

Product generation is the phase where final outputs from the GIS are created. The output products might include statistical reports, maps, or graphics of various kinds. Some of these products are soft copy images, or transient images on television-like computer displays. Others, which are durable since they are printed on paper and film, are called hard copies. Increasingly, output products include computer compatible material: tapes and disks in standard formats for storage in an archive or for transmission to another system.

There are currently several GIS packages and many more are expected to be published in the next few years (Prastacos 1992). For the packages listed below, they are constantly being improved. The listing below, consisting of both government (G) and commercial (C) releases, are for illustrative purposes only as far as the description is concerned. The systems are sampled somewhat randomly and do not represent endorsement on the part of the author:

> ARC/INFO (C): This system is the most widely-used GIS system available for a variety of computers. It is a powerful, command-driven GIS with extensive capabilities for data storage, editing, display, and geographic analysis.

> GRASS (G): The Geographical Resources Analysis Support System is a public domain raster GIS, a vector GIS, an image-processing system, and

a graphics-production system. It is extensively used at government offices, universities, and commercial organizations. It is written mostly in C for UNIX.

MapInfo, Atlas GISs (C): MapInfo and Atlas GISs are menu-based, user-friendly desktop mapping and GIS systems that can store and display street networks and zone boundaries. Both of these packages have sophisticated routines for geocoding. The proprietary data structure is not topological, hence paths and routes, for example, cannot be defined.

SPANS (C): SPANS is a menu-driven, user-friendly GIS with powerful spatial analysis capabilities. It is available on DOS, OS/2, and UNIX platforms. SPANS can handle both vector and raster data. It supports a complete topological network. Networks can be analyzed to model travel distance, travel time and rate of flow. An optimal routing procedure is included in the system, as well as procedures for gravity modeling.[3]

TransCAD (C): TransCAD is a powerful and easy-to-use GIS-based transportation package. The system consists of two parts: a GIS engine and a tool box of transportation models and procedures. The GIS engine is menu driven and, in addition to the standard GIS functions, can directly support transportation data structures such as nodes, links, networks, paths, and tours. TransCAD also provides a platform for users to develop their own transportation related models.

Several trends of GIS-technology development have been observed:

1. The obvious trend is the continued downsizing of computers. Computers are getting more compact and at the same time more powerful. Despite this trend, the speed of input and output on smaller computers remains a concern for data intensive applications like digital mapping. The refinement of data-compaction techniques will help to reduce the amount of data to be transmitted and thus increase the throughput.

2. Another obvious trend is that hardware prices will continue to drop, but programming staff salaries will continue to rise. As systems become more complex, more programmers are required to maintain the system. Many of the digital mapping-software products will probably never become consumer goods. The limited market means that the price for these products will continue to rise as well.

3. In spite of increasing diversity among computer systems used, there is a pressing need to exchange information among users. This will require standardization of data structure among the different systems, a formidable task until there is a period of stability in GIS developments.

4. Many software functions will be integrated into the computer as firmware. One reason for this is to increase speed of processing. It is likely that workstations dedicated to GIS applications will appear in the future given there is increasing demand for GISs.

IV. SELECTING A GIS

Many organizations are faced with the decision to acquire or to upgrade a GIS. This is to be performed in an environment where the technology is rapidly changing (McCrary et al. 1996). Irrespective of the contexts, however, selecting a GIS typically involves answering these fundamental questions:

1. Do you want the ability to access a database and graphics from the same package?
2. Do you want the ability to integrate between software packages, including between GIS and packages that perform analysis?
3. Are you willing to pay the price for integration?
4. Do you have the expertise to use GIS software?
5. Do you want the ability to conduct spatial analysis such as facility location and land use?
6. Is the acquisition or upgrade an efficient use of GIS in your organization?
7. Will your system be networked in the future?
8. Is a topological database needed?

The ultimate driving force behind a GIS selection has to be the problems to which the software is applied. Some of the basic applications can be enumerated below:

1. **Geographic data collection and production:** The fundamental GIS function of collecting geographic data for the purpose of building both spatial and non-spatial databases, as described in the bulk of the current chapter;
2. **Facility and asset management:** Locating, counting, analyzing, and/or reporting on the distribution of facilities and assets that are on, below, or above the earth, for the purpose of inventorying them for usage;
3. **Map and chart publishing:** Producing and publishing maps and charts for the purpose of direct distribution or documentation.
4. **Resource allocation:** Analyzing, allocating, and reporting on a resource's location, quantity, quality, and/or movement, for meeting certain economic, financial, political, social, or other criteria, as illustrated in the spatial interaction and entropy maximization models in Chapters 2, 3 and 4,
5. **Network analysis:** Analyzing, scheduling, routing, and/or reporting the flow of people, goods, or services through a network for optimizing usage, as described in the "Interregional flow" and "Network with gains" sections in Chapters 2 and 4 respectively,
6. **Site selection:** Selecting and reporting on the site desirable based on a set of imposed criteria for optimizing location, as discussed in Chapters 2–4;
7. **Surface and sub-surface assessment:** Modeling, analyzing, and reporting on the natural geophysical phenomena occurring on or below the surface, for understanding, preserving, or exploiting such phenomena.

8. **Tracking and monitoring:** Recording, analyzing, and reporting occurrences over time for understanding the occurrences and/or for developing complementary or corrective responses, as was illustrated in Chapter 5.

It is obvious that depending on the function the GIS is required to perform, very different package(s) may be selected. Among other techniques, multi-attribute utility theory (MAUT)[4] can be the scientific method for evaluating and selecting GIS software. In MAUT, the elements of a decision-making problem are broken down into a hierarchy of objectives, criteria, and attributes. An example of such a hierarchy is shown in Figure 6.13. For a particular application area and a GIS under consideration, the following multi-attribute utility function may yield the necessary metric v for evaluation: $v = v (f, t'', o', c)$ where f' is the functional attribute score, t'' is the technical attribute score, s' is the vendor score, and c is the price. Examples of technical attributes may be user-friendliness, performance, and expandability, while examples of vendor attributes may include experience, reputation, quality of documentation, quality of support, and so forth. Having defined these attributes, a simple additive value function may be $v = w_f f' + w_t t'' + w_s o'$ where w_f, w_t and w_s are weights assigned to the respective attributes. Obviously, there are other forms of value functions. Calibration and implementation of such value functions for GIS selection is situation specific. The detailed MAUT procedure is described in full in Chapter 5. The important point is that MAUT allows for explicit tradeoffs between various criteria and attributes. This is often more important than the single metric v that may fall out of such a procedure.

V. REMOTE SENSING SYSTEMS

GISs are demonstrably powerful tools for the management and analysis of spatial data. Remote sensing systems are equally powerful tools for the collection and classification of spatial data. However, nearly all of the currently operational GISs

Figure 6.13   HIERARCHY OF OBJECTIVES IN GIS SELECTION

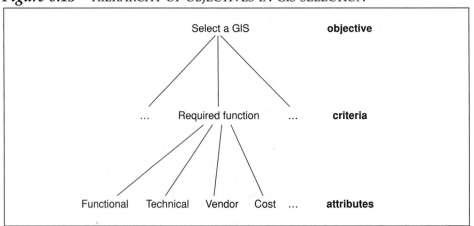

SOURCE: McCrary, Benjamin, and Ambavanekar (1996). Reprinted with permission.

utilize maps as their primary source of spatial data. These complex documents, designed for visual search and retrieval by human operators, are digitized (usually manually) and then entered into the master spatial database of the GIS. Although many of the maps used as input are derived from aerial photography or occasionally other remote sensing devices, there is little use of digital remote platforms as a direct data input. The last few years have seen an increased interest in the direct use of remote sensing data as inputs to GIS, but much of this interest has been centered in the remote sensing community rather than among the potential primary users, those who make operational use of GIS.

A. Interface between Remote Sensing Data and GIS

Perhaps the best way to explain how remote sensing data can serve as input to GIS and vice versa is through a case study. Computer image processing at Caltech's Jet Propulsion Laboratory (JPL) resulted in the development of an Image Based Information System (IBIS) (Marble and Peuquet 1988). Most data entered into IBIS are in raster (image-based) format. However, the system is configured in such a manner that other data types, such as graphical and tabular, may be used in analysis as well. Data input is a three-stage process. The first stage, called **data capture,** includes all operations up to the point where a data file is computer readable. Data capture costs are enormous for many basic kinds of data, such as the demographic and economic data gathered by the U.S. Bureau of the Census. Another common method of data capture is to develop a coordinate digitization of boundaries or linear features from a map. The map is not computer compatible but the digitizer output is and can be used in subsequent processing steps. In order to maintain geometric consistency between all data planes included in the database, an image plane exhibiting good radiometric and planimetric qualities is designed to be the data plane. All other data planes are geometrically corrected to register to the planimetric base. One can integrate various data types to form an IBIS database (see Figure 6.14). Since the primary data structure is a raster format, image data planes are directly entered into the system. Graphical forms of data, usually obtained in Cartesian reference form, must be transformed into image space, but are linked to the image database through a local interface, as shown in Figure 6.14. Graphical or vector data may also be entered into the IBIS database. Graphical data are either produced locally on a coordinate digitizer or are obtained from a data tape. Regardless of the data origin, graphical data are transformed into image space prior to inclusion in the IBIS database.

All tabular files (interface files) are linked to at least one of the geo-reference planes included in the IBIS database. The specific link is obtained by storing the numerical value (gray tone) representing each region of the geo-reference plane with tabular data describing attributes of that region (Figure 6.14). Attribute data may be statistical in origin, an identification code, or may be the result of an image plane comparison routine such as polygon overlay or cross-tabulation. As distinguished from the GIS discussion, remote sensing information is coded in digitized, or **pixel** (picture element) format. This avoids the referencing scheme of Figures 6.11 and 6.12 in storing lines and districts, but it usually increases the data storage and processing costs since more information is being processed.

In previous discussions, we make a distinction between raster versus vector data structures, or cellular versus organizational referencing systems. The traditional advantages and disadvantages of raster versus vector spatial data

Figure 6.14 FORMATION OF AN IBIS DATABASE

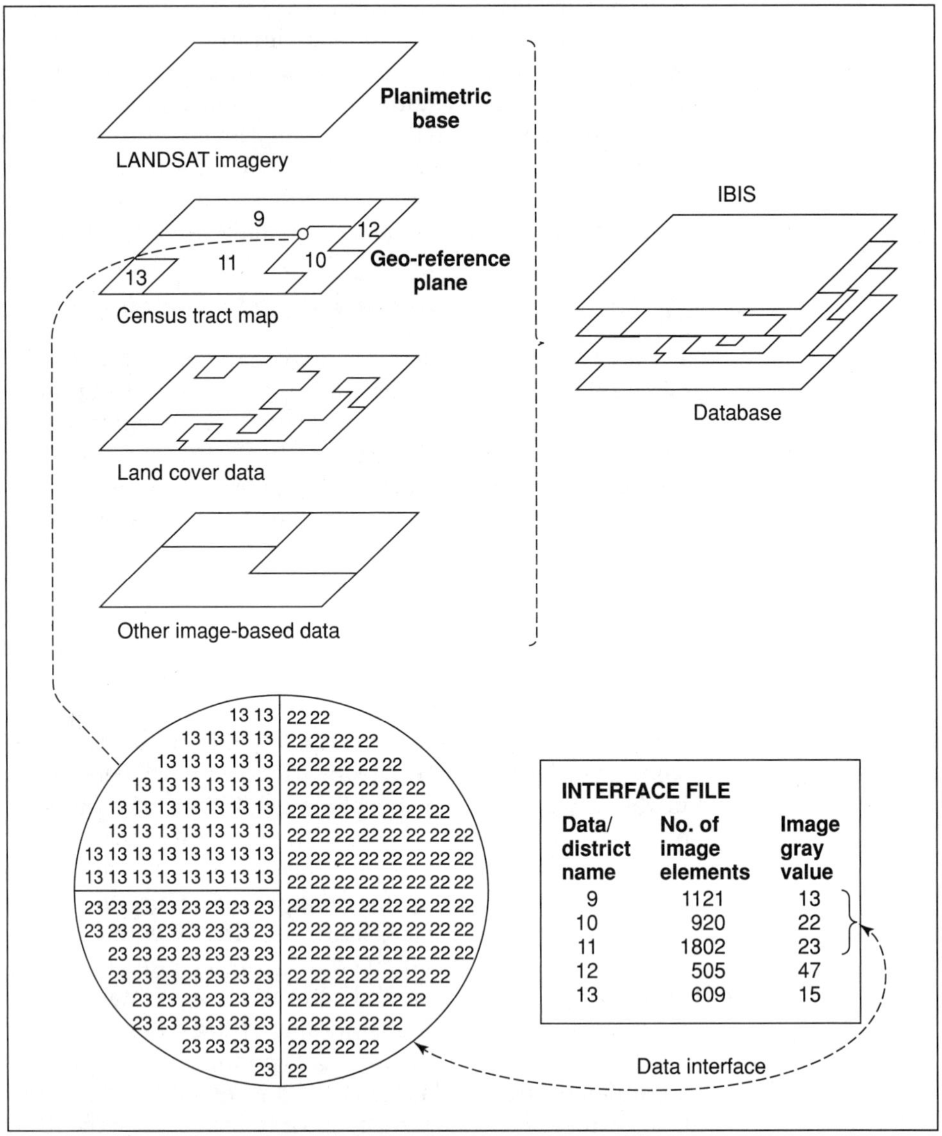

INTERFACE FILE

Data/ district name	No. of image elements	Image gray value
9	1121	13
10	920	22
11	1802	23
12	505	47
13	609	15

SOURCE: Marble and Peuquet (1988). Reprinted with permission.

structures hinge around storage efficiency, retrieval efficiency, robustness to perturbation, data processing efficiency, data accuracy, and data display as mentioned previously. In spite of its raster format, relational data structure such as the one outlined in IBIS has the potential for efficient search among raster and vector data structures, at the expense of data file management complexity. As we have seen, such a system design permits search through either the geometrical entities or the attribute data, without the other getting in the way, since these two kinds of information are stored separately. Thus, one expects better data-retrieval performance for simple kinds of search, which should result in more efficient operations. In any event, such a system can minimize the computer's input/output operations that are required to use the output of one search operation as the input for another. This may be particularly important when working on multi-user systems and is typically done at the expense of more complex file management.

B. An Assessment

An image-based information system is important for the full utilization of satellite imagery data. The future availability of frequent updates of land resource inventory statistics, with a known and acceptable sampling accuracy, should permit the incorporation of these data with the annual updates published by other governmental bureaus. The increasing sophistication of the use of GIS and remote sensing information can be represented by Figure 6.15. At the outset, concerns ranged over geometric fidelity and classification accuracy of satellite imagery. Since those early days, significant progress has been made. We are able to remove noise from images efficiently and delineate boundaries of lakes, forests, constructed facilities, and other land features with confidence. The capacity to perform radiometric enhancement and pattern recognition will be amply illustrated in Section VI of this chapter. The field is now embarking upon database integration and modeling activities that utilize the extended capabilities of remote sensing.

The projected demands to be placed upon GISs will put a strong emphasis on the capability to store and retrieve large amounts of data and to manipulate data sets for portions of the files efficiently. A major drawback facing most geocoding procedures is that they rely on sequential computations applied to tabular data strings and, as such, require a large investment in formatting or processing data that are inherently two-dimensional. Raster scan databases avoid many of these problems and possess additional advantages. The video

Figure 6.15   IMAGE PROCESSING DEVELOPMENT

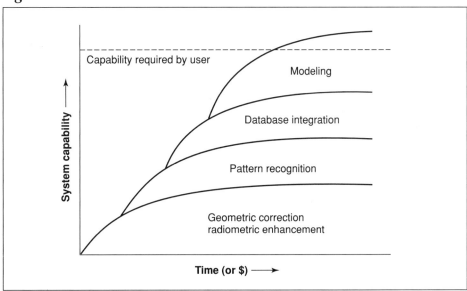

SOURCE: Marble and Peuquet (1988). Reprinted with permission.

communications field has been addressing and continues to address both the problems of mass storage and application of rapid interactive processing that place a minimal reliance upon computer software routines. The specialized requirements of GIS should derive considerable benefit from the image processing field in the future. The outlook is bright in the continuing emphasis on direct image communication. At present, the interface between GIS and remote sensing systems is weaker than it should be, and each side suffers from a lack of critical support of a type that could be provided by the other. The GIS has a continuing need for timely, accurate update of the various spatial data elements held in its system and remote sensing systems could, in many cases, benefit from access to highly precise, ancillary ground data that could significantly improve classification accuracies. In addition, there are a number of significant technical problems that would benefit from a joint, well-planned attack rather than the present disaggregated and disorganized approach. A prime example is data management, since no operational database management system exists that will handle, in a cost-effective and efficient manner, the large volume of spatial data involved in both systems.

C. Remote Sensing Technology

"Photos from space" (Zimmerman 1988), a popularized term for remote sensing from satellites, represents the latest technology for collecting spatial-temporal data. Perhaps the most familiar remote sensing device is a weather satellite, which gives a resolution of one kilometer (0.59 miles) or less. The instruments normally cover areas the size of a continent in a single shot. The National Weather Service (NWS) has defined requirements for the next generation of geostationary operational environmental satellites (GOES), which NOAA has labeled GOES-Next. The emphasis in the NWS during the 1990s has been on improving short-term (0–12 hour) forecasts of severe weather events such as tornadoes, severe thunderstorms, hail, and flash floods. GOES-Next is expected to provide strong support to improving forecasts of these phenomena and will offer improvements in both imagery and vertical-temperature/moisture-sounding capabilities. Imaging capabilities of GOES-Next will be practical to an accuracy of 4 km (2.5 mi) or less.

Another major satellite is the earth-resource monitoring LANDSAT, which has a finer resolution (80 × 80 meters or 87.4 yards × 87.4 yards) on its multispectral scanner (MSS). Similar to (one km) × (one km), the 80 × 80 resolution detail is usually referred to as a pixel. Tremendous progress has been made since LANDSAT's early stages. Pixels of LANDSAT "photos" can be as detailed as 30 × 30 meters (32.8 yards × 32.8 yards) today on its thematic mapper (TM). Satellites with pixels smaller than one meter (1.09 yards) on the side are usually used for military reconnaissance. But the line between military and civilian satellites blurred when the French remote sensing satellite SPOT was able to offer commercially 10-meter (10.9 yard) resolutions in black and white and 20 meters (21.8 yards) in color. In July 1987, the then Soviets offered a 6-meter (6.54 yard) resolution satellite and are in the process of marketing 2-meter (2.22-yard) resolution (Foley 1994). Sweden is now considering a satellite offering one-meter resolution, with the purpose of arms verification in mind.

Some of these satellites can measure infrared radiation, inasmuch as most satellites have several sensors responding to a variety of spectral ranges. LANDSAT and certain Russian satellites can detect the long wavelength radiation produced by heat sources. Both LANDSAT and SPOT can detect short wave-length infrared radiation, which is produced by very hot sources such as the sun. (This includes reflection of the sun's rays by shiny objects.) SPOTs 5, 6, and 7 are planned for the decade from late 1990s through early 2000s. The latest Russian satellite with 6-meter resolution is also capable of detecting these short infrared wavelengths. The Canadian RADARSAT satellite does not have the detailed resolution of the optical image spacecraft. However, it will be able to take pictures at night and through clouds. The Japanese planned to launch a series of Advanced Earth Observing Satellites starting in the late 1990s, continuing earlier attempts at marine sensing and radar satellites. Meanwhile, the U.S. launched LANDSAT 7 successfully on April 15, 1999.

Another factor in remote sensing is the frequency of surveillance. Satellites cannot orbit the Earth faster than once every 90 minutes, since drag would otherwise draw them inside the atmosphere. A camera can photograph only a limited swath of the Earth during each revolution. Hence the best satellite would require a full day to photograph the entire Earth, considering the number of revolutions required to piece the swaths together. This means an average lag time of a half day is required to acquire a specific picture, unless geosynchronized satellites are used, concomitant with their high cost.

The most sophisticated technology has been developed for military applications. Given a two-dimensional data set, such as a satellite picture, if we have the necessary elevation information, which can be derived from a series of satellite pictures at different viewing angles, a geometric model can be constructed in the computer. The output image will be a three-dimensional representation of what started as a two-dimensional scene. This type of image manipulation has many possible intelligence and defense uses. American bomber pilots could rehearse in simulators for low-level bombing missions, becoming familiar with enemy terrain without ever going near it. In February 2000, NASA launched the Endeavour space shuttle, whose crew intended to scan 80 percent of the earth's surface. The all-weather radar image produced a three-dimensional map more accurate and comprehensive than ever before.

So far an average remote sensing satellite has typically cost $300 million (Zimmerman 1988). But with today's off-the-shelf equipment, a five-meter resolution satellite could be built and launched for less than $10 million. Total sales from satellite photography range from hundreds of millions of dollars to $7.4 billion or more, according to KRS Remote Sensing, a Kodak Company. The large range is a reflection of the uncertainty associated with the U.S. Government's national security regulation of commercial use of satellites. This regulation happens in an increasingly international and competitive market, where remote sensing service can be made readily available outside the U.S. at a reasonable cost.

In March 1994, the U.S. Administration removed restrictions on the quality of satellite photos, approving the sale of images able to reveal objects one-meter (1.11 yard) in resolution or possibly smaller (Foley 1994). Liberalizing the policy even further, manufacturers are allowed to sell foreign buyers spacecraft that are roughly equivalent to older U.S. spy satellites. However, companies selling imagery will be subject to conditions that apply to operating licenses granted by the government, conditions designed to maintain government control over the dissemination of such technology. While there are clamors about lost opportunities, license applications mount as major U.S. companies seek a share of the vast potential market. At least three U.S. organizations have 1-meter systems under development with launch dates from late 1997 to 2000 (Amato 1999; Corbey 1996). In October 1999, Space Imaging released the first commercial 1-m black and white image. Developers of the proposed systems expect the availability of high-resolution imagery to touch off a rapid increase in the size of the satellite data user market. They predict that higher resolution is exactly what is needed to convert GIS users who have not yet tried satellite or aerial imagery.

VI. DIGITAL IMAGE PROCESSING

Digital image processing involves the manipulation and interpretation of digital images with the aid of a computer (Lillesand and Kiefer 1987). Digital image processing is an extremely broad subject and often involves procedures that can be mathematically complex, but the central idea behind digital image processing is quite simple. The digital image is fed into a computer one pixel at a time. The computer is programmed to insert these data into an equation, or series of equations, and then store the results of the computation for each pixel. These results form a new digital image that may be displayed or recorded in pictorial format or may itself be further manipulated by additional programs. The possible forms of digital image manipulation are literally infinite. However, virtually all these procedures may be categorized into one (or more) of the following four broad types of computer-assisted operations.

A. Image Rectification and Restoration

These operations aim to correct distorted or degraded image data to create a more faithful representation of the original scene. This typically involves the initial processing of raw image data to correct for geometric distortions, to calibrate the data radiometrically, and to eliminate noise present in the data. Geometric distortion can be induced into the image by sensor operation, orbital geometry, and earth geometry. Examples include the altitude, latitude, and velocity of the platform, earth curvature, atmospheric refraction, and non-linearities in the sensor field of view. All these contribute to distortion. These distortions can be systematic or random. Several techniques exist to correct for geometric distortions. Radiometric correction can be used to address problems caused by scene illumination, atmospheric conditions, viewing geometry, and instrument response. Sun elevation correction can account for seasonal position of the sun relative to the earth. Noise removal can be used to correct striping, boundary, and non-systematic variations that cause the images to be snowy. These can be removed by using a 3×3 or 5×5 median or averaging filter. Thus the nature of any particular image restoration process is highly dependent upon the characteristics of the sensor used to acquire the image data. Image rectification and restoration procedures are often termed preprocessing operations, because they normally precede further manipulation and analysis of the image data to extract specific information.

Fourier Transform Example
This example illustrates how noise can be removed spectrally from an image signal. First, one must remember that any signal can be represented as a combination of sine and cosine waves with different frequency[5], amplitude[6], and phase[7]. One common noise removing technique is the **Fourier transform,** which converts the signal into its frequency domain or into harmonics when one thinks of the

voice signal (Gonzalez and Woods 1992). Inasmuch as noise has a very distinctly different harmonic compared with the regular signal (again think of the voice analogy), it can be recognized and easily removed in the harmonic or the frequency domain. An example would drive this point home. Shown in Figure 6.16 is a made-up signal, to which noise has been added. A Fourier transform has been taken of the signal (with its noise.) It can be seen that the noise has a harmonic quite a bit different from the signal, most of which are at the lower part of the frequency plot in the third frame of the figure. A frequency threshold of 2.5 in this

Figure 6.16   FILTERING A NOISY SIGNAL WITH FOURIER TRANSFORM

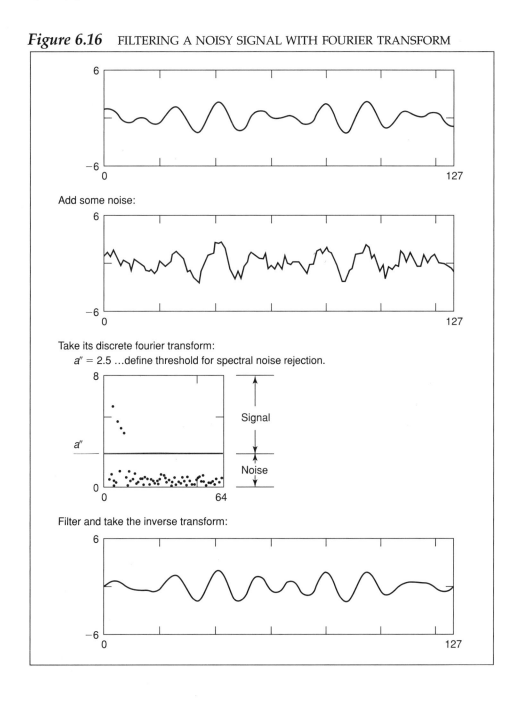

case would form a very clear watershed between the signal and noise. Now we can remove, or "filter" out, any "signal" associated with the frequency below the threshold. This is commonly known as a high-pass noise-filter. An inverse transform is then taken, which reconstitutes the original signal with the noise removed. ∎

1. Discrete Fourier Transform. More formally, let $f(x)$ be a continuous function of a real variable x. The Fourier transform of $f(x)$, denoted by $F(f(x))$, is defined as $F(f(x)) = f(u') = \int_{-\infty}^{\infty} f(x) \exp(-j2\pi u'x) \, dx$ where $j = \sqrt{-1}$, remembering that sine and cosine curves can be represented by a complex exponential function of frequency u. Amplitude, or the Fourier spectrum, in this case is $\| F(u') \|$. Given $F(u')$, $f(x)$ can be recovered by using the inverse Fourier transform $F^{-1}(u') = f(x) = \int_{-\infty}^{\infty} F(u') \exp(j2\pi u'x) \, du'$. Suppose a continuous function $f(x)$ is now discretized into a sequence $\{f(x_0), f(x_0+\Delta x), f(x_0+2\Delta x), \dots, f(x_0+(n-1)\Delta x)\}$ by taking n samples Δx apart, as shown in Figure 6.17. The sequence $\{f(0), f(1), f(2),\dots, f(n-1)\}$ now denotes any n uniformly spaced samples from the corresponding continuous function. The discrete Fourier transform (DFT) pair that applies to the sample functions is then given by

$$F(u') = \frac{1}{n} \sum_{x=0}^{n-1} f(x) \exp(-j2\pi u'x/n)$$

$$f(x) = F^{-1}(u') = n \sum_{u=0}^{n-1} F(u') \exp(j2\pi u'x/n)$$

(6.1)

for $x = 0, 1, 2, \dots, n - 1$.

Application of this equation pair to the signal in Figure 6.17 yields $F(0) = 1/4 \sum_{x=0}^{n-1} f(x)\exp(0) = 1/4 \, [f(0) + f(1) + f(2) + f(3)] = 1/4(2 + 3 + 4 + 4) = 3.25$ and $F(1) = 1/4 \sum_{x=0}^{3} f(x)\exp(-j2\pi x/4) = 1/4(2e^0 + 3e^{-j\pi/2} + 4e^{-j\pi} + 4e^{-j3\pi/2}) = 1/4(-2 + j)$, remembering Euler's formula $e^{j\theta} = \cos\theta + j\sin\theta$ in the last part of the calculation. Continuing with this procedure gives $F(2) = -1/4(1 + j0)$ and $F(3) = -1/4(2 + j)$. All values of $f(x)$ contribute to each of the four terms of the discrete Fourier transform (DFT). Conversely, all terms of the transform contribute in forming the

Figure 6.17   DISCRETE FOURIER TRANSFORM EXAMPLE

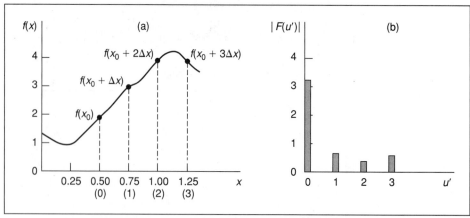

inverse transform via Equation 6.1. The Fourier spectrum is obtained from the magnitude of each of the transform terms: $|F(0)| = 3.25$, $|F(1)| = [(2/4)^2 + (1/4)^2]^{1/2} = \sqrt{5}/4 = 0.56$, $|F(2)| = [(1/4)^2 + (0/4)^2]^{1/2} = 1/4 = 0.25$, and $|F(3)| = [(2/4)^2 + (1/4)^2]^{1/2} = \sqrt{5}/4 = 0.56$. The spectrum is illustrated in frame (b) of Figure 6.7.

2. Fast Fourier Transform. The number of complex multiplications and additions required to implement Equation 6.1 is proportional to n^2, square of the number of discrete intervals. That is, for each of the n values of u', expansion of the summation requires n complex multiplications of $f(x)$ by $\exp(-j2\pi u'x/n)$ and $n - 1$ additions of the results. Proper decomposition of Equation 6.1 can make the number of multiplication and addition operations proportional to $n\log_2 n$. The decomposition procedure is called the fast Fourier transform (FFT) algorithm. The reduction in proportionality from n^2 to $n\log_2 n$ operations represents a significant savings in computational effort. The FFT approach offers a considerable computational advantage over direct implementation of the Fourier transform, particularly when n is relatively large. For that reason, many real-world applications use FFT rather than conventional discrete transform, including the example shown in Figure 6.17.

The above noise-removal procedures, both regular transforms and FFT, were illustrated for a single dimensional case. It can be shown that the same idea can be generalized to a two-dimensional image. The transform now has two arguments instead of one $F(u'_1, u'_2)$, corresponding to the frequencies in both dimensions u'_1 and u'_2. Page limitation prevents further development of the two-dimensional transform here. Readers are referred to Gonzalez and Woods (1992) for an in-depth treatment of the methodology. In accordance with the application flavor of this book, however, we implemented the FFT for image processing in the TS-IP (Training System/Image Processing): a software distributed with this book. The readers are invited to experiment the FFT routine with the image files supplied with the program.

3. Spatial Filter. Rather than developing the two-dimensional Fourier transform, we choose to introduce the concept of the **spatial filter**. It accomplishes a similar noise removal function, but it is based on an entirely different principle. No longer do we need to work in the frequency domain. Considering that noise shows up as outliers in their signal intensity—i.e., either too weak or too strong—spatial filters do their work directly in the signal domain. The **average filter** or the **median filter** are two examples of a spatial filter. Both simply smooth out the outliers, replacing each outlier with a streamlined pixel. While both accomplish the mainstreaming task, they yield different results, as we will demonstrate. Again, the reader is invited to experiment with the average and median filters implemented in TS-IP and verify the results from the following example.

Example

The following example deals with possible outliers in satellite spatial imagery as the result of noise, where several methods could be used to remove the offending point(s). Among these are 3×3 averaging, which compares first- and second-order neighbors, and 3×3 and 5×5 median filtering. Both work on the principle of replacing bad outlier data points with good ones. We use the 5×5 data cell below to answer the following questions with regard to the center point outlier.

31	33	41	44	48
32	39	44	42	45
43	40	92	40	40
46	43	41	42	42
43	44	43	41	42

(a) Using the averaging method, calculate the first- and second-order averages. Describe how you might set threshold in this case and which value you would use as a replacement.

The center-pixel gray value, $v(0)$, is given as 92. The average of first-order neighbors is $v(1) = (44 + 40 + 41 + 40)/4 = 41.25$. The average of second-order neighbors is $v(2) = (42 + 42 + 43 + 39)/4 = 41.50$. One would next want to calculate the absolute differences $|v(0) - v(1)|, |v(0) - v(2)|, |v(1) - v(2)|$ and if some threshold is overcome, substitute either $v(1)$ or $v(2)$ for $v(0)$. In this case

$$|v(0) - v(1)| = |92 - 41.25| = 50.75$$
$$|v(0) - v(2)| = |92 - 41.50| = 50.50$$
$$|v(1) - v(2)| = |41.25 - 41.50| = 0.25$$

One can select any value for the threshold. It depends on how much one wants to smooth the data. One way is to say that if $|v(0) - v(1)|$ or $|v(0) - v(2)|$ is greater than 50 percent of the center outlier 92, then we replace $v(0)$ with $v(1)$ or $v(2)$. In this case $(0.5)(92) = 46.00$. Since 50.75 is larger than the threshold, a replacement is in order, or $v(0)' = v(1) = 41.25$.

(b) Now calculate the 3×3 and 5×5 median estimates of the center point. Describe how you might set the threshold in this case and whether or not you would replace the point.

The 3×3 median, $m(3)$, is 42 from the 9 entries of the 3×3 neighborhood:

39	40	40	41	(42)	42	43	44	92

The absolute difference is $|v(0) - m(3)| = |92 - 42| = 50$. Using the same 50 percent threshold criterion as in (a), the new value for the center point is $v(0)' = 42$. The 5×5 median $m(5)$ is 42 again from the 25 entries of the 5×5 neighborhood:

31	32	33	39	40	40	40	41	41	41	42	42
(42)	42	43	43	43	43	44	44	44	45	46	92

$|v(0) - m(5)| = |92 - 42| = 50$. Again using the same 50-percent threshold criterion as in (a), $v(0)' = 42$.

(c) What advantage does the median approach have over the averaging approach?

A median approach usually produces better results than an average approach because the average approach usually has a much higher replacement value than the median when dealing with noise. The median minimizes the effect of outliers, since they are not weighted more heavily. As a result, the median method does not cause blurring associated with averaging. This works better for noise that consists of spikes, and consequently, it is better in preserving edge sharpness. ∎

Another way of smoothing spatial data is interpolation. Aside from simple interpolation, a family of techniques called **kriging** has been developed, which is designed to minimize the errors in the estimated values (Star and Estes 1990; Cressie 1991). The method is based on estimating the strength of the correlations between known data points, as a function of the distance between the points. This information is then used to select an optimal set of weights for the interpolation. Variations have been developed to include a trend surface model component, which permits estimating values outside the area of known points; this is not possible with simple distance weighted models.[8] Examples of this concept can be found in the "Ratio and correlation method" subsection of Chapter 2 when the time dimension is interpreted as the spatial dimension.

B. Image Enhancement

Enhancement procedures are applied to image data in order to more effectively display or record the data for subsequent visual interpretation. Normally, image enhancement involves techniques for increasing the visual distinction between features in a scene. The objective is to create new images from the original image data in order to increase the amount of information that can be visually interpreted from the data. The enhanced images can be displayed interactively on a monitor or they can be recorded in a hard copy format, either in black and white or in color. There are no simple rules for producing the single best image for a particular application. Often several enhancements made from the same raw image are necessary. Image enhancement can be accomplished by adjusting the contrast or doing spatial feature manipulation and multi-image manipulation. One can also zoom or enhance the resolution of this image. Enhancements involving multiple spectral bands of imagery can be made as well.

Convolution filters can be used for many purposes in image processing. Among them is edge detection, which again can be thought of as an image enhancement technique since it makes an image more crisp. Perhaps the best filters for this purpose come from the family known as Sobel operators, which are a kind of gradient operator to detect discontinuities (Gonzalez and Woods 1992). The gradient of an image $f(x, y)$ at location (x, y) is the vector $\nabla f(x, y) = (G_x, G_y)^T = (\partial f/\partial x, \partial f/\partial y)^T$. The simple gradient δf is the scalar $\delta f = |\nabla f(x, y)| = (G_x^2 + G_y^2)^{1/2}$. A common practice is to approximate the gradient with absolute values $\delta f = |G_x| + |G_y|$. The direction of the gradient vector is an important quantity; it shows whether we are moving from the left to the right or from the right to the left on the x-axis. Likewise, it shows whether we are moving up or down on the y-axis.

At this point, we need to formally define a **mask,** or its alternate names filter, window, or template. A mask is a "window" overlaid on top of an image with a set of specific mathematical operations performed on the pixels underneath this window. The idea behind mask operations is to let the value assigned to a subject pixel be a function of its gray level and the gray level of its neighbors. We have already seen this in the average filter in the last section, where an outlier is replaced by the average of its four first-order neighbors. The first-order neighbors in this case form the 4-element mask for the subject pixel, consisting of a weight of 1/4 each. In other words, the mask looks like

$$\begin{bmatrix} 0 & 1/4 & 0 \\ 1/4 & 0 & 1/4 \\ 0 & 1/4 & 0 \end{bmatrix}$$

Another example can be found in the median filter example, where the outlier is replaced by the median of the 3×3 window (nine pixels) centering around the subject outlier pixel. Instead of a weighted average, the operator is now median computation. In image processing, a mask is normally applied like a moving window across an image, centering around each and every pixel in the image until all pixels have been visited. The result is a processed image with either noise removal or image enhancement accomplished. The Sobel mask can be thought of as a combination of a differencing mask of the weights $(-1\ 0\ 1)$ (or its vertical counterpart) followed by a smoothing mask of the weights $(1\ 2\ 1)$ (or its vertical counterpart), as we will show immediately below. The differencing mask accentuates the gray-value differences among first-order neighbors, while the smoothing mask averages the subject pixel and its first-order neighbors. Because derivatives enhance noise, the smoothing effect is a particularly attractive feature. Given the 3×3 Sobel operators $G_{x\downarrow}$, $G_{y\rightarrow}$, $G_{x\downarrow}$, and $G_{y\leftarrow}$

$$G_{x\downarrow} = \begin{bmatrix} -1 & -2 & -1 \\ 0 & 0 & 0 \\ 1 & 2 & 1 \end{bmatrix} \quad G_{y\rightarrow} = \begin{bmatrix} 1 & 0 & -1 \\ 2 & 0 & -2 \\ 1 & 0 & -1 \end{bmatrix} \tag{6.2}$$

$$G_{x\uparrow} = \begin{bmatrix} 1 & 2 & -1 \\ 0 & 0 & 0 \\ -1 & -2 & -1 \end{bmatrix} \quad G_{y\leftarrow} = \begin{bmatrix} -1 & 0 & 1 \\ -2 & 0 & 0 \\ -1 & 0 & 1 \end{bmatrix} \tag{6.3}$$

and the data cell

$$\begin{bmatrix} z_1 & z_2 & z_3 \\ z_4 & z_5 & z_6 \\ z_7 & z_8 & z_9 \end{bmatrix}$$

derivatives based on the Sobel operator masks are

$$|G_x| = |(z_7 + 2z_8 + z_9) - (z_1 + 2z_2 + z_3)|$$
$$|G_y| = |(z_3 + 2z_6 + z_9) - (z_1 + 2z_4 + z_7)| \tag{6.4}$$

Computation of the gradient at the location of the center of the masks can be performed with these equations, giving one value of the gradient δf. To get the next value, the masks are moved to the next pixel location and the procedure is repeated.

Example
Using the sample 3×3 data-cell

$$\begin{bmatrix} 85 & 112 & 150 \\ 82 & 63 & 115 \\ 84 & 80 & 127 \end{bmatrix}$$

which of the four Sobel filters, $G_{x\uparrow}$, $G_{y\rightarrow}$, $G_{x\downarrow}$, and $G_{y\leftarrow}$, do you think would most likely detect the edge as part of a change in the data pattern? What is the resulting convolved value, or the gradient, for the center pixel using this filter? Visual inspection of the data indicates the brightest line is the third column (150 115 127)^T. The x-axis in G_x is defined in the vertical direction so the strongest response produced by $|G_x|$ is an edge parallel to the x-axis. This data set seems to have an edge perpendicular to the x-axis. So we should use a G_y operator. One can use either the $G_{y\rightarrow}$ or $G_{y\leftarrow}$ since oftentimes, only absolute values are of interest, as shown in Equation 6.4. Using $G_{y\rightarrow}$ of Equation 6.3, it produces a value of $150 + (2)(115) + 127 - 85 - (2)(82) - 84 = 174$ for the center point. The fact that this value is much greater than the values from the $|G_x|$ operators (88) shows that the gradient is working best in the horizontal direction in detecting the edge (150 115 127)^T. ∎

C. Image Classification

The objective of classification operations is to replace visual analysis of the image data with quantitative techniques for automating the identification of features in a scene. This normally involves the analysis of multispectral image data and the application of statistically based decision rules for determining the land cover identity of each pixel in an image. One can perform image classification that will categorize all pixels in an image into land cover classes like grass, water, sand, and so forth. When these decision rules are based solely on the spectral radiances observed in the data, we refer to the classification process as **spectral pattern recognition**. In contrast, the decision rules may be based on the geometrical shapes, sizes, and patterns present in the image data. These procedures fall into the domain of **spatial pattern recognition.** In either case, the intent of the classification process is to categorize all pixels in a digital image into one of several land cover classes or themes. These categorized data may then be used to produce thematic maps of the land cover present in an image, and/or to produce summary statistics on the areas covered by each land cover type.

In both spectral and spatial image classification, the problem can be viewed as grouping similar gray values together in two or more dimensional space. Consider the two-dimensional illustration in Figure 6.18, which can represent both a spectral or spatial image. In the latter case, the entries will simply be gray values in regular raster grid. In the former case, each cell represents a pair of coordinates (x, y), where x is a reading on one spectral band and y is the reading on the second band. Classification amounts to grouping pixels of similar gray values together in the former case or pixels with similar spectral band readings in the latter case. In both cases, we classify image into the logical land cover types.

To illustrate the concept of classification, the region-oriented segmentation algorithm of Gonzalez and Woods (1992) may be of interest. First, a decision criterion describing the image is specified, such as the gray value range that describes, for example, a cornfield, a lake, or a beach. The digital image is then taken as a single region that is partitioned by repeated splitting. One method of dividing the image is by bisection. If the image does not meet the decision criteria, the image is divided into quadrants. If a quadrant does not meet the decision criteria, we divide it into subquadrants and so on. As the image is split into various sized regions, adjacent regions that meet the decision criteria can be merged. This splitting and merging continues until no further merging or splitting is possible. The end result is the objects of interest identified in the image.

In more formal terms, let R'' represent the entire image region. We may view segmentation as a process that spatially partitions R'' into n' subregions, R_1, R_2, ... , R_n' such that (a) $\overset{n'}{\underset{i=1}{\cup}} R_i = R''$; (b) R_i is a connected region, $i = 1, 2, ... , n'$; (c) $R_i \cap R_j = \varnothing$ for all i and j, $i \neq j$; (d) $\mathbf{P}(R_i) = $ TRUE for $i = 1, 2, ..., n'$; and (e) $\mathbf{P}(R_i \cup R_j) = $ FALSE for $i \neq j$ where $\mathbf{P}(R_i)$ is a logical predicate over the points in set R_i such as the range of gray values. Specification regarding no overlaps between two subregions (Condition (c)) may be relaxed for multispectral classifi-

Figure 6.18   DISAGGREGATION AND AGGREGATION OF DIGITAL IMAGE

Step 1

Region I (top-left), Region II (top-right), Region III (bottom-left), Region IV (bottom-right):

36	35	36	36	48	57	57	58
34	36	36	45	51	55	56	54
35	35	38	52	58	56	56	56
35	35	41	53	57	56	56	56
35	35	38	52	56	57	54	53
34	35	38	51	60	59	58	57
35	36	38	49	57	55	55	56
35	35	39	49	60	56	57	58

Step 2

Regions IA, IB, IIA, IIB / IC, ID, IIC, IID / IIIA, IIIB, IVA, IVB / IIIC, IIID, IVC, IVD:

36	35	36	36	48	57	57	58
34	36	36	45	51	55	56	54
35	35	38	52	58	56	56	56
35	35	41	53	57	56	56	56
35	35	38	52	56	57	54	53
34	35	38	51	60	59	58	57
35	36	38	49	57	55	55	56
35	35	39	49	60	56	57	58

Step 3

Regions IB, IIA, ID, IIIB, IIID:

36	35	36	36	48	57	57	58
34	36	36	45	51	55	56	54
35	35	38	52	58	56	56	56
35	35	41	53	57	56	56	56
35	35	38	52	56	57	54	53
34	35	38	51	60	59	58	57
35	36	38	49	57	55	55	56
35	35	39	49	60	56	57	58

Step 4

Regions IB, IIA, IIB, ID, IIIB, IVB, IIID:

36	35	36	36	48	57	57	58
34	36	36	45	51	55	56	54
35	35	38	52	58	56	56	56
35	35	41	53	57	56	56	56
35	35	38	52	56	57	54	53
34	35	38	51	60	59	58	57
35	36	38	49	57	55	55	56
35	35	39	49	60	56	57	58

cation, where the x-axis corresponds to one spectral band and the y-axis another. Notice this algorithm, while conceptually simple, is computationally explosive for any practical image. For this reason, it is good for fixing ideas only.

Example

Use the image cell in Figure 6.18 to demonstrate the concept of classification using the region splitting (disaggregation) technique. Do not split any cell smaller than 2×2 pixels. Show and briefly explain each step of the process. Re-aggregate cells, as necessary, at the end. Your predicate for each region is that the range of pixel gray values must be no greater than five. Be sure your final classification shows each separate region clearly and mark any region that fails to satisfy the predicate. (Note that this should not normally occur in practice).

First, we check the given region. Since $\mathbf{P}(R'') =$ FALSE (or the range of pixel gray values exceeds 5), we subdivide the region into four areas, labeled I, II, III and IV. This procedure was repeated for the second time, resulting in 16 areas, labeled IA, IB, IC, ID, IIA, IIB ... and so forth (see steps 1 and 2 in Figure 6.18). At this point, we have the minimum 2×2 areas, which appear to satisfy the predicate, except for subregions IB, IIA, ID, IIIB, and IIID. Now aggregate the cells, checking to see that all cells assigned to a similar region have values that do not range more than 5 (as shown in step 3 of Figure 6.18). Subregions IA and IC can be recombined with IIIA and IIIC since they together satisfy the predicate. Subregions IIC and IID, together with IVA, IVC, and IVD can be combined, leaving IIB and IVB alone since their inclusion would violate the predicate (step 4). Notice the two subregions IIB and IVB which satisfy the predicate in the final partitions are not contiguous, but it is an acceptable answer as far as illustrating this algorithm is concerned. It is clear that this algorithm leads toward one particular classification and that other combinations are possible should a different partitioning algorithm be used. The classification of the same land cover can also be different should we shift the image by one pixel column to the right. ∎

D. Data Merging

The next set of procedures in image processing is **data merging.** This procedure is used to combine image data for a given geographic area with other geographically referenced data sets for the same area. These other data sets might simply consist of image data generated on other dates by the same sensor, by other remote sensing systems, or an independently assembled data set. Frequently, the intent of data merging is to combine remotely sensed data with other resources of information into a GIS. For example, in urban applications image data are often combined with soil, topographic, ownership, zoning, and assessment information. This forms the basis for a GIS. A simple application of data merging is found in weather forecasts. A weather satellite such as ones launched by NOAA can provide a convenient image of cloud cover and other geographic information. But such information is often of little use unless it is referenced against jurisdictional boundaries such as nations, states, counties, and the like. Figure 6.19 shows the overlay of national, state boundaries, coastlines, and the Great Lakes on a NOAA satellite image of the northeastern United States and east Canada. Such a picture represents the merging of two data layers, one from the satellite and another from an archive storage. It is generated from the TS-IP software that comes with this book.

Figure 6.19   OVERLAY OF JURISDICTIONAL AND NATURAL BOUNDARIES ON WEATHER
INFORMATION

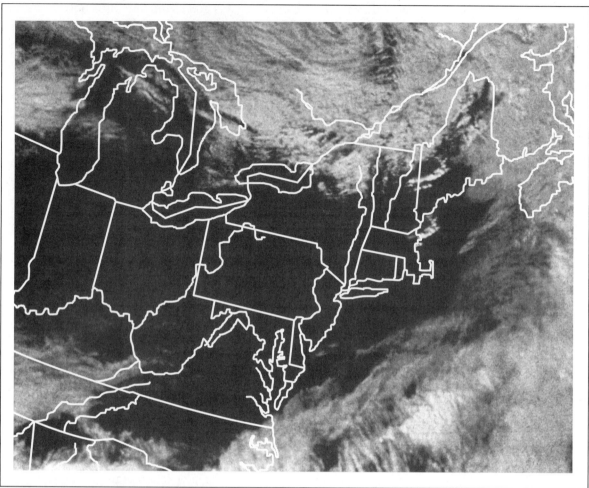

SOURCE: Courtesy of T.S. Kelso. Reprinted with permission.

Example

Another application will show the potential of the data merge function much better (Star and Estes 1990). It is a trafficability problem that addresses the question:
"Can a vehicle travel across a terrain with a certain slope and type of soil?" Figure
6.20 shows the slope and soil data layers which form the information base for
merging. Table 6.3 represents supplementary information regarding how easy it is
for the vehicle in question to navigate a particular combination of slope and surface soil type. For example, when the slope is moderate, the vehicle cannot travel
over sandy soil, but can travel on a gravel surface. This logical table forms a third
data layer, consisting of the translation of nominal information (such as the
rock/sand/clay categories) and ordinal information (such as level/moderate/
steep as well as easy/fair/hard) distinctions into trafficability. It contrasts with
scaled, or interval information typically found in raster files. This layer is input to
the data merging process on top of the two data layers on soil and slope. The

Figure 6.20 A TRAFFICABILITY EXAMPLE OF DATA MERGING

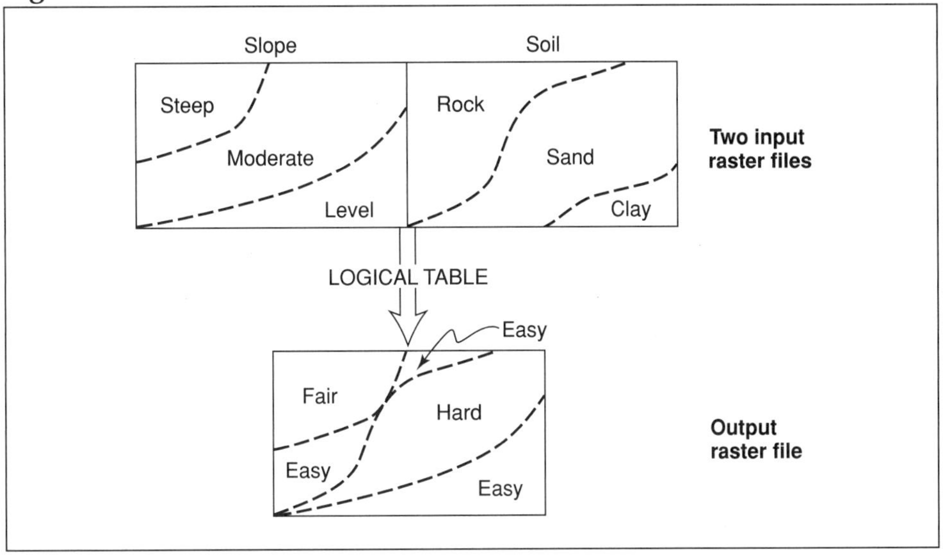

SOURCE: Star and Estes (1990). Reprinted with permission.

resulting derived suitability map for traversal, or the output of the entire exercise, is obtained at the bottom of Figure 6.20.

In a raster-based system, each cell in the input data provides a soil/slope data-tuples input to the trafficability table, which in turn determines the class of trafficability in the output data. We read the value of the first element in the soil array and the first element in the slope array, send these values to a routine that derives the resulting trafficability class, and send this derived value to the first element in the output array. This process continues through all the elements in the raster arrays. While the data merging algorithm is fairly straightforward with raster files, the process is much more involved in vector based files, although the data storage requirement is much more compact in comparison. ■

Although the above treats the four procedures of digital image processing—rectification, enhancement, classification, and merge—as distinct operations, they all interrelate. For example, the restoration process of noise removal can often be considered an enhancement procedure. Likewise, certain enhancement

Table 6.3 INPUT DATA LAYER REGARDING TRAFFICABILITY

		Soil type		
		Rock	**Sand**	**Clay**
Slope	**Level**	Easy	Easy	Easy
	Moderate	Easy	Hard	Fair
	Steep	Fair	Hard	Hard

SOURCE: Star and Estes (1990). Reprinted with permission.

procedures can be used not only to enhance the data, but also to improve the efficiency of classification operations. In a similar vein, data merging can be used in image classification in order to improve classification accuracy as in the combination of multispectral bands. In this regard, we will conduct a case study of merging multispectral bands later on in Section XI. Hence the boundaries between the various operations we discuss separately here are not well-defined in practice.

VII. DIGITAL IMAGE PROCESSING SOFTWARE AND HARDWARE

Image processing is, in general, a special form of two-dimensional, and sometimes three-dimensional, signal processing of scenes collected by sensors. Digital data of these scenes are stored on computers in bits. One bit of information is either on (1) or off (0). If an image had 1 bit of information on it, there will be two gray levels in it: white and black. As more bits of data are added, the number of gray levels in the picture increases. With 6 bits of data, there are 2^6 or 64 gray levels, ranging in value from 0 (black) up to 63 (white). The number of bits in a given pixel determines the number of unique gray values (or colors) available. Eight-bit pixels, for example, provide 256 different gray values in white to black shades or 256 unique colors in a pseudocolor mode.

Computer systems for image processing range from microcomputers to mainframe. Dedicated image processing systems include display memory, a video processor, a parallel interface to a computer, a human-machine interface, digital-analog converters, and a comprehensive software subroutine library. The basic subroutine library should contain all the necessary software for manipulating the internal parts of the image processor. A frame buffer is the key to any image processing system. This bank of memory stores the image data. Most medium size systems are several banks of 512×512 elements. The rows of the frame buffer matrix are the lines of the image, and the columns along each line are the samples. A digital-analog (D-A) converter transforms the contents of the image memory into a form compatible with the monitor. The number of different intensity-levels that a D-A converter can output is related to the number of bits it is designed to handle; the more bits, the more distinct colors or gray levels it can produce. An important part of an image processing system is a look-up table, which is a table of stored data for reference purposes. The look-up table performs a transformation or mapping between each unique input data value and some predefined output values. Table 6.3 represents a more sophisticated example of such a look-up table.

An instructional image processing software is included on the CD-Rom at the back of this book. The TS-IP software (Kelso et al. 1995) runs under Microsoft Windows or MS-DOS on an appropriate PC under a 256 VGA graphics card and a VGA monitor. Several resolution options are available depending on the specific PC, including 640×400 and 640×480. Among the features offered by TS-IP are:

> (a) adding an image to the image in the current window, resulting in an overlay (an example is shown in Figure 6.19);

(b) examining an image by viewing a pixel located at an *x-y* coordinate and displaying its gray value, or viewing a line of pixels and displaying the gray values along the line; when combined with the operation described in (c) below, this allows for image restoration and enhancement;

(c) displaying a histogram of the number of pixels in an image by gray values, which allows for the truncation of the low and/or high gray value range such as that associated with high-level clouds (allowing one to "see through the clouds");

(d) restoring or enhancing an image via such filters as Sobel convolution[9], fast Fourier transform[10], and median filter[11];

(e) performing contour plots of an image where the contours correspond to a specified gray value;

(f) highlighting the image with desired color scheme, including colors of the rainbow or simply a 256 gray value scale.

Real-life satellite images can be handled within TS-IP. The size of the image is limited mainly by the secondary storage device available for filing these images and the display memory. A bank of public domain satellite images is included on the CD that accompanies this text. Instead of being a production line software, TS-IP is mainly intended to demonstrate the power of image processing as described in Section VI, including image rectification and restoration, image enhancement, image classification, and data merging. Through these image processing functions, one can show such interesting features as the capacity to see through clouds. This is achievable through a combination of feature (c) and stretching the remaining gray values to fill in the upper range vacated by the removal of high-level clouds. While the restoration and enhancement functions are accomplished well, the classification feature is yet to be implemented at this time.

VIII. APPLICATIONS OF REMOTE SENSING

It is clear that remote sensing devices have facilitated a fair amount of planning applications. For example, there are documented evidences of its usefulness in environmental, land use, and hazard mitigation studies (Sabins 1987). NOAA satellites, for example, use the advanced very high resolution radiometer (AVHRR), a cross-track multispectral scanner that acquires images with an image swath width of 2700 km (1768 mi) and a ground resolution cell of 1.1 by 1.1 km (0.634 mi). Table 6.4 shows the spectral bands of AVHRR. Spectral ranges of AVHRR bands 1 and 2 were positioned to record significant vegetation properties. As shown by the vegetation reflectance curve in Figure 6.21, the readings in band 1 (B_1) records the chlorophyll absorption of red wavelengths. Band 2 (B_2) records the strong reflection of infrared (IR) wavelengths by the cell structure of leaves. The ratio B_2/B_1 is one index of vegetation. Another is the spectral or normalized vegetation index (NVI), a relationship defined as

Table 6.4   REMOTE SENSING CHARACTERISTICS OF THE ADVANCED VERY HIGH RESOLUTION RADIOMETER

Band	Wavelength, μm	Remarks
1	0.55–0.68	Red: for daytime clouds and vegetation
2	0.73–1.10	Reflected IR: for shorelines and vegetation
3	3.55–3.93	Thermal IR: for hot targets such as fires and volcanoes
4	10.50–11.50	Thermal IR: for sea temperatures and for daytime and nighttime clouds
5	11.50–12.50	Thermal IR: recorded only on NOAA 7 satellites & beyond

SOURCE: Sabins (1987). Reprinted with permission.

Figure 6.21   REFLECTANCE SPECTRA OF VEGETATION AND DRY SOIL

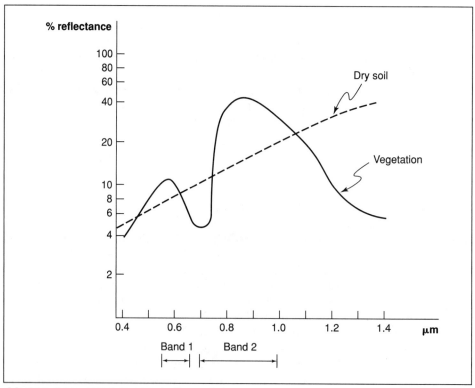

SOURCE: Sabins (1987). Reprinted with permission.

$$NVI = \frac{B_2 - B_1}{B_2 + B_1} \qquad (6.5)$$

This ratio is more useful than individual bands because it brings out the contrast and largely eliminates reflectance variation due to differences in solar elevation. The values for B_1 and B_2 are the average values for the reflectance curves at those wavelength intervals. For the vegetation spectrum in Figure 6.21, the spectral vegetation index is calculated as 0.41. For the dry soil spectrum, the index is only 0.30. Various proportions of soil and vegetation in a ground resolution cell of an AVHRR image will result in intermediate values. Also, different types of vegetation and soil may have different index values from those in Figure 6.21. Individual NVI maps can be used to prepare a vegetation classification map in color codes.

AVHRR images are well suited for studying vegetation distribution and seasonal changes in a continent-wide scale for the following reasons:

(a) The 2700-km (1768 mi) image swath of AVHRR covers a continent such as Africa with a few images, while 1100 LANDSAT MSS (multispectral scanner) or TM (thematic mapper) images are required.

(b) The daily repetition of AVHRR provides a wide selection of images for seasonal changes and for cloud-free coverage. By contrast, LANDSAT TM operates on a 16-day repetition cycle.

(c) The 4-km (2.49 mi) pixels of AVHRR are adequate for regional studies, while the 79-m (259 ft) or 30-m (98.36 ft) pixels of MSS or TM result in far too much data for economical processing.

Another application of remote sensing information is in urban land use. Utilizing the six TM bands of visible and reflected infrared (IR) data, classification of land use can be performed, in much the same manner as the NOAA satellite discussed above. For example, classification may be color coded as follows: violet (residential), orange (commercial), black (streets and parking lots), gray (construction sites), blue (open land), dark green (irrigated vegetation), medium green (mixed rangeland), light green (shrub and brushland), yellow (sand and gravel). Urban areas are so diverse in their land use that even the higher resolution of LANDSAT TM may not be able to represent these diversities adequately. A typical suburban residential lot is approximately the size of one TM 30-by-30-m (98.36-by-98.36 ft) ground resolution cell. The lot will include some or all of the following materials: trees and shrubs, lawns, paving and sidewalks, roofs, and water for a swimming pool. For such a cell, the digital numbers of the TM bands for that pixel are a composite of the spectral reflectance of the various materials. Despite these problems, the LANDSAT classification map portrays quite well the major categories of land use and land cover. Obviously, a multilevel imaging scheme is preferred, ranging from LANDSAT MSS images to low-altitude aerial photographs. Table 6.5 tabulates the spectrum of scale resolutions obtainable from each remote sensing device.

LANDSAT MSS images are excellent for recognizing the continuity and regional relationships of faults. The higher spatial resolution of LANDSAT RBV (return beam vidicon) and TM images records many of the topographic features indicative of active faulting. Stereo viewing of aircraft and large format camera (LFC) photographs provides detailed information on geomorphic features formed by faulting. Thermal IR images of arid and semi-arid areas may record the presence of active faults with little or no surface expression, such as the San Andreas and Superstition Hills faults. The highlighting and shadowing effects on low sun angle aerial photographs can emphasize topographic scarps associated with active faults, such as in the Carson Range, Nevada. Radar images also emphasize subtle features along active fault zones, such as shown in the Spaceborne Imaging Radar, SIR-A, image of the Superstition fault in Iranian Jaya, Indonesia. After a hiatus of nearly 10 years, the most sophisticated imaging radar ever flown in space was launched in 1994 (Shen 1995). Both the Spaceborne Imaging Radar (SIR-C) and X-band Synthetic Aperture Radar (X-SAR) operate in the microwave regime and are able to generate high-resolution images immune to blockage or perturbation from micro particles such as clouds and rain. Like most radar systems, both systems provide their own illumination, enabling 24-hour operation.

Analysis of remote sensing information is directly tied to GIS technology. Infrared images when included in a GIS analysis can reveal considerable information about land use, vegetation growth, and environmental problems. Digitized remotely sensed images can easily become a layer against which other database can be compared, as suggested previously. Given the potential for high-resolution satellite imagery to supplement traditional ground-based data, McCord et al. (1996) estimated the daily highway coverage that could be obtained from a sensor carried on an orbiting satellite. It was found that if a satellite orbit were designed to maximize traffic monitoring coverage, approximately 0.4 percent of the continental U. S. could be imaged daily at 1-meter resolution, a resolution that should be sufficient to distinguish trucks from passenger cars. For orbital inclination angles more typical of earth observation satellites, the coverage drops to approximately 0.2 percent. Coverage could be increased markedly with improved image processing and interpretation and data compression algorithms.

Global navigation satellite systems (GNSS) employ 24 satellites to determine three-dimensioned geocentric positions by distance measurements. They include both the U.S. Global Positioning System (GPS) and the GLONASS of the Commonwealth of Independent States. The accuracy of positions determined by GNSS is highly variable depending on the mode employed. A single receiver only

Table 6.5   CONCEPT OF BASIC VERSUS NONBASIC ACTIVITIES

Level	System	Image Scale
I	Landsat MSS images	1:250,000 and smaller
II	Landsat TM images and high-altitude aerial photographs	1:80,000 and smaller
III	Medium altitude aerial photographs	1:20,000 to 1:80,000
IV	Low altitude aerial photographs	Larger than 1:20,000

SOURCE: Sabins (1987). Reprinted with permission.

provides geodetic positions with an accuracy of about 100 meters (333 ft). With two receivers, one can make use of the differential mode, which yields accuracies of about 1–5 meters (3.3 to 16.7 ft). Most importantly, real time location information of GNSS can be relayed back to a central GIS from a service vehicle in the field, allowing for optimal routing of the vehicle, as is being practiced in Intelligent Transportation Systems (electronic highways). Artificial intelligence programs are being used to assist in data entry, map interpretation, and information retrieval. A spatial data infrastructure can eventually be accessible from the Internet or information superhighway. This would serve as an electronic index of the available geographic databases to anyone with a personal computer. The results is to avoid duplication of effort by knowing what data has already been compiled.

IX. SPECTRAL VERSUS SPATIAL PATTERN RECOGNITION

As mentioned previously, the overall objective of image classification is to categorize all pixels in an image into land cover classes or themes. Normally, multispectral data are used to perform the classification and, indeed, the spectral pattern present within the data for each pixel is used as the numerical basis for categorization. That is, different feature types manifest different combinations of digital numbers (DNs) based on their inherent spectral reflectance and emittance properties. In this light, a spectral pattern is not at all geometric in character. Rather, the term pattern refers to the set of radiance measurements obtained in the various wavelength bands for each pixel. As previously defined, spectral pattern recognition refers to the family of classification procedures that utilizes the pixel-by-pixel spectral information as the basis for automated land cover classification. Spatial pattern recognition, on the other hand, involves the categorization of image pixels on the basis of their spatial relationship with pixels surrounding them. Spatial classifiers might consider such aspects as image texture, pixel proximity, feature size, shape, directionality, repetition, and context. These types of classifiers attempt to replicate the kind of spatial synthesis done by the human analyst during the visual interpretation process. Accordingly, they tend to be much more complex and computationally intensive than spectral pattern recognition.

A. Spectral Pattern Recognition

Spectral pattern recognition forms the backbone of land cover mapping. Supervised classification refers to the process in which numerical description of the various land cover types present in a scene serves as an interpretation key that describes the spectral attributes for each feature type of interest. Each pixel in the data set is then compared numerically to each category in the interpretation key and labeled with the name of the category it most resembles. An example is taken from Lillesand and Kiefer (1987) to illustrate supervised classification. Figure 6.22 shows a single line of an airborne MSS data collected over a landscape composed of several cover types. For each of the pixels shown along this line, the MSS has measured scene radiance in terms of DNs recorded in each of the five spectral bands of sensing: blue, green, red, near-infrared, and thermal infrared. Below the

Figure 6.22   MEASUREMENTS MADE ALONG ONE SCAN LINE

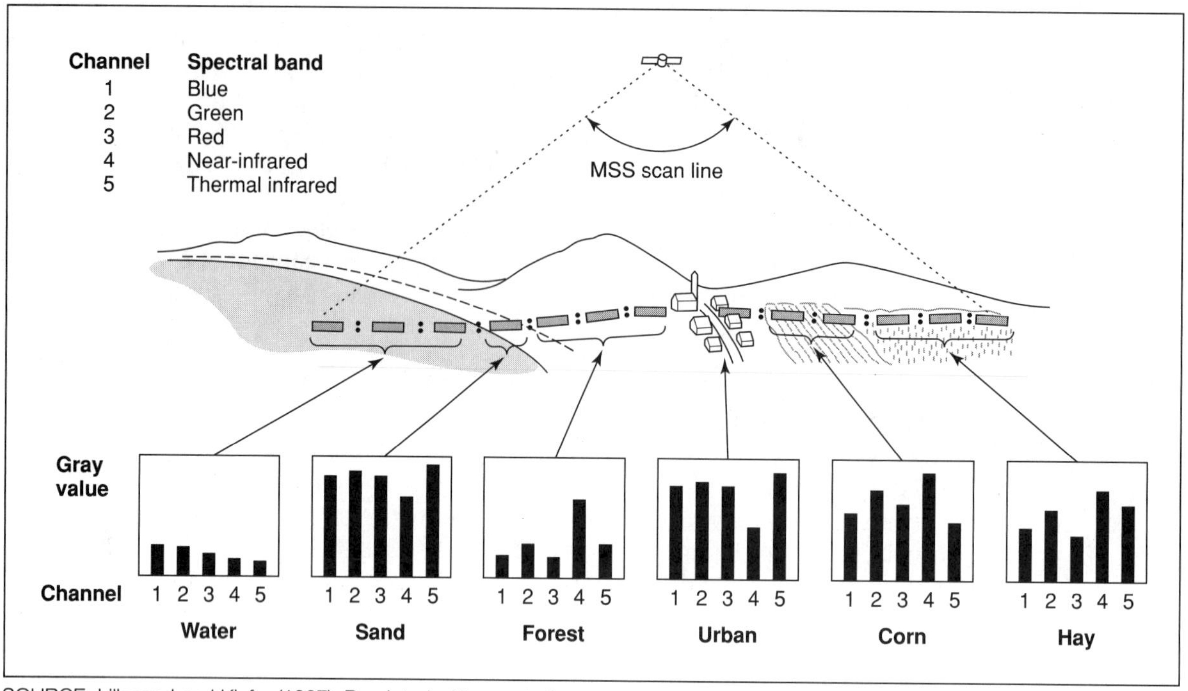

SOURCE: Lillesand and Kiefer (1987). Reprinted with permission.

scan line, typical DNs measured over six different land cover types are shown. The vertical bars indicate the relative gray values in each spectral band. These five outputs represent a coarse description of the spectral response patterns of the various terrain features along the scan line. If these spectral patterns are sufficiently distinct for each feature type, they may form the basis for image classification.

Figure 6.23 summarizes the three basic steps involved in a typical supervised classification procedure. In the training stage, the analyst identifies representative training areas and develops a numerical description of the spectral attributes of each land cover type of interest in the scene. Next, in the classification stage, each pixel in the image data set is categorized into the land-cover class it most closely resembles. If the pixel is insufficiently similar to any training data set, it is usually labeled unknown. The category label assigned to each pixel in this process is then recorded in the corresponding cell of an interpreted data set (an output image). Thus the multidimensional image matrix is used to develop a corresponding matrix of interpreted land-cover category types. After the entire data set has been categorized, the results are presented in the output stage. Figure 6.23 illustrates the classification of an image into its land-cover types, including water, sand, forest, cornfield, and so forth and where the training stage fails, unclassified. Because of the presence of unclassified pixels, this methodology often requires a subjective allocation of these pixels into either their corn field neighbor or forest neighbor. To assist the analyst in making this subjective allocation, systematic procedures have been devised that will be described next.

B. Contextual Allocation of Pixels

The error in classification can come from different sources. It is reported, for example, that 50 percent of the light received by the scanner when pointing at one nominal pixel comes from nearby pixels (McLachlan 1992). Thus, much of the noise that corrupts the signal is spatially correlated. Since the whole observation process has a spatial component, there is a need to use contextual rules in allocating the pixels to the specified spatial groups. Contextual allocation rule means using a model that incorporates the a priori knowledge that spatially neighboring pixels tend to belong to the same group. With a contextual rule, a pixel is allocated not only on the basis of its observed feature vector, but also on the feature data of neighboring pixels. The use of a non-contextual rule that allocates a pixel j solely on the basis of its gray values, or its feature vector x_j representing its multispectral readings, and thereby ignores the information on neighboring pixels, leads to a patchwork quilt of colors representing the different disjoint groups (see Figure 6.25(b). Oftentimes, contiguity of land use categories such as a lake or farmland, for example, is destroyed in the process.

One way of providing a contextual method of segmentation is to consider the allocation of each pixel individually on the basis of its posterior probabilities[12] of group membership given the recorded feature vectors x on all the n' pixels in the scene. Let $\tilde{z}_j$ be the group-indicator vector defining the color of the jth-color pixel with feature vector , where $z_{ij} = 1$ if the jth-color pixel belongs to group i, G_i (i.e., $i = j$). Group i may represent a lake, farmland, and so on—the subregions of colors. The jth-color pixel is allocated then on the basis of the maximum of the posterior probability $P(\tilde{z}_j = z_j \mid x)$ with respect to z_j, where z_j defines the group of origin color of the pixel. A common assumption is to form this posterior probability under the assumption of white noise, that is, the feature vectors x are conditionally independent given their group of origin color z_j. Contextual rules that assume white noise offer less improvement in terms of error rate over non-contextual rules in situations where the feature data are spatially correlated.

Figure 6.23   BASIC STEPS IN SUPERVISED CLASSIFICATION

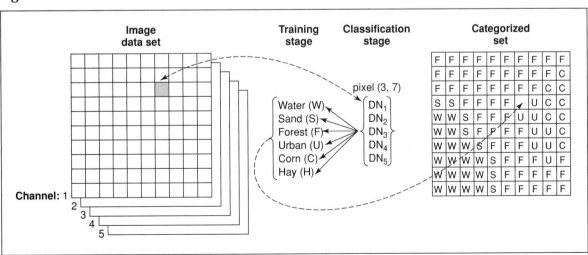

Overall, contextual rules still perform better than non-contextual rules even under this assumption.

We consider a binary example taken from Ripley (as reported by McLachlan [1992]). There are 2 groups representing two colors: white (G_1) and black (G_2). In the ith group G_i, each feature observation x_j is univariate normal with mean μ_i and variance σ^2 $(i = 1, 2)$, where $\mu_1 = 0$ and $\mu_2 = 1$. An assumption on the prior distribution of the image is the Ising model, for which

$$P(z_{1j} = 1 \mid z_j) = \frac{\exp(\beta T_{1j})}{\exp(\beta T_{1j}) + \exp(\beta T_{2j})} \tag{6.6}$$

except at the edges, where T_{1j} is the number of white neighbors of the jth-color pixel, and $T_{2j} = 8 - T_{1j}$ is the number of black neighbors. In other words, the number of black and white neighbor pixels adds up to 8, considering both first-order and second-order neighbors. For known parameters μ_1, μ_2, σ^2, and β, we have from Bayes' Theorem[13] that

$$\log \left[\frac{P(z_{1j} = 1 \mid x, z_i)}{P(z_{2j} = 1 \mid x, z_i)} \right] = -\frac{\left(x_j - \frac{1}{2}\right)}{\sigma^2} + \beta(T_{1j} - T_{2j}) \tag{6.7}$$

Here the probabilities are conditioned upon a vector of feature pixel readings x from a sample band and the two-entry group indicator vector for the jth-color pixel, z_j. An Iterative Conditional Mode (ICM) algorithm is devised whereby the jth-color pixel is allocated on the basis of Equation 6.7 where T_{ij} is replaced by its current estimate $\hat{T}_{1j}$ $(i = 1, 2)$. Assuming equal posterior probabilities, the jth-color pixel is allocated to white, or $z_{1j} = 1$, if

$$x_j < \frac{1}{2} + \beta\sigma^2(\hat{T}_{1j} - \hat{T}_{2j}) \tag{6.8}$$

which is both simple and intuitive. The non-contextual version of this rule, corresponding to $\beta = 0$, would take $z_{1j} = 1$ if $x_j < 1/2$, thereby ignoring the information $\hat{T}_{1j}$ and $\hat{T}_{2j}$ on the color of neighboring pixels. The algorithm can be extended to multivariate features (corresponding to multispectral bands) and multiple groups (colors) as will be illustrated below. (See McLachlan [1992] for further details beyond these two examples).

Two-Class Example

Consider a single-channel 42-pixel image with individual gray values as shown below (Brigantic and Chan 1994; Wright and Chan 1994):

11	5	6	8	13	2	8
2	5	1	1	3	2	3
8	4	6	5	6	6	6
1	4	2	2	6	3	3
4	5	6	5	5	4	5
3	2	2	1	5	2	3

We wish to classify each of these pixels as belonging to either a lake or forest. We will assume each class of pixels, whether lake or forest, are normally distributed with mean μ_i and standard deviation σ_i ($i = 1, 2$). Notice that instead of an overall, common standard deviation σ that applies to both groups, distinction is made between the two groups of pixels, σ_1 versus σ_2. The conditional probability-density function (PDF) of gray value x for the ith class ($i = 1, 2$) given the pixel is in the ith class $\mathbf{z}_i$ is therefore

$$P(x|\mathbf{z}_i) = \frac{1}{\sqrt{2\pi}\sigma_i} \exp\left[-\frac{(x-\mu_i)^2}{2\sigma_i^2}\right] \quad i = 1, 2 \tag{6.9}$$

Unless one class is more likely to occur, the point where the two PDFs are equal constitutes the decision boundary. We show an example of such PDFs in Figure 6.24, where we arbitrarily assume that the lake class has a mean gray value

Figure 6.24   GAUSSIAN PROBABILITY-DENSITY FUNCTION USED IN BAYESIAN CLASSIFIER

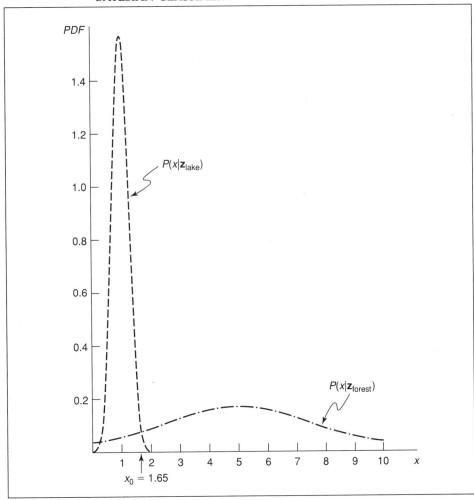

of $\mu_1 = 1$ and a standard deviation of $\sigma_1 = 0.25$. We also assume that the pixels with a gray value of other than 1 represent the forest class. Correspondingly, we compute a mean forest gray value of $\mu_2 = 4.74$ and a standard deviation of $\sigma_2 = 2.50$. From this plot we identify the decision boundary x_0 as 1.65. This means that any pixel with a gray value less than 1.65 is classified as lake and pixels with a gray value greater than 1.65 are classified as forest. The corresponding classified image is shown below, where F stands for forest and L for lake:

F	F	F	F	F	F	F
F	F	L	L	F	F	F
F	F	F	F	F	F	F
L	F	F	F	F	F	F
F	F	F	F	F	F	F
F	F	F	L	F	F	F

Notice this Bayesian classifier here simply computes the probability that a pixel belongs to a class, or it essentially performs a spectral classification (rather than a spatial classification). Contextual classification techniques are now applied to include the relation a pixel has to its neighbors. For example, if a lone pixel had a low gray value that indicates that it belongs to a lake, yet all of its first- and second-order neighbors had a high gray value suggestive of a forest, the contextual classification scheme may well assign the pixel to the forest class despite its low gray value. For our simple problem, we let first- and second-order neighbors have equal weights so that for interior pixels the number of first- and second-order neighbors total 8, or $T_{1j} + T_{2j} = 8$; for corner pixels $T_{1j} + T_{2j} = 3$; and for border pixels $T_{1j} + T_{2j} = 5$. According to Equation 6.8, the decision rule now assumes the form $x_j < 1.65 + \beta(0.25)^2(\hat{T}_{1j} - \hat{T}_{2j})$. So if pixel j had a gray value less than the resulting value as computed, it will be classified as a lake, otherwise it will be classified as forest. It is clear that the parameter β determines the watershed for classification. When $\beta = 0$, the gray values of a pixel's neighbors (and the choice of σ between the two groups) becomes unimportant, non-contextual classification results, as shown in the forest (F) and lake (L) image classification above.

Carrying out the ICM algorithm with values of β greater than zero, a number of classifications were obtained. At 0.25 increments, increasing the value from 0 through 1.5 did not cause a change in the classification. Starting at $\beta = 1.75$, however, the following image was obtained where two of the four lake pixels started to disappear:

F	F	F	F	F	F	F
F	F	F	F	F	F	F
F	F	F	F	F	F	F
L	F	F	F	F	F	F
F	F	F	F	F	F	F
F	F	F	L	F	F	F

Eventually, at $\beta = 2.25$ the predominance of forest pixels causes the lake pixels to disappear altogether:

```
F    F    F    F    F    F    F
F    F    F    F    F    F    F
F    F    F    F    F    F    F
F    F    F    F    F    F    F
F    F    F    F    F    F    F
F    F    F    F    F    F    F
```

Notice that in terms of final result, the difference between a single σ vis-a-vis two σ's is really not that important since it gets to be combined with β in Equation 6.8.

Implementing the contextual classification scheme in conjunction with the Bayesian technique is relatively simple, at least for a single sensor (or one-dimensional problem) and in the case of partitioning pixels into two classes. Extension into several classes and multiple sensors is still straightforward, although computational requirements do go up noticeably, but not dramatically. ∎

Multi-Class Example

In this example, we consider more than two classes in image classification. Take the example of four classes, the decision rule in Equation 6.8 is now based on three watershed points x_0, x_0', and x_0'', where $x_0 < x_0' < x_0''$. A pixel of color j will belong to group 1 if $x_j < x_0 + \beta\sigma_1^2(\hat{T}_{1j} - \hat{T}_{2j} - \hat{T}_{3j} - \hat{T}_{4j})$, to group 2 if $x_j < x_0' + \beta\sigma_2^2(\hat{T}_{2j} - \hat{T}_{1j} - \hat{T}_{3j} - \hat{T}_{4j})$, and to group 3 if $x_j < x_0'' + \beta\sigma_3^2(\hat{T}_{3j} - \hat{T}_{1j} - \hat{T}_{2j} - \hat{T}_{4j})$. While there are numerous ways to classify an image, one way is that the classified pixels are sequentially removed from the image according to this decision rule. Thus after pixels are classified into group 1, they are removed and $\hat{T}_{1j} = 0$ in the decision rule for classifying group 2 pixels. If one does not want to remove pixels from an image after they are classified, an alternate decision rule can be devised.

Figure 6.25   CONTEXTUAL VERSUS NON-CONTEXTUAL IMAGE CLASSIFICATION

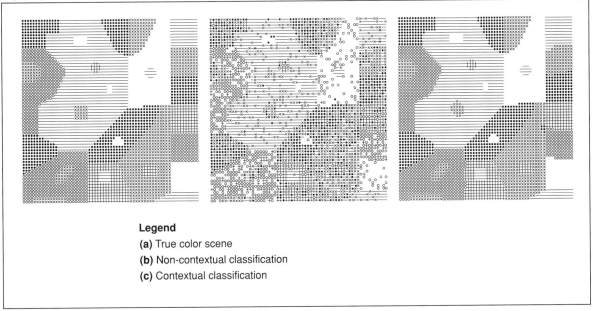

Legend

(a) True color scene

(b) Non-contextual classification

(c) Contextual classification

SOURCE: Besag as cited in McLachlan (1992). Reprinted with permission.

The rule for group 1 remains the same, while that for group 2 becomes $x_j < x_0 + \beta\sigma_2^2(\hat{T}_{1j} + \hat{T}_{2j} - \hat{T}_{3j} - \hat{T}_{4j})$ and that for group 3 becomes $x_j < x_0'' + \beta\sigma_3^2(\hat{T}_{1j} + \hat{T}_{2j} + \hat{T}_{3j} - \hat{T}_{4j})$. The decision rules can easily be generalized to six groups in the following example. We give an artificial example taken from Besag as cited in McLachlan (1992). The true scene contains 6 colors, on a 120×120 array. It was originally hand-drawn and chosen to display a wide variety of characteristics. The univariate feature observations were generated from the color labels by superimposing Gaussian noise with $\sigma^2 = 0.36$. The first 64 rows and the first 64 columns are displayed in Figure 6.25(a) in which the adjacencies are less contrived than in the scene as a whole. A color key, which is part of the pattern, is shown, where the sign "minus" $- = 1$, "cross" $\times = 2$, and so on. The initial reconstruction using the non-contextual classification, i.e., $\beta = 0$, produced an overall misallocation rate of 32 percent, as shown in the patchwork of colors in Figure 6.25(b). With the correct value of σ^2 and with $\beta = 1.5$ throughout, the ICM algorithm gave an overall error rate of 2.1 percent on the eighth cycle. The ICM algorithm, applied with β increased by equal increments from 0.5 to 1.5 over the first six cycles, reduced the overall error rate to 1.2 percent on the eighth cycle, as shown in Figure 6.25(c). ∎

X. A DISTRICT CLUSTERING MODEL

Following the same philosophy, we present here a more general spatial pattern recognition model—sometimes called a districting model—which selects, from a set of candidate pixels, parcels, or cells, the collection that best achieves a pre-specified set of goals or objectives. This is accomplished within specific constraints. The main purpose of most districting models is the design of a predetermined number of territories or districts with contiguous and compact shapes. This compares well with image classification, where we group like pixels together to identify land cover or manmade facilities of interest.

A. A Single Subregion Model

Benabdallah and Wright (1992) present a multi-criteria integer-programming model for selecting a set of cells or parcels from a large set, and identify the complete set of non-inferior or non-dominated[14] solutions on a regular grid configuration. A binary variable x_i takes on a value of 1 if cell i is acquired and 0 otherwise. If we assume that the cost c_i for any particular cell being considered is known, then a criterion function that seeks to minimize overall cost may be written: Minimize $y_1' = \sum_{i=1}^{n'} c_i x_i$. Here costs are broadly defined to include such measures as the gray value of a pixel or subareal population exposed to pollution and so forth. For the example shown in Figure 6.23, application of this criterion function will most likely result in the identification of the previously unclassified pixels as forest. A maximization criterion, on the other hand, will probably identify the pixels as corn.

Similarly, if a_i' —the area of cell i—is also known for all candidate cells, a second criterion function that seeks to maximize total area may be written; Maximize $y_2' = \sum_{i=1}^{n'} a_i' x_i$. The application of this criterion function will support our conjecture that the unclassified pixels in Figure 6.23 will either be identified as forest or corn and not be split between the two, since this criterion fosters as large an acquisition as possible for a land cover type.

A third criterion function may be to induce compactness of the area by tightening the total length of the border surrounding the cells acquired. This premise was based on the observation that, for any given area, the most compact configuration possible is one in which the border surrounding that area is a circle, the border with the shortest length. Define s_{ij} as the length of the border separating cell i from cell j, and variables P_{ij} and N_{ij} to be mutually exclusive binary decision variables that sum to 1 if the border separating cells i and j in the final solution is an external border (a border separating a cell that is acquired from one that is not) and 0 otherwise. The compactness criterion may be written as: Minimize $y'_3 = \sum_{i=1}^{n'} \sum_{j \in T} s_{ij}(P_{ij} + N_{ij})$, where T_i is the set of cells adjacent to cell i, in other words, if cell 11 is adjacent to first-order neighbor cells 7, 10, 12, and 15, then the set T_{11} is {7, 10, 12, 15}.

The combined weighted objective function for the three criterion districting problem is

$$\text{Minimize } z = \lambda'_c \sum_{i=1}^{n'} c_i x_i - \lambda'_a \sum_{i=1}^{n'} a_i x_i + \lambda'_s \sum_{i=1}^{n'} \sum_{j \in T_i} s_{ij} (P_{ij} N_{ij}) \tag{6.10}$$

where $\lambda'_c, \lambda'_a, \lambda'_s$ are weights on the cost, area, and compactness objectives, respectively. By varying the weights, the three criterion functions are emphasized or de-emphasized relative to one another. Thus emphasizing the gray value of the unclassified pixels in Figure 6.23, balanced with maximal acquisition, may result in only part (rather than all) of the pixels being allocated to forest.

A single set of constraints is required to define P_{ij} and N_{ij}

$$x_i - x_j - P_{ij} + N_{ij} = 0 \qquad \forall \; i, j \in T_i \tag{6.11}$$

For any adjacent cells i and j, if only one of the cells is selected ($x_i = 1$, $x_j = 0$; or $x_i = 0$, $x_j = 1$), then either P_{ij} and N_{ij} must equal 0. For example, if cell i is acquired ($x_i = 1$) and cell j is not ($x_j = 0$), then the above equation would be satisfied if $P_{ij} = 1$ and $N_{ij} = 0$. If both cells i and j are acquired ($x_i = x_j = 1$) or neither is acquired ($x_i = x_j = 0$), then P_{ij} and N_{ij} must both equal 1 or both equal 0. Because the external border function is being minimized, the smallest values assigned to P_{ij} and N_{ij} that would satisfy the equation would be 0 ($P_{ij} = N_{ij} = 0$) for all i, j within the same grouping. (Example: If only cell 11 is acquired, or $x_{11} = 1$, such a non-inferior solution will have $P_{11\,7} = P_{11\,10} = P_{11\,12} = P_{11\,15} = 1$, and $N_{7\,11} = N_{10\,11} = N_{12\,11} = N_{15\,11} = 1$.)

While the formulation presented above is a general model, it is computationally difficult due to integrality requirements on the decision variables. Including the second and third criteria as constraints[15], a more compact formulation is obtained:

$$\text{Minimize } y'_1 = \sum_{i=1}^{n'} c_i x_i \tag{6.12}$$

subject to

$$\sum_{i=1}^{n'} x_i = M \tag{6.13}$$

$$x_i - x_j - P_{ij} + N_{ij} = 0 \qquad \forall\, i, j \in T_i \tag{6.14}$$

$$\sum_{i=1}^{n'} \sum_{j \in T_i} s_{ij}\,(P_{ij} + N_{ij}) = L \tag{6.15}$$

$$x_i,\, P_{ij},\, N_{ij} \in \{0, 1\} \tag{6.16}$$

Here, M stands for the number of pixels to be included in the district, and L is twice the boundary of the district[16]—both of which are to be parametrically varied within a range to reflect the change in weights λ'_a and λ'_s. All a_i's are set to unity since pixels are equal in size. The advantage of this formulation is that a non-inferior solution set (or efficient frontier) can be traced out for the allowable range of Equations 6.13 and 6.15. (Again, see Section III in Chapter 5 for details of such a procedure.)

We will illustrate this transformed model through a numerical example. Figure 6.26 shows a 4 × 4 grid of 16 unit squares of the same size. The costs are shown as lower right-hand-side entries of the grid. The cell (or pixel) number is at the left-hand upper corner of each cell. In this example, $M = 2$, indicating an area of 2 units. Also, $L = 12$ represents a boundary line of 6 units in length. The entire formulation is shown in Figure 6.27, prepared in an ASCII input format that will be accepted by many mixed integer programming codes on the market today. The solution, $x_{10} = x_{11} = 1$ and the rest of the variables at zero value, illustrates only one non-inferior solution for the criterion function Equation 6.12 when M and L in Equations 6.13 and 6.15 assume specific values of 2 and 6 respectively. In the general case, there are quite a few number of partitioning possible within permissible range of M and L.

Figure 6.26   A NONINFERIOR SOLUTION SHOWING A SINGLE SUBREGION

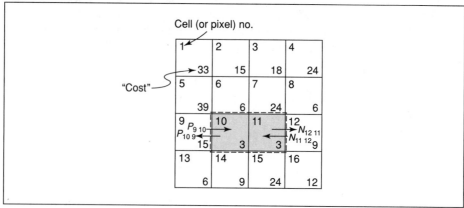

Figure 6.27   EXAMPLE MODEL FORMATION

```
. . OBJECTIVE MINIMIZE
1 ( 33 [ [ x1] ] + 15 [ [ x2] ] + 18 [ [ x3] ] + 24 [ [ x4] ] +
39 [ [ x5] ] + 6 [ [ x6] ] + 24 [ [ x7] ] + 6 [ [ x8] ] +
15 [ [ x9] ] + 3 [ [ x10] ] + 3 [ [ x11] ] + 9 [ [ x12] ] +
6 [ [ x13] ] + 9 [ [ x14] ] + 24 [ [ x15] ] + 12 [ [ x16] ] )
CONSTRAINTS
*constraint for sum (Xi) = M
x1 + x2 + x3 + x4 + x5 + x6 + x7 + x8 + x9 + x10 + x11 + x12 +
x13 + x14 + x15 + x16 = 2

*constraint for Xi − Xj − Pij + Nij = 0

x1 − x2 − p12 + n12 = 0
x1 − x5 − p15 + n15 = 0
x2 − x1 − p21 + n21 = 0
x2 − x3 − p23 + n23 = 0
x2 − x6 − p26 + n26 = 0
x3 − x2 − p32 + n32 = 0
x3 − x4 − p34 + n34 = 0
x3 − x7 − p37 + n37 = 0
x4 − x3 − p43 + n43 = 0
x4 − x8 − p48 + n48 = 0
x5 − x1 − p51 + n51 = 0
x5 − x6 − p56 + n56 = 0
x5 − x9 − p59 + n59 = 0
x6 − x2 − p62 + n62 = 0
x6 − x5 − p65 + n65 = 0
x6 − x7 − p67 + n67 = 0
x6 − x10 − p610 + n610 = 0
x7 − x3 − p73 + n73 = 0
x7 − x6 − p76 + n76 = 0
x7 − x8 − p78 + n78 = 0
x7 − x11 − p711 + n711 = 0
x8 − x4 − p84 + n84 = 0
x8 − x7 − p87 + n87 = 0
x8 − x12 − p812 + n812 = 0
x9 − x5 − p95 + n95 = 0
x9 − x10 − p910 + n910 = 0
x9 − x13 − p913 + n913 = 0
x10 − x6 − p106 + n106 = 0
x10 − x9 − p109 + n109 = 0
x10 − x11 − p1011 + n1011 = 0
x10 − x14 − p1014 + n1014 = 0
x11 − x7 − p117 + n117 = 0
x11 − x10 − p1110 + n1110 = 0
x11 − x12 − p1112 + n1112 = 0
x11 − x15 − p1115 + n1115 = 0
x12 − x8 − p128 + n128 = 0
x12 − x11 − p1211 + n1211 = 0
x12 − x16 − p1216 + n1216 = 0
x13 − x9 − p139 + n139 = 0
x13 − x14 − p1314 + n1314 = 0
x14 − x10 − p1410 + n1410 = 0
x14 − x13 − p1413 + n1413 = 0
x14 − x15 − p1415 + n1415 = 0
x15 − x11 − p1511 + n1511 = 0
x15 − x14 − p1514 + n1514 = 0
x15 − x16 − p1516 + n1516 = 0
x16 − x12 − p1612 + n1612 = 0
x16 − x15 − p1615 + n1615 = 0
*constraint for sum (Pi + Ni)  = L
p12 + n12 + p15 + n15 +
p21 + n21 + p23 + n23 + p26 + n26 +
p32 + n32 + p34 + n34 + p37  + n37 +
p43 + n43 + p48 + n48 +
p51 + n51 + p56 + n56 + p59  + n59 +
p62 + n62 + p65 + n65 + p67  + n67 + p610 + n610 +
p73 + n73 + p76 + n76 + p78 + n78 + p711 + n711 +
p84 + n84 + p87 + n87 + p812  + n812 +
p95 + n95 + p910 + n910 + p913  + n913 +
p106 + n106 + p109 + n109 + p1011  + n1011 + p1014  + n1014 +
p117 + n117 + p1110 + n1110 + p1112  + n1112 + p1115  + n1115 +
p128 + n128 + p1211 + n1211 + p1216  + n1216 +
p139 + n139 + p1314 + n1314 +
p1410 + n1410 + p1413 + n1413 + p1415  + n1415 +
p1511 + n1511 + p1514 + n1514 + p1516  + n1516 +
p1612 + n1612 + p1615 + n1615 = 12
```

To determine the range of L and M to vary in this constrained feasible region, Benabdallah and Wright (1992) offered a formula and subsequently modified by Wright (1994) for determining the minimum value of the L range as a function of M: $B_{min}^M = 4\langle\sqrt{M}\rangle + 2t''$ with

$$t''(M) = \begin{cases} 0 \ if \ M - \langle\sqrt{M}\rangle^2 = 0 \\ 1 \ if \ M \le \langle\sqrt{M}\rangle^2 + \langle\sqrt{M}\rangle \\ 2 \ if \ M > \langle\sqrt{M}\rangle^2 + \langle\sqrt{M}\rangle \end{cases} \tag{6.17}$$

where $<\bullet>$ is the integer part of $\bullet$ The parameter $t''(M)$ monitors the shape of the region, when $t''(M) = 0$, the region is square in shape. When $t''(M) = 1$, the shape becomes a rectangle. For example, an irregular shape will result for $M = 3$, $t'' = 2$, and $B_{min}^M = 8$: ■■/□■. Similar result is obtained for $M = 8$, $t''(M) = 2$, and

$B_{min}^M = 12$: ■■■/■■■/□■■ . When $t''(M) = 2$, the shape will be made up of squares and/or rectangles. Experimentation with small problems will show that the above equations make sense and that for values of L near this lower bound, contiguity of the region will result. When the strict lower bound is used for L, a rectangular or square shape subregion will be formed.

Example

Refer to the numerical example of Figure 6.26 and Figure 6.27. For $M = 2$, and $t'''(M) = B_{max}^M = 6$, and the familiar rectangle consisting of cells 10 and 11 results. The maximum of the range is $B_{max}^M = 4M$, where the region is fragmented and no acquired cell is adjacent to any other acquired cell □■□/■□■/□■□ . In general, the region may be fragmented before reaching $B_{max}^M = 4M$. ∎

B. Multiple Subregion Model

A multiple subregion model can be obtained by introducing another index k, which stands for the subregion number. Thus x_{ik} stands for the binary variable that determines whether the ith cell or pixel is acquired in subregion k. Correspondingly, the mutually exclusive binary-variables associated with the boundary can be extended to include the index k: P_{ijk} and N_{ijk}. Introducing the weight w_k for each subregion, the model now looks like

$$\text{Minimize} \quad z = \sum_{k=1}^{K} w_k \sum_{i=1}^{n'} c_i \, x_{ik} \tag{6.18}$$

subject to

$$\sum_{i=1}^{n'} x_{ik} = M_k \qquad \forall k \tag{6.19}$$

$$x_{ik} - x_{jk} - P_{ijk} + N_{ijk} = 0 \qquad \forall \, i, j \in T_i, k \tag{6.20}$$

$$\sum_{k=1}^{K} x_{ik} \leq 1 \qquad \forall k \tag{6.21}$$

$$\sum_{i=1}^{n'} \sum_{j \in T_i} s_{i_j} (P_{ijk} + N_{ijk}) = L_k \qquad \forall k \tag{6.22}$$

The number of zero-one variables and constraints used in the multiple subregion models can be estimated a priori before one runs the model. Let R be the number of cell rows in the overall region, C the number of cell columns in the overall region, and K the number of subregions being acquired. An estimate of the number of zero-one variables, the number of equality constraints, and less-than-equal-to constraints as a function of R, C, and K can be given.

Number of zero-one variables $\approx 9K^{\bar{R}\bar{C}}$
Number of equality constraints $\approx 2K(1 + \bar{R} + \bar{C} + 2^{\bar{R}}C)$
Number of less-than-or-equal-to constraints $\approx \bar{R}\,\bar{C}$
An example calculation when $R = 3$, $C = 3$, and $K = 2$ Yields 162, 100, and 90 respectively. It can be seen that the size of the problem can grow exponentially large. Either a faster solution algorithm or an alternate model formulation would be necessary to make this an operational procedure.

An example run involving two subregions is shown in Figure 6.28. This table is organized into four groups, corresponding to the size of the first subregion fixed at 1, 2, 3, and 4 pixels respectively, while varying the size of the second subregion. Also included in this table is the various non-inferior solutions when the boundary L is tightened or loosened. This illustrates the usefulness of a model like this in presenting the analyst with various possible cell classifications schemes. The decision maker can then pick and choose among the non-inferior solutions. Figure 6.29 illustrates graphically the non-inferior solutions for the first group in the table. Take the line marked S2_1_2 as an example. The line records a single non-inferior solution to a *two*-subregion model. The first subregion has *one* pixel while the second subregion has *two* pixels. The partitioning is based on the assumption that the first subregion is weighted twice more than the second subregion. Instead of allocating pixel 6 to subregion 1 and pixels 8 and 9 to subregion 2, it can be shown that the better solution is to have pixel 8 assigned to subregion 1 and pixels 6 and 9 to subregion 2. To see this, let us say $w_1 = 1$ and $w_2 = 2$, the solution as shown yields an objective function of $2(1) + (2 + 1) = 5$, which is better than $2(2) + (1 + 1) = 6$.

The model can be further extended to account for shape of a subregion. Let w'_k be the width and h_k be the height of a subregion k. One can specify the shape of each subregion by rewriting Equation 6.22 as two equations:

$$\sum_{i \in n^r} x_{ik} - W'_k y_{rk} = 0 \qquad \forall r, k \tag{6.23}$$

$$\sum_{r=1}^{\bar{R}} y_{rk} = h_k \qquad \forall k \tag{6.24}$$

where y_{rk} is a binary variable equal to 1 if any cell in row r is assigned to subregion k and zero otherwise. The parameter n_r is the set of cells in row r and $\bar{R}$ is the number of rows in the grid. An example of this model is illustrated in

Figure 6.28   MULTIPLE SUBREGION NONINFERIOR SOLUTIONS

File[1]	M_1	L_1	Cost	Cells	M_2	L_2	Cost	Cells	Total Cost
S2_1_1	1	4	1	8	1	4	1	9	2
S2_1_2	1	4	1	8	2	6	3	6, 9	4
S2_1_3	1	4	5	2	3	8	4	6, 8, 9	9
S2_1_4a	1	4	5	2	4	8	17	5, 6, 8, 9	22
S2_1_4b	1	4	5	2	4	10	9	6, 7, 8, 9	14
S2_1_5a	1	4	5	7	5	10	22	2, 5, 6, 8, 9	27
S2_1_5b	1	4	5	7	5	12	15	2, 3, 6, 8, 9	20
S2_1_6a	1	4	5	7	6	10	28	2, 3, 5, 6, 8, 9	33
S2_1_6b	1	4	6	3	6	12	27	2, 5, 6, 7, 8, 9	33
S2_1_6c	1	4	5	2	6	14	23	3, 4, 6, 7, 8, 9	28
S2_1_7a	1	4	6	3	7	12	35	2, 4, 5, 6, 7, 8, 9	41
S2_1_7b	1	4	2	6	7	14	39	2, 3, 4, 5, 7, 8, 9	41
S2_1_7c	1	4	1	8	7	16	38	1, 2, 3, 4, 6, 7, 9	39
S2_1_8a	1	4	1	9	8	12	51	1, 2, 3, 4, 5, 6, 7, 8	52
S2_1_8b	1	4	2	6	8	14	50	1, 2, 3, 4, 5, 7, 8, 9	52
S2_1_8c	1	4	13	5	8	16	39	1, 2, 3, 4, 6, 7, 8, 9	52
S2_2_2	2	6	3	6, 9	2	6	6	7, 8	9
S2_2_3	2	6	6	7, 8	3	8	9	3, 6, 9	15
S2_2_4a	2	6	11	2, 3	4	8	17	5, 6, 8, 9	28
S2_2_4b	2	6	11	2, 3	4	10	9	6, 7, 8, 9	20
S2_2_5a	2	6	11	2, 3	5	10	22	5, 6, 7, 8, 9	33
S2_2_5b	2	6	13	4, 7	5	12	15	2, 3, 6, 8, 9	28
S2_2_6a	2	6	13	4, 7	6	10	28	2, 3, 5, 6, 8, 9	41
S2_2_6b	2	6	2	8, 9	6	12	39	2, 3, 4, 5, 6, 7	41
S2_2_6c	2	6	2	8, 9	6	14	37	1, 2, 3, 4, 6, 7	39
S2_2_7a	2	6	19	1, 4	7	12	33	2, 3, 5, 6, 7, 8, 9	52
S2_3_3	3	8	7	7, 8, 9	3	8	13	2, 3, 6	20
S2_3_4a	3	8	7	7, 8, 9	4	8	26	2, 3, 5, 6	33
S2_3_4b	3	8	13	2, 3, 6	4	10	15	4, 7, 8, 9	28
S2_3_5a	3	8	7	7, 8, 9	5	10	34	2, 3, 4, 5, 6	41
S2_3_5b	3	8	9	3, 6, 9	5	12	30	1, 2, 4, 7, 8	39
S2_3_6a	3	8	22	1, 2, 3	6	10	30	4, 5, 6, 7, 8, 9	52
S2_3_6b	3	8	4	6, 8, 9	6	12	48	1, 2, 3, 4, 5, 7	52
S2_3_6c	3	8	26	4, 5, 7	6	14	26	1, 2, 3, 6, 8, 9	52
S2_4a_4b	4	8	26	2, 3, 5, 6	4	10	15	4, 7, 8, 9	41
S2_4a_5b	4	8	17	5, 6, 7, 8	5	12	35	1, 2, 3, 4, 7	52

[1]Take the first entry under this column, S2 stands for 2 subregions, 1 stands for an area of 1 pixel for subregion 1 and the last 1, stands for an area of 1 pixel for subregion 2 also. The a and b entries specify two different variations on the boundary of the subregion in generating noninferior solutions.

Figure 6.30, in which the first subregion is specified to have a width of 2 and a height of 2, while the second subregion measures 3 by 1. Notice this fundamental formulation is good for subregions of rectangular and square shapes only, where the solution yields the exact specified shape.

     For computational efficiency, this model has been transformed to several more compact formulations. For example, a nonlinear function can be used as a compactness function for a districting model (Benabdallah and Wright 1992). The resulting model is multi-criteria, nonlinear, and discrete. The objective of the model is to maximize the weighted sum of the compactness function of all subregions, subject to the cost limits constraint on each subregion. A heuristic algorithm is developed to generate a solution to the problem. Based on limited experiments, the algorithm converges to a very good solution. However, the solution may not be optimal.

Figure 6.29   MULTIPLE SUBREGION ALLOCATION RESULTS

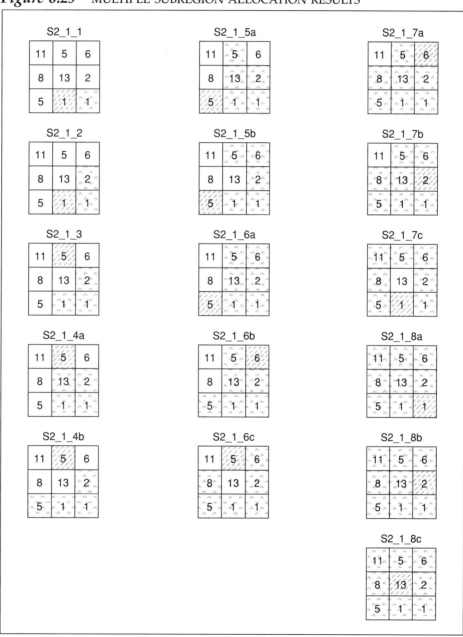

Figure 6.30 MULTIPLE SUBREGION MODEL WITH SHAPE SPECIFICATIONS

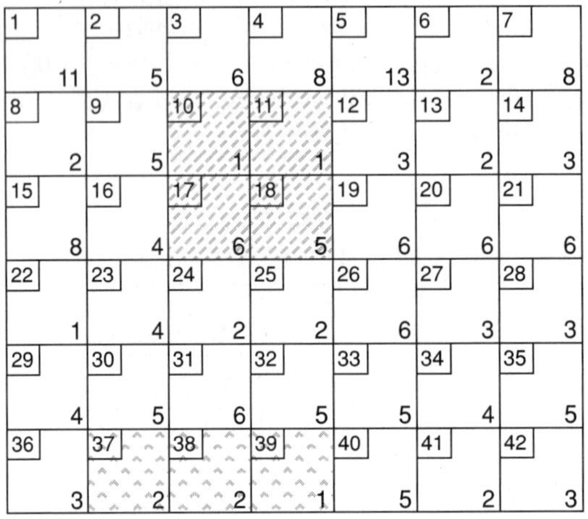

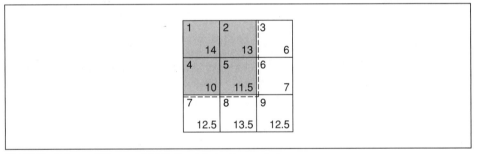

Figure 6.31 DISTRICTING FOR DEMAND EQUITY

SOURCE: Ahituv and Berman (1988). Reprinted with permission.

C. Demand Equity

In providing service to a region, the concept of equity is important. This is particularly true in districting for public service provision. The concept of equity asserts that the entire population of potential clients is treated as equally as possible in terms of the quality of service it receives. Applying the equity criterion will imply that the performance measures by which the quality of service is evaluated will be more or less equal in each subregion. Let us examine the sample region G exhibited in Figure 6.31. Instead of c_i, the region consists of nine cells. The numbers at the lower right-hand corner of each cell indicate the demand at each cell. These are denoted by f_i ($i = 1, \dots, 9$). Suppose we want to partition G into two subregions, G_1 and G_2, where the only guiding criterion is equity. We will certainly not recommend that cells 2 and 3 constitute G_1 while all the rest of the cells are assigned to G_2, since such partitioning will load 81 percent of the total demand on G_2. Rather we will try to divide the cells such that their cumulated demand will be close to 50 percent. For example, $G_1 = \{1, 2, 4, 5\}$ and $G_2 = \{3, 6, 7, 8, 9\}$; this partitioning will split the demand between the two subregions in a ratio of 48.5:51.5.

The principle of equity can be quantitatively formulated as follows: Let K be the desired number of subregions. Perfect equity is obtained if each subregion incurs $1/K$ fraction of the total demand. An additional criterion function to be applied, in addition to compactness, cost, and area, may well be the widely publicized entropy function[17] and max $Q!/\Pi_{k=1}^{K} V_k$ where $V_k = \Sigma_{i=1}^{n'} f_i x_i$, $\Sigma_{i=1}^{K} V_k = Q$ and f_i's are integer valued. Obviously, such a criterion function is nonlinear, even when it is simplified into its Stirling's approximation: $\max \left[-\sum_{i=1}^{k} (V_k \log V_k - V_k) \right]$. The set of constraints are very much similar to Equations 6.19 through 6.22. The model will then partition the study area into service regions of more or less equal demand. Unfortunately, the resulting model is nonlinear, discrete, and huge in size. For this reason, it may further complicate the already computationally demanding Benabdallah/Wright (BW) model. Simpler districting models without the area and border length considerations have been around. They are typically used for effecting equitable redistricting of political subdivisions. Mehrotra and Johnson (1995) provides one of the more recent descriptions of a solution algorithm. A numerical example is included in the "Exercise and Problems" section as Problem III-A.

D. Extensions

The BW model can be further extended in several ways. First, there is an inherent weakness in handling subregions at the border of the grid. The accounting system of the model breaks down at the border. For instance, the border length of a subregion made up of cells 13 and 14 in Figure 6.26 is 3 rather than 6, since the edges at the border do not count. Also a subregion can be broken down into two at the border. The example shown in Figure 6.32 illustrates this fact, where the shaded cells 9, 10, and 16 form one (rather than two) subregion(s) of area 3 and border length 8 ($M = 3, L = 16$). This weakness of the model can be overcome by rewriting the equations governing the subregion length L, distinguishing between the regular interior cells, the corner cells and cells on the border that are not corner cells. A simpler way is to build an artificial border around the region, with values c_i set at a high value. This way, each real cell can be treated the same way without having to distinguish between interior cells, border cells and corner cells. This

Figure 6.32   A SPLIT SUBREGION AT THE BORDER

practice also parallels remote sensing applications, where the pixels at the border are distorted and are of little relevance to the rest of the image.

If there is a single criticism leveled against the BW model, it is about the computational time involved. The current state of the art only allows such a model to be a research tool, rather than an operational one. It is conceivable that better solution algorithms can be devised over time to address this problem. Finally, the shape constraint can possibly be made more elaborate by inclusion of more sophisticated constraints. Research is currently underway to address some of these concerns (Green and Chan 1994; Warrender et al. 1992). Modern GIS technology has developed to the point where exhaustive enumeration algorithms imposed on raster or cell data can solve problems that are much more practical, and in reasonable time, even though these exhaustive algorithms are by definition inefficient. However, for problems that involve clustering of all cells in a field into distinct subregions and the identification of multiple subregions having certain shape or configuration requirements enumeration methods are infeasible.

XI. CASE STUDY OF IMAGE CLASSIFICATION

For this study, a SPOT image of the Washington D.C. area was used as the source of multi spectral data. Land cover types are to be discerned in the image. Rather than attempting to analyze the whole image, this study will be limited to a 48 ×

Figure 6.33   PORTION OF WASHINGTON D.C. MALL UNDER ANALYSIS

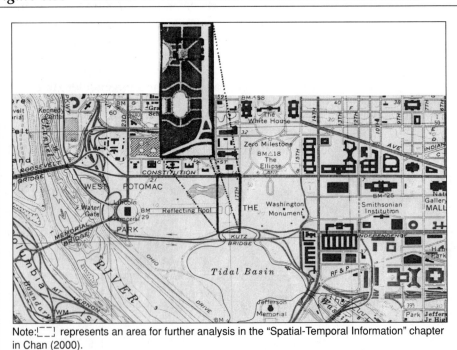

Note:⌐⌐⌐ represents an area for further analysis in the "Spatial-Temporal Information" chapter in Chan (2000).

SOURCE: U.S. Geological Survey (1983). Reprinted with permission.

Figure 6.34   SPOT SUB-IMAGE GRAY VALUES

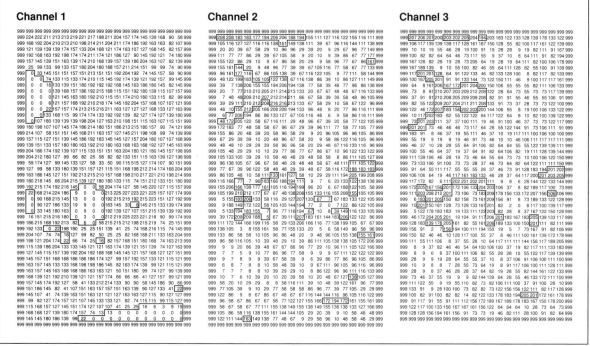

SOURCE: Amrine (1992). Reprinted with permission.

18 pixel sub-image. The area selected is a portion of the Washington D.C. Mall located between the Lincoln Memorial and the Washington Monument (see Figure 6.33). Our objective is to classify the bodies of water found in the Reflecting Pool, Tidal Basin, and Constitution Gardens. The area is chosen because the

Table 6.6   CLASSIFICATION OF WATER IN CHANNEL 1

Gray value	Pixel count		Classification accuracy (%)
	Water areas	Total	
0	57	58	98
3	2	2	100
6	3	4	75
9	4	4	100
13	2	2	100
16	3	5	60
19	2	2	100
22	3	6	50

SOURCE: Amrine (1992). Reprinted with permission.

ground truth regarding the bodies of water is well-known from maps, serving to validate any of our classifications. All three multispectral channels of this sub-image will be used in the analysis. In each channel, the individual pixels are allowed to take on one of 256 shades of gray (Amrine 1992).

A. Digital Image Data

Two assumptions were made regarding this image: (a) No rectification was needed among each of the multispectral images. (b) The processing effects on the image are minimal and do not affect the analysis. The software TS-IP[18] unveils several interesting observations in the images of Figure 6.34 regarding the spectral values. In channel 1, the values ranged from 0 to 227, while in channel 2, the range was 0 to 216, and in channel 3, from 0 to 212. From the processed sub-image based on spectral filters, it is obvious that the spectral range used by these filters identifies water, but not uniquely. For example, the filter uses a spectral range of 0–22 to identify water in channel 1. Table 6.6 documents the overall accuracy in identifying the water contained in the four water subregions of the channel-1 image as 94 percent. In channel 2, the water subregions are not as spectrally distinct. The visual inspection method used in channel 1 could not be used for channel 2. It is first necessary to locate the water subregions from the ground truth so the gray values could be recorded. It is found that the spectral range of water is 5–166. This wide range for water shows why the water is not as spectrally distinct as in channel 1. There is a marked decrease in the overall accuracy when compared to channel 1. In channel 3, the water regions are again spectrally non-distinct. In fact, the problem in locating the water is similar to channel 2 but worse. Any pixels within the 5–200 gray range are labeled as water. Classification accuracy of the water subregions with channel 3 spectral data alone is very low. In fact, channels 2 and 3 are better equipped to pick up land cover types other than water, particularly pavement, when one lays Figure 6.33 and Figure 6.34 side-by-side.

B. Image Classification

Once the gray value ranges are located, we proceed to identify the bodies of water in the image. The BW classification model was extensively modified for this application. An objective function that will work to combine channels p and q is

$$\text{Max} \sum_{k=1}^{K} \left[\lambda_p' \sum_{i=1}^{n'} c_{ip} x_{ik} + \lambda_q' \sum_{i=1}^{n'} c_{iq} x_{ik} \right] \tag{6.25}$$

The size and border-length constraints as specified by the multiple subregion BW model were used (Equations 6.19 to 6.24). However, major improvements can be made to the model. These improvements include the pixel bounds constraint and the multi-criteria functions. The constraint that sets the spectral bound for each channel also sets the value of x_{ik} to zero if the pixel gray-value is out of this range. With these constraints, only the water-type pixels are considered for selection into a water subregion. For channel 1, these pixel-bound constraints look like:

$$c_{i1} x_{ik} \leq 22 \qquad i = 1, \ldots, K$$
$$x_{jk} = 0 \qquad j \neq i, k = 1, \ldots, K \tag{6.26}$$

For channel 2:

$$c_{i2}\, x_{ik} \geq 5 \qquad i = 1, \ldots, n'; k = 1, \ldots, K$$

$$c_{i3}\, x_{jk} \leq 166 \qquad i = 1, \ldots, n'; k = 1, \ldots, K \qquad (6.27)$$

$$x_{jk} = 0 \qquad j \neq i; K = 1, \ldots, K$$

For channel 3:

$$c_{3}\, x_{ik} \leq 5 \qquad i = 1, \ldots, n'; k = 1, \ldots, K$$

$$c_{3}\, x_{jk} \leq 200 \qquad i = 1, \ldots, n'; k = 1, \ldots, K \qquad (6.28)$$

$$x_{jk} = 0 \qquad j \neq i; k = 1, \ldots, K$$

The area and border length constraints are also simplified. Instead of specifying an individual area and border length for each subregion, a total area and border

Figure 6.35　RESULTS OF RUNS FOR AREA $\geq$ 24 AND BORDER LENGTH $\leq$ 64

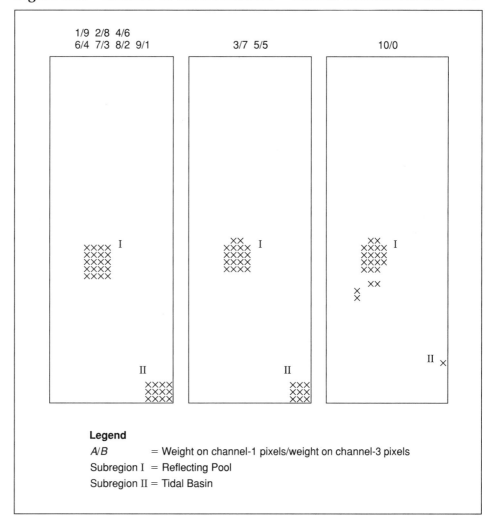

length for all the subregions are specified:

$$\sum_{k=1}^{K} \sum_{i=1}^{n'} x_{ik} \geq M$$

$$\sum_{k=1}^{K} \sum_{i=1}^{n'} \sum_{j \in T_i} s_{ij} (P_{ijk} + N_{ijk}) \leq L$$

(6.29)

Multicriteria optimization is performed using the constraint-reduced feasible-region method[19]. The area is set parametrically at greater than or equal to 24 and the border length restricted to less than or equal to 64. Given these parameters, the modified BW model was run based on the tradeoff of information between channels 1 and 3. In this set of runs, the pixels selected are from the Reflection Pool and the Tidal Basin. The only exception to this statement is the run corresponding to the weights (10/0), where channel-1 is weighted by 10 and channel-3 weighted by 0 (in a scale of 10). In this run the selected pixels also come from the Constitution Gardens Lake and the noise-type pixels. Notice in all the solutions, the model uses the full border length limit of 64. However, the number of pixels selected varies from 24 to 31. Figure 6.35 depicts the results of the complete set of runs.

In a second set of runs, the area has been changed to be greater than or equal to 26 and the border length remains at less than or equal to 64. The model maximizes the objective function by selecting pixels from the Reflection Pool, noise-type pixels, and the Tidal Basin. It is interesting to note that the size of the

Figure 6.36   RESULTS OF RUNS FOR AREA $\geq$ 26 AND BORDER LENGTH $\leq$ 64

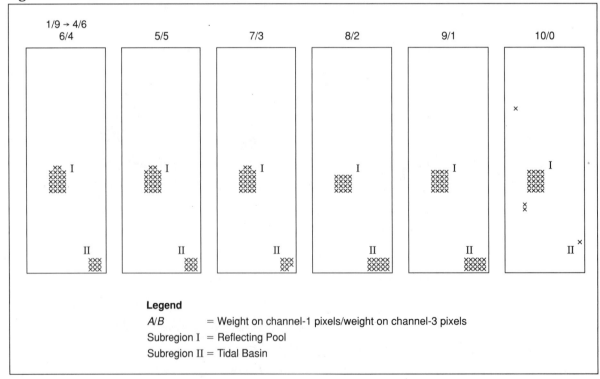

area selected varied from 26 to 32 pixels, but the border length of 64 is maintained. Most of the solutions are the same, except for runs corresponding to weight combinations 7/3, 8/2, and 9/1. For the 10/0 run, the model only identifies the Reflection Pool and a number of noise pixels. These results are very similar to the previous set of runs, including the weight setting 10/0. All these results are plotted in Figure 6.36 for easy reference. Even though only the channel-1/ channel-3 combination is discussed here, the same type of classification can be performed between channels 1 and 2.

C. Lessons Learned

The results are very clear. A combination of two channels has been shown to yield better classification than one single channel. In the two sets of runs above, the 0/10 weight setting corresponds to using only channel-3 while the 10/0 setting corresponds to using only channel-1. In the former setting, the runs never converge. The latter setting also yields unsatisfactory results in that the Tidal Basin is missed altogether, and noise is picked up. Granted that channel 1 is the most suitable of all three channels for identifying water. But the extra information afforded by channel 3 (and for that matter channel 2) will help in the classification, even though we tend to rely more on channel 1 as reflected by the weights. In fact the best classifications came from weighing channel 1 much more heavily than channel 3 as verified by both sets of runs.

An alternative way of classifying the digital image would be to combine two channels into a composite index such as the normalized vegetation index (NVI). Then the BW classification model would operate on a single set of pixels representing the NVI. Such an attempt was followed but to no avail, and the process stops after a futile calculation of the vegetation indices. There are plausible explanations for this shortfall. Recall that the vegetation indices (VI) were defined as the difference between near infra red and red reflectances: $VI = (near\text{-}IR) - (red)$, and the NVI was defined as $NVI = VI/[(near - IR) + (red)]$. The variables in these equations represent the gray value of a pixel in the red and near-IR imaging bands. With SPOT imagery, the red band corresponds to channel 2 and the near-IR band corresponds to channel 3. In general both indices result in high values for vegetation areas due to their relatively high near-IR reflectance and low red reflectance. In contrast, clouds, water, and snow have negative values due to their larger visible reflectance than near-IR reflectance.

Computation of VI and NVI, however, failed to show any negative pixel values in the four major water subregions. Two individual noise-type water pixels did have a negative value. It is suspected that the preprocessing of data in SPOT may have caused this problem. A second explanation is that the vegetation indices were specifically developed for the NOAA AVHRR system and are not applicable to SPOT images. A third explanation for the gray values to be out of the normal range is the imaging conditions. This is a catch-all factor that considers illumination angle/time-of-day, moisture content of gravel and soil, and water. All of these factors can affect the gray values that are recorded for a scene. Thus our initial assumptions about the inherent quality of processed satellite-image data are not supported. This points to the importance of understanding digital image processing as a prerequisite for proper use of remote sensing and GIS.

Computational time for the BW model amounts to hours per run on extreme cases, although most were accomplished around 45 minutes using the

Generalized-Algebraic-Modeling-System/Zero-One-Optimization-Model (GAMS/ZOOM) on a VAX 8550 mainframe computer. Research is under way to find a more efficient solver for the BW model, including the use of network-with-side-constraints routines[20] (Reed 1991; Earl et al. 1992). Simpler model formulations were also attempted (Warrender, Sovaiko, and Chan 1992). Preliminary results look promising.

XII. REMOTE SENSING, GIS, AND SPATIAL ANALYSIS

To the extent that the earth's surface is constantly reflecting and emitting electromagnetic radiation, remote sensing devices such as satellites are capable of measuring this radiation rather accurately and in a timely fashion. The intensities of emissions vary for the different wavelengths of the electromagnetic spectrum. The spectral distribution, or spectral signature, depends upon several factors, of which the most important are surface conditions, type of land cover, temperature, biological activity, and the angle of incoming radiation. Satellites (or equivalent remote sensors) equipped with multispectral scanners are able to measure the intensity in several bands of the spectrum. Since the bands span from infrared to red, such scanners can see beyond the naked eye for a number of geological, urban planning, agricultural, forestry, cartographic, and environmental management applications.

Unfortunately, remote sensing is a new technology that has yet to be fully integrated into GISs. SPOT represents one of the commercial efforts in integrating remote sensing with GIS. An attempt is made to use SPOT images to update GISs, which are typically organized into vector databases. These vector databases consist of digital line graphs (DLGs), TIGER, and DIME files, which are often outdated. Through digital or photographic images, framed in standard USGS map sizes, the company claims that the remote sensing information can be ingested into any major vector/raster GIS or AutoCAD®system.

Among other uses, GIS has been viewed as an integrated information base for analysis. The way in which analysis is linked to the database can be performed in three different ways (Anselin and Getis 1992). One can: (a) fully integrate all spatial analysis within the GIS software; (b) construct models of spatial analysis that efficiently link with the GIS and effectively exploit the spatial information in the database; or (c) leave the GIS and spatial analysis as two separate entities and simply import and export data in a common format between the two.

The third approach ignores the distinctive characteristics of a spatial database for use in spatial analysis. Nevertheless, it seems to be the approach most common in practice, mainly due to the problems with proprietary data formats in commercial GIS and the limited facilities of often awkward macro languages. Examples of this strategy are the joint use of GRASS and S for exploratory data analysis, the combination of SPANS and SYSTAT to carry out stepwise regression, and the use of ARC/INFO and BMDP for logistic regression.

The second approach is similar to the so-called modular design in integrated regional modeling and consists of developing self-contained modules for various types of spatial analyses. These modules are then linked to the specific data structures used in a commercial GIS. They are thus not "generic," but limited to a particular combination of GIS and analysis technique. Most of these modules are written and compiled separately and access the data structure of the GIS by means of proprietary library functions. In general, the use of the GIS macro facilities is avoided, given its poor performance in terms of speed. Even though this second approach links a statistical package to a GIS, it is generally limited to simple descriptive measures, such as univariate measures of spatial association. This has been referred to as Applications Programming Interface (API) (Cronin 1994).

Finally, the first strategy is basically non-existent, due to the lack of analytical capabilities in most commercial GIS, with partial exceptions in SPANS and TRANSCAD. It is most closely approximated by the idea behind a spatial analysis toolkit. To the extent that spatial analysis includes all of the traditional techniques, the determination of an unambiguous set of generic spatial analysis functions in a GIS is an important, yet still largely unresolved question. This philosophy of designing GIS is sometimes referred to as client-server architecture (Cronin 1994).

Looking toward the future, the first strategy can become very useful when eventually implemented. Densham and Rushton (1992) demonstrated that processing cost for the most accurate, heuristic, location-allocation algorithms can be drastically reduced by exploiting the spatial structure of location-allocation problems. The strategy used—preprocessing inter-point distance data as both candidate and demand strings and using them to update an allocation table—allows the solution of large problems (3000 nodes) in a microcomputer-based, interactive decision-making environment. More importantly, these strategies yield solution times that increase approximately linearly (rather than exponentially) with problem size.

Along the same line, Ding, Baveja, and Batta (1994) implemented a facility-location model in GIS. The model locates facilities in a Manhattan metric (l_1-metric)[21] where travel can only take place in the east-west and north-south direction. Furthermore, travel has to avoid such barriers as lakes or other geographic obstacles. Its principal result is that the search for candidate facility-locations can be restricted to a finite, easily identifiable set of points. An example can be found in the "Facility Location" chapter of Chan (2000). Most importantly, the authors found the implementation greatly streamlined by a GIS such as ARC/INFO, assisted by the availability of TIGER files. The Densham and Rushton algorithm described above was employed to perform the location-allocation steps once the candidate facility locations are identified.

According to Bennion and O'Neill (1994), GIS is a very useful tool for defining transportation analysis zones (TAZ). Somewhat parallel to the BW districting model discussed above, they outlined an approach to address homogeneity and shape criteria for developing TAZs. By homogeneity is meant population density, employment density, average income, and so forth. In other words, we wish to group areas of similar population, employment density, and income together. By the same token, we wish to avoid irregular and elongated shapes, and only aggregate adjacent (rather than noncontiguous) geographic units together to form a zone. A fuzzy c-varieties algorithm is offered as a substitute for thematic mapping to model the homogeneity criterion, while analysis of fractal dimensions is used to address shape and compactness criteria. The fuzzy approach explicitly subjects the delineation of zonal boundary to human judgement and hence the boundary is not rigidly mandated by a priori rules. Fractal dimensions are used here to quantify the relationship between the area and perimeter of a polygon—a feature readily compatible with the data structure of most GISs. Bennion and O'Neill discussed future implementation of these procedures for ARC/INFO and ATLAS GIS.

Tomlin (1991) summarizes the cartographic modeling principles that may underpin eventual implementation of an integrated GIS on a digital computer, combining data and problem solving under one roof. He outlines the major conventions, capabilities, and techniques associated with this particular approach. His proposal differs from the competing techniques of relational database and feature- or object-oriented programming. In the widely disseminated relational idiom, geographic entities (such as lines or areas) are explicitly characterized in terms of attributes (such as names or numbers) and are related to one another by way of relations (such as adjacency or inclusion).[22] These relations can also be characterized in terms of their own attributes, and they too can be associated with one another by way of additional relations. The same is true in the now popular feature- or object-oriented idiom. Here, however, primitive entities can be associated with one another not only in terms of relations but in terms of more complex entities as well.

To be distinguished from these approaches, the fundamental spatial entity in cartographic modeling is the location. Unlike the units of data in most relational and object-oriented systems, locations are not units of "what" but of "where." Although locations can be aggregated into set of lines, areas, and surface features, they remain the elemental units for which attributes are recorded. The cartographic modeling approach associates locations with one another not with declarative statements specifying selected relations but with new entities that are generated by applying selected functions. To interrelated entities that are comprised of multiple locations, each is first disaggregated into a set of individual locations. A function is then applied to these locations to generate new attributes that will ultimately be re-aggregated to characterize the original entities or to form entirely new ones.

From this perspective, a question such as "How far is this area from that area?" would be expressed as "What is the minimum distance between any location within this area and any location within that area?" or "What is the distance between the centroid of this area and the centroid of that area?" The fact that there are two interpretations of that initial question reflects the utility of this point of view. It is a view that becomes particularly useful in dealing with more complex spatial relationships such as narrowness, enclosure, spottiness, interspersion, striation[23], and so on. The near future of cartographic modeling will likely be one of both refinement and extension. This is not only true in terms of new software (e.g., the MapBox system) but also in terms of new techniques in areas such as three-dimensional modeling, spatial statistics, interpolation, error tracking, feature extraction, temporal dynamics, flow simulation, and so on. Interoperability standards will make it easier to view, pan, and query geographic images and maps on the web. Efforts are ongoing to merge spatial data with non-spatial data in a single database. Such standardization brings all the advantages of a relational database management system to spatial data.

XIII. CONCLUDING REMARKS

Over the past decades, GIS, automated cartography, and computer-aided design (CAD) have frequently been confused, both in the relative applicability of each technology in various fields and in the direction of basic research. The respective data structures have little in common: the literature of GIS has made little reference to automated cartography or to CAD, and the whole topic has had little relevance to automatic cartography or to CAD, let alone remote sensing. Today the development of technology for digitizing and display has clearly benefited from the influence of a much larger market for CAD. The industry is slowly moving toward this confluence. Similarly, remote sensing developments have been divorced from GIS, with the former being worked on by those involved in space technology and the latter by people involved with databases. However, the connection between the two is quite obvious, and they can greatly benefit from one another. Adams, Vonderobe, and Russell (1992) proposed a scheme to integrate GIS, CAD, facility management, and project management into a facility delivery system centered around spatial data.

Tomlinson and Associates (1987) stated that GIS is a unique field with its own set of research problems, although the entire GIS community would probably not agree with this view. A GIS is a tool for manipulation and analysis of spatial data; it therefore stands in the same relationship to spatial analysis as standard statistical packages such as SAS and SPSS stand to statistical analysis. Perhaps the most useful way of looking at GIS is to treat it as the data merging phase of image rectification, enhancement, classification, and merging. This view integrates remote sensing and information organization efforts very nicely.

Once data are properly organized, it follows that the set of potential applications of GIS is enormous, and is not currently satisfied by any other type of software. Future developments in GIS will depend on better algorithms and data structures, and continuing improvements in hardware. But they also need research in spatial analysis, in the development of better methods of manipulation and analyzing spatial data, and toward a better understanding of the nature of spatial data themselves through such issues as generalization, accuracy, and error and the integration with remote-sensing technology. Thus the future development in GIS needs to be concentrated in three areas: data structures and algorithms, spatial analysis, and spatial statistics. Development of hardware will probably continue to be motivated by larger markets in computer graphics and CAD.

In general, successful data collection, storage and retrieval depend upon (a) clear definition of the problem at hand; (b) evaluation of various data collection procedures; (c) identification of the collection procedures appropriate to the task; and (d) determination of the data interpretation procedure to be employed. In any approach to applying remote sensing, not only must the right mix of data acquisition and data interpretation techniques be chosen, but the right mix of conventional data collection techniques and remote sensing must also be identified. GIS and remote sensing are tools best applied in concert with one another. Their integration permits the synthesis and display of virtually unlimited sources of types of physical and socioeconomic data—as long as they can be computer coded with reference to a common geographic base.

Remote sensing affords us the capability to literally see the invisible. From remote sensing's aerial or space vantage point, we can also begin to see components of the environment on an ecosystems basis, in that remote sensing data can transcend the cultural and political boundaries within which much of our current resource data are collected. Continuing facility location and land use studies require an efficient information system for storing the relevant data. To be effective, information systems must be carefully designed in conjunction with the tasks to be performed by a particular study team. The most important phase of the design of information systems is the identification of the end use of each item of information planned for collection.

Recent development goes one step further to make GIS mobile. Users can transfer GIS databases from a desktop PC to a field unit. In the field, data can be added and edited directly in the GIS. Users can then upload the current database file to their office PC by way of an Internet site. The software also provides support for an optional GPS. Employing encryption technology, the PC can receive open database-compliant formats by way of wireless links from mobile units, and then combine that data into a single database on the office server. Through hand-held mobile devices such as palmtop computers, software exists for users to indentify starting points or destinations to obtain maps and directions. Unlike an existing Internet search engine, it can use proximity to deliver search results, thus automatically providing data relative to the user's current location. This capability lends itself directly to **E-commerce,** defined as selling goods and services on the Web through the exploitation of information technology. Thus a nearby restaurant can interest this user in a meal should he feel hungry. Conversely, this user can have a keen awareness of what is around his current geographic location.

ENDNOTES

[1] See, for example, the "Spatial-Temporal Information" chapter of Chan (2000) under Veronoi diagrams.

[2] For an example, see the "Space Filling Curve" discussion in Chan (2000).

[3] The gravity model was discussed in Chapters 2 and 3.

[4] For a discussion of MAUT, refer to Chapter 5.

[5] Frequency, or how many times a sine wave "wiggles" in a period, is formally defined as the number of waves completed in 360-degree (2π radians) rotation of θ in $\sin\theta$ Thus the sine wave $\sin 2\pi$ has a frequency of one, and the sine wave of $\sin 4\pi$ has a frequency of two and so forth.

[6] Amplitude is the maximum and minimum absolute height of a sine wave. Thus the sine wave $\sin\theta$ has an amplitude of 1 and the sine wave $2\sin\theta$ has an aplitude of 2.

[7] Phase is the horizontal displacement of the sine or cosine wave. For the sine wave $\sin\theta$, for example, the phase is measured in the displacement quantity $\Delta\theta$.

[8] For the relationship between Kriging and Spatial Time Series, see Chan (2000) under the latter.

[9] For an explanation of the Sobel operator, see section VI-B of this chapter. The Sobel filter is a way to detect edges or lines in an image.

[10] For an explanation of the fast Fourier transform, consult Section VI-A of this chapter. The Fourier transform examines the data in its frequency (spectral) domain in order to detect noise. A filter is then applied to remove the noise.

[11] As explained the section VI-A of this chapter, the median filter is used to correct striping and snowy images.

[12] For an explanation of posterior probabilities and the Bayesian classifier, see the "Bayesian Decision Making" section of Chapter 3.

[13] For a review of Bayes' theorem, please refer to Chapter 3 under the "Bayesian Decision Making" section.

[14] For a formal definition of a non-inferior solution (or the analogous terms of a non-dominated solution or efficient frontier), see Chapter 5.

[15] As explained in Chapter 5 under "Exploring the Efficient Frontier" section, this is refered to as the constraint-reduced feasible-region procedure.

[16] Between the two sets of binary decision variables P_{ij} and N_{ij}, each segment s_{ij} is counted twice, and the resulting border length is recorded as twice the actual value.

[17] The entropy function was introduced in Chapter 3.

[18] The TS-IP imaging software was explained in Section VII of this chapter and is included on a CD-ROM at the back of this book.

[19] For an explaination of the constraint-reduced feasible-region method, see Chapter 5 under the "Exploring the Efficient Frontier" section.
[20] For an introduction to network-with-side-constraints, see Appendix 1.
[21] For further explanation of l_1-metric, see Chapter 5 under "Goal setting."
[22] For an example of relational database, see Section III-A of this chapter.
[23] Marking with stripes.

REFERENCES

Adams, T. M.; Vonderohe, A. P.; Russell, J. S. (1992). "Integrating Facility Delivery through Spatial Information." *Journal of Urban Planning and Development* 118, No. 1:13–23.

Ahituv, N.; Berman, O. (1988). *Operations Management of Distributed Service Networks: A Practical Quantitative Approach*. New York: Plenum Press.

Amato, I. (1999). "God's Eyes for Sale." *Technology Review* (March-April):36–41.

American Society of Civil Engineers (1996). "Mapping the Future." *Civil Engineering* (July):18–19.

Amrine, J. M. (1992). Spectral and spatial pattern recognition in digital imagery. Master's Thesis. (AFIT/GSO/ENS/92D-01). Department of Operational Sciences. Air Force Institute of Technology. Wright-Patterson AFB, Ohio.

Anderson, J. R.; Hardy, E. E.; Roach, J. R.; Witmer, R. E. (1976). *A land-use and land cover classification system for use with remote sensor data*. Washington, D.C.: U. S. Geological Survey.

Anselin, L.; Getis, A. (1992). "Spatial statistical analysis and geographic information systems." *The Annals of Regional Science* 26:19–33.

Benabdallah, S.; Wright, J. R. (1992). "Multiple subregion allocation models." *Journal of Urban Planning and Development* 118, No. 1:24–40 .

Bennion, M. W.; O'Neill, W. (1994). Building transportation analysis zones using GIS. (Presentation Paper 94-0476). Paper presented at the 73rd Annual Meeting of the Transportation Research Board, Washington, D. C.

Besag, J. (1989). "Digital image processing: Toward Bayesian image analysis." *Journal of Applied Statistics* 16, No. 3:395–407.

Brigantic, R.; Chan, Y. (1994). A comparison and contrast of Bayesian classification vs. the Benabdallah and Wright procedure of spatial pattern Recognition." Working Paper. Department of Operational Sciences. Air Force Institute of Technology. Wright-Patterson AFB, Ohio.

Bushenkov, V. A.; Chernykh, O. L.; Kamenev, G. K.; Lotov, A. V. (1994). "Multidimensional images given by mappings: Construction and visualization." *Pattern Recognition and Image Analysis* 5:35–56.

Chan, Y. (2000). *Location, transport and land-use: Modeling spatial-temporal information*. New York: Springer-Verlag.

Conner, P. K.; Mooneyhan, D. W. (1985). "Practical applications of LANDSAT Data." In *Monitoring earth, ocean, land, and atmosphere from space*. (Progress in astronautics and aeronautics, Vol 97), edited by A. Schnapf. Washington, D.C.: American Institute of Aeronautics and Astronautics, 371–396

Corbey, K. P. (1996). "One-meter satellites: practical applications by spatial data users." *Geo Info Systems* (Supplement) (July):39–42.

Cressie, N. (1991). *Statistics for spatial data*. New York: Wiley-Interscience.

Cronin, T. (1994). Private communication.

Densham, P. J.; Rushton, G. (1992). "Strategies for solving large location-allocation problems by heuristic methods." *Environment and Planning A* 24:289–304.

Ding, Y.; Baveja, A.; Batta, R. (1994). "Implementing Larson and Sadiq's location model in a geographic information system." *Computers and Operations Research* 21, No. 4:447–454.

Earl, A. J.; McGuiness, J. J.; Chan, Y. (1992). Pixel subregion allocation. Working Paper. Department of Operational Sciences. Air Force Institute of Technology. Wright-Patterson AFB, Ohio.

Eddy, C. A.; Looney, B. (1993). "Three-dimensional digital imaging of environmental data: Selection of gridding parameters." *International Journal of Geographic Information Systems* 7:165–172.

Ehlers, M. (1995). "Integrating remote sensing and GIS for environmental monitoring and modeling: Where are we?" *Geo Info Systems* (July):36–43.

Engelhart, J. (2000). "What's E-commerce have to do with GIS." *Geo Info Systems* (January):58.

Feng, C.; Wei, H.; Lee, J. (1999). WWW-GIS strategies for transportation applications. Paper presented at the 78th annual meeting of the Transportation Research Board, Washington, D. C.

Fischer, M. M.; Nijkamp, P. , eds. (1993). *Geographic information systems, spatial modelling, and policy evaluation.* Berlin, Germany: Springer-Verlag.

Foley, T. M. (1994). "Zooming in on remote sensing markets." *Aerospace America* (October):22–27.

Gonzalez, R. C.; Woods, R. E. (1992). *Digital image processing.* Reading, Massachusetts: Addison-Wesley.

Green, D.; Chan, Y. (1994). "Computational Aspects of the Benabdallah-and-Wright Districting Model." Working Paper. Department of Operational Sciences. Air Force Institute of Technology. Wright-Patterson AFB, Ohio.

Gryder, R. K. (1992). TIGER5-Extraction of geographic information format from the TIGER System. (Report ORNL/TM-12061). Oak Ridge National Laboratory, Martin Marietta. Oak Ridge, Tennessee.

Gualtieri, G.; Tartaglia, M. (1998). "Predicting urban traffic air pollution: A GIS framework." *Transportation Research D* 3, No. 5:329–336.

Heacock, E. L. (1985). "US remote sensing of the earth from space—A look ahead." In *Monitoring earth, ocean, land, and atmosphere from space.* (Progress in astronautics and aeronautics, Vol 97), edited by A. Schnapf. Washington, D.C.: American Institute of Aeronautics and Astronautics, 713–745.

Heagerty, P. J.; Lele, S. R. "A composite likelihood approach to binary spatial data." *Journal for the American Statistical Association* 93, N. 443:1099–1111.

Horowitz, A. J. (1997). "Integrating GIS concepts into transportation network data structures." *Transportation Planning and Technology* 21:139–153.

Huang, Z.; Shin, K. G. (1996). "A new location coding scheme for intelligent transportation systems." *ITS Journal* 3, No. 2:99–109.

Hutchinson, B. G. (1974). *Principles of urban transport systems planning.* New York: McGraw-Hill.

Jusoff, K.; Hassan, H. M. (1998). "An overview of satellite remote sensing for land use planning with special emphasis on Malaysia." *Remote Sensing Review* 16:209–231.

Kelso, T. S.; Chan, Y.; Ursi, R.; Smith, B. (1995). TS-IP Users Guide—Version 2.8 Department of Operational Sciences. Airforce Institute of Technology. Wright-Patterson AFB, Ohio.

Klosterman, R. E. (1991). *TIGER: A primer for planners,* (Planning Advisory Service Report 436). Chicago, Illinois: American Planning Association.

Koch, T. (1999). "GIS: Mapping the OR/MS world." *OR/MS Today* (August):26–30.

Langran, G. (1992). *Time in geographic information systems.* London: Taylor and Francis.

Lazar, B. (1996). "Understanding SDTS topological vector profile implementation." *Geo Info Systems* (June):42–45.

Lee, Y. C.; Zhang, G. Y. (1989). "Development of geographic information systems technology." *Journal of Surveying Engineering* 115, No. 3:304–323.

Leung, Y. (1997). *Intelligent spatial decision support systems.* Berlin, Germany: Springer-Verlag.

Lillesand, M. T.; Kiefer, R. W. (1987). *Remote sensing and image interpretation.* New York: Wiley.

Longley, P.; Batty, M., eds. (1996). Spatial modelling and GIS. Cambridge, England: GeoInformation International.

Marble, D. F.; Peuquet, D. J. (1988). "Geographic information systems and remote sensing." In *Manual of remote sensing,* edited by D. S. Simonett. Bethesda, Maryland: American Society of Photogrammetry, 923–958.

McCord, M. R.; Jafar, F.; Merry, C. J. (1996). Estimated satellite coverage for traffic data collection. Working Paper. Department of Civil/Environmental Engineering and Geodetic Science. Ohio State University. Columbus, Ohio.

McCrary, S. W.; Benjamin, C. O.; Ambavanekar, V. E. (1996). "Consensus building model to select OASIS in small communities." *Journal of Urban Planning and Development* 122, No. 2:46–70.

McLachlan, G. J. (1992). *Discriminant analysis and statistical pattern recognition.* New York: Wiley-Interscience.

Mehrotra, A.; Johnson, E. L. (1995). Taking the politics out of districting. Working Paper. Department of Management Science. University of Miami. Miami, Florida.

Narumalani, S.; Zhou, Y.; Jelinski, D. E. (1998). "Utilizing geometric attributes of spatial information to improve digital image classification." *Remote Sensing Reviews* 16: 233–253.

Nyerges, T. L. (1991). "Geographic information abstractions: conceptual clarity for geographic modeling." *Environment and Planning A* 23:1483–1499.

Nyerges, T. L.; Dueker, K. J. (1988). Geographic information system in transportation. Report to the U.S. Department of Transportation. Federal Highway Administration. Washington, D. C.

O'Neill, W. A.; Harper, E. (1997). Location translation within a GIS. (Presentation Paper No. 97-1246). Paper presented at the 76th annual meeting of the Transportation Research Board, Washington, D. C.

Pace, P. J.; Evers, T. K. (1996). "Oak Ridge National Laboratory develops GISST data server." *Geo Info Systems* (November):32–39.

Prastacos, P. (1992). "Integrating GIS technology in urban transportation planning and modeling." *Transportation Research Record* 1305:125–130.

Reed, T. G. (1991). Binary programming models of spatial pattern recognition: Applications in remote sensing image analysis. Master's Thesis. Air Force Institute of Technology. Wright-Patterson AFB, Ohio.

Sabins, F. F. (1987). *Remote sensing: Principles and interpretation*, 2nd ed. San Francisco: Freeman.

Schweiger, C. L. (1992). Current use of geographic information systems in transit planning. (Report No. DOT-T-92-02). U. S. Department of Transportation. Washington, D. C.

Shaw, D. T.; Maidment, D. R.; Arimes, G. N. (1993). "SITE CODE: Computer-based regulatory information for site development." *Journal of Urban Planning and Development* 119, No. 1:1–14.

Shen, Y. (1995). "SIR-C advanced imaging radar studies the earth." *Aerospace America* (April):38–43.

Shih, S. F. (1988). "Satellite data and geographic information system for land use classification." *Journal of Irrigation and Drainage Engineering* 114, No. 3:505–519.

Star, J.; Estes, J. (1990). *Geographic information systems: An introduction.* Englewood Cliffs, New Jersey: Prentice Hall.

Szekielda, K-H. (1988). *Satellite monitoring of the earth.* New York: Wiley.

Tomlin, C. D. (1991). "Cartographic modeling." In *Geographical information systems: Principles and applications,* edited by M. F. Goodchild, D. J. Mcguire, and D. W. Rhind. Longman Group Ltd.: Essex, England.

Tomlin, C. D. (1990). *Geographic information systems and cartographic modeling.* Englewood Cliffs, New Jersey: Prentice-Hall.

Tomlinson and Associates (1987). "Current and potential uses of geographic information systems—the North American experience." *International Journal of Geographical Information Systems* 1, No. 3:203–218.

Transportation Research Board (1984). "Census data and urban transportation planning in the 1980s." *Transportation Research Record* 981.

U. S. Geological Survey (1983). Map of Washington West, D. C.–MD.–VA., EE-000123. (38077-H1-TB-024).

Ware, R. (1986). Description of the land use suitability assessment implementation evaluation phase: process and procedure. Regional Planning and Coordinating Commission of Greene County, Ohio.

Warrender, C.; Sovaiko, S.; Chan, Y. (1992). Subregion allocation through optimization. Working Paper. Department of Operational Sciences. Air Force Institute of Technology. Wright-Patterson AFB, Ohio.

Werner, P. A. (1974). A survey of national geocoding systems. (Report No. DOT-TSC-OST-74-26). U. S. Department of Transportation, Washington, D. C.

Wright, S. A. (1994). Private discussions.

Wright, S. A.; Chan, Y. (1994). Pure and polluted groundwater classification on a pixel amp. Working Paper. Department of Operational Sciences. Air Force Institute of Technology. Wright-Patterson AFB, Ohio.

Wright, S. A.; Chan, Y. (1994a). Multicriteria decision-making applied to the iterated-conditional-modes contextual image classification technique." Working Paper. Department of Operational Sciences. Air Force Institute of Technology. Wright-Patterson AFB, Ohio.

Zimmerman, P. (1988). "Photos from Space—Why Restrictions Won't Work." *Technology Review* (May–June):45–53.

Zhao, Y. (1997). *Vehicle location and navigation systems.* Norwood, Mass.: Artech House.

Exercises and Problems

These exercises are carefully selected to complement the examples and case studies documented in the main body of the book. In many ways, they also supplement these illustrations, and the answers in the Solution Manual posted on my web site can be thought of as extensions to the main body of the book. Rather than a simple regurgitation of the basic computations, these exercises generally require a bit of thought, and many are open-ended. To provide an integrated view, all the exercises were placed here in this section, rather than at the end of each chapter. The exercises and problems are categorized under the following topics:

I.   Remote Sensing and Geographic Information Systems
II. Facility Location
III. Simultaneous Location and Routing
IV. Activity Derivation, Competition, and Allocation
V.   Land Use Models
VI. Spatial-Temporal Information

We view this as a way to cut across all chapters in the book, emphasizing the main themes that run through this entire volume. For those who are more comfortable with examples (rather than concepts), the Solutions Manual on the web site will serve as a primer on the topics. (Contact the author at ychan@alum.MIT.edu for information about his web site. Students and professionals should enter in the SUBJECT block: "Request for sample solutions." Instructors should enter: "Request for Instructor's Guide.") The exercises also provide the opportunity to try out the software that comes with this book.

I. REMOTE SENSING AND GEOGRAPHIC INFORMATION SYSTEMS

This first group of problems range from the classic Bayesian classifier to image processing schemes such as histogram processing on the Training System/Image Processing (TS-IP) software, which is "Image" on the book's software CD. Two exercises on the Iterative Conditional Mode algorithm are included, illustrating a well-recognized classification technique. A problem is specifically introduced here to illustrate the prescriptive district clustering model advanced in this text. We then finish with a combined classification scheme in which the multicriteria decision-making procedure is explicitly incorporated as an integral part of the algorithm, showing that judgment is part and parcel of remote sensing and geographic information systems.

A. Bayesian Classifier

The Bayesian classifier is one of the ways to group pixels into different patterns—thus the classifier decides that pixel j belongs to a lake while pixel i belongs to a forest. We have illustrated in the "Bayesian Decision-Making" section of Chapter 3 how a decision boundary x_0 can be arrived at when there is only one attribute x such as a pixel's gray value. The concept can be extended to the case when there is more than one attribute for classification (say n attributes). The equations used in this context are as follows the (Gonzalez and Woods 1992). First the Gaussian distribution is extended to multidimensions by

$$P(\mathbf{x} \mid \mathbf{z}_j) = \frac{1}{(2\pi)^{n/2} |\mathbf{C}_j|^{1/2}} \exp\left[1 - 1/2(\mathbf{x} - \boldsymbol{\mu}_j)^T \mathbf{C}_j - 1(\mathbf{x} - \boldsymbol{\mu}_j)\right] \qquad (E.1)$$

where $\boldsymbol{\mu}$ is the mean vector and $\mathbf{C}$ is the covariance matrix respectively defined as

$$\boldsymbol{\mu}_j = \frac{1}{N_j} \sum_{\mathbf{x} \in G_j} \mathbf{x} \qquad \mathbf{C}_j = \frac{1}{N_j} \sum_{\mathbf{x} \in G_j} \mathbf{x}\mathbf{x}^T - \boldsymbol{\mu}_j \boldsymbol{\mu}_j^T \qquad (E.2)$$

where N_j is the number of pattern vectors from class G_j (i.e., the number of pixel vectors belonging to class j), and the summation is taken over these vectors. The multidimensional decision boundary now looks like

$$d_j(\mathbf{x}) = \ln P(\mathbf{z}_j) - \frac{n}{2} \ln 2\pi - \frac{1}{2} \ln |\mathbf{C}_j| - \frac{1}{2} [(\mathbf{x} - \boldsymbol{\mu}_j)^T \mathbf{C}_j^{-1}(\mathbf{x} - \boldsymbol{\mu}_j)] \qquad (E.3)$$

Of course, the second term is equal for all cases, and may be subsequently dropped.

Now consider a two-dimensional reading for a 3×3 set of borings monitoring a groundwater pollution plume, with the gray values shown in italics (Wright and Chan 1994c),

		y-coordinate		
		1	2	3
x-coordinate				
	1	2	3	4
	2	3	8	7
	3	1	7	9

Can you delineate the analytic and precise boundary of the plume based on the above set of equations?

B. Iterative Conditional Mode Algorithm

The iterative conditional mode (ICM) algorithm was described in detail in Chapter 6, under the "Contextual Allocation of Pixels" section. As demonstrated in the numerical example, a β of 0 produces a non-contextual classification, while increasing β accentuates the contextual bias. There is a tradeoff between β and σ^2, where σ^2 is the variance of pixels in a certain class. The σ should be small enough to prevent greatly overlapping regions, and at the same time β will need to be adjusted for the noise level of the image. A 6×6 grid of gray values is given below, with high values representing polluted groundwater and low values representing unpolluted water. Noise is introduced into the data by virtue of the data gathering procedure. For example, a value which has the same approximate gray value as the unpolluted groundwater exists in the center of pixels that are evidently polluted. The second 6×6 data set below shows a 3×3 area of apparently polluted ground water with possible noise on one of the sides of the 3×3 area. Also a single pixel (noise) with a pollution range gray value exists among unpolluted pixels.

3	5	4	3	4	2		3	5	4	3	4	2
3	4	3	2	3	3		3	4	8	6	7	3
4	2	4	8	4	3		4	2	7	8	5	3
5	3	10	9	8	12		5	3	10	9	8	4
3	4	9	4	7	7		3	6	4	4	5	5
2	5	11	12	10	9		2	4	5	4	4	4

Please perform the classification using the ICM on both of these two data sets (Wright and Chan 1994c).

C. Weighted Iterative Conditional Mode Algorithm

In this exercise (Wright and Chan 1994c), the weighted ICM algorithm (rather than the unweighted one used above) is to be applied to illustrate a couple of points. For the second data set above, the noise pixel in the polluted area could be classified as polluted water should a low enough β value be applied, since three of the five neighbors of the pixel are first-order neighbors. It can be shown also that the noise in the unpolluted area would be easier to discern using a weighted procedure. Notice the implementation is almost identical in both the weighted and unweighted cases. The only difference lies in the calculation of the "compare" value in which the summation must be broken into a first-order and a second-order summation. Now carry out the weighted ICM algorithm.

D. District Clustering Model

Shown in Chapter 6 under the district clustering model is a set of noninferior solutions for a small image entitled "Multiple subregion noninferior solutions." Examine the file labeled S2_4a_4b and S2_4a_5b in Figure 6.28, the first of these two code names stands for two subregions, the second and third suggest that an area of four pixels for subregions 1 and 2. The *a* and *b* entries specify two different variations on the boundary of the subregion, generating different non-inferior

Figure E.1   GROUND TRUTH, WELL DATA, AND REMOTELY SENSED DATA

0	0	0	0	0	0	0	0	0	0
0	0	0	0	0	0	0	0	0	0
0	0	0	1	1	1	1	0	0	0
0	0	1	1	1	1	1	0	0	0
0	0	1	1	1	1	1	0	0	0
0	0	1	1	1	1	1	0	0	0
0	0	1	1	1	1	1	0	0	0
0	0	0	1	1	1	1	0	0	0
0	0	0	0	0	0	0	0	0	0
0	0	0	0	0	0	0	0	0	0

$$\begin{bmatrix}
0 & 0 & 0 & 0 & 0 & 0 & 0 & 0 & 0 & 0 \\
0 & 0 & 0 & 0 & 0 & 0 & 0 & 0 & 0 & 0 \\
0 & 0 & 0 & 0 & 4 & 0 & 0 & 0 & 0 & 0 \\
0 & 0 & 0 & 3 & 4 & 5 & 0 & 0 & 0 & 0 \\
0 & 0 & 0 & 5 & 5 & 4 & 0 & 0 & 0 & 0 \\
0 & 0 & 0 & 4 & 3 & 3 & 0 & 0 & 0 & 0 \\
0 & 0 & 0 & 0 & 2 & 0 & 0 & 0 & 0 & 0 \\
0 & 0 & 0 & 0 & 0 & 0 & 0 & 0 & 0 & 0 \\
0 & 0 & 0 & 0 & 0 & 0 & 0 & 0 & 0 & 0 \\
0 & 0 & 0 & 0 & 0 & 0 & 0 & 0 & 0 & 0
\end{bmatrix}
\qquad
\begin{bmatrix}
0 & 0 & 0 & 0 & 0 & 0 & 0 & 0 & 0 & 0 \\
0 & 1 & 0 & 2 & 0 & 0 & 0 & 0 & 0 & 0 \\
0 & 0 & 0 & 3 & 4 & 2 & 4 & 0 & 0 & 0 \\
0 & 0 & 4 & 5 & 0 & 0 & 4 & 0 & 0 & 0 \\
0 & 2 & 3 & 0 & 0 & 0 & 5 & 0 & 4 & 0 \\
0 & 0 & 4 & 5 & 0 & 0 & 4 & 0 & 0 & 0 \\
0 & 0 & 4 & 4 & 4 & 3 & 2 & 0 & 0 & 0 \\
0 & 0 & 0 & 3 & 2 & 4 & 2 & 0 & 0 & 0 \\
0 & 4 & 0 & 0 & 0 & 4 & 0 & 0 & 0 & 0 \\
0 & 0 & 0 & 0 & 0 & 0 & 0 & 0 & 0 & 0
\end{bmatrix}$$

solutions. The two noninferior images are drawn below sequentially, where the bolded gray values stand for one subregion and the italicized stand for another:

11	**5**	**6**		*11*	*5*	*6*
8	**12**	**2**		*8*	**12**	*2*
5	**1**	**1**		*5*	**1**	**1**

Using the "multiple subregion model" outlined in Chapter 6 in the subsection under the same name (Section X-B),

(a) Show the constraint-reduced feasible region model that generated these images;

(b) Verify step by step that we have generated the entire non-inferior solution set;

(c) Show the equivalent weighted objective function model.

E. Combined Classification Scheme

In monitoring groundwater pollution, measurements are made at wells placed discretely around the study area. Interpolation (such as kriging) has been made between these readings, forming a pixel map of the pollution level throughout the study area. Figure E.1 shows a well located at the center of the symmetrical cluster of readings. At the same time, remotely sensed data are available for the entire area. The ground truth data are given as well in Figure E.1.

Can you combine the two sources of information to delineate the pollution pattern more accurately than you would from a single source? Specifically, perform the following:

(a) Employ the ICM algorithm of Chapter 6 with due consideration to proximity as a factor. An inverse relationship is hypothesized between distance and importance in determining the allocation of some internal pixels (i.e., pixels not at the border or fringe of the image). For internal pixels, weights are scaled against eight neighbors. Assuming unitary distance separation between the subject pixel and its first-order neighbor, and a distance of $\sqrt{2} = 1.4142$ with its second-order neighbors. Thus the weight for first-order neighbors is 1.1716 and 0.8284 for second-order neighbors. The sum over all of its neighbors is $(4)(1.1716) + (4)(0.8284) = 8$ and the first-order neighbor is $1.1716/0.8284 = 1.4142$ times as important as the second-order neighbor in determining allocation of a pixel as specified initially.

(b) Employ multicriteria-optimization techniques as outlined in Chapter 5. Define in the decision space a binary variable that labels each pixel as being polluted when the variable is unitary valued. The two criteria in the outcome space—namely the value of the data and the value of contextuality in the ICM classification—are captured by the ground truth and the choice of the β value in the ICM algorithm respectively. Here, β is a measure of forced contiguity, applied parametrically for a 0–1 ranged weight for combining the two sources of information. The two data sets are shown in Figure E.1. Since the water is directly sampled there, one may wish fully to trust the data at the well, thus at the well the weight is unitary for the well reading and zero for the remotely sensed data. Also shown in the same figure is the ground truth, representing a subjective judgment by the decision maker.

(c) Determine the noninferior solutions that identify the most viable image classifications. A preference structure can be adopted whereby the smaller the deviation from the ground truth the more it represents a nondominated solution. Zero deviation is considered Pareto optimal. Deviation in this case is defined as the number of pixels in the ICM-generated solution that are different from the ground truth. Likewise, the less the need for forced contiguity (i.e., the smaller the β value), the better.

F. Histogram Processing

The image brightness histogram shows the number of pixels in the image having each of the 256 possible monochromatic values of stored brightness (Russ 1998; Gonzalez & Woods 1992). Peaks in the histogram correspond to the more common brightness values, which often identify particular structures that are present. Valleys between the peaks and the two tails indicate brightness values that are less common in the image. The flat regions at the two ends of the histogram show that no pixels have those values, indicating that the image brightness range does not necessarily cover the full 0–255 range available. Similarly, the pixels at the two tails of the gray values tend to contain noise, rather than the real image. Figure E.2 shows an example of such a histogram.

In order for the available gray levels to be used efficiently on the display, some will have to be removed (such as those at the two tails of the given histogram). It might be better to spread out the displayed gray levels in the peak areas selectively, compressing them in the valleys (or the two tails) so that the same

Figure E.2   SEVERAL OPTIONS IN HISTOGRAM EQUALIZATION

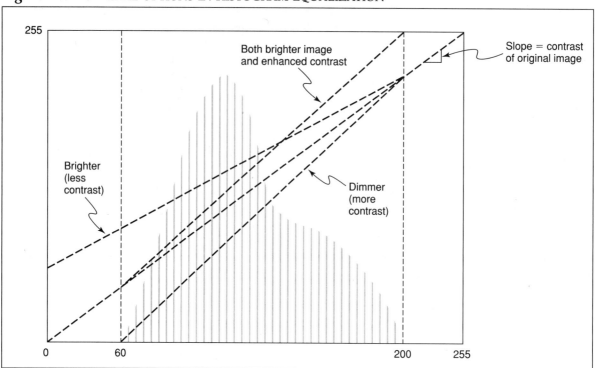

number of pixels in the display shows each of the possible brightness levels. This is called **histogram equalization** or **histogram stretch.** Histogram equalization reassigns the brightness values of pixels. Individual pixels retain their brightness order (i.e., they remain brighter or darker than other pixels) but the values are shifted, so that an equal number of pixels have each possible brightness value. In many cases, this spreads out the values in regions where different regions meet, showing details in areas with a high brightness gradient. The equalization makes it possible to see minor variations within regions that appear nearly uniform in the original image. In this example, we show that the range 60–200 can be stretched out to occupy the entire spectrum, resulting in a dimmer image, but with better contrast.

The process is quiet simple mathematically. For each brightness level j in the original image (and its histogram), the newly assigned value k is calculated as $k = \sum_{i=0}^{j} N_i / n'$, where the summation counts the number of pixels in the image (by integrating the histogram) with brightness equal to or less than j, and n' is the total number of pixels (or the total area of the histogram). This is graphically represented as the dashed straight line plotted from the extreme left gray value to the extreme right value, representing the gray value range we wish to examine in detail.

In Figure E.2 are shown several ways to perform histogram equalization, including controlling brightness and contrast. Using the TS-IP software provided with the CD, please show on the Pentagon image these various options:

(a) dimmer with more contrast,

(b) brighter with less contrast, and

(c) both brighter and with contrast enhanced.

II. FACILITY LOCATION

Facility-location modeling is a key component of this book. Here we cover some less than obvious applications of these models. Following the airport location examples used extensively in the book, we further illustrate the nodal optimality conditions prevalent in not only min-sum location models, but also min-max models as well. The opposite of min-max problems is the max-min problem, commonly found in obnoxious facility location, which includes solid waste facilities. Another challenging facility location model is the quadratic assignment problem, in which interaction between facilities take place.

A. Nodal Optimality Conditions

Consider the cities of Cincinnati and Dayton, Ohio connected by Interstate Highway 75. Cincinnati has a metropolitan population of 2 million and Dayton, 1 million. A regional airport is proposed to serve both cities. It is to be located on I-75 such that the total person miles (PMT) to travel between the two cities is to be minimized. We have shown in Chapters 1 and 4 that the optimal location is Cincinnati. This is an example of nodal optimality conditions.

> **(a)** Per discussions in Chapter 4: if the airport is to be located on I-75 so that the total person decibels of noise pollution is to be minimized, where should the airport be built?

> **(b)** Suppose accessibility and noise exposure are of equal concerns, where should the airport be located? Accessibility is defined as the total PMT while noise exposure is the total person decibel.

> **(c)** Repeat questions (a) and (b) for the three-city case where Columbus is included. Columbus has a population of 2.1 million.

> **(d)** Repeat the whole process for a four-city case in which Indianapolis is included in addition.

B. Solid Waste Facility

In locating a municipal solid waste facility, the analytic hierarchy process (AHP) has often been used. Junio (1994) proposed a hierarchy of attributes as shown in Figure E.3. Discuss the completeness and relevance of such a hierarchy definition. How would you quantify this hierarchy in executing AHP?

C. Quadratic Assignment Problem

Refer to the quadratic assignment problem as introduced in Chapter 4.

> **(a)** Formulate the linearized version of model for the distance separation and flow interaction matrices as shown.

> **(b)** Now solve this linear model.

> **(c)** Is there anything peculiar about the solution to the linear model? If not, simply give the optimal assignment and the objective function. If yes, explain the peculiarity and again give the optimal assignment and the objective function value.

Figure E.3   HIERARCHY OF A MUNICIPAL SOLID WASTE PROBLEM

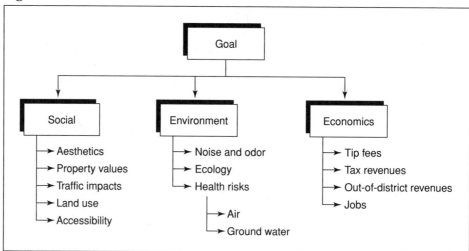

III. LOCATION-ROUTING

The integration of facility location and service delivery is a key feature of this book. We use a simple telecommunication network maintenance problem to lay out the integration. First, we define a region to be served by a maintenance facility using the districting technique. Then we place the facility using the service facility location model, followed by an evaluation of the entire maintenance procedure through a user performance model. To solve a real world problem, the three steps are executed repeatedly in a districting, location, and evaluation triplet. Having laid out this background, we break the problem into the service delivery step and then the combined location routing step. The basic building block of both steps is the quantification of spatial separation. This is illustrated in terms of **Minkowski's metric,** which is also known as l_p-metric—as defined in Chapter 5 under the "Deviational Measures" subsection.

A. Districting

The next three problems demonstrate a solution algorithm for improving maintenance depot location and service delivery operations (Patterson 1995). Here in the first problem, we define the districts each depot is supposed to serve. The model is based upon enumeration and was adapted for network topology by Ahituv and Berman (1988):

$$\text{Min } \Sigma_j C_j x_j$$
$$\text{s. t. } \Sigma_j x_j = p \qquad\qquad\qquad\qquad\text{(E.4)}$$
$$\Sigma_j a_{ij} x_j = 1 \quad \forall i$$

where $x_j = 1$ if subnetwork j is selected to form a district and zero otherwise; $a_{ij} = 1$ if node (zone) i is an element of subnetwork j and zero otherwise; p is the number of districts or subnetworks desired, and the equity measure

$$C_j = \frac{|\Sigma_i f_i - 1/p|}{\alpha/p},\tag{E.5}$$

$0 < \alpha < 1$; and f_i is the fraction of demand at node i.

The algorithm consists of two different phases: Phase I determines all feasible subnetworks (districts) within the larger network, and Phase II determines the final subnetworks based upon our equity objective function in E.4. Contiguity and compactness will be bounding constraints for the first phase. One final requirement is that the p subnetworks must be collectively exhaustive and mutually exclusive. In other words, every node must be within one and only one subnetwork. This is accounted for in Phase II.

> **PHASE I:**   Using a tree search algorithm, we find the feasible set by picking the smallest number node and connecting contiguous nodes while enforcing the compactness requirement until the combined demand becomes redundant. Care must be taken to avoid creating separate enclaves, which are node(s) that are incapable of being separate subnetworks and cannot connect to other subnetworks without going through a previously defined subnetwork. This will prevent impossible solutions.

> **PHASE II:**   The algorithm for node partitioning was developed by Garfinkel and Nemhauser (1970). The following notation is needed: X is the set of fixed variables; $|X|$ is the number of fixed variables; D'' is the set of nodes in the districts, or zones of X; J is the set of districts in the current partial solution; N_j are the nodes J; and $|\cdot|$ is the cardinality of the set $\cdot$ in general.

> The computational steps are briefly outlined below:

> **Step 1:**   Initialization. Set counter $|L| = 0$, and set $J = X$, $N_j = D''$.
> **Step 2:**   Choosing the next list. Pick the smallest number node not in N_j.
> **Step 3:**   Updating set J. Add the node to form subnetworks.
> **Step 4:**   Testing for a solution. Test $|L| = |J| - |X|$. If $|L| = 0$ stop, else $|L| = |L| - 1$.
> **Step 5:**   Finding a solution. Pick the largest cost subnetwork in J as the current solution. Go to Step 2.

Now for the network shown below in Figure E.4, please perform the districting procedure with $\alpha = 0.1$ to arrive at two service regions.

B. Service Facility Location

The current problem is to determine where the maintenance depot should be placed within the network (Patterson 1995). The optimal location is determined using the minimized expected response time for a maintenance call. The development of the stochastic location algorithm comes from Ahituv and Berman (1988) and is also discussed in the "Measuring Spatial Separation" chapter of Chan (2000). Min $\bar{r}(\mathbf{y})$ for all $j \in I$, where the expected response time $(\bar{r}_j)$ is the sum of the mean queuing delay $(\bar{q}_j)$ and the mean travel time $(\bar{\tau}_j)$ and I is the set of nodes.

Figure E.4 SERVICE NETWORK

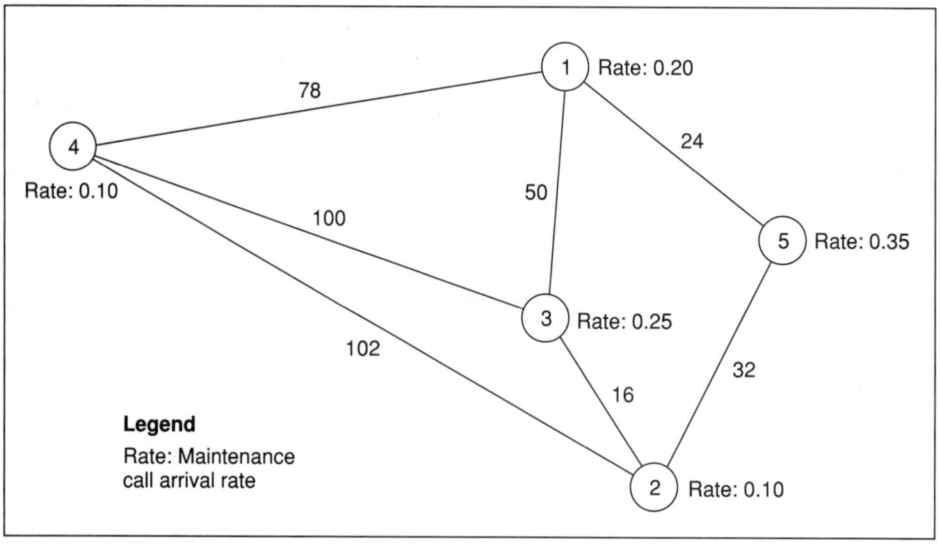

SOURCE: Patterson (1995). Reprinted with permission.

Building on Section IV of Appendix 2, $\bar{q} = \lambda''\sigma_j^2/[2(1 - \lambda''\bar{t}_j)]$ for $\lambda''\bar{t}_j < 1$ and ∞ otherwise. Here σ_j^2 is the variance of service time $\bar{q}_j$ defined in the infinite capacity queue subsection in the "Measuring Spatial-Separation" chapter of Chan (2000), and y is the facility location decision variable. It is important to note that the time to repair a facility and the regeneration time before a next call are zero. This assumption can be made since this amount of time will be treated as a constant. When the objective function for $\bar{r}_j$ is minimized by taking its first derivative, it will be eliminated.

Please locate the service facility in each of the districts obtained in the previous problem.

C. User Performance Model

While the operators might have located the maintenance facility according to their preferences, it does not mean that same sites are necessarily endorsed by the users. The mathematical representation of the model is adapted from Sanso, Soumis, and Gendreau (1991). Patterson's extensions to this model include: the third criterion-function for average link-delay; and the inclusion of link-availability rates to represent maintenance scheduling (Patterson 1995). While a steady-state version is given below, the model can be written for each time period by introducing another superscript t. To introduce the entire model, the first criterion function minimizes the number of lost calls: Min $y'_1 = \Sigma_p\Sigma_q w^{pq}x^{pq}$. Here x^{pq} is the lost traffic between p and q. The second criterion function calls for computing the shortest paths: Min $y'_2 = \Sigma_k\Sigma_p\Sigma_q c_k x_k^{pq}$. The third criterion function minimizes the data transmission delay (or maximizes network availability):

$$\text{Min } y'_3 = \Sigma_k[\Sigma_p\Sigma_q x_k^{pq}/(d_k - \Sigma_p\Sigma_q x_k^{pq})] \qquad \text{(E.6)}$$

This criterion function can be linearized by re-writing it as $\Sigma_k [\Sigma_p \Sigma_q x_k^{pq}/\mu' d_k]/V$, where V is the network throughput and $1/\mu'$ is the average message length. The constraints consist of those on arc capacity $\Sigma_p \Sigma_q x_k^{pq} \leq d_k$ for all k; those on flow conservation

$$\sum_{k \in \boldsymbol{\delta}^+(i)} p^{(k)} x_k^{pq} - \sum_{k \in \boldsymbol{\delta}^-(i)} p^{(k)} x_k^{pq} = \begin{cases} V^{pq} - x^{pq} & for \ i = p \\ -V^{pq} + x^{pq} & for \ i = q \\ 0 & otherwise \end{cases} \qquad (E.7)$$

and non-negativity: $x_k^{pq}, x^{qp} \geq 0$ for all k, p and q. Here $p^{(k)}$ is the availability of arc k. Now perform the network performance evaluation on the same network as given in the last two problems, given the traffic demands as shown below: $A = B = C = D = E = 30$ in Figure E.5.

D. Districting, Location, and Evaluation

The previous three problems highlight how each part of the problem—districting, location, and evaluation—is solved separately. The next step is to show how all the parts are linked together and iterated to find an integrated solution (Patterson 1995).

> **Step 1:** Optimize operator perspective.
> (1.1) Choose number of maintenance depots (p) to be located.
> (1.2) Network partitioning algorithm to create p subnetworks among the $|I|$ nodes.
> (1.3) Use the location algorithm to locate a single facility within the p subnetworks. The optimal solution is chosen according to the minimum-time-to-respond objective.

Figure E.5   MULTICOMMODITY-FLOW

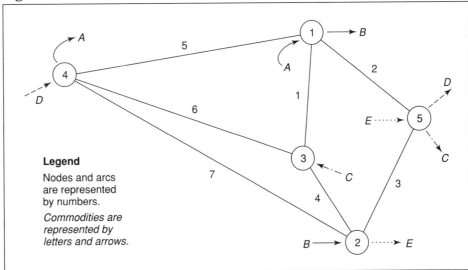

Step 2: Optimize user perspective.
  (2.1) Create network maintenance schedule for solution from Step 1.3
  (2.2) Run network user performance model for solution from Step 1.3 without network delay factor.
  (2.3) If delay factor desired, then create efficient frontier by varying the network delay factor over the desired range.

Please revisit the previous three problems and put the results together in one place.

E. Minkowski's Metric

Consider two points $y^1 = (14, 13)$ and $y^2 = (4, 4)$ in a two-dimensional space. Employing the following general measure of deviation between y^1 and y^2, $r(y; p) = [\Sigma_i |y_i^1 - y_i^2|^p]^{1/p}$, explore the behavior of numerical values of r for parameter p changing from 1 to ∞:

(a) Draw a diagram of function $r = f(p)$. What are the general properties of such a function?

(b) Perform the same analysis for p changing from 0 to 1 and also from $-\infty$ to 0. Do these cases show any meaningful interpretation?

(c) Perform a more difficult but very rewarding exercise: Do these distance measures, especially for p between 1 and ∞, correspond to any particular subfamily of utility (or value) functions? Can you identify such a subclass?

(d) Perform the following graphic exercise: Define a point $y^2 = (0, 0)$ in a two-dimensional space. Plot all such points y^1 whose distance from y^2 is equal to a fixed number r^*, that is, $r = r^*$. Choose $r^* = 1$ and draw such loci of points y^1 for p ranging from 1 to ∞. (Pay special attention to $p = 1, 2, \infty$). Do the resulting "shapes" suggest any connection with utility functions?

(e) Are there some points in (d) which have the same distance from point y^2 regardless of the value of p? What are the other characteristics and possible interpretations of such points?

IV. ACTIVITY DERIVATION, ALLOCATION AND COMPETITION

The transition from facility location to land use models can be marked by activity derivation, allocation, and competition. Thus economic activities such as population and employment are generated at an activity center. Residential neighborhoods then compete to provide housing for these people, resulting in a distribution of residents among these neighborhoods. Here in this group of exercises, we solve a matrix multicriteria game, in which there is more than one payoff among the competitors. The gravity model is a traditional way to analyze competition among geographic areas. Using the gravity versus transportation models exercise, one can see that the gravity model is an extension of the "all or nothing" assignment of activities. Assignment from one single supply exclusively to one single demand is performed by the Hitchcock-Koopman transportation model. This is complemented by the calibration of a doubly constrained model.

A. Multicriteria Game

Consider the following game decision maker 1 (DM1) maximizes his minimum gain while decision maker 2 (DM2) minimizes her maximum loss. Gain of DM1 is exactly equal to the loss of DM2 (i.e., a zero-sum game). Instead of the single metric used in the conventional payoff matrix, there is more than one criterion in measuring payoffs. These multiple payoffs are therefore expressed in terms of a vector (rather than a scalar). An example appears below in Table E.1, where the cells contain the two payoffs for each pair of decisions reached between DM1 and DM2:

Thus if both DMs decide to play their second option, DM1 wins 3 units in the first criterion and 2 in the second. DM2 loses the same number. The symbols p_i' and q_j' denote the probability DM1 and DM2 will play the ith and jth strategy respectively. When p' and q' assume fractional values, the game is a called a **mixed strategy** game. A **pure strategy** is when p's and q's are 1 or 0 in value.

Let each vector payoff $\boldsymbol{a}_{ij} = (a_{ij}^1, a_{ij}^2)^T$ be replaced by a convex combination of both components: $wa_{ij}^1 + (1 - w), a_{ij}^2$, where w is a 0–1 ranged weight. For example, $a_{11} = w3 + (1 - w) 2 = w + 2$, and so on. It can be shown that, similar to a conventional zero-sum two-person game an LP can be set up to solve this problem, where the primal and dual solutions correspond to the strategy taken by the two decision makers. If nonnegative variables p and q are defined such that $p' = pz'$ and $q' = qz'$, the equivalent LP is:

$$\text{Max } q_1 + q_2 + q_3$$
$$\text{s.t.}$$
$$(w + 2)q_1 + (4 - w)q_2 + (5 - 4w)q_3 \leq 1$$
$$(w + 1)q_1 + (w + 2)q_2 + 2q_3 \leq 1$$
$$(3w + 1)q_1 + (3 - 2w)q_2 + (2w + 1)q_3 \leq 1$$

(a) Solve this LP by varying the weights w from 0 to 1.

(b) Is there an equilibrium—defined here as a pair of decisions with which both sides are happy? At this equilibrium, z' is a nonnegative number representing the gain to DM1 and the loss to DM2.

Table E.1   MULTICRITERIA GAME

		DM2		
		q'_1	q'_2	q'_3
DM1	p'_1	(3, 2)	(3, 4)	(1, 5)
	p'_2	(2, 1)	(3, 2)	(2, 2)
	p'_3	(4, 1)	(1, 3)	(3, 1)

B. Gravity versus Transportation Model

Refer to the doubly constrained gravity model as discussed in the subsection bearing the same title in Chapter 3. When the value of α becomes 1 in the propensity function $F(C_{ij})$, the function becomes a special function of travel cost, $F(C_{ij}) = C_{ij}^{-\alpha} = C_{ij}^{-1}$, and the doubly constrained gravity model can be written as

$$V_{ij} = (k_i l_j V_i V_j) F(C_{ij}) = z'_{ij} C_{ij}^{-1} \text{ or } z'_{ij} = C_{ij} V_{ij}$$

$$z = \Sigma_{ij} z'_{ij} = \Sigma_{ij} C_{ij} V_{ij}$$

$$\sum_{i=1}^{n'} V_{ij} = V_j \quad j = 1, 2, \ldots, n'$$

(E.8)

$$\sum_{j=1}^{n'} V_{ij} = V_i \quad i = 1, 2, \ldots, n'$$

z in Equation (E.8) is interpreted as the total travel cost now. By minimizing total travel cost (for instance, veh-min), we have the classical transportation model. Notice this model reflects the system optimum rather than user optimum as obtained by conventional gravity-model calibration. Now answer the following questions:

(a) What value would α assume in the propensity function to have maximum accessibility?

(b) What value would α assume to have minimum accessibility?

(c) For a prescriptive model, what is the resulting trip distribution for case (a)?

(d) For a prescriptive model, what is the trip distribution for case (b)?

(e) Interpret the result of (c) and (d).

C. Calibration of a Doubly Constrained Model

Given the following data on interzonal trips V_{ij} and the associated costs C_{ij}, please calibrate a doubly-constrained gravity model:

$$[V_{ij}] = \begin{matrix} \text{zone 1} \\ \text{zone 2} \end{matrix} \begin{bmatrix} 1 & 2 \\ 100 & 200 \\ 300 & 50 \end{bmatrix} \text{ and } [C_{ij}] = \begin{matrix} \text{zone 1} \\ \text{zone 2} \end{matrix} \begin{bmatrix} 1 & 2 \\ 1 & 2 \\ 2 & 1 \end{bmatrix}$$

Suppose $F(C_{ij}) = c_{ij}^{-2}$, carry out the calculations as far as you can, following the procedure described in the doubly constrained model subsection of Chapter 3. Give the final four equations for the four unknowns, and solve the equations.

V. LAND USE MODELS

Analysis of land use models is a center piece of this book. Here, the economic-base and activity distribution exercise shows how the activity derivation, distribution, and competition concepts can be used to simulate the housing requirements of a college town over time. This set of calculations is then formalized in the iterative Lowry model calculation, which is encoded on the software CD.

A. Economic-Base and Activity Allocation

In a study of a college town, State College, Pennsylvania, Chan and Rasmussen (1979) forecasted housing requirements. Using the basic concepts of the Lowry model, they derived the subareal housing requirement of the town using the university enrollment as the basic activity. Their algorithm follows a two-part procedure:

Part I. Housing Demand Factor
1. Define the zoning types of all residentially zoned developable land.
2. Establish the number of students, blue-collar employees, and white-collar employees from tract i working at employment center c—labeled here as E_{ic}^S, E_{ic}^B, E_{ic}^W respectively.
3. Determine the separation d between each tract centroid and employment center.
4. Obtain the percentage of student, blue-collar, and white-collar commuters traveling a distance of d miles to the related employment center—labeled $f_i^S(d)$, and $f_i^B(d)$, and $f_i^W(d)$ respectively.
5. Determine the percentage of students, blue-collar workers, and white-collar workers in residential type t—labeled p_t^S, p_t^B and p_t^W, respectively
6. Compute the housing demand factor: $V_{it}^d = \Sigma_k \Sigma_c \Sigma_d E_{ic}^k f_i^k (d) p_t^k$.

Part II. Allocation of Housing Demand
1. Determine the excess housing supply in tact i, ΔN_i. The excess is equally distributed among the number of zoning types t_{max}: $\Delta N_{it} = \Delta N_i / t_{max}$.
2. Determine the maximum holding capacity for developable dwelling units: N_{it}^c = (developable average) (average dwelling units per acre).
3. Allocate the total housing demand N to each tract i: $N_{it} = NV_{it}^d / \Sigma_i \Sigma_t V_{it}^d$. The housing demand for housing type t in tract i can either be accommodated by the excess housing supply ΔN_{it} or new construction. Housing demand exceeding the holding capacity of a tract would have to be located elsewhere. The additional developable capacity of a tract for housing type t is $\Delta N_{it}^c = N_{it}^c - N_{it} - \Delta N_{it}$.
4. Additional iterations are necessary as long as one or more δ_{it}^c is negative (i.e., there is spill over from a tract), and excess capacity still exists in the region to accommodate the excess. Otherwise, the algorithm terminates.

Chan and Rasmussen then compared their forecast with the ones by the Centre Region Planning Commission (CRPC). The housing projection performed by the CRPC is computed by a two-step procedure: (1) The future population for the region is computed; and (2) the number of dwelling units is derived from that figure. The derivation process is generally founded on a extrapolation forecasting techniques. The CRPC population forecast takes into consideration a cohort survival model and a straight-line proportional model. (These techniques are discussed in the "Econometrics Modeling" section of Chapter 2.) The following assumptions are made among both studies: (a) No substantial in or out migration would take place, which implies the student enrollment at Penn State University would stabilize at 31,500 by 1985. (b) Existing trends, including birthrates/death rates and other coefficients and ratios, will remain constant over time for each township of the Centre Region.

Since the study, the dwelling units that were actually observed became available. These figures are tabulated beside the Chan and Rasmussen and CRPC forecasts in Table E.2. Can you perform a "before-and-after" analysis as to the accuracy of the forecasts by the Chan-Rasmussen model vis-a-vis the CRPC study?

B. Forecasting Airbase Housing Requirements

Now that you are familiar with the Chan-Rasmussen housing model, can you use the same model to forecast housing requirements for an Air Force base? Similar to the college town model, this new model is based on the hypothesis that the foundation of the local economy is an Air Force base (Bahm et al. 1989). Whiteman Air Force Base (AFB)—near Knob Noster, Missouri—is chosen for the study. Whiteman was picked because the base is a major source of employment for the region and was expected to grow at the time of the study in 1989. The source of the increase in military- and civilian-employment is the new B-2 bomber wing.

Three types of economic activities are envisioned to increase: military and their dependents, civilian Department of Defense (DOD) employees, and civilian non-DOD employees. There are 25 housing tracts or zones in the region. There are four employment centers: Warrensburg, Sedalia, Knob Noster, and Whiteman AFB. Commuting distance is measured in one-mile (1.6-km) increments, with the longest commuting distance being 46 miles (73.6 km). There are five residential types: single family, double family, multiple family, dormitories and non-residential. Additional developable capacities, excess housing, and resident profiles are documented in Table E.3. The information is listed by each tract/zone i. By resident profile we mean the percentage of military, DOD civilian, and non-DOD civilians in each type of housing—whether it be single family, double family, mul-

Table E.2 COMPARISON OF FORECASTS AND OBSERVED HOUSING UNITS

1985 Figures		College	Ferguson	Halfmoon	Harris	Patton	State College
Single family	Chan & Rasmussen	1599	2105	221	960	1434	3316
	CRPC	1599	2505	276	1145	1801	3114
	Observed	1785	2209	303	1124	1768	2650
Multiple family	Chan & Rasmussen	208	544	6	21	790	6207
	CRPC	351	591	6	31	849	6545
	Observed	545	964	19	176	1730	7837

Table E.3   ADDITIONAL DEVELOPABLE CAPACITIES, EXCESS HOUSING*
AND RESIDENT PROFILE

Tract/zone	Single family	Double family	Multiple family	Dormitory
1	0 (2)	0 (2)	–	892
2	181	210	562	–
3	0	0	0	0
4	88	93	92	–
5	45	–	–	–
6	39	–	–	–
7	2490	2495	2492	–
8	24	–	–	–
9	20	27	932	–
10	35	–	–	–
11	38	–	–	–
12	36	–	–	–
13	30 (9)	–	–	–
14	30	–	–	–
15	30 (9)	–	–	–
16	20	–	–	–
17	141	135	893	–
18	35	–	–	–
19	2496	2500 (6)	2500 (2)	–
20	25	–	–	–
21	30 (9)	–	–	–
22	0	0	0	0
23	50 (7)	–	–	–
24	50 (4)	–	–	–
25	31	–	–	–

Resident profile	Single family	Double family	Multiple family	Dormitory
% Military	0.290	0.320	0.073	0.317
% Civilian/DOD	0.645	0.040	0.315	0
% Civilian/non-DOD	0.616	0.031	0.353	0

SOURCE: Patterson (1995). Reprinted with permission.

*Excess housing numbers are in parentheses.

tiple family, or dormitory. Commuting distances from each of the 25 tracts/zones to the four employment centers are shown in Table E.4. The trip distribution, or the percentage of workers traveling distance d to an employment center, is shown in Table E.5. Included in the table are the increases in military, DOD civilian and non-DOD civilian jobs in each of the four employment centers.

Now forecast the housing requirements at the study area based on these assumptions: (a) insignificant projected increase in employment from manufacturing in Warrensburg and Sedalia, (b) insignificant projected increases in

Table E.4   COMMUTING DISTANCES[a] TO EMPLOYMENT CENTERS

Tract/zone	Warrensburg	Sedalia	Knob Noster	Whiteman AFB
1	12	20	3	1
2	10	18	1	3
3	8	22	3	3
4	17	10	8	10
5	25	10	15	17
6	13	23	7	9
7	7	24	4	6
8	17	23	12	10
9	1	28	10	12
10	9	30	17	17
11	7	27	17	19
12	8	32	15	17
13	16	43	23	25
14	20	45	30	30
15	14	43	26	26
16	20	46	30	30
17	28	1	18	20
18	22	12	15	15
19	23	7	14	16
20	24	17	15	17
21	38	15	25	26
22	35	10	23	24
23	35	8	25	26
24	35	8	25	26
25	37	12	28	28

[a]In integral miles (or multiples of 1.6 km).

Table E.5   TRIP DISTRIBUTION AND JOB PROFILES AT THE EMPLOYMENT
            CENTERS

Employment distribution	Military	Civilian/DOD	Civilian/non-DOD
Warrensburg	400	0	400
Sedalia	500	0	800
Knob Noster	100	0	100
Whiteman AFB	2045	355	241

Trip distribution	Military	Civilian/DOD	Civilian/non-DOD
1	0.2	0	0.55
2	0.05	0	0.1
3	0.2	0.08	0.05
4	0.01	0.05	0.03
5	0.01	0.01	0.02
6	0.01	0.05	0.02
7	0.01	0.01	0.02
8	0.01	0.01	0.02
9	0.01	0.01	0.02
10	0.01	0.01	0.02
11	0.08	0.01	0.02
12	0.165	0.25	0.01
13	0.01	0.01	0.01
14	0.01	0.01	0.01
15	0.01	0.01	0.01
16	0.0015	0.01	0.01
17	0.025	0.01	0.01
18	0.05	0.01	0.01
19	0.25	0.01	0.01
20	0.14	0.37	0.01
21	0.005	0.02	0.01
22	0.001	0.01	0.01
23	0.001	0.01	0.01
24	0.001	0.005	0.001
25	0.001	0.005	0.001
26	0.0005	0.005	0.001
27	0.0005	0.005	0.001
28	0	0.001	0.001
29	0	0.001	0.001
30	0.0005	0.001	0.001
31	0	0.001	0.0005
32	0	0.001	0.0005
33	0	0.001	0.0005
34	0	0.001	0.0005
35	0	0.001	0.0005
36	0	0.005	0.0005
37	0	0.005	0
38	0	0.005	0
39	0	0.005	0

employment or student enrollment at Missouri State University, and (c) only a small amount of associated cross-commuting from Whiteman to other points in the study region. All these make Whiteman AFB the major employer in the projected future, attracting the local population to the base.

C. Traditional Lowry Software

One of the most common functions of a land use model is forecasting. In this assignment, you are to forecast the land use of York, Pennsylvania for a forecast-year corresponding to a transportation system improvement. A set of data (named DATA2.DAT) is located in the folder (directory) LOWRY on the software CD. The data file represents the implementation of an ubiquitous Personal Rapid Transit (PRT) system in York. The system operates at a constant speed of 25 miles per hour (40 km/h) on existing streets, replacing all roadway traffic (particularly the automobile) and becoming the city's only means of transportation. Such a precipitous policy (henceforth referred to as the PRT alternative) will undoubtedly redirect land development in York. Compared with the null or "do-nothing" alternative (in which the existing auto-oriented system prevails as shown in DATA1.DAT,) the PRT alternative will probably improve the accessibility at certain congested parts of the city but prolong the travel time at other less congested places. The land use pattern is expected to change dramatically accordingly to the theory of gravitational interaction.

You are commissioned by the city to evaluate the impact of the proposed PRT alternative. Specifically, you are asked to:

(a)   make a forecast corresponding to the PRT alternative;

(b)   compare the forecast with the null or "do-nothing" alternative; and

(c)   explain the development changes from the base year in terms of the difference in transportation policies.

Aside from a graphic plot to show the effects of a policy change for the forecast-year, you are to document your comparison and explanation (parts (b) and (c) above) in a write up of no more than five (double-spaced) typed pages. The following outline for your submission is suggested:

(i)   difference in input,
(ii)   difference in output,
(iii)   accessibility,
(iv)   development opportunity,
(v)   overall interpretation, and
(vi)   visual display.

For part (vi), the data set YORK.DAT, containing both the base-year and the null and PRT alternative forecast-year data, may be useful.

VI. SPATIAL-TEMPORAL INFORMATION

The unifying theme throughout this book is really how one analyzes spatial-temporal information in general. In this last block of problems, we let the data

guide us in the analysis. The first problem eloquently shows the difference between spatial and univariate forecasts, particularly regarding their respective accuracies. Subsequently we worry about the calibration of a spatial forecasting
model, an area so demanding that much more research is still needed.

A. Cohort Survival Method

The cohort survival method is an econometric technique introduced in Chapter 2,
in the "Interregional Growth and Distribution" subsection. Please review the discussions in the text and answer these questions (Jha 1972):

> **(a)** Suppose these statistics are gathered for York County, Pennsylvania
> during the 1940–1945 period. The number of births is 2,000 and the
> number of deaths is 500. The average population for the period is
> 210,000. There were 1,400 people migrating to York and 1,295 migrating
> out. Define the following terms for a certain forecast time period: crude
> birthrate, crude death rate, and net migration.

> **(b)** Check the population for females in 1945 in York County,
> Pennsylvania by the cohort survival method. Use the population statis-
> tics shown in the following table. Note that these numbers are in hun-
> dreds, i.e., 10 means 1000.

Age	0–4	5–9	10–14	15–19	20–24	25–29	Total
1940	10	14	15	18	22	24	103
1945	7	10	12	14	16	21	80

The entries in this table represent the number of people in each age group. The
surviving ratio of the 0–4 year group is 98% and the percentage of female children
is 49%. The fertility rate of the 15–19 year group is 43%; the rate for 20–24 groups
and 25–29 groups is 56%.

B. Calibration of a Spatial Forecasting Model

As cited in Cliff and Ord (1981), Mitchell (1969) studied the pattern of insurgent
control during the Huk rebellion in the Philippines, linking control to a variety of
cultural and economic factors. Doreian and Hummon (1976) pointed out that control of any given area either by the government or by the insurgents has immediate relevance for the control in adjacent areas. In other words, one would expect
the insurgency to spread, or to contract, through adjoining areas. Thus Doreian
and Hummon proposed a regression model with a spatial component to analyze
this phenomenon. The regressor variables are:

> P the proportion of the population speaking the Pampangan dialect,
>
> F farmers as a percentage of the population,
>
> O owners as a percentage of farmers,
>
> S the percentage of cultivated land given over to sugar cane,

M the presence of mountainous terrain (dummy),

X the presence of swamps (dummy).

In the regression equation, P is used multiplicatively with the other variables, so that the exogenous variables are PF, PO, PS, PM, and PX.

Here are three sets of estimates for a linear model linking insurgent (Huk) control to the cultural, demographic, ethical, and physical exogenous variables for each municipality i. Each regression coefficient has an accompanying standard error given in brackets. The coefficient of multiple determination is also shown for each model.

Nonspatial OLS model ($R^2 = 0.73$):

$$Y = \underset{(2.94)}{1.147} + \underset{(0.939)}{3.794F} - \underset{(0.438)}{1.912PO} + \underset{(0.161)}{0.461PS} + \underset{(7.02)}{38.38M} + \underset{(7.94)}{17.17PX}$$

Simultaneous maximum likelihood spatial model ($R^2 = 0.80$):

$$Y = \underset{(2.39)}{1.316} + \underset{(0.008)}{0.571(\mathbf{w}^{(l)})^T(\mathbf{W}^{(l)}\mathbf{y})_{\sim Y}} + \underset{(0.762)}{1.942PF} - \underset{(0.355)}{0.889PO} + \underset{(0.132)}{0.118PS} + \underset{(5.69)}{28.75PM} + \underset{(6.44)}{11.41PX}$$

Conditional OLS spatial model ($R^2 = 0.80$):

$$Y = \underset{(2.62)}{1.382} + \underset{(0.138)}{0.586(\mathbf{w}^{(l)})^T(\mathbf{W}^{(l)}\mathbf{y})_{-Y}} + \underset{(0.928)}{1.892PF} - \underset{(0.453)}{0.862PO} + \underset{(0.164)}{0.108PS} + \underset{(6.51)}{28.49PM} + \underset{(7.01)}{11.26PX}$$

In the above, the non-spatial model is the standard linear model, fitted by OLS without any spatial autoregressive component. In the second model, the simultaneous spatial scheme has been fitted by maximum likelihood. In the third model, conditional OSL has been used to estimate the parameters of a spatial model. In both models 2 and 3, data have been filtered ahead of time by a spatial mask defined by the weight vector $\mathbf{w}^{(l)}$ for each municipality i. As shown in the "Spatial Time Series" and "Spatial-Temporal Information" chapters of Chan (2000), $\mathbf{w}^{(l)} = (\mathbf{w}^{(l)}_{i1}, \mathbf{w}^{(l)}_{i2}, \ldots, \mathbf{w}^{(l)}_{in})^T$ is the vector of spatial weights associated with the lth neighbor. $(\mathbf{W}^{(l)}\mathbf{y})_{-Y}$ is an lth-order filter on data $\mathbf{y}$. It removes the subject Y entry and replaces it with a filtered value. Compare and contrast the results of these three models.

REFERENCES

Ahutuv, N.; Berman, O. (1988). *Operations management of distributed service networks—A practical quantitative approach.* New York: Plenum Press.

Bahm, P.; Ross, M.; Chan, Y. (1989). Forecasting housing requirements for an Air Force installation. Working Paper. Department of Operational Sciences. Air Force Institute of Technology. Wright-Patterson Air AFB, Ohio.

Banaszak, D.; Cordeiro, J.; Chan, Y. (1997). Using the K-medoid and covering approaches in pattern-recognition problems. Working Paper. Department of Operational Sciences. Air Force Institute of Technology. Wright-Patterson Air AFB, Ohio.

Burnes, M. D. (1990). Application of vehicle routing heuristics to an aeromedical airlift problem. Master's Thesis. (AFIT/GST/ENS/90M-3). Department of Operational Sciences. Air Force Institute of Technology. Wright-Patterson Air AFB, Ohio.

Chan, Y. (2000) *Location transport and land-use: Modeling spatial-temperal information.* New York: Springer-Verlag.

Chan, Y.; Rasmussen, W. (1979). "Forecasting housing requirements in a college town." *Journal of the Urban Planning and Development Division* (American Society of Civil Engineers) 105:9–23.

Cliff, A. D.; Ord, J. K. (1981). *Spatial processes: Models and applications.* London: Pion.

Clough, J.; Millhouse, P.; Chan, Y. (1997). The obnoxious facility location problem. Working Paper. Department of Operational Sciences. Air Force Institute of Technology. Wright-Patterson Air AFB, Ohio.

Daskin, M. (1995). *Network and discrete location: Models, algorithms, and applications.* New York: Wiley.

Doreian, P.; Hummon, N. P. (1976). *Modelling social processes.* New York: Elsevier.

Francis, R.; McGinnis, L.; White, J. (1999). *Facility layout and location: An analytical approach*, 3rd ed. Englewood Cliffs, New Jersey: Prentice-Hall.

Garfinkel, R. S.; Nemhauser, G. L. (1970). "Optimal political redistricting by implicit enumeration techniques." *Management Science*, 16:495–508.

Gonzalez, R. C.; Woods, R. E. (1992). *Digital image processing.* Reading, Mass.: Addison-Wesley.

Grosskopf, S.; Magaritis, D.; Valdmanis, V. (1995). "Estimating output substitutability of hospital services: a distance function approach." *European Journal of Operational Research* 80:575–587.

Irish, T.; May, T.; Chan, Y. (1995). A stochastic facility relocation problem. Working Paper. Department of Operational Sciences. Air Force Institute of Technology. Wright-Patterson Air AFB, Ohio.

Jha, K. (1972). Demographic models. Working Paper. Department of Civil Engineering. Pennsylvania State University. University Park, Pennsylvania.

Junio, D. F. (1994). Development of an analytic hierarchy process for siting of municipal solid waste facilities. Master's Thesis. Department of Operational Sciences. Air Force Institute of Technology. Wright-Patterson Air AFB, Ohio.

Kanafani, A. (1983). *Transportation demand analysis.* New York: McGraw-Hill.

Mandl, C. (1979). *Applied network optimization.* New York: Academic Press.

Memis, T.; Eravsar, M.; Chan, Y. (1997). Integer programming solution to Route Improvement Synthesis and Evaluation (RISE). Working Paper. Department of Operational Sciences. Air Force Institute of Technology. Wright-Patterson Air AFB, Ohio.

Mitchell, E. J. (1969). "Some econometrics of the Huk rebellion." *American Political Science Review* 63:1159–1171.

Patterson, T. S. (1995). Dynamic maintenance scheduling for a stochastic telecommunications network: Determination of performance factors. Master's Thesis. Department of Operational Sciences. Graduate School of Engineering. Air Force Institute of Technology. Wright-Patterson Air AFB, Ohio.

Pfeifer, P. E.; Bodily, S. E. (1990). "A test of space-time ARMA modelling and forecasting of hotel data." *Journal of Forecasting* 9:255–272.

Piskator, G. M.; Chan, Y. (1997). Estimating a production function and efficient frontier for the United States Army recruiting battalions. Working Paper. Department of Operational Sciences. Air Force Institute of Technology. Wright-Patterson Air AFB, Ohio.

Russ, J. C. (1998). *Image processing handbook*, 3rd ed. Boca Raton: CRC Press.

Sanso, B.; Soumis, F.; Gendreau, M. (1991). "On the evaluation of telecommunications network reliability using routing models." *IEEE Transactions on Communications* 39, no. 10: 1494–1501.

Steppe, J. M. (1991). Locating direction finders in a generalized search and rescue network. Master's Thesis. Department of Operational Sciences. Air Force Institute of Technology. Wright-Patterson Air AFB, Ohio.

Steuer, R. E. (1986). *Multiple criteria optimization: Theory, computation, and application.* New York: Wiley.

Tapiero, C. S. (1971). "Transportation-location-allocation problems over time" *Journal of Regional Science* 11:377–384.

Wright, S. A. (1995). Spatial time-series: Pollution pattern recognition under irregular intervention. Master's Thesis. Department of Operational Sciences. Air Force Institute of Technology. Wright-Patterson Air AFB, Ohio.

Wright, S. A.; Chan, Y. (1994a). A network with side constraints for the k-medoid method for optimal plant location applied to image classification. Working Paper. Department of Operational Sciences. Air Force Institute of Technology. Wright-Patterson Air AFB, Ohio.

Wright, S. A.; Chan, Y. (1994b). Multicriteria decision-making applied to the ICM contextual image classification technique. Working Paper. Department of Operational Sciences. Air Force Institute of Technology. Wright-Patterson Air AFB, Ohio.

Wright, S. A.; Chan, Y. (1994c). Pure and polluted groundwater classification on a pixel map. Working Paper. Department of Operational Sciences. Air Force Institute of Technology. Wright-Patterson Air AFB, Ohio.

Zelany, M. (1982). *Multiple criteria decision making.* New York: McGraw-Hill.

Appendix 1

Review of Some Pertinent Optimization Schemes

While the main body of the text concentrates on facility location and land use, there are some computational aspects of model solution that readers may wish to review. Four appendices are provided here for that purpose. This first appendix provides an optimization background necessary for a better appreciation of the pertinent chapters. These chapters include location and routing and other prescriptive models of spatial analysis. We assume a background of college algebra and calculus in our presentations below. As with other book appendices, this review is geared toward those specifically interested in the subject of this book. Our audience includes graduate students and professionals possessing a scientific first degree. Science in this case is broadly defined to encompass all physical or social sciences, including engineering, mathematics, economics, regional science, and geography. To the extent that we are trying to cater to all these disciplines, there will be a tendency from time to time, albeit infrequent in nature, to re-state the obvious. This is unavoidable in any attempt to reach a multidisciplinary audience. Each appendix is designed to be self-contained. References to the main body of the book and Chan (2000) are intended for further reading on the subject.

I. LINEAR PROGRAMMING

Linear programming is a procedure used to arrive at the best solution for a set of linear algebraic inequalities and a linear objective function. It should be obvious from Chapter 4 that the graphical method for solving linear programs (LP) is limited to models of two decision variables. An algebraic procedure is needed to solve LPs with numerous variables and inequalities. Also, such an algebraic technique is conducive to computer programming. One algebraic technique for solving LPs is the simplex algorithm. A large number of software packages are available to perform the computation. Because the method has been around for quite some time, most have been refined for computational efficiency. Here we outline the basic concepts mainly for a more coherent discussion of more general and efficient procedures. These include relaxation and decomposition techniques, which form the thrust of this appendix.

A. Simplex Algorithm

Consider the LP

$$\text{Max } z_x = x_1 + x_2$$
$$\text{s.t.} \quad 3x_1 + 6x_2 \leq 1$$
$$5x_1 + 4x_2 \leq 1 \tag{A1.1}$$
$$x_i \geq 0 \quad i = 1, 2$$

First, we solve this graphically as before in Figure A1.1, just for comparison with the algebraic method described below. To start the primal simplex algebraic procedure, the inequalities of the constraint equations are now changed into equalities by the addition of slack variables x_3 and x_4. The adjusted system of equations now looks like

$$z_x - x_1 - x_2 \qquad\qquad = 0$$
$$3x_1 + 6x_2 \qquad + x_4 = 1 \tag{A1.2}$$
$$5x_1 + 4x_2 + x_3 \qquad = 1$$

where the right-hand side (RHS) of $(1, 1)^T$ represents positive resources to be allocated among the decision variables in order to maximize a figure of merit, called the objective function. This operation is an attempt to provide a starting basic feasible solution (BFS) to the LP. As it stands, a solution consisting of $(x_3, x_4) = (1, 1)$ and $(x_1, x_2) = (0, 0)$ is a perfectly good—albeit no where near optimal—solution to the LP. In this solution, (x_3, x_4) are the basic variables, and they form the basis of nonnegative values. The variables (x_1, x_2) are nonbasic variables, assuming zero values. This BFS corresponds to the origin in the graphic plot shown in Figure A1.1.

Figure A1.1 GRAPHIC SOLUTION TO LINEAR PROGRAM

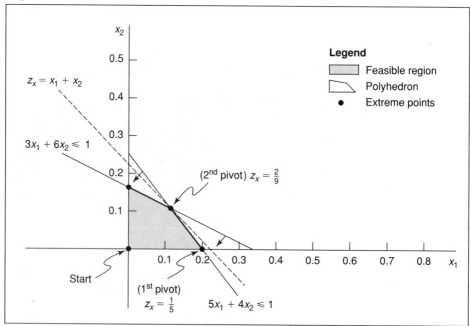

Figure A1.2   LINEAR PROGRAMMING TABLEAUX SHOWING PIVOTING
OPERATIONS

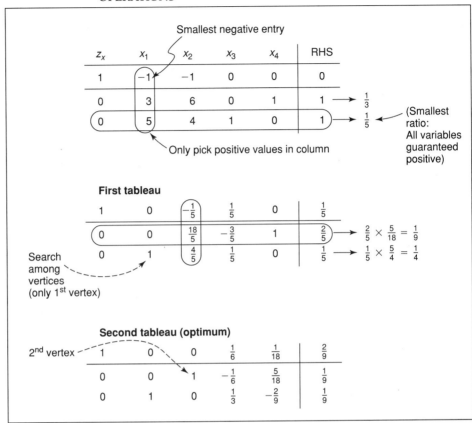

This set of equations is then organized around a tableau, and Gaussian operations are performed as they would be in solving a set of simultaneous equations. As shown in Figure A1.2, the procedure pivots from one extreme point or vertex of the feasible region to another, corresponding to changing the basis in the algebraic context. Figure A1.2 is a good reference for the algebraic operations, showing the movement from extreme point to extreme point as the maximization objective function gets bigger and bigger. Two rules are followed in the pivoting operations. First, the column with the most negative number in the first row is picked to be the variable to enter the basis. For example, x_1 (or x_2) will be the variable to enter in the first pivot. This says that the best way to improve the value of the objective function is to go up the steepest slope, in this case along the x_1-axis. Because the terms have been moved from the right to the left in the objective function during the transformation shown above in Equation A1.2, only by engaging the variables with the negative cost coefficients will the figure of merit z increase. These are the variables j which will provide a net improvement in the objective function in the allocation of limited resources among several activity variables. Such net improvement is often referred to as the reduced cost, $(z_j - c_j)$. It signifies that the engagement of x_j will benefit the objective function by c_j but at an opportunity cost of z_j, reflecting idling other activities x_k $(k \neq j)$.

Once the entering variable has been identified, entries in the column directly under the entering variable (x_1, in this case) will be paired against the RHS. A ratio of the RHS entries and the positive elements in the column will be taken. The row with the smallest ratio will determine the variable to exit the basis. In the first pivot, it is clear that the third row, corresponding to x_3 will exit. This second rule keeps the next solution within the feasible region and also ensures a non-negative solution. The row with the smallest ratio identifies the most confining resource—among the two resources in this example—and keeps us operating "within our means". Choosing only the positive entries in the column of the entering variable is an attempt to stay away from unboundedness—in other words, the endless engagement of an activity variable since it consumes no real resources during its deployment.

Once the column and row have been identified, in this case column 2 and row 3, the element that belongs to both the row and column becomes the pivot. Gaussian operations are performed between all the rows to make this pivot unity in value and the rest of the entries in the column zero. Following our example, we have successfully carried this out in the first tableau. This tableau has a basis made up of x_1 and x_4 recognize that variables outside the basis (the nonbasic variables) are at zero value by definition, corresponds to the extreme point $(1/5, 0)^T$ in Figure A1.1. (Notice that should we pick x_2 as the variable to enter, the basis would be x_2 and x_3 and would correspond to the extreme point $(0, 1/6)^T$. Instead of being at "sea level" ($z_x = 0$) when we started at original vertex $(0, 0)$, the new altitude at $(1/5, 0)^T$ is now 1/5.

A second pivot will introduce x_2 into the basis and elevate the altitude further to 2/9 at the new vertex (1/9, 1/9). We know we have arrived at the optimum since none of the entries in the first row are negative any more. Should we engage any of the variables to enter the basis, we will be descending, instead of ascending, the slope. In fact, the disappearance of all negative entries in the first row constitutes the termination rule. The readers probably recognize that these pivots are essentially effected by basis inverses in linear algebra. Matrix formulation of pivots will be shown below.

B. Some Other Key Concepts

The simplex procedure works because there is a finite number of extreme points, a convex combination of which will define all points in the feasible region, or polyhedron, of the LP. In other words, if x^1 and x^2 are two extreme points, the convex combination $x^1 + (1 - w)x^2 (0 \leq w \leq 1)$ forms a point that will be within the polyhedron. Furthermore, an optimum has to occur at an extreme point. This is clear from the graphical plot of this LP example in Figure A1.1, in which the reader is challenged to show otherwise, excepting for the case when the objective function parallels one of the constraints. The same concept can be demonstrated in the unbounded polyhedron shown in the dual space of this LP.[1] In Figure A1.3, we have extreme directions d^1 and d^2 in addition to extreme points λ^1, λ^2 and λ^3. It is clear from this figure that we can represent every point in the set as a convex combination of the extreme points plus a non-negative linear combination of the extreme directions. Consider the point λ, which can be represented as λ^0 plus a positive multiple of the extreme direction d^1. Notice that $\lambda^0 - \lambda$ points in the direction d^1. But λ^0 itself is a convex combination of the extreme points λ^1 and λ^3. Hence $\lambda^0 = \lambda + \mu d^1 = w\lambda^1 + (1 - w)\lambda^3 + \mu d^1$ where $0 \leq w \leq 1$ and $\mu \geq 0$.

Figure A1.3   DUAL OF LINEAR PROGRAMMING EXAMPLE

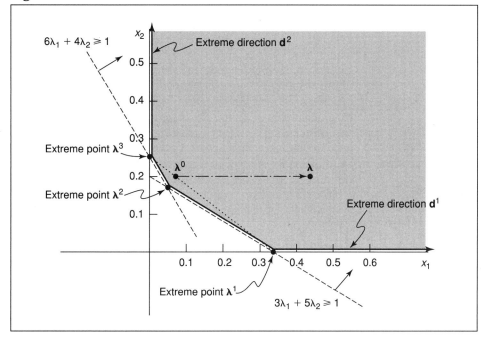

Notice this version of the simplex algorithm works only for these specific conditions:

(a) maximization of the objective function,

(b) less-than-or-equal-to in all the constraint equations, with positive RHSs,

(c) non-negativity in all the decision variables.

But it is also a general procedure since many LPs can be cast into this form. For example, any minimization objective function can be converted to a maximization format:

$$\text{Min } z = \sum_{j=1}^{n} c_j\, x_j \text{ becomes Max } z' = \sum_{j=1}^{n} c_j\, x_j$$

(Such a conversion suggests that the termination rule for a minimization LP should be when the first row of the simplex tableau consists of all non-positive entries.) Similarly, constraints not in the correct form can be converted:

$$\sum_j a_{ij}\, x_j \le b_i \quad \text{becomes} \quad \sum_j -a_{ij}\, x_j \le -b_i$$

Equalities can be expressed in terms of two inequalities. Thus

$$\sum_j a_{ij}\, x_j = b_i \quad \text{becomes} \quad \sum_j a_{ij}\, x_j \le b_i \text{ and } \sum_j a_{ij}\, x_j \ge b_i$$

Finally, a negative RHS can be converted to a positive value by multiplying both sides of the constraint by a negative one. The simplex algorithm proceeds similarly as in the previous case once the model is cast into the form shown in Equation A1.1. Notice that there is really no magic in the form encapsulated in Equation A1.1. It is simply a convenient way to obtain a BFS, and it also allows us to explain the logic behind the simplex steps easily in terms of resource allocation. Should there be any difficulty in this conversion—and it will arise sometimes—other means for obtaining an initial BFS are necessary. There are several ways to do so, including solving the dual instead of the primal problem, wherein a minimization problem is converted to a maximization problem. An artificial variable may be added (with zero cost coefficient) to an equality constraint to make up the full rank of a BFS. Another way is to look for an initial solution based on existing operating conditions in practice. Interested readers may wish to consult Winston (1994) or Hillier and Lieberman (1990) regarding the precise procedures for doing this. In most applications, however, software packages are available to take care of the entire computational procedure, leaving more time for the user to formulate the LP and perform the analysis and to discern abnormalities in the computation when one occurs.

C. Theory of Simplex

We can summarize the simplex method as a set of matrix operations. First, we cast Equation A1.2 into an equation form:

$$\text{Min } z$$
$$s.t. \quad z - \mathbf{c}_B^T\mathbf{x}_B - \mathbf{c}_N^T\mathbf{x}_N = 0 \tag{A1.3}$$

$$\mathbf{A}_B\mathbf{x}_B + \mathbf{A}_N\mathbf{x}_N = \mathbf{b}$$
$$\mathbf{x}_B, \quad \mathbf{x}_N \geq \mathbf{0} \tag{A1.4}$$

Equation A1.4 is transformed in pivoting operations by pre-multiplying by $\mathbf{A}_B^{-1}$

$$\mathbf{x}_B + \mathbf{A}_B^{-1}\mathbf{A}_N\mathbf{x}_N = \mathbf{A}_B^{-1}\mathbf{b} \tag{A1.5}$$

Multiplying Equation A1.5 by $\mathbf{c}_B$ and adding to Equation A1.3:

$$z + \mathbf{0}\mathbf{x}_B + (\mathbf{c}_B\mathbf{A}_B^{-1}\mathbf{A}_N - \mathbf{c}_N)\mathbf{x}_N = \mathbf{c}_B\mathbf{A}_B^{-1}\mathbf{b} \tag{A1.6}$$

By setting the nonbasic variables to zero $\mathbf{x}_N = 0$, Equation A1.5 yields $\mathbf{x}_B = \mathbf{A}_B^{-1}\mathbf{b}$ and Equation A1.6 yields $z = \mathbf{c}_B\mathbf{A}_B^{-1}\mathbf{b}$. The tableau looks like the following in each iteration, including the last and optimal iteration:

	Z	$\mathbf{X}_B$	$\mathbf{X}_N$	RHS	
Row 0	1	0	$\mathbf{c}_B^T\mathbf{A}_B^{-1}\mathbf{A}_N - \mathbf{c}_N^T$	$\mathbf{c}_B^T\mathbf{A}_B^{-1}\mathbf{b}$	(A1.7)
Row 1→m	0	I	$\mathbf{A}_B^{-1}\mathbf{A}_N$	$\mathbf{A}_B^{-1}\mathbf{b}$	

Consult the example worked out below for an illustration. To do this it is conve-nient to rearrange the slack variables in Equation A1.2 in terms of an identity ma-trix $\mathbf{I}$ by reversing rows 1 and 2 in the constraints.

Example

Given the following maximization LP tableau that has been rearranged into the format of Equation A1.3, where the basis $\mathbf{A}_B$ is the identity matrix:

z	x_3	x_4	x_2	x_1	RHS
1	0	0	-40	-10	0
0	1	0	1	1	10
0	0	1	5	2	30

Here $\mathbf{c}_B = (0\ 0)^T$, $\mathbf{c}_N = (40\ 10)^T$, $\mathbf{A}_N = \begin{bmatrix} 1 & 1 \\ 5 & 2 \end{bmatrix}$ and $\mathbf{b} = (10\ 30)^T$. The reduced cost for column 2 is $\mathbf{c}_B^T \mathbf{A}_B^{-1} \mathbf{A}_N(x_2) - \mathbf{c}(x_2) = 0 - 40 = -40$, which constitutes the pivot column to enter the basis. Now $\mathbf{A}_B = \begin{bmatrix} 1 & 1 \\ 0 & 5 \end{bmatrix}$, $\mathbf{c}_B = (0\ 40)^T$, $\mathbf{c}_N = 0\ 10)^T$, and $\mathbf{A}_N = \begin{bmatrix} 0 & 1 \\ 1 & 2 \end{bmatrix}$.

According to the format of Equation A1.7, the inverse of the basis $\mathbf{A}_B$ is taken, and the refreshed tableau becomes

z	x_3	x_2	x_4	x_1	RHS
1	0	0	8	10	240
0	1	0	$-1/5$	$3/5$	4
0	0	1	$1/5$	$2/5$	6

This illustrates one pivot of the simplex. If Equations A1.3 and A1.4 are viewed as the initial tableau where $\mathbf{A}_N$ is an identity matrix and Equation A1.7 the optimal tableau (as in a 2×4 example tableau), then $\mathbf{c}_N$ is a zero vector and $\mathbf{c}_B^T \mathbf{A}_B^{-1} \mathbf{A}_N = \mathbf{c}_B^T \mathbf{A}_B^{-1}$ is simply the dual vector. In general, $\lambda_i = \mathbf{c}_B \mathbf{A}_B^{-1} \mathbf{A}_N(s_i) - \mathbf{c}_N(s_i)$ for the nonbasic variable s_i and zero for the basic variables, where s_i is the slack for inequality i. Thus in this example, the dual vector can be read from the first row of the last tableau, directly above the identity matrix where the slack variables were in the initial tableau. This means $\lambda_1 = 0$ and $\lambda_2 = 8$ as the readers can verify. Furthermore, $\mathbf{B}^{-1}$ can be found where the identity matrix for the slacks was, namely $\mathbf{B}^{-1} = \begin{bmatrix} 1 & -1/5 \\ 0 & 1/5 \end{bmatrix}$. ∎

II. NETWORK-WITH-SIDE-CONSTRAINTS

While the simplex procedure is a good way to introduce optimization procedures, there are more efficient techniques to solve such a model, depending on the struc-ture of the tableau. Network-flow programming is an excellent way to attack large-scale models, when the tableau can be cast into special formats.[2] A generalized network-flow algorithm is network-with-side-constraints (NSC), which can be applied toward problems having the following structure:

$$
\begin{aligned}
\min \quad & \mathbf{w}^T\mathbf{x} + \mathbf{c}^T\mathbf{y} \\
\text{s.t.} \quad & \mathbf{A}\mathbf{x} = \mathbf{b} \\
& \mathbf{B}\mathbf{x} + \mathbf{C}\mathbf{y} = \mathbf{b}' \\
& 0 \le \mathbf{x} \le \mathbf{d}, \ 0 \le \mathbf{y} \le \mathbf{d}'
\end{aligned}
\tag{A1.8}
$$

where $\mathbf{A}$ is the network matrix, $\mathbf{B}$ and $\mathbf{C}$ are arbitrary matrices. $\mathbf{d}$ and $\mathbf{d}'$ are arc capacity vectors on flow variables $\mathbf{x}$ and other variables $\mathbf{y}$ respectively. The algorithm takes advantage of the nice properties of the network matrix $\mathbf{A}$, which is assumed to be the more prominent part of the tableau in comparison to $\mathbf{B}$ and $\mathbf{C}$, and achieves computational efficiency that way. Let us call NETSIDE the off-the-shelf program available in SAS/OR, CPLEX, and other production codes to solve NSC problems.

A. Multicommodity-Flow Problem

A good way to illustrate NSC is through a well-known special case: the multicommodity-flow problem. Consider the two-commodity ($r = 1, 2$) problem illustrated in Figure A1.4, where the supply for nodes 1, 2 and 3 for both commodities is at most 2, and the demand at nodes 4, 5, and 6 for both commodities is at least 2. The individual bounds d_k^r are infinite for all arcs and both commodities ($r = 1, 2$), and the mutual capacity for arc 1 (d_1) is 2 and all other arcs (d_j, $j \ne 1$) have a capacity of 3. A corresponding tableau for this problem is shown in Figure A1.5. It is clear that the tableau can be partitioned into $\mathbf{A}$, $\mathbf{B}$, and $\mathbf{C}$ matrices, with $\mathbf{A}$ being the block-diagonal network matrix containing the two commodities, while $\mathbf{B}$ and $\mathbf{C}$ constitute the arc flow constraints, $\mathbf{x}$ is the regular network flow vector and $\mathbf{y}$ the slack flow vector.

Figure A1.4 SAMPLE MULTICOMMODITY-FLOW NETWORK

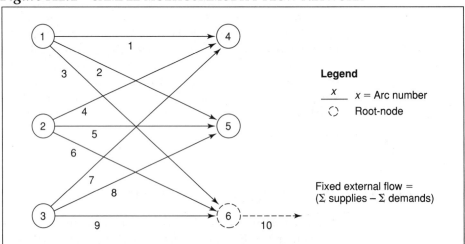

SOURCE: Kennington and Helgason (1980). Reprinted with permission.

Figure A1.5   BLOCK DIAGONAL MATRIX CORRESPONDING TO AN ORIENTATION SEQUENCE

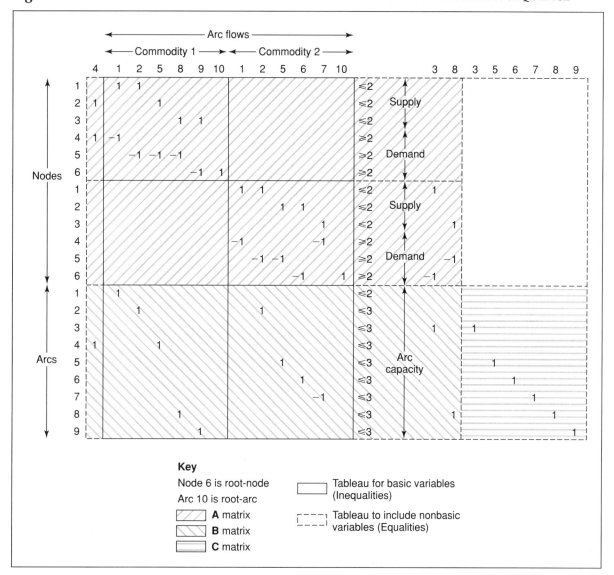

Specialization of the primal simplex algorithm for network programs results in the simplex on a graph algorithm, where there is a graphic/labeling replacement for each step of the simplex. The tableau with a basic solution looks like Figure A1.5, where the basic variables are boxed within the solid lines and the nonbasic variables to enter the basis are housed in dashed lines. The process in which a nonbasic variable enters the basis, or the incremental method of inverting a basis, is performed by an orientation sequence. For example, see the first column of the tableau in Figure A1.5, where the NETSIDE algorithm (Kennington and Helgason 1980) is being illustrated. Notice arc 4 of commodity 1 is introduced into the basis by an orientation sequence. The example illustrates

Figure A1.6   BASIS TREES SHOWING ORIENTATION SEQUENCE

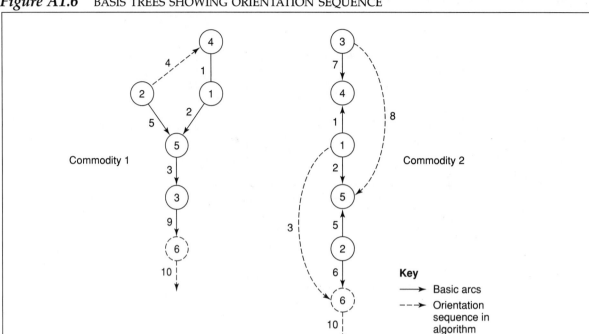

SOURCE: Kennington and Helgason (1980). Reprinted with permission.

this algorithm in the tableau, where primal feasibility is maintained and complementary slackness relaxed.[3]

By way of a definition, the orientation sequence of a path P of length k, $O'(P)$, is specified by a sequence of these numbers:

$$O'_i(P) = \begin{cases} +1 & \text{if } e_{j_i} = (i, i+1) \\ -1 & \text{if } e_{j_i} = (i+1, i) \end{cases} \quad i = 1, \ldots, k \tag{A1.9}$$

where e_{j_i} is the arc j associated with node/vertex i. The associated basis trees for the tableau in Figure A1.5 are sketched in Figure A1.6 where the nonbasic network flow variables are arcs 4, 3, and 8. An example of the orientation sequence for $P = \{3, 5, 2, 6\}$ is $O'(P) = \{1, -1, 1\}$. In household terms, the orientation sequence records whether the path is with the direction of the arrow or against the direction of the arrow. This is recorded using a $+1$ and -1 respectively. The orientation sequence $O'(P)$ performs a series of computations on the graph similar to basis inversion in simplex. In Figure A1.6, we can show how a nonbasic vector in the commodity-1 tree can be represented in terms of basic vectors by way of an orientation sequence. For example, the nonbasic arc-4 considered for entering the network basis can be represented in terms of three basic arcs 5, 2 and 1, and the algebra proceeds as follows:

$$\mathbf{A}(4) = \mathbf{A}(5) - \mathbf{A}(2) + \mathbf{A}(1)$$
$$= (\mathbf{e}^{2(4)} - \mathbf{e}^{5(4)}) - (\mathbf{e}^{1(4)} - \mathbf{e}^{5(4)}) + (\mathbf{e}^{1(4)} - \mathbf{e}^{4(4)})$$

$$= \mathbf{e}^{2(4)} - \mathbf{e}^{4(4)} = \begin{bmatrix} 0 \\ 1 \\ 0 \\ 0 \\ 0 \\ 0 \end{bmatrix} - \begin{bmatrix} 0 \\ 0 \\ 0 \\ 1 \\ 0 \\ 0 \end{bmatrix} = \begin{bmatrix} 0 \\ 1 \\ 0 \\ -1 \\ 0 \\ 0 \end{bmatrix} \qquad (A1.10)$$

Here $\mathbf{A}(j)$ stands for the column vector in the simplex tableau for arc j, $\mathbf{e}^{i(j)}$ is the unitary column vector for arc j with the unitary entry in the ith row. Care should be exercised in distinguishing the arc notation e_{ji} from the unitary column notation $\mathbf{e}^{i(j)}$.

B. The Network-with-Side-Constraints Algorithm

Having illustrated some basic ideas, we will show an NSC algorithm—NET-SIDE—step by step through an example (Kennington and Helgason 1980). The following problem is of the same format as Equation A1.8:

Min			$10x_2$	$+2x_3$		$+3x_5$	$+4x_6$					
s.t.	x_7	$+x_1$	$+x_2$					$\vert$		$=$	10	
		$-x_1$		$+x_3$	$+x_4$	$-x_5$		$\vert$		$=$	0	
			$-x_2$	$-x_3$		$+x_5$	$+x_6$	$\vert$		$=$	0	
					$-x_4$		$-x_6$	$\vert$		$=$	-10	$(A1.11)$
		$10x_1$		$-2x_3$	$+3x_4$	$-2x_5$		$\vert +y_1$		$=$	16	
	x_1			$+4x_3$		$+x_5$		$\vert$	$+y_2$	$=$	10	

Recall that regular LP simplex starts with a full rank m for the constraint matrix, where m is the number of nodes in the node-arc incidence matrix. But in Chapter 4, we suggested that the rank of the node-arc incidence matrix $\mathbf{A}$ is of rank $m - 1$. An artificial variable is added to make up the full rank of m as required in LP. An artificial variable is added to one of the nodes, say node m. The augmented constraint matrix now looks like $[\mathbf{A}, \mathbf{e}^{m(m)}]$, with the additional unitary column vector corresponding to the mth root-arc in a basis of $(m - 1)$ arcs. This arc is added to root-node m. Since any basic LP solution must contain m linearly independent columns, the artificial variable must appear in every basic simplex-on-a-graph solution (in other words, every tree). An artificial variable in LP is added to an equality constraints in LP merely to provide a starting BFS; correspondingly this artificial arc carries with it a zero cost. We have already seen examples of a root arc, namely arc 10, and root node 6 in Figure A1.4 through Figure A1.6. More examples will be forthcoming in the following computation steps. For the current example (Figure A1.7), all variables are bounded as indicated in the table below, with x_7, the root arc flow, bounded between 0 and ∞, and the slack flows also uncapacitated $0 \le y_j \le \infty$.

Arc j	1	2	3	4	5	6
d_j	12	18	5	12	1	16

1. Initialization Step.

Equation A1.11 shows that the tableau for the example problem can be partitioned into matrices **A**, **B**, and **C** as was the case with the multicommodity flow problem. The initial basis for this tableau is a 6×6 matrix $\bar{\textbf{B}}$.

The algebraic representation is the matrix $\bar{\textbf{B}} = \begin{bmatrix} \textbf{G} \ \textbf{H} \\ \textbf{D} \ \textbf{F} \end{bmatrix}$ which is

	x_7	x_2	x_5	x_6	x_1	x_3
	1	1			1	
			−1		−1	1
			−1	1	1		−1
				1		
			−2		10	−2
			1		1	4

where **G** is a square sub-matrix of the network matrix **A** carrying the same rank, with $\det(\textbf{G}) \neq 0$, constituting a rooted spanning tree. The corresponding graphical representation is a tree, which is shown in Figure A1.8.

Inverse of this matrix takes on special form, requiring only two inverses $\textbf{G}^{-1}$ and $\textbf{Q}^{-1}$:

$$\bar{\textbf{B}}^{-1} = \begin{bmatrix} \textbf{G}^{-1} + \textbf{G}^{-1}\textbf{H}\textbf{Q}^{-1}\textbf{D}\textbf{G}^{-1} & -\textbf{G}^{-1}\textbf{H}\textbf{Q}^{-1} \\ -\textbf{Q}^{-1}\textbf{D}\textbf{G}^{-1} & \textbf{Q}^{-1} \end{bmatrix} \quad i = 1, \ldots, k \quad (A1.12)$$

Figure A1.7   EXAMPLE TO ILLUSTRATE NETWORK-WITH-SIDE-CONSTRAINT ALGORITHM

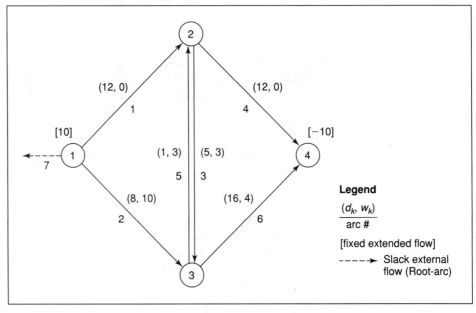

where $\mathbf{Q} = \mathbf{F} - \mathbf{DG}^{-1}\mathbf{H}$. Even though the $\mathbf{G}^{-1}$ can be arrived at by graphical means, we show the straightforward inversion below as a start:

$$\mathbf{G}^{-1} = \begin{bmatrix} 1 & 1 & 1 & 1 \\ 0 & -1 & -1 & -1 \\ 0 & -1 & 0 & 0 \\ 0 & 0 & 0 & -1 \end{bmatrix}, \quad \mathbf{Q}^{-1} = \begin{bmatrix} 1/12 & 1/15 \\ 0 & 1/5 \end{bmatrix} \text{ and the initial } \mathbf{B}^{-1} \text{ looks like}$$

1	1	1	1		
	$-9/10$	-1	-1	$-1/12$	$-1/15$
	$-7/10$			$-1/12$	$-2/15$
			-1		
	$-1/10$			$1/12$	$1/15$
	$1/5$				$1/5$

The current solution, as evaluated by $\mathbf{B}^{-1}\begin{bmatrix} \mathbf{b} \\ \mathbf{b}' \end{bmatrix}$, is

$$(x_1^B, x_2^B, x_3^B, x_4^N, x_5^B, x_6^B, x_7^B, y_1^N, y_2^N) = (2\ 8\ 2\ 0\ 0\ 1\ 0\ 0\ 0)$$

where the superscript B marks a basic variable and N a nonbasic variable.

After guessing at an initial basis $\overline{\mathbf{B}}$, and hence $\mathbf{G}$ (or the basis tree T_B) for $\mathbf{A}$, we proceed with the two basic steps of LP simplex: entry and exit of variables into $\mathbf{G}$. The pricing step selects the entry variable while the ratio test selects the exit variable.

Figure A1.8   TREE REPRESENTING INITIAL BASIS

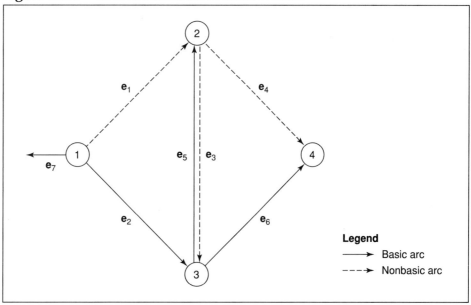

2. Pricing Step. An integral part of obtaining the reduced costs in the top row of the simplex tableau is computing the dual variable. The dot product of the dual vector, representing nodal potentials or "odometer readings" v_j for network flow, and the column vector under consideration will obtain the reduced cost $\mathbf{v}^T \mathbf{N}(k) - w_k$ of the column concerned. Notice the column for the kth arc (i, j) is in the nonbasic matrix outside $\overline{\mathbf{B}}$. In a network, the reduced cost is the potential difference across the arc $(v_j - v_i)$ that overcomes the arc cost w_{ij}, $\overline{v}_{ij} = (v_j - v_i) - w_{ij}$. To obtain the dual variable v_j in a network with side constraints:

$$(\mathbf{v}^1 \mid \mathbf{v}^2)^T = (\mathbf{w}^1 \mid \mathbf{w}^2)^T \overline{\mathbf{B}}^{-1} = [\{(\mathbf{w}^1)^T + (\mathbf{w}^1)^T \mathbf{G}^{-1} \mathbf{H} \mathbf{Q}^{-1} \mathbf{D}$$
$$- (\mathbf{w}^2)^T \mathbf{Q}^{-1} \mathbf{D}) \mathbf{G}^{-1} \mid ((\mathbf{w}^2)^T - (\mathbf{w}^1)^T \mathbf{G}^{-1} \mathbf{H} \} \mathbf{Q}^{-1}]$$

according to Equation A1.12 distinguishing between the spanning tree and non-spanning tree parts of $\overline{\mathbf{B}}^{-1}$. We will compute this in several steps utilizing graphical means where feasible. In this effort, we utilize two well-known facts. The rows and columns of the node-arc incidence matrix of any spanning tree can be rearranged to be lower triangular. The converse is the well-known result that every basis matrix defines a spanning tree.

   Step 1. First, we calculate $(\pi^1)^T = (\mathbf{w}^1)^T \mathbf{G}^{-1}$ as follows. Let $\mathbf{G}$ be the basis with corresponding basis tree T_B. By virtue of Equation A1.5, any the kth component of dual variable can be obtained by first solving $\mathbf{G}\mathbf{y}' = \mathbf{A}(k) = \mathbf{e}^i(k) - \mathbf{e}^j(k)$ for the updated column $\mathbf{y}'$. Here $\mathbf{e}^i(k)$ and $\mathbf{e}^j(k)$ are the unitary vectors for arc k made up of $+1$ and -1 in the columns of the node-arc incidence matrix corresponding to the beginning node of starting arc and the ending node of the terminating arc in a path P, as illustrated in Equation A1.10. The dual variable is simply $(\mathbf{w}^B)^T \mathbf{y}'$. The basis of a min-cost-flow network program $\mathbf{G}$ (or the tree T_B) can be put in lower triangular form with $+1$ or -1 on the diagonals. This means the system of equations $\mathbf{G}\mathbf{y}' = \mathbf{A}(k)$ can be solved by simple forward substitution process. Since $\mathbf{G}$ is triangular, $\mathbf{y}'$ may be obtained directly and hence algebraic inverse $\mathbf{G}^{-1}$ is not required. We further make use of T_B to solve this triangular system. Let $P = \{1, 2, \ldots, n + 1\}$ be the unique path in T_B linking node $i(k)$ to node $j(k)$, then

$$\sum_{i=1}^{n} O_i'(P) \mathbf{A}(j_i) = \mathbf{e}^{i(k)} - \mathbf{e}^{j(k)}$$

In other words, if the arcs in T_B are ordered as $\mathbf{e}_{k_1}, \mathbf{e}_{k_2}, \ldots, \mathbf{e}_{k_j}$ corresponding to the columns of $\mathbf{G}$, then the pth component of $\mathbf{y}'$ can be determined by the orientation sequence

$$y_p = \begin{cases} O_i'(P) & \text{if } \mathbf{e}_{k_p} = \mathbf{e}_{j_i} \in P \\ 0 & \text{otherwise} \end{cases} \tag{A1.13}$$

A clarification note is in order at this point. Decision variable $\mathbf{y}$ is to be distinguished from updated column $\mathbf{y}'$, and $\mathbf{A}(j)$ here refers to the jth column in $\mathbf{A}$.

   Now the arcs in the tree T_B is already ordered in the columns of

$$\mathbf{G} = \begin{matrix} e_7 & e_2 & e_3 & e_6 \\ \begin{bmatrix} 1 & 1 & 0 & 0 \\ 0 & 0 & -1 & 0 \\ 0 & -1 & 1 & 1 \\ 0 & 0 & 0 & -1 \end{bmatrix} \end{matrix}$$

which is triangular. For column 2 of the network matrix in Equation A1.11, we have a column vector $\mathbf{A}(2) = (1 - 1\,0\,0)^T = (1\,0\,0\,0)^T - (0\,1\,0\,0)^T$. This is converted to $\mathbf{y}'$ by mapping path $P = \{1, 3, 2\}$ in the tree T_B in Figure A1.8 against the orientation sequence, resulting in $(0\,1\,1\,0)^T$ according to Equation A1.13. In other words, we go down the vector entries corresponding to nodes 1, 2, 3, and 4 and ask where the arrow on the arrival node points. Is it with the path orientation (hence a +1 is assigned) or is it against (hence a −1 is assigned)? Notice $\mathbf{y}'$ checks out the matrix inverse algebra of

$$\mathbf{G}^{-1}\mathbf{A}(2) = \begin{bmatrix} 1 & 1 & 1 & 1 \\ 0 & -1 & -1 & -1 \\ 0 & -1 & 0 & 0 \\ 0 & 0 & 0 & -1 \end{bmatrix} \begin{bmatrix} 1 \\ -1 \\ 0 \\ 0 \end{bmatrix} = \begin{bmatrix} 0 \\ 1 \\ 1 \\ 0 \end{bmatrix}$$

as computed by "brute force" method above.

Now that the updated column $\mathbf{y}(2)$ in the network part of network-with-side-constraint tableau has been computed by graphical means as $(0\,1\,1\,0)^T$, the dual variable associated with node 2—or the "odometer reading" at node 2—of the network $\pi_2^1 = (\mathbf{w}^B)^T\mathbf{y}(2)$ can readily be computed. This is done by summing up the mileage $-3 - 10 = -13$, using the convention that flow goes from the root node (0 potential) to lower potentials (negative "odometer readings") at the other nodes. More formally, the dual variable $(\mathbf{w}^B)^T\mathbf{y}'$ for each updated column $\mathbf{y}'$, or $(\mathbf{w}^B)^T\mathbf{G}^{-1}$, is simply

$$\pi_j = \sum_{i=1}^{n} w_{ji}O_i'(P)$$

where the orientation sequence $O_2'(P)$ *and* $O_3'(P)$ are taken as -1's, a convention which will be explained shortly. Thus the complete pricing vector $\boldsymbol{\pi}^1 = (\pi_1^1, \pi_2^1, \pi_3^1, \pi_4^1) = (0 - 13 - 10 - 14)^T$ can be represented in Figure A1.9, where the superscript 1 is the extra notation that identifies this as the duals associated with the network part of the network-with-side-constraint tableau.

Notice that in this figure, it can be deduced also from the sequence $x_7\,x_2\,x_5\,x_6$ in $\mathbf{G}$ that

$$\mathbf{G}^{-1} = \begin{bmatrix} 1 & 1 & 1 & 1 \\ 0 & -1 & -1 & -1 \\ 0 & -1 & 0 & 0 \\ 0 & 0 & 0 & -1 \end{bmatrix} \begin{matrix} e_7 \\ e_2 \\ e_5 \\ e_6 \end{matrix}$$

which checks out with the algebraic inverse shown earlier. Here the first row are all ones corresponding to the orientation sequence of the root node, which is

Figure A1.9   CALCULATION OF $\boldsymbol{\pi}^1$ FOR PRICING

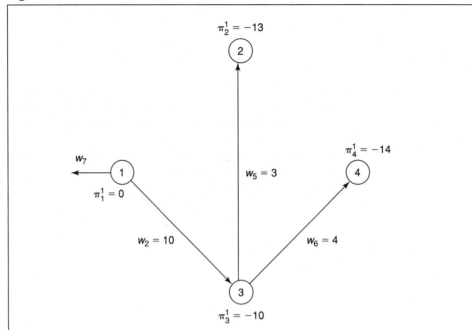

taken as +1 by convention. The other arcs, if pointing in the opposite direction, would have a negative orientation sequence. This explains a dual variable π_2^1 of -13 instead of $+13$ and $\pi_3^1 = -10$ instead of $+10$.

Step 2. Going back to the matrix expression for the dual variables $(v^1 \mid v^2)$ at the beginning of this pricing step discussion. Let $\pi^2 = [(\mathbf{w}^1)^T + (\mathbf{w}^1)^T \mathbf{G}^{-1}\mathbf{H}\mathbf{Q}^{-1}\mathbf{D} - (\mathbf{w}^2)^T \mathbf{Q}^{-1}\mathbf{D}] = [(\mathbf{w}^1)^T + \pi^1 \mathbf{H}\mathbf{Q}^{-1}\mathbf{D} - \mathbf{w}^2)^T \, \mathbf{Q}^{-1}\mathbf{D}]$. From this formula, we can compute $\pi^2 = (0\ 10\ 7/10\ 4)^T$ as:

$$(\boldsymbol{\pi}^2)^T = (0\ 10\ 3\ 4) + (0\ -13\ -10\ -14) \begin{bmatrix} 1 & 0 \\ -1 & 1 \\ 0 & -1 \\ 0 & 0 \end{bmatrix} \begin{bmatrix} 1/12 & 1/15 \\ 0 & 1/5 \end{bmatrix} \begin{bmatrix} 0 & 0 & -2 & 0 \\ 0 & 0 & 1 & 0 \end{bmatrix}$$

$$\hspace{6cm} (A1.14)$$

$$-(0 \quad 2) \begin{bmatrix} 1/12 & 1/15 \\ 0 & 1/5 \end{bmatrix} \begin{bmatrix} 0 & 0 & -2 & 0 \\ 0 & 0 & 10 & 0 \end{bmatrix}$$

Step 3. $(\mathbf{v}^1)^T = (\pi^2)^T \mathbf{G}^{-1}$ is equivalent to step 1 in which π^2 replaces $\mathbf{w}^B$. This is again solved graphically in Figure A1.10 by computing nodal potentials, resulting in $v^1 = (v_1^1\ v_2^1\ v_3^1\ v_4^1)^T = (0\ -10\ 7/10\ -10\ -14)^T$.

Step 4. $(v^2)^T = [(\mathbf{w}^2)^T - (\pi^1)^T \mathbf{H}]\mathbf{Q}^{-1}$

$$(\mathbf{v}^2)^T = \left\{ (0\ 2) - (0\ -13\ -10\ -14) \begin{bmatrix} 1 & 0 \\ -1 & 1 \\ 0 & -1 \\ 0 & 0 \end{bmatrix} \right\} \begin{bmatrix} 1/12 & 1/15 \\ 0 & 1/5 \end{bmatrix} = (-1\ \tfrac{1}{12}\ \tfrac{1}{15}) \quad (A1.15)$$

Figure A1.10   CALCULATION OF v^1

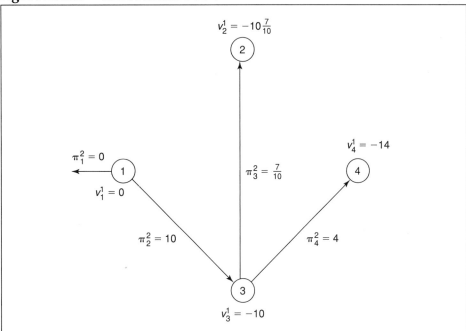

We now calculate the reduced costs using the dual variables $(\mathbf{v}^1 \mid \mathbf{v}^2)^T$ by examining the nonbasic column under x_4, the nonbasic variable under consideration: $\mathbf{N}(4) = (0 \; +1 \; 0 \; -1 \; +3 \; 0)^T$, where the reduced cost is $(\mathbf{v}^1 \mid \mathbf{v}^2)^T \mathbf{N}(4) - w_4$. For x_4: $v_2^1 - v_4^1 + 3v_1^2 - w_4 = -10 \; 7/10 - (-14) + 3(-1 \; 1/12) - 0 > 0$. This means entering of x_4 into the basis.

3. Ratio Test. Now is the time to pick an exit variable. Before the ratio test for exist variable selection is done, however, column updates need to be performed according to the revised simplex method, wherein only the columns of interest $\mathbf{y}'$ and $\mathbf{b}$ (i.e., column k of the tableau and the RHS) are updated. Here $\mathbf{y}' = \overline{\mathbf{B}}^{-1}\overline{\mathbf{A}}(k)$, where we write

$$\mathbf{y}' = \begin{bmatrix} \mathbf{y}^1 \\ \mathbf{y}^2 \end{bmatrix} \quad \text{and} \quad \overline{\mathbf{A}}(k) = \begin{bmatrix} \mathbf{A}(k) \\ \mathbf{B}(k) \end{bmatrix}$$

If the entering column corresponds to arc[4], then

$$\begin{bmatrix} \mathbf{y}^1 \\ \mathbf{y}^2 \end{bmatrix} = \begin{bmatrix} \mathbf{G}^{-1} + \mathbf{G}^{-1}\mathbf{H}\mathbf{Q}^{-1}\mathbf{D}\mathbf{G}^{-1} & -\mathbf{G}^{-1}\mathbf{H}\mathbf{Q}^{-1} \\ -\mathbf{Q}^{-1}\mathbf{D}\mathbf{G}^{-1} & \mathbf{Q}^{-1} \end{bmatrix} \begin{bmatrix} \mathbf{A}(k) \\ \mathbf{B}(k) \end{bmatrix}$$

$$= \begin{bmatrix} \mathbf{G}^{-1}\{\mathbf{A}(k) + \mathbf{H}\mathbf{Q}^{-1}\mathbf{D}\mathbf{G}^{-1}\mathbf{A}(k) - \mathbf{H}\mathbf{Q}^{-1}(k)\} \\ \mathbf{Q}^{-1}\{\mathbf{B}(k) - \mathbf{D}\mathbf{G}^{-1}\mathbf{A}(k)\} \end{bmatrix}$$

(A1.16)

Step 1. Considering the entering variable x_4, perform the intermediate column update $\mathbf{y}_1 = \mathbf{G}^{-1}\mathbf{A}(4)$ using part of Equation A1.16. This calculation is shown in Figure A1.11. Here $P = \{2 \; 3 \; 4\}$, which when matched against the arrows at the arrival node, shows that $\mathbf{y}_1 = (0 \; 0 \; -1 \; +1)^T$.

Figure A1.11 y_1 CALCULATION IN RATIO TEST

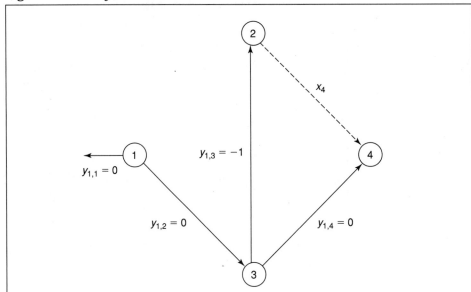

Step 2. From the first entry of the vector in Equation A1.16, define $y_2 = A(4) + HQ^{-1}Dy_1 - HQ^{-1}B(4)$

$$
y_2 = \begin{bmatrix} 0 \\ 1 \\ 0 \\ -1 \end{bmatrix} + \begin{bmatrix} 1 & 0 \\ -1 & 1 \\ 0 & -1 \\ 0 & 0 \end{bmatrix} \begin{bmatrix} 1/12 & 1/15 \\ 0 & 1/5 \end{bmatrix} \begin{bmatrix} 0 & 0 & -2 & 0 \\ 0 & 0 & 1 & 0 \end{bmatrix} \begin{bmatrix} 0 \\ 0 \\ -1 \\ 1 \end{bmatrix} - \begin{bmatrix} 1 & 0 \\ -1 & 1 \\ 0 & -1 \\ 0 & 0 \end{bmatrix} \begin{bmatrix} 1/12 & 1/15 \\ 0 & 1/5 \end{bmatrix} \begin{bmatrix} 3 \\ 0 \end{bmatrix} = \begin{bmatrix} -3/20 \\ 19/20 \\ 1/5 \\ -1 \end{bmatrix} \quad \text{(A1.17)}
$$

Step 3. Again, from the first entry of the vector in Equation A1.16, $y^1 = G^{-1}y_2$, where the basis G is inverted by graphic means in Figure A1.12. In these figures, we show the computations of y_1^1 by tracing the path from node 1 to node 1 in T_B, y_2^1 by tracing from 2 to 1, y_3^1 from 3 to 1, and y_4^1. Notice that instead of from node 1 to all other nodes, we are starting from other nodes to node 1, since we have the system $G^{-1}y$ rather than $\pi^T G^{-1}$ to solve.

From the graphs, or referencing the orientation sequences already contained in

$$
G^{-1} = \begin{bmatrix} 1 & 1 & 1 & 1 \\ 0 & -1 & -1 & -1 \\ 0 & -1 & 0 & 0 \\ 0 & 0 & 0 & -1 \end{bmatrix}
$$

we write

$$
y^1 = \begin{bmatrix} -3/20 \\ 0 \\ 0 \\ 0 \end{bmatrix} + \begin{bmatrix} 19/20 \\ -19/20 \\ -19/20 \\ 0 \end{bmatrix} + \begin{bmatrix} 1/5 \\ -1/5 \\ 0 \\ 0 \end{bmatrix} + \begin{bmatrix} -1 \\ 1 \\ 0 \\ 1 \end{bmatrix} = \begin{bmatrix} 0 \\ -3/20 \\ -19/20 \\ 1 \end{bmatrix}
$$

Figure A1.12   CALCULATION OF $\mathbf{y}^1$

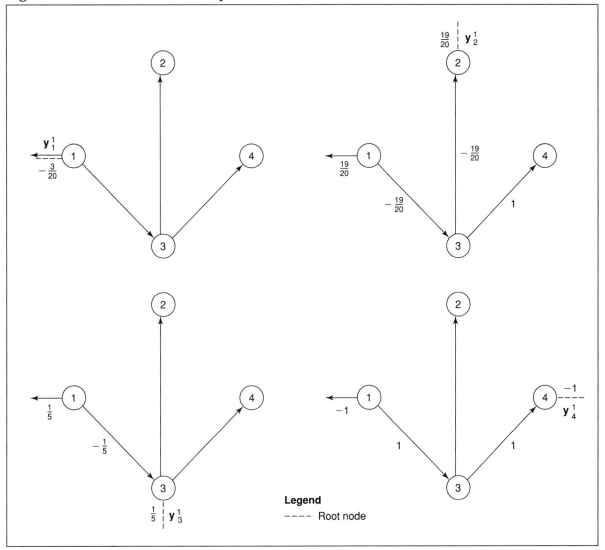

Step 4. According to Equation (A1.16), $\mathbf{y}^2 = \mathbf{Q}^{-1}[\mathbf{B}(4) - \mathbf{D}\mathbf{y}_1]$. Hence

$$\mathbf{y}^2 = \begin{bmatrix} 1/12 & 1/15 \\ 0 & 1/5 \end{bmatrix}\left\{\begin{bmatrix} 3 \\ 0 \end{bmatrix} - \begin{bmatrix} 0 & 0 & -2 & 0 \\ 0 & 0 & 1 & 0 \end{bmatrix}\begin{bmatrix} 0 \\ 0 \\ -1 \\ 1 \end{bmatrix}\right\} = \begin{bmatrix} 3/20 \\ 1/5 \end{bmatrix}$$

$$\begin{bmatrix} \mathbf{y}^1 \\ \mathbf{y}^2 \end{bmatrix} = (0 \ -3/20 \ -19/20 \ 1 \ 3/20 \ 1/5)^T.$$

Similarly

$$\overline{\mathbf{B}}^{-1}\begin{bmatrix} \mathbf{b} \\ \mathbf{b'} \end{bmatrix} = (0 \ 8 \ 0 \ 10 \ 22) \tag{A1.18}$$

For the column corresponding to the entering variable, we perform two types of ratio tests, since we have both a lower bound, 0, and upper bound, d_k, on the decision variables. The following tests correspond to the condition under which the basic variable drops to its lower bound or reaches its upper bound respectively:

$$\Delta_1 = \min_{1 \le j \le m} \left\{ \frac{x_j^B - 0}{|y_j|}, \infty \right\} = \left\{ \frac{x_j^B}{|y_j|}, \infty \right\} = \min \left\{ \frac{10}{1}, \frac{2}{\frac{3}{20}}, \frac{2}{\frac{1}{5}} \right\} = 10 \qquad \text{(A1.19)}$$

for positive entries in $\mathbf{y}'$, and

$$\Delta_2 = \min_{1 \le j \le m} \left\{ \frac{d_j^B - x_j^B}{|y_j|}, \infty \right\} = \min \left\{ \frac{18 - 8}{\frac{3}{20}}, \frac{1 - 0}{\frac{19}{20}} \right\} = \frac{20}{19} \qquad \text{(A1.20)}$$

for negative entries.

Considering the case when the entering variable x_k can reach its upper bound and hence be the restricting variable, the tolerable increase in resource engagement overall is

$$\Delta = \min\{\Delta_1, \Delta_2, d_4\} = \min\{10, 20/19, 12\} = 20/19 \qquad \text{(A1.21)}$$

In this case, the leaving variable will be x_5 remembering the order of the variables in $\overline{\mathbf{B}}$ *and* $\overline{\mathbf{B}}^{-1}$ is x_7, x_2, x_5, x_6, x_1, and x_3.

This completes a simplex-on-a-graph iteration, consisting of one pricing operation and one ratio test for the sample problem. The network-with-side-constraint algorithm is used in locating satellite tracking stations in the "Facility Location" chapter under the "Generalized p-Median Problem" section in Chan (2000).

III. LAGRANGIAN RELAXATION

As can be seen from network with side constraints, for large-scale linear programs (LPs) or mixed integer programs (MIPs) with a special structure decomposition methods can be employed for computational efficiency. The central idea is to exploit the nice properties of the well-structured part of the mathematical program (such as a network matrix) and to set aside the more complicated part in the interim. Hence the term relaxation is sometimes used in the general decomposition procedure of this kind.

A. Illustration of Basic Concepts

A more general way to introduce decomposition is through Lagrange relaxation, which we will explain through an integer programming (IP) example (Fisher 1985)

$$\begin{aligned}
\min z_{IP} = {}&{-16x_1} \quad {-10x_2} \qquad\qquad {-4x_4} \\
\text{s.t.} \quad &{-8x_1} \quad {-2x_2} \quad {-x_3} \quad {-4x_4} \ge -10 \\
&{-x_1} \quad {-x_2} \qquad\qquad\qquad \ge -1 \qquad\qquad \text{(P)} \\
&\qquad\qquad\qquad {-x_3} \quad {-x_4} \ge -1 \\
&x_j = 0 \text{ or } 1 \text{ for all } j
\end{aligned}$$

which has the form

$$\min z_{IP} = \mathbf{c}^T\mathbf{x}$$
$$\mathbf{A}^1\mathbf{x} \geq \mathbf{b}^1$$
$$\mathbf{A}^2\mathbf{x} \geq \mathbf{b}^2 \tag{A1.22}$$

The first constraint is judged to be the complicated one and we form the relaxed Lagrangian by dualizing it:

$$
\begin{aligned}
z_{LR}(\lambda) &= \min\,[-16x - 10x_2 - 4x_4 + \lambda(-10 + 8x_1 + 2x_2 + x_3 + 4x_4)]\\
&= \min\,[-x_1(16 - 8\lambda) - x_2(10 - 2\lambda) - x_3(0 - \lambda) - x_4(4 - 4\lambda) - 10\lambda]\\
\text{s.t.}\quad & -x_1 - x_2 \geq -1\\
& -x_3 - x_4 \geq -1\\
& x_j \in \{0, 1\}\quad \text{for all } j
\end{aligned}
\tag{LR(λ)}
$$

Here we have formed the Lagrangian relaxation problem

$$
\begin{aligned}
z_{LR}(\boldsymbol{\lambda}) &= L(\mathbf{x}, \boldsymbol{\lambda}) = \min_x\,[\mathbf{c}^T\mathbf{x} + {}^{\lambda T}(\mathbf{b}^1 - \mathbf{A}^1\mathbf{x})]\\
\text{s.t.}\ & \mathbf{A}^2\mathbf{x} \geq \mathbf{b}^2\\
& \mathbf{x}_j = \{0, 1\}\quad \text{for all } j
\end{aligned}
\tag{LR($\boldsymbol{\lambda}$)}
$$

Notice that a network-with-side-constraints model can be formulated as a Langrangian relaxation problem when $\mathbf{A}^2 = \mathbf{A}$ and $\mathbf{A}^1 = [\mathbf{B}\ \mathbf{C}]$.

For the dual variable $\boldsymbol{\lambda}$ fixed at some non-negative value this problem is easy to solve (as a network flow problem for example), as shown in Figure A1.13 where the dual variable is fixed at its optimal value λ^*. The mathematical program reduces to minimizing over $\mathbf{x}$ (a discrete variable), yielding the optimal

Figure A1.13   MIN IN x AND MAX IN λ FOR A WEAK DUALITY

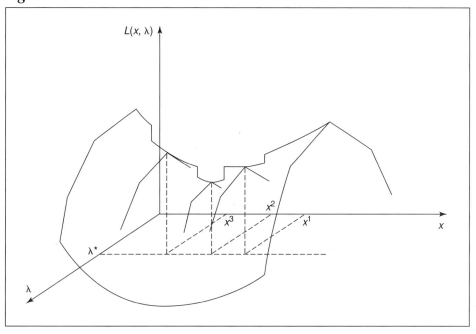

value at $x^* = x^2$. (Notice this includes the case of multiple optima.) For any other values of λ, a weak duality results, which says that the resulting optimization over x will yield a z value smaller than before relaxation—some kind of a super optimum. The inequality $z_{LR}(\lambda) \leq z_{IP}$ allows LR(λ) to be used in place of LP to provide lower bounds (cuts) in a branch and bound (B&B) algorithm for IP, where the bounds are usually tighter than LP relaxation.[5] The solution x^* is optimal to IP if there is a λ^* such that $z_{LR}(\lambda^*) = z_{IP}$.

B. Underlying Theory

Restating the above in more formal terms:

$$z_{LR}(\lambda) = \min_x \{z(\lambda, x): x \in \text{conv}(\tilde{Q}')\} \tag{LR}$$

where the convex hull $\text{conv}(\tilde{Q}')$ is formed from a convex combination of discrete points defined by $A^2 x \geq b^2$. An example of this can be shown in Figure A1.14 below. It is interesting to contrast this with LP relaxation, in which $z_{LP} = \min_x \{c^T x: x \in S\}$ where $S = \{x \in R_+^n: Ax \geq b\}$. Here R_+^n is the domain of continuous non-negative variables, rather than the discrete variables that are of real interest. We can now view the Lagrangian relaxation problem as minimization over a set of discrete points:

Figure A1.14   OPTIMIZING OVER A CONVEX HULL

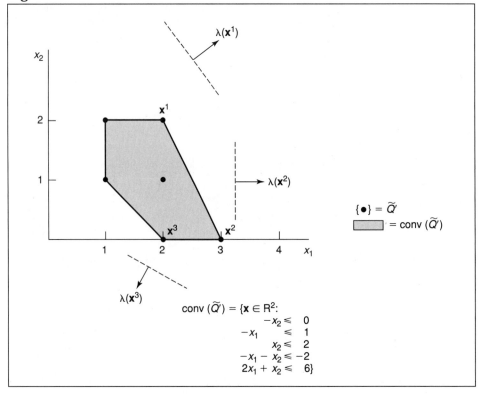

$$z_{LR}(\boldsymbol{\lambda}) = \min_{x_i \in \tilde{Q}'} z(\boldsymbol{\lambda}, \mathbf{x}')$$

and to observe that for fixed $\mathbf{x}^i$, $z(\boldsymbol{\lambda}, \mathbf{x}^i) = \mathbf{c}^T \mathbf{x}^i + \boldsymbol{\lambda}(\mathbf{b}^1 - \mathbf{A}^1 \mathbf{x}^i)$ is a function of $\boldsymbol{\lambda}$.

Ideally, $\boldsymbol{\lambda}$ should solve the Lagrangian dual problem z_{LD} in accordance with expression (LD) below, which provides the best choice of λ.

$$z_{LD} = \max_{\boldsymbol{\lambda} \leq 0} z_{LR}(\boldsymbol{\lambda}) \tag{LD}$$

z_{LD} is always linear in $\boldsymbol{\lambda}$. Based on the constraints of the relaxed program, a finite number of combinations for x_j are admissible, $\mathbf{x}^1, \mathbf{x}^1, \ldots, \mathbf{x}^{|J|}$. These values and the resultant piecewise linear function are shown in Figure A1.15. Contrast this with LP relaxation in which $z_{LP}(\mathbf{u}) = \max_{\mathbf{u}}\{\mathbf{b}^T \mathbf{u} : \mathbf{u} \in P_D\}$ where $P_D = \{\mathbf{u} \in R_+^m : \mathbf{A}^T \mathbf{u} \leq \mathbf{c}\}$ and $z_{LP}(\mathbf{u}) \leq z_{IP}$. Here, columns are appended to the dual of the LP corresponding to the imposition of integer values in the branching process. Until all variables are integerized, LP relations will yield super-optima. In Lagrangian relaxation, we are expressing LD formally as an LP with many constraints:

$$z_{LR}(\boldsymbol{\lambda} = \max_{\boldsymbol{\lambda} \geq 0} \{z' : z' \leq z(\boldsymbol{\lambda}, \mathbf{x}^i) \text{ for } i = 2, \ldots, |J|\} \tag{LD'}$$

In other words:

$$
\begin{aligned}
\text{Max } & z' \\
\text{s.t. } & {-20 + 2\lambda \geq z'} \quad {-10 - 8\lambda \geq z'} \\
& {-16 - 2\lambda \geq z'} \quad\quad\;\; {-10\lambda \geq z'} \\
& {-14 - 4\lambda \geq z'} \quad\quad\quad\;\; {\lambda \geq 0}
\end{aligned}
$$

This problem is sketched out in Figure A1.15. Problem (LD') makes it apparent that $z_{LR}(\boldsymbol{\lambda})$ is the lower envelope of a finite family of linear functions. The function $z_{LR}(\boldsymbol{\lambda})$ has all the nice properties, like continuity and concavity, that lend themselves to hill climbing algorithms (specifically subgradient optimization) (Ahuja et al. 1993; Nemhauser and Wolsey 1988).

C. Subgradient Optimization

It is appropriate at this juncture to explain the subgradient optimization algorithm (Fisher 1985). At differentiable points of Figure A1.15, the derivative of $z_{LR}(\boldsymbol{\lambda})$ with respect to λ is given by $\mathbf{A}^1 \mathbf{x} - \mathbf{b}^1$ or $8x_1 + 2x_2 + x_3 + 4x_4 - 10$ in our example, where $\mathbf{x}$ is an optimal solution to LR($\boldsymbol{\lambda}$). These facts also hold in general with the gradient of the $z_{LR}(\boldsymbol{\lambda})$ function at differentiable points given by $\mathbf{A}^1 \mathbf{x} - \mathbf{b}^1$, where $\mathbf{x}$ may not be optimal. This observation suggests it might be fruitful to apply a gradient search method to maximize $z_{LR}(\boldsymbol{\lambda})$ with some adaptation at the points where $z_{LR}(\boldsymbol{\lambda})$ is nondifferentiable. The subgradient method chooses arbitrarily from the set of alternative optimal Lagrangian solutions $\mathbf{x}^i$ at these nondifferentiable points and use the vector $\mathbf{A}^1 \mathbf{x} - \mathbf{b}^1$ for this solution as though it were the gradient of LD'. The result is a procedure that determines a sequence of values for $\boldsymbol{\lambda}$ by beginning at an initial point $\boldsymbol{\lambda}^0$ (such as zero) and applying the following formula. We illustrate this problem for the case where $\boldsymbol{\lambda}$ is scalar:

Figure A1.15   MAXIMIZATION IN DUAL VARIABLE

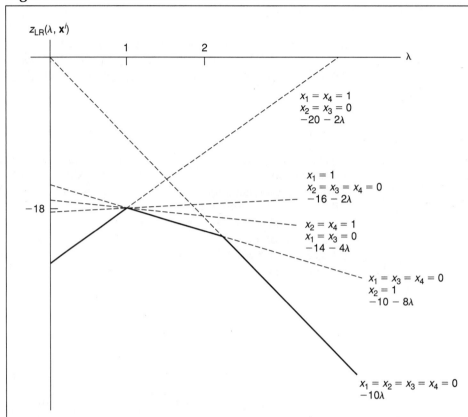

$$\lambda^{k+1} = \max \left[0, \lambda^k - t_k(\mathbf{b}^1 - \mathbf{A}^1\mathbf{x}^k) \right] \tag{A1.23}$$

In this formula, t_k is a scalar step size and $\mathbf{x}^k$ is an optimal solution to LR(λ^k), the Lagrangian problem with dual variables set to λ^k. Equation A1.23 can be thought of as a generalization of the method of steepest ascent in nonlinear programming when the objective function is piecewise linear (See Section III-F in Chapter 4). The choice is between staying put and moving along a gradient, whichever is better. Even though we have illustrated subgradient optimization only through the scalar example, multiple dimension generalization of Equation A1.23 can be found in the formalization below and in Nemhauser and Wolsey (1988) and Reeves (1993).

The nondifferentiability also requires some variation in the way the step size is normally set in a gradient method. A formula for t_k that has proven effective in practice is

$$t_k = \frac{\tau_k(z_{\text{LR}}(\lambda^k) - z^*_{\text{IP}})}{\displaystyle\sum_{i=1}^{m^1} \left(b_i^1 - \sum_{j=1}^{n} a_{ij}^1 x_j^k\right)^2} = \frac{\tau_k(z_{\text{LE}}(\lambda^k) - z^*_{\text{IP}})}{\left\| \mathbf{b}^1 - \mathbf{A}\mathbf{x}^k \right\|} \tag{A1.24}$$

In this formula, z_{IP}^* is the objective function value of the best known feasible solution to the original problem P and τ_k is a user defined scalar chosen between 0 and 2. It is assumed here that there are m^1 complicated constraints in $\mathbf{A}^1\mathbf{x} \geq \mathbf{b}^1$. Notice Equation A1.24 measures the difference between z^* and the current Lagrangian objective against the Euclidean norm (or the l_2-norm as described in Chapter 5 of this book and the "Measuring Spatial Separation" chapter in Chan (2000). When the difference is large relative to the norm, a larger step size is taken and vice versa. Frequently, the sequence τ_k is determined by starting with $\tau_k = 2$ and reducing τ_k by a factor of two whenever LR($\boldsymbol{\lambda}^k$) has failed to increase in a specified number of iterations. The feasible value z^* initially can be set to 0 and then updated using the solutions that are obtained on those iterations, in which the Lagrangian problem solution turns out to be feasible in the original problem P. Unless we obtained a $\boldsymbol{\lambda}^k$ for which LR($\boldsymbol{\lambda}^k$) = z_{IP}^*, there is no way of proving optimality in the subgradient method. To resolve this difficulty, the algorithm is usually terminated upon reaching a specified iteration limit.

Example
Here is an example of the subgradient method illustrating the judicious choice of step sizes:

k	Dual variable λ_k	Step size t_k
0	0	1
1	max[0, 0 − (1)(−2)] = 2	1/2
2	max[0, 2 − (1/2)(8)] = 2	1/4
3	max[0, 0 − (1/4)(−2)] = 1/2	1/8
4	max[0, 1/2 − (1/8)(−2)] = 3/4	1/16
5	max[0, 3/4 − (1/16)(−2)] = 7/8	1/32
6	max[0, 7/8 − (1/32)(−2)] = 15/16	etc.

As can be seen, the algorithm converges nicely to the optimal value of $\lambda = 1$. ∎

Subgradient Optimization Algorithm
The subgradient algorithm can now be applied to the Langrangian relaxation problem as follows:

> **Step 1:** Solve the Lagrangian relaxation problem LR($\boldsymbol{\lambda}^k$) to obtain the optimal $\mathbf{x}^k$.
> **Step 2:** Evaluate the subgradient $\mathbf{g}(\boldsymbol{\lambda}^k) = \mathbf{b}^1 - \mathbf{A}^1\mathbf{x}^k$. If $\mathbf{g}(\boldsymbol{\lambda}^k) = \mathbf{0}$, stop; ($\boldsymbol{\lambda}^k$, $\mathbf{x}^k$) is an optimal solution.
> **Step 3:** Let $\boldsymbol{\lambda}^{k+1} = \boldsymbol{\lambda}^k + t_k\mathbf{g}(\boldsymbol{\lambda}^k)$, which is a m^1-entry vector generalization of Equation A1.23. Increment counter $k + 1 \to k$, and go to step 1.

From Figure A1.15, it is easy to see that $\lambda = 1$ maximizes $z_{LR}(\lambda)$. Thus the lower bound is $z_{LR}(1) = -18$ and a corresponding feasible solution of $z_{IP} = -16$ by inspection, namely one of three feasible solutions[6] $\mathbf{x} = (1, 0, 0, 0)$, $(0, 1, 0, 0)$, or $(0, 1, 0, 1)$, $(1, 0, 0, 0)$ yields $z_{IP}(1, 0, 0, 0) = -16$. Formally, the lower bound -18 should now be used in B&B to arrive at the optimal solution $\mathbf{x}^*$. In other words, by taking a convex combination of points in $\tilde{Q}'$, we obtain a point x^* in conv($\tilde{Q}'$) satisfying the complicating constraint, for which $\mathbf{c}^T\mathbf{x}^* = z_{LD}$. This shows that for the example we obtain $z_{LD} = \min\{\mathbf{c}^T\mathbf{x}:\mathbf{A}^1\mathbf{x} \geq \mathbf{b}^1, \mathbf{x} \in \text{conv}(\tilde{Q}')\}$. The major result is as follows: The primal LP problem of finding a convex combination of points in $\tilde{Q}'$ that also satisfies the complicating constraint $\mathbf{A}^1\mathbf{x} \geq \mathbf{b}^1$ or $-8x_1 - 2x_2 - x_3 - 4x_4 \geq -10$ is dual to the Lagrangian dual, or the solution is optimal.

D. Branch and Bound (B&B) Solution

While we showed above how the optimum can be obtained, this is not simple in general. Oftentimes, we need to resort to a tree search (B&B) procedure to resolve the problem (as explained in Section III-B of Chapter 4). We use the traditional B&B procedure in which a tree of solution alternatives is constructed with certain variables fixed to specified values at each node of the tree, representing a proposal $\mathbf{x}^{i_k}$. Shown below is a tabular display of the various contending solutions at $\lambda = 1$ in Figure A1.15. It serves to illustrate a B&B tree that can lead toward the optimal solution via pruning rules such as infeasibility, dominance, and incumbency[7]:

λ	Lagrangian solution					z_{IP}
	x_1	x_2	x_3	x_4	$z_{\text{LR}}(\lambda)$	
1	1	0	0	0	-18	-16^*
1	1	0	0	1	-18	Infeasible
1	0	1	0	0	-18	-10
1	0	1	0	1	-18	-14

Figure A1.16   GENERIC LAGRANGIAN RELAXATION ALGORITHM

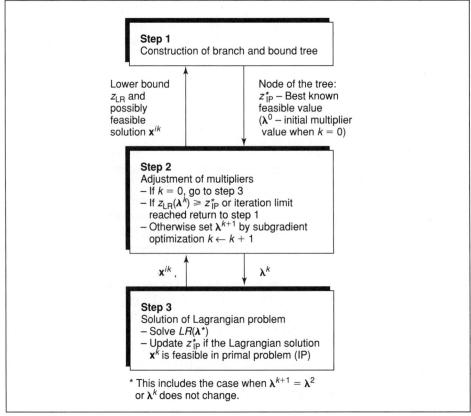

SOURCE: Fisher (1985). Reprinted with permission.

For example, a B&B tree will be pruned at the infeasible solution node as represented by the second line of the table. Similarly, the solutions on the third and fourth lines are dominated by the solution of -16 in the first line. All things said and done, here the solution at the first line is the optimum, yielding $\mathbf{x}^* = (1\ 0\ 0\ 0)$ and $z^*_{IP} = 16$.

Insightful as this example may be, left unexplained is the procedure to generate the $\mathbf{x}^i$, from which the constraints of (LD$'$) can be generated. For a totally unimodular matrix, such as the one shown in $\mathbf{A}^2$, the $\mathbf{x}^i$s are discernable. However, this is not the case in general, when the extreme points of the polyhedron $\mathbf{A}^2\mathbf{x} \geq \mathbf{b}^2$ are not integer valued. Suppose we start out with a couple of integer points $\mathbf{x}^{i_0}$ on an integer convex-hull $\tilde{Q}'$, from which $z_{LD}(\boldsymbol{\lambda})$ can be maximized at $\boldsymbol{\lambda}^0$. Then for $\boldsymbol{\lambda}^{0'} \neq \boldsymbol{\lambda}^0$ we solve for $z_{LR}(\boldsymbol{\lambda}^{0'}, \mathbf{x})$ according to (LR) for additional $\mathbf{x}^{ij}$ with which (LD$'$) can be solved again, often with the help of a B&B tree. The process then gets repeated again for the $\boldsymbol{\lambda}^1$ so obtained, until two subsequent iterations yield the same $z_{LR}(\boldsymbol{\lambda}^*, \mathbf{x}^*)$. The generic Lagrangian-relaxation algorithm is illustrated in Figure A1.16. This figure shows the complete Lagrangian relaxation algorithm consisting of three major steps. The first step is the standard B&B process in which a tree of solution alternatives $\{\mathbf{x}^k\}$ is generated with certain variables fixed to specified values at each node of the tree, namely the $\boldsymbol{\lambda}^k$ values. These specified values are passed from block 1 to block 2 together with z^*_{IP}, the objective function value of the currently best-known feasible solution. In the initial step, we set $k = 0$ and the value of the starting multipliers $\boldsymbol{\lambda}^0$ (normally to $\mathbf{0}$).

We iterate between blocks 2 and 3, adjusting the multipliers $\boldsymbol{\lambda}^k$ with the vector generalization of the subgradient update and obtaining a new Lagrangian solution $\mathbf{x}^k$ respectively. This process continues until we either reach an interation limit or discover an upper bound that is less than or equal to the current best-known feasible solution z^*_{IP}. At this point, we pass back to block 1 the best upper-bound together with any feasible solution z^*_{IP} that may have been obtained as a result of solving the Lagrangian problem LR($\boldsymbol{\lambda}^k$).

According to Fisher (1985), it is not uncommon in large-scale applications to terminate the process depicted in Figure A1.16 before the B&B tree has been explored sufficiently to prove optimality. Beasley shared many of his computational experiences in Reeves (1993). In this case, the Lagrangian algorithm is really a heuristic—similar to LP relaxation—with some nice properties, such as the maximum amount by which the heuristic solution z^*_{IP} deviates from optimality. Related discussions on Lagrangian relaxation can be found in Chapter 4, Section V in this book and in the "Facility Location" chapter in Chan (2000) under "Median Location Problems."

IV. BENDERS' DECOMPOSITION

Lagrangian relaxation takes care of complicating constraints by incorporating them in the objective function. Here we consider the allied problem of complicating variables. Suppose we have the following mixed integer program (MIP)

$$z = \max \mathbf{g}^T\mathbf{y} + \mathbf{c}^T\mathbf{x}$$
$$\text{s.t.} \quad \mathbf{B}\mathbf{y} + \mathbf{A}\mathbf{x} \leq \mathbf{b}$$

where $\mathbf{x}$ are non-negative discrete variables of dimension n ($\mathbf{y} \in Y'' \subseteq Z''_+$), *and* $\mathbf{x}$ are continuous non-negative variables of dimension p ($\mathbf{x} \in R^p_+$). We think of the discrete variables $\mathbf{y}$ as complicating variables to what would otherwise be a linear program (LP), or we can view the continuous variables $\mathbf{x}$ as complicating variables to what would have been a pure integer program. Instead of Lagrangian relaxation, an allied procedure called Benders' decomposition is employed to solve this MIP.

A. Example

Let us illustrate with a numerical example (Nemhauser and Wolsey 1988).

$$
\begin{aligned}
\text{Max} \quad & 5y_1 - 2y_2 + 9y_3 + 2x_1 - 3x_2 + 4x_3 \\
\text{s.t.} \quad & 5y_1 - 3y_2 + 7y_3 + 2x_1 + 3x_2 + 6x_3 \leq -2 \\
& 4y_1 + 2y_2 + 4y_3 + 3x_1 - x_2 + 3x_3 \leq 10 \\
& y_j \leq 5 \text{ for } j = 1, 2, 3 \\
& \mathbf{y} \in Z_+^3, \mathbf{x} \in R_+^3
\end{aligned} \qquad (A1.25)
$$

Here

$$
Y = \{\mathbf{y} \in Z_+^3 : y_j \leq 5 \text{ for } j = 1, 2, 3\}
$$

As a first step, we suppose that the integer variables $\mathbf{y}$ have been fixed, in other words, projecting on $\mathbf{y}$. The resulting LP is:

$$
z_{LP}(\mathbf{x}) = \max\{\mathbf{c}^T\mathbf{x}: \mathbf{A}\mathbf{x} \leq \mathbf{b} - \mathbf{B}\mathbf{y}, \mathbf{x} \in R_+^p\} \qquad (A1.26)
$$

and its dual is

$$
\text{Min}\{(\mathbf{b} - \mathbf{B}\mathbf{y})\,\boldsymbol{\lambda} : \mathbf{A}\boldsymbol{\lambda} \geq \mathbf{c}, \boldsymbol{\lambda} \in R_+^m\} \qquad (A1.27)
$$

which forms a subproblem. For our current example, we have the dual polyhedron $\{\mathbf{A}\boldsymbol{\lambda} \geq \mathbf{c}, \boldsymbol{\lambda} \in R_+^2\}$ of dimension 2 or

$$
\begin{aligned}
2\lambda_1 + 3\lambda_2 &\geq 2 \\
3\lambda_1 - \lambda_2 &\geq -3 \\
6\lambda_1 + 3\lambda_2 &\geq 4 \\
\boldsymbol{\lambda} &\in R_+^2
\end{aligned}
$$

This polyhedron is sketched out in Figure A1.17, where the extreme points and extreme directions are shown. A bounded optimal solution can be represented by these extreme points and directions.

Let $\boldsymbol{\lambda}^1, \boldsymbol{\lambda}^2, \ldots, \boldsymbol{\lambda}^{|K|}$ be the extreme points and $\mathbf{d}^1, \mathbf{d}^2, \ldots, \mathbf{d}^{|J|}$ be the extreme directions of the dual polyhedron D''. Then any point $\boldsymbol{\lambda}$ in D'' can be represented by the extreme points and directions as we explained in Section I-B:

$$
\boldsymbol{\lambda} = \sum_{k \in K} w_k \boldsymbol{\lambda}^k + \sum_{j \in J} \mu_j \mathbf{d}^j
$$

$$
\sum_{k \in K} w_k = 1; \quad w_k, \mu_j \geq 0 \quad k \in K, j \in J \qquad (A1.28)
$$

If $z = \max_{x,y}\{\mathbf{g}^T\mathbf{y} + \mathbf{c}^T\mathbf{x}\}$, then $z = \max_y\{\mathbf{g}^T\mathbf{y} + \min\{\mathbf{b} - \mathbf{By}\}\boldsymbol{\lambda}\}$ for each $\boldsymbol{\lambda} \in D''$, *or* $z = \max_y\{\mathbf{g}^T\mathbf{y} + \min_{j\epsilon J}(\mathbf{b} - \mathbf{By})\boldsymbol{\lambda}^{j\cdot}$ Here λ^j includes both extreme points and extreme directions. But if $(\mathbf{b} - \mathbf{By})\mathbf{d}^j < 0$ for some j, we can choose μ_j large enough so that

$$z = \max_y\{\mathbf{g}^T\mathbf{y} + \min_{\lambda \in D}\{(\mathbf{b} - \mathbf{By})\boldsymbol{\lambda}\}$$

becomes infeasible. Hence we must impose the additional constraints $(\mathbf{b} - \mathbf{By})\mathbf{d}^j > 0$. [For those $(\mathbf{b} - \mathbf{By})\mathbf{d}^j > 0$, naturally we would gravitate toward the extreme points and move away from the extreme directions by setting the appropriate μ_j to zero.] The MIP can now be rewritten as

$$z = \max_y\{\mathbf{g}^T\mathbf{y} + \min_{k \in K}(\mathbf{b} - \mathbf{By})\boldsymbol{\lambda}^k\} \tag{A1.29}$$
$$(\mathbf{b} - \mathbf{By})\mathbf{d}^j \geq 0 \quad \text{for } j \epsilon J$$
$$\mathbf{y} \in Y''$$

and the problem can be reformulated as the master problem

$$z = \max z'$$
$$s.t. \ z' \leq \mathbf{g}^T\mathbf{y} + (\mathbf{b} - \mathbf{By})\boldsymbol{\lambda}^k \quad \text{for } k \in K \tag{A1.30}$$
$$(\mathbf{b} - \mathbf{By})\mathbf{d}^j \geq 0 \quad \text{for } j \in J$$
$$\mathbf{y} \in Y''$$

In our case for the finite number extreme points $\boldsymbol{\lambda}$ and extreme directions $\mathbf{d}$, the complete master problem (which is an all-integer program) looks like

Figure A1.17   DUAL POLYHEDRON FOR BENDERS' EXAMPLE

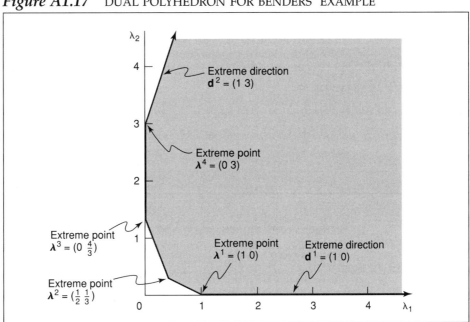

$$z = \max z'$$

$$s.t. \quad z' \leq 5y_1 - 2y_2 + 9y_3 + \quad (-2 - 5y_1 + 3y_2 - 7y_3)$$

$$z' \leq 5y_1 - 2y_2 + 9y_3 + \tfrac{1}{2}(-2 - 5y_1 + 3y_2 - 7y_3) + \tfrac{1}{3}(10 - 4y_1 - 2y_2 - 4y_3)$$

$$z' \leq 5y_1 - 2y_2 + 9y_3 \qquad\qquad\qquad\qquad + \tfrac{4}{3}(10 - 4y_1 - 2y_2 - 4y_3)$$

$$z' \leq 5y_1 - 2y_2 + 9y_3 \qquad\qquad\qquad\qquad + 3(10 - 4y_1 - 2y_2 - 4y_3)$$

$$-2 - 5y_1 + 3y_2 - 7y_3 \qquad\qquad\qquad\qquad\qquad \geq 0$$

$$-2 - 5y_1 + 3y_2 - 7y_3 + 3(10 - 4y_1 - 2y_2 - 4y_3) \geq 0$$

$$y_j \leq 5 \text{ for } j = 1, 2, 3$$

$$\mathbf{y} \in Z_+^3$$

It can be verified that an optimal solution is $\mathbf{y} = (0\ 3\ 1)^T$ and $z' = 3$. Using this information, it can be easily verified that $\mathbf{x} = (1\ 0\ 0\ 0)^T$ is part of the optimal solution to the example. This can be seen by substituting $\mathbf{y} = (0\ 3\ 1)^T$ into Equation A1.25 and solve the resulting LP in $\mathbf{x}$ as represented by Equation A1.26.

B. Convergence

In practice, there are an enormous number of constraints in the above master problem. A natural approach is to consider relaxations obtained by generating only those constraints corresponding to a small number of extreme points $k = 1$, $2, \ldots, k'$ and extreme directions, $j = 1, 2, \ldots, j'$. We call these the relaxed master problems, yielding an optimal solution $(z', \mathbf{y}'')$, which is an upper bound on z. The solution $(z', \mathbf{y}'')$ is optimal if and only if it is feasible to all constraints in the master problem. In other words, we wish to check the subproblem shown in Equation A1.27 where $\mathbf{y}$ is obtained from the optimal solution of the relaxed master problem [Equation A1.30]. Given a finite number of extreme points $k = 1, \ldots, |K|$ and a finite number of extreme directions $j = 1, \ldots, |J|$, an optimal solution $(z^*, \mathbf{y}^*)$ exists. Let $\boldsymbol{\lambda}'^*$ be an optimal extreme point corresponding to an iteration where $k' + 1$ extreme points and $j' + 1$ extreme directions have been generated. If the optimum is obtained, $z^* = \mathbf{g}^T\mathbf{y}^* + (\mathbf{b} - \mathbf{By}^*)\boldsymbol{\lambda}'^*$. Then $z' \leq \mathbf{g}^T\mathbf{y}^* + (\mathbf{b} - \mathbf{By}^*)\boldsymbol{\lambda}'^*$ for all k and j. Otherwise, generate additional extreme points and directions as necessary in accordance with the relaxed master problem. Notice the iterations are schematically represented in Figure A1.15 if we read $z_{LR}(\boldsymbol{\lambda}, \mathbf{x}^i)$ as $z(\boldsymbol{\lambda}, \mathbf{y}^k)$ according to Equation A1.30, even though the figure was drawn initially for Lagrangian relaxation.

An example illustrating the Benders' convergence process is found in the "Measuring Spatial Separation" chapter in Chan (2000) under the "Scheduling Restrictions" subsection. This is supplemented by a homework problem in which each step of the algorithm is spelled out in detail.

C. Extension

The discussion above can easily be extended to the case where the linear term $\mathbf{gy}$ in the objective function is a nonlinear function $f(\mathbf{y})$. In the above algorithm, simply replace $\mathbf{gy}$ with $f(\mathbf{y})$ throughout. The only difference is in the way we solve the master problem, which may involve a nonlinear solver. Nonlinear integer programming is not an easy task, however. In principle, the Benders' scheme can still be applied, taking full advantage of the part of the mathematical program which can be solved as a subproblem by LP.

Benders' decomposition is sometimes referred to as a resource-directive decomposition method. It starts with an initial solution consisting of, for instance, the discrete variable **y** and dual variable and adjusts the common resource available **b** by fixing the next **y** through master problem (30) and the corresponding (and hence **x**-variable) values through the dual subproblem (27). As suggested by Figure A1.15, this resource directive decomposition scheme can be viewed as an alternative approach to the subgradient search used in Lagrangian relaxation.

Benders' decomposition is also a competing approach for solving the multicommodity flow problem, formerly formulated in Section II-A as a network with side constraints. In this regard, the common flow capacity linking constraint is **By** and the commodity-flows are modeled by **Ax**. The Benders' approach decomposes the problem into a separate single commodity flow problem for each commodity by allocating the scarce bundle capacities to the various commodities. Finding the optimal allocation (in other words, the one that gives the overall lowest cost in this case) is an optimization problem with a simple constraint structure and a (complicated) convex cost objective function. Using sensitivity information about the single commodity subproblems, however, we can generate subgradient information about the resource allocation cost function and solve the allocation problem by a version of the subgradient optimization technique. Interested readers are referred to Ahuja et al. (1993) for further details. Benders' decomposition is an important and viable technique in solving location-routing models, as illustrated in the "Generalized Benders' Decomposition" subsection in the "Simultaneous Location-and-Routing Models" chapter in Chan (2000).

V. ALGORITHMS AND COMPLEXITY

Throughout this book, particularly in the discussions in this appendix, we are concerned with the efficiency of solution algorithms, which led to network-with-side-restraints and Benders' decomposition. The theory of computational complexity yields insights into how difficult a problem may be to solve and hence how much computational savings are obtainable from more efficient algorithms. For example, we may be able to show that in the order of $O(l^k)$ time, for some fixed k and data-input length l, an optimal solution is obtained. In this section, we wish to define some commonly used terms and to fix some basic notions.

- **Class P problems:** Most efficient min-path algorithms, for example, are polynomial P in execution time. As shown in the literature, the complexity is $O(m)$ for a path, $O(m^2)$ for a tree and $O(m^3)$ for a point-to-point computation, where m is the number of nodes in a network. The polynomial order makes min-cost-flow network algorithms an attractive alternative to more computationally demanding methods such as regular simplex, as illustrated in Section II-B.
- *NP problems:* In contrast, simplex LP is a non-deterministic polynomial (*NP*) problem. In the simplex algorithm, the number of elementary steps required to solve the $m \times n$ LP is $O(mn)$ arithmetic operations for each pivot iteration, since it can be viewed as a matrix vector multiplication. The simplex algorithm can, at worst, visit all

basic feasible solutions, and there are at most $\binom{m+n}{m}$ basic feasible solutions, requiring therefore $\binom{m+n}{m}$ pivots. All together, simplex is an $O(mn\binom{m+n}{m})$ algorithm. Notice this makes the simplex a much less efficient algorithm than network flow. The relationship between class P and NP is illustrated in Figure A1.18, in that polynomial problems are a subset, and a special case, of non-deterministic problems.

- **NP-completeness:** An *NP*-complete (*NPC*) problem is a computational problem that is as hard as any reasonable problem; specifically, an *NPC* problem is characterized by:

  1. No *NPC* problem can be solved by any known polynomial algorithm.
  2. If there is a polynomial algorithm for any *NPC* problem, then there are polynomial algorithms for all *NPC* problems.

Figure A1.18 shows the class of *NP* and the two subsets *P* and *NPC*, which are disjoint unless $P = NP$, which put us in the category of item 2 above. If $P \neq NP$, it can be shown that $P \cup NPC \neq NP$.

Example
The (symmetric) traveling salesman problem (TSP) seeks to find the lowest cost tour among m nodes and return home.[8] There are $(m-1)!/2$ possible tours in a network, where a tour (or Hamilton circuit) is a path traversing each node in the network exactly once. There is a solution to TSP if and only if a Hamilton circuit exists. TSP is an *NPC* problem (even though the Hamilton circuit problem may be a *P* problem). Finding the TSP tour among the 50 state capitals in the United States, for instance, could require many billions of years, with the fastest computer available. ∎

NP-hard problems: One problem polynomially reduces to another if a polynomially bounded number of calls to an algorithm for the second will always solve the first. Sometimes we may be able to show that all problems in *NP* polynomially reduce to some problem α''. But we are unable to argue that $\alpha'' \in NP$. So α''

Figure A1.18   TYPES OF COMPLEXITY

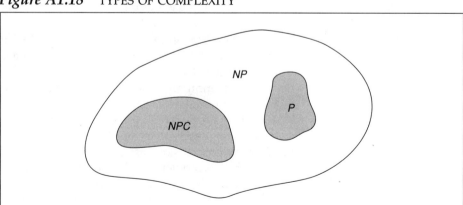

does not qualify to be called *NP*-complete. Yet undoubtedly α'' is as hard as any problem in *NP*, and hence most probably intractable. It is for these problems that we have reserved the term *NP*-hard. A polynomial algorithm for an *NP*-hard problem implies $P = NP$. Problems that are both *NP*-hard and member of the class *NP* are called *NPC* (Figure A1.18.). It has turned out that the family of *NP*-hard problems is amazingly rich, including 0-1 integer/mixed integer programming (polynomial backtracking)[9].

To date, complexity theory is still evolving and may continue to do so for quite some time. With or without complexity theory, however, practitioners will continue to be confronted by significant discrete problems in all sorts of management and engineering settings. To date, the main value of the theory for practitioners has been to provide a theoretical base that confirms long held suspicions. Most importantly, it allows us to gauge the worst-case scenarios of efficiency independent of computer hardware and software—both of which are evolving too rapidly to allow for meaningful comparisons across diverse computational platforms. One must note that the worst-case behavior of an algorithm might be markedly different from its behavior in practice. Indeed, several *NP* and *NPC* algorithms can be solved very efficiently in practice. An example is the simplex algorithm, which has undergone generations of streamlining to make it competitive with polynomial LP solvers. However, in the words of Ahuja et al. (1993), we can safely say *NPC* problems sometimes do not have algorithms that can solve large practical instances in reasonable time, whereas problems in class *P* often have.

VI. CONCLUDING REMARKS

This appendix describes some fundamental optimization algorithms that are applicable to the solution of facility location and land use problems. Of particular interest is the notion of decomposition, which can greatly accelerate an algorithm, including the case of mixed integer programs. Decomposition is broadly defined to mean the exploitation of special structure of the problem. Thus in a network-with-side-constraint model, we take advantage of the network part of the tableau by using efficient labeling algorithms in lieu of regular simplex. In this fashion, basis inverses—the more computationally intensive part of the process—are cut down to a minimum.

In Langrangian relaxation, we set aside the complicated part of the constraints and concentrate on the nice ones first. Likewise, in Benders' decomposition, we defer facing the complicated variables in preference for the better behaved ones. We bridged the gap between Lagrangian relaxation and Benders' decomposition by pointing out that both can be best illustrated by a plot of both the primal and dual space. The iterative procedure can be portrayed as a series of adjustments on the pricing scheme, represented as different slopes on the objective functions. Alternatively, the computations can be viewed as a sequence of cuts in the dual space, where each cut brings the solution closer to the optimal resource allocation. These are equally convenient and insightful ways of looking at the problem. An example of the pricing scheme can be found in Figure A1.14. There the slope of the objective functions is obtained for each extreme point defined either by **x** in Lagrangian relaxation or **y** in Benders' decomposition. An example of the cutting scheme can be found in Figure A1.15, where the dual variable is λ for the respective examples for Lagrangian relaxation and Benders' decomposition. Of equal importance here is the relationship between bounding techniques, decomposition, and duality. They represent promising analytical solution techniques in dealing with complicating constraints or decision variables in a mathematical program.

We conclude with a discussion on computational complexity—a taxonomy to categorize algorithmic efficiency. Drawing upon the examples worked out in this appendix, we have defined the commonly used terms such as polynomial, non-deterministic polynomial *(NP)*, *NP*-complete, and *NP*-hard. These terms are used extensively in the literature. Through this taxonomy, we are able to comfortably justify the efficient algorithms introduced in this appendix, showing how they compare with the more traditional approaches. While computational complexity is a useful concept, we must point out that there are issues that go beyond the categorizations. It is possible to classify algorithms and problems by their data structure. This final point is particularly relevant as we design geographic information systems to support facility location and land use models. (See Chapter 6 in this book and the "Spatial-Temporal Information" chapter in Chan [2000]).

ENDNOTES

[1] The dual of an LP is defined, according to Chapter 4, as $\min\{(\lambda_1 + \lambda_2): 3\lambda_1 + 5\lambda_2 \geq 1, 6\lambda_1 + 4\lambda_2 \geq 1\}$, where λ_1 and λ_2 and non-negative dual variables.

[2] For a review of basic network-flow terminology, the reader is referred to Chapter 4, Section IV.

[3] Complementary slackness is explained in Chapter 4, Section III-C.

[4] When the entering variable is **y** instead of **x**, similar algebra applies. For details, see Kennington and Helgason (1980).

[5] LP relaxation is a common way to solve IP problems by ignoring integrality and solve the resulting LP. The integrality requirements are subsequently re-introduced through a branch and bound on the fractional variables. For a discussion and illustration of LP relaxation, see Chapter 4 (Section II-B) and the "Facility Location" chapter in Chan (2000) respectively.

[6] Notice the fourth extreme point (1, 0, 0, 1) is infeasible since it violates the complicated constraint $-8x_1 - 2x_2 - x_3 - 4x_4 \geq 10$.

[7] The terms infeasibility, dominance, and incumbency are defined in Chapter 4, Section II-B.

[8] For a complete discussion of the traveling salesman problem, see the chapter on "Measuring Spatial Separation" in Chan (2000).

[9] For a discussion of 0–1 integer/mixed integer programming algorithms, including backtracking and branch and bound, see Chapter 4.

REFERENCES

Ahuja, R. K.; Magnanti, T. L.; Orlin, J. B. (1993). *Network flows: Theory, algorithms, and applications.* Englewood Cliffs, New Jersey: Prentice-Hall.

Bazaraa, M. S.; Jarvis, J. J.; Serali, H. D. (1990). *Linear programming and network flows,* 2nd ed. New York: Wiley.

Chan, Y. (2000). *Location, transport, and land-use: Modelling spatial-temporal information.* New York: Springer-Verlag.

Fisher, M. S. (1985). "An applications oriented guide to Lagrangian relaxation." *Interfaces* (Operations Research Society of America) 15, no. 2:10–21.

Hillier, F. S.; Lieberman, G. J. (1990). *Introduction to mathematical programming.* New York: McGraw-Hill.

Kennington, J. L.; Helgason, R. V. (1980). *Algorithms for network programming.* New York: Wiley.

Nemhauser, G. L.; Wolsey, L. A. (1988). *Integer and combinatorial optimization.* New York: Wiley.

Reeves, C. R., ed. (1993). *Modern heuristic techniques for combinatorial problems.* New York: Halsted Press.

Winston, W. L. (1995). *Introduction to mathematical programming: Applications and algorithms,* 2nd ed. Belmont. California: Duxbury Press.

Appendix 2

Review of Pertinent Markovian Processes

In making locational decisions over time, we face a world of uncertainty. In this appendix, we put together the basic concepts behind time-dependent probabilistic processes (or stochastic processes), including Poisson (random), queuing, Markov, and state-transition procedures in general. Particularly of interest is optimizing a Markovian decision system. A basic building block of these methodologies is the Markovian (or memoryless) property, which suggests independence among sequential outcomes. By discussing the "memoryless properties" that govern many of these phenomena, reference is made to dynamic programming, non-Markovian processes and compartmental models as well. All these are extensions to the basic concepts. While compartmental models will be discussed in detail in Appendix 4, their relationship to Markov process is delineated here. This appendix logically follows Appendix 1 by addressing the question of prescriptive modeling under uncertainty.

I. POISSON PROCESS

One of the motivations to study stochastic process is to address problems of congestion. Congestion is often manifested in terms of waiting lines (or queues) at a service facility such as a fire station, which has to respond to probabilistic demands over the entire neighborhood it serves. Given demands are usually random and there is a limited number of fire engines, the fire station can be taxed to its limit on occasions. Stochastic process helps us to understand such situations and to offer possible solutions.

A. State Transition Equations

The first step in the analysis process is to understand how random demands arrive. To represent random demands, consider the state transition diagram shown in Figure A2.1, where each state stands for the number of demands arriving in the period of time t. Let p_{ij} stand for the probability of transitioning from state i to j or that the demand changes from i to j. The differential equations governing the evolution of the system over time, when demands arrive at an average rate of λ'', becomes

$$
\begin{aligned}
\dot{p}_{00}(t) &= -\lambda'' p_{00}(t) \\
\dot{p}_{01}(t) &= \lambda'' p_{00}(t) - \lambda'' p_{01}(t) \\
\dot{p}_{02}(t) &= \lambda'' p_{01}(t) - \lambda'' p_{02}(t) \\
&\ . \\
&\ . \\
&\ .
\end{aligned}
\tag{A2.1}
$$

etc.,

Figure A2.1   CUMULATIVE ARRIVAL PATTERN AND ASSOCIATED STATE-TRANSITION DIAGRAM

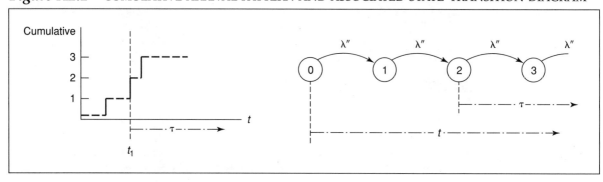

or $\dot{p}_{0k}(t) = \lambda'' p_{0k-1}(t) - \lambda'' p_{0k}(t)$ for $k = 0, 1, \dots , n$; where $\dot{p}_{0i}'(t)$ is the time derivative of the probability of transitioning to state i. The subscript 0 simply suggests the system starts empty. In matrix form,

$$
\begin{bmatrix}
\dot{p}_{00}(t) \\
\dot{p}_{01}(t) \\
\dot{p}_{02}(t) \\
\cdot \\
\cdot \\
\cdot \\
\dot{p}_{0n}(t)
\end{bmatrix}
=
\begin{bmatrix}
-\lambda'' \\
\lambda'' & -\lambda'' \\
& \lambda' & -\lambda'' \\
& & & \cdots \\
& & & & \cdots
\end{bmatrix}
\begin{bmatrix}
p_{00}(t) \\
p_{01}(t) \\
p_{02}(t) \\
\cdot \\
\cdot \\
\cdot \\
p_{0n}(t)
\end{bmatrix}
\tag{A2.2}
$$

or $\dot{\mathbf{p}}_0(t) = \mathbf{\Pi} \mathbf{p}_0(t)$, which describes the system evolving over time increments dt. Here $\mathbf{\Pi}$ is the matrix of transition rates from state 0 to state x.

Figure A2.2   INTERARRIVAL TIME DISTRIBUTION FUNCTION

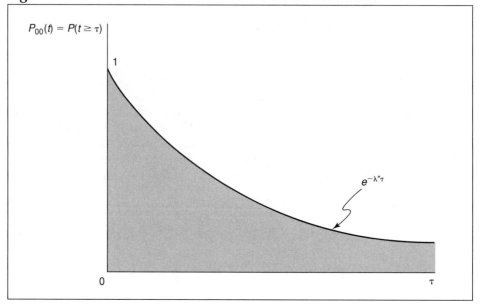

Figure A2.3   POISSON-ARRIVAL DISTRIBUTION FUNCTION

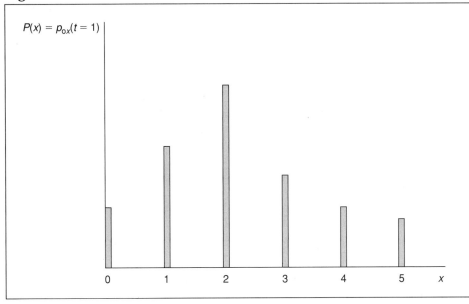

$P(x) = p_{0x}(t = 1)$

B. Solution to Random Process

Solving the first line of Equation A2.1 by integration, with the constant of integration $p_{00}(0) = 1$, we have $p_{00}(t) = e^{-\lambda''\tau}$. This curve is plotted in Figure A2.2 for illustration. Notice this is the probability that there is no event in time τ, or the interarrival time t is greater than τ: $P(t \geq \tau)$. Substituting this integration result into the second equation and integrating again yields $p_{01}(t) = e^{-\lambda''t}$. Repeating the process one more time for the next equation, we have: $p_{02}(t) = (\lambda''t)^2 e^{-\lambda''t}/2$. In general, $p_{0x}(t) = (\lambda''t)^x e^{-\lambda''t}/x!$, for $x = 0, 1, 2, ..., n$. Thus for a given time period $t = \tau$, the vector $\mathbf{p}_0$ gives the probability distribution of the various states, and the sum of the entries in the vector is unity by definition of a probability distribution. Such a Poisson distribution is plotted in Figure A2.3. When τ is normalized to one time unit, we have the alternate expression for Poisson distribution:

$$P(x) = \frac{(\lambda'')^x e^{-\lambda''}}{x!} \quad x = 0, 1, 2, ..., n. \tag{A2.3}$$

II. FIELD DATA FROM AIR TERMINAL

The somewhat abstract ideas above can be illustrated with concrete data (Morlok 1978). Suppose we collected the information of Table A2.1 at an air terminal during an eight-hour day. Here in this figure one time unit represents a half hour. For the time being, we only examine the first column—arrival time of an aircraft—since we are interested in the demands placed upon the terminal. In this case, the first aircraft arrives 1/2 hour after the day begins, the second one arrives one hour after the day starts and so on. The average arrival rate λ'' is computed as 12/16 or 0.75 vehicles per unit time.

Table A2.1   AIRCRAFT ARRIVAL AND DEPARTURE FIELD DATA

Aircraft	Arrival time*	Depart time*	Wait time	Total time in system	Service time	Total in system	Interarrival time
#1	1	2	0	1	1	1	—
2	2	3	0	1	1	1	1
3	3	4	0	1	1	1	1
4	5	6	0	1	1	1	2
5	8	9	0	1	1	1	3
6	8.1	10	0.9	1.9	1	2	0.1
7	9	11	1	2	1	2	0.9
8	9.5	12	1.5	2.5	1	3	0.5
9	11	13	1	2	1	2	1.5
10	12.5	14	0.5	1.5	1	2	1.5
11	14	15	0	1	1	1	1.5
12	16	17	0	1	1	1	2

*Data to be collected, rest can be derived.

SOURCE: Morlok (1978). Reprinted with permission.

A. Exponential Distribution

From the discussions in Section I-B, if arrivals are random, interarrival times are exponentially distributed: $P(t \geq \tau) = e^{-0.75\tau}$ for $0 \leq \tau \leq \infty$, where $P(t \geq \tau)$ is the probability that the interarrival time t is greater than τ. Now we can compare the field data with a theoretical exponential interarrival time distribution. If the two match, then we can conclude that interarrivals are truly random. Table A2.2 shows how this can be conducted. For example, in the first row of the second column, there are clearly the entire 11 (12-1) interarrival times that are larger than 0 unit in duration, considering that an interarrival time is defined for each pair of aircraft. In the second row, we counted only eight interarrival-times that are one unit or longer and so on. Now we plot the theoretical curve against the experimental curve in Figure A2.4, which allows for a visual inspection of the two curves side by side. Notice the average interarrival time, $1/\lambda''$ or 1.333 units, is also graphed in Figure A2.4 for reference.

B. Poisson Distribution

Again from Section I-B, if arrivals are random, the number of aircraft arriving in a unit of time (1/2 hour) constitutes a Poisson distribution: $P(X = x) = (e^{-[0.75]x})/x!$ for $x = 0, 1, 2, 3, \ldots$, where $P(X = x)$ is the probability that x aircraft arrive in the time unit. Table A2.3 shows both theoretical and field data side by side. For example, there are six occurrences in which no aircraft arrive in a time unit, and eight occurrences in which one aircraft arrives in a time unit and so on. All these come from the first data column of Table A2.1. Comparison between theoretical and empirical curves in Figure A2.5 does not seem to support the assumption of

Table A2.2   THEORETICAL AND FIELD DATA ON INTERARRIVAL TIME DISTRIBUTION

| Time intervals t | Experimental | | Theoretical |
	No. interarrival times that exceed the time interval $t > \tau$	Frequency distribution	$P(t > \tau) = e^{-0.75\tau}$
0	11	1.00	1.00
1	8	0.73	0.47
2	3	0.27	0.22
3	1	0.09	0.11
4	0	0	0.05
5	0	0	0.02
6	0	0	0.01
7	0	0	0.01
8	0	0	0

Figure A2.4   INTERARRIVAL TIME DISTRIBUTIONS

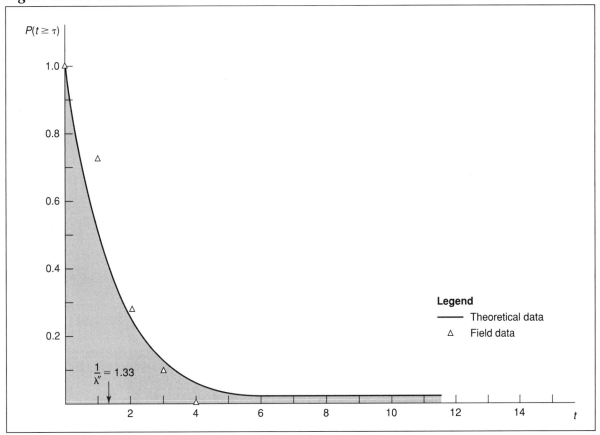

Table A2.3   THEORETICAL AND FIELD DATA ON POISSON DISTRIBUTION

| | Experimental | | Theoretical |
No. of arrivals per unit time x	No. of occurrences (time intervals)	Frequency distribution	$P(X = x) = \dfrac{e^{-0.75}[0.75]^x}{x!}$
0	6	0.375	0.47
1	8	0.500	0.35
2	2	0.125	0.13
3	0	0	0.03
4	0	0	0.01
5	0	0	0

Figure A2.5   POISSON DISTRIBUTIONS

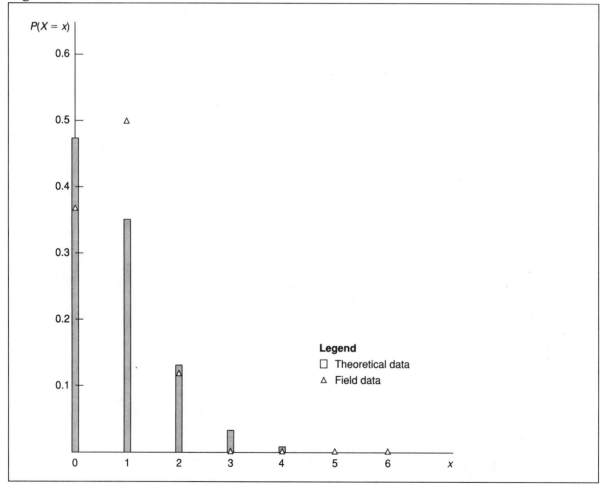

a random process, even though the previous test using exponential function resulted in a more positive visual verification. Rigorous, scientific goodness-of-fit statistics such as the chi-square should be used in lieu of a manual, visual process.[1]

III. M/M/1 QUEUE

Instead of just the demand arrival pattern, one can use similar state transition equations to derive the full set of waiting-line or queuing equations. This covers both arrivals and departures after receiving service at the terminal. We assume random arrivals and random service here, or more specifically Poisson arrivals with an average rate of λ'' and exponential service time averaging $1/\mu'$. Let $P_i(t)$ be the probability that the system is in state i at time t. In Figure A2.6, we have the transition diagram to describe random arrivals and random service at a single server. The usual convention is to use $M/M/1$ designation where the first M stands for random arrival, the second M stands for random service, and 1 stands for a single server.

Starting with an empty system, or state $i = 0$, the transition differential-equation set is

$$\dot{P}_0(t) = -\lambda'' P_0(t) + \mu' P_1(t)$$
$$\dot{P}_1(t) = -(\lambda'' + \mu')P_1(t) + \lambda'' P_0(t) + \mu' P_2(t)$$
$$\dot{P}_2(t) = -(\lambda'' + \mu')P_2(t) + \lambda'' P_1(t) + \mu' P_3(t)$$

$$\cdot$$
$$\cdot$$
$$\cdot$$

etc.

(A2.4)

where $\dot{P}_i(t)$ is the time derivative of the probability of being in state i. In general, $\dot{P}_{0i}(t) = -(\lambda'' + \mu')P_i(t) + \lambda'' P_{i-1}(t) + \mu' P_{i+1}(t)$ for $i = 0, ..., \infty$. Expressed in matrix form:

Figure A2.6   CUMULATIVE ARRIVAL AND DEPARTURE CURVES AND ASSOCIATED TRANSITION DIAGRAM

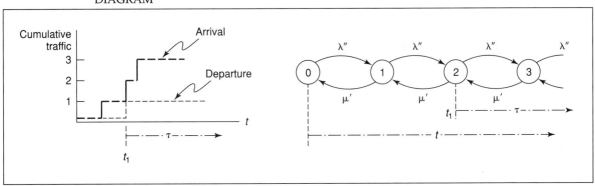

$$
\begin{bmatrix} \dot{P_0}(t) \\ \dot{P_1}(t) \\ \dot{P_2}(t) \\ \cdot \\ \cdot \\ \cdot \\ \dot{P_n}(t) \end{bmatrix} = \begin{bmatrix} -\lambda'' & \mu' & & & \\ \lambda'' & -(\lambda'' + \mu') & \mu' & & \\ & \lambda' & -(\lambda'' + \mu') & \mu' & \\ & & \cdots & & \\ & & & \cdots & \\ & & & & \cdots \end{bmatrix} \begin{bmatrix} P_0(t) \\ P_1(t) \\ P_2(t) \\ \cdot \\ \cdot \\ \cdot \\ P_n(t) \end{bmatrix} \tag{A2.5}
$$

or $\dot{\mathbf{P}}(t) = \tilde{\Pi}\ \mathbf{P}(t)$, where $0 \le t \le \infty$, and the system evolves over the time increments dt.

For the steady-state (or average) situation, all derivatives are zero, and we have the following equation set after dropping the t argument:

$$\lambda'' P_0 = \mu' P_1$$
$$(\lambda'' + \mu') P_1 = \lambda'' P_0 + \mu' P_2$$
$$(\lambda'' + \mu') P_2 = \lambda'' P_1 + \mu' P_3$$
$$\cdot$$
$$\cdot$$
$$\cdot$$

etc.

Solving these equations yields $P_1 = \rho'_0$, where $\rho' = \lambda''/\mu'$; $P_2 = \rho'^2 P_0$; $P_3 = \rho'^3 P_0$; ... etc. Substituting into the relationship that $P_0 + P_1 + P_2 + P_3 + ... = 1$, we have $P_0(1 + \rho' + \rho'^2 + ...) = 1$, or $P_0 = (1 - \rho')$. Now, re-substituting back $P_1 = \rho'(1 - \rho')$, $P_2 = \rho'^2(1 - \rho')$, $P_3 = \rho'^3(1 - \rho')$, ... and so forth. The average length of a waiting line or queue, including the one being served, is therefore

$$\bar{L} = 0P_0 + 1P_1 + 2P_2 + ...$$
$$= (1 - \rho')(\rho' + 2\rho'^2 + 3\rho'^3 + ...)$$
$$= (1 - \rho')\rho'(1 + 2\rho' + 3\rho'^2 + ...)$$
$$= (1 - \rho')\rho'(1 - \rho')^{-2} = \rho'/(1 - \rho')$$

From the queue length, other queuing statistics can be derived. For example, the total time in the system, which is the amount of time for the last arrival to spend in line plus the time being served is simply $(1/\mu')\bar{L}$, or $= \rho'/\mu'(1 - \rho')$.

IV. QUEUING SYSTEMS

The above derivations are based on a set of state transition equations that describe a Markov process—especially, a continuous-time Markov process. Similar processes can be used to model other types of queues. For example, if we have established that the arrivals are not random in the air terminal example, some other distributions may fit the data better, and the $M/M/1$ queue may not be an appropriate model to use in this case. We wish to present several queuing models below. But due to space limitation, we will not show the detailed steps of derivation, as we have done in the case of $M/M/1$ queue. Interested readers should refer to standard texts on queuing for details (See Cooper [1980] for example).

A. Basic Theory

The basic idea behind queuing is really quite straightforward. We have a stream of demands coming in, and they are being met by a service facility. The demand traffic eventually exits after being served at the end of the process. A schematic describing this phenomenon can be sketched: $\lambda'' \to \mu' \to ...$ where in the air terminal example both parameters λ'' and μ' are measured in vehicles/time-unit. λ'' is called the average rate of arrival, and μ' is the average rate of service. As defined in Section III, λ''/μ' is called the utilization factor ρ', or the traffic intensity, signifying the percentage of time the server is busy on the average. Broadly speaking, there are two types of queuing: deterministic and probabilistic. A deterministic queue is straightforward; it is analogous to a sink with a running faucet. Water enters the sink via the faucet at a precise rate of λ'', and the sink drains at a precise rate of μ'. Unless the water comes in faster than going out, or $\lambda'' > \mu'$, there is no water backup, which is analogous to saying that no queue is formed. When $\lambda'' > \mu'$, water backs up in the sink and the water level keeps on rising, resulting in a wet floor when water eventually overflows. In the case of a probabilistic process, a queue may be formed even though that on the average $\lambda'' < \mu'$, since the water is coming in and going out at fluctuating rates. Thus on occasions, the water gushes out of the faucet while the drain is sluggish, causing water backup, even though on the average, the sink is supposed to drain faster than the incoming rate at the faucet.

We can summarize the probabilisic situation with the following table:

λ''	μ'	delay W_q
random	random	worst
random	constant	medium
constant	random	least

which says that if the faucet runs randomly, and the drain works randomly, the water backs up and the water in the sink takes a long time to clear on the average. If the faucet runs randomly, but the drain is perfectly reliable, the situation is more under control. The best is when the incoming water is steady, even though the drain may be haphazard. All these refer to the situation when $\lambda'' < \mu'$. Obviously, we are guaranteed an infinite backup and a wet floor when $\lambda'' \geq \mu'$ to begin with. Standardized short-hand notations for random is M (as mentioned previously) and for constant D. Based on this notation, the queuing system above in the second line of the table is an $M/D/1$ model, where the last number again denotes one single server, similar to the case of $M/M/1$ queue. The average system-behavior is summarized in Figure A2.7, which shows the steady-state (or stationary) behavior of the queues. On the average, the delay is at its worst for $M/M/1$ queue, and least for $D/D/1$ (until the water spills over beginning at $\lambda'' \geq \mu'$). Notice the figure is dimensionless, in that both scales of the horizontal and vertical axes are independent of any particular unit of measurement. First of all, the utilization factor is clearly dimensionless. Total time in the system (in units/unit) is scaled with the average service time being 1 unit. In our air terminal example, it simply means that everything is a multiple of $1/2$ hour. The total time W_T is the sum of the delay time in queue W_q and the service time $1/\mu'$. It refers to the time spent by a single vehicle unit to be served at the terminal.

Figure A2.7   AVERAGE PERFORMANCE OF VARIOUS QUEUING DISCIPLINES

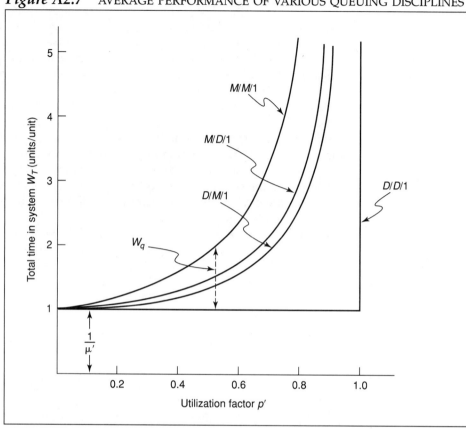

In the case of multiple servers, a schematic can be drawn as follows:

$$\lambda'' \rightarrow \begin{cases} \mu' \rightarrow \\ \mu' \rightarrow \\ \cdot \\ \cdot \\ \cdot \\ \mu' \rightarrow \end{cases}$$
(A2.6)

The more servers, the less the delay time, as illustrated by $M/M/p$, or the p-server system shown in Figure A2.8. For example, for a utilization factor $\rho' = 0.6$, the single-server queue incurs the largest system delay (at 2.5 units/unit), the two-server queue less (at 1.8 units/unit) and the three-server queue the least (at 1.3 units/unit).

B. Queuing Formulas

Now back to the single-server system. For a first-come-first-served (FIFO) system, the following queuing equations can be obtained:

Figure A2.8   PERFORMANCE OF MULTI-SERVER QUEUES

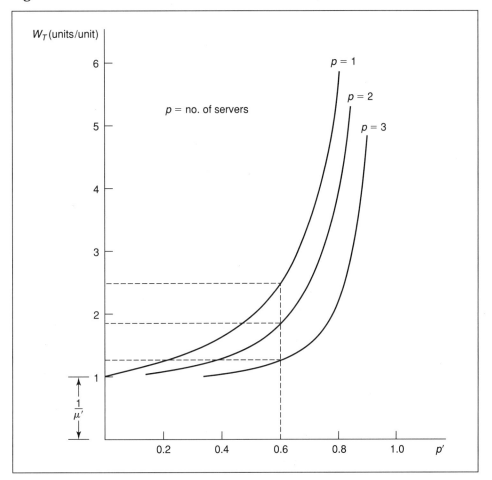

queue discipline	queue length (L_q)	delay (W_q)
$D/D/1$	0	0
$D/M/1$	(Intractable analytically, resort to simulation)	
$M/D/1$	$\rho'^2/2(1 - \rho')$	$\rho'/2\mu'(1 - \rho')$
$M/M/1$	$\rho'^2/(1 - \rho')$	$\rho/\mu(1 - \rho')$

Notice the average queue length and queuing delay for an $M/D/1$ queue is half of that for an $M/M/1$ queue, as confirmed by the plot in Figure A2.7. Several other observations are also worthy of note. First, the percentage of idle time $= 1 - \rho' = P(\text{system empty}) = P_0$. For an $M/M/1$ system, $P(i \text{ units in the system}) = P_0\rho'^i = P_i$. Second, total time in system (W_T) is the combination of queuing delay and service time as mentioned, or $W_q + (1/\mu')$. Third, it is seen that the total number of demands on the system is the combination of those in the queue and those being served $= L_q + \rho'$, and queuing delay is simply $W_q = L_q/\lambda''$. Finally, of significance is that most queuing systems are not subject to closed-form solutions, as already alluded to in the case of $D/M/1$ queue, not to say more complicated ones.

Example
Suppose demand arrives at a rate of $\lambda'' = 0.75$ veh/unit-time and $\rho' = 1$ veh/unit-time, setting aside economic and other considerations, is it more desirable to have constant service time or random service time?

According to the formulas given above, we construct this tabular calculation:

queue	W_q
$M/D/1$	$\dfrac{0.75}{2(1)(1-0.75)} = 1.5$
$M/M/1$	$\dfrac{0.75}{1(1-0.75)} = 3$

Thus the obvious answer is to go for constant service time since it results in half of the wait time (and queue length) alluded to earlier. The astute reader would have arrived at this conclusion directly from the queuing formula table above, without substituting any numbers. ■

An example of a multi-server system is the random-arrival, random-service $M/M/p$ queuing model, where the percentage of idle time is

$$P_0 = \frac{1}{\displaystyle\sum_{i=0}^{p-1} \frac{(\lambda''/\mu')^i}{i!} + \frac{(\lambda''/\mu')^p}{p!}\frac{1}{1-\lambda''/\mu'p}}$$

(A2.7)

$$P_i = \begin{cases} [(\lambda''/\mu')_i/i!]P_0 & \text{if } 0 \le i \le p \\ [(\lambda''/\mu')^i/p!p^{i-p}]P_0 & \text{if } i \ge p \end{cases}$$

$$L_q = \frac{(\lambda''/\mu')^i(\lambda''/\mu'p)P_0}{p!(1-\lambda''/\mu'p)^2}$$

(A2.8)

Example
Given $\lambda'' = 2$ veh/min, and $\mu' = 3$ veh/min and $p = 2$, what is the percentage time the system is empty? How about with one vehicle in the system and with two vehicles in the system?

$$P_0 = \frac{1}{\displaystyle\sum_{i=0}^{1} \frac{(2/3)^i}{i!} + \frac{(2/3)^2}{2!}\frac{1}{1-(2/(2)(3))}} = 0.5$$

(A2.9)

$P_1 = [(2/3)^1/1!](0.5) = 0.333$ and $P_2 = [(2/3)^2/2!2^{2-2}](0.5) = 0.111$. ■

In many queuing systems, an arrival who finds all servers occupied is, for all practical purposes, lost to the system. For example, suppose someone calls in a fire alarm and no fire engines are available; an engine has to be called in from a neighboring town or the fire will simply burn out of control. The result is that the demand evaporates from the local fire station. Thus, a request for a fire engine that occurs when no engines are available may be considered lost to the system. If demand arrivals who find all servers occupied leave the system, we call the system blocked-demands cleared. Assuming that interarrival times are exponential, such a system may be modeled as an $M/G/p/p$ system, where G stands for general distribution (which includes the above cases of random and constant service) and all p servers are identically distributed. The extra p at the end of the notation stands for a capacity of serving up to p demands only.

For an $M/G/p/p$ system, L', W_T, L_q and W_q are of limited interest. Since a queue can never occur, hence $L_q = W_q = 0$. We let $1/\rho'$ be the mean service time and λ'' be the arrival rate. Then $W_T = 1/\mu'$. In most blocked-demands cleared systems, primary interest is focused on the fraction of all demand arrivals who are turned away. Hence an average of $\lambda''P(p)$ arrivals per unit time will be lost to the system, where $P(p)$ is generally referred to as the loss probability. Since an average of $\lambda''(1 - P(p))$ arrivals per unit time will actually enter the system, we may conclude that the average queue length in the system (including the ones being served) is

$$L' = \frac{\lambda''(1 - P(p))}{\mu'}$$

For an $M/G/p/p$ system, it can be shown that $P(p)$, the percentage time p-servers are occupied, depends on the service time distribution only through its mean $1/\mu'$. This fact is known as Erlang's loss formula. In other words, any $M/G/p/p$ system with an arrival rate λ'' and service time of $1/\mu'$ will have the same value of $P(p)$ (Winston 1994) and

$$P(p) = (\rho'^p/p!)\left/\sum_{k=1}^{p} \rho'^k/k!\right.$$

The Erlang loss formula, including the loss probability $P(p)$, has been computed in terms of nomographs for everyday use (Cooper 1980). The Erlang loss formula is important in locating such facilities as fire stations, as shown in the "Stochastic Facility Location" subsection of the "Measuring Spatial Separation" chapter in Chan (2000).

C. Choosing a Queuing Discipline

With so many queuing disciplines, the logical question at this juncture is "Which model best describes our situation?" Obviously, the answer is not simple, since this is where theory meets application. Perhaps the best way to answer this question is to return to the field data we collected in Table A2.1 for the air terminal. In this data set, we assume that only one ground crew is available, who takes exactly a half hour to service an aircraft. Notice that only the first two columns need to be compiled, the rest can be calculated. Take the first row for example. Since it is the first aircraft that arrived, no wait is necessary for it to be serviced. The total time in the system consists of only the service time, which is a half hour. The only demand traffic is this first aircraft, which constitutes the total number of vehicles in the system. Since this is the only aircraft thus far, there is no interarrival time yet. Following this line of logic, the reader is invited to go through another few lines and derive the rest of the columns from the first two in Table A2.1. From the discussions in Section II, we were inconclusive about whether demand arrivals are random. The service pattern, however, appears to be deterministic, since it takes precisely one half hour to service an aircraft. Remember that the average arrival rate was 0.75 vehicles per unit-time. We compute the rest of the parameters below: service rate = $\mu' = 1$ veh/unit, utilization factor = $\rho' = 0.75$, total time in system = 16.9/12 = 1.41 units, and (interarrival time = 15/11=1.26). Based on these calculations, both the theoretical curve and empirical data point can be plotted. We now overlay the experimental data point on the $M/D/1$ theoretical plot of W_T against ρ' in Figure A2.9. Now the question that arises is: How good is the $M/D/1$ model in predicting field data? The answer is again inconclusive, since only one data point is available. Additional information is required for a more definitive answer to the question. This example, simple as it may be, shows that choosing a queuing discipline to fit the data—one of the most important tasks— is by no means straightforward.

Figure A2.9   FIELD DATA ON $M/D/1$ CURVE

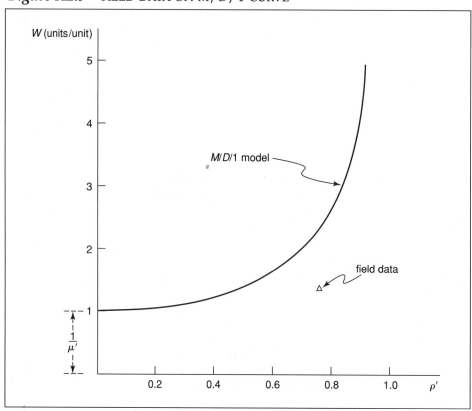

One obvious solution is to collect more data. This will allow more validation points to be plotted, not just the one shown in Figure A2.9. This does not, however, address the validation question any better than what has been illustrated. Use of statistical tests, such as the chi-square goodness-of-fit statistic, would help. But again the answer ultimately rests with the judgment of the model builder. Even if the data pass the statistical test, there remains the following question: "Are the data collected in isolation or are they part of a larger queuing system (such as a system preceded by aircraft landing patterns)?" If it is part of a larger system, the input rate to the gate cannot be random in spite of the statistical tests. The input stream in this case is likely to be influenced by the landing policy, or technically speaking, conditioned upon the landing pattern. This opens the question of whether two queues—aircraft landing and service at the gate—are actually in tandem. It is easy to see, again through this simple example, that choosing the appropriate queuing discipline remains an art (not a science.)

V. MARKOVIAN PROPERTIES

Regarding the state transition equations shown above in Sections I and III, both examples are special cases of the continuous time Markov process, where the following Markovian properties are discerned:

1. The conditional probability of any future state $X(t_{k+1}) = j$, given any past state $X(t_0) = i_0, \dots, X(t_{k-1}) = i_{k-1}$ and the present state $X(t_k) = i_k$ is independent of past states and depends only on the present state of the process:

$$P[X(t_{k+1}) = j \mid X(t_k) = i_k, X(t_{k-1}) = i_{k-1}, \dots, X(t_0) = i_0] =$$
$$P[X(t_{k+1}) = j \mid X(t_k) = i_k]$$

This is usually referred to as the memoryless property.

2. The process is stationary if the transitional probabilities above depend only on the time interval between the events rather than on absolute time t: $P[X(t_2) = j \mid X(t_1) = i] = P[X(t_2 - t_1) = j \mid X(0) = i]$, for all $i, j, t_1, t_2 (t_1 < t_2)$. In other words, the starting time of the process is unimportant in comparison to the amount of time that has elapsed $t = t_2 - t_1$. Given these two properties, a Markov process is completely described by its transition probabilities $p_{ij}(t) = P[X(t) = j \mid X(0) = i]$. Notice the concept of stationarity is similar to that in time series (see the "Spatial Time Series" chapter in Chan [2000]).

Examples
Consider a Poisson process in which $X(0) = 0$ gives rise to a distribution $p_{0x}(t) = (\lambda''t)^x e^{-\lambda''t}/x!$, for $x = 0, 1, 2, 3, \dots, n$. Suppose for $X(t_1) = 2$, $p_{2x}(\tau) = (\lambda''\tau)^{X'} e^{-\lambda''\tau}/X'!$, where $\tau = t - t_1$ and $X' = x - 2$. For the time interval t or τ, both are the same distribution function in spite of different start times (0 vs. t_1) and different initial conditions ($X(0) = 0$ vs. $X(t_1) = 2$). Having two vehicle arrivals already merely shifted the cumulative curve up by 2 for the initial state, irrespective of past history of the arrival

pattern. With a transformation of state variables, $X^i(t_1) = 0$, which is the same as $x(0) = 0$. In diagrammatic form, the same cumulative and state transition diagram for Poisson process can be overlaid on top of Figure A2.6: one starts at time 0 and the other at t_1. This example illustrates the memoryless and stationary properties of a Markovian system. Also for the same example, $p_{00}(\tau) = p_{22}(\tau) = e^{-\lambda''\tau}$ for $0 \leq \tau \leq \infty$; or the times between events in a Poisson process are all negative exponentially distributed with the same parameter λ''. This is irrespective of whether we start with $t = 0$ (when the system is idle) or $t = t_1$ (after two arrivals have been logged).

Similarly, for $M/M/1$ queue, the initial state can be $X(0) = 0$ or $X(t_1) = 2$, and the identical distribution $P_i = \rho'^i(1 - \rho')$ results in the steady state. Graphically speaking, cumulative and state transition diagrams for both $M/M/1$ queues can again be overlaid on top of Figure A2.6 to illustrate the memoryless and stationary properties. In this Figure, both cumulative/departure and state transition diagrams look the same to the right of the starting point. The only difference is that two arrivals and one departure have occurred in the latter case. Again, the history of the process is adequately represented by the initial state. $X(0)$ and $X(t_1)$ and does not depend on the history prior to $t = 0$ and $t = t_1$. ∎

VI. MARKOVIAN PROPERTIES OF DYNAMIC PROGRAMMING

Perhaps we can illustrate Markovian property even better with regular dynamic programming (DP), which is a set of deterministic state transition equations in which a decision variable is built into a Markovian system for optimization purposes. The best way to describe DP is through examples.

A. Vehicle Dispatching Example

We are to construct a timetable for dispatching a cargo aircraft toward the end of a business day. The cargo carrying capacity of the vehicle is 30,000 lbs (15,000 kg). Due to space limitations, we do not allow more than a vehicle load of cargo (30,000 lbs) to accumulate at the loading dock. Our objective is to minimize the cost-of-operation and delay cost experienced by the cargo consignee (who either receive the cargo early or late). One can think of constructing a timetable as making a series of decisions as to whether or not to dispatch at each instance when 10,000 lb (5,000 kg) of cargo are accumulated. Figure A2.10 shows a demand-arrival pattern from 4:30 pm to 6:30 pm. We define stages k as the times at which dispatching decisions are made; and states X_k as the accumulated inventory of cargo at the loading dock when a dispatching decision is reviewed. The rules of engagement are that when the vehicle is filled up, it has to be dispatched. At the end of the business day, all cargo has to be dispatched in order to clear the dock. The decision variable y_k is a binary 0-1 variable: 1 stands for "dispatch" and 0 for "hold". The operating cost function $c(y_k)$ can be represented by Table A2.4. Thus if the decision is to dispatch, it will invariably cost 6,000 dollars to fly the aircraft. On the other hand, the delay cost is varying depending on the shape of the demand arrival curve shown in Figure A2.10. These delay costs can be calculated below.

1. Markovian Properties. Delay to consignee can be represented in pound-minutes (kg-min), graphically depicted as the shaded wedges in Figure A2.10 if the

Figure A2.10   DEMAND ARRIVAL PATTERN

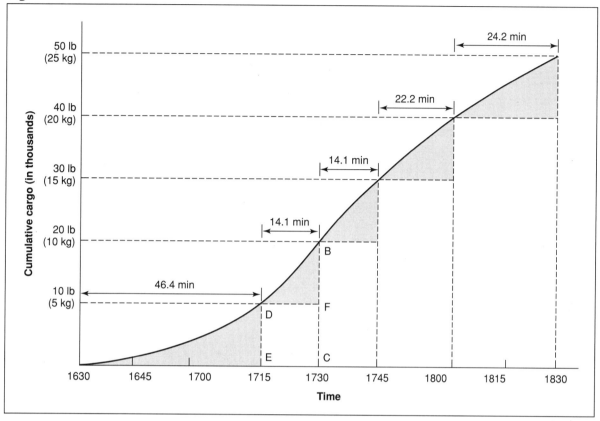

decision is always to dispatch at each decision point. Assume a delay wedge, measured in lb-min (kg-min), can be approximated by a triangle. When the decision is no at the first decision point *E*, the delay cost will be the bigger triangle *ABC* rather than the two smaller triangles *ADE* and *DBF*. Would this refer us two stages back rather than just one stage, thus destroying the Markovian property? Graphical examination seems to confirm this, since between the two the rectangle *DFCE* is missing. But a little transformation of the cost accounting procedure will guarantee the Markovian property. To show this, a little calculation will help:

Table A2.4   OPERATING AND DELAY COSTS FOR DISPATCHING EXAMPLE

		Incremental cost ($) of operation $c(y_k)$ for decision point (stage) k					
		0	1	2	3	4	5
$y_k =$ {	1 dispatch	—	6000	6000	6000	6000	6000
	0 hold	4640	1410	1410	2220	2420	—

Average delay-cost for a vehicle load of cargo in dollars
= (avg delay to a lb [kg]) (value of time for a veh load of cargo)
= (abscissa/2) (time value for an avg veh load of 10,000 lb [5,000 kg])
    ↑   ↑

    in min   in $/min
= (abscissa/2) ($200/min)

Average delay for triangle *ABC*
= *AC*/2
= *AE*/2 + *EC*/2
= (avg delay of triangle *ADE*) + (avg delay of triangle *DBF*).

This transformation effectively measures delay in terms of time on the horizontal axis. By accounting for an *average* load of cargo, the missing rectangle dilemma disappears. Each decision y_k over time interval $(t_k - t_{k-1})$ is now separable, and costs are cumulative (incremental from the last "running sum.") Notice the assumption on the size of an average cargo load is unimportant, as long as we use the same vehicle load consistently. For an average load of 10,000 lb., the delay costs are shown in Table A2.4.

Here in this example, all arc costs are anticipatory and discretionary. However, there is an unavoidable overhead cost of $(4640 + 1410 + 1410 + 2220 + 420) = $12,000, in other words the sum of all shaded triangles in Figure A2.10. They are the result of our policy that a dispatch decision will not be reviewed until 10,000 pounds of cargo have arrived. Notice the $12,100 is implicit and does not need to appear in our objective function. Instead of measuring anticipatory delay by a triangular wedge, however, it can be shown that a retrospective delay can be measured by such rectangles as that formed by the points *DFCE*. In this case, only historic cost is accounted for and the anticipatory overhead-cost evaporates. The return function is now both a function of the decision variable x_k and the state variable X_k: $c(x_k, X_k)$. The Markovian property is automatically upheld, and hence no cost transformation is necessary.

2. Solution Algorithm. Now that we have established a Markovian system, the problem is ready for solution. To properly solve this problem, however, a state-stage diagram needs to be constructed. This diagram—pictured in Figure A2.11—is derived from the demand arrival curve, but the linkage stops at that point. Similar to the Markovian state-transition diagram depicted in Figure A2.1 and Figure A2.6, the state stage diagram can be described by a set of state transition equations. The steady-state equations (for measuring cargo in pounds) look like

$$X_k = X_{k-1} + 10000(1 - y_{k-1}[X_{k-1}/10000]) \tag{A2.10}$$

where X_k is the state variable (in lbs of cumulative cargo at the dock) at decision point k. These equations are subject to boundary conditions at $k = 0$ and 5: when $k = 0$, $y_k = 0$; and at $k = 5$, $y_5 = 1$. Numerical examples of these steady-state transition equations can be provided. For a hold decision at decision point 0, the accumulated cargo at the next decision point will be 10000 lbs. as confirmed by $X_1 = X_0 + 10000(1 - y_0[X_0/10000]) = 0 + 10000(1 - 0[0/10000]) = 10000$. Another hold decision at $k = 1$ will result in 20,000 lb cargo at the dock by decision point $k = 3$:

Figure A2.11   STATE STAGE DIAGRAM

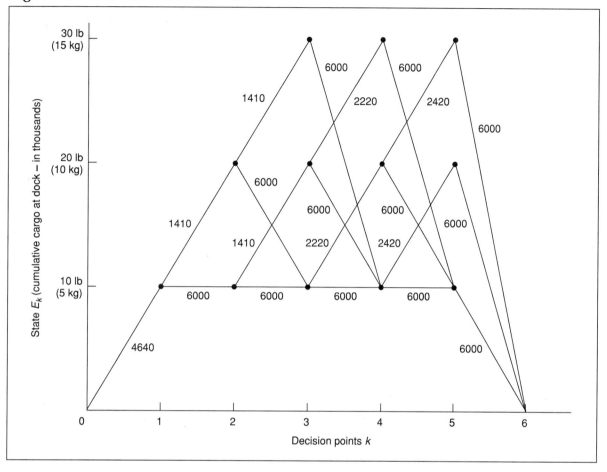

$X_2 = X_1 + 10000(1 - y_1[X_1/10000]) = 10000 + 10000(1 - 0\,[10000/\,10000]) = 20000$, and so forth.

Solution of the system of equations can be carried out working backwards:

$$f_5^*(X_5 = 10000) = 6000, \text{ where } y_5 = 1$$
$$f_5^*(X_5 = 20000) = 6000, \text{ where } y_5 = 1$$
$$f_5^*(X_5 = 30000) = 6000, \text{ where } y_5 = 1$$

where f_k is the running sum or the criterion function. In tabular form

$k = 6$	X_5	$f_5^*(X_5)$	y_5
	10000	6000	1
	20000	6000	1
	30000	6000	1

$$f_4^*(10000) = [c(y_4) + f_5^*(X_5)]$$
$$= \min\{[6000 + f_5^*(10000)], [2420 + f_5^*(20000)]\}$$
$$= \min[(6000 + 6000), (2420 + 6000)] = 8420, \text{ where } y_4 = 0$$

$$f_4^*(20000) = \min\{[6000 + f_5^*(10000)], [2420 + f_5^*(30000)]\}$$
$$= \min(6000 + 6000, 2420 + 6000) = 8420, \text{ where } y_4 = 0$$

$$f_4^*(30000) = \min[6000 + f_5^*(10000)] = 12000, \text{ where } y_4 = 1$$

The recursive function for these three equations is the common form

$$f_4^*(X_4) = \min_{y_4=1,0}[f_4(X_4, y_4)] = \min_{y_4=1,0}[c(y_4) + f_5^*(X_5)]$$

In tabular form:

$k = 5$	X_4	$f_4^*(X_4)$	y_4
	10000	8420	0
	20000	8420	0
	30000	12000	1

The remaining iterations can be tabulated as follows:

	X_{k-1}	$f_{k-1}^*(X_{k-1})$	y_{k-1}
	10000	10640	0
$k = 4$	20000	14220	0
	30000	14420	1
	10000	15630	0
$k = 3$	20000	15830	0
$k = 2$	10000	17240	0
$k = 1$	0	21880	0

In general, the recursive equation is $f_{k-1}^*(X_{k-1}) = \min_{y_{k-1}=1,0}[c(y_{k-1}) + f_k^*(X_k)]$ for $k = 5, 4, \ldots, 1$. We trace back using the state transition Equation A2.10, with the assistance of the tabular computations for $k = 5, 4, 3, 2, 1$ above. Starting with the boundary condition at $k = 1$: $X_0 = 0, y_0 = 0 \rightarrow X_1 = 10000, y_1 = 0 \rightarrow X_2 = 20000$, $y_2 = 0 \rightarrow X_3 = 30000, y_3 = 1 \rightarrow X_4 = 10000, y_4 = 0 \rightarrow X_5 = 20000, y_5 = 1$. Thus the dispatch timetable is to send an aircraft out at decision points 3 and 5. This translates to about 5:40 p.m. and 6:30 p.m. While the example has been worked out using backward recursion, it can be shown that it can be solved equally well using forward recursion.

B. Principle of Optimality

In summary, a Markovian system such as the example above can be optimized using the principle of optimality, which we shall recap simply: After k decisions have been made, the effect of the remaining $n - k$ stages on the total criterion-function f depends only on the state at stage k and the final $n - k$ decisions. In other words, an optimal policy for the remaining stages is independent of the policy adopted in previous stages. This principle is the basis of many solutions to an optimal control problem such as the vehicle dispatching one under discussion.

The general forward recursion equations of DP can now be expressed as follows (backward recursion is similar):

$$f_k^*(X_k) = \text{opt}_x [r_k(x_k) \circ f_{k-1}^*(X_{k-1})]$$
$$\text{s.t. } X_{k-1} = h'(x_k, X_k) \quad k = 1, 2, \ldots, n$$

where *opt* is a subproblem of maximization or minimization, $\circ$ stands for addition or multiplication, X is the state variable, k is the stage variable, x is the decision variable, f is the criterion function, $r(x_k)$ is the return function[2], and h' is the state transition function. In the vehicle dispatching example, these terms can be illustrated below. Notice that each minimization subproblem can be solved by simple arithmetic calculations:

Formal terms	Illustration in the vehicle-dispatching example
$X_{k-1} = h'(X_k, x_k)$	$X_k = X_{k-1} + 10000 (1 - x_{k-1}[X_{k-1}/10000])$
$r_k(x_k)$	$c(y_k)$
f_k	$c(y_k) + f_{k+1}$
subproblem solution	arithmetics

Based on this example, these general observations can be made regarding the optimization of a Markovian system. First the system has to be decomposable:

$$f_n(x_n, X_n) = f_0(x_0, X_0) \circ r(x_1, X_1) \circ r(x_2, X_2) \circ \ldots \circ r(x_n, X_n)$$

where the return function r is separable or $r(X, Y) = r_1(X, r_2(Y))$, in other words, return at each stage is independent of previous decisions and subsequent decisions, and r_1 is monotonically nondecreasing (or nonincreasing) relative to its second argument. Then local decision at each stage "adds up" to an overall multistage decision. An example of a separable function is $(x_1 + x_2^3)$, or x_1x_2. As an opposite example $(x_1 \ln x_2 + x_2)$ illustrates a non-decomposable function.

Second, the system has to be Markovian:

$$f_n^*(x_n, X_n) = \underset{x_1,\ldots, x_n}{opt} \{f_n(x_n, X_n)\} = \underset{x_n}{opt} \{ \underset{x_1,\ldots, x_{n-1}}{opt} [f_{n-1}(x_{n-1}, S_{n-1})]\}$$

$$= \underset{x_n}{opt} \langle \underset{x_{n-1}}{opt} \{ \underset{x_1,\ldots, x_{n-2}}{opt} [f_{n-2}(x_{n-2}, S_{n-2})]\} \rangle \ldots \text{ etc.}$$

This says that after k decisions have been made, the effect of the remaining $n - k$ stages on the total criterion function depends only on the state X_k, and the final $n - k$ decisions $x_{k+1}, ..., x_{n-1}, x_n$. Put it in a different way, an optimal policy for the remaining stages is independent of the policy adopted in previous stages.

These two properties—separability and memorylessness—are prerequisites to the optimization of a Markovian system. We have described them above in terms of forward recursion. Similar arguments can be made for backward recursion as well.[3] Even though a deterministic system was used in the DP example, we will show below how this can be generalized to a probabilistic system.

VII. *MARKOVIAN DECISION PROCESSES*

Infinite-horizon probabilistic dynamic-programming problems are called **Markovian decision processes** (MDP) (Winston 1994). An MDP is described by four types of information: state space, decision set, transition probabilities, and expected rewards. At the beginning of each period, the MDP is in some state i, where i is a member of the state space $X' = \{1, 2, . . ., n\}$. For each state i, there is a finite set of allowable decisions, $D(i)$. Suppose a period begins in state i, and a decision $d'' \in D(i)$ is chosen. Then with probability $\pi(j \mid i, d'')$, the next period's state will be j. The next period's state depends only on the current period's state and on the decision chosen during the current period (and not on previous states and decisions). During a period in which the state is i and a decision $d'' \in D(i)$ is chosen, an expected reward of $r(i, d'')$ is received.

A. *Policy Iteration*

In an MDP, what criterion should be used to determine the correct decision? Answering this question requires that we discuss the idea of an optimal policy for an MDP. A policy is a rule that specifies how each period's decision is chosen. A policy $\tilde{\delta}$ is a stationary policy if whenever the state is i, the policy $\tilde{\delta}$ chooses (independently of the period) the same decision (call this decision $\delta(i)$). If a policy δ^* has the property that for all $i \in X'$, the optimal expected value of the decision at state i, $Z(i)$, is the same as that obtained from the policy δ^*, $Z_{\delta^*}(i)$, or $Z(i) = Z_{\delta^*}(i)$, then δ^* is an optimal policy.

1. Value Determination. Let us determine a system of linear equations that can be used to find $Z_\delta(i)$ for $i \in X'$ for any stationary policy δ. If $\delta(i)$ stands for the decision chosen by the stationary policy δ whenever the process begins a period in state i, then $Z_\delta(i)$ can be found by solving the following system of n linear equations, the value determination equations:

$$Z_\delta(i) = r(i, \delta(i)) + \ell' \sum_{j=1}^{n} \pi(j \mid i, \delta(i))Z_\delta(j) \quad i = 1, . . ., n \qquad (A2.11)$$

Here we are discounting rewards by assuming that a dollar reward received during the next period will have the same value as a reward of ℓ' dollars $(0 < \ell' < 1)$ received during the current period. This is equivalent to assuming that the decision maker wishes to maximize expected discounted reward. Then the expected discounted reward earned during an infinite number of periods consists of $r(i, \delta(i))$ (the expected reward earned during the current period) plus ℓ' times the expected discounted reward. This discounted value includes the reward to the beginning of the next period, earned from the next period onward. But with probability $\pi(j \mid i, \delta(i))$, we will begin the next period in state j and earn an expected discounted reward, back to this next period, of $Z_\delta(j)$. Thus the expected discounted reward, discounted back to the beginning of the next period and earned from the beginning of the next period onward, is given by $\sum_{j=1}^{n} \pi(j \mid i, \delta(i)) Z_\delta(j)$. Equation A2.11 now follows. Notice its similarity to the recursion equation in deterministic dynamic programming.

Example

To illustrate the use of the value determination equations, let us consider a site relocation example characterized by Table A2.5, which shows the probable degradation of a site over time as demand patterns change. We consider the following stationary policy for the site relocation example: $\delta(E) = \delta(G) = N$ and $\delta(A) = \delta(B) = Y$, where Y stands for relocation and N stands for no relocation. This policy relocates a bad (B) or average (A) site to an excellent (E) site at a cost (negative reward) and does not relocate a good (G) or excellent (E) site. For this policy and the given rewards and discount factor, Equation A2.11 yields the following four equations:

$$Z_\delta(E) = 100 + 0.9(0.7\,Z_\delta(E) + 0.3\,Z_\delta(G)) \qquad Z_\delta(A) = 100 + 0.9(0.7\,Z_\delta(E) + 0.3\,Z_\delta(G))$$
$$Z_\delta(G) = 80 + 0.9(0.7\,Z_\delta(G) + 0.3\,Z_\delta(A)) \qquad Z_\delta(B) = -100 + 0.9(0.7\,Z_\delta(E) + 0.3\,Z_\delta(G))$$

The last two equations suggest that with probabilities 0.7 and 0.3, the excellent site will remain "excellent" or become "good" respectively at the beginning of the next period. Solving these equations yields $Z_\delta(E) = 687.81$, $Z_\delta(G) = 572.19$, $Z_\delta(A) = 487.81$, and $Z_\delta(B) = 487.81$. In other words, following the stationary policy as outlined above, the expected value of having an excellent, good, average, and bad site can be uniquely determined. ∎

2. Howard's Method for Optimal Policy. We now describe Howard's (1960) policy iteration method for finding an optimal stationary policy for an MDP.

Table A2.5   TRANSITION MATRIX OF SITE-RELOCATION EXAMPLE

Present state of site	Probability that site begins next year as			
	Excellent (E)	Good (G)	Average (A)	Bad (B)
Excellent (E)	0.7	0.3		
Good (G)		0.7	0.3	
Average (A)			0.6	0.4
Bad (B)				1.0[a]

[a]A "bad" site remains "bad" until relocation takes place.

Step 1. Policy evaluation: Choose a stationary policy $\tilde{\delta}$ and use the value determination equations to find $Z_\delta(i)$, $i = 1, ..., n$.
Step 2. Policy improvement: For all states $i = 1, ..., n$, compute

$$Z_\delta' = \max_{d'' \in D(i)} (r(i, d'') + \ell' \sum_{j=1}^{n} \pi(j \mid i, d'')Z_\delta(j)) \qquad \text{(A2.12)}$$

Since we can choose $d'' = \delta(i)$ for $i = 1, ..., n$, $Z_\delta'(i) \geq Z_\delta(i)$. If $Z_\delta'(i) = Z_\delta(i)$ for $i = 1, ..., n$, then $\tilde{\delta}$ is an optimal policy. If $Z_\delta'(i) > Z_\delta(i)$ for at least one state, $\tilde{\delta}$ is not an optimal policy. In this case, modify $\tilde{\delta}$ so that the decision in each state is the decision attaining the maximum in Equation A2.12 for $Z_\delta'(i)$. This yields a new stationary policy δ' from which $Z_\delta'(i) \geq Z_\delta(i)$ for $i = 1, ..., n$, and for at least one state i', $Z_\delta(i') > Z_\delta(i')$. Return to Step 1, with policy δ' replacing policy $\tilde{\delta}$. The policy iteration method is guaranteed to find an optimal policy after evaluating a finite number of policies. We now use the policy iteration method to find an optimal stationary policy for the site relocation example.

Example
We begin with the stationary policy as mentioned: $\delta(E) = \delta(G) = N$ and $\delta(A) = \delta(B) = Y$. For this policy, we have already found that $Z_\delta(E) = 687.81$, $Z_\delta(G) = 572.19$, $Z_\delta(A) = 487.81$, and $Z_\delta(B) = 487.81$. We now compute $Z_\delta'(E)$, $Z_\delta'(G)$, $Z_\delta'(A)$, and $Z_\delta'(B)$. Since N is the only possible decision in E according to Table A2.5, $Z_\delta'(E) = Z_\delta(E) = 687.81$ and $Z_\delta'(E)$ is attained by the decision N. State G can become state E with a relocation (Y) or stay at G with no relocation (N):

$$Z_\delta'(G) = \max \begin{cases} -100 + 0.9(0.7 Z_\delta(E) + 0.3 Z_\delta(G)) = 487.81 & (Y) \\ 80 + 0.9(0.7 Z_\delta(G) + 0.3 Z_\delta(A)) = Z_\delta(G) = 572.19^* & (N) \end{cases} \qquad \text{(A2.13)}$$

Thus, $Z_\delta'(G) = 572.19$ is attained by the decision N which incurs a larger reward. State A can become E or remain at A involving a Y or N decision respectively:

$$Z_\delta'(A) = \max \begin{cases} -100 + 0.9(0.7 Z_\delta(E) + 0.3 Z_\delta(G) = 487.81 & (Y) \\ 50 + 0.9(0.6 Z_\delta(A) + 0.4 Z_\delta(B)) = Z_\delta(A) = 489.03^* & (N) \end{cases} \qquad \text{(A2.14)}$$

Thus $Z_\delta'(A) = 489.03$ is attained by the decision N. B can be upgraded to E or remain at B:

$$Z_\delta'(B) = \max \begin{cases} -100 + 0.9(0.7 Z_\delta(E) + 0.3 Z_\delta(G)) = 487.81^* & (Y) \\ 10 + 0.9 Z_\delta(B) = 449.03 & (N) \end{cases} \qquad \text{(A2.15)}$$

Thus $Z_\delta'(B) = Z_\delta(B) = 487.81$.
    We have found that $Z_\delta'(E) = Z_\delta(E)$, $Z_\delta'(G) = Z_\delta(G)$, $Z_\delta'(B) = Z_\delta(B)$, and $Z_\delta'(A) > Z_\delta(A)$. The policy δ is not optimal, and the policy δ' given by $\delta'(E) = \delta'(G) = \delta'(A) = N$, $\delta'(B) = Y$, is an improvement over δ. Notice the new policy relocates only when the site is bad. We now return to Step 1 and solve the value determination equations for δ'. From Equation (A2.11), the value determination equations for δ' are

$$Z_\delta(E) = 100 + 0.9(0.7 Z_\delta(E) + 0.3 Z_\delta(G)) \quad Z_\delta(A) = 50 + 0.9(0.6 Z_\delta(A) + 0.4 Z_\delta(B))$$
$$Z_\delta(G) = 80 + 0.9(0.7 Z_\delta(G) + 0.3 Z_\delta(A)) \quad Z_\delta(B) = -100 + 0.9(0.7 Z_\delta(E) + 0.3 Z_\delta(G))$$

Solving these equations, we obtain $Z_\delta(E) = 690.23$, $Z_\delta(G) = 575.50$, $Z_\delta(A) = 492.35$, and $Z_\delta(B) = 490.23$. Observe that in each state i, $Z_\delta(i) > Z_\delta(i)$. We now apply the policy iteration procedure to δ'. We compute $Z'_{\delta'}(E) = Z_\delta(E) = 690.23$, N being the only decision.

$$Z'_{\delta'}(G) = \max \begin{cases} -100 + 0.9(0.7\,Z_\delta(E) + 0.3\,Z_\delta(G)) = 490.23 & (Y) \\ 80 + 0.9(0.7\,Z_\delta(G) + 0.3\,Z_\delta(A)) = Z_\delta(G) = 575.50^* & (N) \end{cases} \quad (A2.16)$$

for transitions to E and G respectively. Thus, $Z_{\delta'}'(G) = Z_\delta(G) = 575.50$ is attained by the decision N.

$$Z'_{\delta'}(A) = \max \begin{cases} -100 + 0.9(0.7\,Z_\delta(E) + 0.3\,Z_\delta(G)) = 490.23 & (Y) \\ 50 + 0.9(0.6\,Z_\delta(A) + 0.4\,Z_\delta(B)) = Z_\delta(A) = 492.35^* & (N) \end{cases} \quad (A2.17)$$

for transitions to E and A. Thus $Z_{\delta'}'(A) = Z_\delta(A) = 492.35$ is attained by the decision N.

$$Z_{\delta'}(B) = \max \begin{cases} -100 + 0.9(0.7\,Z_\delta(E) + 0.3\,Z_\delta(G)) = 490.23^* & (Y) \\ 10 + 0.9\,Z_\delta(B) = 451.21 & (N) \end{cases} \quad (A2.18)$$

for states E and B. Thus $Z_{\delta'}'(B) = Z_\delta(B) = 490.23$ is attained by Y.

For each state i, $Z_{\delta'}'(i) = Z_\delta(i)$. Thus δ' is an optimal stationary policy. In order to maximize expected discounted rewards (profits), a bad site should be relocated, but an excellent, good, or average site should not be relocated. If we began period 1 with an excellent location, an expected discounted reward of $690.23 dollars could be earned and so on. ∎

B. Reward Per Period

Linear programming can be used to find a stationary policy that maximizes the expected per-period rewards earned over an infinite horizon. Consider a decision rule or policy δ that chooses decision $d'' \in D(i)$ with probability $P_{id''}$ during a period in which the state is i. A policy δ' will be a stationary policy if each $P_{id''}$ equals 0 or 1. To find a policy that maximizes expected reward per period over an infinite horizon, let $P_{id''}$ be the fraction of all periods in which the state is i and decision $d'' \in D(i)$ is chosen. Then the expected reward per period is to be optimized:

$$\text{Max} \sum_{i=1}^{n} \sum_{d'' \in D(i)} P_{id''} r(i, d'')$$

What constraints must be satisfied by the $P_{id''}$? First, all $P_{id''}$s must be non-negative, or $P_{id''} \geq 0$ for $i = 1, ..., n$ and $d'' \in D(i)$. Second, sum of the probabilities must add up to unity:

$$\text{Max} \sum_{i=1}^{n} \sum_{d'' \in D(i)} P_{id''} = 1$$

Finally, the fraction of all periods during which a transition occurs out of state j must equal the fraction of all periods during which a transition occurs into state j. This is identical to the restriction on steady-state probabilities for Markov chains (see Equations A2.1 and A2.4):

$$\sum_{d''\epsilon D(j)} P_{jd''}(1 - \pi(j|i,d'')) = \sum_{d''\epsilon D(i)}\sum_{i \neq j} P_{id''} - \pi(j|i,d'') \quad j = 1, \ldots, n \quad \text{(A2.19)}$$

which, after rearranging, yields

$$\sum_{d''\epsilon D(j)} P_{jd''} = \sum_{d''\epsilon D(i)}\sum_{i=j} P_{id''}\pi(j|i,d'') \quad j = 1, \ldots, n \quad \text{(A2.20)}$$

It can be shown that this LP has an optimal solution in which for each i, at most one $P_{id''} > 0$. This optimal solution implies that the expected reward per period is minimized by a solution in which each $P_{id''}$ equals 0 or 1. Thus the optimal solution to the LP will occur for a stationary policy. For states having $P_{id''} = 0$, any decision may be chosen without affecting the expected reward per period.

Example
For the relocation example above, the corresponding LP looks like

$$
\begin{aligned}
\text{Max} \quad & 100P_{EN} + 80P_{GN} + 50P_{AN} + 10P_{BN} - 100(P_{GY} + P_{AY} + P_{BY}) \\
\text{s.t.} \quad & P_{EN} + P_{GN} + P_{AN} + P_{BN} + P_{GY} + P_{AY} + P_{BY} = 1 \\
& P_{EN} = 0.7(P_{EN} + P_{GY} + P_{AY} + P_{BY}) \\
& P_{GY} + P_{GN} = 0.3(P_{GY} + P_{AY} + P_{BY} + P_{EN}) + 0.7P_{GN} \\
& P_{AY} + P_{AN} = 0.3P_{GN} + 0.6P_{AN} \\
& P_{BY} + P_{BN} = P_{BN} + 0.4P_{AN}
\end{aligned}
$$

with all $P_{id''}$ non-negative. It was found that the optimal objective function is at \$60. The only non-zero decision variables are $P_{EN} = 0.35$, $P_{GN} = 0.50$, and $P_{AY} = 0.15$. Thus the system is optimized by not relocating from an excellent or good site, but relocating from an average site. Since we are relocating from an average site, the action chosen during a period in which the site is bad is of no importance. It is not surprising the optimal policy reached here is different from those in response to maximizing expected discounted rewards. ■

Additional locational examples of the Markovian decision process can be found in Chapter 3 under the "Stochastic Process" subsection and in "Measuring Spatial Separation" chapter under the "Approximate versus Exact Measure" subsection in Chan (2000).

VIII. RECURSIVE PROGRAMMING

Related to Howard's policy iteration method is recursive programming, an analogue spearheaded by economists (Day 1973). We will introduce recursive programming via an example here. More general computational treatment is found in the sub-subsection bearing the same name in the "Location Routing" chapter of Chan (2000). Suppose a firm is planning on a multiyear production of two products. Let $x_1(t)$, $x_2(t)$ be the amounts to be produced on each of the two commodities over year $t = 1, 2$, and so forth. Let $I_1(t)$ and $I_2(t)$ be the profits per unit at the end of year t. Let c_1 and c_2 be the resource requirements of one unit of the two commodities. Let b_1 be the yearly combined production quota of the two commodities, as limited by, labor availability for instance. Finally, let $b_2(t)$ be the production budget available at the beginning of year t. Assuming constant return to scale, or c_1 and c_2 are independent of x_1 and x_2, the decision problem at the beginning of year t can be represented by the linear programming problem:

$$I(t) = \max_{x_1, x_2} [I_1(t)x_1 + I_2(t)x_2] \tag{A2.21}$$

s.t.

$$\begin{aligned} x_1 + x_2 &\leq b_1 \\ c_1x_1 + c_2x_2 &\leq b_2(t) \\ x_1, x_2 &\geq 0 \end{aligned} \tag{A2.22}$$

The optimal solution of this LP, $x_1(t)$ and $x_2(t)$, will give the production of each commodity in period t.

The expected marginal net-revenue values of the two factors, labor and capital, are given by the dual variables $u_1(t)$ and $u_2(t)$, obtainable from the dual program:

$$I_D(t) = \min_{u_1, u_2} [b_1u_1 + b_2(t)u_2] \tag{A2.23}$$

s.t.

$$\begin{aligned} u_1 + c_1u_2 &\geq I_1(t) \\ u_1 + c_2u_2 &\geq I_2(t) \\ u_1, u_2 &\geq 0 \end{aligned} \tag{A2.24}$$

A. Existence of Solutions

Let $p_i(t)$ be the market price at the end of year t for each commodity, then the profit from each commodity unit is the net between revenue and cost:

$$I_i(t) = p_i(t - 1) - c_i \qquad i = 1, 2 \tag{A2.25}$$

Working capital now is limited to the sales minus overhead (say at a constant amount of C_0 for each period):

$$b_2(t) = \sum_i p_i(t - 1) x_i(t - 1) - C_0 \tag{A2.26}$$

For each year, the existing supply is sold at a uniform price in a perfectly competitive market. The price received for each commodity is a function of the total amount of commodity supplied. When a commodity is sold at a positive market price, its price is determined by a linear demand-function, defined by intercept a and slope b:

$$p_i(t) = \max\{0,\, a_i + b_i x_i(t)\} \quad i = 1, 2 \tag{A2.27}$$

The system of Equations A2.21–A2.27 is defined as a recursive program. The primal-dual LP problems Equations A2.21–A2.24 describe the optimization component, as driven by profitability. Equations A2.26–A2.27 together with the definition (Equation A2.25) describe the feedback mechanism, in other words how the market dynamics work. It is a closed, discrete time, dynamic system of which one may ask such traditional questions as: Do equilibria exist? Are they stable?

The dual LP at any time t are dual feasible so long as

$$\sum_i \left[\max\left\{0,\, a_i + b_i x_i(t - 1)\right\} \right] x_i(t - 1) \geq C_0 \tag{A2.28}$$

In other words, if total revenue in the preceding year is insufficient to cover the overhead, then no surplus remains to finance the current year's production. The system goes bankrupt. So long as each dual program in the sequence is feasible in the above sense, then optimal solution values $x_1(t)$, $x_2(t)$, $u_1(t)$ and $u_2(t)$ exist at each time t. When this occurs, $I(t) = I_D(t)$ by the duality theorem of LP.

It is important to emphasize that the solution values $x_1(t)$, $x_2(t)$, $u_1(t)$ and $u_2(t)$ describe and do not prescribe behavior in our model. That is, these values are not necessarily optimal ex post. For the industry as a whole, the actual optimum is the monopoly solution given by the quadratic programming problem[4] that arises when a perfect knowledge of the demand curves (Equation A2.27) is accounted for by the decision makers over time.

B. Phase Solutions

If a solution of the problem at the time t is unique, it lies at an extreme point of the LP feasible region. If there is more than one solution, then extreme point solutions are among them. Consequently, a solution at any time t can be represented by a set of equated constraints corresponding to the duality conditions. These equations give the algebraic description of the extreme point. Because of the recursive character of the sequence of programs, these sets of equated constraints identify difference equations that describe the behavior of the production variables and marginal value for a given time period. Since these sets may change from time to time, the system as a whole is a multiple-phase system. Questions concerning growth, cycles and equilibrium consequently boil down to an analysis of the conditions for the occurrence of specific phases (sets of difference equations) and the dynamic properties of each phase.

By examining the extreme solution possibilities we find the following six cases:

Phase 0 (Null phase): nothing produced, no imputed value.

Phase 1-s: fixed-factor constraints equated, the first commodity produced.

Phase 2-s: fixed-factor constraints equated, the second commodity produced.

Phase 1-r: financial constraints equated, the first commodity produced.

Phase 2-r: financial constraints equated, the second commodity produced.

Phase 12-rs: both constraints equated, both commodities produced.

To each of these extreme solutions corresponds a set of equations:

Phase 0: $x_1(t) = 0$, $x_2(t) = 0$, $u_1(t) = 0$ and $u_2(t) = 0$

Phase 1-s: $x_1(t) = 1$, $x_2(t) = 0$, $u_1(t) = a_1 + b_1 x_1(t - 1) - c_1$, $u_2(t) = 0$

Phase 2-s: $x_2(t) = 1$, $x_1(t) = 0$, $u_1(t) = a_2 + b_2 x_2(t - 1) - c_2$, $u_2(t) = 0$

Phase 1-r: $x_1(t) = (1/c_1)[\Sigma_i\{a_i + b_i x_i(t - 1)\}x_i(t - 1) - C_0]$, $x_2(t) = 0$,
$$u_2(t) = (1/c_1)[a_1 + b_1 x_1(t - 1) - c_1], u_1(t) = 0$$

Phase 2-r: $x_2(t) = (1/c_2)[\Sigma_i\{a_i + b_i x_i(t - 1)x_i(t - 1) - C_0]$, $x_1(t) = 0$,
$$u_2(t) = (1/c_2)[a_2 + b_2 x_2(t - 1) - c_2], u_1(t) = 0$$

Phase 12-rs:
$$\begin{bmatrix} x_1(t) \\ x_2(t) \end{bmatrix} = \left(\frac{1}{c_1-c_2}\right)\begin{bmatrix} -c_2 & 1 \\ c_1 & -1 \end{bmatrix}\begin{bmatrix} 1 \\ \Sigma_i\{a_i + b_i x_i(t - 1)\}x_i(t - 1) - C_0 \end{bmatrix}'$$
$$\begin{bmatrix} u_1(t) \\ u_2(t) \end{bmatrix} = \left(\frac{1}{c_1-c_2}\right) - \begin{bmatrix} -c_2 & c_1 \\ 1 & -1 \end{bmatrix}\begin{bmatrix} a_1 + b_1 x_1(t - 1) - c_1 \\ a_2 + b_2 x_2(t - 1) - c_2 \end{bmatrix}$$

Which phase holds in a given time period depends on the solution in the preceding time period and the relative positions of constraints and objective functions that the preceding solution brings about. Various possibilities are shown to occur, including phase and production periodicity, convergence to a stationary state and so on. It is important to note that solutions are multi-phase; they satisfy different sets of dynamic equations at various times during their evolution. Recursive programming is the problem of optimizing an infinite set of recursively generated linear functionals subject to an infinite set of recursively generated linear constraints. This could be expressed as the search for a set of functions that satisfy a system of nonlinear simultaneous difference inequalities (duality conditions). Among the possible solutions of a given system are sometimes one that exhibit an optimality property, in other words, they converge to some desirable state. Notice this is not always the case in practice, and it is in this respect that recursive programming is different from dynamic programming.

IX. CONCLUDING REMARKS

We have illustrated in this appendix several examples of a Markovian system, including Poisson or random demand pattern and queuing. These are both time-dependent probabilistic processes, or what is commonly known as stochastic processes. An equally common Markovian system is regular dynamic programming (DP), which can be both a deterministic and probabilistic process. All the above mentioned processes can be described by state transition equations, characterized by memoryless properties. This property suggests that the entire history of the process can be encapsulated in the last state of the system. A hybrid of a Markovian system and DP is found in Markovian decision processes, in which a stochastic process is optimized through time. We bring out the stationarity property of these processes, which allows steady-state equations to be written. A distinction is made, however, regarding optimizing the expected reward over the complete time horizon of a system and the expected reward per time period. While both policies can be stationary, they are intrinsically different since the former is specified for the entire life span while the latter is by definition time-period dependent. Although less known outside the economic literature, recursive programming (RP) is an allied concept to dynamic programming. It is a robust solution algorithm for sequential processes. Unlike DP, however, RP yields only local optimum where it exists, since it lacks the Markovian properties that allow decomposition of the optimization procedure into stages.

Admittedly we have only touched on a few fundamentals in this appendix, but it serves as an adequate prerequisite to understanding much of the discussions on stochastic facility location problems, one of the main topics in this text. It also allows understanding of the optimality conditions for certain heuristics in simultaneous location routing models, particularly the Route Improvement Synthesis and Evaluation (RISE) algorithm contained in the software CD and described also in the "Location-Routing" chapter of Chan (2000).

ENDNOTES

[1] An explanation of goodness of fit and chi-square is contained in Appendix 3 on "Statistical Tools" and the "Descriptive Tools" chapter respectively.

[2] Note that the return function can also be a function of both the decision variable and the state variable, $r_k(x_k, S_k)$. This is the case when delay is measured by a rectangle such as DFCE rather than a line segment such as AE/2 in Figure A2.10.

[3] DP is used to solve a multi-period capacitated location problem in the "Facility Location" chapter under the "Long-run Location Production Allocation Problems" section of Chan (2000).

[4] A quadratic program has an objective function that is a quadratic function of the decision variables, subject to a set of linear constraints. An example is the quadratic assignment problem in Chapter 3. Also, a monopolistic market model is given in the "Alternative Models of Spatial Competition" section of the "Spatial Equilibrium" chapter in Chan (2000), showing a nonlinear objective function.

REFERENCES

Chan, Y. (2000). *Location. transport and land-use: Modelling spatial-temporal information.* New York: Springer-Verlag.

Cooper, R. B. (1980). *Introduction to queuing theory.* New York: Elsevier Science Publishing.

Day, R. H. (1973). "Recursive programming models: A brief introduction" In *Studies in economic planning over space and time,* edited by G. G. Judge and T. Takayama. Amsterdam: North-Holland and New York: American Elsevier Publishing Co.

Howard, R. (1960). *Dynamic programming and Markov processes.* Cambridge, Massachusetts: Technology Press of Massachusetts Institute of Technology.

Morlok, E. F. (1978). *Introduction to transportation engineering and planning.* New York: McGraw-Hill.

Winston, W. L. (1994). *Operations research: Applications and algorithms,* 3rd ed. Belmont, California: ITP Duxbury Press.

Appendix 3

Review of Some Pertinent Statistical Tools

This appendix puts in one place a few basic statistical analysis techniques, including estimators, goodness of fit parameters, ordinary and stepwise regression, analysis of variance, and the general idea behind statistical modeling. As with the previous two appendices, we strive to provide a self-contained account through numerical examples, rather than formal developments. It paves the way for chapters such as Chapter Three and these chapters in Chan (2000): "Generation, Competition and Distribution," "Spatial Econometrics," "Spatial Time Series," and "Spatial Temporal Information." It also proves to be convenient in places in the current book where statistical knowledge is assumed.

I. STATISTICAL ANALYSIS: BASIC CONCEPTS

For the purpose of this discussion, statistics can be thought of as dealing with representative indicators of figures, when a huge number of figures need to be summarized in terms of a more compact set of information. An estimator such as the mean or average is a good example, wherein n numbers are represented in terms of a single one:

$$X = \sum_{t=1}^{n} \frac{x_i}{n}$$

Here capital X stands for the random variable for the data and x_is are the data observations themselves. Similarly, one can define the spread of the data about the mean, an estimator called standard deviation:

$$s = \sqrt{\frac{\sum_{t=1}^{n} (x_i - \overline{X})^2}{(n - 1)}} \tag{A3.1}$$

Variance is the square of standard deviation, such that the sign of standard deviation—indicating whether the specific figures are smaller than or bigger than the mean—is set aside. To summarize the two estimators, mean and standard deviation, one can define the coefficient of variation, which compares the magnitude of the spread with the average $s/\overline{X}$. A small coefficient suggests a sharp distribution, while a large one implies a flat distribution.

A normal distribution is representative of many large samples of data—data on anything from income to population. The mean and standard deviations are overlaid on top of the normal distribution in Figure A3.1. It shows that about 68.3 percent of the sample will be within one standard deviation from the mean and about 95 percent within two standard deviations. Inasmuch as the normal distribution describes any large sample, such numbers are very useful in detecting abnormalities such as outliers.

It is appropriate at this time to introduce the concept of **degree of freedom** (*dof*). Notice that in computing the standard deviation, we divide the sum of the data by $n - 1$ instead of n, which makes it different from computing the mean. While there is a lengthy explanation possible for such a practice, there is an informal way to rationalize it here. We can think of the degree of freedom as the number of useful, or contributory, pieces of information. Imagine that a piece of information is no longer useful once it has been used. If there are n data points to begin with, or n useful pieces of information. We extract from the pool of data one piece of information, for instance, say the mean. The number of unused ones or contributory data remaining will be $n - 1$. Viewed in this light,

$$dof = (number\ of\ observations - number\ of\ coefficients\ estimated)$$

It goes without saying that the larger the degree of freedom, the more representative the estimator, since it is based on a large pool of useful information, instead of a meager sample. In practice, there are often more data pieces than the number of estimated parameters; the precise *dof* becomes less important and the difference between $(n - 1)$ and n in the denominator of Equation A3.1 is minute. We suggest that the sample estimator [using $(n - 1)$ division] approximates the population estimator [using nth division].

Figure A3.1   ILLUSTRATING MEAN AND STANDARD DEVIATION IN A NORMAL DISTRIBUTION

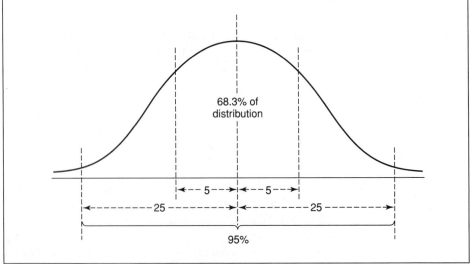

II. GOODNESS OF FIT MEASURES

If one generalizes from a single dimension to two or more dimensions, we start to worry about the relationship between the data represented in these dimensions. For example, we may have families in the study area for which we are interested in the linkage between the number of work trips made and the population density in each of the subareas. Likewise, we may want to study the relationship between the employment level and the population, suspecting that the two may be related; in other words, the more people around, the larger the number of people working and hence the more work trips made. We call these the degrees of correlation, and the more one variable is related to another, the larger the correlation between them. The correlation coefficient, r, between retail land use random variable (Y) and retail employment random variable (X), for example, may be 0.96, which indicates a close relationship between the two variables, considering that by convention, 1 is the largest correlation possible;

$$r_0 = \frac{\Sigma_t (x_t - \overline{X}) (y_t - \overline{Y})}{s_X s_Y}$$

where x, s and y, s are data observations. A close examination of this expression will suggest that a plot of the retail land use (in acres or hectares) against retail employment will yield a linear relationship, in that retail land use goes up as retail employment goes up. One can readily see this in a shopping mall, as illustrated in the correlation coefficient plot in Chapter 3.

In forecasting applications, we often distinguish two situations. The first is when the relationship between two variables are sought, both of which are known for a future year. The second is when we want to forecast a variable from an independent variable that we know. The relationship between the latter pair of variables is called the partial correlation coefficient while the relationship between the former is simply the correlation coefficient. Another way of saying this is that the partial correlation coefficient measures the linear association between the dependent and independent variables, while the correlation coefficient does the same job between two independent variables. While we want a high value for the partial correlation coefficient, the exact opposite is true for the correlation coefficient. The reason is that a high partial means good explanatory power of the independent variable in predicting the dependent variable, but a high correlation among two independent variables means that there is some kind of double counting. In other words, the same information is used twice to predict the dependent variable. For example, one should be careful in using both population and employment as independent, or explanatory, variables for the number of work trips generated from a subarea simply because they are related. Including both variables will lead toward a statistical fallacy known as colinearity.

If we generalize the concept to two or more independent variables and one dependent variable, we have broadened the concept of a partial correlation coefficient to a multiple correlation coefficient. This pertains to the explanatory power of several independent variables in predicting the dependent variable. For example, if land use development is to be forecasted, one way to do this is to relate land development in the future to the population and per capita income in the area. The stronger the relationship between land development and both population and income, the more accurate the forecast is likely to be. In other words, a multiple correlation coefficient R close to unity is preferred to one that is smaller. When there is only one dependent and one independent variable, the multiple correlation coefficient R becomes the partial correlation coefficient r'_0.

III. LINEAR REGRESSION

The concept of multiple correlation coefficient, the square of which is sometimes known as coefficient of multiple-determination, brings us to the subject of linear regression. Linear regression can be thought of as the structural postulation between dependent and independent variables that can be supported by sound goodness of fit parameters, where goodness of fit parameters are simply multidimensional extension of estimators like mean and variance. Take the example of work trip forecasting. Suppose the following structural relationship is postulated: $Y = a + bX$ where Y is the number of total trips predicted and X is the household income (in thousands of U. S. dollars), and a, b are calibration coefficients, which take on the values of 29.33 and 1.150 respectively for the data shown in Table A3.1. These values are calculated on the basis of these formulas:

$$b = \frac{\sum_{t=1}^{n} (x_t - \overline{X})(y_t - \overline{Y})}{\sum_{t=1}^{n} (x_t - \overline{X})^2}$$

and

$$a = \overline{Y} - b\overline{X}$$

In other words, b is calculated as

$$\frac{(30 - 20)(65 - 52.333) + (20 - 20)(50 - 52.333) + (10 - 20)(42 - 52.333)}{(30 - 20)^2 + (20 - 20)^2 + (10 - 20)^2}$$

and a as $52.333 - (1.15)(20)$. These formulas determine a and b on the basis of minimizing the sum of the deviations of the dependent variable from the regression line. To show this concept, a plot of the regression line is given in Figure A3.2, in which the deviations, sometimes referred to as residuals, are highlighted. Here the multiple correlation coefficient, R, is 0.985. This is close enough to 1.000. In an applicational context, however, this coefficient is often much less than unity. The toy problem we have been using, as illustrated in Figure A3.2, shows a definite relationship between work trip and population. In most regression applications, the square of the figure is used, R^2, such that

$$R^2 = \frac{\sum_{t=1}^{n} (\hat{y}_t - \overline{Y})^2}{\sum_{t=1}^{n} (y_t - \overline{Y})^2}$$

Table A3.1   DATA FOR THE REGRESSION EXAMPLE

Households	Household income X (in thousands)	No. of trips per week Y	Estimated no. of trips $\hat{Y}$	Error ϵ
Jones	30	65	63.833	1.167
Browns	20	50	52.333	−2.333
Robinsons	10	42	40.833	1.167

where $\hat{y}_t$ is the estimated number of trips for family t ($t = 1, 2, 3$) from the equation

$$\hat{Y} = 29.33 + 1.15X$$

In other words, they are the values read off from the regression line itself (Figure A3.2) for a given household income x. $R^2 = 0.970$ is then calculated as

$$R^2 = \frac{(63.833 - 52.333)^2 + (52.333 - 52.333)^2 + (40.833 - 52.333)^2}{(65 - 52.333)^2 + (50 - 52.333)^2 + (42 - 52.333)^2}$$

Figure A3.2   REGRESSION LINE OF EXAMPLE

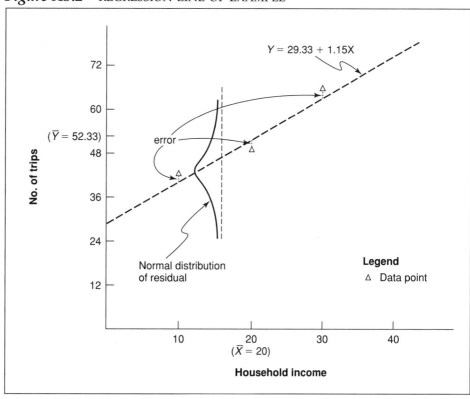

One can think of $\hat{Y}$ as a two-dimensional generalization of the mean estimator. The difference between the data point y_t and the estimated value $\hat{y}_t$ is called the error of estimation a_t. Viewed in this light, one can write $y_t = y_t + a_t$, and the regression equation can be written as $Y = a + bX + \epsilon$ where ϵ is the error term random variable (see Figure A3.2 and Table A3.1).

R^2 has the interpretation of the percentage of variation explained by the regression. In other words, the amount of relationship that is captured by the linear model itself in terms of the structural equation $Y = a + bX$, with the remaining part due to random error associated with any statistical analysis. A moment's reflection will show that R^2 can also be expressed in terms of these alternative expressions

$$R^2 = \frac{(source\ of\ variation\ due\ to\ regression)}{(total\ source\ of\ variation)}$$

or

$$R^2 = \frac{(variance\ explained\ by\ the\ regression)}{(total\ unconditional\ variance)}$$

The higher the R^2 value, the more significant the regression equation is. The only exception is over-fitting, which is best exemplified by fitting two data points with a regression line. This results in $R^2 = 1$, but $dof = 0$, meaning there is no allowance for statistical analysis. As seen from this toy problem and will be shown in the analysis of variance discussion later, including a large number of independent variables (in comparison to the number of data points) decreases the dof and increases the R^2. The increase in R^2 purely due to a larger number of independent variables is not necessarily helpful. First, there is an extra cost of data collection. Aside from data collection, there is also an extra burden in using a more complicated model. Second, including two independent variables that are strongly correlated does not contribute to the explanatory power of the equation. As a matter of fact, it will detract from it. There is a delicate tradeoff, therefore, between having a perfect statistical fit and simplifying a model by minimizing the number of explanatory variables. We often refer to this tradeoff as the art of parsimony.

The standard error of estimate (SEE) is a measure of the dispersion of the observed data about the regression line. This can again be thought of as a two-dimensional generalization of the standard deviation about the mean. The smaller the SEE, the tighter the fit of the regression line about the data:

$$SEE = \sqrt{\sum_{t=1}^{n} \frac{(y_t - \hat{y}_t)^2}{dof}}$$

It can be verified that the *SEE* in this case is 2.858, which is calculated as

$$SEE = \sqrt{[(65 - 63.333)^2 + (50 - 52.333)^2 + (42 - 40.833)^2]/(3 - 2)}$$

Two dimensional generalization of the coefficient of variation can also be made. It is simply

$$\left(\frac{SEE}{\overline{Y}}\right) 100\%$$

It measures how accurately the dependent variable can be estimated by the regression equation, relative to the mean of the dependent variable observations. Obviously, the smaller the ratio, the more accurate the estimate tends to be. In our case, the ratio is $(12.858)/(52.333) = 5.46\%$, reflecting quite a high degree of accuracy.

A last set of goodness of fit measures pertains to the regression coefficients. The t-ratio or t-statistic shows how well the coefficient b is calibrated. Statistically, it is simply defined as

$$t_b = \frac{b}{s_b}$$

where

$$s_b = \frac{SEE}{s_X \sqrt{n}}$$

when n is a large number. Notice this is again a two-dimensional generalization of the concept of

$$s_{\overline{X}} = \frac{s_X}{\sqrt{n}}$$

This is a test on the null hypothesis that the coefficients should be zero, in other words, the regression equation has no explanatory power since the data has no pattern, or the data represent total randomness. In this toy example, t_b is calculated as

$$t_b = \frac{1.150}{2.858/(10)(\sqrt{3})} = 6.969$$

While the first equation in this paragraph may be inappropriate for a small number of data points ($n = 3$) in this case, the formula should be a good approximation for large samples in general. To assess how significant the calibration coefficient b is, we examine the t-table, which shows that $t\,(1, 0.90) = 6.314$, or the t-value for a Student t distribution at 1 dof and 90 percent confidence level is 6.314. Since $t_b = 6.969$ is larger than 6.314, we reject the null hypothesis and state that the coefficient b is significant at 90 percent confidence level. In other words, the linear regression model is useful in explaining the variation of the Y random variable in terms of the X random variable. Implicit in the definition of the t-statistic is the assumption that the error is normally distributed. This is illustrated in Figure A3.2 by the normal distribution drawn around the regression line. The technical way of describing this assumption is to say that the residuals are homoscedastic.

F-ratio or F-statistic measures how well the coefficients perform as a whole, in this case only the parameter b itself. F is computed as

$$F = \frac{mean\ variance\ due\ to\ regression}{mean\ variance\ about\ regression} = \frac{\sum\limits_{t=1}^{n} (\hat{y}_t - \overline{Y})^2 / dof}{SEE} \qquad (A3.2)$$

Here the *dof* refers to the regression coefficient data pool rather than the observation data pool. The F-statistic is then calculated as

$$F = \{[(63.833 - 52.333)^2 + (52.333 - 52.333)^2 \\ + (42 - 53.333)^2]/(2 - 1)]\}/(2.858)^2 = 32.388$$

Since there is only one coefficient b in a bivariate regression, the square of the t-ratio is the same as the F-value. To show the significance of the calibration, we examine the F-statistic, $F(1,1,0.90) = 39.9$ (or the F-ratio at 90 percent confidence level with 1 *dof* at the numerator and the denominator, supports the null hypothesis, suggesting that the calibration parameters are insignificant. However, with 32.388 being bigger than $F(1, 1, 0.75) = 5.83$, it says that the calibration parameters are significant at a reduced confidence level of 75 percent, if in fact 75 percent confidence level is acceptable. Thus by lowering the confidence level, a formerly unacceptable regression model may now be acceptable.

IV. ANALYSIS OF VARIANCE

To gain better insight, an analysis of variance can be performed on linear regression. Analysis of variance (ANOVA) breaks total variance of a set of data into two components: data dispersion from local mean and local mean deviation from global mean. Placed in the context of regression, one can explain the sum of squares of the deviations of y_ts about Y'' in terms of the sum-of-squares of the deviations of y_ts from the regression line and the sum-of-squares of deviations of the estimated values $\hat{y}_t$ about $\overline{Y}''$:

$$\sum_t (y_t - \overline{Y})^2 = \sum_t (y_t - \hat{Y})^2 + \sum_t (\hat{y}_t - \overline{Y})^2 \qquad (A3.3)$$

This equation is best illustrated by Figure A3.3, which breaks down total variance into its two components for an illustrative data point (x_t, y_t). Another way to explain ANOVA for regression is that

(total [corrected] sum of squares) = (error sum of squares)
+ (explained sum of squares)

or

(total source of variation) = (source of variation about regression)
+ (source of variation due to regression)

Figure A3.3   ANALYSIS OF VARIANCE AS APPLIED TO LINEAR REGRESSION

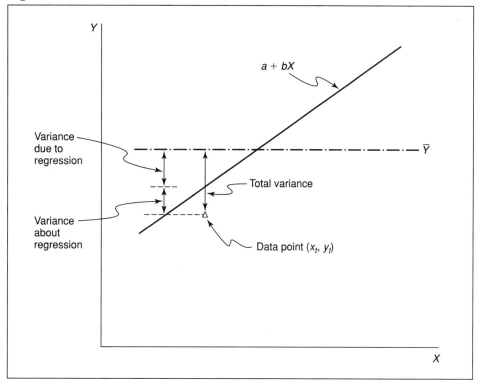

The word corrected is used to distinguish between raw data y_t and data corrected for the mean $(y_t - Y)$. The degrees of freedom for each of the above three terms are $n - 1$, $n - k$, and $k - 1$ respectively, where k is the number of parameters estimated in the regression equation.

A typical ANOVA table is shown in Table A3.2 for the example problem we have been using thus far. It can be verified that the F-ratio is computed as $264.5/8.167 = 32.388$, which is exactly the same as Equation A3.2. When the numerator (mean variance due to regression) possesses only one *dof*, as in the case of a bivariate regression, F will be the same as t^2 (as mentioned). This is checked out in this case, where the t-statistic was computed as 5.691 ($t^2 = 32.388$).

Table A3.2   EXAMPLE ANALYSIS OF VARIANCE TABLE

Source of variation	Degree of freedom	Sum of squares	Mean square	F-ratio
Due to regression	1	246.500	264.500	32.388
About regression	1	8.167	8.167	
Total	2	272.667		

V. USING THE REGRESSION EQUATION

Earlier, we made a distinction between sample estimator and the population estimator. An analogy can be drawn for the regression line here. A model can be constructed to estimate the "true" Y values from a population regression line $E[Y \mid X = x^*] = \alpha' + \beta' X$ (Crow, Davis, and Maxfield 1960). This contrasts with an estimate obtainable from a regression line $y = a + bx$ based on sample observations (x^*, y^*). Since a and b are observations from random variables $\hat{a}$ and $\hat{b}$, the estimator for y^* is $\hat{y} = a + bx^*$. In the absence of a true population, we are interested in the accuracy of estimating $E[Y]$ at $X = x^*$.

A. Confidence Interval

In practical applications, the ordinate of the sample regression line for any given x^* (which need not be any of the observed $x_i's$) is calculated as $Y = a + bX$. This Y necessarily differs from the true or population mean ordinate at $X = x^*$, which would be obtained if an infinite number of observations could be made with the same value x^*. We can show how good our estimate Y of the true mean ordinate $E[Y \mid X = x^*]$ is by calculating the $100(1 - \alpha)\%$ confidence limits

$$\hat{Y} \pm t_{\alpha/2,n-2}\sigma_{M^*} \cong \hat{Y} \pm t_{\alpha/2,n-2}s_Y \sqrt{\frac{1}{n} + \frac{(x^* - \overline{X})^2}{(n-1)s^2_X}} \tag{A3.4}$$

$$= \hat{Y} \pm t_{\alpha/2,\, n-2}s_Y \sqrt{\frac{1}{n} + \frac{(x^* - \overline{X})^2}{(n-1)s^2_X}}$$

where $t_{\alpha/2,n-2}$, is the t-statistic (at $100(1 - \alpha)\%$ confidence-level and $(n - 2)$ *dof* obtainable from any statistical tables and σ_{M^*} is the variance of a normally distributed set of residuals around the sample regression line at $X = x^*$. In this way, we can construct a confidence interval for any particular ordinate of interest. Stated in another way, there is now a way to tell how good any $\hat{Y}$ is.

Example
Using the data of Table A3.1, we calculate a 95 percent confidence-interval for the ordinate to the regression line of Figure A3.2 for the household income $x^* = 20$ thousand. First, $\hat{y}^* = 29.33 + 1.15(20) = 52.333$ (which is the same as Y).

$$\sigma_{M^*} \sim (11.676) \sqrt{\frac{1}{3} + \frac{(20 - 20)^2}{(3 - 1)(10)}} = (11.676) \sqrt{\frac{1}{3}} = 6.741 \tag{A3.5}$$

95 percent confidence interval on $E[Y \mid x = 20]$ is therefore $t_{0.025,1}\sigma_{M^*} \cong (12.706)$ $(6.741) = 85.651$. In other words, for the household with the average income of \$20,000, 95 percent of the number of trips made will fall within the band 52.333 ± 85.651. Admittedly, this is a very wide band, reflecting the questionable validity of this toy regression model and the validity of the implicit assumption of having a large number of data points. This is particularly suspect since the band is at its narrowest when $x^* = \overline{X}$, as seen by the calculations in Equation (A3.5). A check on less central positions such as $x^* = 10$ and 30 will verify that the band widths are $\pm$ 342.60 on either side of the regression line! ∎

B. Prediction Interval

Suppose a regression line has been estimated. We obtain another observation $X = x'$, and we are interested in the confidence interval on the estimated Y for this new observation. This typically arises in forecast applications. For instance, future trips (Y') are generated from a target year population (x'). In other words, the best estimate of $y' = a + bx'$ is to be obtained. The total variance of Y' is made up of two components. The first is the uncertainty of y itself, σ^2, corresponding to the inherent error term ϵ independent of x' in the true regression line $Y' = \alpha' + \beta'x' + \epsilon$. The second is the statistical estimate on the line that changes with the observations x. As the database pool increases, this second variance term, corresponding to the tilting effect of an additional data point, will go down. Expressed more formally, we have

$$\sigma^2_{Y'} = \sigma^2 + \sigma^2_{M'} \tag{A3.6}$$

Let us look at this another way. For any given x', the individual values of Y are scattered above and below both the true and the sample regression lines. In practice, it may often be of interest to know how closely one can predict an individual value of Y rather than just the accuracy of the mean value given by the regression line. The formula for a $100(1 - \alpha)\%$ prediction interval for Y is

$$\hat{Y} \pm t_{\alpha/2,n-2}s_Y \sqrt{1 + \frac{1}{n} + \frac{(x' - \overline{X})^2}{(n - 1)s_x^2}}$$

Notice this expression is very similar to Equation A3.4, except that we have identified two components of the variance as shown in Equation A3.6—one corresponding to the inherent uncertainty and the second associated with the additional data point x'.

Example
Continuing the same trip generation example, the 95 percent prediction interval for a single trip observation Y at income $x' = 25$ thousand is

$$58.08 + (12.706)(11.676) \sqrt{1 + \frac{1}{3} + \frac{(25 - 20)^2}{(3 - 1)(10)}} = 58.08 \pm 238.432 \tag{A3.7}$$

Again, this toy problem is for illustration only, since the prediction interval is far too huge to be of any use. ∎

C. Summary

The entire interval problem can be viewed in terms of two graphical illustrations. Figure A3.4 shows the inherent probabilistic element of data. Even if a true regression is obtained by virtue of an infinite number of data points in the sample, there is still a spread of the data, the residuals, around the regression line. In other words, Y is a random variable that follows a probabilistic distribution. The residual, ϵ, is assumed to be normally distributed with a variance of σ^2. In practice, such a true regression line is never obtainable. In its place, an estimated regression line is calibrated based on the model $\hat{Y} = \tilde{a} + \tilde{b}x$, for given values of x.

Here $\tilde{a}$ and $\tilde{b}$ are random variables, with specific values of $\tilde{a}^*$ and $\tilde{b}^*$ calibrated by a sample of data points. To predict a value of Y for a given x^* or x' value in practice, two types of errors can be involved: the inherent error σ^2 as discussed above, and the error due to randomness of the regression coefficients themselves, $\sigma^2_{\hat{Y}}$ (that is, tilting of the regression line). In other words,

$$\sigma^2_Y = \sigma^2 + \sigma^2_{\hat{Y}} \tag{A3.8}$$

Figure A3.5 shows that there is randomness in the calibration coefficients a and b, which result in a family of regression lines that are contained in the error envelope defined by Equation A3.8. This band is a combination of both random and estimation errors. Thus the confidence band is reduced to the prediction band when the data sample is so huge that it encompasses the entire population. In this case the term $\sigma^2_{\hat{Y}}$ becomes zero, taking away the curvature of the error envelope and reducing it to a constant band σ^2 around the true regression line as shown in Figure A3.4.

VI. STEPWISE REGRESSION

Stepwise regression is a procedure to search for the best equation automatically. In the case of multiple regression where there are a number of possible explanatory variables (instead of just one as in the toy problem used for illustration so far), it is

Figure A3.4   PREDICTION BANDS FOR A "TRUE" REGRESSION LINE

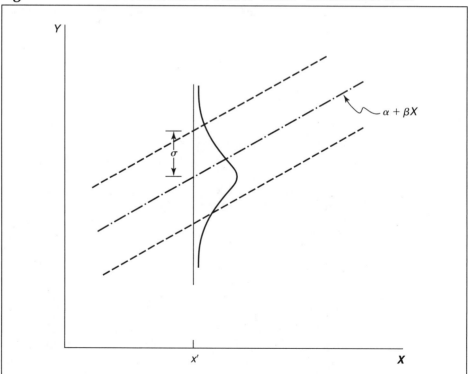

Figure A3.5   CONFIDENCE BANDS FOR AN ESTIMATED REGRESSION LINE

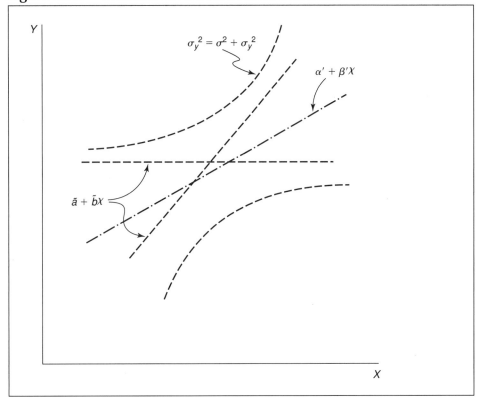

not at all clear which of them will contribute the most in the regression. Take the following example, which is a trip generation analysis based on stepwise regression for a 29-zone[1] study area (Hutchinson 1974). Here, trips are generated from land use information, including zonal population and employment activities:

$$Y = 69.92 + 1.71X_3 \quad (R^2 - 0.735, t_3 - 8.7)$$
$$Y = 78.63 + 0.78X_2 + 1.24X_3 \quad (R^2 - 0.888, t_2 - 5.8, t_3 - 8.0) \tag{A3.9}$$
$$Y = 58.36 + 1.24X_1 + 0.76X_2 + 0.71X_3 \quad (R^2 - 0.938, t_1 - 4.7, t_2 - 7.6, t_3 - 4.4)$$

Here the notation for *t*-statistics is referenced against the explanatory variable. Thus t_1 is the *t*-statistic for the first explanatory variable X_1, t_2 the second explanatory variable X_2 and so on. With $t(25 - 27, 0.99) \approx 2.8$, the question is: How many of the explanatory variables should be included and which of the three equations is the best?

A. Backward and Forward Regression

To generate these equations, two stepwise regression procedures are commonly found in many statistical packages: the backward elimination procedure and the forward selection procedure (or a combination of both). Specifically, the backward elimination procedure does the following:

1. It includes all variables in the equation to start with.
2. The partial F-test value is then calculated for every variable that is treated as though it were the last variable to enter the equation.
3. The lowest partial F-test value F_L is compared to a pre-selected significance level F_0.
4. If $F_L < F_0$, the variable X_L (which gives rise to F_L) is removed from consideration and the equation re-computed in the remaining variables. Go to step 2.
5. If $F_L > F_0$, adopt the equation as calculated.

The forward selection procedure, on the other hand, performs the following steps:

1. Select the explanatory variable X most correlated with Y (for instance, X_1) and calibrate the equation $Y - f(X_1)$.
2. Find the partial correlation coefficient between X_j ($j \neq 1$) and Y (after allowances for X_1). The X_j with the highest partial correlation coefficient is selected (say X_2) and a second equation $Y - f(X_1, X_2)$ is fitted. Repeat this step until $X_1, X_2, \ldots, X_q$ are in the regression.
3. As each variable is entered into the regression, the following values are examined: R^2 and the partial F-test value for the variable most recently entered. The latter shows whether the variable has taken up a significant amount of the variation over that removed by variables previously in the regression.
4. As soon as the partial F-value related to the most recently entered variable becomes insignificant, the process is terminated.

Example

A regression model for home-based non-work trips in York, Pennsylvania, is to be constructed. Variables are added into the model one at a time. The order of insertion is determined by using the partial correlation coefficient as a measure of the importance of a variable not yet in the equation. The selection stops when the contribution of such a variable ceases to be significant at a predetermined level, as measured by the increase in partial F. Table A3.3 summarizes the results of the regression procedure. It can be seen that the variables enter the equation in the order that the one with the largest partial correlation coefficient (indicating the most significant) would enter the equation first. The R value increases significantly from the equation with one variable to the one with two variables, indicating a better fit. Adding the third variable to the equation did not change the R value that much, which means that this third variable is not helping the equation to a better fit since the R value would have a tendency to go up as the number of variables increases (due to a decrease in *dof*). Thus the increase in R^2 can be attributable to statistical properties rather than explanatory power of a variable.

The partial F-value decreases as more variables are added to the equation, which is normally the case. But the decrease of the partial F-value from the total employment explanatory variable of the first equation to the housing land use variable in the second is significant, while that from the second to the third (with the housing density explanatory variable) is even more significant in comparison. This indicates that by adding the housing land use variable, our confidence level

Table A3.3   CALIBRATION RESULTS OF THE FORWARD REGRESSION PROCEDURE

Step		1	2	3
Independent variables		Total employment	Housing land use, Total employment	Housing land use, Total employment, Housing density
New variable		Total employment	Housing land use	Housing density
Partial correlation coefficient of new variables		0.5861	0.5133	0.3290
Partial *F*-value		20.9306	13.953	4.6139
Multiple correlation coefficient (R)		0.5861	0.71863	0.75422
Standard error / Average *Y* observations		0.7957	0.6916	0.6616
Analysis of variance	*F*-ratio (for the whole equation)	20.9306	20.831	16.7121
	Confidence interval[a]	$F(1, 40, 0.99) = 7.31$	$F(2, 39, 0.99) = 5.20$	$F(3, 38, 0.99) = 4.35$

[a] $F(V_1, V_2, 0.99)$ where v_1 is the degree of freedom for the numerator and v_2 for the denominator.

to reject the null hypothesis did not decrease. However, we cannot say the same for the housing density variable. These facts point toward favoring the equation in step 2, resulting in the equation trip-*f* (housing land use, total employment). This is confirmed by the sharp drop of the overall *F*-ratio from step 2 to step 3. ∎

B. Goodness of Fit Parameters for Stepwise Regression

A number of goodness of fit parameters are used to measure the significance of the stepwise regression equation. In the backward elimination procedure, the goodness of fit parameter used to terminate further deletion of explanatory variables, as pointed out above, is the partial *F*-value. It is defined as

$$\frac{variance\ due\ to\ regression\ with\ one\ variable\ eliminated}{variance\ about\ regression\ with\ none\ eliminated}$$

This is the same as

$$\frac{(explained\ sum\text{-}of\text{-}squares)/(k-1)-(explained\ sum\text{-}of\text{-}squares)/[(k-1)-1]}{(unexplained\ sum\text{-}of\text{-}squares)/(n-k)}$$

This indicates the contribution of the coefficient b_i corresponding to the *i*th independent variable. More precisely, the partial *F*-value is

$$\frac{sum\text{-}of\text{-}squares\ (b_i/b_{0j},\ b_1,\ \ldots,\ b_{i+1},\ \ldots,\ b_k)/1}{error\text{-}sum\text{-}of\text{-}squares/(n-k)}$$

where the value of the ith variable is the marginal explained sum-of-squares due to the extra degree of freedom. It is, by definition, different from the regular F-value, which is

$$\frac{(explained\ sum\text{-}of\text{-}squares)/(k-1)}{(unexplained\ sum\text{-}of\text{-}squares)/(n-k)}$$

In the forward selection procedure, the square of the partial correlation coefficient is the contribution to explained variation by the candidate variable X_j. It is defined as

$$\frac{explained\ sum\text{-}of\text{-}squares\ (with\ X_j\ in)-explained\ sum\text{-}of\text{-}squares\ (with\ X_j\ out)}{total\ sum\text{-}of\text{-}squares\ (with\ X_j\ out)}$$

This is the same as

$$\frac{sum\text{-}of\text{-}squares\ (X_j\mid X_1,\ X_2,\ \ldots,\ X_{j-1,}\ X_{j+1,\ldots,}\ X_k)}{total\ sum\text{-}of\text{-}squares\ (X_1,\ X_2,\ \ldots,\ X_{j-1,}\ X_{j+1,\ldots,}\ X_k)}$$

More precisely, it can also be thought of as the percentage of variance in Y not accounted for by other variables explained by the variable in question (Kane 1968):

$$\frac{R^2_Y\mid X_1,\ X_2,\ \ldots,\ X_k - R^2_Y\mid X_1,\ \ldots X_{j-1,}\ X_{j+1,}\ \ldots,\ X_k}{1 - R^2_Y\mid X_1,\ X_2,\ .\ ,\ X_{j-1,}\ X_{j+1,}\ \ldots,\ X_k} \tag{A3.10}$$

Recall that partial correlation describes the extent of linear association that is obtained between a particular pair of variables when other specified variables are held constant. Computationally speaking, it is more convenient to use the following iterative relationship:

$$r_{Y\mid X_i}(X_j) = \frac{r(Y,\ X_i) - r(Y,\ X_j)\ r(X_i,\ X_ji)}{\sqrt{(1 - r^2(Y,\ X_j))(1 - r^2(X_i,\ X_j))}} \tag{A3.11}$$

where the notation $r_{Y\mid X_i}(X_j)$ denotes the partial correlation between Y and X_j given X_i is in the equation already, $r\ (Y,X_i)$ is the unconditional partial correlation of Y with X_i, and $r\ (X_i,\ X_j)$ is simply the correlation between two independent variables. Should independent variable k be now introduced into the equation, its partial correlation coefficient can simply be calculated from the ones already known:

$$r_{Y\mid X_i X_j}(X_k) = \frac{r_{Y\mid X_i}(X_k) - r_{Y\mid X_i}(X_j)\ r_{X_j\mid X_i}(X_k)}{\sqrt{(1 - r^2_{Y\mid X_i}(X_j))(1 - r^2_{X_j\mid X_i}(X_k))}} \tag{A3.12}$$

Notice any unknown quantity in the right-hand side above can be calculated by Equation A3.11 recognizing that i and j can be interchanged, and the definition of the Y variable is also relative.[2]

Partial Correlation Example

For estimating home-based non-work trips, let us calculate, via Equation A3.11, the partial correlation coefficient for housing land use given total employment is already in the regression equation. Using the notations and the correlation matrix given in Table A3.4, we are interested in

$$_{x_1}(X_2) = \frac{r(Y, X_2) - r(Y, X_1)r(X_1, X_2)}{\sqrt{(1 - r^2(Y, X_1))(1 - r^2(X_1, X_2))}} = \frac{0.2492 - (0.5861)(-0.2600)}{\sqrt{(1 - (0.5861)^2)(1 - (-0.2600)^2}} = 0.51 \quad \text{(A3.13)}$$

This result agrees with that reported in Table A3.3. It can be seen from Equation A3.12 that second-order partial correlation coefficients, such as that for housing density, involve a lot more calculations than the first-order coefficient calculated above, since they build upon the results of Equation A3.11. ∎

The partial F-value for forward regression, similar to the backward regression, is defined as

$$\frac{\textit{variance due to regression with another variable added}}{\textit{variance about regression with existing variables}}$$

or

$$\frac{(\textit{explained sum-of-squares})/((k-1)+1) - (\textit{explained sum-of-squares})/(k-1)}{\textit{unexplained sum-of-squares}/(n-k)}$$

Table A3.4   CORRELATION MATRIX FOR CALCULATING PARTIAL-CORRELATION

	Home-based non-work trips (Y)	Total employment (X_1)	Housing land use (X_2)	Housing density (X_3)
Home-based non-work trips (Y)		0.5861	0.2492	0.1213
Total employment (X_1)			−0.2600	0.0188
Housing land use (X_2)				−0.2610
Housing density (X_3)				

or

$$\frac{\text{sun-of-squares } (b_{k+1} \mid b_0, b_1, b_2, \ldots, b_k)/1}{\text{error sum-of-squares}/(n - K)} \tag{A3.14}$$

It can be seen, again, that the partial F used in forward-regression is different from the regular F. While there are computational shortcuts in calculating partial F, the central ideas are captured in the above discussions and the following example. ∎

Partial F Example
Consider the home-based non-work trip forward regression $Y = f(X_1, X_2)$ again. Let b_1 be the calibration coefficient for X_1 and b_2 for X_2. While the partial F's are part of the output, it can also be gleaned from the analysis-of-variance tables according to the definition of partial F above. Notice the partial F for b_2 or due to X_2 is computed in the last column of Table A3.5, second entry from the bottom. Of further interest is the fact that the third entry from the bottom as indicated is not the partial F for b_1. It agrees with the partial F as documented in Table A3.3. Both are 13.953 in value. ∎

It should be noted that the goodness of fit parameter, the coefficient of multiple determination (R^2), is not comparable between the various steps of the stepwise regression. The reason is that the (dof) change from one step to another. Recall that

$$R^2 = 1 - \frac{\text{error sum-of-squares}}{\text{total sum-of-squares}} = \frac{\Sigma_i(y_i - \hat{Y})^2}{\Sigma_i(y_i - \overline{Y})^2} \tag{A3.15}$$

where the numerator has $n - k$ dof while the denominator has $n - 1$. As more and more explanatory variables are added on, k becomes larger or $n - k$ becomes smaller. There is a tendency for the numerator to become smaller as there is less variability (remember the case of zero dof when a regression line is fitted on two points.) One way to compensate for this is to adjust Equation A3.14 as follows
Adjusted $- R^2 = \overline{R}^2 = 1 - (1 - R^2)\frac{n-1}{n-k}$.

Table A3.5   EXAMPLE OF PARTIAL F FOR FORWARD-REGRESSIVE

Source of variation	Degree of freedom	Sum of squares	Mean square	F-value
Total (corrected)	41	1.95392×10^3		
Due to regression $\mid b_0$	2	1.00920×10^3	5.04602×10^7	2.08310×10^b
Due to b_1 $b_0 \mid$	1	6.71205×10^c	6.71205×10^7	2.09306×10
Due to b_2 b_1, b_0	1	3.38000×10^d	3.38000×10^7	1.39531×10^e
Residual	39	9.44723×10^7	2.42237×10^6	

[a]Unless indicated otherwise, all figures are from the analysis of variance table of $Y = f(X_1, X_2)$.
[b]F-value for the entire regression $Y = f(X_1, X_2)$.
[c]From the analysis of variance table of $Y = f(X_1)$.
[d]Computed from equation A3.14.
[e]Partial F for b_2 due to X_2.

Adjusted-R^2 Example

In the home-based non-work trip regression $Y = f(X_1, X_2)$ shown in Table A3.3, $R^2 = 0.5164$. The adjusted R^2 becomes $R^2 = 1 - (1 - 0.5164)[(42 - 1)/(42 - 3)] = 0.4916$. As expected, $\bar{R}^2$ is smaller than the R^2. Put in another way, R^2 is inflated in comparison to the $\bar{R}^2$ due to the diminished *dof*. ∎

VII. MATRIX APPROACH TO LINEAR REGRESSION

In the context of multiple linear regression, it is convenient to generalize our parameter estimation discussions in terms of matrix notations. $\mathbf{Y}$ is defined to be the vector of n observations y_t where $t = 1, 2, \ldots, n$; $\mathbf{X}$ is the $nx(k + 1)$ matrix of independent variables constituting the observations x_{tj} (where $t = 1, 2, \ldots, n$ and $j = 1, 2, \ldots k$; $\mathbf{b}$ is the vector of parameters to be estimated (consisting of intercept a and coefficients $b_1, b_2, \ldots, b_k$; and $\epsilon = (\epsilon_1, \epsilon_2, \ldots, \epsilon_n)$ is the vector of errors. Our bivariate toy problem can be put in matrix notation as follows:

$$\mathbf{Y} = (65, 50, 42)^T, \mathbf{X} = \begin{bmatrix} 1 & 30 \\ 1 & 20 \\ 1 & 10 \end{bmatrix}, \mathbf{b} = (a\ b)^T, \epsilon = (\epsilon_1, \epsilon_2, \epsilon_3)^T$$

Now we can write the matrix regression equation as

$$\mathbf{Y} = \mathbf{Xb} + \epsilon \tag{A3.16}$$

This is simply a compact way of writing

$$\begin{bmatrix} 65 \\ 50 \\ 42 \end{bmatrix} = \begin{bmatrix} 1 & 30 \\ 1 & 20 \\ 1 & 10 \end{bmatrix} \begin{bmatrix} a \\ b \end{bmatrix} + \begin{bmatrix} \epsilon_1 \\ \epsilon_2 \\ \epsilon_3 \end{bmatrix} \tag{A3.17}$$

which constitutes a simultaneous set of three equations. A set of normal equations can be defined from Equation A3.16 by first writing $\mathbf{Xb} = \mathbf{Y}$ (leaving out the error vector) and then pre-multiplying by $\mathbf{X}^T$, resulting in $\mathbf{X}^T\mathbf{Xb} = \mathbf{X}^T\mathbf{Y}$. From these normal equations, the coefficients $\mathbf{b}$ can be solved, yielding the least square estimates (a, b): $\mathbf{b} = (\mathbf{X}^T\mathbf{X})^{-1}\mathbf{X}^T\mathbf{Y}$.

It can be seen that

$$\mathbf{X}^T\mathbf{X}^{-1} = \begin{bmatrix} 1 & 1 & 1 \\ 30 & 20 & 10 \end{bmatrix} \begin{bmatrix} 1 & 30 \\ 1 & 20 \\ 1 & 10 \end{bmatrix} = \begin{bmatrix} 1+1+1 & 30+20+10 \\ 30+20+10 & 30^2+20^2+10^2 \end{bmatrix} = \begin{bmatrix} n & \Sigma x_t \\ \Sigma x_t & \Sigma x_t^2 \end{bmatrix} \tag{A3.18}$$

It can also be shown that

$$(\mathbf{X}^T\mathbf{X})^{-1} = \frac{1}{n\Sigma(x_t - \bar{X})^2} \begin{bmatrix} \Sigma x_t^2 & -\Sigma x_t \\ -\Sigma x_1 & n \end{bmatrix} = \begin{bmatrix} 2.333 & -0.1 \\ -0.1 & 0.005 \end{bmatrix} \tag{A3.19}$$

In addition,

$$X^TY = \begin{bmatrix} 1 & 1 & 1 \\ 30 & 20 & 10 \end{bmatrix} \begin{bmatrix} 65 \\ 50 \\ 42 \end{bmatrix} = \begin{bmatrix} 65+50+42 \\ (30)(65)+(20)(50)+(10)(42) \end{bmatrix} = \begin{bmatrix} \Sigma y_t \\ \Sigma x_t Y_t \end{bmatrix} = \begin{bmatrix} 157 \\ 3370 \end{bmatrix} \quad \text{(A3.20)}$$

Thus

$$\mathbf{b} = \begin{bmatrix} 2.333 & -0.1 \\ -0.1 & 0.005 \end{bmatrix} \begin{bmatrix} 157 \\ 3370 \end{bmatrix} = \begin{bmatrix} 29.28 \\ 1.15 \end{bmatrix}$$

Within the numerical round-off errors of a basis inversion and the number of significant figures carried, this agrees with previous calculated values of $a = 29.33$ and $b = 1.15$.

VIII. NONLINEAR REGRESSION

Regression models need not be linear (Draper and Smith 1966). Suppose the postulated model is of the form

$$Y = f(X_1, X_2, \ldots, X_k; \delta_1, \delta_2, \ldots, \delta_r) + \epsilon \quad \text{(A3.21)}$$

where δjs are the estimated parameters. If we write $\mathbf{X}^T = (X_1, X_2, \ldots, X_k)$; $\delta^T = (\delta_1, \delta_2, \ldots, \delta_r)$, Equation A3.21 can be rewritten compactly as

$$Y = f(\mathbf{X}, \delta) + \epsilon \quad \text{(A3.22)}$$

Notice that k is not necessarily the same as r—that the number of estimated parameters r do not necessarily have to be equal to the number of independent variables k in general. We shall assume that errors ($\in$s) are uncorrelated, that $\text{var}(\epsilon) = \sigma^2$, ϵ's are independent and normally distributed with a mean of zero and variance σ^2.

When there are n observations of the form $Y_t, X_{1t}, X_{2t}, \ldots, X_{kt}$ for $t = 1, 2, \ldots, n$, we can write the model (22) as

$$Y_t = f(\mathbf{X}_t, \delta) + \epsilon_t \quad t = 1, 2, \ldots, n \quad \text{(A3.23)}$$

where $\mathbf{X}_t = (X_{1t}, X_{2t}, \ldots, X_{kt})^T$. The assumption of normality and independence of the errors can now be written compactly as $\epsilon \sim N(\mathbf{0}, \mathbf{I}\sigma^2)$ where bold $\epsilon = (\epsilon_1, \epsilon_2, \ldots, \epsilon_n)^T$, and as usual $\mathbf{0}$ is a vector of zeros and $\mathbf{I}$ is an identity matrix. We define the error sum-of-squares for the nonlinear model and the given data as

$$S(\delta) = \sum_{t=1}^{n} [y_t - f(\mathbf{X}_t, \delta_0)]^2 \quad \text{(A3.24)}$$

The above is also referred to as the sum-of-squares surface. Notice that since y_t and $\mathbf{X}_t$ are fixed observations, the sum of squares is simply a function of δ. The δ

so obtained is referred to as the conditional estimate, in the sense that they are conditioned upon the given values of y_t and $\mathbf{X}_t$. We shall denote by $\hat{\boldsymbol{\delta}}$ a least squares estimate of $\boldsymbol{\delta}$—a value of $\boldsymbol{\delta}$ that minimizes $S(\delta)$. It can be shown that under the conditional assumptions, the least squares estimate of is also the maximum likelihood estimate.[3] This is because the likelihood function for this problem can be written as $L(\boldsymbol{\delta}, \sigma^2) = (2\pi\sigma^2)^{-n/2} \exp[-S(\delta)/2\sigma^2]$, so that if σ^2 is known, maximizing $L(\boldsymbol{\delta}, \sigma^2)$ with respect to δ is equivalent to minimizing $S(\boldsymbol{\delta})$ with respect to δ.

To find the least squares estimate $\hat{\boldsymbol{\delta}}$, we need to differentiate Equation A3.24 with respect to $\hat{\boldsymbol{\delta}}$. This provides the r normal equations, which must be solved for $\boldsymbol{\delta}$:

$$\sum_{t=1}^{n} \left\{ [y_t - f(\mathbf{X}_t, \boldsymbol{\delta})] \left[\frac{\partial f(\mathbf{X}_t, \boldsymbol{\delta})}{\partial \boldsymbol{\delta}_i} \right] \right\}_{\boldsymbol{\delta} = \hat{\boldsymbol{\delta}}} = 0 \quad i = 1, 2, \ldots, r \tag{A3.25}$$

Notice the derivative in square brackets is evaluated at the corresponding estimated values δs, which have the same subscript. When the function $f(\mathbf{X}_t, \delta)$ is linear

$$f(\mathbf{X}_t, \boldsymbol{\delta}) = \delta_1 X_{1t} + \delta_2 X_{2t} + \ldots + \delta_r \mathbf{X}_{rt} \tag{A3.26}$$

this derivative is a function of the $\mathbf{X}_t$ only: $\frac{\partial f}{\partial \delta_i} = X_{it}$ for $i = 1, 2, \ldots, r$ and does not involve δ at all. This leaves the normal equations in the form of linear equations in δ as discussed in the previous section.

$$\sum_{t=1}^{n} [y_t - f(\mathbf{x}_t, \hat{\boldsymbol{\delta}})] x_{it} = \sum_{t=1}^{n} (y_t - y_t) x_{it} = 0 \quad i = 1, 2, \ldots, r \tag{A3.27}$$

which is equivalent to $\mathbf{X}^T(\mathbf{Y} - \mathbf{X}\hat{\delta}) = \mathbf{0}$, where the estimated parameters $\hat{\delta}$ is the same as $\mathbf{b}$ in linear regression. While this is a simple set of equations to solve for linear regression, it is quite complicated for nonlinear cases, as demonstrated by the example below. Unfortunately, nonlinear regression is the rule rather than the exception in spatial time series, as demonstrated in the "Space Time Modeling" section of the "Spatial Time Series" chapter of Chan (2000).

Example

Suppose we wish to find the normal equation(s) for obtaining the least squares estimate $\hat{\boldsymbol{\delta}}$ *of* δ for the model $Y = f(\delta, \tau) + \epsilon$ where $f(\delta, \tau) = \exp(-\delta\tau)$ and where n pairs of observations $(y_1, t_1), (y_2, t_2), \ldots, (y_n, t_n)$ are available. We take the derivative $\frac{\partial f}{\partial \delta} = -\tau e^{-\delta\tau}$. Applying Equation A3.25 yields a single normal equation

$$\sum_{j=1}^{n} [y_j - \exp(-\delta t_j)] [-t_j \exp(-\hat{\delta} t_j)] = 0 \tag{A3.28}$$

We can see that even with one parameter and a comparatively simple nonlinear model, finding $\hat{\delta}$ by solving the only normal equation is not easy. When more parameters are involved and the model is more complicated, the solution of the normal equations can be extremely difficult to obtain; iterative methods must be employed in nearly all cases. To compound the difficulties, multiple solutions may exist, corresponding to multiple stationary values of the surface function $S(\hat{\delta})$. ∎

IX. CONCLUDING REMARKS

This appendix reviewed some of the basic statistical concepts. We discussed estimators in their single, two-dimensional, and multidimensional contexts, covering linear regression, stepwise regression, and nonlinear regression. Aside from the current volume, this introduction is meant to supplement such other chapters as "Generation, Competition and Distribution" and "Spatial Time Series" in Chan (2000), with pertinent fundamental principles. It does not pretend to replace excellent texts such as those listed in the references. However, care has been taken to make the presentation as self-contained and tutorial as possible, and to include as many toy examples as necessary—conducted sometimes at the sacrifice of mathematical rigor. The focus is on model calibration.

In linear regression, we pointed out that no single statistic can by itself speak for the overall quality of the regression equation. A number of statistics need to be considered together in assessing the quality of a calibration. Goodness of fit parameters are confirmations of a priori professional judgment on the hypothesized structural equation. The ultimate quality of a regression equation depends critically on the judicious choice of a sound structural equation, not just on statistical tests. Hypothesis about such a regression equation should therefore be re-examined all the time during a regression exercise to ensure a sound model.

Stepwise regression procedures are by no means perfect ways to automate the selection of a best equation. They are heuristic ways based on selective statistics such as partial-F or partial correlation coefficient. As pointed out in the text, the values of partial-F and partial correlation coefficients are conditioned on what variables are already included in the equation. A different sequence with which explanatory variables are introduced in the equation will result in different values for the same coefficient. Thus the use of partial-correlation coefficients in an iterative application of forward and backward regression fails to test whether the elimination of a variable, for instance, X_j might not have made it possible for it to qualify for readmission.

In practical applications, it is desirable to have a parsimonious equation, meaning a simple model that is statistically significant. Too many explanatory variables will not only introduce the problems associated with a diminishing degree of freedom, it will often pose prohibitive data collection requirements. Let us replace the first equation in Equation 9 with $Y = 50.02 + 0.84X_4$ ($R^2 = 0.93$, $t_4 = 19.2$). The goodness of fit statistics are similar between the first and third regression equations. Both are superior to the second equation; however, since the first equation is more parsimonious, it is preferred to the third. It can be seen therefore that the selection of the best equation is not a purely statistical exercise. It requires the combination of statistical tests with professional judgement in an artful manner.

Matrix notation for regression is convenient, particularly in the case of multiple regression and nonlinear regression. Through such a notation, one can more easily see the relationship, such as the one between linear and nonlinear calibration. It was shown that while calibration of linear regression is relatively straightforward, calibration of nonlinear regression is not. One of the state-of-the-art issues in this field is, in fact, the availability of stable and accurate nonlinear calibration procedures (Seber and Wild 1989). Unfortunately, the real world is replete with examples of nonlinear models. In spite of valiant attempts to provide generalized calibration tools, practical computational experiences tend to be case-specific, as we can see in the main body of the text.

ENDNOTES

[1] A zone (or more accurately traffic zone) is a subregion of a study area, each of which has its zonal attributes such as population and employment.

[2] This procedure can be generalized to an autoregressive time series, as explained in the "Estimating the Parameters" subsection of the "Spatial Time-Series" Chapter in Chan (2000).

[3] The maximum likelihood estimation procedure is explained in Chapter 3.

REFERENCES

Chan, Y. (2000). *Location, transport and land-use: Modelling spatial-temporal information.* New York: Springer-Verlag.

Crow, E. L.; Davis, F. A.; Maxfield, M. W. (1960). *Statistics manual: With examples taken from ordinance development.* New York: Dover.

Draper, N. R.; Smith, H. (1966). *Applied regression analysis.* New York: Wiley

Freeman, H. (1963). *Introduction to statistical inference.* Reading, Massachusetts: Addison-Wesley

Hutchinson, B. G. (1974). *Principles of urban transport systems planning.* New York: McGraw-Hill.

Kane, E. J. (1968). *Economic statistics and econometrics: an introduction to quantitative economics.* New York: Harper and Row.

Seber, G. A. F.; Wild, C. J. (1989). *Nonlinear regression.* New York: Wiley.

Wallace, T. D.; Silver, J. (1988). *Econometrics: An introduction.* Reading, Massachusetts: Addison-Wesley.

Appendix 4

Control, Dynamics, and System Stability

In this appendix, we review the basic theories that govern the evolution of complex systems, wherein systems transition from one state to another over time. Systems may evolve on their own or external influence may be brought to bear upon their development. In both cases, there can be smooth transitions as well as precipitous happenings. We discuss the conditions under which a system may change between these two types of evolution—namely from smooth to precipitous changes and vice versa. Most importantly, we wish to effect these changes where we can, so as to direct the development toward a desired goal.

I. CONTROL THEORY

The concept of control theory was introduced in Appendix 2, where an example of inventory control was worked out in the context of vehicle dispatching. In the example, trucks deliver a stock of cargo $X(t)$ at the loading dock over the afternoon between hours t_0 and t_1. The cargo is to be airlifted to a destination. We wish to construct a schedule to minimize operating cost and schedule delay. The problem was solved by discrete dynamic programming, wherein the optimal dispatch schedule as indicated by the control variable $U(t)$ is determined. Here we will generalize and formalize the results in a more systematic way using control theory (Silberberg 1990).

The general form of a control theory problem is expressed as a maximization problem instead of minimization:

$$\max_{U(t)} \int_{t_0}^{t_1} f(X(t), U(t), t) \, dt \tag{A4.1}$$

subject to the state equation[1]

$$\dot{X}(t) = g(X(t), U(t), t) \tag{A4.2}$$

with end-point conditions

$$X(t_0) = X_0, \, X(t_1) = X_1 \qquad (\text{or } X(t_1) \text{ free})$$

and some control set $\{U(t)\}$ or the set of decision variables. The time between t_0 and t_1 is called the planning period. In many important problems, t_1 tends to infinity, or the planning horizon is far out into the future. End-point conditions vary depending on the problem context. Typically the initial stock of the state variable X is fixed,

453

although the final stock may not be. In addition, there may be restrictions on the variables, such as non-negativity on the state X, and perhaps inequality bounds on the control variable U. An example of such inequality bounds is the 0–1 valued dispatch or hold policy $0 \leq U \leq 1$ at each time the dispatch decision is renewed.

Let us ignore for the moment how the control problem is solved, but assume that finite interior solution $(U^*(t), X^*(t))$ does exist, in other words, a time path that leads from $X_0(t_0)$ to $X_1(t_1)$ as defined by the control set $\{U(t)\}$. The value $(U^*(t), X^*(t))$ represents the optimal time paths of the control variable U and the state variable X. Although we are suppressing it in the notation, X^* and U^* in fact depend on the initial parameters X_0, t_0, and so forth. Thus in the cargo dispatching example, the amount of cargo at the dock at the starting time t_0 defines the ultimate dispatching policy. Denote the resulting value of the objective functional (objective function) as $F(X_0, t_0)$, that is

$$F(X_0, t_0) = \int_{t_0}^{t_1} (X^*(t), U^*(t), t) \, dt \tag{A4.3}$$

where a functional $f(\cdot)$ is defined as a function that has a domain whose elements are functions, sets, or the like, and that assumes numerical values. Although Equation A4.1 requires us to find an actual path as specified by the function $(U^*(t), X^*(t))$, this maximizes an integral function, which once found results in some ordinary maximum expressed in terms of the parameters of the model. (Notice we suppress t_1 here in Equation A4.3, as the parameter is not germane to the present discussion).

Given the initial state X_0, a marginal value of the stock exists for any time t between the initial time t_0 and the terminal time t_1. Denote this imputed value by the equivalent of the Lagrange multiplier (or the dual variable) $\lambda(t) \times F_x(X^*(t), t)$, where F_X stands for the derivative of F with respect to X. This marginal value of the stock, $\lambda(t)$, is often referred to as the costate or adjoint variable in control theory. The change in the value of the stock caused by dispatching is $d[\lambda(t)X(t)]/dt = \lambda \dot{X} + X\dot{\lambda}$. The true net benefit of dispatching at some schedule $U(t)$ is the sum of the benefits in the present, $f(X, U, t)$, and the change in the maximum value of the stock caused by executing that schedule in the present. The optimal path is obtained by always setting the true marginal net benefits equal to zero along the entire optimal path of values $(U^*(t), X^*(t))$. Thus, we can characterize this solution to the control problem as requiring that, at each time instance t ($t_0 \leq t \leq t_1$), the first derivative of F with respect to t be maximized, or for a continuous function F

$$\max_{U, X} f(X, U, t) + \lambda \dot{X} + X\dot{\lambda} \tag{A4.4}$$

Using the state Equation A4.2, this becomes

$$\max_{U, X} f(X, U, t) + \lambda g(X, U, t) + X\dot{\lambda} \tag{A4.5}$$

We suppress the dependence on t at this point because we have not yet found the functions $(U^*(t), X^*(t))$ and expressed them as functions of t. Differentiating with respect to the control variable U and the state variable X yields

$$f_u + \lambda g_u = 0 \qquad\qquad\qquad (A4.6)$$

$$f_x + \lambda g_x + \dot{\lambda} = 0 \qquad\qquad\qquad (A4.7)$$

Equation A4.6 is called the maximum principle; Equation A4.7 is called the costate or adjoint equation. These two conditions plus the state equation $\dot{X} = g(X, U, t)$ are the necessary conditions for an optimal path $(U^*(t), X^*(t))$ of control and state variables over the planning period. Also determined is the path of marginal values of the stock, $\lambda(t)$.

Equations A4.6 and A4.7 are generally expressed in terms of the expression $H = f + g$, called the **Hamiltonian.** The maximum principle is $\partial H/\partial U = 0$ (assuming an interior solution to the problem) while the adjoint equation is $\partial H/\partial X = -\dot{\lambda}$. In the original problem, given the initial stock level, X_0, choosing $U(t)$ determines the state equation $\dot{X}(t)$ and thus the state variable $X(t)$. There is really only one independent variable, U in this control problem. However, the introduction of the new variable $\lambda(t)$ adds another degree of freedom; as in static Lagrangian analysis, we pretend the problem has one more dimension than it actually has.

Using the maximum principle, Equation A4.6, which is not a differential equation (in other words, equation containing derivatives of t), and invoking the implicit function theorem of calculus, we can solve for U: $U \times k(X, \lambda, t)$. Substituting this into the state and adjoint equations produces two first-order equations and

$$\dot{X} = g(X, k(X, \lambda, t), t) \qquad\qquad\qquad (A4.8)$$

and

$$\dot{\lambda} = -f_x(X, k(X, \lambda, t), t) - \lambda g_x(X, k(X, \lambda, t), t) \qquad\qquad (A4.9)$$

Solving these differential equations (and using the relevant end-point conditions to evaluate the constants of integration) yields the optimum path of X and λ. Using the solutions to these equations—by substituting them into $k(X, \lambda, t)$—yields the optimum path of the control variable, U. The reader can see the close parallel between control theory and dynamic programming as explained in Appendix 2.

Example
Consider the optimal control problem

$$\max \int_0^t (-X - \frac{1}{2}\alpha U^2)\, dt$$

subject to $\dot{X} = U$, $X(0) = X_0$, $X(1) = X_1$, where $\alpha > 0$ is a parameter for this problem. The Hamiltonian for this problem is $H(X, U, \lambda) = -X - \frac{1}{2}\alpha U^2 + \lambda U$. Assuming an interior solution, the necessary conditions are $\frac{\partial H}{\partial U} = -\alpha U + \lambda = 0$ and $\frac{\partial^2 H}{\partial U^2} = -\alpha = 0$. By assumption $\alpha > 0$, so $\partial^2 H/\partial U^2 < 0$. Solving $\partial H/\partial U = 0$ for U gives $U = \lambda/\alpha$. The other necessary conditions are the state and adjoint equations $\dot{X} = \frac{\partial H}{\partial \lambda} = U$, $\dot{\lambda} = -\frac{\partial H}{\partial X} = 1$. Using $U \times \lambda/\alpha$ in these equations yields, $\dot{X} = \lambda/\alpha$, $X(0) = X_0$, $X(1) = X_1$, and $\dot{\lambda} = 1$. Integrating $\dot{\lambda} = 1$ directly gives $\lambda^*(t) = t + c_1$, where c_1 is an unknown (as of yet) constant of integration. Substitute $\lambda^*(t)$ in λ/α to get $\dot{X} = (t + c_1)/\alpha$. Integrating this equation yields $X^*(t) = t^2/2\alpha + c_1 t/\alpha + c_2$ where c_2 is another constant of integration. The constants of integration c_1 and c_2 are determined by using the initial and terminal conditions $X(0) = X_0$ and $X(1) = X_1$, respectively. Use $X(0) = X_0$ in $X^*(t)$ to get $X^*(0) = c_2 = X_0$. Now use $X(1) = X_1$ to obtain the value of c_1: $X^*(1) = \frac{1}{2\alpha} + c_1/\alpha + X_0 = X_1$; thus $c_1 = \alpha(X_1 - X_0) - \frac{1}{2}$. These constants of integration are then substituted in (X^*, λ^*) to yield their optimal paths, and then λ^* is substituted into $U = \lambda/\alpha$ to give the control's optimal time path. Doing this gives the solution of

$$X^*(t; \alpha, X_0, X_1) = \frac{t^2}{2\alpha} + \left[(X_1 - X_0) - \frac{1}{2\alpha}\right] t + X_0 \qquad (A4.10)$$

$$\lambda^*(t, \alpha, X_0, X_1) = t + \alpha(X_1 - X_0) - \frac{1}{2} \qquad (A4.11)$$

$$U^*(t; \alpha, X_0, X_1) = \frac{t}{\alpha} + (X_1 - X_0) - \frac{1}{2\alpha} \qquad (A4.12)$$

Notice how the state, control, and marginal values are all expressed as functions of one single variable, time t, in the final solution. ∎

II. CALCULUS OF VARIATIONS

Let us consider a special case of the control problem where $\dot{X} = g(X, U, t) = U$. That is, the time rate of change of the stock is identical to the control variable, rather than some general function $g(\cdot)$ that might also include the stock itself and time. Simply put, control activity is in direct proportion to (and equal to) the rate of accumulation or depletion. Control in this case is the degenerate case of "going with the flow." Now substitute this state equation $U = \dot{X}$ into the integrand $f(\cdot)$ in Equation A4.1. The result is the following objective functional

$$\max \int_{t_0}^{t_1} f(X, \dot{X}, t) \, dt \qquad (A4.13)$$

We call this problem the calculus of variations (Silberberg 1990). In this problem, we determine a function $f(\cdot)$ such that a certain definite integral involving that function and certain of its derivatives takes on a maximum or minimum value. Notice this special case of the general control theory problem has been illustrated by the numerical example worked out above, where U is exactly set to $\dot{X}$. The corresponding solution maps out an optimal path as specified by the state variable $X(t)$ in Equation A4.10.

In this special case, the necessary conditions for a maximum (or minimum) are as follows. Remember the maximum principle is $H_U = H_X th = f_X + \lambda g_{\dot{X}} = 0$. However, $g_X = g_u \cong 1$ here, so this condition becomes

$$f_X = -\lambda \qquad (A4.14)$$

Similarly the adjoint or costate equation is

$$H_X = f_X + \lambda g_X = f_X = -\dot{\lambda} \qquad (A4.15)$$

recognizing $g_X = \partial U/\partial X = \partial\dot{X}/\partial X \cong 0$. Since the right-hand side of the adjoint Equation A4.15 directly above is the time derivative of the right-hand side of Equation A4.14, these two equations can be combined into $\frac{d}{dt}f_{\dot{X}} = \frac{\partial f}{\partial X}$. Carrying out the differentiation in the above equation results in the equivalent expression

$$f_X(X, \dot{X}, t) \cong f_{\dot{X}t} + f_{\dot{X}\dot{X}} + f_{\dot{X}\dot{X}}\ddot{X} \tag{A4.16}$$

This is the classic Euler-Lagrange equation defining the necessary condition for an optimal path. Solutions of this equation are known as extremals and an extremal which satisfies the appropriate end conditions at t_0 and t_1 is called a stationary function. Application of Equation A4.16 results in a second-order differential equation (except for special cases), whereas the necessary conditions of control theory result in the first-order simultaneous Equations A4.8 and A4.9. There is no uniform computational advantage to one approach over the other. However, the Euler-Lagrange equation is difficult to interpret, while the control theoretic equations often provide useful characterizations of the dynamics of spatial economic models.

Example

Take the control theoretic numerical example shown in the above section, where $f(\cdot) = -X - \frac{1}{2}\alpha\dot{X}^2$. According to the Euler-Lagrange equation one can verify by regular calculus that $f_{\dot{X}} = -\alpha\dot{X}$ where $f_X = -1$. Solving the second-order differential equation $\ddot{X} = 1/\alpha$ with the end-point conditions $X(0) = X_0$ and $X(1) = X_1$ yields the same solution as worked out previously. The solution is identical to Equation A4.10, as one would expect. ∎

III. VARIATIONAL INEQUALITY

Obviously, both control theory and the calculus of variation are tools to analyze the optimality conditions of functionals. A general condition that encompass both of these techniques can be stated: Let $f(\mathbf{x})$ be a functional on a normed (regular) vector space Ω, it has a directional derivative at $\mathbf{x}_q$, and $\Omega_q \subset \Omega$ be convex. A necessary condition for $\mathbf{x}_q \in \Omega$ to be a maximum of f on Ω_q is that for all $\mathbf{x}_q \in \Omega_q$, the gradient $\nabla f^T(\mathbf{x}) = (\frac{\partial f}{\partial x_1}, \dots, \frac{\partial f}{\partial x_n})$ (or the generalization of the first derivative) of $f(\mathbf{x}_q, \mathbf{x} - \mathbf{x}_q)$ is less than or equal to a zero vector ($\leq \mathbf{0}$). This condition is illustrated for the maximization and minimization two-dimensional case in Figure A4.1. In the unconstrained case, the necessary optimality conditions are that the gradient of $f(\mathbf{x}_q, \mathbf{y})$ is equal to a zero vector ($\mathbf{0}$) for all $\mathbf{y}$ in Ω, where $\mathbf{y} = (\mathbf{x} - \mathbf{x}_q)$. We call these **variational equalities.** In the constrained case, the optimality condition is called **variational inequalities** (Minoux 1986). Though these results are straightforward to establish, they constitute the foundation of the calculus of variation. In fact it can be shown that they make it possible for us to derive the necessary optimality conditions known as the Euler-Lagrange equation for an interior (unconstrained) optimum.

A. Fundamentals

We can provide a formalization of the above discussion: Let f be a smooth real valued function on the closed interval $\Omega_q = [a, b]$. We seek the points $x_q \in \Omega_q$ for which $f(x_q) = \underset{x \in \Omega_q}{\min}\, f(x)$ (Kinderlehrer and Stampacchia 1980). Three cases can occur for

Figure A4.1   ILLUSTRATION OF VARIATIONAL INEQUALITY

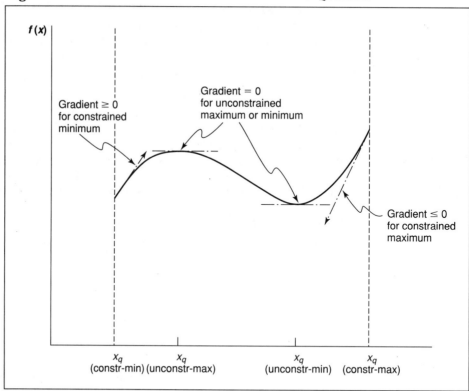

the two-dimensional case as shown in Figure A4.1: (a) if $a < x_q < b$, then $\dot{f}(x_q) = 0$; (b) if $x_q = a$, then $\dot{f}(x_q) \geq 0$, and (c) if $x_q = b$, then $\dot{f}(x_q) \leq 0$. These statements can be summarized by writing

$$\dot{f}(x_q)(x - x_q) \geq 0 \qquad \forall x \in \Omega_q \qquad (A4.17)$$

Such a set of relationships will be referred to as variational inequality illustrated here in two dimensions.

Let f be a smooth real valued function defined on the closed convex-set Ω_q of Euclidean n-dimensional space. Again we shall characterize the points $x_q \in \Omega_q$ such that $f(x_q) = \min_{x \in \Omega_q} f(x)$. Assume x_q is a point where the minimum is achieved and let $x \in \Omega_q$. Since Ω_q is convex, the segment $(1 - w)x_q + w(x - x_q)$, $0 \leq w \leq 1$, lies in Ω_q. The function $F(w) = f(x_q + w(x - x_q))$, $0 \leq w \leq 1$, attains its minimum at $w = 0$. Analogous to the two-dimensional case above, $\dot{F}(0) = \nabla f^T(x_q)(x - x_q) \geq 0$ for any $x \in \Omega_q$. Consequently, the point x_q satisfies the variational inequality

$$x_q \in \Omega_q: \nabla f^T(x_q)(x - x_q) \geq 0 \qquad \forall x \in \Omega_q \qquad (A4.18)$$

If Ω_q is bounded, the existence of at least one x_q is immediate.

It should be noted that the above two cases—two and n-dimensional—can be solved by means of calculus since they depend on a finite number of variables.

Many optimization problems have unknowns beyond a finite number of n variables. Consider a function $u(t)$ of the real variable t on some interval $[a, b]$. Since the graph of the function u is defined by infinite pairs of $[t, u(t)]$, we shall say that we are dealing with an optimization problem in infinite dimension. We have already encountered this in control theory, where $u(t) = U(t)$ is the control variable over time t. In this case, there are an infinite number of control paths $U(t)$ between the initialpoint $t = a$ and end-point $t = b$. More generally, we shall see that such problems can be formulated in the following way. Given a vector space Ω of (infinite dimension) and a functional f on Ω, find u^* such that for a minimization problem, $f(u^*) \leq f(u)$, $u \in \Omega$, for unconstrained optimization, or such that $f(u^*) \leq f(u)$, $u \in \Omega_q \subseteq \Omega$, for constrained optimization over a convex region. At this point, we will illustrate an application of variational inequality in an infinite dimensional space. The following example is similar to a problem of the calculus of variations.

Example
Let Ω be a bounded domain with boundary $\delta\Omega$ and let ψ be a given function on $\Omega = \Omega \cup \delta\Omega$ satisfying $\max_\Omega \psi \geq 0$ and $\psi \leq 0$ on $\delta\Omega$. Define $\Omega_q = \{y \geq \psi$ in Ω and $y = 0$ on $\delta\Omega\}$, where y is a function continuously differentiable in Ω. Notice this is a convex set of functions that we assume is not empty. We seek a function $u \in \Omega_q$ for which $\int_\Omega |\nabla u|^2 dx = \min_{y \in \Omega_q} \int_\Omega |\nabla y|^2 dx.$[2] Assuming such a y function to exist, we argue analogously to our previous discussion relying again on the convexity of Ω_q. For any $y \in \Omega_q$, the sequence $u + w(y - u) \in \Omega_q$, $0 \leq w \leq 1$, whence the function $f(t) = \int_\Omega |\nabla(u + w(y - u))|^2 dx$, $0 \leq w \leq 1$, attains its minimum at $w = 0$. This implies that $\dot{f}(0) \geq 0$, which leads to the variational inequality

$$u \in \Omega_q: \int_\Omega \nabla u^T \nabla(y - u)\, dx \geq 0 \qquad \forall y \in \Omega_q \qquad (A4.19)$$

Intervening here is the point set $\{x \in \Omega: u(x) = \psi(x)\}$. Its presence distinguishes u from the solution of a boundary value problem such as the end-point conditions imposed on the Euler-Lagrange second-order differential equation. As mentioned, one can interpret u as the height function of the equilibrium position of a thin membrane constrained to lie above the body $\{(x, x_{n+1}):x_{n+1} \leq \psi(x), x \in \Omega\}$ and with fixed height zero ($\psi \times 0$) on the boundary $\delta\Omega$. In spatial economics, we may have a market defined within a geographic boundary. The consumers in this market are charged a price of ψ, which is to be maximized. Conventional business practice dictates, however, that the price be as uniform as possible within the defined market such that market equilibrium results. ∎

B. Existence and Uniqueness

Variational inequalities are general formulations that encompasses a plethora of mathematical problems, including, but not limited to, optimization and complementarity problems. Variational inequalities were originally developed as a tool for the study of certain classes of partial differential equations (equations containing partial derivatives) such as those that arise in mechanics. A membrane example has been shown above. Such problems were defined over infinite dimensional spaces. We focus here, however, on the finite dimensional variational inequality problem, mainly defined for economic equilibrium applications (Nagurney 1993).

In geometric terms, variational inequality, Equation A4.18, states that the gradient $\nabla f^{T}(\mathbf{x})$ is orthogonal to the feasible convex set Ω_q at the point $\mathbf{x}_q$. This formulation is particularly convenient because it allows for a unified treatment of equilibrium problems and optimization problems. For example, the variational inequality problem can be shown to contain the complementarity problem as a special case. The nonlinear complementarity problem, introduced earlier as part of the Karash-Kuhn-Tucker condition in Chapter 4, is a system of equations and inequalities stated as: Find $\mathbf{x}_q \geq \mathbf{0}$ such that

$$\nabla f(\mathbf{x}_q) \geq \mathbf{0} \ \text{ and } \ \nabla f^{T}(\mathbf{x}_q)\, \mathbf{x}_q = \mathbf{0} \tag{A4.20}$$

Whenever $\nabla f(\mathbf{x}) = \mathbf{A}'\mathbf{x} + \mathbf{b}$, where $\mathbf{A}'$ is an $n \times n$ matrix and $\mathbf{b}$ is an $n \times 1$ vector, Equation A4.20 is then known as the linear complementarity problem.

Variational inequality theory is also a powerful tool in the qualitative analysis of equilibria. Existence of a solution to a variational inequality problem follows from continuity of the function $\nabla f(\mathbf{x})$ entering the variational inequality, provided that the feasible set Ω_q is defined in the real space. It can be shown that variational inequality (A4.18) admits a solution if and only if there exists a bounded solution $\mathbf{x}_q$. Qualitative properties of existence and uniqueness become easily obtainable under certain monotonicity conditions. For example, if $\nabla f(\mathbf{x})$ is strictly monotone on Ω_q, then the solution is unique, if one exists.

Monotonicity is closely related to **positive definiteness**, in other words, the generalization of a positive second derivative, where positive definiteness is defined to be the value of

$$\mathbf{x}^{T}\nabla^{2}f(\mathbf{x})\,\mathbf{x} = \mathbf{x}^{T}\left[\frac{\partial^{2}f(\mathbf{x})}{\partial x_i \partial x_j}\right]\mathbf{x} \tag{A4.21}$$

Let $\mathbf{x} = (\leftarrow x_I \rightarrow)^{T}$ be a vector of decision variables and $\mathbf{F}'(\mathbf{x}) = (\leftarrow F_i(\mathbf{x}) \rightarrow)^{T}$ be a vector of functions for $i = 1, \ldots, n$. These functions are characterized by asymmetric interactions $\partial F'_i(\mathbf{x})/\partial x_j \neq \partial F'_j(\mathbf{x})/\partial x_i\,(i \neq j)$. Suppose that $\nabla \dot{\mathbf{F}}'(\mathbf{x}) = \dot{F}'(\mathbf{x})$ is continuously differentiable on Ω_q and the Jacobian matrix (or the generalization of the gradient for asymmetric interactions)

$$\dot{F}'(\mathbf{x}) = \begin{bmatrix} \dfrac{\partial F'_1}{\partial x_1} & \dfrac{\partial F'_1}{\partial x_n} \\ . & . \\ . & . \\ . & . \\ \dfrac{\partial F'_n}{\partial x_n} & \dfrac{\partial F'_n}{\partial x_n} \end{bmatrix}$$

which need not be symmetric, is positive semi-definite (or the expression A4.21 for $F'_i(\mathbf{x})$ is greater than or equal to zero), then $\dot{F}(\mathbf{x})$ is monotone. If the function is positive definite (or expression A4.21 is strictly greater than zero), then $\dot{F}(\mathbf{x})$ is strictly monotone.

Example
Given the Jacobian matrix

$$\nabla F'(\mathbf{x}) = \dot{F}'(\mathbf{x}) = \begin{bmatrix} \dfrac{\partial F'_1}{\partial x_1} & \dfrac{\partial F'_1}{\partial x_2} \\[2mm] \dfrac{\partial F'_2}{\partial x_1} & \dfrac{\partial F'_2}{\partial x_2} \end{bmatrix} = \begin{bmatrix} 2x_1^2 + 3x_2^2 + 6x_2 + 6 \\ \cdot \quad \cdot \end{bmatrix}$$

and the Hessian is

$$\nabla^2 F_1(\mathbf{x}) = \begin{bmatrix} \dfrac{\partial^2 F'_1}{\partial x_1^2} & \dfrac{\partial^2 F'_1}{\partial x_1 \partial x_2} \\[2mm] \dfrac{\partial F'_1}{\partial x_2 \partial x_1} & \dfrac{\partial^2 F'_1}{\partial x_2^2} \end{bmatrix} = \begin{bmatrix} 4 & 0 \\ 0 & 6 \end{bmatrix}$$

$$\mathbf{x}^{T} \cdot \nabla F'_1(\mathbf{x})\mathbf{x} = (x_1 \ x_2)\begin{bmatrix} 4 & 0 \\ 0 & 6 \end{bmatrix}\binom{x_1}{x_2} = 4x_1^2 + 6x_2^2 > 0$$

excluding the origin (0, 0). If it can be shown that the Hessian of the other three entries of matrix $\dot{F}'$ is also positive definite, then $\dot{F}'$ is strictly monotone. If this is true for the entire convex feasibleregion Ω_q, then the solution to the corresponding optimization problem is unique. ∎

IV. CATASTROPHE THEORY

Let $\mathbf{X}$ be a set of state variables describing some system—the dependent variables to be predicted in a model—and let $\mathbf{U}$ be a set of variables one can control (Wilson 1981; Lorenz 1993). Then in a gradient system,[3] the equilibrium position is determined by

$$\underset{\mathbf{X},\,\mathbf{U}}{\text{Min}} \ f(\mathbf{X}, \mathbf{U}) \tag{A4.22}$$

This concept has been introduced in the previous section on control theory. The dynamics of the process is given by $\frac{\partial f}{\partial \mathbf{X}} = \nabla f$ and the minimum of f, of course, occurs when

$$\nabla f = \mathbf{0} \tag{A4.23}$$

The appearance of the gradient ∇, of the potential function f explains the name of this type of system.

The solution to Equation A4.23 gives the equilibrium point, which minimizes the potential function in Equation A4.22, and, as $\mathbf{U}$ varies, determine a surface in the space $(\mathbf{X}, \mathbf{U})$. This is a surface representing possible equilibrium states of the system. If, for example, there is a single state variable X and two control variables U_1 and U_2, then this will be a surface in the three-dimension space (X, U_1, U_2).

In this context, distinction is often made between a slow variable and a fast variable. Correspondingly, one may attach the time argument t behind the variables, which now read as $\mathbf{X}(t)$ and $\mathbf{U}(t)$. By convention $\mathbf{X}(t)$ is a fast variable and $\mathbf{U}(t)$ a slow variable. Correspondingly, one can think of $\mathbf{U}$ as a set of parameters influencing $\mathbf{X}$. For a smooth, slow and small change in one or more of the $\mathbf{U}$ variables, a corresponding smooth change in the state variables $\mathbf{X}$ can be anticipated. For this to occur, the surface in $(\mathbf{X}, \mathbf{U})$ space of equilibrium solutions has to be itself smooth and not folded in any way. It has long been recognized that when, for a given $\mathbf{U}$, there are multiple solutions for $\mathbf{X}$, then something more complicated can occur. The essence of catastrophe theory is the classification of these complications and the proofs that, in a number of cases, they fall into a small group of basic types.

A. Basic Concepts

The solutions of Equation A4.22 or equivalently Equation A4.23 are the stationary points of the function f or, more precisely, of a family of functions of $\mathbf{X}$ (the fast variables), parameterized by $\mathbf{U}$ (the slow variables). Stationary points are often maxima or minima, which are distinguished by, in the single state variable case, the second derivative of f being negative or positive respectively. (In the multi-state variable case, the corresponding result is that the Hessian matrix or the generalized version of second derivative is negative or positive definite, respectively, as mentioned earlier in this appendix.) When stationary points are not maxima or minima, the second derivative is zero or the Hessian matrix is singular. Such equilibrium points are known as singularities and it is at and near such points that unusual system behavior is observed. What catastrophe theory does is to classify the kinds of singularities that can occur. It has been shown that, for a number of control variables in the vector $\mathbf{U}$ up to or equal to four, the types of singularities, in a topological sense, are relatively few. For example, in the case of a single state variable and two control variables, the surface of equilibrium points around a singularity must be topologically equivalent to the cusp surface, which is illustrated in Figure A4.2. Application of the cusp catastrophe is found in the "Chaos, Catastrophe, Bifurcation and Disaggregation" chapter of Chan (2000) under the "Spatial Dynamics" section.

We can illustrate the possibilities of catastrophe theory using this figure. The surface of possible equilibrium values describes all possible states of the system. A particular behavior of the system is a trajectory on the surface. The study of such surfaces for particular systems, therefore, allows us to investigate possible types of behavior, and we know that the surface must in a topological sense be of the form shown in the figure. The italicized qualification is an important one in practice and should be emphasized. It means that the surface of possible equilibrium values for a system can be forced into the form of Figure A4.2 after some smooth transformation of the variables, where necessary. This is known as a standard, or canonical form. The achievement of the appropriate transformation in applied work is often likely to be a very difficult task, though insights can often be gained without it being carried through explicitly.

Three types of behavior that we are not accustomed to expect are shown in sample trajectories on Figure A4.2:

(1)   a sudden jump (or catastrophe);
(2)   hysteresis—a reverse path to some point not being the same as the starting point; and

Figure A4.2   THE CUSP SURFACE

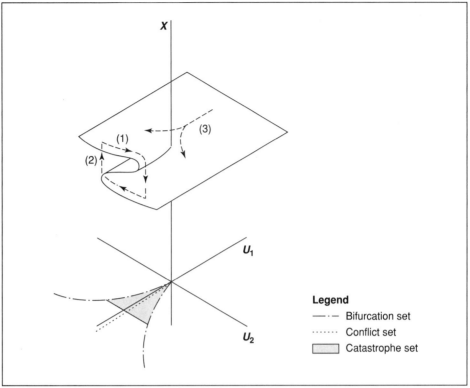

SOURCE: Wilson (1981). Reprinted with permission.

> **(3)**   divergence—a small difference in approach toward, in this case, a cusp point, leads the system to the upper or lower surface and hence to a very different state.

It can easily be seen that the jump behavior arises from a path in the **U**-plane that leads the system to fall from the upper surface to the lower one at a fold (in other words, a change in state)—or vice versa.

It can also be seen that a fold, and hence jump behavior, arises because in some regions of **U**-space, there are multiple equilibrium solutions for **X**. In the particular case of Figure A4.2, there is a region in the central part of the diagram (at the fold) where there are three possible solution sets for **X**. It turns out that the upper and lower surfaces represent stable minima (and hence are observable) while the central part of the fold represents maxima and hence unstable (and unobservable) states. If this fold region is projected vertically downwards onto the **U**-plane, we obtain the familiar cusp-shaped section of that plane. This contains the set of values of **U** that are critical. Outside the shaded region, the system only has one state available to it; inside there are two possible observable states and hence possible conflict; as the boundary of the critical region is crossed, jumps can take place. We will see later in this section, and also in Section VI, how this preliminary analysis can be formalized into various concepts of stability. We will also see explicitly that, as noted above, the function *f* is singular at critical parameter values and that geometrically this can be identified with folds in the equilibrium surface. In the critical region, where there are multiple states, some rule has to be assumed, or discovered, about which state the system actually adopts. This involves a delay convention, which will be pursued later.

B. Elementary Catastrophes

We can examine the types of singularity in relation to canonical forms of functions and exploit the fact that other functions of the same co-rank[4] and co-dimension[5] can then be transformed (locally, in the neighborhood of a point) into the same form. In general, the canonical forms are polynomials consisting of a single state variable X, and assuming the form

$$f(\mathbf{X}) = X^m + U_1 X^{m-2} + U_2 X^{m-3} + \ldots + U_{m-2} X \tag{A4.24}$$

The first term, in this case X^m, captures the degeneracy and type of singularity. If all the $\mathbf{U}$-variables are zero, this can be considered as the lowest order non-zero term in a Taylor expansion. As the $\mathbf{U}$-variables vary from zero values, the right hand side of Equation A4.24 approximates the Taylor expansion of a whole family of functions. Catastrophe theory essentially says that all other families of functions with the same number of parameters have singularities of the same type as the canonical, truncated Taylor expansion. This form is said to represent a universal unfolding of singularities of this type. Thom's theorem says that for m up to six (that is, up to four control variables) this models all functions f that co-dimension and the structure of the singularities, in this neighborhood of the function. The canonical form can then be used as a model for the singularities of all the functions of this type.

     The notion of unfolding can also be expressed in another way, based on the concept of structural stability, which provides another route into catastrophe theory. Consider the function

$$f(X) = X^3 + UX \tag{A4.25}$$

which is a special case of Equation A4.24 with $m = 3$. This is plotted in Figure A4.3 for the cases $U < 0$, $U = 0$, $U > 0$. When $U = 0$, $f(X) = X^3$ is not structurally stable in the sense that the addition (or substraction) of a term UX, however small U is, changes the shape of the curve in a basic way in the neighborhood of the origin. The function $f(X)$ in Equation A4.25 when $U \neq 0$, however, is structurally stable: it retains its shape under small perturbations. However, $f(X) = X^3$ is said to have a degenerate singularity at $X = 0$, and the addition of the term UX is the simplest way to make the function structurally stable.

     We noted earlier that catastrophes occur because of the existence of multiple minima of the potential function. The behavior manifold is defined as the surface in $(\mathbf{X}, \mathbf{U})$ space that contains the minima of the potential function, the possible equilibrium states of the system. We can usefully classify different possible types of system behavior by focusing on the control manifold, the equilibrium surface in the smaller dimensional $\mathbf{U}$-space. For each point on the control manifold, consider the point or points (if any) to which it gives rise on the behavior manifold. We can identify regions of the control manifold as follows:

Figure A4.3 ILLUSTRATING STRUCTURAL STABILITY

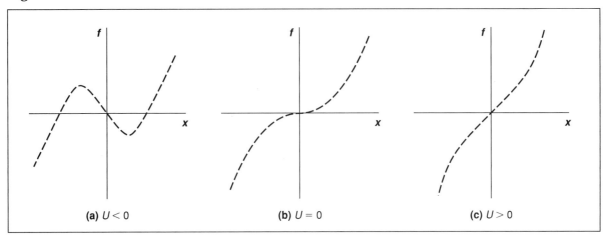

(a) $U < 0$ (b) $U = 0$ (c) $U > 0$

(1)   The region where those values of the control variables generate only one equilibrium solution, and the behavior of the system is then well-determined.

(2)   The region where there is more than one solution, discounting for the time being any region where there may be no solution. (This is known as the catastrophe set, and it is not immediately clear which state the system adopts, additional information must be supplied.)

(3)   The bifurcation set, which is the set of points that separates the catastrophe set from the "single solution" set. (It is the critical set of points at which a minimum disappears. It is at such points that the system must jump to another state, and hence branch or bifurcate).

Notice these concepts have been illustrated in the cusp surface Figure A4.2. The precise behavior of the system for control points within the catastrophe set is determined by a delay convention as mentioned. This is a rule that must be supplied to determine which of the multiple possibilities the system adopts. The two most common are first, perfect delay, which means that the system stays in its original state until that state disappears as the trajectory leaves the bifurcation set; and second, the Maxwell convention, which assumes that if more than one minimum is available, the system chooses the state that represents the lowest. In the perfect delay case, jumps take place as the trajectory crosses the bifurcation line, as noted. In the Maxwell case, the region of interest is the so-called conflict set, defined as the points on the control manifold at which two or more minima take equal values. This has been illustrated in Figure A4.2 for the cusp case. With perfect delay, system behavior can be associated with thresholds that the system must cross before a change. In the case of the Maxwell convention, the conflict set can be seen as a traveling wave that is the basis for morphogenesis (or structural development), which is particularly important where the control variables are taken as representing space and time (three space coordinates and one time coordinate). It is in this context that the traveling wave concept plays a key role in applications.[6]

C. The Fold Catastrophe as an Example

The simplest of elementary catastrophes is the fold. It is the universal unfolding of the singularities of X^3 and its potential function is $f = X^3/3 + UX$ for a single state variable X and a single control variable U. The possible equilibrium states of this system are those for which f is a minimum, and we can find this by setting the derivative to zero: $df/dX = X^2 + U = 0$. This has solutions $X = \pm \sqrt{-U}$, and we note that the second derivative is $d^2f/dX^2 = 2X$. Since the derivative is positive for positive values of X and negative for negative values, the minima occur for the positive values and the maxima for negative values. The solution also shows that real roots only exist for negative U. This information is displayed in Figure A4.4, which shows a parabola. The top half has been shown as a solid curve, because it represents the minima and the stable, observable states of the system. The bottom half is in dashed lines; it represents the maxima, which are unstable and unobservable.

We can now illustrate the general argument in the previous subsection by this simple example. The function f is a canonical representation for any function with a singularity of co-rank 1 at the origin and of co-dimension 1. (In other words, $d^2f/dX = 2X$ is a first-order polynomial that vanishes at the origin, and there exists only one control variable.) In this case, since we have only one state variable and one control variable, the whole picture of possible equilibrium values—the singularities of f in the neighborhood of the origin, can be represented in two dimensions as shown in Figure A4.4. The control manifold, the projection of the $(\mathbf{X}, \mathbf{U})$-manifold onto the $\mathbf{U}$-manifold is in this case simply the horizontal axis. There is no catastrophe set because there are no points on the horizontal axis at which there are two or more values of X for which f is a minimum, and the bifurcation set is also very simple: it is the single point at the origin, because here an observable minimum disappears. It is at this point, therefore, that jump be-

Figure A4.4   EXAMPLE OF A FOLD CATASTROPHE

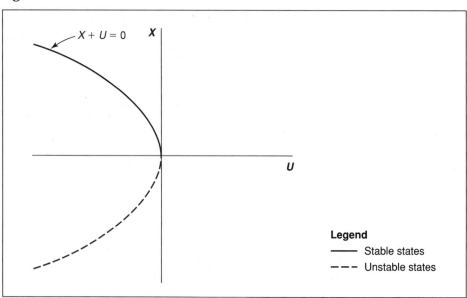

SOURCE: Wilson (1981). Reprinted with permission.

havior can be observed—if the system is in a state given by negative U and on a trajectory in which U is increasing, then as U passes through zero, the stable minimum equilibrium state disappears, and the system will have to take up some other state not accounted for by this diagram.

Because there is no area of the control manifold that produces multi-valued solutions, we cannot illustrate directly the concepts of delay conventions, conflict sets, and so on. However, we can see by reference to the fold catastrophe example in the "Activity Allocation and Derivation" chapter of Chan (2000) that even in this case, states can be added in the particular application that do create multi-valuedness. The example mentioned was concerned with the emergence or otherwise of spatial structure, namely whether or not to develop a housing project. Obviously delay conventions and associated concepts for thresholds are very important in this context.

One other technique can be introduced at this stage that gives more insight into the workings of catastrophe theory. Plots such as Figure A4.4 give the equilibrium values for X and U but do not show what is happening to the function f in the neighborhood of these values. This can be depicted on another form of diagram as illustrated in Figure A4.3: structural stability. For typical values of the control variable—in this case $U < 0$, $U = 0$ and $U > 0$—we can plot f against the state variable, in this case X. In the $U < 0$ case, the minimum (occurring at a positive value of X) can easily be seen as can the way in which the plot of f against X changes as U increases from a negative value. At $U = 0$, the graph is an obviously limiting case: the maximum and minimum have fused to form a point of inflexion, while for $U > 0$, the stationary points have clearly disappeared.

D. Higher Order Catastrophes

Aside from the fold and cusp catastrophes, there are other potential functions where catastrophes could occur. Of these, the seven elementary catastrophes are listed in Table A4.1. The table gives the number of state variables, the number of control variables, and the potential function that gives the universal unfolding of

Table A4.1   THE SEVEN ELEMENTARY CATASTROPHES

Name	State variables	Control variables/ Co-dimension	Potential function
Fold[a]	1	1	$X_1^3/3 + U_1 X_1$
Cusp	1	2	$X_1^4/4 + U_1 X_1^2/2 + U_2 X_1$
Swallow tail[a]	1	3	$X_1^5/5 + U_1 X_1^3 + 3 + U_2 X_1^2/2 + U_3 X_1$
Hyperbolic[a] umbilic	2	3	$X_1^3/3 + X_2^3/3 + U_1 X_1 X_2 - U_2 X_1 - U_3 X_2$
Elliptic[a] umbilic	2	3	$X_1^3/3 - X_1 X_2^2/2 + U_1(X_1^2 X_2^2)/2 - U_2 X_1 - U_3 X_2$
Butterfly	1	4	$X_1^6/6 + U_1 X_1^4/4 + U_2 X_1^3/3 + U_3 X_1^2/2 + U_4 X_1$
Parabolic umbilic	2	4	$X_1^2 X_2/2 + X_2^4/4 + U_1 X_1^2/2 + U_2 X_2^2/2 - U_3 X_1 - U_4 X_1$

[a] These unfolding functions are self-duals.

SOURCE: Wilson (1981). Reprinted with permission.

that type of singularity. Only the fold and cusp can be given a fully geometrical treatment because in other cases four or more dimensions would be needed for equivalent presentations. However, it is possible to generate pictures by portraying two or three dimensions as slices of higher order diagrams. The full treatment of the remaining elementary catastrophes are, however, now available in many other sources that can be used for reference (Wilson 1981).

The list of elementary catastrophes can be extended slightly by looking at duals. These exist for three of the entries in Table A4.1: the cusp, the butterfly and the parabolic umbilic; the rest of the list are self-duals. Duals are constructed by replacing the function being unfolded by its negative. In effect, this means that the positions of maxima and minima are reversed as the control manifold is covered. The self-duals are such because the negative sign can be produced by a change of coordinates. In effect, a review of Table A4.1 shows that functions that are wholly even powered polynomials have duals which are different, while the rest, including at least one odd powered term, are not, as replacing X by $-X$ produces the required minus sign. (For example, in the case of the fold, X^3 simply becomes $-X^3$ on this transformation.)

We illustrate briefly the concept of a dual by reference to the cusp. The potential function in Table A4.1 is replaced by $f = -X^4/4 + U_1 X^2 + U_2 X$ and the equivalent of Figure A4.4 can be used to see what happens when maxima are turned into minima and vice versa. The only maxima for the cusp surface were on the middle sheet of the folded section, and so this part of the surface in the dual becomes the only set of minima and therefore the only observable states. Thus there is a unique minimum inside the shaded areas of the control manifold and no stable states outside it. The possible behaviors of the system are therefore less interesting than that of the basic cusp surface. This particular example of catastrophe is also sometimes known as the false cusp.

Finally, we note the existence and importance of what is called constraint catastrophes. These arise as, in effect, extensions of Thom's theorem. The theorem is concerned with maxima and minima determined by points of the potential function where the derivative varnishes. If a model is constructed that includes constraints, then observable minima may be determined by the constraint rather than by vanishing derivatives. This point is illustrated by the curve shown in Figure A4.5, which shows the effect of a non-negativity constraint on a variable. In this case, local maxima or minima often occur on the boundary imposed by the constraint, and the derivative of the potential function does not vanish at that point.

E. Remarks

The reader will recall that the title of this appendix is "Control, Dynamics, and System Stability." While catastrophe theory contributes toward the subject of this chapter qualitatively, our focus is really on the more general discussion of system stability. Toward this goal, we will find that bifurcation theory is more quantitative in its applications. Indeed it is likely that sudden changes addressed by bifurcation theory are most important in applied work, inasmuch as most dynamic systems of interest are not gradient systems. In other words, the corresponding differential equation cannot be reduced to the optimization form $\nabla f(\mathbf{X}) = \mathbf{0}$. Typically, such differential equations have a small number of isolated equilibrium points, and information about system behavior is presented as trajectories on

Figure A4.5   LOCAL OPTIMA CREATED BY A CONSTRAINT

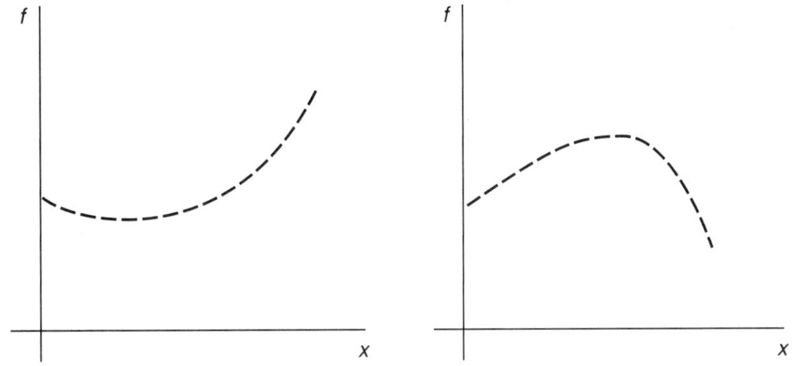

(a) Local max at $X = 0$ (b) Local min at $X = 0$

state space diagrams. A continuous network example is shown in the "Chaos, Catastrophe, Bifurcation, and Disaggregation" chapter in Chan (2000). We will turn to these subjects sequentially in the sections below, starting with time trajectories on state space. Meanwhile, it is interesting to note that variational inequality may help identify the existence and uniqueness of equilibria.

V. COMPARTMENTAL MODELS

We have made a distinction throughout this book between prescriptive and descriptive analysis procedures. While the pevious sections of this appendix have dealt with prescriptive procedures, the techniques involved here are specific to the description of systems in terms of processes. Indeed, in this case, no variational principle, characteristic of the prescriptive approach, seems to apply. The models currently used can be subdivided in two classes: the deterministic models in terms of differential or difference equations and the stochastic models in terms of Markov processes or chains. More recently, quasi-deterministic models in terms of differential or difference stochastic equations have been developed. These concepts apply readily to compartmental models, subject of our present discussion (dePalma and Lefèvre 1987; Godfrey 1983; Seber and Wild 1989).

A. Basics

A compartmental model is concerned with the description of a system divided into a finite number of subsystems called compartments between which the fundamental units of the system move. The purpose of this model is to describe the temporal evolution of the state of the system, which is defined as the number of units in the different compartments. The compartmental models defined here are intrinsically dynamic because the state of the system is the consequence of the various past transitions. The results derived describe the transient (finite time) and stationary (infinite time) regimes of the models. Moreover, the systems considered are concerned with characterizing the state variable in terms of populations or units, and special attention is paid to macroscopic behaviors and collective phenomena.

The most general form of compartmental equations for a system with n compartments is:

$$\frac{dX_i}{dt} = -H'_{i0} - \sum_{j \neq i} H'_{ij} + \sum_{j \neq i} H'_{ji} + H'_{0i} \quad i = 1, \ldots, n \quad \text{(A4.26)}$$

where X_i is the number of units in compartment i; H'_{ij} is the flow rate from compartment i to compartment j and the subscript 0 denotes the environment. Notice here that the flow rate H' is usually a function of the state variables, in other words, $H'(X_1, X_2, \ldots, X_n)$. If the flow rates from all compartments to the environment are zero ($H'_{i0} = 0$, $i = 1, \ldots, n$), the system is said to be closed; otherwise it is open. Equation A4.26 is illustrated for two of the n compartments in Figure A4.6.

Compartmental models typically involve rate constants like h in the growth model $dX(t)/dt = hX(t)$, where the growth rate is proportional to the population size $X(t)$ at time t. Thus $h = \frac{dX(t)/dt}{X(t)}$ or $dX(t) = hX(t)\, dt$. The reader can easily check using calculus that this single compartment model has solution $X(t) = X(0) \exp(ht)$. The example shows that compartmental models typically involve linear combinations of exponential terms, being solutions to differential equations. Consider the three-compartment model as shown in Figure A4.7, where an open system is portrayed, with both flow rates from and to the environment. Notice the input rate h_{01} from the environment is exemplified previously by the control variable U in our discussion of control theory. Here in this example, the change in the population in compartment 1 is $dX_1(t) = h_{21}X_2(t)\, dt + h_{01}dt - h_{13}X_3(t)\, dt - h_{12}X_1(t)\, dt$. Correspondingly, the rate of change is given by

$$\dot{X}_1 = \frac{dX_1(t)}{dt} = h_{21}X_2(t) + h_{01} - (h_{13} + h_{12}) X_1(t) \quad \text{(A4.27)}$$

Thus the whole system of Figure A4.7 is described by the set of differential equations

$$\begin{aligned}
\dot{X}_1 &= (h_{13} + h_{12})X_1(t) + h_{21} X_2(t) + h_{01} \\
\dot{X}_2 &= h_{12}X_1(t) - h_{21}X_2(t) \\
\dot{X}_3 &= h_{13}X_1(t) - h_{30}X_3(t)
\end{aligned} \quad \text{(A4.28)}$$

Figure A4.6 ILLUSTRATING TWO COMPARTMENTS OF A GENERAL COMPARTMENTAL MODEL

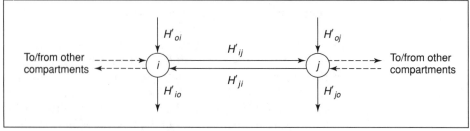

SOURCE: Godfrey (1983). Reprinted with permission.

Figure A4.7   ILLUSTRATING A THREE-COMPARTMENT MODEL

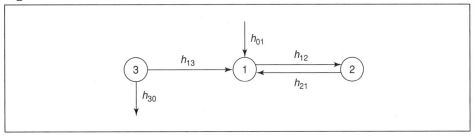

SOURCE: Seber and Wild (1989). Reprinted with permission.

We see that compartmental models, in their fundamental form, are simply sets of constrained first-order differential equations, the constraints being the physical requirement that flow rates are non-negative. Two qualitatively different situations occur in this type of modeling. In the linear systems, the individuals have independent behaviors and consequently, the state of the population can be deduced simply from the behavior of their units. This applies to migration models, for example, where each migrant is supposed to make his/her decision independent of other migrants. In nonlinear models, the individuals have interdependent behaviors whose aggregation can give rise to qualitatively new situations. This applies to individual choice models in collective systems, where individual decisions are often made conditioned upon the state of the system. In other words, linear (time invariant compartmental models) have flow rates that are directly proportional to the quantity in the donor compartment, with the constant of proportionality being referred to as a rate constant. Nonlinear systems, on the other hand, have some of the flow rates specified as a function of the state vector $\mathbf{X}$ instead of being constants.

B. Stochastic Models

While the above examples are illustrated for a deterministic case to fix ideas, the concept carries over readily to the stochastic case. For a stochastic compartmental model, we make here the Markov assumption that states that the individuals move from compartment to compartment with probabilities that depend on the characteristics of these compartments but not on the previously occupied compartments. In other words, it has the typical Markovian property that the future depends on the present but not on the past[7]. The situation is exactly analogous to deterministic models. In the linear case, the transition probabilities do not depend on the state of the system (that is to say, on the number of individuals in the compartment). In the nonlinear case, they do.

1. The Master Equation. Let us consider a compartment model with n compartments. $X_j(t)$ will denote the number of individuals in compartment j at time t, $t \geq 0$, and X_j^* a positive realization of $X_j(t)$, $j = 1, \ldots, n$. Let $\mathbf{X}(t)$ be the $n \times 1$ column vector $(X_1(t), \ldots, X_n(t))^T$ and $\mathbf{X}^*$ a possible realization of $\mathbf{X}(t)$. We define by $\pi_{ij}(\mathbf{X}^*, t)dt$, $1 \leq i \neq j \leq n$, the probability that during the infinitesimal time interval $(t, t + dt)$, a given individual moves from compartment i to compartment j when the system is in the state $\mathbf{X}^*$ at time t. Let $P(\mathbf{X}_0^*, \mathbf{X}^*, t)$ denote the probability that $\mathbf{X}(t) = \mathbf{X}^*$ given the initial condition $\mathbf{X}(0) = \mathbf{X}_0^*$. Let $\delta_j = (\delta_{j1}, \ldots, \delta_{jr})$,

$j = 1, \ldots, n$, be an orthonormal[8] base of the transition rate space Π^n, which maps out the possible transitions from the current jth compartment.

The Kolmogorov forward differential equations[9] give the temporal evolution of the probability distribution of the system's state. This accounts for the gain terms allowing for transition to the state $\mathbf{X}^*$, and the loss terms allowing for transitions *from* the state $\mathbf{X}^*$. These equations take the following form where the gain terms are positive and the loss terms negative:

$$\dot{P}(\mathbf{X}_0^*, \mathbf{X}^*, t) = \sum_{i=1}^{n} \sum_{j \neq i} P(\mathbf{X}_0^*, \mathbf{X}^* + \boldsymbol{\delta}_i - \boldsymbol{\delta}_j, t)(X_i^* + 1)\pi_{ij}(\mathbf{X}^* + \boldsymbol{\delta}_i - \boldsymbol{\delta}_j, t)$$

$$+ \sum_{j=1}^{n} P(\mathbf{X}_0^*, \mathbf{X}^* + \boldsymbol{\delta}_j, t)(X_j^* + 1)\pi_{j0}(\mathbf{X}^* + \boldsymbol{\delta}_j, t)$$

$$+ \sum_{j=1}^{n} P(\mathbf{X}_0^*, \mathbf{X}^* - \boldsymbol{\delta}_j, t)\pi_{0j}(\mathbf{X}^* - \boldsymbol{\delta}_j, t) \qquad \text{(A4.29)}$$

$$- P(\mathbf{X}_0^*, \mathbf{X}^*, t)\left[\sum_{i=1}^{n} \sum_{j \neq i} X_i^* \pi_{ij}(\mathbf{X}^*, t) \right.$$

$$\left. + \sum_{j=1}^{n} X_j^* \pi_{j0}(\mathbf{X}^*, t) + \sum_{j=1}^{n} \pi_{0j}(\mathbf{X}^*, t) \right]$$

The above constitute the master equations for the multi variate birth and death process. The notations used are consistent with those in Appendix 2. These equations are difficult to solve in general. Short of a solution, however, there are means to obtain information on the evolution of the system's state, as we will demonstrate.

2. A Special Nonlinear Case.

In the nonlinear case, the transition rates $\pi_{ij}(\mathbf{X}^*, t)$, $\pi_{j0}(\mathbf{X}^*, t)$, $\pi_{0j}(\mathbf{X}^*, t)$ depend explicitly on the state of the system. The presence of the argument $\mathbf{X}^*$ in the transition rates makes Equation A4.29 even more difficult to solve. However, we will discuss two examples that permit the derivation of analytical results. Let us consider a population of N individuals, each individual having to select one between two choices (1 and 2). The choice behavior of the individuals is described by a compartmental model, each choice corresponding to a compartment in the system. Assuming the system was initially empty, we will describe the state of the system with one of the two variables, $X_i(t)$, whose realizations are denoted by $\mathbf{X}^*$. Let us now give the structure of the transition rate $\pi_{ij}(\mathbf{X}^*, t)$, $1 \le i, j \le 2$.

We will suppose that an individual decides to review and modify the choice through two successive steps. First, during $(t, t + dt)$, an individual reviews his or her present choice i with a probability $\pi^{(i)}dt$; then, he or she selects a choice j with a probability $p^{(j)}(\mathbf{X}^*)$ which has the following *logit* form:[10]

$$p^{(j)}(\mathbf{X}^*) = \frac{\exp\left[v^{(j)}(\mathbf{X}^*)/\mu^{(j)}\right]}{\exp\left[v^{(1)}(\mathbf{X}^*)/\mu^{(1)}\right] + \exp\left[v^{(2)}(\mathbf{X}^*)/\mu^{(2)}\right]} \quad (j = 1, 2) \qquad \text{(A4.30)}$$

where $v^{(1)}(\mathbf{X}^*)$ and $v^{(2)}(\mathbf{X}^*)$ represent the utility functions of choices 1 and 2 respectively, and μ is a positive parameter tht expresses the degree of uncertainty in the individual's behavior. Specifically, we add an error term $\epsilon^{(j)}$ to the deterministic value function $v^{(i)}$: $v^{(i)}(\mathbf{X}^*) + \mu^{(i)}\epsilon^{(i)}$, where $\mu^{(i)}$ is a constant measuring the importance of the error term. Thus $\mu^{(i)}$ can be thought of as a scaling constant; the larger it is, the higher the uncertainty.

It is clear that the process for determining $X_i(t)$ is reduced to a birth-death process[11]. The global distribution of individual choices strongly depends on the structure of the utility functions. For illustration, we will examine the cases where the utilities of each choice is a linear or logarithmic function of the number of individuals who have adopted this choice (that is, $v^{(1)}(\mathbf{X}^*)$ and $v^{(2)}(\mathbf{X}^*)$ are linear or logarithmic functions of X^* and $N-X^*$ respectively).

Let us first consider the case where the utility functions are linear:

$$\left.\begin{array}{l} v^{(1)}(\mathbf{X}^*) = a + bX^* \\ v^{(2)}(\mathbf{X}^*) = c + d(N - X^*) \end{array}\right\} \ X^* = 0, \ldots, N \qquad (A4.31)$$

The Markov process is then irreducible (that is to say, all compartments intercommunicate), $\lim_{t\to\infty} P(X_0^*, X^*, t) \cong P(X^*)$ exist and are independent of the initial condition X_0^*. Define the generating function[12] $G(\boldsymbol{\xi}, t) = \sum_{X^*} \boldsymbol{\xi}^{x^*} P(X_0^*, \mathbf{X}^*, t)$ where the nth-derivative exists for $G(\boldsymbol{\xi}, t)$ $|\xi_j| < 1, 1 \le j \le n; \boldsymbol{\xi}^{x^*} \cong \xi_1^{x_1^*}, ..., \xi_n^{x_n^*}$. The generating function for the probability distribution $P(X_0^*, \mathbf{X}^*, t)$, where $\mathbf{X}^* = [X_1^*(t), X_2^*(t), \ldots, X_n^*(t)]^T$, can be written out in long hand for a stationary, irreducible Markov process. It assumes the form $P(X_0^*) + \xi_1^{X_1^*}P(X_1^*) + \xi_2^{X_2^*}P(X_2^*) + \cdots + \xi_n^{X_n^*}P(X_n^*)$. Suppose there are no arrivals and departures. Then for the stationary solution $\lim_{t\to\infty} G(\boldsymbol{\xi}, t) = (p^T\boldsymbol{\xi})^{X_0^T u''}$ where $\mathbf{p}$ is a $n \times 1$ Perron vector whose components are positive and of sum equal to 1, and $\mathbf{u}''$ is an $N \times 1$ column vector $(1, \ldots, 1)^T$ Consequently, at the stationary state, G is the generating function of a multinomial vector of exponent $\mathbf{X}_0^T\mathbf{u}''$ and of parameter $\mathbf{p}$ (Cox and Miller 1965). In longhand,

$$G(\boldsymbol{\xi}, t) = [p^{(1)}\xi_1^{X_1^*} + p^{(2)}\xi_2^{X_2^*} + \ldots + p^{(n)}\xi_n^{X_n^*}]^{\text{constant}}$$

We will now examine the symmetrical situation where $\pi^{(1)} = \pi^{(2)}$, $a = c$, and $b = d$ to illustrate in a simple way the importance of nonlinearities. Clearly, the stationary distribution is symmetrical, and $\mu^{(1)} = \mu^{(2)} = \mu$. When $b = 0$ (linear case), the stationary state can be shown via the above generating function result to be a binomial distribution of exponent N and parameter 0.5,

$$P(X^*) = \binom{N}{X^*}[\exp(-0.5)]^{X^*}[1 - \exp(-0.5)]^{N-X^*}$$

The values of b tht are positive (negative) express a behavior of imitation (antilimitation). It can be proved that if the imitation behavior becomes sufficiently important (or when $b > 2\mu/N$), the stationary distribution passes from a unimodal to a bimodal shape: the state $N/2$ is no longer the mode of the distribution and corresponds now to a local minimum of the distribution. This is illustrated in Figure A4.8.

Let us now consider the case where the utility functions are logarithmic:

$$\left.\begin{array}{l} v^{(1)}(\mathbf{X}^*) = a + b\ln X^* \\ v^{(2)}(\mathbf{X}^*) = c + d\ln N - X^* \end{array}\right\} < \ X^* = 0, \ldots, N \qquad (A4.32)$$

Figure A4.8   STATIONARY DISTRIBUTION IN THE NONLINEAR CASE
WHEN $\mu = 1$

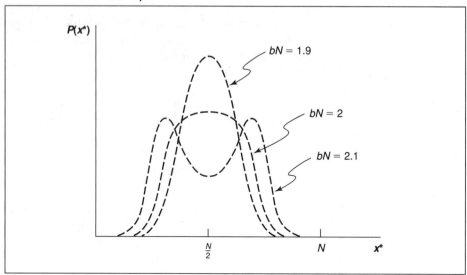

SOURCE: dePalma and Lefèvre (1987). Reprinted with permission.

The Markov process is then either irreducible or absorbing in relation to the sign of the coefficients b and d. For example, when b and d are positive, there exists two absorbing states 0 and N. In other words, the transitional probability $\pi_{00} = 1$ and $\pi_{NN} = 1$. In this case, it is quite plausible that one of these two states, 0 for example, is in fact preferable to the other, N. As the absorption probabilities depend on μ, it is then natural to consider this parameter (interpreted here as the information level accessible to individuals) as a control parameter to maximize the probability of absorption in state 0. It can be proved that here exists an optimal stationary policy that consists of taking for μ the largest possible value when the choice distribution X^* favors choice 1 to the detriment of choice 2 (that is when $v^{(2)}(X^*) < v^{(1)}(X^*)$) and the smallest possible in the contrary case. This is illustrated in Figure A4.9.

The above two models represent examples of an epidemic model. Such ecological models are related to the Lotka-Volterra predator-prey model as well as nonlinear, dynamic, Lowry derivative models[13]. They typically describe the interacting (often conflicting) relationship between two or more populations. More importantly, they illustrate the asymptotic behavior of stochastic models. Often, a stationary solution is obtained that can be adequately modeled by a deterministic framework.

C. Deterministic Models

A deterministic version of Equation A4.29 can be written in terms of the following differential equations:

$$\frac{dX_i(t)}{dt} = \sum_{j \neq i} X_j(t) H'_{ji}[\mathbf{X}(t), t] - X_i(t) \sum_{j \neq i} H'_{ij}[\mathbf{X}(t), t]$$

$$-X_i(t) H'_{i0}[\mathbf{X}(t), t] + H'_{0i}[\mathbf{X}(t), t] \qquad i = 1, \ldots, n$$

(A4.33)

Figure A4.9   LOGARITHMIC UTILITY FUNCTION

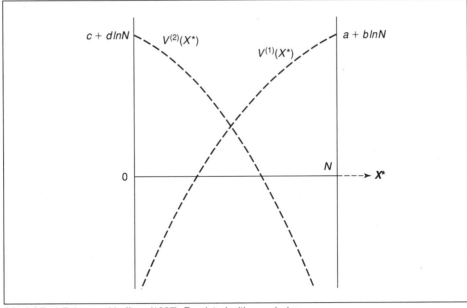

SOURCE: dePalma and Lefèvre (1987). Reprinted with permission.

where $\mathbf{X}(t) \cong [X_1(t), \ldots, X_n(t)]^T$ is the $n \times 1$ column vector of the state of the system at time t, and $H'_{ij}(\mathbf{X}, t)$'s represent the deterministic flow rates defined before. In the linear case, the systems of differential equations can be written in the form

$$\dot{\mathbf{X}}(\mathbf{t}) = \mathbf{A}'\mathbf{X}(\mathbf{t}) + \mathbf{U}(\mathbf{t}) \tag{A4.34}$$

subject to $\mathbf{X}(0) = \mathbf{X}_0$. Here $\mathbf{U}(t)$ can refer to an input vector or control variables. Such equations are discussed in many books on differential equations and dynamical systems. They involve the use of matrix exponential exp $(\mathbf{A}')$ for a square matrix $\mathbf{A}'$. This is defined as exp $(\mathbf{A})' = \mathbf{I} + \mathbf{A}' + \frac{\mathbf{A}'^2}{2!} + \frac{\mathbf{A}'^3}{3!} + \cdots$ and this series converges for any $\mathbf{A}'$. If $\mathbf{A}'$ is any square matrix, the general solution of the homogeneous[14] equation $\dot{\mathbf{X}} = \mathbf{A}'\mathbf{X}$ is given by $\mathbf{X} = $ exp $(\mathbf{A}'t)\mathbf{c}$ for any constant vector $\mathbf{c}$. A particular solution[15] is $\int_0^t$ exp $(\mathbf{A}'(t - \tau))\mathbf{U}(\tau) \, d\tau$. Thus the complete solution to Equation A4.34 that satisfies the initial conditions is

$$\mathbf{X}(t) = \exp (\mathbf{A}'t)\mathbf{N}_0 + \int_0^t \exp (\mathbf{A}'(t - \tau))\mathbf{U}(\tau) \, d\tau \tag{A4.35}$$

When the $n \times n$ matrix $\mathbf{A}'$ has n linearly independent eigenvectors[16], it is possible to form the spectral decomposition $\mathbf{A}' = \mathbf{P}''\mathbf{Q}''\mathbf{P}'^{-1}$, where $\mathbf{Q}''$ is an $n \times n$ matrix with n eigenvalues on its diagonal, or $\mathbf{Q}'' = $ diag $(q'_1, q'_2, \ldots, q_n')$, and the kth column of P' is a right eigenvector of $\mathbf{A}'$ corresponding to q_k'. In particular, this is possible if all the eigenvalues of $\mathbf{A}'$ are distinct, as this implies that the eigenvector are all linearly independent.

In the linear case the state of the system in the deterministic version is the expected state in the Markovian version for identical initial conditions. In the nonlinear case, this result is no longer true. The Kurtz theorem establishes a connection, under certain hypotheses, between the deterministic and Markovian models. This result can be applied when the total population is important, say proportional to a large number N'(large). In addition, it supposes that the arrival rates in the system take the form N'(large)H'_{0i}, and that the rates, H'_{0i}, H'_{i0} and H'_{ij} $(1 \le i, j \le n)$, depend on the state of the system through the relative frequencies X/N'(large) (and not on the absolute values X).

Let $Z(t)$[large] denote the relative frequency (or density for short) X/N'(large) and $Z^*(t)$ the density $X^*(t)/N'$(large) for the stochastic and deterministic versions respectively. Kurtz has proved the following theorem: Under the hypothesis given above, if $\lim_{N'(\text{large}) \to \infty} Z(0)[N'(\text{large})] = Z^*(0)$, then for every τ ($0 \le \tau \le \infty$) $\lim_{N'(\text{large}) \to \infty} \sup_{t \le \tau} |Z^*(t[N'(\text{large})] - Z^*(t)| = 0$. That is to say, the normalized state in the Markovian version converges almost always to the normalized state in the deterministic version. This allows one to use the deterministic model to approximate the stochastic.

D. Deterministic Example

Consider an example as illustrated in Figure A4.10, where the constant transition rates h are shown. In this open system, there is an initial quantity of $N_1^*(0)$ in compartment 1 and nothing elsewhere. The rate of change equations can be written as

$$
\begin{aligned}
\dot{N}_1 &= -h_{12}N_1 \\
\dot{N}_2 &= h_{12} + h_{32}N_3 - h_{23} + h_{20})N_2 \\
\dot{N}_3 &= h_{23} - h_{32}N_3
\end{aligned}
\tag{A4.36}
$$

with initial conditions $N_1^*(1, 0, 0)^T$ and the parameters

$$\{N_1^*, h_{12}, h_{23}, h_{32}, h_{20}\}^T$$

Hence

$$
\mathbf{A}' = \begin{bmatrix} -h_{12} & 0 & 0 \\ h_{12} & -(h_{23} + h_{20}) & h_{32} \\ 0 & h_{23} & -h_{32} \end{bmatrix}
$$

$$
\mathbf{A}' - q'\mathbf{I} = \begin{bmatrix} -h_{12} - q' & 0 & 0 \\ h_{12} & -h_{23} - h_{20} - q' & h_{32} \\ 0 & h_{23} & -h_{32} - q' \end{bmatrix}
$$

Figure A4.10   EXAMPLE OF A DETERMINISTIC COMPARTMENTAL MODEL

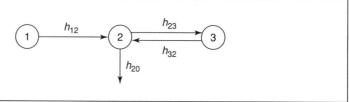

SOURCE: Seber and Wild (1989). Reprinted with permission.

The characteristic polynomial[17] for the eigenvalues q' is

$$|\mathbf{A}' - q'\mathbf{I}| = -(h_{12} - q')[q'^2 + (h_{23} + h_{32} + h_{20})q' + h_{32}h_{20}] = 0 \quad (A4.37)$$

with eigenvalues q' equal to $-h_{12}$ and $-\frac{1}{2}\{h_{23} + h_{32} + h_{20} \pm [(h_{23} + h_{32} + h_{20})^2 - 4h_{32}h_{20}]^{1/2}\}$. For simplicity, we will write the last two eigenvalues (out of three) as a and b, where $a + b = -(h_{23} + h_{32} + h_{20})$ and $ab = h_{32}h_{20}$.

The adjoint matrix is obtainable by replacing each element of a square matrix by its co-factor[18] and then interchanging rows and columns:

$$\text{adj}(\mathbf{A}' - q'\mathbf{I}) = \begin{bmatrix} (h_{23}+h_{20}+q')(h_{32}+q')-h_{23}h_{32} & 0 & 0 \\ h_{12}(h_{32}+q') & (h_{32}+q')(h_{32}+q') & h_{32}(h_{12}+a') \\ h_{12}h_{23} & h_{23}(h_{12}+y') & (h_{12}+q')(h_{12}+h_{20}+q) \end{bmatrix} \quad (A4.38)$$

It can be shown that *any* non-zero column of adj$(\mathbf{A}' - q'\mathbf{I})$ is a right eigenvector $\mathbf{x}_R$ of $\mathbf{A}'$ in the set of homogeneous equations $\mathbf{A}'\mathbf{x}_R = q'\mathbf{x}_R$. Similarly, *any* row is a left eigenvector $\mathbf{x}_L$, or $\mathbf{x}_L^T\mathbf{A}' = \mathbf{x}_L q'$. Thus the right eigenvectors corresponding to eigenvalues $-h_{12}$, a and b respectively (after some slight manipulation and canceling common column factors), are

$$\mathbf{R}' = \begin{bmatrix} | & | & | \\ \mathbf{x}(-h_{12}) & \mathbf{x}(a) & \mathbf{x}(b) \\ \downarrow & \downarrow & \downarrow \end{bmatrix} = \begin{bmatrix} (h_{12}+a)(h_{12}+b) & 0 & 0 \\ h_{12}(h_{32}+h_{12}) & h_{32}+a & h_{32}+b \\ h_{12}h_{23} & h_{23} & h_{23} \end{bmatrix} \quad (A4.39)$$

The left (row) eigenvectors using rows 1 and 3 of the adjoint matrix yield

$$\mathbf{L} = \begin{bmatrix} 1 & 0 & 0 \\ h_{12}h_{23} & h_{23}(h_{12}+a) & (h_{12}+a)(h_{23}+h_{20}+a) \\ h_{12}h_{23} & h_{23}h_{12}+b & (h_{12}+b)(h_{23}+h_{20}+b) \end{bmatrix} \quad (A4.40)$$

From linear algebra (Noble 1969), if $\mathbf{A}'$ has n independent right eigenvectors $\mathbf{x}_R$, then to each $\mathbf{x}_R$ there corresponds a left eigenvector $\mathbf{x}_L$ for the same eigenvalue such that $\mathbf{x}_L^T\mathbf{x}_R = 1$. We can thus normalize the rows of $\mathbf{L}$ using

$$\mathbf{x}(q') = \mathbf{x}_L(q')/\mathbf{x}_L(q')^T\mathbf{x}_R(q') \quad (A4.41)$$

The resulting vector $\mathbf{x}(q')$ is a row vector of $\mathbf{R}'^{-1}$ since $\mathbf{R}'^{-1}\mathbf{R}' = \mathbf{I}$:

$$\mathbf{R}'^{-1} = \begin{bmatrix} \dfrac{1}{(h_{-12}+a)(h_{12}+b)} & 0 & 0 \\ \dfrac{h_{12}}{(h_{12}+a)(a-b)} & \dfrac{1}{a-b} & \dfrac{{}^*h_{23}+h_{20}+a}{h_{23}(a-b)} \\ \dfrac{h_{12}}{(h_{12}+b)(b-a)} & \dfrac{1}{b-a} & \dfrac{h_{23}+h_{20}+b}{h_{23}(b-a)} \end{bmatrix} \quad (A4.42)$$

The solution to homogeneous equations $\dot{\mathbf{X}} = \mathbf{A}'\mathbf{X}$ with initial condition $\mathbf{X}(0) = \mathbf{X}^*(0)$ can be written as $\mathbf{X}(t) = \exp{(\mathbf{A}'t)}\mathbf{X}^*(0) = \sum_{j=1} \beta_j \exp{(q'_j t)}$ where $\beta_j = [\mathbf{x}(q')^T\mathbf{X}^*(0)]\mathbf{x}_R(q')$ and q is the number of eigenvalues. This has been referred to as the sum of exponential model, and is typical of linear systems. Given $\mathbf{X}(0) = N_1^*(0)(1, 0, 0)^T$, the solution $\mathbf{X}(t)$ in this case is

$$\mathbf{X}(t) = N_1^*(0)\sum_{j=1}^{3} \exp{(q'_j\, t)}\left(\mathbf{x}_R(q'_j)\right)\left[\left(-\mathbf{x}(q'_j)\rightarrow\right)\begin{pmatrix} 1 \\ 0 \\ 0 \end{pmatrix}\right] = N_{1(0)}^*\begin{pmatrix} w'_1 \\ w'_2 \\ w'_3 \end{pmatrix} \quad \text{(A4.43)}$$

Here,

$$w'_1 = \exp{(-h_{12}t)}$$

$$w'_2 = h_{12}\left[\frac{h_{32} - h_{12}}{(h_{12} + a)(h_{12} + b)}\, \exp{(-h_{12}t)} + \frac{h_{32} + a}{(h_{12} + a)(a - b)}\, \exp{(at)}\right.$$
$$\left. + \frac{h_{32} + b}{(h_{12} + b)(b - a)}\, \exp{(bt)}\right] \quad \text{(A4.44)}$$

$$w'_3 = h_{12}h_{23}\left[\frac{1}{(h_{12} + b)(a + b)}\, \exp{(-h_{12}t)} + \frac{1}{(h_{12} + b)(a - b)}\, \exp{(at)}\right.$$
$$\left. + \frac{1}{(h_{12} + b)(b - a)}\, \exp{(bt)}\right]$$

We note that $X_1(t) = N_1^*(0)\exp{(-h_{12}t)}$ corresponds to a simple exponential decay.

E. Stochastic Example

Shown in Figure A4.11 is a two-compartment open model. For this model, the parameters $\{\pi_{12},\ \pi_{21},\ \pi_{10},\ \pi_{20}\}$ are given. Notice the flow rates are now denoted by π's instead of h's to show the stochastic nature of the current model, consonant with the notation used in Equation A4.29. In lieu of the rate of change matrix $\mathbf{A}'$, we write its stochastic counterpart as $\mathrm{II} = [\pi_{ij}]$. Here the matrix takes on the form

$$\mathrm{II} = \begin{bmatrix} 0 & \pi_{10} & \pi_{20} \\ 0 & -\pi_{10} - \pi_{12} & \pi_{21} \\ 0 & \pi_{12} & -\pi_{20} - \pi_{21} \end{bmatrix}$$

where the first row and column refer to transitions to and from the environment. For this model the explicit form for $\mathbf{P}(t) = \exp{(\mathrm{II}t)}$ is readily obtainable. The eigenvalues of II are $q'_0 = 0$ and $q'_1,\ q'_2 - \frac{1}{2}\{\pi_{10} + \pi_{12} + \pi_{20} + \pi_{21} \pm [(\pi_{10} + \pi_{12} - \pi_{20} - \pi_{21})^2 + 4\pi_{21}\pi_{12}]^{1/2}\}$. Now

$$\mathbf{P}(t) = \begin{bmatrix} 1 & p_{01}(t) & p_{02}(t) \\ 0 & p_{11}(t) & p_{12}(t) \\ 0 & p_{21}(t) & p_{22}(t) \end{bmatrix}$$

Figure A4.11   EXAMPLE OF A STOCHASTIC COMPARTMENTAL MODEL

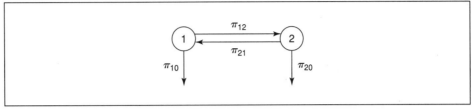

SOURCE: Seber and Wild (1989). Reprinted with permission.

and using the method of the deterministic example above, including normalization via Equation A4.41, we find that

$$p_{11}(t) = \frac{1}{q'_2 - q'_1} \left[(\pi_{01} + \pi_{21} + q'_2) \exp(q'_1 t) - (\pi_{01} + \pi_{21} + q'_1) \exp(-q'_2 t) \right]$$

and   (A4.45)

$$p_{21}(t) = \frac{\pi_{21}}{q'_2 - q'_1} \left[\exp(q'_2 t) - \exp(q'_1 t) \right]$$

The terms $p_{22}(t)$ and $p_{21}(t)$ are obtained by symmetry, and the values of $p_{01}(t)$ and $p_{02}(t)$ follow from the fact that the column sums of **P** are unity.

F. Discrete Time Models

Let us revisit a compartmental system where a discrete time scale $t = 0, 1, 2, \ldots$ is used instead of a continuous time axis. First, let us consider the stochastic model. We are interested in the linear case where the transition rates $\pi_{ij}(\mathbf{X^*}, t)$, $\pi_{0j}(\mathbf{X^*}, t)$ and $\pi_{j0}(\mathbf{X^*}, t)$ are independent of $\mathbf{X^*}$. If $p_{ij}(t)$ denote the probability that an individual in compartment i at time 0 is in compartment j at time t, $\mathbf{P}(t)$ is the $n \times n$ matrix of these $p_{ij}(t)$'s as mentioned. Equation A4.29 can be written in a compact form as $\mathbf{P}(t + 1) = \mathbf{P}(t)\text{II}(t)$ where $\text{II}(t)$ is the $n \times n$ matrix of the $\pi_{ij}(t)$'s. We note that if $\text{II}(t)$ is a constant matrix II, then

$$\mathbf{P}(t) = \text{II}^t \qquad\qquad\qquad (A4.46)$$

It can be shown through the use of generating functions that expected values of **X** can be written asymptotically ($t \to \infty$) as the difference equation

$$E[\mathbf{X}(t + 1)] = \text{II}' E[\mathbf{X}(t)] + \text{II}_0(t) \qquad\qquad (A4.47)$$

where $\text{II}_0(t) = [\pi_{10}(t), \ldots, \pi_{n0}(t)]^T$.

The deterministic version associated with the Markov model above is constructed formally by putting $\mathbf{X^*}(t + 1) \cong E[\mathbf{X}(t + 1) | \mathbf{X}(t)]$ and $\mathbf{X^*}(t) \equiv \mathbf{X}(t)$. Thus $\mathbf{X^*}(t)$ is solution of the following system of difference equations:

$$\mathbf{X^*}(t + 1) = \mathbf{A}'^{t[\mathbf{X}(t), t]}\mathbf{X^*}(t) + \mathbf{A}_0[\mathbf{X}(t), t] \qquad (A4.48)$$

where we replace II with $\mathbf{A}'$. In the linear case, the above equation reduces to Equation A4.47. This says that, as in the continuous time version, the state of the deterministic model is asymptotically equal to the expected state of the Markovian model (for identical initial conditions).

We have demonstrated above and in Section V-C that the normalized Markovian process converges to its associated deterministic version almost surely as the population size becomes very large. In applications, it is then natural to approximate the stochastic model by the deterministic one, in view of the computational advantage. However, the Kurtz theorem does not give any information on the quality of this approximation over time. It is possible to express the stochastic process as the sum of the deterministic process and a stochastic diffusion (epidemic) process[19]. The result allows us to judge the validity of the approximation as a function of time. Moreover, it is also very useful for statistical inference because a likelihood function can then be easily constructed from the data. We call this procedure the quasi-deterministic approach. While we will show an example, the reader is referred to dePalma and Lefèvre (1987) for details of this procedure.

Comparing the deterministic with the probabilistic evolution, Haag (1989) notes that the latter is the more general formulation, since the case of incomplete knowledge about the system comprises complete knowledge as a limit case while the converse is not true. The limit case of almost complete knowledge of the dynamics is revealed by the shape of the probability distribution $P(\mathbf{X_0}^*, \mathbf{X}^*, t)$ itself in the master equation A4.29. In this case, the master equation leads to an evolution in such a way that it develops one outstanding mode sharply peaked around the most likely state $\mathbf{X}^*_{max}(t)$. This means that the system assumes state $\mathbf{X}^* = \mathbf{X}^*_{max}(t)$ with overwhelming probability at time t, while all the other states $\mathbf{X}^* \neq \mathbf{X}^*_{max}$ are highly improbable at the same time. Evidently this particular case descries a quasi-deterministic evolution of the system along path $\mathbf{X}^*(t) \approx \mathbf{X}^*_{max}(t)$.

G. Example of a Quasi-Deterministic Analysis

Consider a closed system solution to the linear version of difference Equation A4.48 in which $\mathbf{A_0} = \mathbf{B_0} = 0$ and Equation A4.48 represents the individual terms of the geometric series[20]

$$\mathbf{I} + \tilde{\mathbf{B}} + \tilde{\mathbf{B}}^2 + \cdots + \tilde{\mathbf{B}}^k \qquad k \to \infty \qquad (A4.49)$$

It can be shown that this deterministic approximation of the stochastic Equation A4.47 may or may not converge under certain circumstances (Yi 1986; Noble 1969). Here we will investigate the circumstances where convergence is guaranteed. Through this exercise, we wish to arrive at a stationary solution to Equation A4.49 and in the process show an example of how a seemingly complex stochastic model can be approximated asymptotically by a simple deterministic model.

Before we start, several basic concepts in matrix algebra need to be reviewed. Matrix norm on square matrix $\tilde{\mathbf{B}}$ is defined as $\|\tilde{\mathbf{B}}\| = \max_{\|z\|=1} \|\tilde{\mathbf{B}}z\|$ where $\mathbf{z} = \mathbf{x}/\|\mathbf{x}\|$, $\mathbf{x}$ is any vector, and $\|\mathbf{z}\| = 1$. In this spirit, the matrix norm $\|\tilde{\mathbf{B}}\|$ is parallel to the concept of a vector norm $\|\mathbf{x}\|$. On the other hand, the spectral radius of matrix $\tilde{\mathbf{B}}$, $\breve{\rho}(\tilde{\mathbf{B}})$, is defined as $\max_k |q'_k|$ where q'_ks are eigenvalues of $\tilde{\mathbf{B}}$. For example, let $\tilde{\mathbf{B}} = \begin{bmatrix} 1 & c \\ 0 & 1 \end{bmatrix}$ for any real c. $\|\tilde{\mathbf{B}}\| = [1\backslash 2c^2 + 1 + 1\backslash 2c(c^2 + 4)^{1/2}]^{1/2}$ and the spectral radius $\breve{\rho}(\tilde{\mathbf{B}}) = 1$.

Now according to the definition of matrix norm, we can state for the ∞-norm

$$\|\tilde{\mathbf{B}}\|_{\infty} = \max_{\|\mathbf{z}\|=1} \|\tilde{\mathbf{B}}\mathbf{z}\|_{\infty} \geq \|\tilde{\mathbf{B}}\mathbf{x}_i\|_{\infty} \tag{A4.50}$$

where $\mathbf{x}_i$s are any normalized eigenvector (in other words, $\|\mathbf{x}_i\|_{\infty} = 1$). Introducing eigenvalues, $\|\tilde{\mathbf{B}}\mathbf{x}_k\|_{\infty} = \|q_k'\mathbf{x}_i\|_{\infty} = |q_k'| \; \|\mathbf{x}_i\|_{\infty} = |q_k'|$ where q_k''s are any eigenvalues. Combined with the spectral radius definition, $\rho(\tilde{\mathbf{B}}) = \max_k |q_k'|$ $= \max_k \|\tilde{\mathbf{B}}\mathbf{x}_k\|_{\infty}$. From the result of Equation A4.50, $\rho(\tilde{\mathbf{B}}) \leq \|\tilde{\mathbf{B}}\|_{\infty}$ for any eigenvalue. This means we have an easily calculable bound of the spectral radius. Thus in the example above, we have $\rho(\tilde{\mathbf{B}}) \leq \|\tilde{\mathbf{B}}\|_{\infty} = 1 + |c|$. This illustrates one of the characteristic features of analysis using norms.

According to the definition of the norm of a vector, if $\|\mathbf{x}\|_{\infty} = 1$, this means that $\max_i |z_i| = 1$. In this case, the ∞-norm of a matrix is defined as $\|\tilde{\mathbf{B}}\mathbf{x}\|_{\infty} = \max_i |\Sigma_j \tilde{\mathbf{b}}_{ij} x_j| \leq \max_i \Sigma_j |\tilde{\mathbf{b}}_{ij}| \; |x_j| \leq \max_i \Sigma_j |\tilde{\mathbf{b}}_{ij}|$ (Noble 1969). Hence

$$\|\tilde{\mathbf{B}}\| = \max_{\|\mathbf{x}\|=1} \|\tilde{\mathbf{B}}\mathbf{x}\|_{\infty} \leq \max_i \sum_{j=1}^{n} |\tilde{\mathbf{b}}_{ij}| \tag{A4.51}$$

Suppose the maximum sum occurs at row k^*, then we construct a vector $\mathbf{x}$ with $x_j = 1$ if $\tilde{\mathbf{b}}_{k^*j} \geq 0$, and $x_j = -1$ if $\tilde{\mathbf{b}}_{k^*j} < 0$. For this $\mathbf{x}$, equality is obtained in Equation A4.51.

Next, define $\mathbf{P}' = [\mathbf{x}_1, \ldots, \mathbf{x}_n]$ consisting of linearly independent eigenvectors. We also define the eigenvalue matrix

$$\mathbf{Q}'' = \begin{bmatrix} q'_1 & 0 & . & . & . & 0 \\ 0 & q'_2 & 0 & . & . & . \\ 0 & 0 & q'_3 & . & . & . \\ . & . & . & . & . & 0 \\ 0 & . & . & . & 0 & q'_n \end{bmatrix} . \; \tilde{\mathbf{B}}\mathbf{x}_k = \mathbf{Q}''_k(\mathbf{x}_k \neq \mathbf{0}$$

We have $\tilde{\mathbf{B}}\mathbf{P}' = \tilde{\mathbf{B}}(\mathbf{x}_1, \ldots, \mathbf{x}_n) = (\tilde{\mathbf{B}}\mathbf{x}_1, \ldots, \tilde{\mathbf{B}}\mathbf{x}_n) = (q'_1\mathbf{x}_1, \ldots, q'_n\mathbf{x}_n) = \mathbf{P}'\mathbf{Q}''$. It follows that $\tilde{\mathbf{B}} = \tilde{\mathbf{B}}\mathbf{P}'\mathbf{P}'^{-1} = \mathbf{P}'\mathbf{Q}''\mathbf{P}'^{-1}$. Correspondingly,

$$\tilde{\mathbf{B}}^2 = (\mathbf{P}'\mathbf{Q}''\mathbf{P}'^{-1})(\mathbf{P}'\mathbf{Q}''\mathbf{P}'^{-1}) = \mathbf{P}'\mathbf{Q}''^2\mathbf{P}'^{-1}, \ldots, \tilde{\mathbf{B}}^r = \mathbf{P}'\mathbf{Q}''^r\mathbf{P}'^{-1}$$

$$= \mathbf{P}' \begin{bmatrix} q''_1 & 0 & 0 & . & 0 \\ 0 & q''_2 & 0 & . & . \\ . & . & . & . & . \\ 0 & . & . & 0 & q''_n \end{bmatrix} \mathbf{P}^{-1} .$$

Obviously, if $\breve{\rho}(\tilde{\mathbf{B}}) < 1$, in other words, $|q'_k| < 1$ for all k, $q_k''^r \to 0$ as $r \to \infty$. One can conclude therefore that $\lim_{r \to \infty} \tilde{\mathbf{B}}^r = \mathbf{0}$ if $\breve{\rho}(\tilde{\mathbf{B}}) < 1$.

For matrix series $\tilde{\mathbf{I}} + \tilde{\mathbf{B}} + \tilde{\mathbf{B}}^2 + \cdots + \tilde{\mathbf{B}}^k$ we have $(\mathbf{I} - \tilde{\mathbf{B}})(\mathbf{I} + \tilde{\mathbf{B}} + \tilde{\mathbf{B}}^2 + \cdots + \tilde{\mathbf{B}}^k) = \mathbf{I} - \mathbf{B}^{k+1}$. From what have been shown, $\rho(\tilde{\mathbf{B}}) < \|\tilde{\mathbf{B}}\|_{\infty} = \max_i \Sigma_j \tilde{\mathbf{b}}_{ij} < 1$

for $\tilde{\mathbf{b}}_{ij} \geq 0$. It follows that $(\mathbf{I} - \tilde{\mathbf{B}})(\mathbf{I} + \tilde{\mathbf{B}} + \tilde{\mathbf{B}}^2 + \cdots + \tilde{\mathbf{B}}^k) = \mathbf{I}$, as $k{\to}\infty$. Notice $(\mathbf{I} - \tilde{\mathbf{B}})$ is non-singular, inasmuch as there exists another matrix, namely the matrix series $(\mathbf{I} + \tilde{\mathbf{B}} + \cdots + \tilde{\mathbf{B}}^k)$ such that their product is $\mathbf{I}$ (non-zero). Hence, we can formally express the series as a finite quantity: $\mathbf{I} + \tilde{\mathbf{B}} + \tilde{\mathbf{B}}^2 + \cdots + \tilde{\mathbf{B}}^k = \mathbf{I}/(\mathbf{I} - \tilde{\mathbf{B}})$ as $k{\to}\infty$. The division $\mathbf{I}/(\mathbf{I} - \tilde{\mathbf{B}})$ provides an asymptotic stationary solution to Equation A4.49. It should also be emphasized that the solution is no longer stationary if the spectral radius is equal or bigger than unity. The watershed value of 1 for the spectral radius is referred to as a bifurcation point—a key concept in analyzing system stability. Application of such quasi-deterministic analysis is found in the Garin-Lowry model" sections in the "Chaos, Bifurcation" chapter of Chan (2000).

VI. SYSTEM STABILITY

We have demonstrated the concept of bifurcation in the above sections, in which critical values of a parameter determine totally different behavior of the system under study. We will generalize these concepts in the current section, where system stability is discussed (dePalma and Lefèvre 1987). First we examine the autonomous case of Equation A4.33, in other words, the situation when the system $d\mathbf{X}/dt = \mathbf{F}(\mathbf{X}, \mathbf{H}', t)$ is independent of time, or $d\mathbf{X}/dt = \mathbf{F}(\mathbf{X}, \mathbf{H}')$. With this simplification, we will rewrite Equation A4.33 as

$$\frac{dX_j(t)}{dt} = F_j[X_1(t), \ldots, X_n(t)] \qquad j = 1, \ldots, n \qquad (A4.52)$$

In general, it is not possible to solve this system explicitly. Nevertheless, mathematical methods do exist to obtain some information on the solution. Among these methods, we mentioned bifurcation theory, catastrophe theory, and stability theory. The stationary states of Equation A4.52, denoted by $\mathbf{X}'' = (X_1'', \ldots, X_n'')^T$, are defined by $d[X_j(t)]/dt = 0$ $(j = 1, \ldots, n)$ and are solutions of the following algebraic system:

$$F_j(X_1'', \ldots, X_n'') = 0 \qquad j = 1, \ldots, n \qquad (A4.53)$$

In other words, these are solutions to the system when motion ceases.

A. Basic Types of Trajectory

The solution as sketched out in Equation A4.53 can be classified into a handful of trajectory types (Wilson 1981). It is also most common for a system to have a small number of single equilibrium points. If they are stable, trajectories lead into them, and they are called attractors. If they are unstable, trajectories are repelled by such points, and they are called repellers. When there are two or more state variables as shown in Equation A4.53 and sketched out in Figure A4.12, the equilibrium point may be saddle points, which represent a special kind of instability. In this case, most trajectories are repelled by such points, but there can be two trajectories (in opposite directions) that pass through the saddle, and these play an important role in sketching trajectories in general. They separate the state space into two regions with trajectories on each side being directed to different stable equilibrium points. For this reason, such a trajectory is known as a separatrix, and it plays an important role in bifurcation behavior.

To make it perfectly clear, consider a system described by state variables X_1 and X_2. First, we distinguish two kinds of behavior in the neighborhood of a

Figure A4.12   STABLE AND UNSTABLE EQUILIBRIA

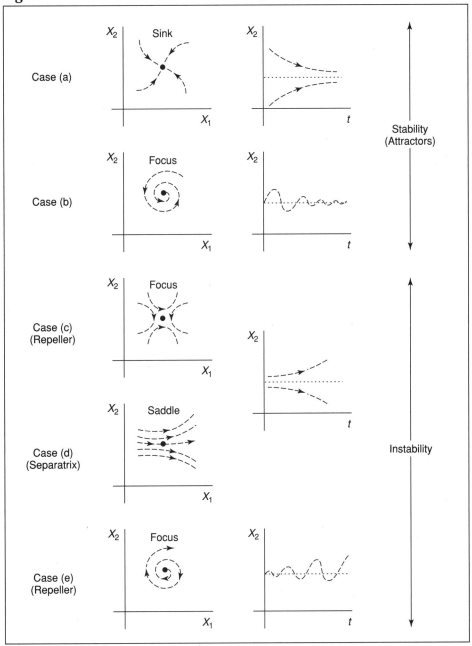

stable equilibrium point. These are shown on a state space plot in Figure A4.12. In case (a), the trajectories lead directly to the equilibrium point and represent an exponential convergence. Such attractors are also called a sink. In case (b), the trajectories spiral into it and represent oscillatory convergence. Such an attractor is also called a focus. Typical time plots for X-against-*t* are shown also for the two cases side by side.

Corresponding plots exist for unstable equilibrium points. Here saddle points behave like unstable case (c) points, but with the addition of the trajectories that form the separatrix as shown in (d). If behavior is neither convergent to a stable point nor divergent, then it may be periodic. There are two basic types as shown in Figure A4.13. Case (a) is a closed orbit periodicity, when the trajectory never leaves one of many possible such orbits (the particular one being determined by the initial conditions). Case (b) is limit cycle behavior: a typical trajectory winds in and out of a closed orbit and may become asymptotically close to it. It turns out that closed orbit behavior is structurally unstable while limit cycle behavior is structurally stable.

Finally, there are examples of system behavior characterized by neither stable or unstable equilibrium points, nor by oscillating behavior of any regular periodicity. Such behavior is called chaotic and is demonstrated by irregular looking time plots of state variables. Furthermore, particular (complicated) systems may exhibit a number of different kinds of solution for different starting values of the variables and for different parameter values. As a result, a state space diagram may be a mixture of trajectories related to different kinds of equilibrium values and may change character as the parameters change.

B. Bifurcation Theory

Bifurcation theory studies the multiplicity of the solutions of Equation A4.53 as a function of some parameters H' of the model (Dendrinos and Mullully 1985; Hildebrand 1962). A bifurcation point $[H', \mathbf{X}''(H')]$ is a point such that in its neighborhood, the multiplicity of the stationary state changes, as discussed

Figure A4.13   PERIODIC TRAJECTORIES IN STATE SPACE

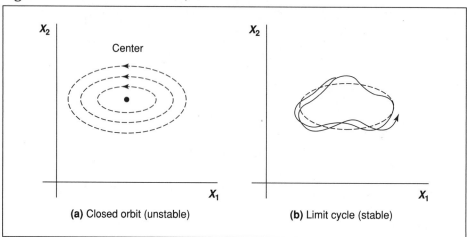

SOURCE: Wilson (1981). Reprinted with permission.

above in conjunction with the trajectories and illustrated by the Section V-G above. Consider a dynamical system of the form $d\mathbf{X}/dt = \mathbf{F}(\mathbf{X}, \mathbf{H'})$ where $\mathbf{X}$ and $\mathbf{F}$ are n-dimensional vectors and $\mathbf{H'}$ is an m-dimensional vector of parameters. As $\mathbf{H'}$ changes, the phase plane[21] also changes. Usually the change is continuous, but at certain bifurcation points the change in dynamic trajectories is abrupt.

The simplest bifurcation is found in the univariate system equation $dX/dt = aX$ as a varies from $-\infty$ to $+\infty$. Negative a generates a set of negative exponential (stable) trajectories, while positive a depicts exponential (unstable) growth. At zero the trajectory bifurcates. These three trajectories and the associated (simple) phase diagram for a is shown in Figure A4.14. In each case, a family of trajectories are shown, corresponding to different initial conditions. A slightly more complicated example is the following two-state system

$$\dot{F}_1 = \dot{X}_1 = X_2$$
$$\dot{F}_2 = \dot{X}_2 = X_1^2 - X_2 - a \qquad (A4.54)$$

The equilibrium solution is approximated by the matrix linear system $d\mathbf{X}/dt = \mathbf{A'}\mathbf{X}(t)$ where the stability setting Jacobian-matrix $\mathbf{A'}$ has elements A'_{ij} where

$$A'_{ij} = \left.\frac{\partial F_i}{\partial X_j}\right|_{\mathbf{X''}} \qquad i, j = 1, 2, \ldots, n \qquad (A4.55)$$

In other words, for a two-dimensional case,

$$\mathbf{A'} = \left.\begin{bmatrix} \dfrac{\partial F_1}{\partial X_1} & \dfrac{\partial F_1}{\partial X_2} \\[2ex] \dfrac{\partial F_2}{\partial X_1} & \dfrac{\partial F_2}{\partial X_2} \end{bmatrix}\right|_{\mathbf{X''}}$$

Figure A4.14   EXAMPLE OF A SIMPLE BIFURCATION

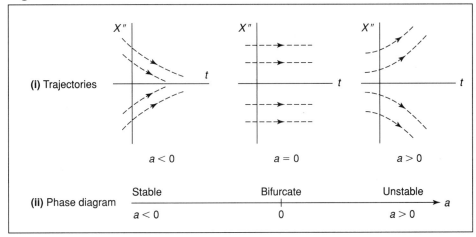

(i) Trajectories

$a < 0$ $a = 0$ $a > 0$

(ii) Phase diagram

Stable   Bifurcate   Unstable

$a < 0$ 0 $a > 0$

We follow the solution procedure outlined by Equation A4.35, and the deterministic example worked out in the same Section (V-D). Letting $X_i(t) = X_i'' + \epsilon_i(t)$ and expanding the Taylor series around the equilibrium state X_i'', the solution to the above system is $\mathbf{X}(t) = \mathbf{N}_0 \exp(\mathbf{q}'t)$, where the matrix $\mathbf{N}_0$ contains constants that depend on the initial values $\mathbf{X}(0)$, and $\mathbf{q}'$ is the vector of the eigenvalues of $\mathbf{A}$.

Here in this example, solution to the equations yield $\mathbf{X}'' = (X_1'', X_2'') = (I\sqrt{a}, 0$. If a is negative, there are no real valued equilibria, since the square root of a negative number yields an imaginary root. If a is positive, there are two real valued equilibria: $(\sqrt{a}, 0)$ and $(-\sqrt{a}, 0)$. Linearizing around these points, one obtains the matrix

$$\mathbf{A}' = \begin{bmatrix} 0 & 1 \\ \pm 2\sqrt{a} & -1 \end{bmatrix}$$

according to Equation A4.55 with eigenvalues $q'_1 = \frac{1}{2}[-1 \pm (1 + 8\sqrt{a})^{1/2}]$ and $q'_2 = \frac{1}{2}[-1 \pm (1 + 8\sqrt{a})^{1/2}]$. Solution of such system of equations in general yields eigenvalues that are complex or real numbers. The complex part induces an oscillating behavior while the real part gives rise to an exponentially increasing or decreasing solution according to its sign being positive or negative. Consequently, the stationary state $\mathbf{X}''$ is asymptotically stable if all the real parts are negative; the state $\mathbf{X}''$ is unstable if there exists at least one positive real part. In addition, the state $\mathbf{X}''$ is marginally stable if there is at least one eigenvalue whose real part is null and if all the other eigenvalues have a negative real part.

Consider the ordinary differential equation $dX/dt = F(X, t)$. Remembering isoclines are the family of curves defined by the equation $F(X, t) = K$, where K is a constant. In the autonomous case under consideration, this becomes simply $dX(t)/dt = F(X(t))$ and $F(X(t)) = K$. The differential equation states that at any point $X(t)$ for which $F(X(t))$ is defined, the slope of any integral curve passing through that point is given by $F(X(t))$. If we plot the family of isocline curves, $F(X(t)) = K$ for a series of values of the constant K, it then follows that all integral curves of the differential equation intersect a particular curve of the family of isocline curves with the same slope angle α, where $\tan \alpha$ is given by the value of K specifying the isocline. Thus if on each isocline a series of short parallel segments having the required slope is drawn, an infinite number of integral curve can be drawn by starting in each case at a given point on one isocline and sketching a curve passing through that point with the indicated slope and crossing successive isoclines with the slopes associated with them. This method can always be used to determine graphically the particular solution of the differential equation that passes through a prescribed point $X^*(t)$ when the function F is single valued and continuous. The procedure is illustrated in Figure A4.15.

Applying the above procedure to the current two-state example, the first intersection of isoclines always implies a saddle, since $1 + 8\sqrt{a} > 0$. One eigenvalue is positive whereas the other is negative. However, in the second intersection $1 - 8\sqrt{a}$ could be positive, zero, or negative. At the point where it is zero, ($a = 1/64$), the nature of the dynamic path changes. As a increases the system's trajectories are transformed from a stable sink (q_1', q_2' negative, real, unequal) to a stable focus (q_1', q_2' complex, with negative real parts). Another illustration is found under the "Synergetic Models of Spatial Interaction" subsection of the "Activity Allocation and Derivation" chapter in Chan (2000).

Figure A4.15   GRAPHICAL SOLUTION OF A DIFFERENTIAL EQUATION

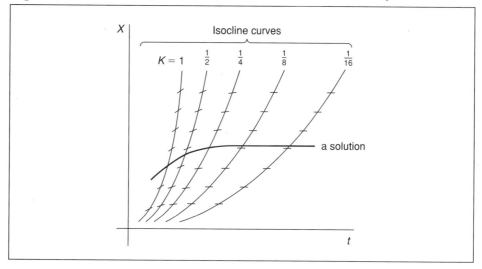

C. Comments

The above example is cited for illustrative purposes only. In real systems, problems tend to be nonlinear, and the solution procedure becomes a lot more complex. It is not unusual to resort to numerical simulation, which is often the only feasible means to solve the problem. Insights can be obtained, however, by developing a qualitative theory in which the topological nature of the model's equilibrium point is studied. In the preceding subsections, we have explored how the main types of solutions for dynamical systems described by differential equations are constructed and how to get some insights by representing them graphically or through simple examples. It should already be clear by implication that the possible types of bifurcation behavior are richer than indicated in the canonical forms of catastrophe theory. We now summarize several cogent observations (Wilson 1981).

First, we note that the solutions (for equilibrium points) to Equations A4.52 will typically involve multiple solutions because of any nonlinearities in the functions F_js. Hence, the manifold of equilibrium solutions in the space of $(\mathbf{X}, \mathbf{H}')$ variables will be folded. This can lead to the same broad kinds of bifurcation as in catastrophe theory, as suggested in the introduction to Section IV.

Second, we observe that the types of solutions to the differential equations can be determined by parameter values. There can be critical parameter values at which a stable sink becomes a focus, as shown in the numerical example above. Similarly, one can envisage situations in which a stable equilibrium point becomes unstable or disappears, or at which a periodic solution could disappear and be replaced by a stable equilibrium point, or vice versa. (These changes are collectively known as the **Hopf bifurcation**). In theory, all the possible interchanges between the kinds of solution (or trajectory) listed in Section VI-A are possible, and it is useful to be alert to this in applied work.

Finally, we also note here in passing a completely different type of possible bifurcation. Suppose a system is disturbed from an equilibrium position and moves to a non-equilibrium state in the neighborhood of a separatrix in state space. Then if the separatrix is crossed, the return to equilibrium could be to a state other than the original one. This is analogous to the cusp catastrophe discussion in Subsection IV-A.

VII. CONCLUDING REMARKS

In this appendix, we have reviewed the theories that govern the evolution of complex systems over time, including the influence of external factors. It can be seen that the body of knowledge in this area is huge and has diverse roots among a number of disciplines. We can, at best, provide only an overview in the limited number of pages here. While the theories hold great promise in modeling facility location and land use, their present status can often only allow us to computationally solve small problems. In limited cases, the theories can be best used qualitatively to gain insights, rather than used quantitatively to yield computational results, even for small problems. Many larger systems need to be modeled by numerical simulation, even though such systems can be set up analytically as equation sets. This point is demonstrated in some detail in the main body of this book. Under certain circumstances, stochastic systems can be approximated by deterministic systems, effecting a fair amount of computational savings. Overall, the aim of this appendix is to provide the basics and a road map for readers to relate these diverse theories to one another, particularly in the context of problem solving, including the appropriate references to the vast amount of literature for further investigation.

ENDNOTES

[1] For the dynamic programming problem, this is called the state transition equation.
[2] Those who are familiar with the calculus of variations of deformable bodies will recognize this as the variational form of a thin membrane, often written as $\delta \int \Omega^{1/2} (\nabla u)^2 \, d\mathbf{x} = 0$, where u is the amplitude of such small deformation as oscillation. Here u takes on a prescribed function along the boundary. In this context, the variational equational equation simply prescribes that the potential energy stored in the membrane must be in equilibrium. In the two-dimensional $x_1 - x_2$ case, for example, the potential energy $\frac{1}{2}(\nabla u)^2$ is simply $\frac{1}{2}(u_x^2 + u_y^2)$.
[3] Suppose that a function $f(X(t), U(t))$ exists such that $fX \equiv F(X, U) = \partial X/\partial t = \dot{X}$. A dynamic system that can be derived from such a function $f(X, U)$ is formally called a gradient system.
[4] The co-rank measures the degree of degeneracy of the worst kind of singularity that can occur in the particular family of functions. For nth-order polynomial functions of one variable, for example, the degree of degeneracy is n, where all derivatives up to the nth order vanish.
[5] The co-dimension of a family of functions is the number of control variables U that parameterize these functions.
[6] An example of such an application can be found in the "Chaos, Catasrophe, Bifurcation and Disaggregation" chapter in Chan 2000 under the "Spatial Dynamics" section.
[7] For a discussion of the Markovian process, see Appendix 2.
[8] When the column vectors in a square matrix are mutually orthogonal and of unit length, we say that the matrix is orthonormal. Specifically, if the dot product of vector $\mathbf{x}$, $\mathbf{x}^T\mathbf{x} = \|\mathbf{x}\|^2 = 1$, the vector $\mathbf{x}$ is said to be normalized. If a set of vectors $\mathbf{x}_1, \ldots, \mathbf{x}_n$ is orthogonal and normalized (in other words, $\mathbf{x}_i^T\mathbf{x}_j = 0$, $i \neq j$; $\mathbf{x}_i^T\mathbf{x}_i = 1$), then the vectors are said to be orthonormal.
[9] An example of such equations has been illustrated in Appendix 2 in the derivation of the Poisson process.

[10] The logit model is explained in Chapter 3.

[11] An example of the birth-death process has been illustrated in the derivation of the $M/M/1$ queue as part of Appendix 2.

[12] Consider a random variable taking on the values $\xi = 0, 1, 2, \ldots$ with the associated probabilities $P_0, P_1, P_2, \ldots$. The generating function for this probability distribution is $G(\xi) = P_0 + \xi P_1 + \xi^2 P_2 + \cdots = \Sigma_x \xi^x P_x$. This function has several useful properties. First $G(1) = 1$, $G(0) = P_0$, and $dP/d\xi = \Sigma_x \mathbf{x} \xi^{x-1} P_x$. Notice that $\frac{dG}{d\xi}\big|_{\xi=1} = \sum_{x=0}^{\infty} x P_x = E(x)$, which yields the mean of the random variables x. By the same token, $\frac{d^x G}{d\xi^x}\big|_{\xi=0} = x! P_x$ which yields the individual terms of the distribution. The generating function is often used to derive many analytical results in stochastic processes.

[13] Both the predator-prey and the dynamic Lowry derivative models are explained in the "Lowry-based Models" and "Chaos, Catastrophe, Bifurcation and Disaggregation" chapters of Chan (2000).

[14] A homogeneous equation is one that does not have an input or forcing function $U(t)$ on the right-hand side. In the case of linear algebraic equations, this means the right-hand side is a zero vector. For a linear homogeneous equation, any linear combination of individual solutions is also a solution.

[15] A particular solution to a differential equation is that part of the solution in response to the input or control function $\mathbf{U}(t)$.

[16] Consider the homogeneous set of equations: $\mathbf{AX} = q'\mathbf{X}$. Values of q' for which non-trivial solutions exist are called eigenvalues, and corresponding vector solutions $\mathbf{X}$ are known as eigenvectors. More specifically, $\mathbf{X}$ here is a right eigenvector.

[17] If $(\mathbf{A}' - q'\mathbf{I})\mathbf{x} = \mathbf{0}$ where $\mathbf{x} \neq \mathbf{0}$, and we set the determinant to zero, in other words, $|\mathbf{A}' - q'\mathbf{I}| = 0$, then the scalar roots q'_k of the resulting polynomial are eigenvalues of $\mathbf{A}'$.

[18] If the row and column containing an element (i, j) in a square matrix are deleted, the determinant of the remaining square array is called the minor of (i, j), and is denoted by M_{ij}. The co-factor of $i, j)$ is then defined by $(-1)^{i+j} M_{ij}$.

[19] This can be likened to a time series that consists of a structural part and a noise term. See the "Spatial Time Series" chapter of Chan (2000) for a more complete discussion.

[20] This is witnessed by the solution to the Garin-Lowry model as shown in the "Chaos, Catastrophe, Bifurcation, and Disaggregation" chapter of Chan. In the un-capacitated case, a constant transition matrix II is assumed, resulting in the special solution of Equation A4.46.

[21] Also known as a phase diagram, this is an analytic device to characterize the solution without necessarily writing out the system solution explicitly. An example will be illustrated shortly in Figure A4.14.

REFERENCES

Belensky, A. S. (1998). Operations research in transportation systems: Ideas and schemes of optimization methods for strategic planning and operations management. Boston: Kluwer Academic Publishers.

Chan, Y. (2000). *Location, transport and land-use: Modeling spatial-temporal information*. New York: Springer-Verlag.

Cox, D. R.; Miller, H. D. (1965). *The theory of stochastic processes*. London: Chapman and Hall.

De Palma, A.; Lefèvre, C. L. (1987). "The theory of deterministic and stochastic compartmental models and its applications." In *Urban systems: Contemporary approaches to modelling*, edited by C. S. Bertuglia, et al. London: Croon Helm.

Dendrinois, D. S.; Mullally, H. (1985). *Urban evolution: Studies in the mathematical ecology of cities*. Oxford and New York: Oxford University Press.

Godfrey, K. (1983). *Compartmental models and their application*. New York: Academic Press.

Haag, G. (1989). *Dynamic decision theory: Applications to urban and regional topics.* Boston: Kluwer Academic Publishers.

Hildebrand, F. B. (1965). *Advanced calculus for applications.* Englewood Cliffs, New Jersey: Prentice-Hall.

Kinderlehrer, D.; Stampacchia, GT. (1980). *An introduction to variational inequalities and their applications.* New York: Academic Press.

Lorenz, H. W. (1993). *Nonlinear dynamical economics and chaotic motion,* 2nd ed. New York: Springer-Verlag.

Minoux, M. (1986). *Mathematical programming-theory and algorithms.* (Translated by Stephen Vajda). New York: Wiley.

Nagurney, A. (1993). *Network economics: A variational inequality approach.* Boston: Kluwer Academic Press.

Noble, B. (1969). *Applied linear algebra.* Englewood Cliffs, New Jersey: Prentice-Hall.

Seber, G. A. F.; Wild, C. J. (1989). *Nonlinear regression.* New York: Wiley.

Silberberg, E. (1990). *The structure of economics: A mathematical analysis,* 2nd ed. New York: McGraw-Hill.

Wilson, A. G. (1981). *Catastrophe theory and bifurcation: Applications to urban and regional systems.* London: Croom Helm and Berkeley, California: University of California University Press.

Yi, P. (1986). Infrastructure management: A bifurcation model in urban regional planning. Master's Thesis. Department of Civil and Environmental Engineering. Washington State University. Pullman, Washington.

Appendix 5

Discussion of Technical Concepts

This appendix consists of technical words or concepts that are not necessarily familiar to the general audience, mainly words that are not found in a standard English dictionary. The main thrust of this book is to show the relationship between technical concepts from different disciplines—this emphasis is particularly apparent in this section. It complements, rather than competes with, the comprehensive index compiled at the back of this book. While each term is defined in as plain a language as possible, on rare occasions one technical term is explained in terms of another. When a related technical term in this glossary is used within an explanation, it is italicized, alerting the user that the related term is defined elsewhere in the glossary. Naturally, this glossary is best used in conjunction with the book index as suggested earlier.

Accessibility, impedance, propensity functions, and trip frequency curves: In this book, we discuss the importance of spatial costs in organizing the economic activities in a study area. Spatial costs are defined in many different terms. For example, spatial separation is measured in both time and cost. When we wish to convert these diverse measures into a single unit such as utiles, we face some challenges. Aside from the conventional apples versus oranges conversion problem, utiles is usually construed as the more the merrier, while time and cost, or impedance in general, is defined as: "small is beautiful." To resolve this problem, we often take an inverse function of impedance to convert it from disutility to utility. This conversion function is sometimes called the propensity function, which takes on the form of a negative power function—(impedance)^b—or an exponential function—$\exp[-\beta(\text{impedance})]$—among others. Here both b and β are positive calibration coefficients. Irrespective of the form of the propensity function, it is usually calibrated by trip distribution curves, defined as the frequency with which a trip of certain duration is being executed in the study area. Propensity functions and trip distribution curves have similar shapes, differing only in their scaling constants. Sometimes, it is useful to normalize these propensity functions against a regional total. In a region consisting of two zones, for example, the propensity to zone 1, $\exp[-\beta_1(\text{impedance})_1]$, is normalized against the total propensities to zones 1 and 2, or $\{\exp[-\beta_1(\text{impedance})_1] + \exp[-\beta_2(\text{impedance})_2]\}$, resulting in the accessibility to zone-1 : $\exp[-\beta_1(\text{impedance})_1]/\{\exp[-\beta_1(\text{impedance})_1] + \exp[-\beta_2(\text{impedance})_2]\}$. While these terms are strictly defined here, they are often used loosely and interchangeably.

Additive versus multiplicative utility/value function: In defining a multi-attribute utility/value function, many mathematical forms can be used. For ease of calibration, it is proposed that we broadly classify the functions into two types: additive and multiplicative. The former is linear while the latter is nonlinear with the former being more straightforward to work with than the latter. The additive form is completely satisfactory when all we need is an ordinal ranking among alternatives, in other words, to rank them in decreasing order of preference. However, when preference intensity is required, or when we wish to know exactly by how much alternative A is preferred to alternative B, it is often necessary to deal with the latter function.

Aggregate versus disaggregate: A model can be either simple or elaborate, depending on the context of the study. A simple model has the advantage of transparency for policy decisions, yet often lacks the details to support actual implementation. Simplicity is often attained by aggregation where an aggregate model assumes homogeneity among the data within the unit. For example, all travelers within a zone are expected to value travel time equally. A disaggregate model retains the specific valuation of each individual traveler. Aside from application-oriented contexts, the specific analysis approach is dictated by data availability. When only average conditions are reported, an aggregate analysis is often the only feasible option. When more detailed information is available, a disaggregate model can be constructed and is often more useful. The secret is the judicious and consistent match between application, data, and models. In disaggregate land use models, for example, individual parameters such as the labor force participation rate (the ratio between service employment and population) can be calibrated individually for each zone, instead of for the entire region. This results in a more descriptive version of zonal level development.

Allocation or distribution: The ultimate goal of facility location or land use is to serve the demands or the customers. Thus a fire station is located for the sole purpose of putting out fires quickly, while a city master plan will provide all the services to the local population in the best way possible. The way these demands are served reflects the merit or drawbacks of a spatial decision. This service pattern is often referred to as the demand allocation or activity distribution. For example, a compact city form cuts down on commuting time from home to work. A single facility or a combination of facilities may provide service. Sometimes, specialized services may only be provided by a facility capable of delivering such services. There may be interaction among facilities that provide these services. For example, the facilities may reinforce each other in stimulating additional demands in aggregate. At the same time, they may compete for a market share of the customers. The way the services are delivered has a direct bearing upon how well customers are served. For example, a driver and vehicle may have a specific delivery route each day and make deliveries in order according to the location of customers along that route, or a dedicated driver and vehicle may make an out-and-back delivery. These two delivery patterns have very different efficiencies and customer satisfaction, with the former being more efficient and the latter being more pleasing to the customer.

Area, subarea, tessellation, and Voronoi diagram: In regional science, information is often sought for each location within a study area, rather than for the entire region in aggregate. There are quite a few ways to divide up the area depending on the problem context. We may divide it up by school districts, census tracts, traffic zones or political jurisdictions, just to name a few ways. To cut across all these subdivisions, we prefer to use the word subarea, to be distinguished from the entire study area. Thus we use the word subareal population and employment rather than, for instance, zonal population and employment, since the mathematical models apply equally well across the different ways to subdivide a study area. A natural way to divide an area into subareas is to use tessellations such as the Voronoi diagram. In this representation, each activity center is defined as the generator, for which a zone of influence is defined, representing the demands that are naturally attracted to this activity center. It has been shown that such a tessellation is consistent with the central place theory, which hypothesizes that interregional trade leads toward natural market place settlements.

Asymtotics: A powerful tool in analysis is the asymptotic behavior of a process or procedure. Many examples of this are documented in this book. We have seen how location routing models can be solved by heuristics that converge toward the optimum. In system dynamics, convergence and divergence of a process are analyzed in terms of attractors and repellers. In statistics, the central limit theorem suggests that many probability density functions converge toward a normal distribution given a large enough sample is taken. In spatial processes, however, things are more complex. The central limit theorem may not apply. This prevents borrowing ideas from classical time series models and applying them wholesale spatial processes. In our discussions in this book, we have tried to highlight both the commonality and differences between spatial statistics and classical statistics. We draw analogies where we can between them, and at the same time point out some unique behavior of spatial information not found in classical statistics.

Attractivity and lattice structure: The two paradigms used in facility location and land use are discrete versus continuous modeling. Irrespective of the type of models used, there exists a central location where activities are generated from or attracted to, which takes on such names as centroids or generators. The system of centroids or generators often form a lattice structure, which shows the proximity and relationship between them. Now the demands within the zone of influence of a centroid or generator are expected to interact with the respective centroid or generator. The zones of influence or market area can be defined by a Voronoi polygon or other representation. The interaction between centroids or generators can in turn be described by a number of different models. Among them are the gravity model, the weight matrices or spatial masks, or the Delaunay triangles. The gravity model suggests that nearby and more intense activities interact more than distant or low intensity activities. The spatial mask simply summarizes these inter-centroid interactions in a matrix form. Should spatial interaction be modeled by tile-like structures such as Voronoi diagram, the Delaunay triangles are simply the most direct paths of interaction between generators.

Attractor, repeller, and separatrix: A dynamic system is said to be stationary when its behavior does not change over time. Close study of the stationary behavior reveals some commonalities among them. The trajectories can be attracted to a sink or a focus, reaching a stable solution. Alternatively, the trajectory can be repelled from a focus or they can be separated at a saddle point, suggesting instability. A sink and stable focus are categorized as an attractor while an unstable focus and saddle point are called a repeller and a separatrix respectively.

Average versus marginal cost: Average cost is the total production cost apportioned among the number of units produced, and marginal cost is the cost of producing an additional unit. A firm is most efficient, and is most profitable, if it produces at the level where marginal revenue (the unit price charged to consumers) is set equal to marginal cost. In contrast, it would be less efficient and only breaks even when marginal revenue (price) is set equal to average cost. While these basic definitions are well understood, its application in the public sector is more controversial. An example is marginal cost pricing of transportation services. It can be shown that it prevents Braess' paradox from happening. In this regard, marginal cost pricing is desirable in that the average travel cost for the user is less. Marginal cost pricing, however, may result in less total usage of the transportation facility. Another example showing the controversial effects of pricing is in the development of a new community. Accessibility may be provided to a new community at the expense of the existing communities. But consumers' surplus is increased for the entire population. In all these examples, the basic average and marginal cost concepts carry over to transportation when spatial equilibrium is considered. Notice that transportation cost is added on top of production cost in determining interregional trade. In addition, demand for transportation is modeled as a function of the transportation cost. Trade occurs when transportation cost is compensated by the difference in price between the production point and the consumption destination.

   Backshift operator, transfer function, lag operator, and image processing mask: In analyzing time series data, the backshift operator is a useful concept. It affords a compact notation and tool for writing and analyzing time shifted data. In its simplest form, the backshift operator simply lags a time series by one or more period. Linear combinations of these lagged series are then formed by putting different weights among each series. In a more involved usage, algebraic manipulations such as divisions can be performed on these operators, allowing powerful analysis of time series. In a similar vein, a transfer function consists of a set of weights placed upon an input time series and transforms it to a different output series. Often, the input series is white noise, or uncorrelated random shocks, and the output series consists of correlated information. If the input series is not white noise, its underlying pattern can be taken away by prewhitening the time series. When these concepts are applied toward spatial data, we have the spatial lag operator, which performs a similar function to that of the backshift operator, except in two dimensions. In image processing, we call this a mask, defining how a subject data point (such as a pixel) relates to its surrounding data (or next door neighbors). An image processing mask consists of a set of two-dimensional spatial weights to be applied toward each data point. This transforms the two-dimensional data set (an image) into a different one, often making it less noisy or giving it more definition.

   Basic versus nonbasic activities: According to economic-base theory, basic activities are the goods and services that are seeds of economic development for a local area. They are generally consumed outside the study area. Nonbasic activities are derived from basic activities. They are the result of the multiplier effect of basic activities upon the local economy. For that reason, nonbasic activities are for local consumption. The difficulty of this paradigm, however, lies in how defensible these definitions of basic versus nonbasic activities really are. While the fundamental concept upon which the Lowry model is built can be traced to economic-base theory, the explanation becomes blurred once subareal allocation of activities becomes a key element. The distinction is further complicated by economic development over time. In the local versus outside world paradigm of economic-base theory, it is fairly easy to distinguish between export versus local consumption (the location quotient definition), or the requirements one economic sector places upon another (the minimum requirement definition). However, it is not so clear in applying this concept to subareas in the local economy over time, where basic employment is supposed to be exogenously fixed, while other service employments are located within the study area in relation to these basic activities. The interaction among these activities can relocate basic employment. Development over time can also change the requirement one economic activity places on another, particularly when the zonal level of detail is required.

Bayesian or subjective probability: According to Bayes, all probabilities are subjective. However, the more sampled information one has, the better one can determine the underlying probability with precision. Classic decision analysis builds upon this fundamental idea and extends it into multiple attributes in recent years. In remote sensing, this concept is used in classifying pixels in a satellite image of land cover, to discern whether a pixel belongs to a lake or a forest for example. In time series, it is used to update the mean, variance, or model form as new data become available. In accordance with Bayes, while we can get a good approximation, there really is no practical way to obtain the true probability distribution.

Capacitated versus uncapacitated: In facility location and land use models, distinction is made between whether or not a capacity exists in a geographic unit. The model tends to be a great deal simpler to solve if there is no capacity, but this is often a simplifying assumption. The demand increments are then allocated or distributed exclusively to the closest facility. However, when capacity is present, demands or activities above and beyond the facility or zonal capacity must be assigned somewhere else. No longer is there a binary pairing between demand and facility (or zone). Fractional assignments take place, in which only part of the demand is accommodated by a single facility. In other words, more than one facility is assigned to a demand.

Cardinality versus ordinality: In ranking alternatives, we can be satisfied with a simple preferential ordering, in which the ones from the top of the list are picked over those at the bottom. If the preferential intensity is required, or we wish to assess by how much alternative A at the top of the list is better than B at the bottom, a scale or cardinality is involved. Obviously, the former preference structure is simpler than the latter since less information is required to capture the preferential intensity.

Catastrophe, hysteresis, and divergence: The trajectories of a chaotic system can be categorized. Among them is the sudden jump (or catastrophe), hysteresis, and divergence. A sudden jump is fairly self-explanatory. Hysteresis is defined as a trajectory in which a path, if reversed, ends up at a point other than the starting point. A divergence suggests that a small difference in approach leads the system to a very different state. These counter intuitive phenomena are different manifestations of a catastrophe theory in general, characterized by such unusual trajectories as sudden jumps, irreversibility, and divergence.

Center versus anticenter: A center is the facility location that ensures that the furthest demand is kept closest. The best example is a fire station, which should be close to any fire that may flare up even at the most remote location. An anticenter, on the other hand, is a location that keeps the closest demand as far away as possible. Thus it is desirable to put a landfill as far away as possible from the most exposed residence. Formally, we minimize the maximum distance between demand and the facility in the center problem, and we maximize the minimum distance in the anticenter problem.

Centroid or generator: Two paradigms are used throughout facility location and land use: a geographic representation can be continuous or discrete. One way to compromise discrete versus planar models of land use is through the use of centroids. Population and employment distribute continuously over a map. However, there is advantage in modeling the zonal or subareal population or employment as concentrating in a single node called centroid. Centroid is an imaginary node/vertex amid a plane through which activities (for example, trips) originating from or destined for the subarea are loaded or unloaded from the map. In this case, the centroid is the geographic center or center of gravity for the economic activities in this zone (or subarea). The use of centroids can also be thought of as a more aggregate representation than its counterpart. Viewed in this light, the question really boils down to how big one should define a zone (or subarea), and correspondingly the accuracy of using relatively few number of centroids (vis-a-vis the extra computation involved with a larger number.) In this text, centroids and generators are used interchangeably. The word generator comes from the concept of Voronoi diagrams, representing the natural gathering place for a subarea. (See also internodal versus intranodal.)

Collinearity: When two random variables are related to one another statistically, we say that they are collinear. Problems arise when both of these two variables are included as independent or explanatory variables in a regression model. This amounts to double counting the same explanatory variable in a model. The result may be spurious correlation, or statistical relationships that are chancy and not well supported by the facts and figures.

Combinatorial: Among discrete alternatives, one way to account for the various options available is by combining them in different ways. In obnoxious facilities location, for example, a combination of landfill, incinerator, and transfer station may be desirable to dispose of solid wastes. When there are many alternatives, the combinations can become huge very quickly. Finding an efficient way to choose among these combinations is mandatory. Modern mathematics has provided many guidelines to achieve this goal, as evidenced by recent advances in combinatorics, the branch of mathematics that addresses this type of combinational problem.

Complementarity problem: An optimization problem is often characterized by complementarity conditions, or the relationship between the primal and dual representation of the problem. For both linear and nonlinear optimization, the gradient of an objective function or functional is orthogonal to the feasible convex set at the point of interest. In other words, the product of the gradient and the feasible solution is always zero. For example, in the first row of a simplex tableau, the rate of ascent (gradient) for a particular basic (non-zero) variable is zero, while the rate of ascent for a nonbasic (zero) variable is non-zero. In both cases, the product of the two pertinent quantities—gradient and variable—is always zero. In facility location and land use, spatial price equilibrium, or the way that trade takes place between any two points, can be best formulated as a complementarity problem.

Complementarity versus substitutionality: According to classic microeconomic theory, goods or services are either complements or substitutes of one another. In our context, users either view alternative facilities as catering to their needs in an aggregate or the goods and services offered by individual facilities are replaceable among themselves. In most cases, the facilities play both roles, although not equally. The relative dominance among these roles results in interesting spatial activity derivation and allocation results that serve as extensions and generalizations of classic facility location models. These extensions and generalizations eventually bring us a land use model.

Condorcet versus Simpson points: In discrete facility location models, a Condorcet point is any point in the network that is closest to most of the demands. A Simpson point, on the other hand, is the least objectionable place where the maximum demand closer to another point is at its minimum. Both Condorcet and Simpson points are relative, rather than absolute, concepts.

Contextuality: In discerning spatial patterns, whether they be land use or satellite images, one can obtain a fair amount of information by observing the neighborhood of what one is examining. Thus a noise pixel can be detected quite clearly as an outlier and subsequently removed when context is taken into account. Similarly, a facility location decision cannot be divorced from the community in which the facility is to be sited. In this latter case, the local context of the problem drives the location decision.

Control, state, slow, and fast variables: The term decision variables used in operations research becomes control variables in control theory. Dependent variables, on the other hand, are labeled state variables. In using catastrophe theory to analyze system stability, control and state variables are called slow and fast variables respectively. When more than one control variable is present, we refer to the set a control point.

Convex versus nonconvex programming: In optimization, one has either a single (unique) global optimum or more than one local optimum. The former is associated with a convex mathematical program while the latter a nonconvex program. A convex program is characterized by a number of nice mathematical properties that satisfy strict duality conditions. On the other hand, nonconvex programs are characterized by less rigorous conditions, making the solution algorithms more ad hoc. In the majority of network facility location models, integrality (or discreteness) dictates an integer programming formulation, which is nonconvex. For this reason, facility location models, besides being challenging to apply, are also at the frontier of discrete optimization research.

Cross-sectional versus time series data: In the context of spatial-temporal information, data points within the same time period are called cross-sectional data. A time series, on the other hand, is the tracking of spatial data over multiple periods. In household terms, the former can be thought of as a snapshot, while the latter is a movie.

Curvilinear: An efficient frontier is defined as the set of nondominated solutions when judged in terms of two or more criteria. In competitive or group decision making, an efficient frontier can either be linear or bounded by curved lines. The latter, or the curvilinear case, poses more computational challenge than the former.

Dependent versus independent, criterion versus predictor, endogenous versus exogenous variables: In regular regression, a dependent variable is explained statistically by a number of independent variables. The dependent variable appears on the left-hand side and the independent variables on the right-hand side of the equation. Independent variables are also called explanatory variables or regressors. The dependent variable is sometimes called response variable. In canonical correlation, one ascertains if a set of criterion variables are possibly affected by a set of predictor (input) variables. Often, the number of criterion and predictor variables can be collapsed or reduced to enable a simpler, more tractable analysis. In econometrics, simultaneous equations are used to pose the relationship between a number of endogenous variables and exogenous variables. Endogenous variables appear on both the left-hand side and right-hand side of the equations, while exogenous variables only appear on the right-hand side.

Deterministic versus probabilistic: Traditionally, the location literature has been modeling spatial analysis in a sequence of deterministic events. Thus we know exactly where the demands are, and we locate a service facility that will be proximal to these demands. Recent decades have witnessed a broadening of view when the demands are no longer known precisely ahead of time. Rather, they are random or probabilistic. For example, a fair amount of progress has been made in recent years in locating fire stations when there is little knowledge about when and where a fire may break out. In this example, it is not easy to lay down a set of rigid rules one follows in selecting a fire station site. One way to site a fire station is to think of all possible ways fires can break out and locate the fire station such that it will respond to these fires the fastest way. This is obviously not a straightforward process and may take a huge amount of computer time (if it is at all possible.) A better way is to model the fire outbreaks in terms of a random process (stochastic process) and marshall our knowledge on random processes in modeling the situation. The challenge obviously is to carry this in a spatial context, posing additional analytical intricacies beyond the difficulty with modeling standard random processes.

Differencing: Finding the change in values among discrete points in a grid is the numerical equivalent of finding the differential in continuous variables. It is a much more general technique in that we can solve a much larger class of problems, particularly when assisted by modern day computing. In spatial analysis, it is often used to restore and enhance an image, such as in edge detection. Statistically, it also induces a homogeneous set of data, which allows for more insightful analysis to be performed (see separate entry in this glossary for the definition of homogeneity). In time series, data are differenced to achieve stationarity, for similar purposes. Differencing in this case removes the trend from the data, resulting in a constant mean. It allows us to concentrate on discerning the underlying pattern in the data.

Dimensionless analysis: Oftentimes, it is insightful to display analysis results that are independent of the physical units used. An example is the nomographs used in queuing handbooks. For comparison among queuing disciplines, it is most insightful to emphasize the relative performances among these queuing disciplines without regard to whether a metric or English system of weights and measures is used. Thus, instead of worrying about measuring total time in the system in minutes, hours, or seconds, it is best to display it as a multiple of the service time. A total time in the system being one means the only time required is the service time and the system is totally congestion free. No wait is involved in this case, and the customer receives service right away. On the other hand, a total time bigger than one would suggest congestion, in which some wait in line is inevitable. The amount of wait is again quantified in multiples of the service time. Queuing delay of 0.5, for example, means the customer waits in line half as much time as being served.

Discrete versus continuous: Distinction is made between continuous and discrete variables. When a variable assumes integer values such as 1, 2, 3 . . . , for example, we say that it is a discrete variable. On the other hand, when the variable can assume any rational value to as accurate a decimal point as needed, we call this a continuous variable. In facility location and land use, we can either locate the facility in a network of arcs and nodes/vertices or on a plane. When facility is to be located in a network, it ends up at a node/vertex or on an arc; we call this discrete facility location. In contrast, if a facility can be anywhere on a plane, we refer to it as a planar location or continuous facility location problem. Ranking discrete alternatives such as the candidate sites of an airport is a complex task. Unlike its continuous counterpart, multicriteria simplex procedure is no longer valid. We may miss some discrete alternatives that form the efficient frontier. Under these circumstances, implicit enumeration among pairs of alternatives is a viable solution option. *ELECTRE,* for example, is a computer program advanced by Roy (1977) to rank-order a set of discrete alternatives. Consisting of a graph theoretic outranking procedure, it identifies the set of noninferior solutions. Since its inception the software has gone through at least two new releases to the public.

Discriminant: A yardstick is often required in classifying a population into groups. This decision boundary is often represented in a discriminant function, which includes the important attributes that distinguish one group into another. For example, a properly defined discriminant will allow us to tell whether a picture element (pixel) belongs to a lake or a forest.

Disjunctive graph: In a mathematical program, a set of constraints is called disjunctive if at least one of the constraints has to be satisfied but not necessarily all. Consider a multiple traveling salesmen example, there are n demand locations to be visited. To cover each location i, m salespersons are to be used in a given order. The total time of the visit at location i by salesperson k is finite and is known. The problem consists of finding a fixed order of visiting the demand locations sequentially by each salesperson so as to finish visiting these n locations as soon as possible. For a given salesperson k, the tours (i, k) for $i = 1, \ldots, n$ can be represented in a potential task graph called a disjunctive graph (a clover leaf graph in this case). Here there are m such graphs (clover leafs), one by each salesperson.

Dissipative structure and self-organizing systems: The term dissipative structure stems from physical systems with a permanent input of energy that dissipates through the system. If energy input is interrupted, the system collapses to its equilibrium state. This stands in contrast to conservative dynamical systems in classical mechanics. In a conservative system, there is neither an additional input nor a loss of energy, implying that no friction exists. As part of the development of socio-spatial dynamic theory, G. Nicolis and I. Prigogine proposed a theory of self-organization that was observed in phase transitions in physical chemistry. Departing from conservative systems, they illustrated various self-organizing and non-equilibrium systems well beyond physical sciences, ranging from dissipative structures to order through fluctuations. (See also equilibrium and disequilibrium.)

Duality: In facility location and land use, duality has several meanings. The first, perhaps the simplest, is the mathematical programming usage of the word. It provides everything from computational bounds to economic interpretations. An example is the game theoretic interpretation, as in simple games that can be analyzed as a primal dual linear program. Primal and dual variables give significant insight into location problems. Dualization of a mathematical program also allows more efficient algorithms to be implemented. Then there is the application of duality in spatial tessellation, or the analysis of space in terms of tile-like units, ranging from squares to polygons. A dual graph can be constructed for every tessellation that is presented, giving significant insights to and again allowing for computational savings in location decisions.

Duopoly, triopoly, quadropoly, and oligopoly: In competitive facility location, each provider is locating a facility to capture as large a geographic market share as can possibly be managed. When there are two competitors, we have a duopoly. When we have three competitors, we have a triopoly. When there are quite a few number of competitors, we have an oligopoly. Unlike monopoly or pure competition, oligopolies are quite complex. While an oligopolistic market is challenging to model to begin with, the spatial version of it certainly does not make it any easier. It turns out that the land use modeling literature has a much richer knowledge base to offer than the discrete/network facility location analysts on this subject. It represents an area where the land use and facility location models may yield synergistic benefits from one another.

Econometric(s): The discipline of economics used to be quite a bit more qualitative than it is today. Recent years have witnessed tremendous emphasis on quantifying a number of concepts commonly used in classic economics, including estimating demand and supply functions. As an adjective, econometric describes any undertaking in estimation and measurement. As a noun, econometrics is the science and art of estimation and measurement. This typically involves analyzing historical information in support of a statistical hypothesis. There are two common types of land use models, one is based on deterministic simulation and the other on econometric models. There is a relationship between time series and econometric models wherein a specialization of the coefficients in a multivariate time series yields an econometric system of equations.

Eigenvalue/eigenvector or characteristic value/characteristic vector: A model in equilibrium is often described by a system of homogeneous linear equations. The behavior of the model is characterized by a parameter, which we call the eigenvalue. In a mechanical system, for example, the eigenvalue is its natural vibration frequency. In a multicriteria decision-making model such as the analytic hierarchy process, the principal eigenvalue measures the consistency with which the pairwise comparison survey is completed by the decision maker. The eigenvector here is the set of weights the decisionmaker places upon each attribute as implied by the completed survey. In adjusting a time series to change, the eigenvalues of the variance-covariance matrix of the estimation error may also be required. In this case, the correlative properties of the time series are captured in the variance covariance matrix.

Elliptic, hyperbolic, and parabolic umbilic: As the control variables change, a system can transition from a stable to unstable pattern at bifurcation points. One type of such transition can be described by an elementary catastrophe called an umbilic, which geometrically suggests a depression in the center of a surface through which potential can be transferred. Depending on the number of control and state variables, we can have an elliptic, hyperbolic, or parabolic umbilic. The former two are variations of the parabolic umbilic, obtainable, say, by replacing the potential function by its negative. As with other elementary catastrophes such as the cusp and the butterfly, they are canonical models rather than actual description of the system under study. They allow us to understand the qualitative behavior, rather than the quantitative behavior, of catastrophes in the system being studied.

Emittance: Most remote sensing devices work on signals that are reflected off the object being observed. We say that they process the emittance from these objects. The emittance is different depending on the reflective angle, and the type of energy source used to illuminate the object. The emittance data are often processed and filtered for best detection by selected sensors.

Entropy: Borrowing from its Greek origin meaning "change," entropy is best interpreted in the spatial context as a measure of the frequency with which an event occurs within a closed system. In an aggregate statement of a travel pattern, for example, it is sometimes useful to have a description that is robust enough to accommodate as many possible detailed patterns as possible. This is called entropy maximization, and is applied often to capture all possible patterns. In the absence of any additional information, for example, this results in equally likely detailed travel toward each destination given a fixed number of trips emanating from a central location. Any additional information would obviously modify the homogeneous travel to a pattern other than uniform, to be consistent with the newly acquired knowledge. Additional information would include such knowledge as the relative trip lengths, which provide the percentages of short, medium, and long trips. When interpreted this way, entropy maximization is equivalent to the information minimization principle. (See also micro-, meso- and macro states.) Entropy can also be interpreted as spatial uncertainty. It measures the degree of diversity in the dominance of destinations. For a regular triangular lattice of equal size and with no boundary effect, the spatial uncertainty is at a minimum at the points themselves and at a maximum in the intervening space.

Enumeration: One of the ways to identify the best alternative is to examine each and every alternative. Comparison among their figures of merit will reveal the best alternative. For example, we may wish to select the least costly alternative. In the real world, however, such enumeration is either impractical or impossible due to the large number of alternatives that exist. Here is when a mathematical model of the problem may become useful. Solution to the model automatically sorts out only the most promising alternatives or the very best alternative in an efficient way, without having to enumerate them exhaustively.

Equilibrium versus disequilibrium: Equilibrium is a stable state of a system in which there is no immediate tendency for change. Small perturbation would not dislocate the equilibrium state. The opposite situation is disequilibrium, in which the system is characterized by instability. Disequilibrium can take on many forms, including a cyclic pattern and truly chaotic patterns that do not have any discernible order. (See also dissipative structure and self-organizing systems.)

Exponentiation: An exponent is the power to which a mathematical variable or a mathematical term is raised. To exponentiate is to raise the entity to its power. In spatial-temporal analysis, spatial cost is often measured in terms of an exponentiated function of distance or time. For example, an exponent of one gives a linear spatial cost function; an exponent bigger than one a convex function, and an exponent of less than one a concave function. Whether a unique optimum is obtained or where it is found depends on the shape of this function. It also turns out the value of this exponent can transform one class of spatial problem to another seemingly unrelated class. (See also parameterization.)

Externality: Microeconomics accounts for the transactions between various parts of the economy via the price system. The price system is the mechanism by which supply and demand of goods and services are cleared in the marketplace. It becomes quite clear that not every transaction can be regulated by price. An example is pollution, which industries often incurred as part of the production process. Yet its cost to society in terms of health hazards is not often charged toward the industry. These costs are external to the accounting system and therefore unaccounted for.

Extremal and extremal solution: A well-known fact in linear programming is that the optimal solution has to occur at an extreme point (or corner point) of the feasible region. This property is carried over to network facility location models. For example, the optimal siting is often found at a node/vertex (or an intersection) of, for instance, the street network on which a fire station is to be sited. This is not an intuitive result by any means, since there is no reason a priori why the optimal location cannot be on an arc or at any other place. This nodal optimality property, where identified, does allow us to design some computationally efficient solution algorithms. Available evidence suggests that certain extreme conditions also exist in planar location models, in which the facility can be sited at any point in the Euclidean space. For example, the optimal airport among three cities is often located at one of the cities. In other words, the optimal site is at a vertex of the triangle formed by the three cities as vertices, rather than somewhere inside the triangle. In a calculus of variations problem, or a special case of a control problem, the solution for an optimal path that satisfies the initial and end conditions is called an extremal or a stationary function. This usage should not be confused with extremal point optimality mentioned above.

Factorization: As explained under frequency domain, Fourier transform is a convenient way for analysis of a signal over time. In Fourier analysis of discrete, mass probability distributions, the transform is expressed as, or factorized into, a polynomial of functions of complex variables. Unfortunately, this cannot be carried over to the spatial domain directly. In a random or Poisson field, joint probability mass functions can be factorized into conditional probabilities only under stringent positivity conditions, where the positivity condition is a prerequisite property for a random field. Under this situation, conditional probability models for data of this kind cannot be of the simple nearest neighbor variety commonly used to analyze spatial data.

Fractiles and fractile method: Fractal comes from the Latin word fractus, meaning "broken," describing objects that are too irregular to fit into traditional geometrical setting. Many fractiles have some degree of self-similarity, they are made up of parts that resemble the whole in some way. The similarity may be approximate or statistical. A space-filling curve used in routing is an example of fractiles. The space-filling curve transforms a two-dimensional map into a single dimension. By observing the clusters in the single-dimension line instead of proximity in two dimensions, vehicle tours can be constructed much more conveniently for each cluster of demand points. Fractal method is really a very different concept altogether. The word fractal is used only because we split a line up into fractions in this method. In constructing the univariate utility function, one common way is to have the decision maker play a lottery. The objective is to locate an indifference point by which the decision maker is undecided between playing the lottery and being awarded a fixed sum. Based on preference for the lottery or the fixed sum, the decision maker is either identified as risk-prone, risk-neutral, or risk-adverse, and the corresponding convex, linear, or concave function defined. When enough lotteries are played, a sufficient number of points are obtained to plot the univariate function. Drawing upon the common coin tossing experience, it is natural to design a 50-50 lottery. Such a lottery also has the nice property of dividing the vertical axis of the univariate utility function into halves, quarters and so forth each time an additional point is defined on the curve. Such a survey procedure is referred to as the fractile method.

Frequency domain, Fourier transform, line spectrum, periodogram, and time/image domain: A signal or data emitting from a source can be analyzed in a couple of ways. We can analyze the signal directly (in its time domain), whether it be a time series or a spatial image, or we can examine its frequency. Each of these two methods has its advantage. The time domain is more intuitive, since it describes the signal directly. The frequency domain, typically represented in terms of a line spectrum or periodogram, is convenient for noise-removal, as noise has a distinctly different frequency than a regular signal. By examining the line spectrum or periodogram, outlying frequencies corresponding to those from noise, can be easily discerned and removed. Fourier transform is a common technique used to analyze the frequency of the signal and reconstruct the signal once the noise is removed in the frequency domain. Among other uses, seasonal data patterns can also be easily picked out from a line spectrum or periodogram. This will help in identifying the correct time series model. Fourier transform is a convenient way to analyze signals in the frequency domain. In two-dimensional images, there are parallel, and sometimes more superior techniques for performing similar functions when stringent assumptions are made. Not only is the noise removed in this case, often the image is made more crisp also by virtue of sharpening the outlines.

Feng shui: In Chinese mythology, facility location should fit into the harmony of the natural environment. This includes orientation of the facility with respect to the topology and layout of the surrounding land. Literally translated, feng means "wind" and shui means "water," referring to the elements. Should a facility be placed the wrong way, bad luck will follow, while proper placement will bring good luck. Increasingly, the western world has caught on to these qualitative factors in facility location. The idea of feng shui is introduced in this book to highlight its scope (and limitations). Instead of using a holistic view like feng shui, we are often concentrating on the effect of one factor at a time. For example, what is the effect of highway construction (specifically) upon facility location and land use?

Gaming: Many factors in facility location and land use cannot be quantified precisely, particularly the rivalry between stakeholders. Although the state of the art has progressed significantly, the analytical techniques advanced in this text—including game theory—are limited in their utility. This is the reason why we discussed gaming. Gaming is an exercise that immerses the interested parties in a replica of the real world scenario. Divorced from the dangers of failing, a player can step through the many faceted situations of spatial decisions and learn from the experience in a game. CLUG, the Community Land Use Game, is one such game. Originated by Alan Feldt, the game simulates the real world of land development, complete with monetary transactions, urban renewal, and politics. It is a forerunner of many subsequent efforts in this area.

Gradient versus subgradient search: Gradient search is the most general way to solve regular nonlinear optimization problems. It is also known as the method of steepest ascent/descent. When the slope is not smooth, but piecewise linear, an equivalent scheme, called subgradient search is employed. In the former case, a gradient is computed in each step. In the latter case, a Lagrangian relaxation problem needs to be solved first to determine the subgradient. In both cases, a step size is computed to show the distance along which one climbs the slope. Both algorithms terminate when either the gradient or subgradient approaches zero.

Graphs and networks: Graphs are convenient, visual ways to represent the relationships between land use entities such as population and employment. For example, employment opportunities will bring in dependent population into the community. This can be represented as an arrow drawn from employment to population. Other combinatorial relationships can likewise be sketched, from which mathematical models can be constructed. An advantage of such representation is that certain mathematical properties can be readily discerned in the graph. In constructing an econometric model between population and employment, for example, we can easily postulate the correlation coefficients between variables. The graph helps to identify the expected values of some of these correlation coefficients. When flows are introduced in directed graphs, or a graph with arrows drawn on the arcs, a network is obtained. Again, a network can unveil useful mathematical properties of the model. An example is the representation of a facility location model as a network. Here, the incidence relationship in a tree graph is directly equivalent to the basis matrix of the corresponding linear programming formulation of the facility location problem. Instead of inverting a basis matrix, we can now accomplish the same thing by manipulating the graph. In this book, we show that many facility location models can be solved more efficiently when represented as a network (rather than as a formal mathematical program.) Also useful are the inherent properties of the network constraints, which lends itself to an integer solution for integer right-hand sides of the mathematical program.

Homogeneity versus heterogeneity: Spatial data are said to be homogeneous if the statistical inference made at unit i is the same irrespective of where i is. On the other hand, the data are heterogeneous if this is not so, or the inference is different dependent upon where i is. The stochastic-process approach to spatial data means that essentially only one observation is variable at each instance, in other words, the process of allocating values to the random variables in space or space time is performed one at a time. This gives rise to a computationally imposing situation, and there are some operational difficulties. Since this is not particularly practicable, some restrictions need to be imposed on the degree of dependence and heterogeneity that can be allowed. Only in this way can one handle on the spatial stochastic process. Essentially, in order to infer certain characteristics of the underlying process, a degree of stability needs to be assumed among the spatial data.

Homoscedasticity, stationarity, ergodicity and isotropy: In ordinary least squares regression, the model is homoscedastic if the residuals are uniformly distributed about the dependent variable means as shown by the regression line. In time series, where we regress a series against its lagged series, the same property is named stationarity. Similarly, a time-varying (stochastic) process is said to be stationary if it has become regular in its behavior (or reached a steady state). In this situation, the dependent variable would have a constant average value. Often, we prefer to model the underlying stationary process (rather than, say, the evolving process or the raw data) for a couple of reasons. First, it is more insightful (and therefore more valuable) to understand the underlying behavior. Second, it is easier to model than its non-stationary counterpart. Once the underlying process is understood, we could always map the results back to the dynamics of evolving process. When spatial data are involved, it is often advantageous to model it as a random or Poisson field. While stationary concept still carries over in general, the process is much more complex. One other useful property here is ergodicity, a concept borrowed from a memoryless random process called Markov chain. Ergodicity ensures that, on the average, two events will be independent in the limit. Now recall that by definition a Markov chain is ergodic if all states in the state transition chain are recurrent, aperiodic, and communicate with each other. An ergodic assumption allows for consistent estimation of the joint probability of various variables in a spatial time series.

Hypercube model: The model dispatches a fleet of service vehicles in response to calls. A vehicle at a depot is either free or busy, as represented by the binary 0–1 variable. For two depots with a vehicle at each, (0, 0) denotes both vehicles are free and available for service, (0, 1) means only the vehicle from the first depot is free; (1, 0) means only the vehicle at the second depot is available; (1,1) says both are busy. The four states of the system—(0, 0), (0, 1), (1, 0), and (1, 1)—can be plotted as four nodes/vertices in a graph that describes the possible transitions between these states. Such a state transition graph resembles a rectangle, characterized by the four nodes/vertices and arcs representing the possible transitions between the states. When there are three depots, the graph resembles a cube. In the general case when there are any number of depots, the graph is a hypercube, and hence the name hypercube model. Technically speaking, it is a spatial queuing model that caters to random calls or demands at an average arrival rate.

Inflexion point: Change of a graph from convex to concave or vice versa. In the context of a simple elementary catastrophe, the inflexion point could show the transition from stable solutions to unstable solutions. Thus in a plot of the functional against a control variable, a negative control variable may signify the existence of stationary solutions, while a non-negative value signifies instability.

Infrastructure: The functioning of society is supported by a number of facilities that are critical. Examples include utilities, transportation, and water supply. They constitute a web of basic building blocks essential to a standard of living. This book is concerned with the judicious configuration of such facilities in achieving certain goals.

Integrality: Many spatial-temporal models require the decision variables to assume binary or integer values. For example, we either locate a facility at a node/vertex or we do not, a decision often represented by a binary 0–1 variable. Similarly in image processing of satellite photos, we either classify a pixel (picture element) to belong to the lake or the forest, but not to both. Unfortunately, the computational requirement to solve this type of problem is often explosive. This requires careful model formulation as well as fast algorithms, not to say advanced computational machinery. When formulated as a binary or integer program, many nice mathematical properties associated with, for instance, a continuous variable model are also absent. For all these reasons, integrality requirements are challenging (and often impossible) to fulfil. In locating a facility on a network consisting of nodes/vertices and arcs, the optimal location is often found at a node/vertex. This is a desirable property since it saves computational efforts. Nodal optimality can be thought of as an analogue of the familiar extreme point optimality condition for linear programming. Both nodal optimality and extreme point optimality are not obvious in many models and a fair amount of attention has been paid by researchers to identify the conditions under which nodal optimality holds. Nodal optimality conditions can be identified in median, center, deterministic and stochastic facility location problems (See also extremal solution.)

Internodal versus intranodal: In spatial representation, approximation is often necessary. Thus we may consider all the population or employment in a zone to concentrate at a node (often called a centroid), while in reality, they are distributed among every part of the zone. Under this abstraction, trips executed by the residents or employees will take a finite amount of time to come out of the origin node in their journey toward a destination. Once they are in the destination zone, it will also take a finite amount of time to get to its ultimate destination. We refer to this finite egress and access time as the intranodal travel time, with the time covering the line haul journey from origin to destination zones as the internodal travel time. (See also centroid.)

Interregional transactions: Much of economic development and land use is concerned with the trade between geographic regions of interest, including imports and exports. Interregional transactions form the driving force behind spatial evolution. It is not sufficient only to model trade between economic sectors such as manufacturing, service, and household. Much of our concern here in this book is on where these manufacturers, service providers, and households are located, since their locations determine how much interaction is expected between them.

Intersectoral transactions: An economy is made up of sectors such as the manufacturing sector, the service sector, the household sector, and so on. Each sector trades with another in the conduct of business. Thus a manufacturer purchases auditing service from the service sector and hires labor from the household sector. Similarly, the household sector purchases manufactured products from the manufacturer and buys entertainment from the service sector. This results in intersectoral transactions, which in turn makes the economy go round and round.

Intransitivity: To the average person, if alternative A is preferred to alternative B and alternative B is preferred to alternative C, then alternative A is preferred to alternative C. Contrary to intuition, however, such transitivity between alternatives does not necessarily hold. While many such transitive cases exist, the world is replete with intransitive alternatives. One can easily construct an example that under a democratic voting process (based on majority), cyclic ranking can result. In this case, A is preferred to B, B is preferred to C, and C is in turn preferred to A. We say that intransitivity is observed. Intransitivity often arises when one is judging along conflicting stimulus dimensions.

Isocost, iso-utility and isoquant curve: For a fixed amount of capital outlay, various combinations of resources can be purchased. The tradeoffs among these resources form the isocost curve. Thus for a fixed household budget, one may wish to trade off between spending it on housing and transportation. Living further out of town will presumably lower housing cost, but this is done at the expense of higher commuting expenses. The isocost curve forms the frontier of the purchasing power of a fixed budget outlay. The household settles on a combination that maximizes its aggregate utility. The combination is often determined by an indifference curve on which the household gets equal pleasure on each point on the curve. Thus the curve represents a constant utility to this household. Viewing from the producer's side, certain combination of input factors, such as labor and raw materials, will achieve a certain level of production. Several combinations of input factors will accomplish the same level of production. The line drawn linking these combinations is the isoquant curve. A market equilibrium is determined by the consuming households and the producing industries.

Lagrange multipliers, dual, costate, or adjoint variables: In an optimization problem, it is often of interest to impute the marginal value of a resource. Various disciplines have different terminology for the same concept. Economists may call it the opportunity cost. Mathematicians call it the Lagrange multiplier or dual variable. Control theorists call it the costate or adjoint variable. The Lagrange multiplier or dual variable is usually associated with the relaxation of a limited resource, whether it be a budget or other constraints. It answers the question: What will another dollar in the budget buy me when my budget has been exhausted. Costate or adjoint variables, on the other hand, refer to the marginal value of a stock. Thus for an inventory problem, this amounts to the opportunity cost of a unit of inventory shortage.

Linearity: In its simplest form, a linear function has its dependent variable directly proportional to the independent variable. A linear system does not have reinforcing effects among the inputs, in other words, the response is directly proportional to the applied excitation. A linear operator has the property that the effect on the sum of two components is similar to that of each component. A linear filter, for example, takes a weighted sum of a time series to transform it into another time series. Thus a simple filter may just delay a time series by a constant number of periods. These linearity properties allow superposition of the effects of each of the individual excitations to form the resultant system response. A linear system is, therefore, much easier to analyze than a nonlinear one. Computationally speaking, it is desirable to approximate a nonlinear system by linearizing it under specific, local conditions. For example, nonlinear regression is typically a computationally imposing task in statistics. Fortunately, it can be performed by conditional least squares linear regression techniques. This is accomplished by estimating the regression coefficients for a given set of observations, hence the word conditional.

Location factors: In spatial-temporal analysis, we try to discern those factors that have spatial implications. For example, transportation is a significant factor in residential decisions. In these decisions, one trades off housing cost with transportation cost. Together with housing cost, transportation becomes part of the location expenditures in the household budget. This contrasts with non-location expenditures, such as food, clothing and savings, for example.

Macrostate, mesostate, and microstate: A travel pattern can be described conveniently in terms of these three states. Macrostate is the most aggregate description of a travel pattern, while microstate is the most detailed. For example, a macrostate description would only indicate the total number of trips originating or terminating in a zone. In contrast, a microstate description would identify each trip individually about where it is heading. Correspondingly, the former requires the least information and the latter the most. Suppose we wish to characterize the travel pattern in terms of the macro and meso states. The most likely mesostate or macrostate is assumed to be one with the greatest number of possible microstates. Thus we maximize the possible microstates in an aggregate description of travel pattern (see entropy maximization.) In other words, we ask for the least amount of information (information minimization) to characterize the travel pattern consistent with some givens, such as the total number of trip originations.

Maximum principle and adjoint equation: In control theory, we optimize the performance of a system by manipulating the control variables and theoretically the state variable over time. The optimization procedure can be executed by first optimizing with respect to the control variable and then the state variables. The first optimization equation is termed the maximum principle and the second the costate or adjoint equation. These two conditions plus the state equation are the necessary conditions for optimality over time.

Median versus antimedian: A median is a location that is the closer to the demands on the average. Thus, a retail chain may wish to open a store close to the population. An antimedian is just the opposite. It puts the facility away from the demands. An example is to locate an airport away from the population for noise considerations. In short, the median problem minimizes the distance to the total regional demand, while the antimedian problem maximizes the distance to the demand. Medianoid refers to a median on a tree (which is a network without any closed loops or cycles).

Medicenter versus anti-medicenter: A medicenter, also known as centian (which stands for *center* and med*ian*), is a hybrid between a median and a center. It takes care of both the proximity to demands as well as the reduction of the most adverse exposure. One can argue this is the best criterion for locating a landfill—close in general but not too close for the most irritated. Anti-medicenter is just the opposite of medicenter. It maximizes the sum of the weighted distance where the demands serve as weights. Yet at the same time, we minimize the maximum weighted distance. It may be the best for locating an airport, which should be a reasonable distance away from the regional population, yet within reach for the most remote residents.

Mini-max versus mini-sum: There are two traditional criteria in locating facilities. One is the mini-max criterion and the other is the mini-sum criterion. The mini-max (or min-max) criterion results in a center, wherein the farthest demand is to be brought as close to the service facility as possible. The mini-sum (or min-sum) criterion, on the other hand, results in a median, a facility that is as close to the demands as possible on the average. Within these two general criteria, quite a few variations are possible, giving rise to a rich array of facility location models.

Model versus submodel: A model is a mathematical abstraction of a problem. In building large-scale mathematical models, it is often convenient to break down the model into its parts, called submodels. The model is now made up of several submodels. The art of modeling then becomes a matter of how to account for the interaction between these submodels accurately. This to ensure that analyzing each submodel, one at a time, will not lose any property or behavior of the overall model.

Model identification and specification: In fitting an econometric model statistically, there has to be an appropriate match between the available data, the structural equations describing the model, and the corresponding ability to calibrate model coefficients. Classical literature points toward the proper balance between endogenous (dependent) and exogenous (independent) variables. Otherwise, a model can be overspecified and overfitted. A regression line that is fitted over two data points, for example, is both a mis-specified and overfitted model. In spatial econometric models, we are explaining spatial dependence between the variables defined at various locations. Spatial data come in different levels of aggregation, with some geographic units bigger and others smaller. To calibrate a homogeneous model, we properly define spatially lagged variables with predefined weights. In image processing, we refer to these weights as masks. Through these lagged or weighted variables, a model can be readily calibrated consonant with the proper data format. Here, some lagged variables may become endogenous variables, while others become exogenous variables. Combined with other explicitly given spatial variables, a meaningful econometric model can correspondingly be constructed. Mis-specification of a model can give rise to unreasonable results that may look fine statistically, but has little meaning in modeling the system at hand.

Monocentric: Classic regional science literature has idealized a typical city as having a single downtown with the highest development density, and the rest of the development thins out toward the fringes. This simple monocentric city form is constructed obviously for convenience. But it yields a number of insights, based on which more complex models can be built.

Monotonic/monotonicity: A monotonic function is either non-increasing or non-decreasing. It has a nice analytic property for a number of spatial-temporal applications. Among these is the economic activity generation process in a study area, in which the seed of economic development germinates multiplier effects on the local economy. Barring any catastrophic intervention, the resulting population employment activity level is shown to be non-decreasing. In the absence of bifurcation, the growth stabilizes in time to a limit. This process, and its monotonicity property, forms the basic building block of a surprising number of land use models.

Multi-attribute/multicriteria/multi-objective: Utility theory is the foundation of economics and operations research. The basic premise is that a number of disparate metrics can be translated into a common unit called utiles. Once this is done, cross comparison can then be made among alternatives with seemingly incommensurate attributes or criteria. This is generally accomplished by a multi-attribute utility function, which combines the incommensurate attributes or criteria through weights and scaling constants. Cross comparison among alternatives can still be possible without a multi-attribute utility function, although in a more limited sense. For example, a shirt that is cheaper and better quality is always preferred to one that is more expensive and inferior in quality. Here, no utility function needs to be constructed to combine price and quality, the two different attributes, into utiles before a decision can be made between them.

Multicommodity or multiproduct: Rather than monolithic, often one differentiates the type of service provided, or the purpose of tripmaking. Multicommodity or multiproduct flow results in such a situation, with each type of service or trip tagged. The analyst needs to decide the most parsimonious model commensurate with the problem at hand, wherein the complexity is justifiable on the grounds of model realism. In many cases, the multicommodity or multiproduct model is a simple extension of the single commodity/product case, at least mathematically speaking.

Multinomial logit model: Often we wish to classify entities into multiple groups based on their attributes. A statistical model is often formulated with a response variable having two or more categories. In the case of two responses, the model is called binomial, and with three or more responses, it is called multinomial. An example is to find a neighborhood in which one locates a home. The multinomial logit model is a common way to do this and over recent years has found its way into the location and transportation literature. In many ways, it is related to the venerable gravity model that is pervasive among those involved in regional science. Instead of using power functions to describe accessibility, the logit model prefers exponential utility functions. Among the advantages of the logit model is that it is based on some widely accepted behavioral assumptions regarding the utility associated with belonging to each group, such as the accessibility to various opportunities in the study area should one locate a home in a particular neighborhood. The logarithm of the model is linear, making it convenient for the application of ordinary least squares regression.

Multispectral sensors: Today's remote sensing devices, such as satellites, are equipped with more than one sensor. Several sensors are used to collect different emittance wavelengths, resulting in a signature of an object being observed as characterized by the different waves the object emits. A much more positive identification of the object can be obtained this way compared with a single sensor that captures only one type of wavelength. For example, the human eye is a sensor that is limited to see the visual wavelengths, which is but a minute fraction of the signals emitted from an object. For this simple reason, multispectral sensors can see the invisible.

Non-dominated, efficient, or Pareto optimal solutions versus supremum:
A cornerstone of multicriteria optimization is the concept of dominance. Thus site
A, which is cheaper and more functional, is a better site than B which is more
costly and less functional. Here, A is the non-dominated solution or the Pareto optimum, and B is the dominated one. This idea can be easily generalized to many
alternative sites, as long as we compare only two at a time. After an exhaustive
comparison between all pairs and discarding all dominated alternatives, those remain form the non-dominated, efficient, or Pareto optimal solution set. In contrast, the supremum of a function refers to either the maximum or the minimum.

NP, NP-complete: *NP* stands for non-deterministic polynomial, characterizing problems that have not been shown to be solvable within execution time
that goes up polynomially with the size of the problem. *NP*-complete (*NPC*) problems constitute a subset of *NP* problems. The implication is that once a member
of the *NPC* class of problem is solvable within polynomial time, the entire class of
problem will also be solvable within polynomial time. Being an integer program,
discrete facility-location models are at best an *NPC* problem, making it a difficult
problem to solve.

Object-oriented programming: One can think of solution algorithms for a
mathematical model as a set of computational procedures to process a set of input
data, resulting in a set of output data. The solution algorithm is as efficient as how
fast one can process the data. It follows that when the data are organized in the
right format, they can be processed faster than otherwise. Efficiency can also be
achieved if a set of computational procedures can be used time and again for a
number of purposes. This avoids coding a separate routine for each application.
Object-oriented programming is one good way to accomplish these objectives.
In location allocation models, this means preprocessing of inter-point distance
data as both candidate and demand strings, which serves to update an allocation
table. In a data transfer protocol for geographic information systems, this means
that we define precisely such objects as a node/vertex and a chain in a vector
data structure. Specifically, they are stored in relation to other related node/
vertex-chain information. In this way, the efficient transfer of complete chains is
facilitated.

Objective function or functional: In optimization problems, a figure of
merit is usually maximized or minimized. For example, profit is to be maximized
while cost is to be minimized. This figure of merit is expressed in terms of an objective function or functional. Thus profit or cost is expressed in terms of a set of
decision variables or control variables respectively. The two terms—function and
functional—are traditionally used in different disciplines, but are in fact equivalent. Both define a domain whose elements are functions, sets, and the like.
According to traditional usage, objective functionals (the integration of a functional overtime) normally have a time element associated with them, while objective functions are generally static expressions.

Optimality and stationarity: A function satisfies its optimality conditions when it is maximized or minimized at a point within the feasible region. A
continuously differentiable function is optimized when it has a relative maximum
or minimum at a point assuming a stationary value. This value again lies at an interior point of the feasible region. At this point, the function is said to be stationary. A stationary point is obtained by setting the gradient of the functional to zero.
For this reason, it also includes an inflexion point of the function, which is not a
local optimum.

Orthogonal/orthogonality: Independence among attributes is necessary for the construction of a meaningful multi-attribute utility model, since we will not be double counting an attribute. If two attributes are independent, they are also orthogonal. Orthogonality is a more general term than independence, however, since there are several types of independence in multi-attribute utility theory, while orthogonality is pretty much a monolithic concept.

Orthonormal vectors: If a set of vectors is orthogonal and normalized, the vectors are said to be orthonormal. These vectors form a convenient algebraic basis for referencing. For example, in a stochastic compartmental model, the transition rate space can be conveniently characterized by a set of orthonormal vectors. These vectors map out the possible transitions from the current jth compartment (state) to other compartments (states). Thus the transition rate to a neighboring compartment is changed by a unit increase or decrease of activity level or price. Here the increase or decrease is implemented by adding or subtracting a unit vector from the current activity or price level.

Parametric versus non-parametric statistics: Means and variances are typical ways to summarize statistical information. The use of the parameters such as means and variances is a good example of parametric statistics. Data description can take on other forms, however. In a very small sample, means and variances are no longer meaningful, since there are simply too few data points for these parameters to become representative of the entire data set. Dispensing with the use of parameters, non-parametric statistics serves to characterize the data under these circumstances. An example of non-parametric statistics is entropy, defined here as the various representations of the data permissible within some givens. In the example of a small data set, the givens may be the precious few observed values of the data. There are obviously quite a few underlying data populations that could manifest themselves in these observed values. The number of possible underlying data sets in this case is called entropy. One normally asks for the maximum number of characterizations of a data pattern that requires the least amount of information (minimal information), or entropy maximization. This means we seek the largest possible number of underlying data populations that are consistent with the few observed values. Notice here that not only is parameter estimation not required, no knowledge of the underlying data distribution is necessary. Non-parametric statistics plays a significant role in spatial statistics—statistics that arise in facility location and land use.

Parameterization: In spatial allocation models such as the gravity model, a key term is the accessibility factor, defined roughly as the inverse function of distance. It turns out that the exponent associated with spatial separation is a critical parameter. It determines the importance of interaction between origins and destinations vis-a-vis the dispersion or the distribution of activities such as population and employment among neighbors. As it turns out, when this exponent is infinite, there is nothing but interaction, or the assignment of supplies to demands. When the exponent is very small, there is predominantly continuous allocation of activities among its neighbors. One can say that this exponent is the key to characterizing a model as discrete facility location or continuous activity allocation (land use) models. One of the aims of this book is to show that through the transformation of distance measures, one can relate apparently different spatial-temporal models to one another. Another parameterization example is the relationship between a median model and a center model in facility location. It has been established that upon appropriate transformation of the spatial-separation function through the exponent, a center model can be reduced to a median model. There are several other examples, but these two cases serve as graphic illustrations. (See also exponentiation above.) In time series, parameterization means specifying the degree of differencing and the number of time lags built into the data, and so forth. It characterizes the time series.

Pluralistic/pluralism: One of the challenges of facility location and land use is the multiplicity of viewpoints held by a diversity of stakeholders. Often citizens have a viewpoint opposite from that of the local government, and industries have different objectives from environmentalists. Analysis techniques need to explicitly recognize this pluralism and produce useful information for all stakeholders in the decision-making process.

Polyhedron and polytope: Many discrete facility location problems are solved by mathematical programs. The simplest mathematical program is linear programming, which can be solved readily by off-the-shelf software. These programs work on the principle of searching among the faces of a polyhedron, or a many sided multi dimensional body defined by the linear constraint inequalities of the linear program. A polytope is simply a bounded (or finite) polyhedron. It can be proved that one only needs to examine the extreme points or edges of a polyhedron for an optimal solution, where an extreme point or edge is the place where two or more faces come together. (See Appendix 1; see also extremal conditions.) The same concept can be carried over to other types of mathematical programs, such as integer programs and nonlinear programs, except the search for optimality becomes much more complex.

Queuing: In this book, service vehicles are often lined up at the depot to respond to calls or demands during busy periods. Until a vehicle has finished servicing a demand, it cannot be dispatched to another demand location. In this case, one has to wait for a vehicle to become available; the vehicle then takes time to travel to the scene; it spends time servicing the demand; and finally returns to the depot ready for assignment again. Typical queuing literature, or the study of waiting lines, is now extended to a spatial context, concomitant with the greatly expanded analytical complexity.

Recursive operation, recursion, and recursive programming: In the temporal dimension of spatial-temporal analysis, one wishes to lay out the evolution of development from one time stage to another. To design the most desirable plan in the long run, the question is whether it is sufficient to do the right thing at each stage. Irrespective of whether it is or not, one can only execute a local decision at each stage, and he or she does it repeatedly for each time stage. We call this repetitive process recursion. The same idea applies to stagewise decisions in which only the spatial dimension is involved. An example is planning airline flights. A corporate planner starts out with candidate nonstop flights, then configures a one-stop flight made up of a new leg attached to an existing nonstop, and finally configures a two-stop flight by adding yet another leg to a one-stop. Again, the overall decision is broken down into a series of recursive decisions. Many computations are recursive in nature, including the filtered and one-step ahead recursions in adjusting a time series to a new pattern. When successive optimal recursions result in an overall optimum, we are dealing with a Markovian process. When global optimality is not guaranteed, we are merely dealing with a recursive program.

Satisficing: There are two types of achievements. The first is "the more the merrier." An obvious example is money; few would argue against having more money. The second achievement is more precise. When a standard or goal is achieved, we have obtained a satisficing solution. The concept of satisficing is therefore related to a threshold. Once a threshold is exceeded, there is no preference between the resulting solutions, no matter whether one barely exceeds it or exceeds it by a large margin.

Scaling and re-scaling: In spatial allocation of activities, it is necessary to ensure the sum of the zonal allocations add up to the grand total for the region. As one derives population from employment and vice versa, the sum of the derived zonal allocations does not necessarily agree with the forecast regional total. A scale factor simply ensures this happens. Another example of scaling is the calibration of a multi-attribute utility function. Survey of the decision maker will yield a set of weights among the criteria. But there is no guarantee that the utility function so obtained will be 0–1 ranged, the convention for utility functions. A scale factor simply makes it happen.

Single versus multiple periods: At times, it is important to consider the expansion of a facility or facilities over time. When a facility is treated as a discrete entity with a location and a service capacity, this multiperiod expansion problem is anything but trivial. To the extent that we have to build upon existing facilities already in place, we may not be able to do the very best we can if start with a clean slate every period. The goal of facility planning is to provide such continuity between single-period decisions and to come out with the most desirable evolution over time. Again, while an aggregate statement of such a problem, such as in terms of total service capacity to be provided, is relatively straightforward, the spatial statement of the problem compounds the complexity rapidly.

Single versus multiple products: A facility can provide only one type of service or that it can provide different ones. Closely related to this is the hierarchy of service provision. For example, a facility can provide up to a certain level of service and no more, or it can provide all types of services. Once distinction is made regarding the types of services, only an appropriate facility can render a particular service. At the same time, more than one capable facility may cater to the needs of a demand or customer. Facility B can serve as a backup in case facility A can no longer deliver the demand, or both A and B can satisfy the total needs of a customer together. This tremendously complicates the one service provider for one customer paradigm. This idea is not new in urban land use. There we have the equivalent concept of trip purpose, or the type of trip that is being executed. For example, office buildings take work trips while parks and recreational facilities take nonwork trips. They provide different products or services. We find mostly work trips during peak hours of the day and nonwork trips during off peaks. Among recreational facilities are state parks, movie theaters, and bowling alleys that can offer an alternative form of entertainment should a particular recreational facility become unavailable. For example, the seat capacity at a theater may dictate a substitute, or backup, recreational alternative, either a theater at a different location or perhaps a bowling alley.

Siting: In this book, the term siting is used interchangeably with facility location. With only minor exceptions, we do not deal with site layout in detail (although the theory is similar). Rather, we are concerned with the location of the facility in relation to other facilities and the aggregate design parameters of the facility, such as size and capacity.

Software or computer programs: In today's analysis world, seldom does the analyst perform tasks without the aid of computer programs or software.

There really is no centralized software package for facility location and land use to date. The computer disk that comes with this book is only a sample of what would eventually be a generalized software suite for this field. Such a suite may be similar to the office suites for various office functions offered with today's personal computers. Clearly the eventual package should contain quite a few elements, including remote sensing/geographic information system, location allocation procedures, location routing algorithms, and land use forecasting tools. Supporting or utility routines should include optimization procedures (such as CPLEX), statistical routines (such as SAS), and stochastic/simulation programs. Part of the aim of this volume is to provide the interested readers with food for thought for the design of an eventual facility location/land use software package.

Source and sink: In the location literature, sources are equated with a service or production facility, while sinks are demand locations, where the customers are located. Thus in both discrete and continuous (planar) location problems, they are the places where service or commodity flows originate and terminate respectively. This concept comes naturally with the discrete network flow literature, which traditionally has similar terminologies in place. In continuous problems, sources and sinks are among several stable or unstable fixed points, singularity points, or equilibrium points. These points in general characterize the flow patterns on a plane. Existence of these points introduces discreteness of facility and demand locations in an otherwise homogeneous pattern. This lessens the idealized distinction between discrete and continuous location problems.

Spatial versus aspatial analysis: A distinguishing feature of this book is that it explicitly considers geographic attributes, network effects, and interaction between economic activities among different areas within a region. In other words, it analyzes problems with full recognition of the spatial dimensions. In contrast, aspatial analysis deals only with aggregate attributes such as the population and employment in the entire region, the total amount of retail floor space, the total acreage of parks and recreation areas, the total number of hospitals, and perhaps their growth over time. It does not disaggregate by zones or other subareal units, neither does it deal with interzonal interactions such as commuting between employment centers and population centers. Naturally, spatial analysis is much more complex that aspatial analysis. (See also area and subarea.)

Spatial dependence and independence: When a spatial unit influences or is being influenced by its neighbors, the subject unit is said to be spatially dependent on its neighbors and vice versa. On the other hand, if all spatial units are truly random, they are said to be independent of one another. In this case, the assumed value of a spatial unit i has no relationship to the value of unit j. Spatial dependence is usually expressed in terms of weights w_{ij} between units i and j, where a larger weight connotes a heavier dependence. A totally independent set of spatial units is referred to as random field.

Stability and instability: A key property of a dynamical system is structural stability or instability. Inherent in the system is the innate ability to return to equilibrium after perturbation or that it transforms into disequilibrium. We refer to the former as a stable system and the latter unstable. In terms of spatial structures, the flow pattern of services and commodities between facilities and demands is a result of the economy that governs the study area. Locations of these facilities can either be stable or unstable. Example of a stable facility location is a source (where flows originate naturally), while certain saddles (with the associated separatrices or the dividing flow lines separating flows so that they are not converging on the saddle point) are unstable. Flows can be periodic or cyclic. In this case, a family of concentric circles around a fixed center suggests instability. On the other hand, a limit cycle—in spite of slight irregularities in its orbit—will always return to its starting point and hence it is stable. (See also equilibrium and disequilibrium.)

Statics versus dynamics: When a phenomenon is the same irrespective of time, it is said to be static. By contrast, a dynamic phenomenon changes over time. In this book, traditional facility location models are often static in nature. Recent advances in stochastic facility location models have extended the horizon to time-varying location decisions. By contrast, land use models are often used to forecast population and employment for a target date. In that light, they are dynamic in nature as one forecasts iteratively over, say five-year increments into the future.

Total unimodularity: If the constraint matrix of a linear program (LP) is totally unimodular, and the right-hand side is an integer vector, the LP will yield integer solutions. A network LP has exactly such property. To the extent that a facility location problem can often be formulated as a network LP, the desired integrality property is most valuable in computational solution procedures.

Trip and route, versus tour: Much of a location decision is the result of considering accessibility to economic, social, and recreational opportunities. To reach these opportunities, trips may have to be executed either by the population or the provider. In this case, the population follows a route to the goods and services, or the goods or services have to be routed by the provider to the population. When a special delivery is made by the provider, the vehicle used for the delivery may be productive only in one direction, namely on the way to the demands when carrying the goods and services. The return trip is often empty and not productive, unless another load is backhauled to the provider. On the other hand, if the population combines several errands in a trip, these errands can be completed in a round robin visit to several service providers. We call this a tour, which can likewise be executed by the provider to deliver the goods or services.

Unimodal, bimodal, or multimodal: In a frequency distribution, there may be only one single peak. We call this distribution unimodal. When there are two peaks, it is bimodal. In general, there can be multiple peaks, constituting a multimodal frequency distribution.

Univariate, bivariate, and multivariate models: For pedagogic reasons, most subjects are introduced in its simplest form, often involving one single variable. Multivariate models, however, are common in spatial-temporal analysis since each unit (for instance, a zone in a region or pixels in a photo) is usually represented by separate variables. As a result, there are many entities to analyze. Bivariate models are often used as a transition from univariate to the more complex multivariate case.

Univariate spatial time series: A time series is a sequence of observations on a single or multiple variables. This book is particularly interested in the latter when several spatially related variables are examined. It is often of interest to analyze the underlying pattern of such a time series, so that one can forecast future trends. One such analysis is to regress the time series with its lagged series, and the quality of such a model is measured by a goodness of fit parameter such as autocorrelation, the temporal counterpart of regular Pearson correlation in classical statistics. When each of these spatial variables is expected to behave similarly, one can simply construct a univariate time series. Once calibrated, such a time series would describe every spatial variable equally well over time. One pattern that exists in such a time series is seasonality. For example, people travel more in the summer months than winter months annually. While differencing may remove seasonality from a time series, a seasonal pattern may still remain in stationary data. This poses an additional challenge in model identification. Not only does one need to identify the lags for the autoregressive and moving average components (usually denoted by p and q respectively), additional specifications on the season length for the two components (s_p and s_q) need to be made. These two tasks, identification of p/q and s_p/s_q, are performed in the sequence as stated. There is a close parallel between the identification of a seasonal non-spatial model and the identification of a univariate spatial time-series. Normally, the spatial time series can be analyzed as a scalar sequence of observations that in all appearances, resemble a seasonal time series. One can employ steps similar to the seasonalized procedure to identify a spatial-temporal model.

Utiles: Utiles are the common currency of exchange among incommensurate quantities. Through the construction of a multi-attribute utility/value function, for example, one can combine apples and oranges together in a common unit called fruit. The common unit allows cross comparison to be made among two very different quantities, including tradeoffs among them. Utiles is the basic building block among most operations research and econometric analyses.

Variance, covariance, correlation, and autocorrelation: Variance (or standard deviation) of a single random variable is the spread of the data around the mean. When two or more variables are involved, the metric is broadened to measure the scatter of data around the trend line explaining the relationship between the two (or a dependent and several independent) variables. The less the scatter, the more the variables are correlated via a trend line (surface). The more the scatter, the more questionable the correlation. Formally, covariance between a pair of variables is the product of the standard deviations of the two given variables and the correlation between them. Thus one can see it reduces to the variance of a single variable when the two random variables are identical, or when the correlation between the two is unity. Where the concept is carried over to the spatial (multivariate) and temporal dimension, we have variance-covariance matrix and autocorrelation. A variance-covariance matrix has the variances along its diagonal for the same variable and covariances at off diagonal elements for a pair of different variables. Autocorrelations are correlations between a time series and itself shifted by a certain period of time, the former series forms the dependent variable and the latter the independent variable. In analyzing time series, the use of autocovariance and auto-correlation functions aids in the identification and estimation of the models.

Vector versus raster spatial data storage: Spatial data can be stored in two generic formats: vector and raster. The former is the traditional way, advanced long before the digital computer and satellite images. It exploits relations among points, lines, and areas. It has a more compact storage requirement and can be even be more precise in selected applications. However, the latter, because of its grid or lattice structure, has the distinct advantage of format uniformity when various data sources are merged, as long as the data are discretized into a grid. It is also amenable to a wide variety of image restoration and enhancement routines. Many of today's spatial data are digitized for storage, precisely for these reasons. Obviously, the problem drives the logical format for data storage and no single format is inherently superior to another. The data stored in vector or raster format can be socioeconomic attributes such as population and employment, or they can be gray values in a panchromatic image. For uniformity, we choose to use the generic term activity in this book to describe any spatial data value.

Weighting: In evaluating alternatives, it is desirable to combine several criteria or attributes into a single metric called utiles. In doing so, it is common to weigh each criterion/attribute differently according to its importance and then add them together, by means of a weighted sum for example. Obviously, the overall utile of an alternative is different depending on the specification of weights. The ranking among alternatives according to utile is therefore different depending on the assignment of weights.

Work versus non-work trips: Transportation planning is a major factor in land development. In transportation, distinction is made between trips made to employment location and trips for other purposes. Generally speaking, work trips are inelastic, while nonwork trips are much more elastic and are often discretionary. Work trips determine factory and other employment locations with respect to residential locations. Nonwork trips, on the other hand, determine the siting of shopping malls and other services, again vis-a-vis residential neighborhoods.

Appendix 6

Acronyms

2SLS	two-stage least squares (calibration procedure)
ACF	autocorrelation function
AHP	analytic hierarchy process
AIC	akaike information criterion
ANOVA	analysis of variance
API	application programming interface
ARIMA	auto regressive integrated moving average (model)
ARMA	auto regressive moving average (model)
AVHRR	advanced very high resolution radiometer
B & B	branch and bound
BFS	basic feasible solution
BW	Benabdallah and Wright (algorithm for districting)
CAD	computer-aided design
CBA	capacitated basic algorithm
CD-ROM	compact disk-read only memory
CDF	cumulative density function
CFLOS	cloud-free line of sight
CI	consistency index
CLUG	Community Land Use Game
CSPE	classical spatial price equilibrium
CW	Clarke-Wright (routing heuristic)
D-A	digital-analog
DCPLP	dynamic capacitated plant-location-problem
DCS	Defense Courier Service
DEA	data envelopment analysis
DIME	dual independence map encoding
DLG	digital line graph
DLG-E	digital line graph-enhanced
DM	decision maker
DMU	decision-making unit (in data envelopment analysis)
DN	digital number (of a pixel)
DOF, *dof*	degree of freedom
DP	dynamic programming
DPM	downtown people mover
ETAC	Environmental Technical Applications Center
FFT	fast Fourier transform
FI	full industries
FIFO	first-in-first-out (queuing discipline)
FIPS	Federal Information Processing Standard
F-W	Frank-Wolfe (method)
GAMS	Generalized Algebraic Modeling System
GASP	General Activity Simulation Program

GBF	geographic base file
GEODSS	ground-based electro-optical deep-space surveillance
GIS	geographic information systems
GMI	Gray-McCrary index
GMP	generalized median problem
GNSS	Global Navigation Satellite Systems
GOES	Geostationary Operational Environmental Satellites
GPS	Global Positioning System
GPSS	General Purpose Simulation System
GRASS	Geographical Resource Analysis Support System
GS	goal setting
GSARP	generalized search and rescue problem
GUF	group utility/valve function
HFDF	high frequency direction finder
IBIS	image based information system
IC	information criterion (decision rule)
IOM	intervening opportunity model
ICM	iterative conditional mode (algorithm)
IGUF	individual group utility function
IMSL	International Mathematical and Statistical Library
IP	integer programming
KKT	Karash-Kuhn-Tucker (condition)
LD	Lagrangian dual
LP	linear program, linear programming
LR	Lagrangian relaxation
LRP	location-routing problem
MADA	multi-attribute decision analysis
MARMA	multivariate auto-regressive moving-average model
MAUT	multiattribute utility theory
MCDM	multicriteria decision making
MCLP, MLP	multicriteria linear program
MCO	multicriteria optimization
MC-SIMPLEX	multicriteria simplex
MCSLP	maximum consumers' surplus location problem
MDMTSFLP	multi-depot multi-traveling salesmen facility location problem
MDP	Markovian decision process
MDVRP	multi-depot vehicle-routing problem
MIP	mixed integer programming
MNBLP	maximum net-benefit location problem
MOLIP	multiple objective linear integer program
MPSX	Mathematical Programming System extended
MSF	minimum spanning forest
MSFC	multiple space filling curve
MSS	multispectral scanner
MTC	marginal transportation (economic) cost
MTSFLP	multiple traveling salesmen facility location problem
MTSP	multiple traveling salesmen problem
MULSTARMA	multivariate spatial-temporal auto-regressive moving-average model
NASA	National Aeronautics and Space Administration

NDCDB	National Digital Cartographic Database
NIMBY	not in my backyard (syndrome)
NLIP	Nonlinear integer program
NOAA-n	National Oceanic and Atmospheric Administration n-series (meteorological satellites)
NP	non-deterministic polynomial
NPC	*NP*-complete
NSC	network-with-side-constraints
NVI	normalized vegetation index
NWPA	Nuclear Waste Policy Act
NWS	National Weather Service
OBE	operating basic earthquake
OLS	ordinary least squares
P	polynomial
PACF	partial autocorrelation function
PC	personal computer
PDF	probability-density function
PI	partial industries
PMT	person-miles-of-travel
PMTSFLP	probabilistic multiple-traveling salesmen facility location problem
PMTSP	probabilistic multiple-traveling salesmen problem
PRT	personal rapid transit
PTSFLP	probabilistic traveling salesmen facility location problem
PTSP	probabilistic traveling salesmen problem
PTST	probabilistic traveling salesman tour
PVRL	probabilistic vehicle-routing location
QAP	quadratic assignment problem
RP	recursive programming
RIOM	regional input-output model
RISE	route improvement synthesis and evaluation (algorithm)
SAR	seasonal auto-regressive (model); search and rescue
SARMA	seasonal auto-regressive moving-average (model)
SDTS	spatial data transfer standard
SEE	standard error of estimate
SFC	space filling curve (heuristic)
SIR	spaceborne imaging radar
SMA	seasonal moving average (model)
SMSA	Standard Metropolitan Statistical Area
SPE	spatial price equilibrium
SPLP	simple plant-location problem
SSM	subregional simulation model
SSR	sum of squared residuals
SSTMA	seasonal spatial-temporal moving-average (model)
STACF	spatial-temporal autocorrelation function
STARMA	spatial-temporal auto-regressive moving-average (model)
STMA	spatial-temporal moving average (model)
STPACF	spatial-temporal partial autocorrelation function
TAZ	transportation analysis zone
TCTSP	time-constrained traveling salesman problem

TCVRP	time-constrained vehicle routing problem
TIGER	Topologically Integrated Geographic Encoding and Referencing (system)
TM	Thematic Mapper
TS-IP	Training System-Image Processing
TSFLP	traveling salesman facility location problem
TSP	traveling salesman problem
TST	traveling salesman tour
TUM	totally unimodular
TVP	topological vector profile
UNEP	United Nations Environment Programme
USGS	United States Geological Survey
USPE	univariate stochastic model preliminary estimation (program)
VARMA	vector auto-regressive moving-average (model)
VGA	video graphics adapter
VI	vegetation index
VRP	vehicle routing problem
WMTS-1	Wisconsin Multiple Time Series (program)-1st edition
X-SAR	X-band Synthetic Aperture Radar
ZOOM	Zero-One Optimization Model

Other Abbrieviations

ADBASE	multicriteria linear programming model code
AMDAHL	type of main frame computer
AMPL	modeling programming language
ARC/INFO	geographic information system
ATLAS	geographic information system
CPLEX	linear and integer programming code
ELECTRE	discrete alternative multicriteria optimization software
EMPIRIC	linear econometric land use model
FANAL	Factor analysis program in the EMPIRIC model
FORCST	Forecast program in the EMPIRIC model
FSCORE	Factor Scores program in the EMPIRIC model
GLONASS	navigation satellite system operated by the Commonwealth of Independent States
IGDS	geographic information system
INFORMAP	geographic information system
LANDSAT	earth surveillance satellite
MICROSOLVE	operations-research software suite
MIP83/XA	linear and integer programming software
NETSIDE	network with side constraints software
PAR	calibration parameters of the auto-regressive terms in an ARMA model
PMA	calibration parameters of the moving average terms in an ARMA model
POLYMETRIC	nonlinear econometric model
PROC	procedure in the SAS software
RADARSAT	Canadian satellite with all weather and night-time capability
SAS/OR	operations research software suite
SCA	integrated time series analysis computer program
SIMAN	discrete event simulation language
SIMSCRIPT	discrete event simulation language
SLAM	discrete event simulation language
SPANS	geographic information system
SPOT	French commercial-satellite
SPSS	statistical software system
STATESPACE	procedure within the SAS software
SYSNLIN	procedure within SAS for vector time series analysis
SYSTAT	statistical software
TRANSCAD	geographic information system for transportation applications

Index

525